W9-APC-179

BOTTOM LINE YEAR BOOK 2022

BY THE EDITORS OF

Bottom Line
PERSONAL

BottomLineInc.com

Bottom Line Yearbook 2022

10 9 8 7 6 5 4 3 2 1

ISBN 978-0-88723-001-1

Bottom Line Books® publishes the advice of expert authorities in many fields. These opinions may at times conflict as there are often different approaches to solving problems. The use of this material is no substitute for health, legal, accounting or other professional services. Consult competent professionals for answers to your specific questions.

Telephone numbers, addresses, prices, offers and websites listed in this book are accurate at the time of publication, but they are subject to frequent change.

Bottom Line Books® is a registered trademark of Belvoir Media Group, LLC.
535 Connecticut Avenue, Norwalk, CT 06854-1713

Belvoir.com || BottomLineInc.com

Bottom Line Books® is an imprint of Belvoir Media Group, LLC, publisher of print and digital periodicals, books and online training programs. We are dedicated to bringing you the best information from the most knowledgeable sources in the world. Our goal is to help you gain greater wealth, better health, more wisdom, extra time and increased happiness.

Printed in the United States of America

Contents

3 • CURES FOR COMMON AILMENTS

4 • DIET, NUTRITION, AND FITNESS

5 • NATURAL CURES

6 • AGING WELL

7 • VERY PERSONAL

PART TWO • YOUR MONEY

8 • INVESTMENT INSIDER'S GUIDE

9 • MONEY MANAGEMENT

10 • TAX SAVVY

11 • RETIRE RIGHT

12 • CONSUMER SAVVY SECRETS

13 • INSURANCE ALERTS

PART THREE • YOUR LIFE

14 • EMOTIONAL RESCUE

Preface

We are happy to bring you our *2022 Bottom Line Yearbook*. Here you will discover numerous helpful and practical ideas for yourself and for everyone in your family.

At Bottom Line Books, it is our mission to provide all of our readers with the best information to help them gain better health, greater wealth, more wisdom, extra time, and increased happiness.

The *2022 Yearbook* represents the very best and the most useful Bottom Line articles from the past year. Whether you are looking for ways to get the most from your money or ensure the retirement of your dreams...boost your immunity or get fit in just a few minutes a day...get your marriage back on track or do-it-yourself repair trouble spots in your house, you'll find it all in this book...and a whole lot more.

Over the past 40 years, we have built a network of thousands of expert sources.

When you consult the *2022 Yearbook*, you are accessing a stellar group of authorities in fields that range from natural and conventional medicine...to shopping, investing, taxes, and insurance...to house and garden care and self-improvement. Our advisers are affiliated with the premier universities, financial institutions, law firms, and hospitals. These experts are truly among the most knowledgeable people in the country.

As a reader of a Bottom Line book, you can be assured that you are receiving reliable, well-researched, and up-to-date information from a trusted source.

We are very confident that the *2022 Bottom Line Yearbook* can help you and your family have a healthier, wealthier, wiser life. Enjoy!

The Editors, *Bottom Line Personal*
Norwalk, CT

1

Health Alerts

COVID-19 Symptoms Can Linger for Months

COVID-19 has been a moving target since it was first identified. And just as we've learned that many parts of the body are points of attack during the active phase, we've found over time that many symptoms linger for weeks or months after tests to detect the virus come back negative. The good news is that a lot can be done to help you feel better.

The array of lingering symptoms suggests that patients develop a form of postviral chronic fatigue syndrome/fibromyalgia, sometimes also referred to as myalgic encephalomyelitis/chronic fatigue syndrome (ME/CFS).

In fact, half of ME/CFS cases in general are triggered by infections. For instance, it occurs in about 40 percent of people who contract the SARS virus and up to 11 percent of severe cases of mono (Epstein-Barr virus, EBV).

Researchers are finding the same type of postviral fatigue can occur after COVID-19 with the addition of problems related to lung, heart, and brain inflammation.

Why does this happen? Numerous infections can trip key "circuit breakers" in your body as they respond to the stress of the illness, and that leads to a cascade of symptoms.

Because numerous systems are malfunctioning, there is no single "magic bullet." Rather, a large mix of natural and pharmaceutical treatments is needed to strengthen the system. Most can be discontinued six to nine months after the person has recovered from COVID-19.

Jacob Teitelbaum, MD, holistic physician and nationally recognized expert in the fields of pain, sleep, chronic fatigue syndrome, and fibromyalgia. He is author of numerous books, including *Real Cause, Real Cure* and *From Fatigued to Fantastic!* and is the creator of the app Cures A-Z. He runs the websites EndFatigue.com and Vitality101.com

OVERWHELMING FATIGUE WITH INSOMNIA

These common lingering symptoms also are the hallmarks of ME/CFS. The paradox of having insomnia despite exhaustion tells you that you have tripped the "hypothalamic circuit breaker" in your brain. That is what distinguishes ME/CFS from other causes of fatigue. Anything that overwhelms your body's energy reserves can trip this circuit breaker. And this circuit breaker controls sleep, blood pressure, pulse, and hormone function.

Meanwhile, low energy in your muscles causes them to get stuck in the shortened position. (That is also why your muscles go tight after a vigorous workout.) Persistent tight muscles then trigger chronic pain.

The end result? Insomnia, fatigue, widespread pain, and brain fog. Countless other symptoms, including shortness of breath and palpitations, also are common.

Fortunately, our published research shows that all of these postviral ME/CFS symptoms are very treatable, with an average 90 percent improvement in quality of life. *The way to address these lingering symptoms is with a protocol that I developed to ease ME/CFS called SHINE, the acronym for…*

- **Sleep.** The goal is to get eight to nine hours of sleep each night. Because your sleep center isn't working correctly, however, you will need some sleep support. Chamomile tea at bedtime can help, along with 200 milligrams (mg) of magnesium…an herbal sleep blend (such as the Revitalizing Sleep Formula from Enzymatic Therapy)…and 5 mg of melatonin.* Also talk to your doctor about a low-dose prescription sleep aid such as *trazodone* (Desyrel/25 mg to 50 mg) or *gabapentin* (Neurontin/100 mg to 600 mg).

- **Hormones.** When your hypothalamus is affected, your entire hormonal system will be malfunctioning, despite normal blood tests. Feeling "hangry" (irritable when hungry) is a clue that you could need adrenal support.

Helpful supplement: Adrenaplex from Terry Naturally, which contains vitamins B-6 and C, adrenal extract, and licorice root.

If you're tired, abnormally sensitive to cold temperatures, and experience weight gain, you could need thyroid support. Supplements may help, such as Thyroid Care Plus (Terry Naturally), which contains iodine, L-tyrosine, and selenium. If you have symptoms of low thyroid despite normal blood tests, you may need a holistic physician to get the necessary prescription for your thyroid.

- **Infections.** Though you may have been treated for COVID-19, you want to rule out other preexisting infections especially candida, or reactivation of other viruses (e.g., EBV and herpes simplex virus, HSV-1), which can contribute to your ongoing symptoms. Talk to a holistic doctor for proper evaluation and testing.

- **Nutritional support.** COVID-19 and secondary ME/CFS both trigger nutritional deficiencies (e.g., zinc) and result in increased nutritional needs (e.g., ribose, B vitamins, and magnesium) to enhance energy production. A high-potency multivitamin with at least 50 mg of B complex, 200 mg of magnesium, 1,000 international units (IU) of vitamin D, 15 mg of zinc, and 500 mg of vitamin C is recommended. Getting sunshine also is critical for optimal vitamin D production—aim for at least 30 minutes a day. *In addition, our research has shown that…*

  - Ribose (preferably in the form of SHINE D-Ribose) increased energy by an average of 61 percent.

  - Recovery Factors (RecoveryFactors.com), a unique serum-derived polypeptide, helped in 60 percent of cases with an average 69 percent increase in both energy and quality of life. This study was recently submitted for publication.

In general, your diet should be high in salt and protein to support adrenal function, and low in added sugars, which suppress immunity. Also, drink plenty of water.

- **Exercise.** Though you feel exhausted, a graduated increase in walking can help

*Check with a holistic doctor before taking any of the supplements mentioned in this article, especially if you take any medication and/or are being treated for another health condition. Dr. Teitelbaum has a financial tie to the SHINE D-Ribose and Recovery Factors supplements.

maintain conditioning. Start at a level that is comfortable, and increase by just one minute each day. Too much exercise can cause post-exertional malaise, a reaction that leaves you feeling as though you were hit by a truck, and it can last for days. If your exhaustion gets worse, that's a sign you're doing too much.

COUGHING AND BREATHLESSNESS

For most people, COVID-19 affects the lungs and heart to some degree, and that can lead to ongoing symptoms in your respiratory and cardiovascular systems. It's important to ramp up antioxidants to combat the damage done to these organs by the virus. In addition to a multivitamin high in antioxidants, take NAC (N-acetyl cysteine, 2,000 mg a day) to boost your respiratory system and the body's production of glutathione, the body's key antioxidant...and Clinical Glutathione (from Terry Naturally)—take one to two tablets dissolved under the tongue twice daily. This is the only glutathione that I use because it is highly absorbed and comes in the reduced form (most brands are already oxidized and therefore don't work).

Important: Use a fingertip pulse oximeter to check your oxygen saturation rate. A reading over 96 percent shows that you're getting enough oxygen, making significant lung or heart problems less likely to be the cause of the shortness of breath. If the reading goes down more than two to three percentage points (e.g., to 93 percent) during exercise rather than staying the same or going up a little, check with your doctor.

Breathlessness can come from heart issues, too. Your heart muscle can get stunned by COVID-19. The nutrients discussed above, along with coenzyme Q10 (200 mg), also markedly improve cardiac function. I also recommend a high-quality omega-3 supplement such as Vectomega (from Terry Naturally, one to two capsules daily).

Important: Check your blood pressure. Low blood pressure, or hypotension, is a major contributor to chronic fatigue. Adding adrenal support, drinking more water, and adding salt to your diet helps.

EASY TO DO...

Mask Up in the Restroom

Physicists studying fluid dynamics discovered that flushing a public urinal releases a large spread of aerosol particles that can contain viruses and bacteria. More than 57 percent of those particles travel away from the urinal—and toward other people.

American Institute of Physics

GI ISSUES

If diarrhea, nausea and vomiting were among your primary COVID-19 symptoms, your gastrointestinal tract could now benefit from probiotics and 2 g of glutamine twice a day. Glutamine can help your intestinal lining heal faster. After six to 12 weeks, these supplements can improve intestinal function. In addition, I suspect candida overgrowth if you also have nasal congestion or sinusitis. Yeast grows by fermenting sugar, so a low-sugar diet and a good probiotic are especially important if these are present.

LOSS OF SMELL AND TASTE

In other infections, these symptoms are thought to stem from inflammation around the olfactory nerve. But this is not the case in COVID-19. Rather, it is suspected that the loss of smell comes from zinc deficiency. Many viruses trigger the body to excrete zinc, which is critical for both immune function and the ability to smell and taste. Take 50 mg of zinc daily for one month to rebuild stores and then 15 mg a day for ongoing maintenance. This amount is usually present in a good multivitamin.

Roll Down Car Windows

Roll down car windows to protect against COVID-19 if you're in a car with someone outside your household—such as an Uber or Lyft drive. While it's safest to open all the windows, that can be impractical.

One beneficial configuration: Open front passenger-side and rear driver-side windows. This creates an "air curtain" type of flow, which can flush out some of the airborne particles in the cabin.

Varghese Mathai, PhD, assistant professor of physics at University of Massachusetts-Amherst. His study, with colleagues at Brown University, was published in *Science Advances*.

Too Much Salt Lowers Your Immune Defenses

Volunteers ate a high-salt diet—just over double the daily suggested limit of nearly six grams—equivalent to two regular fast-food burgers and fries every day. After one week, blood samples revealed a reduced ability to fight bacterial infections such as *listeria* and *E. coli*. And mice on a high-salt diet cannot defend as well against uropathogenic E. coli and listeria.

Best: Cap salt intake at six grams (about one teaspoon) a day.

Christian Kurts, MD, director of the Institute of Experimental Immunology, University Hospital Bonn, Germany, and coauthor of the study published in *Science Translational Medicine*.

Go to the Park to Help Your Heart

Researchers have discovered that people who spend more time around trees, grass, and other green spaces have a lower risk of dying from heart disease. In their study, for every 0.10 unit increase in greenness, deaths from heart diseases decreased by 13 per 100,000 adults. The relationship is likely linked to lower air pollution in green spaces.

American Heart Association

You're More Likely to Die from the Cold Than from the Heat

Based on the records on 48,000 temperature-related hospitalizations, 94 percent of the deaths were from cold weather and 6 percent from the heat. Hypothermia is difficult to reverse, while recovering from excessive heat usually just means getting to a cooler place and rehydrating.

Study by researchers at University of Illinois, Chicago, published in *Environmental Research*.

All About Resting Heart Rate

Jessica DeLuise, MHS, PA-C, CCMS, a physician assistant at American Family Care in Conshohocken, Pennsylvania. She is a wellness expert, TV personality, and certified culinary medicine specialist. Her TV show, *Eat Your Way to Wellness*, is now streaming on Amazon Prime.

Resting heart rate (RHR), the number of times your heart beats per minute (bpm) while you're at complete rest, serves as an indicator of overall physical fitness and can help predict your future risk of cardiovascular disease.

You can easily measure your RHR at home. According to the American Heart Association, the best time to test your RHR is first thing in the morning, before you've gotten out of bed, ideally after a good night's sleep. Use your index finger and middle finger to find the pulse in your wrist, just below your thumb (in the radial artery). When checking your pulse, do not use your thumb. It carries its own pulse, which can be confusing and provide an inaccurate RHR.

Count the number of beats you feel in one minute to determine heart rate. Or count for 15 seconds and multiply by four.

You can also use a heart rate monitor device, such as a Fitbit or Apple Watch, to measure heart rate. Once per week, check your pulse manually and match it up to the reading on the device to ensure accuracy. For healthy adults, 60 to 100 bpm is considered a normal heart rate range.

WHEN RHR IS TOO HIGH

Stress levels, caffeine consumption, and over-the-counter or prescription drugs may cause RHR to go up temporarily, but if your rate is consistently or frequently over 100 bpm, alert your physician. This may be an indication that you have a fast sinus rhythm known as tachycardia or an irregular rhythm.

If you do not have an underlying health issue, here are some simple ways to lower your RHR...

- **If your physician approves, exercise at a moderate level for about 30 minutes on most days of the week.** Exercise can increase cardiovascular health and, in turn, may lower heart rate.

- **Lose weight if necessary.** If you need any resources and referrals, talk to your health-care practitioner or visit TheWellnessKitchenista.com.

- **Reduce stress through relaxation exercises,** journaling, or lifestyle changes. People have found success through daily meditation, tai chi, and other stress-busting techniques.

- **Avoid tobacco products,** and limit alcohol, processed and refined foods, and caffeinated beverages.

WHEN RHR IS TOO LOW

Some professional or seasoned athletes may have RHRs that safely dip as low as 40 to 50 bpm, but if you're not an athlete and have an RHR under 60 bpm, I recommend being evaluated by your health-care provider. Slow heart rate, or bradycardia, may cause insufficient blood flow and result in fatigue, dizziness, or shortness of breath.

USING RHR FOR EXERCISE

Once you know your RHR, you can use it to determine your maximum heart rate (MHR) and to set a goal range to attain during exercise. MHR varies by age, exercise tolerance, cardiovascular status, and heart arrhythmia.

Ideally, you should talk to your health-care provider to determine your safe ranges and goals, but you can also estimate your target zone with a series of calculations called the Karvonen method (see table).

TABLE: THE KARVONEN METHOD

Calculate MHR by subtracting your age from 220.	**Example: Age 50, RHR 70** 220-50 years old = 170
Subtract your RHR from your MHR.	170-70 = 100
Multiply the number from step 2 by 50 percent, and then add your RHR back in. That number is the lowest heart rate that would be considered moderate activity.	100 x 50 percent = 50 50 + 70 (RHR) = 120 bpm
Redo the calculation from step three but use 70 percent to calculate the upper level of moderate exercise.	100 x 70 percent = 70 70 + 70 = 140 bpm
Do it one more time but use 85 percent to determine the top end of the vigorous exercise goal	100 x 85 percent = 85 85 + 70 = 155 bpm
Monitor your heart rate during exercise to gauge intensity.	Moderate: 120 to 140 bpm Vigorous: 141 to 155 bpm

Sudden Cardiac Arrest May Not Be So Sudden

More than half the people who suffered cardiac arrest contacted doctors with symptoms such as shortness of breath, chest discomfort, and heart palpitations during the two weeks before the event. A statistical analysis found that, on average, 26 percent of patients who eventually had cardiac arrest were in contact with their primary physician each week—and at two weeks before cardiac arrest, the percentage rose to 54 percent. Cardiac arrest, an electrical malfunction that causes a sudden loss of heart function, is fatal within minutes if left untreated—less than 10 percent of victims survive.

Study of 28,955 people who had cardiac arrest outside a hospital between 2001 and 2014 by researchers at Copenhagen University Hospital Herlev and Gentofte, Hellerup, Denmark, presented at the European Society of Cardiology Congress 2020 in Sophia Antipolis, France.

Silent Heart Attacks

Rekha Mankad, MD, a noninvasive cardiologist. She is the director of the women's heart clinic and the director of the cardio-rheumatology clinic at Mayo Clinic in Rochester, Minnesota.

When we think of heart attacks, a common image comes to mind—a person clutching his or her chest, doubled over in pain. But it's quite possible to have a heart attack without chest pain. In fact, it's possible to have no symptoms at all.

The lack of symptoms doesn't mean these events are insignificant, though. They can cause long-lasting damage that goes untreated and increases the risk for a second—and potentially fatal—cardiovascular event.

HOW CAN IT BE SILENT?

Often, people learn they experienced a silent heart attack only when imaging shows evidence of previous heart damage. While some people recall no symptoms at all, others look back and recognize that they felt something—just not a classic heart attack symptom.

They may have felt indigestion, a pulled chest muscle, or flu symptoms. They may have had sweating, lightheadedness, nausea, or shortness of breath. Or they may have had very mild classic symptoms—chest pain and pressure, or pain in the arm, neck, or jaw—that didn't feel severe enough to cause alarm.

GENDER DIFFERENCES IN SILENT HEART ATTACKS

Women more commonly experience these kinds of nontraditional symptoms, possibly because they are more likely to have blockages in the smaller arteries that supply blood to the heart, in addition to the main arteries.

But while the symptoms of a silent heart attack may be different, the underlying process is the same: Blood flow to the heart is blocked, potentially damaging the heart muscle.

RISK FACTORS

The risk factors for a silent heart attack are no different from a traditional one…

- **Advanced age.** Men ages 45 or older and women ages 55 or older are more likely to have a heart attack.
- **Excess weight.** Even being somewhat overweight is a risk factor, and the risk rises along with body mass index.
- **High blood pressure.** The excess strain from high blood pressure causes the coronary arteries to stiffen and narrow.
- **High cholesterol.** Strive to keep your total cholesterol under 200 milligrams per deciliter (mg/dL) and your LDL ("bad) cholesterol under 100 mg/dL. If you have coronary artery disease, aim for less than 70 mg/dL.
- **Lack of exercise.** You need 150 minutes per week of moderate-intensity aerobic activity or 75 minutes per week of vigorous aerobic activity, or a combination of both.
- **Tobacco use.**
- **Family history of heart disease.** This is a significant risk factor, but it does not increase the likelihood of symptoms being vague or silent.
- **People with diabetes** may have a higher likelihood of silent events, particularly if they also have neuropathy.

FUTURE RISK

A person who has experienced a silent heart attack has an elevated risk of having another attack. Because they didn't know they had an event, they had no medical intervention to limit damage to the heart. Further, there are no clues to guide ongoing monitoring. If you are concerned that you may have had a silent heart attack, talk to your doctor about your symptoms to see if you should undergo testing.

Whether that testing reveals a prior heart attack or not, you can immediately begin to lower your risk of a first or subsequent event by following a heart-healthy diet, reducing stress, exercising, losing weight, and managing other conditions like diabetes and high blood pressure.

If you are concerned that you may have had a silent heart attack, talk to your doctor. A medical professional can review your symptoms and health history, and a physical exam can help determine if you need more tests.

Aortic Aneurysm: A Silent Killer

Grace Wang, MD, clinical director of the vascular laboratory at the Hospital of the University of Pennsylvania.

Most of us don't walk around thinking our body's largest blood vessel might have a dangerous, balloon-like bulge that could potentially rupture. But when the aorta, which is normally the diameter of a grape, develops an aneurysm that can swell a portion of this artery to the size of a tennis ball, the risk is real.

With the aorta snaking through the chest and abdomen, aneurysms in this vital vessel occur in either the thoracic (chest) region or, more commonly, the abdomen. And, like many health issues, the risk rises as people age. Between three and 10 percent of adults older than 50 have an abdominal aortic aneurysm (AAA). The condition is diagnosed in about 200,000 people in the United States each year. It's not a problem to be ignored, since ruptures claim the lives of about 14,000 Americans annually.

Most of these deaths are sudden and unexpected: Ruptured AAAs kill up to 90 percent of those they strike, and up to half of these patients don't even make it to a hospital. Thoracic aortic aneurysms are far more rare, affecting six to 10 of every 100,000 people, but they are similarly deadly.

All told, about 47,000 Americans die of aortic disease each year—surpassing deaths from auto accidents and breast cancer, among other conditions considered more "common" and familiar to the general public.

In the midst of these shocking statistics, however, there is good news: Awareness can save your life. Knowing the risk factors for aortic aneurysms, as well as signs to watch for, can help reveal the condition at a stage where monitoring is all that is needed. And if an aortic aneurysm continues to expand despite vigorous control efforts, early referral to a vascular surgeon can allow for cutting-edge surgery to be performed, proactively averting a lethal outcome.

PINPOINTING THE PROBLEM

Admittedly, figuring out you have an aortic aneurysm can prove challenging, which is why many aren't detected until patients come to the emergency room with intense abdominal or back pain. Symptoms of either type are often vague at first, becoming more noticeable as the aneurysm grows.

Look for unusual back or belly pain, or feeling full early while eating for AAA, or chest pain and shortness of breath for thoracic aortic aneurysms. These signs can point to many different problems, but they should be checked out in any case.

Even without symptoms, certain people should be screened for aortic aneurysms. Medicare covers a one-time abdominal ultrasound screening for AAA if patients 65 or older have a family history of aortic aneurysms, or if men have smoked more than 100 cigarettes in their lifetime.

A careful palpation of your belly by a doctor can reveal some AAAs, which can feel like a second beating heart just below the ribcage. But most aortic aneurysms detected before they rupture are done so through imaging tests such as ultrasound, MRI, or CT scans. Bear in mind that it may fall on you to be proactive about undergoing such tests. But you have to ask for it—so don't be shy. The odds of surviving an aortic aneurysm are exponentially higher if it's caught before it ruptures.

SURGICAL STRIDES

Another benefit of early detection is that an aortic aneurysm might be small enough to leave alone, provided it stays that way. "Watchful waiting" through periodic checkups and imaging scans can monitor the bulge, which may never grow to a size requiring repair. Only an estimated five to 10 percent of AAAs end up needing surgical intervention.

Who oversees this? Vascular surgeons, who treat all arteries and veins aside from those in the brain and heart, provide everything from noninvasive tests to minimally invasive procedures and open surgeries when needed. These surgeons can also help prevent aneurysms from enlarging by referring patients to smoking cessation programs, coordinating care to ensure blood-pressure optimization, offering lifestyle guidance, such as avoiding heavy lifting (for those with thoracic aortic aneurysms), and recommending physical activity.

While AAA repair is managed by vascular surgeons, if complex surgery spanning both the thoracic and abdominal aorta is deemed necessary, vascular surgeons sometimes work with other specialists to carry out these repairs. Open surgeries using large incisions are sometimes unavoidable. But increasingly, newer, cutting-edge procedures incorporating endovascular repairs—requiring only tiny incisions and navigating within blood vessels—can offer a much quicker recovery.

RISK FACTORS

Who's most likely to experience an aortic aneurysm? The odds are unquestionably stacked against men, who suffer from AAAs five times more often than women and thoracic aneurysms nearly twice as often.

Other noteworthy risk factors include...

- **Smoking.** Much research points to this habit as the greatest modifiable hazard for both types of aortic aneurysms.
- **Age.** AAAs are more likely to occur in those over 65.
- **Genetics.** Aneurysms can run in families, with 20 percent of those with an AAA having a family history of the condition. Thoracic aortic aneurysms are more often linked to inherited disorders such as Marfan or Ehlers-Danlos syndromes, which weaken connective tissues such as blood vessels.
- **Lifestyle.** Aside from smoking, habits such as holding your breath when lifting heavy weights (the Valsalva maneuver) or using stimulants can greatly increase the odds for an AAA.
- **Health conditions.** Chronic medical problems raise your risks, most notably high blood pressure and continued smoking.

GOOD TO KNOW...

Having a Consistent Bedtime Is Better for Your Heart

Good sleep hygiene goes beyond getting the right amount of sleep. Going to bed just 30 minutes past your normal bedtime can raise your resting heart rate, an indicator of heart health, as you sleep and into the next day. To protect your ticker, tuck yourself in at the same time every night—even on weekends.

Nitesh Chawla, PhD, director of Center for Network and Data Science, University of Notre Dame, Indiana, and a lead author of the study published in *npj Digital Medicine.*

Confirmed: Omega-3s Protect Against Heart Attack and Heart Disease

In a massive analysis of previous studies, researchers concluded that the fatty acids in omega-3 supplements reduce risk for coronary heart disease events by 10 percent, coronary heart disease mortality by 9 percent and heart attack by 13 percent. Further, each additional gram of omega-3 consumed daily cuts heart attack risk by 9 percent. Talk to your doctor about taking one to two grams of omega-3 each day.

Analysis of 40 studies led by researchers at University of Queensland School of Medicine, New Orleans, Louisiana, published in *Mayo Clinic Proceedings.*

Heart Attack or Passing Panic?

Sam S. Torbati, MD, emergency medicine physician and medical director of the Ruth and Harry Roman Emergency Department at Cedars Sinai Hospital in Los Angeles.

You have a sudden onset of chest pain, trouble breathing, sweating, nausea, dizziness, and a terrifying sense of impending doom—the classic symptoms of a life-threatening heart attack. But they are also classic symptoms of a passing panic attack.

If you are having a heart attack, time is not on your side. The sooner you get to the emergency room (ER), the sooner they can get a stent in your heart and restore blood flow. Any delay means more damage to your heart muscle.

The worst mistake you can make is to assume you are having a panic attack and show up at the ER hours later or the next day still having chest pain. By this time the damage is done. You may still get a stent placed, but the consequences of your heart attack may affect the rest of your life. It would have been much wiser to show up at the ER without any symptoms. You might feel a bit embarrassed, but your ER doctor would rather see you embarrassed than debilitated.

DON'T DRIVE YOURSELF

Don't ever take a chance on driving to the ER. Calling 911 gets you there safely and quickly. Traffic will move out of the way. Paramedics can start treatment in the ambulance, and they can call ahead to get the ER and the stent room ready for you. This is the only way to get the help you need when you might be having a heart attack.

WHEN TO WAIT

A panic attack usually peaks and passes quickly. If you are under age 40 with no history of heart disease or risk factors, and you have a history of panic attacks in the past, you can try some relaxation techniques and deep breathing to see if your symptoms will pass. If they last longer than 20 to 30 minutes, call 911.

A panic attack is a sudden episode of intense fear when there is no apparent danger. Panic attacks are not life-threatening, even though they may feel that way. Symptoms peak within minutes. After the attack you may feel tired and drained. Even though you did not need to call 911, you should still call your doctor. Panic attacks tend to get worse and more frequent without treatment.

BEWARE THIS MYTH

You may have heard that panic attacks come out of the blue when you are resting, but a heart attack usually occurs during exercise. That is true for chest pain called angina, but not for a heart attack. Most heart attacks occur without exertion or warning.

Finally, remember that the difference between a heart attack and a panic attack is not like the difference between a sprained ankle and a broken ankle. As they say in the ER, time is muscle. If in doubt, call 911.

Blood Pressure Mistakes

Raymond R. Townsend, MD, professor of medicine and director of the Hypertension Program at the Hospital of the University of Pennsylvania in Philadelphia.

Depending on the type of error that could occur when your blood pressure is taken, you could be misdiagnosed with high blood pressure (hypertension)...or you could have hypertension that goes undetected and untreated, increasing your risk for a heart attack or stroke.

Most of these errors raise the systolic (top number) reading—the one that doctors watch most closely as you age. That's because diastolic (bottom number) readings peak around age 50 to 55 and may decline thereafter. Systolic numbers, on the other hand, may keep going higher.

There are guidelines for getting accurate blood pressure readings, but most people don't know them and they're often overlooked by health-care providers. In research published in *The Journal of Clinical Hypertension*, my colleagues and I studied how well medical students followed the guidelines. Only one of the 159 participants followed all 11 steps looked at in our research.

Other research found that even seasoned medical providers make the same mistakes, especially those using a sphygmomanometer, a blood pressure monitor with an inflatable cuff, a manually operated bulb, and an aneroid (nonmercury) gauge that the doctor uses with a stethoscope. (Mercury sphygmomanometers have traditionally been the "gold standard.") Human errors still are being made even with meters using the oscillometric method that relies on an automated electronic pressure sensor that is interpreted by the person conducting the test.

Among oscillometric monitors, fully automated electronic devices are the most reliable. They record multiple readings as you sit undisturbed without any medical staff in the room. Yet even if your doctor's practice has this state-of-the-art device, testing guidelines need to be followed to get the most accurate measurement.

STEPS FOR BP ACCURACY

To ensure your blood pressure is being measured accurately, follow these steps from the American Heart Association (AHA) and the American Medical Association (AMA)…

1. On the day of your test, avoid caffeine, exercise, and smoking (there's never a good time to smoke!) for at least 30 minutes beforehand.

2. Empty your bladder. Waiting in an exam room with a full bladder can increase your blood pressure.

Helpful: When you arrive at the doctor's office, ask if a urine sample is needed. If not, heed nature's call before going into the exam room. If a sample is necessary, request a cup so that you can empty your bladder before seeing the doctor.

3. Sit in an armchair with your back supported…uncross your legs…and place both feet flat on the floor or on a low stool.

4. Support your forearm on the arm of the chair. Blood pressure is lower when the measurement site is above heart level…and higher when the measurement site is below heart level.

5. Rest for five minutes before the test. This is essential to get blood pressure to its baseline (the treatment target).

6. Make sure the correct cuff size for your weight is used. Many practices have only the one size cuff that came with the equipment. But a small, medium, large, and extra-large cuff should be available to account for differences in body weight. Though less common than getting a too high blood pressure reading, an inaccurate low reading can result if a medium or large cuff is used on a petite woman, for instance, and high blood pressure could be missed.

7. Make sure the cuff is placed over a bare arm or nothing more than very thin fabric—slip your arm out of your clothes if necessary. Thick shirts and sweaters reduce the oscillations detected by the blood pressure device. The cuff should be placed on the upper arm, level with your heart.

8. No chitchat. Talking can raise blood pressure by up to 15 mm Hg—likely due to activation of the brainstem centers that govern our focusing of attention.

9. Don't use or even look at your cell phone. And skip the magazines. Such activities activate the brain centers that govern blood pressure and heart rate.

Important: Have your blood pressure taken in both arms if you've never had that done before—there can be a 10 mm Hg to 15 mm Hg difference between the right and left arms. The arm that gives the higher reading is the one to use for future readings.

CORRECTING MISTAKES

Once you know how your blood pressure should be measured, you (as the patient) should speak up if missteps are being made. It's your health at risk.

What's more, that blood pressure reading is going into your medical record. If the numbers are incorrect, it can result in a misdiagnosis of hypertension when it is not present, for example, or overtreatment, which can result in dizziness and light-headedness.

Talk to the doctor if the guidelines weren't followed when he/she, a nurse, or medical assistant tested your blood pressure. If your doctor doesn't listen, get a new one.

BEST AT-HOME BP TESTING

We all benefit from keeping an eye on our blood pressure, but it's especially important to monitor it if you've been diagnosed with hypertension.

There are good oscillometric devices for home use. You can buy a high-quality device online for less than $100. Manufacturers such as Omron and Welch Allyn have developed monitors that have been scientifically validated. For a list of validated blood pressure devices, go to the AMA site ValidateBP.org.

If you don't yet know which arm has the higher reading, take your blood pressure in both arms and use the higher one for future measurements.

Keep a log, and bring it with you to doctor appointments. Once a year, bring along your home monitor and have it checked for accuracy against a mercury sphygmomanometer or comparable device. Readings from a device that is not properly calibrated may be consistently 5 mm Hg or more higher or lower. Aneroid devices can be sent back to the manufacturer for recalibration, while oscillometric devices will need to be returned or replaced.

Be sure to ask your doctor how often you should check your blood pressure at home. He may advise you to take it daily, for example, starting two weeks after you have changed blood pressure medications.

What to do: Before taking any blood pressure medication, take two measurements one minute apart in the morning...and two readings, also a minute apart, in the evening, and average the two sets.

If the readings aren't in line with your doctor's office reading—especially if they are higher at home—it could be a sign that you need more medication or coaching to better stick with your regimen. Not taking medications as directed is the biggest problem among people with hypertension.

Busting the Cholesterol Myth

Stephen Sinatra, MD, an integrative cardiologist and the founder of the New England Heart Center in Manchester, Connecticut. Dr. Sinatra is author of *The Great Cholesterol Myth* and *Reversing Heart Disease.* HeartMDInstitute.com and HealthyDirections.com/dr-stephen-sinatra

Every year, doctors in America write 240 million prescriptions for statins, such as *simvastatin* (Zocor) or *atorvastatin* (Lipitor), to lower "bad" LDL cholesterol and reduce the risk of heart disease.

But here's a little-known fact: Although statins lower LDL, as advertised, for most people, that reduction doesn't translate to a lower risk of heart disease.

LOOKING AT THE DATA

In new research published in the *British Medical Journal* (*BMJ Evidence-Based Medicine*), three cardiologists analyzed the results of 35 studies on lowering LDL cholesterol with statins or other cholesterol medications. Nearly half of the studies failed to show that taking statins or other LDL-lowering medications reduced the risk of developing cardiovascular disease (CVD), and 75 percent showed no reduction in rates of death from heart disease.

What's more, there was no consistent correlation between lowering LDL and cardiovascular protection. In many of the studies, large drops in LDL levels produced no reduction in heart attacks, strokes, or deaths from CVD. In others, failure to significantly decrease LDL did not lead to more heart attacks, strokes, and deaths from CVD. In fact, in 14 of the 35 studies, a failure to decrease LDL reduced the risk for heart attacks and strokes. The researchers noted that, in the United States, cardiovascular deaths are increasing despite the rising use of statins and lower levels of cholesterol overall.

The only proven and reliable benefit of statins for CVD is for men under 75 with heart disease or a previous heart attack or stroke. Statins work in this case by thinning the blood and reducing inflammation, not by lowering LDL.

QUESTIONING THE PREVAILING THEORY

The study authors concluded that using statins and other drugs to reduce the risk of CVD is a failed strategy. They wrote: "Considering that dozens of randomly controlled trials of LDL-cholesterol reduction have failed to demonstrate a consistent benefit, we should question the validity of this theory. In most fields of science, the existence of contradictory evidence usually leads to a paradigm shift or modification of the theory in question, but in this case, the contradictory evidence has been largely ignored, simply because it doesn't fit the prevailing paradigm."

HOW DID THE EXPERTS GET IT SO WRONG?

The main factor behind the persistence of the prevailing paradigm is profit—for the food industry and for drug companies. In the 1960s, the dietary causes of heart disease were still a matter of debate—with many scientists asserting that cholesterol-raising saturated fat found in meat, dairy, and eggs was the culprit, and others pointing to artery-damaging sugar. The debate was largely decided by a seemingly definitive 1967 study conducted by Harvard scientists and published in the prestigious *New England Journal of Medicine*. It reviewed the link between sugar and heart disease and concluded sugar did not play a role in heart disease, and that the only dietary factors of importance were fat and cholesterol.

But recent investigative research revealed that the study was secretly funded, designed, and directed by the Sugar Research Foundation—a trade group dedicated to the profitability of sugar—that is now called The Sugar Association.

LDL-lowering statins came on the market in the 1990s and were heavily promoted by drug companies as the answer to heart disease. However, the results of statin-supported research were consistently exaggerated by those same drug companies and the scientists they funded—as demonstrated by the new *BMJ* study.

THE REAL RISK

What is significantly more worrisome than high cholesterol is insulin resistance. This condition doesn't account for 100 percent of heart disease, but it predicts CVD better than any other variable studied. Research by the late Gerald Reaven, MD, of Stanford University, showed that insulin resistance dramatically increases the risk of heart disease. Other researchers found that insulin resistance was the only significant predictor of a second heart attack, while LDL cholesterol had no predictive value.

A hormone manufactured by the pancreas, insulin ushers blood sugar (glucose) out of the bloodstream and into muscle cells, where it is used for energy. But in an estimated 50 percent of Americans, insulin doesn't work that way. That's because excessive stress and a daily diet rich in refined carbohydrates trigger the pancreas to pump out unnatural amounts of insulin—so much that the muscle cells begin to resist the hormone. Instead, the glucose is stored in fat cells. Those cells release a flood of inflammatory chemicals—and inflammation is one of the major causes of CVD. It makes arteries vulnerable to artery-clogging plaque. Insulin resistance also causes high blood pressure; increases triglycerides; lowers heart-protective HDL cholesterol; and increases small, dense LDL particles. This subtype of LDL is dangerous because—in contrast to large, fluffy LDL particles—it can burrow into arteries.

ARE YOU INSULIN RESISTANT?

Fortunately, there is a simple way to figure out if you're insulin resistant: Measure your waist. Men with waist sizes of 40 inches or more are almost certainly insulin resistant, as are women with waist sizes of 35 inches or more. However, about one in 10 people with insulin resistance are slim—their sugar-generated fat isn't right under their skin, but invisibly wrapped around their abdominal organs, a form of fat scientists call visceral.

Another giveaway is the ratio of your triglycerides divided by your HDL. An ideal ratio is 2 or under.

ADDRESSING INSULIN RESISTANCE

The best way to eliminate insulin resistance is by changing your diet.

- **Sugar is the biggest threat** to your heart. Cut out soda, processed cereals, pasta, bread, cakes, candies, pastries, and doughnuts.

• **Avoid trans fats,** a highly inflammatory form of fat that has been removed from much of the food supply, but may still be found in non-dairy creamers, margarine, ramen noodles, energy bars, and fast food.

• **Don't eat processed meats,** such as salami, sausages, hot dogs, luncheon meats, and bacon. They contribute to inflammation and heart disease.

• **Cut back on omega-6 fats,** which are found in vegetable oils such as corn, canola, and soybean. They're also pro-inflammatory.

EAT THIS INSTEAD

Research shows the higher the average daily consumption of vegetables and fruits, the lower the chances of developing CVD.

• **Eat five to nine half-cup servings of vegetables and fruits each day.** The most protective are green, leafy veggies, such as spinach and kale, and cruciferous veggies, such as cauliflower and broccoli. Berries and cherries are also loaded with anti-inflammatory compounds.

• **Wild Alaskan salmon, sardines, and anchovies** are loaded with anti-inflammatory omega-3 fatty acids and are low in mercury. Eat these at least twice a week.

• **Eat more nuts.** Five large studies have found a consistent 30 to 50 percent lower risk of heart disease or heart attacks linked to eating nuts several times a week.

• **Eat more beans.** One study found that one serving of beans daily lowered the risk of a heart attack by 38 percent. Eat a serving of beans or lentils at least four times a week.

• **Favor dark chocolate for dessert.** It's rich in flavanols, a heart-protecting antioxidant. Research has found that regular chocolate consumption reduces CVD by 37 percent. Look for a product with no less than 60 percent cocoa. Eat one or two squares four to six days a week.

• **Use only olive oil.** Dozens of studies show it's one of the healthiest fats for the heart.

• **Use more garlic.** It lowers blood pressure and thins the blood. In one study, people who used garlic powder regularly for four years had a 2.6 percent regression in arterial plaque—while people who used a placebo powder had a 15.6 percent increase.

SUPPLEMENT SUPERSTARS

I've used these two science-backed nutritional supplements (and many others) in my practice for decades—and they're superb for protecting and restoring the health of the heart.

Coenzyme Q10 (CoQ10) helps create cellular energy from nutritional fuel. And the heart—which beats more than 100,000 times a day—is dependent on the energy-generating power of CoQ10. It also helps protect against the side effects of energy-depleting statins.

Recommended dose: At least 100 milligrams (mg), twice a day.

Medications That Raise Diabetes Risk

Statins...

Data on 4,683 subjects showed that prolonged use (two years or more) of the cholesterol-lowering drugs more than tripled the risk for type 2 diabetes.

But: Statins are very effective at preventing cardiac events among patients with indications for their use (both primary and secondary prevention). So discuss risks and benefits with your doctor.

Victoria Zigmont, MPH, PhD, assistant professor of public health at Southern Connecticut State University in New Haven. Her peer-reviewed research was published in *Diabetes/Metabolism Research and Reviews.*

Proton Pump Inhibitors...

Researchers examined data on 204,689 participants from the U.S. Nurses' Health Study and the Health Professionals Follow-up Study and discovered that people who regularly used PPIs for at least two years were 26 percent more likely to develop type 2 diabetes than those who didn't. Using PPIs for less than two years was associated with a five percent increased risk.

Jinqiu Yuan, PhD, Clinical Research Center, The Seventh Affiliated Hospital, Sun Yat-Sen University, Shenzhen, Guangdong, China.

The mineral magnesium can help prevent and manage both insulin resistance and high blood pressure. It also helps stop the calcification that underlies clogged arteries.

Recommended dose: 400 mg daily. (Magnesium supplementation is not recommended for anyone with kidney disease.)

STRESS IS HARD ON YOUR HEART

Chronic stress is a major instigator of inflammation and high blood pressure and weakens your heart. Use the relaxation response exercise every day for 10 to 20 minutes to decrease heart rate, lower blood pressure, slow breath, and relax the muscles. Sit quietly in a comfortable position with your eyes closed. Deeply relax all your muscles, beginning at your feet and progressing up to your face. Breathe through your nose. Become aware of your breathing. As you breathe out, say one word silently to yourself.

Weak Grip Strength Can Predict Type-2 Diabetes Risk

Exact grip thresholds depend on body weight, sex, and age. Grip strength, measured by an electronic handgrip device, can be performed during annual checkups in order to identify patients who may need further diabetes diagnostic testing and lifestyle intervention.

Elise Brown, PhD, assistant professor of wellness and health promotion at Oakland University, Rochester, Michigan, and leader of an analysis of data on more than 5,000 patients, published in *American Journal of Preventive Medicine.*

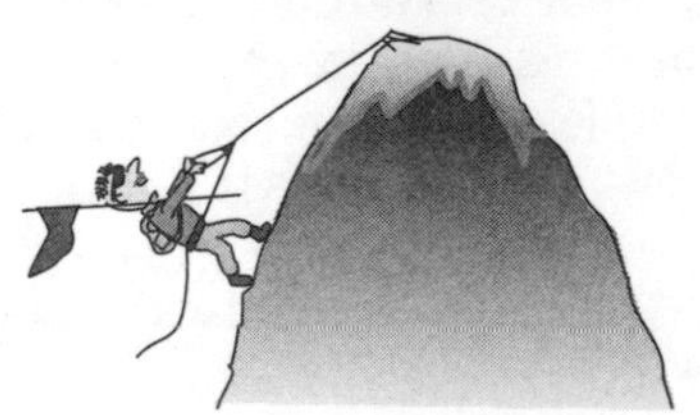

New Option for Preventing Diabetes

Michael Hochman, MD, MPH, associate professor of clinical medicine at Keck School of Medicine and director of Gehr Family Center for Health Systems Science and Innovation at University of Southern California, Los Angeles.

Are pharmaceuticals the answer to America's diabetes problem? One group of diabetes researchers recently reported on a novel approach—give people with prediabetes, those who are close to developing full-blown diabetes, three different drugs, including one that needs to be self-injected as often as twice a day.

It sounds extreme, but it worked. In the study, published in *The Lancet,* 81 overweight participants took the diabetes drugs *metformin, pioglitazone* (Actos), and a GLP-1 receptor agonist (Byetta, Victoza, and others). On average, they were treated for 32 months. None of them got diabetes. In contrast, 11 percent of those in the study's "lifestyle only" group, who were given diabetes-prevention advice on diet, weight loss, and exercise and followed for 32 months, on average, developed diabetes.

So is lifestyle a failure? Don't jump to conclusions from this study. Some of the people in the lifestyle group lost weight, but others gained weight. And losing weight if you are too heavy is a linchpin of preventing diabetes.

Maybe changing your diet, exercising, and therefore losing weight—and keeping it off—is hard. But taking three medications for the rest of your life has plenty of downsides. Metformin often causes gastrointestinal problems... pioglitazone is associated with fluid retention and heart failure...and the GLP-1 medications may trigger nausea and headaches.

And the lifestyle changes above give you benefits well beyond keeping your blood sugar "number" down. They help prevent heart disease, stroke, and other "complications" of prediabetes. It's good that we have the prediabetes drugs for people who need them. But it's better to improve our health ourselves and not have to take them.

The Hidden Risks of Normal-Weight Obesity

John A. Batsis, MD, a staff geriatrician at Dartmouth-Hitchcock Medical Center in Lebanon, New Hampshire, and an associate professor of medicine at Geisel School of Medicine at Dartmouth. He is also director of clinical research at Dartmouth-Hitchcock Weight & Wellness Center.

Normal-weight obesity (NWO) may sound like an oxymoron, but that doesn't make it any less harmful.

Obesity (or, in many cases, simply being overweight) is a well-established risk factor for a slew of health problems, including hypertension, elevated cholesterol, and high blood sugar—which, in turn, increase your odds of having a heart attack, stroke, type 2 diabetes, and other serious medical conditions.

The grim link between excessive body weight and poor health is why scientists have carefully defined who is overweight and who isn't, creating three main categories—normal weight, overweight, and obesity—based on a formula called the body mass index, or BMI.

Here's the rub: Your BMI can be normal, but you can still have the same weight-related health risks as a person with obesity—something known as normal-weight obesity, or NWO.

For important insights on this commonly overlooked phenomenon, we spoke with John A. Batsis, MD, a noted authority on NWO...

UNDERSTANDING BODY WEIGHT LABELS

NWO occurs when a person has excess body fat that the BMI fails to take fully into account. The type of fat found in NWO is almost always excess abdominal fat, commonly called "central obesity" or "visceral fat" because it surrounds the viscera, or the internal organs of the abdominal cavity.

There are varying estimates on the extent of this problem in the US, but a scientific paper published in *Nutrition Reviews* stated that 30 million Americans have NWO.

A RISKY TYPE OF FAT

The scientific evidence linking NWO to poor health is very strong...

- **Metabolic syndrome, cardiovascular disease, and diabetes.** Metabolic syndrome is a cluster of conditions—including hypertension, high blood sugar, elevated cholesterol or triglycerides, and central obesity—that increases your risk for heart disease, stroke, and type 2 diabetes. In a study published in *European Heart Journal,* people with NWO were four times more likely to have metabolic syndrome than those without NWO.

- **Functional decline.** As one ages, function—the ability to get out of bed, walk, do everyday activities, and take care of yourself—is paramount. As function declines, risk increases for frailty, falls, fractures...and placement in a nursing home. When researchers at Dartmouth-Hitchcock Medical Center analyzed six years of health data for nearly 4,500 adults age 60 and older, they found that women with NWO had a much greater decline in function than women with a normal BMI and waist circumference.

- **Premature death.** Among more than 7,000 patients age 65 and older with heart disease, those with NWO were 29 percent more likely to die during a 7.1-year period than those without NWO, according to a study published in *Mayo Clinic Proceedings.* In research published in *Annals of Internal Medicine,* men with NWO were twice as likely to die over a 14-year period as men who were overweight or obese.

Why would NWO be even more harmful than obesity alone? The main reason is that the component of central obesity that characterizes NWO is particularly inflammatory—and inflammation drives chronic disease, such as heart disease, diabetes, cancer, kidney disease, fatty liver disease, autoimmune disease, and neurodegenerative disorders such as Parkinson's disease.

DO YOU HAVE NWO?

NWO is common, but most people don't know they have it because primary care physicians rarely diagnose it. NWO can be identified by determining your BMI and measuring your waist circumference.* If your BMI is

*To determine your BMI, go to NIH.gov and search "BMI Calculator."

"normal"—between 18.5 and 24.9—but your waist circumference is greater than 40 inches (for men) or more than 34.6 inches (for women), you have NWO.

That may sound like an easy determination, but measuring waist circumference accurately is not that simple. Ideally, a nurse or other trained health professional should do it. But you also can measure your waist circumference by using a cloth tape measure and following these steps (*caveat*: this method may not be 100 percent accurate)...

Put the tape measure at the top of your hip bone. Loop the tape measure around your waist, level with your belly button and level all the way around your body, front, and back.

Important: Make sure the tape measure is snug but not too tight...breathe easily while measuring—and don't hold your breath...take the measurement right after you exhale.

HOW TO PREVENT OR REVERSE NWO

If you have NWO or are concerned about belly fat, you can reverse the condition—or prevent it. *My advice...*

• **Diet.** Follow a nutritionally balanced, evidence-based weight-loss and weight-maintenance diet, such as a Mediterranean-style diet or the DASH (Dietary Approaches to Stop Hypertension) diet. Both plans emphasize fruits and vegetables, whole grains, beans, poultry, fish, and low-fat dairy products, with a minimum of lean, red meat and avoidance of fried foods, refined carbohydrates, and processed foods.

Important: When losing weight, it's important to lose fat, not muscle. To do that, you need to consume enough muscle-building protein—typically a daily protein intake of 15 percent to 25 percent of total calories. Good protein sources include chicken, meat, and nuts.

Caution: Avoid very low-calorie diets for weight loss, which in older adults can cause imbalances in fluids and electrolytes (calcium, magnesium, potassium, and sodium). Never consume less than 1,200 calories daily unless your doctor recommends this and you are under medical supervision.

• **Exercise.** Aim for 150 minutes of moderate-to-vigorous exercise every week.

Examples: Walking for moderate exercise...and jogging for vigorous exercise. Ideally, your routine should also include resistance-training two to three times weekly, along with stretching and balance training.

• **Take vitamin D.** This nutrient is crucial for maintaining muscle mass and strength. Ask your doctor to test your blood level, which should be no lower than 30 ng/mL. If your level is low, your doctor can recommend a supplement dosage tailored to your needs and recheck your vitamin D levels in about eight weeks.

• **Set and monitor goals.** Making and sustaining behavioral changes is difficult, but it can be done. You must decide what you're going to do...track your progress with a daily diary...and adjust your routine to stay on track.

Gum Disease Raises Cancer Risk

After reviewing the records of nearly 150,000 adults, researchers found that periodontal (gum) disease and tooth loss were associated with a 43 percent increased risk for cancer of the esophagus and a 52 percent higher risk for stomach cancer.

Mingyang Song, MD, assistant professor of clinical epidemiology and nutrition at Harvard T.H. Chan School of Public Health and Harvard Medical School, Boston, and leader of a study published in *BMJ Gut.*

Colorectal-Cancer Screening Should Start Sooner Than You Think

Colorectal-cancer screening should start at 45, not 50, which has been the standard recommendation for many years. Most colorectal cancers are found in people age 50 and older, but there has been a significant rise in disease incidence among younger people—12 percent of colorectal cancers diagnosed in 2020 are expected to be in adults under age 50. Black men and women especially should be encouraged to be screened at 45, since African-American communities have high rates of the disease and higher death rates than other groups.

Recommendation by US Preventive Services Task Force to the American Cancer Society. Cancer.org

---

Don't Ignore Bloody Stools If You're Taking a Blood Thinner

Doctors often assume that these drugs cause the bleeding, but four percent to eight peercent of atrial fibrillation patients who have gastrointestinal bleeding while being treated with an oral anticoagulant tested positive for colorectal cancer compared with less than one percent of anticoagulant users without bleeding.

If you see blood in your stool: Consult your doctor and ask about getting a colonoscopy to test for cancer.

Peter Vibe Rasmussen, MD, PhD, research fellow, department of cardiology, Herlev-Gentofte University Hospital, University of Copenhagen.

How to Protect Your Colon: The 5 Essentials

Robert Bresalier, MD, vice chair for research in the department of gastroenterology, hepatology, and nutrition at University of Texas MD Anderson Cancer Center, Houston. He has been a member of several national and international advisory committees aimed at reducing mortality from colorectal cancer.

With the recent death of actor Chadwick Boseman at age 43 from colorectal cancer and the early retirement of Japanese Prime Minister Shinzo Abe at age 65 due to ulcerative colitis, colon health is on many people's minds. How can you best take care of your colon?

That's not a simple question. The colon is not just a simple tube. It is a living, constantly changing organ whose microbiome (the mix of bacteria that call it home) is associated with many forms of serious disease besides cancer and colitis, including neurodegenerative disorders such as Alzheimer's and psychiatric conditions such as depression and anxiety. I'm happy to report that colon health is a very active area of medical research, but mostly what we have now are associations between lifestyle choices and outcomes rather than hard, scientifically proven causations.

Still, with each new finding, recommendations continue to focus in the following very basic areas to give your colon the best fighting chance...

• **Pay attention—even if it's gross or embarrassing.** In recent years, young-onset colorectal cancer (affecting people under age 50) has been on the rise. It is both a preventable disease and one that is highly treatable when it's caught early—but too many young people ignore symptoms that would allow for early intervention.

Understand that when it comes to bowel habits, there is a wide spectrum of "normal" in terms of how often you move your bowels, what the consistency is, and so on. Feeling like you're outside of the norm is not cause for alarm, but seeing a dramatic change in what is normal for you should get your attention. Don't ignore significant and persistent changes in bowel habits such as blood in the stool, constipation, or abdominal pain, any of which could indicate a problem. If a close family member—parent, grandparent, sibling—has had colorectal cancer, be especially vigilant.

• **Get screened.** Even if you have no symptoms, you still should be screened for colon cancer. If you're age 50 or older, most private insurance will cover a colonoscopy every 10 years or less. If you're between ages 40 and 50, check with your provider—colonoscopy typically is covered earlier when there is a family history and then again every five years. Medicare will pay for screening (including colonoscopy) in people age 65 and older or otherwise Medicare-eligible.

You may have heard of alternative screening methods such as fecal immunochemical testing (FIT), which looks for hidden blood in the stool..."virtual colonoscopy" (actually called CT colonography)...or at-home stool tests such as Cologuard, which analyze stool DNA in addition to FIT. These types of tests avoid the small risk associated with the invasive colonoscopy, and the stool tests avoid the unpleasant prep process. Those are fine if you're not in a high-risk group and are symptom-free. Note that insurance usually won't pay for virtual colonoscopy as a first test and coverage varies for Cologuard, but the cost may be substantially less than for colonoscopy. If you don't have insurance or if you have a high deductible that you never meet, you may come out ahead financially with one of these tests, assuming that you are a good candidate for them. Depending on the results, you may need to follow up with an actual colonoscopy. Whatever you do, don't put this off. Early detection is the best tool we have for fighting these cancers.

• **Don't stir up the microbiome unnecessarily.** Doctors are learning more and more about treating bacterial infections such as C. difficile and conditions like irritable bowel syndrome with "good" bacteria (probiotics or, in the case of C. difficile, fecal transplantation from a healthy donor). That has led some people to consume probiotics religiously, thinking that they'll proactively promote bacterial diversity and correct imbalances between "good" and "bad" bacteria in their gut. But they do so without any baseline knowledge about their existing levels and composition of bacteria before they start messing with it. While most probiotics are safe, they vary in their mix of bacteria, and it is unclear what the effects will be on your system and how long they will persist.

Other people undertake "colon cleanses" thinking that they'll flush out bad bacteria and make room for more good bacteria to grow. In fact, what tends to happen after a colon cleanse is that the exact same mix of bacteria grows back. So you may be wasting your money and putting yourself through discomfort for nothing.

Now, if you've been on an antibiotic and experience bowel issues such as diarrhea, it may be worth trying a live-culture yogurt or probiotic supplement to help get things back in balance. But even that is something the medical community needs to learn more about. Although there is a large body of research, the evidence is far from definitive. Persistent symptoms, however, require evaluation by your physician to rule out more serious disease.

• **Engage in physical activity and get plenty of sleep.** We know there's a strong association between regular exercise and colon health, and researchers currently are studying the link between sleep and a healthy colon. As a rule of thumb, things that are good for your heart also are good for your colon, and aerobic exercise is the best example of that. Research shows that physical activity in the form of regular exercise may prevent up to 15 percent of colon cancers and is effective in reducing symptoms of irritable bowel syndrome and other digestive issues.

• **Watch your diet.** It should come as no surprise that what you put into your body matters. Nutrition affects every cell of your body, of course, but it has a direct impact on the gut. Eat a diet with plenty of fruits, vegetables, whole grains, and the omega-3 fatty acids found in fish oil and olive oil. Limit intake of red and processed meats and alcohol. Fiber intake in the form of fruits, vegetables, and whole grains is associated with a lower risk for colorectal cancer across populations, but the reason for this is multifaceted. Other dietary components such as calcium, folate, and vitamin D have been found beneficial. A general "eating well" approach is preferable to targeting specific nutrients. In one study, adherence to a Mediterranean-style diet, as described above, lowered risk for colorectal cancer by up to 11 percent.

• **Limit—or eliminate—unhealthy fats** such as from fried foods, red meat, refined sugars, and processed foods.

If you are a young person, don't cheat yourself by waiting until you're older to clean up your diet. Nutritional interventions are not only most effective when you're young, they also lay the groundwork for a healthier future.

Seaweed May Treat Skin Cancer and MRSA

Studies titled "Bioactive Molecular Networking for Mapping the Antimicrobial Constituents of the Baltic Brown Alga Fucus vesiculosus" and "Pyrenosetin D, a New Pentacyclic Decalinoyltetramic Acid Derivative from the Algicolous Fungus Pyrenochaetopsis sp. FVE-087," both by researchers at GEOMAR Helmholtz Centre for Ocean Research Kiel, Germany, published in *Marine Drugs.*

Among the many resources the sea offers humans are drugs—including life-saving cancer drugs—derived from marine organisms. Unfortunately, the process for developing such drugs is complicated, expensive, and time-consuming, making it impractical to take better advantage of this rich resource.

Breakthrough: Thanks to cutting-edge new technology, scientists were able to dramatically shorten the research process...and discovered compounds that can treat skin cancer and a deadly skin infection in a common type of seaweed.

Normally, it takes up to four years to discover and identify bioactive compounds extracted from algae that might be effective against human diseases. But research scientists at Helmholtz Centre for Ocean Research in Kiel, Germany, used automated computer algorithms to map and analyze the massive chemical and molecular complexity of a type of seaweed called bladder wrack in just months. The algorithms also allowed the team to quickly and accurately identify known and new compounds...and to predict the bioactivity of molecules.

Bladder wrack (*Fucus vesiculosus*) is a brown alga that grows along coastlines of many oceans, including Kiel Fjord, an inlet of the Baltic Sea in Germany and the source for the bladder wrack used in the study. Bladder wrack and other algae living in intertidal zones of oceans develop protective molecules to defend against constant attack from millions of microorganisms found in seawater. Some of these molecules also happen to be active against human bacteria.

GOOD TO KNOW...

HPV Vaccination Should Start at Age Nine Rather Than 12

The vaccine protects against the human papillomavirus. Almost everyone who is not vaccinated will get the sexually transmitted virus at some point. It usually causes no symptoms and goes away on its own. But in some cases, HPV can cause genital warts or even lead to cancer. The American Cancer Society says boys and girls should get the vaccine.

American Cancer Society recommendations, reported at Cancer.org.

Study results: Some of the molecules in bladder wrack were found to inhibit the growth of methicillin-resistant Staphylococcus aureus (MRSA), skin bacteria that cause a potentially deadly infection. In another study, the researchers also examined the symbiotic fungi called Pyrenochaetopsis that naturally grow on bladder wrack and found important bioactive microorganisms that were able to efficiently kill melanoma skin cancer cells.

The researchers pointed out that bladder wrack's therapeutic potential is not limited to drugs. The seaweed is edible and also could be used to make food supplements.

They further predicted that computer-aided learning tools such as used in their study will accelerate the discovery of other active marine compounds that can be used for drug development—and may lead to an unprecedented number of new medications.

Leukemia Breakthrough

A phase 3 clinical trial showed that an experimental drug called CC-486 improved survival in people over age 55 who have acute myeloid leukemia, according to a report in the *New England Journal of Medicine.* Among 472 patients in the trial, those receiving the drug had an average survival from remission of almost 25 months compared with 15 months in the placebo group. The medication was well tolerated and can be taken as a tablet at home. The U.S. Food and Drug Administration has fast-tracked its approval.

New England Journal of Medicine

Irritable Bowel Syndrome Eased by Walking

College students "mildly affected" with IBS reduced the severity of their symptoms from a five to a four (on a scale of one to seven—with anything above five indicating severe symptoms) simply by walking. Those who walked 9,500 steps a day had 50 percent less severe symptoms compared with those who walked 4,000 steps.

Study by researchers at Graduate School of Health Science, Saitama Prefectural University, Japan, published in *PLOS One*.

ALS and the Gut-Brain Connection

In recent years, medical researchers have established a connection between gut health and neurological conditions such as Alzheimer's and Parkinson's. Now they have uncovered a similar connection regarding amyotrophic lateral sclerosis (ALS, also called Lou Gehrig's disease). Comparing two populations of laboratory mice that both had genetic mutations making them vulnerable to ALS, scientists found that ALS development was associated with the mix of bacteria in the gut and that the inflammation associated with ALS could be reduced through the use of antibiotics and fecal transplants from mice with healthy gut biomes.

Study by researchers at Harvard University, Boston, published in *Nature*.

Dangerous Carbohydrate Transformation

Gut bacteria can change carbs into alcohol, possibly contributing to nonalcoholic fatty liver disease (NAFLD), in which excess fat accumulates in the liver. This may explain why some people develop a more severe form of NAFLD known as nonalcoholic steatohepatitis, which can lead to liver scarring and cancer. The bacteria studied essentially act as miniature fermentation vats—which means a test could be developed for the effects of the bacteria, making it possible to diagnose NAFLD in early stages, when it is reversible.

Study led by researchers at Capital Institute of Pediatrics, Beijing, China, published in *Cell Metabolism*.

Your Heartburn Could Be Caused By an Allergy

If you experience heartburn symptoms that don't respond to antacids, it's possible you're suffering from a condition called eosinophilic esophagitis (EoE), a buildup of disease-fighting white blood cells in the esophagus reacting to a food allergy (often milk, wheat, or eggs) or even seasonal allergies. People who have the condition experience pain and difficulty when swallowing, chronic cough, and, for some, heartburn.

A gastroenterologist can diagnose EoE through an endoscopy and a biopsy. Once the culprit allergens have been identified, diet changes and/or allergy medication can be effective treatments.

George Kroker, MD, retired allergist, formerly of Allergy Associates of La Crosse, Onalaska, Wisconsin, quoted on AllergyChoices.com.

Know the Symptoms of a Lung Emergency

Kevin McQueen, MHA, RRT, director of respiratory care, sleep diagnostics, hyperbarics, and wound care at University of Colorado Health, Colorado Springs.

Most respiratory illnesses share the same set of symptoms, making it difficult to determine if you have pneumonia, flu, vaping-related illness, or the coronavirus (COVID-19).

Many people recover with a little rest at home, fever reducers, and fluids. But others progress to a dangerous point before they seek medical care. In fact, five of the 30 most common causes of death are related to lung diseases, according to the World Health Organization.

Individuals who notice a slow progression in their shortness of breath should contact their primary care provider or go to an urgent-care facility.

If symptoms come on rapidly or are severe, seek care at a hospital emergency department. *Key symptoms...*

- **Respiratory distress.** You may climb a flight of stairs and feel "winded," or wheeze or grunt as you inhale and exhale. You might breathe better if you change positions, such as leaning forward. You may sweat but feel cool and clammy. Sometimes, air becomes trapped inside the lungs so you can't take in a normal breath.
- **Significant shortness of breath.** This usually is the key sign that a respiratory illness may be worsening to the dangerous level. Shortness of breath may worsen quickly—sometimes within hours. Stay aware of significant changes in your ability to complete normal daily activities. If you can usually walk several blocks or climb a flight of stairs without becoming winded but your illness makes you short of breath just walking across the room or if you can say only one or two words between breaths, you need medical care.
- **Signs of decreased oxygen levels.** Rapid, shallow breathing or sharp pain when you breathe, especially associated with a bluish tinge in your fingertips or lips, could indicate low oxygen in your blood—seek medical attention.

Having an underlying medical condition, such as cardiovascular disease or lung disease or undergoing treatment for cancer, puts you at greater risk. It's better to err on the side of caution and seek medical attention should you start developing symptoms.

TAKE NOTE...

Danger of Using Petroleum Jelly in the Nose to Moisturize

Breathing in tiny particles of products such as Vaseline or Vicks VapoRub can cause a pneumonia-like reaction called lipoid pneumonia that can cause significant shortness of breath. The condition is rare but in extreme cases can cause significant lung inflammation. Using edible oils—such as vegetable oil—as nasal lubricants also can cause lung problems.

Safer alternative: Saline nasal spray or water-based gel.

Terry Graedon, PhD, medical anthropologist and cofounder of PeoplesPharmacy.com.

Recreational Cannabis Use Can Impair Driving Even After the High Wears Off

Recent finding: Cannabis users who had not used it for at least 12 hours did more poorly on a driving-simulator test than nonusers—they were more likely to exceed the speed limit, run red lights, cross the center line, and hit pedestrians. The effect was most pronounced among those who had begun using cannabis regularly before age 16.

Staci Gruber, PhD, director, marijuana investigations for neuroscientific discovery program, McLean Hospital, Belmont, Massachusetts, and senior author of a study published in *Drug and Alcohol Dependence*.

The Role of Cannabis in Pain Management Is Unclear

Among 295 legal users who were surveyed on their pain levels, health trajectories, and frequency of use, daily cannabis use among those with severe pain was associated with decreased health over a year.

Unknown: Whether more frequent users had more severe health problems to begin with or certain conditions respond better to medical marijuana than others.

Alexis Cooke, PhD, MPH, postdoctoral fellow in psychiatry at University of California, San Francisco. Her study was published in *International Journal of Drug Policy.*

Beware Uncommon Symptoms of Jaw Problems That Lead to a Temporomandibular Joint Disorder (TMJ)

Lesser known signs: Headaches...painful earaches or feeling stuffed up with trouble hearing...neck pain...discomfort when swallowing.

Surprising causes—beyond tooth grinding and clenching: Poorly adjusted orthodontia and dental restorations...trauma, such as whiplash or an upper-body sports injury... cracking your neck...nail biting...chewing on only one side.

Jeffrey Bassman, DDS, director of the Center for Headaches, Sleep & TMJ Disorders in Davenport, Iowa. JBassmanTMJ.com

Maybe It's a Migraine

Deborah I. Friedman, MD, MPH, director the of Headache and Facial Pain Program, University of Texas Southwestern Medical Center, Dallas.

About one-quarter of migraine sufferers have visual symptoms that can look like spots, sparkles, squiggles, zig zags, or flashes.

These are not the same thing as eye floaters, and they don't even originate from the eye: They come from the brain. They can precede migraine pain, occur along with it, or even occur with no headache pain.

It can be hard to tell if what you're seeing is coming from the eye or brain, but one trick is to close one eye at a time. If closing one eye makes no difference in what you're seeing, it suggests that the spots are coming from your brain. If you see something different in each eye, however, it's likely an eye issue. It is possible to have migraine symptoms from one eye only, but it is rare.

Further, when you close both eyes, you can still see migraine aura symptoms, but not floaters. Migraine-related visual symptoms are short-lived. They last for about five to 60 minutes, most often for 30 minutes or less.

Other migraine visual symptoms include fragmented vision (like looking through cracked glass), inability to see the right or left side of the world, tunnel vision, and complete vision loss.

Fight the Rise of Autoimmune Disease

Susan Blum, MD, MPH, an assistant clinical professor in the department of preventive medicine at the Icahn School of Medicine at Mount Sinai, and the founder and director of the Blum Center for Health in Rye Brook, New York. She is author of *The Immune System Recovery Plan* and *Healing Arthritis.* Blum HealthMD.com and BlumCenterFoHealth.com

The immune system is constantly working to fend off viruses, bacteria, and other invaders, but when it becomes overzealous, it can attack the very body it's defending. As a result, runaway inflammation wreaks havoc throughout the body. From rheumatoid arthritis to multiple sclerosis, there are more than 100 conditions attributed to what's called autoimmune disease.

And the problem appears to be growing: According to researchers from the National Institutes of Health, nearly 16 percent of Americans have a biomarker of autoimmunity called antinuclear antibodies, a significant rise from 11 percent a few decades ago.

Research suggests that this increase could be attributed to a handful of factors that are common in the 21st century—a diet loaded with processed foods, chronic stress, an imbalance in the gut microbiota, and a deluge of environmental toxins. Addressing those factors, then, is a good place to start to lower your risk of developing an autoimmune disease or, if you already have one, to get it under control. Here's a look at some of the steps I used to eliminate my own Hashimoto's thyroiditis.

EAT A MEDITERRANEAN DIET

In a recent review paper in the journal *Biomedicines*, Greek researchers reported that the Mediterranean diet is linked to a lower incidence of multiple sclerosis, less severe psoriasis, and better quality of life in patients with rheumatoid arthritis and lupus. This anti-inflammatory diet calms rather than overstimulates your immune system. This diet emphasizes nutrient-rich vegetables and fruits, beans, nuts and seeds, fatty fish, and olive oil, and eliminates white sugar, white flour, and processed foods.

Some people may also want to eliminate foods that contain gluten, a combination of two proteins found in wheat, barley, and rye. In people with celiac disease, gluten triggers an immune response that damages the lining of the small intestine, interfering with the absorption of nutrients from food. A related condition called gluten sensitivity can cause symptoms similar to celiac disease. It's not enough to just cut out bread, though, as gluten can be found in everything from beer to soy sauce.

RELAX

Studies show that stress is a risk factor for autoimmune disease. In October 2020, researchers reported that people who were diagnosed with a stress-related disorder, such as post-traumatic stress disorder, were more likely to be diagnosed with an autoimmune disease and were more likely to develop multiple autoimmune diseases.

To turn off stress, practice a relaxation technique every day. I teach many of my patients a simple, stress-relieving exercise, and use it myself. Sit up in a chair or bed, as erect as possible. Get comfortable and close your eyes. Loosen any clothing that feels restrictive. Breathe deeply, in through your nose and out through your mouth. Now, imagine your belly is soft. This will deepen the breath and improve the exchange of oxygen, even as it relaxes your muscles. Say to yourself in your mind "soft" as you breathe in and "belly" as you breathe out.

As you breathe in, imagine your belly puffing out. As you breathe out, imagine your belly flattening in. Sit quietly and practice "soft belly" breathing for five to 10 minutes. If you notice your mind wandering away, just come back to "soft belly."

HEAL YOUR GUT

About 70 percent of your immune system resides in your gut. The two most important ways to keep your gut healthy are to eat a Mediterranean diet and to take a daily probiotic supplement, which supplies friendly, gut-balancing bacteria. Look for a gluten-free and dairy-free probiotic supplement with 25 to 50 billion colony-forming units of six or more strains of probiotics, with an emphasis on lactobacillus and bifidus strains. Also try to eat more fermented foods and beverages, such as sugar-free yogurt with live cultures, miso (fermented soy paste), kimchee (Korean sauerkraut), and kombucha (fermented green and black tea).

DETOX YOUR ENVIRONMENT

From personal care products to cleaning supplies, our world is filled with toxins. To reduce your exposure, always use natural cleaning supplies and household products Use a HEPA air filter to remove toxins from indoor air.

Don't spray pesticides around or in your home. Look for cosmetics and skincare products that don't contain synthetic fragrances, parabens, or phthalates. Go organic when it comes to fruits and vegetables, and opt for free-range, organic meats and eggs. Filter your tap water. Avoid using plastic bottles and containers with the numbers 3, 6, and 7 on them as they may leach chemicals into their contents. Support your liver, your most powerful detoxifying organ with 600 to 1,200 milligrams of N-acetyl-cysteine each day.

MY STORY

When I was diagnosed with Hashimoto's thyroiditis, I began using the principles of functional medicine to heal myself. Genetic testing showed that I also had an issue with clearing out mercury, resulting in high levels in my body. To take my unique biological patterns into account, I went on a gluten-free diet, stopped eating fish that was high in mercury, had my mercury dental fillings removed and replaced, drank an inflammation-reducing protein shake every day, and took small amounts of thyroid hormone. Two years into my new regimen, my level of thyroid-attacking antibodies had returned to normal. I was energetic instead of fatigued. Maintaining my weight was no longer a struggle. I no longer had any evidence of Hashimoto's.

AUTOIMMUNE DISEASE THROUGHOUT THE BODY

Autoimmune diseases seem different from each other, but that's because antibodies are targeting and attacking tissues in different parts of the body...

- **Thyroid.** When the immune system attacks the thyroid gland, it can cause either Graves' disease (overactive thyroid) or Hashimoto's disease (underactive thyroid).
- **Nerve cells.** When it attacks the myelin sheathing around nerve cells, a process called demyelination, patients can develop multiple sclerosis.
- **Joints.** The immune system can attack the joints, causing the tissue damage and inflammation known as rheumatoid arthritis.
- **Intestines.** If the immune system attacks the microscopic, finger-like protrusions called villi that line the small intestine, it can cause Celiac disease.
- **Mucus-secreting glands.** In Sjogren's syndrome, the immune system attacks mucus-secreting glands, leading to symptoms such as dry eyes and dry mouth.
- **Multiple systems.** In systemic lupus erythematosus, the immune system attacks the skin, joints, kidneys, and nervous system.

Strange Sleep Disorders

Carlos Rodriguez, MD, neurologist and sleep medicine specialist at the Cleveland Clinic's Sleep Disorders Center.

You wake up to find a stranger standing at the end of your bed. You are terrified but unable to move or cry out. This isn't a nightmare—it's sleep paralysis, a type of sleep disorder called a parasomnia. Night terrors, sleepwalking, and exploding head syndrome may sound like something from a science fiction movie, but they are real disorders that can be simply upsetting or downright dangerous.

NREM PARASOMNIAS

When you first fall asleep, you enter non-rapid-eye-movement (NREM) sleep. Your brain cells march in sync, creating slow brain waves and a deep sleep that is hard to wake from. Parasomnias that occur in NREM sleep are called disorders of arousal. You are not sleeping, but your brain is not fully awake either. You usually have no memory of your actions or experiences during an NREM parasomnia.

Sleep terrors strike about three percent of adults and may be triggered by alcohol consumption. They occur when you are suddenly aroused from a deep sleep in a state of fear. You may scream or thrash around in bed. You may be having a fight-or-flight experience with a rapid heartbeat, sweating, and quick breathing. Although your eyes are wide open, you are not fully awake. Sleep terrors usually last a few minutes but can last for up to

40 minutes. When the arousal subsides, the sleeper usually goes back to sleep without remembering the terror. Trying to wake someone from a sleep terror may prolong it.

Confusional arousals are like night terrors without the terror. You may sit up in bed in a foggy state of mind. Although you may seem to be awake, you respond to questions slowly or weirdly. You may act strangely or have a fit of crying. If someone tries to wake you up, you may lash out violently. Like sleep terror, this arousal may be prolonged if someone interferes.

Sleepwalking includes getting out of bed and walking. Although your eyes are open, you are not awake. Your body is switched on, but your brain is still off. You may walk around the house or even go outdoors. Waking a sleepwalker is not dangerous for the walker, but he or she may strike out at you. Sleepwalking tends to run in families. If sleepwalking includes eating, it is called sleep-related eating disorder, which can lead to weight gain or the consumption of odd or dangerous items. There have been reports of people sleep driving.

REM PARASOMNIAS

Later at night, you switch into rapid eye movement (REM) sleep, which is when you dream.

Brain waves during REM are similar to awake brain waves because your brain neurons are more active. During REM sleep, your body is mostly paralyzed, except for breathing and eye movements. This is to prevent you from acting out your dreams. Because your brain is active, it is easy to wake up and remember a REM parasomnia.

Nightmares are different from sleep terrors. Because they occur during REM sleep, they tend to wake you up fully, and you remember them. Although fear is common, nightmares may also cause strong emotions like anxiety or sadness. You may not be able to get back to sleep and may develop insomnia. Frequent nightmares are often a sign of emotional stress or trauma. Repeated nightmares that have the same theme are common with post-traumatic stress disorder (PTSD) and may require treatment with psychotherapy or medication.

Sleep paralysis occurs when REM sleep invades wakefulness and the paralysis of REM sleep invades along with it. In about 50 percent of people, the paralysis also includes a visual hallucination. This parasomnia may be a sign of the disorder called narcolepsy and tends to run in families. Interference from another person with a touch or a noise may help a person break free of this parasomnia.

REM sleep behavior disorder (RBD) may be the most dangerous parasomnia for a sleep partner. RBD occurs when normal sleep paralysis—called atonia—does not prevent you from moving during an action dream. You may act out your dream physically by thrashing, kicking, or punching. RBD may be an early warning of Parkinson's disease. It is more common in people over age 50 and in smokers. It may also be triggered by the use of antidepressants. RBD can be diagnosed with a sleep study and responds well to medication.

Exploding head syndrome (EHS) is a rare parasomnia that occurs in the twilight zone just before falling asleep or waking up. A very loud sound is imagined, like a gunshot or explosion. EHS often occurs in people who are overly tired or stressed. It is more common in women and people over age 50. EHS often responds to restful sleep or stress reduction, but medication may be needed for people with severe sleep disturbance from EHS.

GETTING HELP

The cause of many parasomnias remains mysterious. Some have a strong genetic component and tend to run in families. Parasomnias are more common if you have a disorder that interferes with sleep like sleep apnea, congestive heart failure, or Parkinson's disease. You may be at higher risk if you drink alcohol, are experiencing emotional stress, or if you are not getting enough sleep. Some sleep medications, such as *zolpidem* (Ambien), antidepressants, antianxiolytic, and antipsychotic medications also increase your risk.

If your sleep partner tells you that you are having signs of a parasomnia, take it seriously. Injuries can occur to you or your partner. A parasomnia may also interfere with your ability to get a good night's sleep. These are all good reasons to talk to your doctor. You may need to see a sleep medicine specialist to diagnose your parasomnia and find the right treatment.

Diagnosis may include keeping a sleep diary, getting input from a sleep partner, or having a sleep study. Treatment may include lifestyle changes, creating a safe sleep environment, working with a sleep psychologist, or medications. You may also need to treat an underlying condition like sleep apnea or PTSD.

Multiple Sclerosis Symptoms Improve with Mindfulness Meditation

Studies titled "Mindfulness training for emotion dysregulation in multiple sclerosis: A pilot randomized controlled trial," published in *Rehabilitation Psychology*...and "Effects of 4-week mindfulness training versus adaptive cognitive training on processing speed and working memory in multiple sclerosis," published in *Neuropsychology,* both by researchers at The Ohio State University, Columbus.

People who have multiple sclerosis (MS) deal with more than just physical problems—the disease also causes emotional and cognitive problems. Now, thanks to a new study, there may be an easy way for MS patients to improve both their mental and emotional health.

Bonus: It costs nothing and is drug-free.

Multiple sclerosis (MS) is a neurodegenerative disease that damages the central nervous system. It affects nearly one million Americans, causing among other symptoms, unsteady gait, slurred speech, numbness, tingling, cognitive changes that make it take longer to understand and complete mental tasks, and emotion dysregulation—difficulty managing negative emotions such as depression and anxiety. In fact, up to half of people with MS experience some type of psychiatric disorder.

In a small pilot study, researchers at The Ohio State University looked at whether people with MS would benefit from mindfulness meditation. This kind of meditation, which is known to help with depression and anxiety, focuses perception on awareness and acceptance of the present moment.

Study: Three groups of people with MS (61 total) received four weeks of either mindfulness meditation training...or adaptive cognitive training...or they were placed on a wait list and received no training (the control group). All participants had their cognitive impairment and self-reported emotional control evaluated before and after the four-week intervention.

Mindfulness training consisted of two hours of in-person training each week, plus 40-minutes of daily exercises to perform at home—such as breathing awareness, body scanning, sitting meditation, and focusing on thoughts, emotions, and sensations.

Adaptive cognitive training also included two hours weekly of in-person training plus 40 minutes of different daily exercises to perform at home—reading and video games focused on processing speed (time it takes to understand and react to information), attention, working memory (capacity for retaining information short-term in order to perform mental operations using the information), and executive function.

Results: At the end of four weeks, participants in the mindfulness meditation group were significantly better able to manage negative emotions than the participants of other two groups.

An additional analysis looked at processing speed and working memory. While working memory was unchanged for all three groups, the researchers were surprised to find that the meditation group showed significant improvement in processing speed—surpassing adaptive cognitive training, currently a common and considered effective therapy for MS-caused cognitive impairment.

Since this research involved only a small number of participants, the researchers are hoping to do a larger study to test their findings. Meanwhile, results of the current study are encouraging. Mindfulness meditation is easy to learn and practice—and shows potential to be an important tool to improve the quality of life for people with MS.

2

Medical Matters

How to Survive the Hospital Now

Even before the extensive pandemic that taxed all medical resources, hospitals have been a scary labyrinth of bureaucracy and dangers. New systems such as electronic health records and "hospitalists" theoretically improve things but are far from infallible. *Steps to take whether you are going for a planned surgery or other procedure...*

PRESURGERY/PREPROCEDURE CONSULT

This crucial meeting gives your doctor information about you and your medical history to help your procedure go well and informs you about how to best prepare for it. It typically is held about one week before...but schedule it farther out if you have a serious medical problem, such as COPD or uncontrolled blood pressure or blood sugar. *At this meeting...*

- **Review the hospital's electronic health record (EHR),** updating your current medication and supplement list as well as filling in missing information, such as an omitted specialist, dietary restrictions, and emergency contacts.
- **Bring a written snapshot of your medical history.** This information may not be in your EHR if the doctor doing the surgery or procedure, the hospital/surgical center, and your primary medical doctor are not all in the same network. *Include...*
  - Current supplements and medications with product name, dosage, frequency, and the name of the prescribing doctor.
  - Contact info for all your doctors and what each treats you for.

David Sherer, MD, an anesthesiologist now retired from clinical practice whose career spanned 40 years. He is author of the newly updated *Hospital Survival Guide: The Patient Handbook to Getting Better and Getting Out* and the Bottom Line blog, "What Your Doctor Isn't Telling You" at BottomLineInc.com.

• Other critical facts such as food or latex allergies...medications that have caused negative reactions...past hospital difficulty, such as with intubation or anesthesia...artificial implants, pins, or other foreign objects in your body.

Smart: Also bring copies of this snapshot to the hospital for your anesthesiologist and other medical personnel.

Ask these key questions at this procedure consult...

• **Can I have an early-morning time slot?** The operating staff will be fresher, and you'll have less time to feel hungry or anxious. Also, avoid scheduling surgery in July, when new med-school grads begin their hands-on hospital learning.

• **Which medications and supplements should I take the morning of my procedure?** And how far in advance should I stop others, such as low-dose aspirin, blood thinners, or fish oil, due to bleeding concerns? Don't start anything new to avoid potential interactions with medications you'll be given at the hospital.

• **Should I donate blood in case I need a blood transfusion?** This will depend on whether you're healthy enough to do so and the potential for blood loss.

• **What will my recovery be like?** Ask for an honest assessment of the healing process...whether you'll need special rehab or equipment at home...and any likely side effects.

• **Am I a candidate for *bupivacaine* (Exparel)?** This local, time-released anesthetic injection now is approved for use during many surgical procedures. It may eliminate the need for post-op opioids.

• **What is the hospital/facility policy regarding patient advocates or companions?** Having someone with you is ideal, and fortunately, many facilities now allow a companion to accompany the patient as the coronavirus eases up.

GETTING READY

You know not to drink alcohol the night before a surgery and often you can't eat after midnight. It's also important not to overeat. You don't want bloating and discomfort to spoil your sleep. Your stress levels will be much higher if you don't rest well the night before.

• **Skip all cosmetics and skin-care products the morning of the procedure.** Makeup could get on the surgical team's gloves and into your body. Nail polish could prevent a fingertip pulse oximeter from accurately measuring the oxygen in your blood. Body lotion could keep surgical tape from adhering. *Note*: If your skin is thin or frail, ask that paper tape be used.

• **Pack smart.** For better sleep—thereby better healing—bring eyeshades, ear plugs, your favorite pillow, and a white-noise machine. Personal items, from body wash and lip balm to a tablet computer loaded with books and other diversions, can make the hospital stay less unpleasant. Bring throat lozenges to soothe any soreness from the breathing tube during sedation. Many people feel nauseous after surgery, so consider a wearable antinausea device such as Reliefband or ginger supplements (get the doctor's OK before using).

AT THE HOSPITAL

During check-in, review your EHR again. Yes, it's redundant but still worthwhile.

When you meet with your anesthesiologist before your procedure, alert him/her to reactions you've had to narcotics such as sedatives, your typical pain threshold, and any allergies. The more information you provide, the better he can tailor your anesthesia. Ask about possible side effects and how to get relief. Make him aware of loose teeth, crowns, and other dental work, and if you're used to sleeping with your head on two or more pillows—lying flat for a long time could cause breathing difficulties.

AFTER YOUR PROCEDURE

Answering the same questions every time a staff member enters your room is tedious but helps avoid mistakes, including administering wrong tests and medications. *To stay on top of your care...*

• **Get to know your care givers.** Hospitalists are doctors who work exclusively for the hospital and may be responsible for your post-op care rather than your primary doctor. Chances are you won't meet the hospitalist until you're in your hospital room. Some hospitals rotate hospitalists, so you may have more than one. Engage doctors and staff in pleasant conversation so that they relate to you as a person rather than by your ailment.

There are more staffing shortages than ever before, and some tasks may have been offloaded to untrained nurse assistants—their badges might read "patient care associate" or "patient care partner." Make sure that only qualified nurses insert IVs, catheters, and gastric tubes, change sterile dressings, treat damaged skin, and give injections.

• **Don't be shy.** When an unfamiliar staffer enters your room, check his/her badge and ask about his credentials and why he's there. If you have a legitimate concern, politely but firmly say, "I'd like to speak with my doctor first to be sure this is something I'm supposed to have."

Confirm that you're getting the right doses of the right meds—generics of your daily medications can look different from what you take at home. Any time you're given a medication, ask what it is and why. Also, remind the doctor or nurse about any allergies. Write down the drug name, dosage, and frequency for your records.

If many doctors are involved in your care, when one orders a major procedure or changes your treatment, make sure the hospitalist(s) and your own doctor are notified.

• **Watch when your dressings are changed so you'll know how to care for yourself at home.**

• **Ask if telemedicine can be used to contact specialists at other institutions if your case needs an expert consult and also for your follow-up visits.**

• **Transition to recovery at home as soon as you can.** Even before COVID-19, hospitals were hotbeds of germs. A silver lining of the pandemic is that many safety practices, such as frequent handwashing, single-use gloves, gowns, and face masks or shields are now standard, but ask all staff to follow these measures if they aren't.

Don't Let Medical Care Take Over Your Life

Mary Tinetti, MD, professor of medicine and public health and chief of geriatrics at Yale University School of Medicine in New Haven, Connecticut. She is the author of more than 200 peer-reviewed papers, a MacArthur Foundation Fellow, and a leader of the Patient Priorities Care initiative, which conducts research into and disseminates information about Patient Priorities Care. PatientPrioritiesCare.org

If you've got a chronic illness such as heart disease, diabetes, cancer, or arthritis, staying on top of your medical care is essential. But the truth is, it also can take a lot out of you.

A trip to the doctor or lab can take up to half a day when you include transportation and waiting time. Medications can sap your energy and cloud your thinking, while special diets and exercises can put a crimp in your lifestyle.

If you have more than one chronic condition—as do 67 percent of adults age 65 and older—you can double, triple, or quadruple your doctor visits, tests, and medications. It's no small wonder that many patients feel overburdened by their medical care.

Your health is precious to you, because it allows you to live your life the way you want—to do activities that bring you pleasure and to connect with people you love and give meaning to your life. If you must sacrifice whatever makes life worth living, you may wonder what's the point of that health care?

In an ideal world, medical care would fix our health problems and allow us to have full, rewarding lives without any hassle or discomfort. But in reality, trade-offs are almost always necessary. We must decide what's truly important to us and what we're willing to give up for the sake of our health.

Better way: A new approach looks at the way a person's medical care fits with his/her life priorities so that smart choices can be made by patients and their doctors. *Here's how...*

WHAT ARE YOUR PRIORITIES?

Everyone's priorities are different. For one person, it means being free enough from pain to be able to walk more. Another wants to keep a clear head and remain alert enough to drive—even at the price of some discomfort.

While you are the expert in what matters most and what you're willing to do or give up in a trade-off, your doctors are experts in how to achieve your goals. That's why you need to work together. Helping people do that is the idea behind "Patient Priorities Care," a program designed and developed by a research team that includes patients, doctors, and scientists at Yale University, New York University, and Baylor College of Medicine.

In a pilot study, the research team showed that this approach, which incorporates the patient's assessment of how his/her life priorities fit into treatment decisions, can work in a busy medical practice. A member of the health-care team can help patients identify their health priorities—what they want to focus on in their health care while clinicians can learn how to align their care with these priorities—all without much extra time. Patients and clinicians report liking this approach.

Based on the program's principles, the American Geriatrics Society has recommended that doctors put these ideas into action when working with older adults who have multiple medical conditions. And the research group is working to expand the program into the health-care community at large.

PUTTING PATIENTS FIRST

When using this program, patients are guided by a nurse or other health-care professional through a systematic process to specify their personal health outcome goals and identify the aspects of their medical care that they feel either advance these goals or are too difficult, burdensome, or unhelpful.

Participants begin by identifying their "core values" that don't change as life circumstances and health change—things that mean the most to them, such as relationships, independence, longevity, and physical and mental capacity. They then pinpoint specific, achievable activities linked to their core values. For one person, it may be seeing her grandchildren every week...for another, it may be a desire to be strong and clear-headed enough to travel.

Doctors and other health-care professionals are trained to elicit and respond to patients' concerns...and to tailor treatment to what they value. Communication in both directions—patients getting their needs and values across, and doctors making it clear what goals are realistic and what trade-offs will be involved—is essential.

TRY THIS AT HOME

Even though Patient Priorities Care was designed for use with professional guidance, you can gain many of the same benefits on your own.

***STEP 1:* Start by creating a road map of your own priorities by considering what aspects of life you value most.**

For example, ask yourself...

- What relationships mean the most to you?
- What gives you particular pleasure?
- What aspects of function do you value most highly—for example, independence... keeping your mind sharp...maintaining physical abilities...and/or learning new things?
- What do you most want from medical care? For example, is a long life or highest quality of life more important? What about freedom from pain?

***STEP 2:* Consider three specific, realistic activities that allow you to realize these core values—ones that you'd hate to give up.**

Examples: Walking to the park daily to see friends...driving yourself to your weekly poker or bridge game...traveling abroad with a loved one.

***STEP 3:* Consider what aspects of your health care help you achieve these goals—** for example, medication that relieves pain so you can walk or regular exercise that boosts your mood.

***STEP 4:* Consider three aspects of your health care** (for example, medications, health-care visits, tests or procedures, or self-management tasks) that get in the way of achieving your goals or that you find too difficult or burdensome. Examples might include drugs that make you too tired to socialize...or a prescribed diet that forbids your favorite foods.

***STEP 5:* Once you have identified your personal priorities, work with your doc-**

tor—or doctors—to align your health-care goals with them. Your task is to make your doctor understand that even though optimal results for each of your diseases are desired, other things also matter—maybe even more—to you.

These conversations may be challenging. Doctors are trained to focus on diagnosing diseases and then choosing effective treatments for them. But if you say very explicitly what you care about, they will find it hard to ignore.

Be simple and direct: "I really want to focus on being able to visit my family regularly, so what should we work on to enable me to do this?"

Also, share what aspects of your health care you think make it hard to achieve your goals. The more information the doctor has, the better you can work out trade-offs with acceptable risks and optimal benefits. For example, if you have diabetes, you may be willing to stick to a diet that helps stabilize your blood sugar but want to forgo taking insulin shots because of the inconvenience of the shots and difficulty that you have self-administering them. You are willing to consider oral medications that help control your blood sugar.

Another trade-off might be to reduce blood pressure medications that make you too tired or dizzy to complete your desired exercise routine even if it means a small increase in your risk of having a stroke down the road.

It's an ongoing process. Whenever the doctor prescribes new medication or orders tests, ask, for example, "Staying physically active is what really matters to me. Is this treatment/test likely to help me do it better?" Keep your goals flexible, too. A change in your condition, such as a stroke or worsening of arthritis, may alter what you can realistically expect to achieve.

Lead Shielding Does Not Protect During X-rays

It has been recommended since the 1950s to guard patients' testicles and ovaries. But new studies show shielding has unintended negative effects. Shields are hard to position properly and often miss the areas they are meant to protect. Even when placed correctly, they can obscure the areas doctors need to see...they can cause machines' automatic exposure controls to increase radiation in an attempt to see through the shield...and they do not protect against radiation scatter, in which radiation ricochets inside the body and ends up affecting internal tissues. The amount of radiation needed for a modern X-ray is about one-twentieth what it was in the 1950s, and no measurable harm from it has been found after a search through decades of data. Several physicians' groups now recommend that shielding be discontinued as a routine practice.

Roundup of experts on lead shielding and X-rays, reported at KHN.org.

Build Your Team of Medical Experts

Charles B. Inlander a consumer advocate and health-care consultant based in Fogelsville, Pennsylvania. He was the founding president of the nonprofit People's Medical Society, a consumer-advocacy organization credited with key improvements in the quality of U.S. health care, and is author or coauthor of more than 20 consumer-health books.

We encounter and rely on a number of medical professionals to maintain our health or recover from an illness or surgery. For example, aside from the doctors I see regularly, members of my team include my local pharmacist, several nurse practitioners (NPs) and physician assistants (PAs) who work in medical practices I use, a psychologist who helped me with some post-surgical depression, and a physical therapist who helped me recover from brain surgery. I call them my team of experts because I know I can call upon any of them to answer my medical questions or help guide me to the information I need.

This approach has worked well for me, so let me give you some tips on creating and using your own team.

• Assembling your team. Creating your team is easy. First, make a list of physicians you see on a regular basis, such as your primary care doctor, and any specialists you use, such as a cardiologist, dermatologist, or oncologist. Next list any non-physician practitioners you see at any of those practices, such as an NP or PA. For example, I regularly see an NP at my dermatologist's practice, so she is on my list. Now list any other medical professionals you use, such as a psychologist, medical social worker, or chiropractor. Put the pharmacist (or pharmacy) you use most often on the list.

• Using your team. Your team should be your primary resource when you have a medical issue. If you have a question about a medication you are taking or are experiencing some unexpected side effects, your pharmacist might be the first person to contact. More than anyone, a pharmacist is likely to have the information to deal with your issue. Quite often, he or she would be the ideal person to contact your prescribing doctor and discuss it.

When I have a question about following home treatment prescribed by my doctor, I usually call the NP or PA for help. Again, they will consult with my doctor if necessary. This is especially useful if you are home recovering from surgery.

• Coordinate your care. Because we see numerous medical professionals, and all of them are busy, important information about your care or treatment is often not shared between your doctors. That puts the onus on you to make sure your team is up-to-date. Inform each member of your team if you have a medication change, new diagnosis, or are undergoing treatments. Coordinated care helps avoid unnecessary duplicate tests or expensive office visits, and can help your care team make better decisions. Most practices now have online portals where you can enter this information, but you can also simply call or write your team members with any updates.

Make the Most of Video Visits with Your Doctor

John L. Bender, MD, family medicine physician and senior partner at Miramont Wellness Center in the Fort Collins, Colorado area, past president of the Colorado Medical Society and a pioneer in the implementation of telemedicine in his state. He has written various pieces of legislation governing telemedicine. Miramont.us

Telemedicine technology has been ramping up for some time, but the need for health-care alternatives in the face of the coronavirus pandemic led to it being adopted at warp speed. Even some injuries can be managed by video chat.

Whether your telemedicine visit is with one of your existing providers or via a telehealth-service doctor you have never met, here are the steps to take before and during your appointment to get the most out of it.

• Test out the software. Health systems and medical practices have various telemedicine applications to choose from, so unless all your specialists belong to the same network, the software may be different from one provider to another. You may need to install a mobile app—some software works only on a tablet or a smartphone rather than on a computer—or sign up for an online account with a telemedicine platform.

Once an appointment has been made, you may receive a text or an e-mail with a link and directions for you to test the system and fill out forms. Don't wait until the last minute in case you need time to troubleshoot. You'll be guided through a few screens to make sure your camera and speakers can be accessed... that you can see and hear the doctor...and that you can be seen and heard by him/her.

In order for some telemedicine programs to work correctly, you may be prompted to exit other programs or close out of other websites. If your home Internet connection is spotty, you might try running the test on your various devices to see if the platform works better on one than on another.

• Take your vital signs. With a few moderate-cost devices, you can perform many of the health checks a nurse would do in the office and report them to your provider. *Depending on the nature of your call, these can be very helpful...*

- Thermometer
- Bathroom scale
- Blood pressure cuff (you may have a lower reading at home because you're more relaxed).

You can take your pulse on many gadgets and track atrial fibrillation on an Apple Watch.

If you're managing a chronic condition and haven't invested in monitoring tools—such as an advanced blood glucose monitor for diabetes that can store and relay information to your doctor's office or a fingertip pulse oximeter for measuring blood oxygen if you have COPD—now may be the time. Some or all may be covered by insurance. Getting these readings from you in advance helps the doctor prepare for your appointment.

- **Create a script of your symptoms and concerns.** This will help you stay focused and ensure that you don't omit any details or questions, especially if it feels awkward to communicate through a screen. State your list of concerns at the beginning of the appointment so that issues can be prioritized, and the time will be well-managed from the start. If you have a visible issue, such as a swollen joint or a rash, take clear, straight-on photos and send them to the doctor as a text or e-mail attachment. This is usually a lot easier than trying to find the right angle at which to hold the affected area up to your device's camera during the appointment.
- **Have a written health history to refer to.** Of course, this is essential if you're talking to a telemedicine-service doctor you've never met, but even if you're meeting with a member of your existing medical team, be prepared to succinctly communicate the pertinent parts of your medical history as a reminder for your provider. While all of this information should be in your doctor's records on you, reviewing it all helps prevent errors. It should include a detailed medication list with product names, dosages, and frequency and the names of the prescribing doctors...any allergies (this will help to prevent drug interactions if the telemedicine doctor e-prescribes a new drug)...a list of significant hospital stays and surgeries...and any other information that could be pertinent to why you're being seen. If there's a chat box, you can use it to type in complex drug names.
- **Be patient.** As in a real office, you might experience a wait time.
- **Get past any self-consciousness.** As surprising as this sounds, even when sick, some people suddenly worry about how they look when they see their face on the screen. One of my patients actually aimed the camera at her feet! Remember that we've seen it all before and we want to see you—eye contact and nonverbal cues assist in making a diagnosis.
- **Have your care advocate with you.** Just as your spouse or another loved one—or your caregiver—might accompany you to an office visit, he/she can be on the virtual visit, too, whether to describe symptoms, provide tech help, or take notes.
- **Take and read back notes.** This is important because you can't just turn to the nurse for clarification after the doctor leaves the examination room as you might if you were in the office. Ask if any instructions can be e-mailed to you.
- **Clarify the follow-up.** A virtual visit might lead to an in-person checkup if your condition doesn't improve or if your problem needs a physical examination. If it is a check-in to see how you're managing a chronic condition, you may be able to schedule your next visit virtually as well. If your next step is a lab test, ask whether the script will be sent to you or straight to the lab and how the results will be communicated to you.

As telemedicine technology continues to advance and as patients and doctors get better at using it, it will become even easier to access care without leaving your home.

Best Health-Monitoring Devices to Have at Home

Andrea Chymiy, MD, MPH, a family physician in private practice in Poulsbo, Washington. She is a Medical Reserve Corps coordinator, an Urban Search & Rescue team physician and an emergency-preparedness blogger. LeftyPrepperMom.com

When it comes to routine health care these days, you're more likely than ever to meet virtually with your doctor. Having the right home health devices can help you provide necessary data to your doctor. *What everyone should have...*

HEART-RATE APP

Why own one: A suddenly elevated or reduced pulse may signal a severe medical problem. And while phone apps lack the accuracy of professional equipment, they can give you a close idea.

What to look for: A highly rated app with an easy-to-use interface that works off your phone's camera—it takes pictures of your fingertip to calculate your heart's rhythm.

Top pick: For iOS, Cardiograph Classic ($0.99, App Store). For Android, Instant Heart Rate (free to use for heart-rate monitoring, but other features cost $9.99 per month, Google Play).

PULSE OXIMETER

Why own one: Normally you wouldn't need this fingertip blood-oxygen–measuring device unless you had a lung disease. But low blood oxygen has been linked with COVID-19, so pulse oximeters have been flying off shelves.

What to look for: Easy use (single button)...large display.

Top pick: ClinicalGuard CMS-50DL Finger Pulse Oximeter (about $15, widely available).

BLOOD PRESSURE MONITOR

Why own one: Blood pressure is an important statistic in medical emergencies as well as routine virtual visits.

What to look for: One-touch operation, a clear display and mobile/cloud data storage

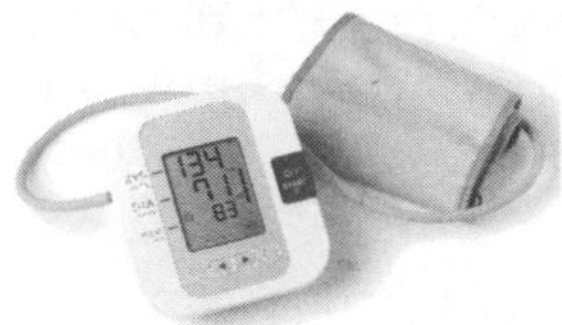

and sharing. Get a cuff that goes over your bicep, not your wrist, and choose an established brand with a track record of reliability.

Top pick: Omron 7 Series ($89.99, Omron HealthCare.com).

BATHROOM SCALE

Why own one: Sudden weight gain or loss can indicate serious illness. Weight change of five percent or more up or down in less than a week, assuming you're not trying to lose weight, should be discussed with your doctor.

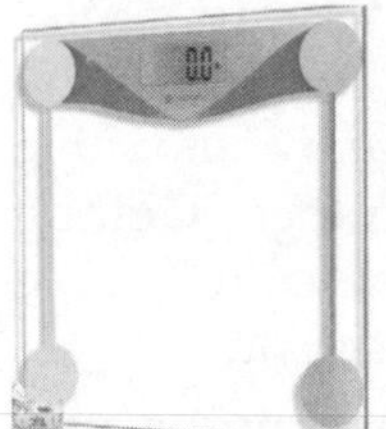

Measure your weight weekly to know your baseline and so you don't miss dramatic changes.

What to look for: Simplicity, sturdiness, and a backlit display.

Top pick: Etekcity Digital Body Weight Bathroom Scale ($19.99, widely available).

THERMOMETER

Why own one: To diagnose fever. A temperature greater than 100.4°F is considered a fever.

What to look for: Something practical and easy to use. The general consensus among doctors is that oral thermometers are most accurate. If you prefer something faster, go for an in-ear or on-forehead, also called temporal, model. All are accurate, but in-ear temperature usually is 0.5°F higher than oral, and forehead temperature is usually 0.5°F lower.

Top picks (all widely available): For an oral thermometer, iProven Digital Thermometer (about $10). For in-ear measurements, Braun ThermoScan 7 ($59.99). For a forehead thermometer, iHealth Non Contact Infrared Thermometer ($24.99).

OTOSCOPE

Why own one: This device is recommended for parents of young children and for adults who are prone to ear infections. A quick YouTube search for an explanatory video will give you enough know-how to discern between healthy ear tissue and infection.

What to look for: 5X magnification and a glass lens for greater clarity.

Top pick: Dr. Mom 4th Generation LED Pocket Otoscope ($28.92, DrMomOtoscope.com).

Images: GettyImages

The Right Way to Measure Your Blood Oxygen

Timothy Connolly, MD, medical director of respiratory care services at Houston Methodist Hospital. HoustonMethodist.org

Pulse oximeters, which use infrared light to painlessly measure blood-oxygen levels, became popular during the pandemic, since some COVID-19 sufferers experience dramatic—and dangerous—drops in blood oxygen without realizing it. *Here's what you need to know about using this device...*

- **Pulse oximeters can't diagnose COVID-19.** A normal reading is not evidence that you don't have COVID-19. The majority of people who are infected never see any change in their blood-oxygen levels. But if you have been diagnosed with COVID-19, low blood-oxygen levels could be a sign that the infection has led to a potentially dangerous pneumonia and that you should contact your doctor to see if you should head to the hospital.

- **Some people have low blood-oxygen levels all the time.** That's especially common among people suffering from chronic lung diseases such as COPD, pulmonary fibrosis, and congestive heart failure. If you consistently get readings below 94, mention it to your doctor and ask him/her what pulse oximeter reading you should consider problematic, especially following a COVID diagnosis.

- **To ensure an accurate reading, take your blood-oxygen levels at least a few times when you're healthy to establish your normal level.** Before you put the device on your finger, spend a few minutes moving around to get your blood pumping...and warm up your hand, such as by putting it under your armpit—cold hands are a common cause of inaccurate, low readings. Which finger you use doesn't matter.

Warning: Fake fingernails or dark nail polish—black, purple, or dark blue, in particular—interfere with accuracy. Remove these from at least one finger before using a pulse oximeter...or use the device on a toe.

- **A single low pulse oximeter reading doesn't necessarily mean a problem.** Take a few readings from both hands to rule out a bad reading before calling your doctor or visiting the emergency room—one hand might have better blood circulation than the other. If you can get one reading within normal range, there's no reason for concern—when pulse oximeters provide varied results, the highest reading is most likely to be a true reflection of your blood-oxygen levels.

HOW OFTEN TO CHECK?

I do not recommend that the general public routinely monitor their oxygen levels. Individuals with chronic health conditions that may involve low oxygen levels should discuss monitoring programs with their health-care providers.

If an individual has been diagnosed with COVID-19 and is recovering at home, there is no perfect recipe for how often to check. Taking a reading every few hours while awake is reasonable. Make sure to check both at rest as well as during activity such as walking around. Furthermore, if new symptoms develop at any point such as chest pain or worsening cough, a quick oxygen check won't hurt.

EASY TO DO...

Trusted Health Resources

The National Institutes of Health has a directory of hotlines for help with Alzheimer's disease, arthritis, burns, stroke, and many other medical topics. Visit NIH.gov/health-information/health-info-lines.

NIH.gov

Expert Update: Aspirin for Heart Attack Prevention

Gregory S. Thomas, MD, MPH, FACC, MASNC, the medical director of cardiovascular program development for the MemorialCare Heart & Vascular Institute in Southern California.

Nearly 30 million Americans over the age of 40 take a daily "baby aspirin" to prevent a first heart attack or stroke, a strategy medical experts call primary prevention. That includes about half of Americans ages 70 and older who don't have cardiovascular disease (CVD), or about 10 million people. But many of those 30 million people might be making a debilitating—or even fatal—mistake. Here's why.

Your blood clots when microscopic, plate-shaped blood cells called platelets stick to one another, a process called platelet aggregation.

Ordinarily, that's a crucial biological function: Without it, you could bleed to death. But artery-clogging blood clots are also the cause of most heart attacks and strokes.

Daily, low-dose aspirin—typically 81 milligrams (mg)—reduces platelet aggregation, thereby reducing the risk of a heart attack or stroke. A major study published in the *Journal of the American Medical Association* found that taking low-dose aspirin cut the risk of a heart attack by 32 percent in men 45 and older, and the risk of a stroke by 24 percent in women 55 and older.

That's the benefit. Here's the risk: Aspirin's antiplatelet action can cause major internal bleeding, which can be debilitating or even deadly. In one survey, 82 percent of patients who stopped taking aspirin did so because of gastrointestinal (GI) bleeding, such as a stomach ulcer, and 33 percent stopped because of cerebral (brain) bleeding. Forty-four percent had major bleeding in other parts of the body.

Medical experts think that the bleeding risk is reasonable when taking low-dose aspirin to prevent a second heart attack or stroke (or if you're at very high risk for a first)—a medical strategy called secondary prevention. But experts are now saying low-dose aspirin is often not worth the risk in primary prevention. What's changed?

THE DECLINE OF ASPIRIN

Twenty years ago, the risk of heart attack and stroke in the United States was 25 percent higher than it is today. Healthier lifestyles, less smoking, the use of statins, better medical control of blood pressure and blood sugar, and other medical advances have led to this remarkable decrease in risk.

When the risk of cardiovascular disease was higher, taking a daily, low-dose aspirin benefited middle-aged and older people—even healthy people without a previous heart attack or stroke.

But today, the risk of aspirin for primary prevention outweighs the benefits. Many recent studies support that conclusion.

THE LATEST RESEARCH

In one study, published in the *New England Journal of Medicine*, more than 15,000 people with diabetes but without cardiovascular disease took either a daily 100-mg dose of aspirin or a placebo. After seven years, those taking the aspirin had a 12 percent lower risk of "major cardiovascular events," such as a heart attack or stroke. But they also had a 29 percent higher risk of major bleeding events, such as GI bleeding from an ulcer, sight-threatening eye-bleeding, or brain bleeding from a hemorrhagic stroke.

In another study of more than 19,000 healthy people in their 70s, those who took 100 mg of aspirin a day were at increased risk of death from any cause, compared with people who took a placebo. They did not have fewer heart attacks and strokes.

In fact, the study was ended early because aspirin wasn't showing any benefit. But it showed plenty of risk, with a higher incidence of major bleeding among the aspirin-takers, leading to transfusions, hospitalizations, surgery, or death.

Researchers reported in *The Lancet* in 2018 that healthy people age 55 and older who took 100 mg of aspirin daily for many years had no reduction in CVD. In a sample of 12,000 people, they found no reduction in angina, heart attacks, mini-strokes, or deaths from CVD.

Looking at 67 other studies on the benefits and risks of aspirin, an international team of researchers concluded that taking aspirin for primary prevention lowered the risk of a first, non-fatal heart attack or stroke by 17 percent—and increased the risk of GI bleeding by 47 percent and the risk of brain bleeding by 34 percent.

The results from these and other recent studies led the American Heart Association and the American College of Cardiology to recommend that most healthy people over 70 with bleeding risk (such as peptic ulcer disease, which afflicts one in 10 Americans) should not take low-dose aspirin to prevent CVD.

Similarly, the Canadian Cardiovascular Society no longer recommends aspirin for primary prevention in healthy people. In fact, the U.S. Food and Drug Administration (FDA) has released a statement saying it "does not believe the evidence supports the general use of aspirin for primary prevention of heart attack or stroke" because of the "increased risk of bleeding in the stomach and brain."

BOTTOM LINE

For most people, taking aspirin for primary prevention is no longer the right choice: The risks outweigh the benefits. If you're currently taking aspirin for primary prevention, discuss the treatment with your primary care physician or a specialist.

IS PRIMARY PREVENTION FOR YOU?

There are several key factors to take into account when deciding whether or not to take low-dose aspirin for primary prevention.

- **How old are you?** People under age 45 rarely have a high enough risk of CVD to justify taking low-dose aspirin for primary prevention. Similarly, the newest research shows that low-dose aspirin is unlikely to benefit people ages 70 and older.

- **Do you have metabolic syndrome?** About 40 percent of Americans over the age of 40 have metabolic syndrome, a combination of high blood pressure, high blood sugar, excess body fat around the waist, and abnormal cholesterol and triglyceride levels. People with the condition have about a one in six chance of having a first heart attack within 10 years—the same level of risk for a second heart attack in people taking aspirin for secondary prevention.

- **What's your 10-year risk of a heart attack or stroke?** Anyone who has a 10 percent or higher risk of having a first heart attack or stroke in the next 10 years should probably take low-dose aspirin.

- **Are you taking another nonsteroidal anti-inflammatory drug (NSAID)?** Aspirin is in a class of drugs called NSAIDs, all of which increase the risk of GI bleeding. If you're taking another NSAID daily—for example, *ibuprofen* for arthritis—it is not a good idea to also take low-dose aspirin. (For those taking aspirin for secondary prevention, the risk of combining an NSAID and aspirin daily also may be too high.) Corticosteroids and selective serotonin reuptake inhibitors, such as *sertraline* (Zoloft), *citalopram* (Celexa), and *escitalopram* (Lexapro) also increase the risk of bleeding.

- **Have you experienced bleeding from a stomach ulcer?** If so, adding low-dose aspirin to the mix is not a good idea for primary prevention (and it's borderline for secondary prevention). Likewise, severe kidney or liver disease puts you at much higher risk for an internal bleed.

---

3 Questions to Ask Before You Start Statins

Jamal S. Rana, MD, PhD, award-winning heart researcher, preventive cardiologist and chief of cardiology at Kaiser Permanente's Oakland Medical Center and president-elect of American College of Cardiology, California Chapter.

Cardiovascular disease remains the leading cause of death in the U.S. To help combat unnecessary deaths, national guidelines by the American College of Cardiology/American Heart Association (ACC/

AHA) suggest that in addition to a healthy lifestyle, people at risk should talk with their doctors about taking cholesterol-lowering statin drugs. Research shows that these drugs help stop buildup of plaque in arteries, a main risk factor for heart attack and stroke, and may stabilize already built-up plaque.

Although statins were initially approved to reduce high cholesterol levels, the definition of "high cholesterol" has changed through the years, as has the consideration of statins for other related health concerns. In addition to those with established heart disease, statins now are recommended for people ages 20 to 75 with an LDL-cholesterol level of 190 mg/dL or higher...patients with diabetes ages 40 to 75 (have a risk-benefit discussion with your doctor if you're younger or older)...or with a 10-year calculated risk for heart disease of 7.5 percent or higher (more on this factor below). Some of these criteria are clear-cut, but others are more of a gray area. *Here's what you need to know before you say "yes" to a statin prescription...*

TWO TYPES OF PREVENTION

When considering statins to prevent heart attack and stroke, there really are two types of prevention. Primary prevention relates to people who have never had either of these events and are trying to prevent one from happening in the first place. Secondary prevention relates to people who already have had a stroke or heart attack, which puts them at high risk for a second one in the future.

There's no controversy regarding the benefits of statins for secondary prevention. All people who have had a heart attack or stroke, in addition to striving for a healthy lifestyle with exercise and a healthy diet, should be taking statins. For these patients, it is a lifelong commitment as they remain at high risk for a future event.

The statin decision is more nuanced when it comes to primary prevention. The guidelines recommend them for a broader range of people than ever before due to our better understanding of risk enhancers. But the value of statins has to be evaluated in the context of your personal health history and weighed against the concern surrounding side effects, such as muscle pain or weakness, headaches, and dizziness. A careful evaluation of the combined answers to three key questions can help clarify whether these statins are right for you.

THE 3 QUESTIONS

1. What is my ASCVD Risk Score? At the heart of the widening scope of who should take statins is the Atherosclerotic Cardiovascular Disease (ASCVD) Risk Calculator, created by the ACC/AHA and used by doctors to evaluate their patients. You can take it online at ClinCalc.com/cardiology/ASCVD/PooledCohort.aspx.

After plugging in information—such as cholesterol (total, HDL, and LDL), blood pressure, age, race, gender, and whether you have diabetes or are or were a smoker—the tool rates your 10-year risk of having a heart attack or stroke. You'll note that there are no questions about diet or exercise in this questionnaire. If you are exercising regularly and eating well, your blood pressure and cholesterol levels would reflect the impact of those healthful behaviors.

Results fall into four categories...

Low: Below 5 percent

Borderline: 5 percent to 7.4 percent

Intermediate: 7.5 percent to 19.9 percent

High: 20 percent or greater.

Interpreting the low and high scores is very easy. If you have a low score, statins generally are not recommended—you can feel reassured that you're in good shape. If you're at high risk, many doctors recommend starting a statin—its preventive benefits have been proven. You may be able to lower the dose over time by making healthy lifestyle changes.

If your score is borderline or intermediate, the statin decision is more nuanced. Also, no risk calculators are perfect. In research conducted at Kaiser Permanente, we found that there was risk overestimation among adults without diabetes between ages 40 and 75, which could lead to unnecessary statin therapy. In fact, at Kaiser Permanente, we are in the process of implementing our own calculator that will address this problem. But for now, the ACC/AHA ASCVD Risk Calculator is a useful tool.

Benefits to knowing your ASCVD Risk Calculator score: Your result can trigger a useful discussion with your doctor and encourage you to look at lifestyle habits that could help reduce your risk for heart disease. A healthy lifestyle remains the cornerstone of prevention of heart disease and stroke. Rather than starting statins, you might try to lower your risk through improved diet, exercise and, if you smoke, quitting.

2. Do I have any "risk enhancers"? These factors increase your heart attack and stroke risk but currently are not part of the ASCVD Risk Calculator questionnaire...

- Having a family history of premature heart disease—before age 55 in men...age 65 in women
- Having LDL cholesterol of more than 160 mg/dL
- Having metabolic syndrome, a group of risk factors that include high triglyceride levels, high blood sugar, high blood pressure, and excessive body fat around the waist
- Having chronic kidney disease
- Having an inflammatory condition such as rheumatoid arthritis, psoriasis, or HIV/AIDS
- Menopause before age 40
- Having had a pregnancy-related circulatory condition such as preeclampsia
- Being part of a high-risk ethnic group, such as South Asian
- Having a biomarker such as Lp(a) (a type of low-density lipoprotein—LDL—cholesterol) levels of 50 mg/dL or higher.

3. What is my CAC score? A low-radiation imaging test detects the level of coronary artery calcium (CAC) buildup in your arteries. The presence of such plaque buildup is associated with risk for future heart attacks. If there is a question about the merits of taking a statin, having this test may help indicate whether you will benefit. Results are given as a number, from zero to, in some cases, more than 1,000.

0: This shows no calcium or calcified plaque buildup so no statin would be recommended in the absence of diabetes, family history of premature heart disease, and smoking.

1 to 99: You have some degree of calcium buildup that can help guide the statin decision-making process. Having a lower number might allow you to put off statins and adopt a lifestyle of good habits. However, if you're over age 55 and have plaque development and are at the higher end of this range despite a healthy diet and regular exercise, taking a statin merits consideration.

100 and over: This score suggests that statin therapy should be considered.

A recent study published in *Circulation: Cardiovascular Imaging* added to our understanding of the CAC score and differences in how it predicts heart attack and stroke. *It found that...*

- **The 10-year risk level for both heart attacks and strokes for those with scores of 1 to 99 is below 6 percent.**
- **At scores of 1 to 99, stroke risk is higher than heart attack risk for women...and the reverse for men.**
- **With a CAC score of 100 or higher, the 10-year heart attack risk jumped above 12 percent for men and 8 percent for women.** Stroke risk averaged 8 percent, with a woman's risk again higher than a man's.

Benefits to knowing your CAC score: As a real-time snapshot, the CAC is a visual reinforcement of your risks and can help encourage lifestyle changes even if you've been resistant.

IF YOUR DOCTOR SUGGESTS STATINS...

If statins seem wise for you, ask your doctor if you can take a low dose to minimize any side effects.

While natural practitioners may recommend supplements of CoQ10 and/or vitamin D to help prevent statin side effects, their effectiveness has not been demonstrated in randomized control trials. However, both have good safety profiles, so there is no harm in trying them to see if they help.

WHEN THERE'S TIME TO PUT OFF STATIN THERAPY

The first and foremost step in preventive cardiology is lifestyle changes—following a plant-based diet focused on vegetables, fruits, whole grains, nuts and seeds, and unsaturated fats (such as olive oil)...eating less animal protein and minimal added sugars...getting more exercise...and losing weight if needed. Losing just five percent to 10 percent of excess body weight can lead to significant improvement in cholesterol as well as blood pressure.

We know these changes are more difficult than taking a pill, but remember that statin therapy is not an alternative to healthy eating and exercise—it's an added preventive measure to consider when those steps aren't enough.

Robotic Device Helps Stroke Survivors Move

Scientists have developed a computer program that can capture brain activity to determine how a person wants to move. The program relays the information to a robotic exoskeleton that moves the affected limb. The device is fully controlled by the user's intentions.

University of Houston

GOOD TO KNOW...

Speech Therapy After Stroke Does Not Have to Be Rushed

When a stroke survivor loses the ability to speak, there's a perceived need to give intense therapy to help him/her recover communication ability as quickly as possible, and therapy often ends within 12 weeks. New research shows no benefit to this approach. While early intervention is important, spreading out therapy over many months may be better.

Erin Godecke, PhD, senior research fellow in speech pathology at Edith Cowan University, Joondalup, Australia, and leader of a study published in *International Journal of Stroke.*

Don't Be Misdiagnosed

David E. Newman-Toker, MD, a professor of neurology, ophthalmology, and otolaryngology at the Johns Hopkins University School of Medicine in Baltimore. He is also the president of the Society to Improve Diagnosis in Medicine.

An 83-year-old woman had diarrhea, which her doctor said was a side effect of her diabetes medication. She was treated with a change in medication and diet but received no further tests. Several years later, she was diagnosed with incurable metastatic colon cancer. A 36-year-old man suffering from fatigue and lethargy was diagnosed by different doctors with depression and anemia. Months later, an examination showed he had endocarditis, a bacterial infection that had destroyed one wall and two valves of his heart.

A nurse had a severe headache that radiated to her shoulders and waistline. A doctor diagnosed her with a tension headache and prescribed pain medication. She collapsed several days later, after which doctors discovered she had a ruptured blood vessel in her brain.

DEFINING MISDIAGNOSIS

These are true stories of misdiagnosis, or diagnostic error.

In general, there are two types of misdiagnoses: Doctors miss the opportunity to treat a dangerous disease, or they mistakenly treat a person for a disease or health problem they don't have. Most diagnostic errors occur in primary care, though some happen at the hospital. And they're very common. Experts say most people will experience at least one diagnostic error in their lifetime.

DIFFERENT TYPES OF HARM

Yearly, an estimated 500,000 to one million people suffer permanent disability or death because of a misdiagnosis. Millions more aren't disabled or killed, but they are permanently harmed. Others endure serious short-term suffering, such as ending up in an intensive-care unit for weeks on end. Still others deal with lower levels of suffering for longer periods. For example, a patient of mine suffered from near-constant dizziness. She had seen two neurologists, two ear-nose-and-throat specialists, and two psychiatrists, all of whom concluded that she had psychological problems. But I was able to diagnose her with vestibular migraine, an unusual form of migraine that may cause dizziness without headaches.

There's also psychological harm. As with my patient, many misdiagnosed patients have been told they are imagining it or their problem is all in their head—an insensitive comment that can cause psychological trauma. Patients may lose faith in doctors and the health-care system.

THE BIG THREE

Health problems that affect tens of millions of people, such as fractures and high blood pressure, are commonly misdiagnosed. But some rare problems are misdiagnosed, too, such as spinal abscess, with 20,000 to 30,000 yearly cases and a misdiagnosis rate of 65 percent; and aortic dissection, with 50,000 to 100,000 yearly cases and a misdiagnosis rate of 25 to 35 percent.

New research by my colleagues at the John Hopkins University School of Medicine and I show that diagnostic errors in three categories of illness generate 50 percent of all disability and death from misdiagnoses. *In fact, just 15 diseases in those three categories are the main causes of serious, permanent harm...*

- **Vascular events,** including stroke, heart attack, venous and arterial thromboembolism (blood clots in the legs, feet, arms, or groin), and aortic aneurysm and dissection (a bulge or tear in an arterial lining);
- **Infections,** including sepsis, meningitis, encephalitis, spinal abscess, pneumonia, and endocarditis; and
- **Cancer,** including lung cancer, breast cancer, colorectal cancer, prostate cancer, and melanoma.

BEFORE, DURING, AND AFTER

Avoiding misdiagnoses in these three categories could save 100,000 lives every year, including your own. *And you can help your doctor do it by taking three steps...*

- **Come prepared.** Before your primary care visit, put together a one-page, easy-to-read list of your symptoms and the timeline during which they occurred. This helps you avoid a common mistake—talking about what previous doctors have said. The executive summary also saves precious time. Instead of the doctor spending 10 to 15 minutes finding out about your symptoms, he or she can spend that time thinking about what caused your problem.
- **Ask this key question.** As a patient, you have to guide the doctor in giving you a detailed explanation about what he or she thinks is going on.

To do that, ask this question: "What is the worst problem this could be and why is it not that problem?"

This forces the doctor to give you specific information. For instance, if your major symptom is dizziness, you're hoping to hear something like this: "The pattern of my findings is consistent with vestibular neuritis, an inflammation of a nerve in your ear, which causes dizziness. The problem I'm most worried about is stroke, but there is substantial evidence that my findings in this exam confirm your problem is vestibular neuritis."

This shows that the doctor is thinking clearly and systematically about the problem and can articulate the rationale for the diagnosis. It also shows that he or she is thinking about making sure you don't get harmed by a diagnostic error.

However, if the doctor says something like, "You don't need to worry about that," or "I see a lot of this, and it is very common," you should immediately find another doctor or at least get a second opinion. Research from the Mayo Clinic shows that 87 percent of patients who seek a second opinion leave with a refined or changed diagnosis (66 percent refined, 21 percent changed, and 12 percent confirmed).

- **Stay vigilant.** During your visit, your doctor will give you a treatment plan, such as, "This problem should go away by itself in a week," or "Take this pill, which should solve the problem." However, when things don't go according to plan, patients tend to think they have received the wrong treatment. If you've been given a pill, you might think you need a higher dose or a different medication.

But you may not have the wrong treatment for the right disease: You might have the right treatment for the wrong disease.

If you're not getting better, it's time to make sure your diagnosis is correct and to keep the possibility of diagnostic error on the physician's radar by giving the office a call.

Checking Out Hospitals

Charles B. Inlander, a consumer advocate and health-care consultant based in Fogelsville, Pnnsylvania. He was the founding president of the nonprofit People's Medical Society, a consumer-advocacy organization credited with key improvements in the quality of U.S. health care, and is author or coauthor of more than 20 consumer-health books.

There is an old saying that the last place you want to be when you are sick is in a hospital. While there is a lot of truth to that statement, it's likely that, at some time in your life, you will need a hospital, and a little research now can make sure you go to the best facility.

As recently as 30 years ago, there was virtually no publicly available information about the safety and quality of individual hospitals. Patients went to the facilities where their doctors put them, not knowing if it was the right hospital for their needs. As a result, facilities had no impetus to improve.

But because of consumer demand, that has all changed. Today, consumers can access numerous sources that rate and even compare hospitals by patient safety, quality of care, and outcomes.

PATIENT SAFETY

Patient safety is a major problem in many hospitals. Up to 20 percent of patients leave a hospital with a condition they did not have when they entered. That includes potentially deadly infections (called nosocomial or hospital-acquired infections), injuries because of falls, or reactions to inappropriate or wrongly administered medications. Hospitals are required by law to keep track of these issues and make them public. An independent, nonprofit organization called the Leapfrog Group uses that information to give hospitals patient safety grades that you can access for free. Just go to HospitalSafetyGrade.org and enter a city or zip code.

QUALITY OUTCOMES

The federal government and most states have excellent websites that help you compare the quality of hospitals. Go to Medicare.gov and click the Providers & Services drop-down menu and you will find ratings of just about every hospital in the country. There, you can see an overall quality score, recent patient ratings and comments, and inspection data related to specific procedure outcomes, such as coronary bypass surgery.

The site also provides ratings for nursing homes, home care agencies, and medical practices. Most states also provide hospital outcome data. Do an online search asking for hospital outcomes and your state name. You can also call your state or local health department to help you find information.

ASK QUESTIONS

Don't be afraid to ask questions at your local hospitals. If you are contemplating surgery, contact the hospital's medical director and find out how many of the same surgeries they perform each year. While the same information is important about your doctor, remember that most care in a hospital is provided by nurses and technicians. The more a procedure is done at a hospital, the better they get at it.

THE BEST HOSPITALS

Several websites purport to rank the best hospitals in the country by areas of specialty, such as heart disease, cancer, or pediatrics, but no two sites use the same criteria. The magazine *US News & World Report* publishes one of the most popular and extensive surveys at https://health.usnews.com/best-hospitals. It's a good source to review as part of an overall assessment strategy.

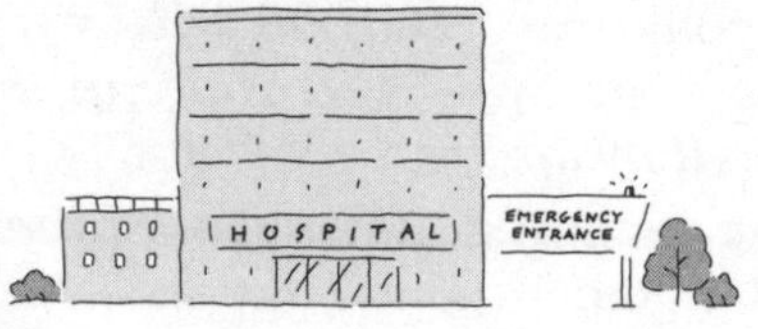

TAKE NOTE...

Before You Say "Yes" to Outpatient Surgery

Make sure the outpatient facility has medications for anesthesia-induced complications on hand and the health-care providers know how to use them. *Dantrolene* treats malignant hyperthermia, a reaction to general anesthesia. Intralipid treats reactions to local anesthetics. Such dangerous reactions are rare, but patients have died when doctors were not properly trained in their use...or when the meds were expired or not on hand at the facility.

David Sherer, MD, retired anesthesiologist and author of *Hospital Survival Guide: The Patient Handbook to Getting Better and Getting Out.*

Cannabis Use Before Surgery

If you use cannabis (including THC and/or hemp-derived CBD products), tell your doctor and anesthesiologist before surgery. In a study of 118 patients undergoing surgery to repair leg fractures, regular cannabis users required more anesthesia, reported more pain, and received 58 percent more daily opioids during their hospital stays. Regular cannabis use may affect pain tolerance.

Ian Holmen, MD, an anesthesiology resident at University of Colorado School of Medicine, Aurora. His research was presented at the annual meeting of the American Society of Anesthesiologists.

Beware of AFib After Any Surgery

David Sherer, MD, retired anesthesiologist and author of *Hospital Survival Guide: The Patient Handbook to Getting Better and Getting Out.*

Atrial fibrillation, the most treated heart rhythm abnormality in the United States, is a worrisome and sometimes complex medical issue. It occurs when the atrial upper chambers of the heart's four chambers (two atria or auricles and two ventricles) beat erratically and ineffectively. Patients who suffer this often describe a "skipping," "flip-flop" sensation or other unusual feeling in their chests and can complain also of fatigue, dizziness, and lightheadedness. Some patients have no symptoms at all. Atrial fibrillation (abbreviated AF or AFib), affects 2.7 million Americans and places people who leave it untreated at a five times greater risk of stroke and a doubled risk of cardiac-related death.

The traditional treatments for AF have been effective in lowering these risks, and they include medication, cardioversion (a non-invasive surgical option), and ablation (a more invasive surgical option).

Many of the medications are structured to control the heart's ventricular rate, which often gets accelerated due to the spastic and disorganized activity in the atria. The atria in a normal heart conducts electrical impulses to the lower chambers, the ventricles, so that the heart beats in an organized and effective way.

Cardioversion is an electrical shock to the heart designed to restore normal heart rhythm (also known as "normal sinus rhythm," named for the sinus node in the heart, the bundle of nerves that help regulate the heartbeat).

Ablation is a surgical procedure formulated to electrically excise the abnormal focus of tissue that is causing the atria to go into spasm. It requires general anesthesia to accomplish that. Another less invasive option is a new technique that removes a part of the atrium, the "appendage," that is responsible for the faulty electrical signals. Finally, there is invasive treatment for AF, usually associated with other cardiac surgery.

But while AF alone is of concern, there has been increased attention paid to the presence of AF following surgical procedures, and this is something to look out for. *The Journal of the American Medical Association* (JAMA) has reported that after non-cardiac surgery, a number of patients present with a new onset of AF, which places them at a 2.69 increased hazard ratio for subsequent stroke or transient ischemic attack (the so-called mini-strokes).

The National Institutes of Health in an older report (1995) found that between 0.4 percent and 26 percent of post-operative patients, depending on the study, developed AF. This post-surgical AF can be temporary or permanent. It requires monitoring and follow up to know which. And if permanent, it requires treatment.

Researchers postulated that there were a number of factors that contributed to that, including increased pain, increased sympathetic nervous system activity, low blood oxygen, low blood or plasma volume, too much acidity to the blood, abnormally low blood glucose, inflammation, and other factors. That's why it is so important for doctors, nurses, and the rest of the medical team keep these parameters as normal as possible in the immediate after-surgery period. It's also vital that patients and their loved ones inquire whether these abnormal factors are present.

The good news: If AF does not develop within days of surgery, most likely it will not occur because the contributing factors mentioned above will have abated. Some higher risk patients may want to consider the advice in this new study presented at the American Heart Association's Scientific Sessions 2020 concerning 24-hour-a-day monitoring for 30 days after heart surgery.

So the next time you go in for surgery, particularly if you are older, have existing significant medical history (high blood pressure, heart disease, diabetes, inflammatory diseases, or cancer, among others), have an advocate, family member, friend, or other trusted person ask the staff if your heart rhythm has remained stable in the after-surgery period. This is an often overlooked but vital parameter that requires attention should any abnormalities arise. In these days of over-stressed healthcare and hospital systems, it behooves you to be your own advocate, especially in something as important as your beating heart.

Reduce Delirium Risk After Surgery

Background: Up to 65 percent of older adults develop postoperative delirium—sudden and severe confusion after undergoing surgery.

Recent finding: Patients who regularly exercised (walking, sports, cycling, dancing, etc.) five to six days a week before surgery were 73 percent less likely to develop postoperative delirium than those who were sedentary, according to a study of 132 men and women older than age 60 who underwent orthopedic surgery.

Even better: Those who were mentally active (for example, by knitting or doing crossword puzzles) had an 81 percent lower risk.

Susie S. Lee, MD, MS, assistant professor of anesthesiology, Albert Einstein College of Medicine, New York City.

Alcohol and the Brain

Bankole A. Johnson, MD, DSc, the Dr. Irving J. Taylor professor and chair of the department of psychiatry and the pharmacology director of the Brain Science Research Consortium Unit at the University of Maryland School of Medicine. He is author of *Six Rings: Preparedness and Restoration: Beyond Imagined Borders of Brain Wellness and Addiction Science.* SixRingsBooks.com

Many people may be surprised to learn that a moderate level of alcohol is just one drink per day for women and two for men. Just eight drinks for women and 15 for men over the course of a week is considered excessive, and research shows that it's associated with a host of illnesses, from gastrointestinal disorders to liver disease, high blood pressure to increased cholesterol, and heart attack to many cancers.

Drinking heavily can affect the part of the brain that is responsible for motivation, appetite, emotions, and memory. Over long periods, it can cause short- and long-term brain damage that manifests as dementia, confusion, visual disturbance, hallucinations, and delusions. It can actually alter brain chemistry, creating psychological conditioning that limits a person's ability to control the desire to drink.

If excessive drinking becomes uncontrollable, it can tip into alcohol use disorder (AUD). People with AUD develop tolerance to the effects of alcohol, suffer from withdrawal symptoms when they are not drinking, and may experience cravings and a compulsion to keep drinking after starting.

IN THE BRAIN

People drink because it feels good. It can ease stress, lower shyness, and make things more fun. All of those positive feelings come from an increase in the neurotransmitter dopamine. As the production of dopamine molecules rises, receptors in the brain rush to meet them. This helps stimulate a system in the brain that governs emotions the cortico-mesolimbic system. Three structures in this system are crucial elements in producing pleasure and can move some people from casual drinking to AUD.

- **The hippocampus** can remember everything about the experience of drinking alcohol with extreme clarity. It will capture the "high" as well as the people, places, objects, smells, and tastes associated with drinking. When a person drinks, the hippocampus triggers the production of dopamine by firing off another neurotransmitter, glutamate. Glutamate helps the brain receive a signal that it is about to experience something good.

- **The amygdala** then goes into overdrive, producing a strong, emotional response.

- **The insular cortex** plays a role in the way people consciously seek pleasure from food, alcohol, or drugs.

Over time, alcohol can damage this system and other parts of the brain, creating an imbalance between neurotransmitters, like dopamine, and their receptors. The brain's ability to interpret and respond to dopamine becomes dulled, so the cortico-mesolimbic system responds by demanding more input. For someone with AUD, that can translate to a craving for more alcohol.

RETHINKING TREATMENT

Excessive drinking, then, is a brain disorder. The most common approach to treating AUD, however, is based on talk therapy and self-help, which ignores the biological underpinning of the disease. About 60 percent of AUD is biological. The most successful treatments address both biology and psychology with the use of medication.

NALTREXONE

Drinking activates opioid receptors, and *naltrexone* (ReVia, Depade, Vivitrol) is an opioid antagonist. It blocks those receptors and prevents the pleasurable response to drinking. If a person drinks while taking the medication, they simply won't get the high feeling. As a result, naltrexone can help reduce the number of days a person drinks each month, as well as the number of drinks consumed.

A course of the treatment can last three months to one year or longer. With several months of abstinence strung together, naltrexone essentially gives the brain a chance to reconfigure itself, separating good signals from bad ones and making more logical connections. A person whose life used to revolve around alcohol has an ever-increasing chance of long-term abstinence.

The Combining Medications and Behavioral Interventions for Alcoholism (COMBINE) study showed that a combination of the medication naltrexone and brief counseling curtailed drinking and enhanced abstinence among people with AUD. Side effects can include sleep problems, tiredness, anxiety, headache, joint and muscle pains, abdominal pain and cramps, nausea, and vomiting.

TOPIRAMATE

Topiramate (Topamax) was developed to treat epilepsy, and it is approved by the U.S. Food and Drug Administration to prevent migraines. Psychiatrists have used it to treat bipolar disorder and counteract the weight gain associated with some antidepressants. It has also been investigated for use in treating obesity, binge eating, post traumatic stress disorder, bulimia, obsessive-compulsive disorder, smoking cessation, cocaine dependence, and AUD.

Topiramate appears to be particularly effective for reducing cravings and increasing abstinence in people who are still drinking. First, it blocks the ability of glutamate to increase dopamine. Since glutamate is involved in the process of long-term memory, blocking it holds back the pleasurable feelings associated with memories of drinking. Second, topiramate enhances the production of gamma-aminobutyric acid, which suppresses dopamine output, reducing the pleasurable effects of drinking.

What's in a Drink?

In the United States, one drink contains roughly 14 grams of pure alcohol, which is found in…

- **12 ounces of regular beer**
- **8 to 9 ounces of malt liquor**
- **5 ounces of wine**
- **3 to 4 ounces of sherry or port wine**
- **1.5 ounces of distilled spirits**
- **2 to 3 ounces of cordial liqueur.**

For different types of beer, wine, or malt liquor, the alcohol content can vary greatly. Check labels or the bottler's website for specific information.

In two large-scale clinical trials, topiramate helped improve all drinking outcomes. One of the studies reported that heavy drinkers were six times more likely to remain abstinent for a month when taking topiramate even in small doses. Participants taking topiramate had fewer drinks during a drinking day, fewer heavy drinking days, more days abstinent, and were less likely to binge drink when compared with the placebo group. Half of everyone in the topiramate group reported less craving for alcohol.

Topiramate is most effective when it is paired with brief counseling on a weekly basis. Most patients need to be treated for six months to one year to decrease the possibility of full-blown alcohol relapse. Topiramate can have side effects that include weight loss, fatigue, a feeling of pins and needles, mental slowness, and kidney stones.

ONDANSETRON

Ultra-low-dose *ondansetron* (AD04, in development) is a serotonin-3 receptor antagonist. Serotonin helps to regulate appetite, sleep, memory, learning, and mood. The serotonin system modulates the effects of other neurotransmitter systems, including the cortico-mesolimbic dopamine system. Many antidepressant drugs act by regulating serotonin levels in the brain.

Blocking serotonin receptors decreases dopamine release and, as a result, lessens the craving for alcohol. This treatment is targeted for people with a specific genetic composition. It was shown to work for the subpopulation of 35 percent of people of European or Hispanic descent who have a specific genotype of key genes in the serotonin system. In a pivotal phase 2b clinical trial, ultra-low-dose ondansetron reduced the number of drinks per drinking day, increased abstinent days, and decreased the percentage of heavy drinking days in that specific population.

Ondansetron is currently used for the treatment of vomiting, but the lowest dose currently available commercially is 12 times higher than the dose required to treat AUD. That ultra-low dose of ondansetron is not commercially available, but it is in a phase 3 trial that is scheduled to be completed in 2022. Side effects can include headache, constipation, and fatigue.

ACAMPROSATE

Acamprosate (Campral) works as a relapse-prevention drug. The glutamate system remains highly active and seeks out additional stimulation even after alcohol intake stops, causing negative emotions and sometimes withdrawal symptoms. Acamprosate is thought to restore normal glutamate activity in the brain. Acamprosate has been found to be most effective when combined with behavioral interventions focused on preventing relapse.

Side effects can include diarrhea, constipation, nausea, stomach pain, loss of appetite, headache, drowsiness, dizziness, weight changes, muscle/joint pain, change in sexual desire, or decreased sexual ability.

Breakthroughs in Migraine Relief

Alexander Mauskop, MD, founder and director of the New York Headache Center (NYHeadache.com), and a professor of clinical neurology at SUNY Downstate Medical Center. He is author of the books *The Headache Alternative* and *What Your Doctor May Not Tell You About Migraines.*

Up to 40 million Americans suffer from migraine headaches, 75 percent of them women. Symptoms can include throbbing head pain, nausea, vomiting, sensitivity to light and sound, fatigue, and dizziness.

Sobering statistic: According to the World Health Organization, migraine is the second-leading cause of disability, with only back pain causing more downtime.

To prevent or relieve migraines (which can strike as often as every couple of days), doctors prescribe two types of drugs—preventive, to stop attacks before they start; and abortive, to stop attacks once they've begun.

PREVENTIVE DRUGS

Preventive drugs have plenty of problems. None of them were developed specifically to prevent migraines. Drug by drug, each was accidentally discovered to block migraines—which means they deliver a host of unwanted side effects. *These problematic drugs originated for a variety of conditions...*

• **Beta-blockers,** such as *propranolol* (Inderal) and *timolol* (Blocadren), are usually prescribed for hypertension. Common side effects include fatigue, lightheadedness, shortness of breath and, in migraineurs, low blood pressure.

• **Anti-seizure drugs,** such as *topiramate* (Topamax), are used for epilepsy. They can cause memory loss, osteoporosis, and hair loss. They can also cause birth defects—a big risk for premenopausal women.

• **Antidepressants,** such as *amitriptyline* (Elavil) and *nortriptyline* (Pamelor), can cause insomnia, weight gain, and loss of libido, as well as distressing withdrawal symptoms if you suddenly stop taking the medication.

• **Botox** is best known as the anti-wrinkle drug. For migraines, the dose is five to six times higher than that used for cosmetic purposes. It's injected once a month in the back of the head, in the neck, and in the shoulders. Botox is the safest and most effective of the preventive drugs, but the U.S. Food and Drug Administration (FDA) has approved it only for chronic migraineurs who have 15 or more migraine days per month.

Because of the many downsides, only 20 percent of migraineurs who are prescribed preventive therapy stay on the drug long term.

NEW DEVELOPMENT

Twenty-five years ago, scientists discovered that a chemical called calcitonin gene-related peptide (CGRP) is released in the brain during a migraine. CGRP's exact causative role in migraines isn't yet understood, but it may stimulate the sensory nerves that cause or contribute to the pain.

After decades of research by drug manufacturers, with hundreds of millions of dollars invested, six CGRP-blocking drugs were approved by the FDA in 2019 and 2020. They're proving to be reasonably effective and mostly safe in preventing migraines. About 30 percent of people who try them get good results—with one out of five of those experiencing dramatic relief (75 percent to 100 percent reduction in migraines), and one out of two experiencing a 50 percent reduction.

So far, CGRPs have been used by more than 300,000 migraineurs, with very few side effects. For some people, they work when no other drug does.

Here's what you need to know about this new class of drugs and how they might work for you or your loved ones...

CURRENT OPTIONS

There are currently four preventive CGRP drugs on the market, with a fifth likely to be approved within a year or so. There are also two migraine-abortive CGRPs.

• **The injectable preventive CGRPs.** Three drugs, *fremanezumab* (Ajovy), *erenumab* (Aimovig), and *galcenezumab* (Emgality), are self-administered by a push-button device where you don't have to see the needle.

Aimovig and Emgality are injected once a month. Ajovy is injected either once a month or as a triple dose once every three months.

Sometimes, the results are cumulative: The second treatment is more effective than the first, and the third treatment is even better.

The three drugs have slightly different mechanisms of action. Aimovig blocks the CGRP receptor on cells, whereas Ajovy and Emgality block CGRP itself. While none of these drugs consistently works better than the others, in about 10 percent to 20 percent of cases, Ajovy or Emgality might work better than Aimovig. If you're taking a monthly drug, try it for at least three months before giving up on it.

Warning: Some people develop constipation on Aimovig. In about 100 cases, the constipation was so severe that surgery was necessary to resolve the problem. If you have constipation, don't take this drug.

- **The intravenous preventive CGRP.** *Eptinezumab* (Vyepti) is delivered intravenously at the doctor's office once every three months. This might be the right drug for you if you don't like injecting yourself and because there's only one treatment every three months.
- **The oral abortive CGRPs.** *Rimegepant* (Nurtec) and *ubrogepant* (Ubrelvy) stop a migraine that's starting. They are prescribed only if the gold standard for abortive drugs—the triptans, such as *sumatriptan* (Imitrex)—have failed.
- **An oral preventive CGRP.** Atogepant is a migraine-abortive drug that is expected to be FDA-approved sometime in late 2021.

Here's the rub: These drugs are very expensive—around $600 per treatment. Currently, they're covered by insurance only after every other preventive drug has failed.

A DIFFERENT TYPE OF DRUG

- ***Lasmiditan* (Reyvow).** This new migraine abortive drug was approved by the FDA in December 2019.

Like the triptans, it works on serotonin receptors: Triptans work on 1B and 1D receptors, while Reyvow works on 1F.

Why this matters: Reyvow doesn't cause vasoconstriction of blood vessels so, unlike Imitrex, it's not contraindicated for people with cardiovascular disease.

If you have cardiovascular disease, don't respond to a CGRP abortive drug, or have side effects from a triptan, this may be the abortive drug for you.

Caution: Reyvow can cause drowsiness. Don't drive a car for eight hours after taking the drug.

NON-DRUG OPTIONS

- **Nerivio** is a new, FDA-approved electrostimulator that eased migraine pain in two out of three people who tried it in a clinical trial. Placed under the upper arm for 45 minutes at the first sign of a migraine, it generates a low-level electrical current that activates nerve fibers to block pain messages from reaching the brain.

A prescription product, it costs $99 for 12 self-care treatments. It isn't covered by insurance. Many patients find it very effective when combined with an abortive drug such as Imitrex, and some find the device useful on its own to abort a migraine. You can find out more about the Nerivio device at Theranica.com.

- **Allay Lamp.** This non-prescription lamp was invented by Harvard-based migraine researcher Rami Burstein, PhD. Knowing that migraineurs are affected by light, he studied each color in the spectrum, first in rats and then in people, to see which worsened migraine and which made it better. He discovered that green light was the only color that eased migraine—and created the green-generating Allay Lamp.

How to use it: When you feel a migraine coming on, go into a room, close the shades, turn off all other sources of light (including your smartphone, computer, and TV screens), and spend an hour or two with the Allay Lamp turned on. (It provides enough light to read or work.) The lamp costs $149. You can learn more at AllayLamp.com.

Steroids for Asthma Linked to Osteoporosis

Patients receiving the most oral steroids had 4.5 times higher odds for osteoporosis...1.6 times higher from inhaled steroids. This steroid risk has been known in other health conditions but not for asthma.

Asthmatics: Use steroids sparingly. If you take steroids orally for two months or more, ask your doctor if a bone-protection treatment using bisphosphonates is for you, though there are reports of osteonecrosis of the jaw and atypical fractures with them. Vitamin D and calcium may protect bones, but data are scarce.

Christos Chalitsios, MSc, a PhD candidate at University of Nottingham, UK, and leader of a study published in *Thorax*.

Popular Drugs That Can Lead to Eye Problems

Theresa M. Cooney, MD, associate professor of ophthalmology at University of Michigan Kellogg Eye Center in Ann Arbor and Michigan Medicine's Kellogg Eye Center in Milford. Her research has been published in *British Journal of Ophthalmology* and other leading professional journals.

When your doctor writes you a prescription for, say, a blood pressure medication, a drug for prostate problems or even a nasal spray for your allergies, you probably don't think about your eyes. But you should.

Medications that treat a wide variety of medical conditions can lead to blurry vision, cataracts, glaucoma, and even blindness.

To help protect yourself, you should get a baseline eye exam before taking one of the medications below and schedule follow-ups at the frequency recommended by your ophthalmologist (typically annually or every four to six months, depending on the drug).

Important: Be sure to report any eye-related side effects, including distorted vision or eye pain, to your ophthalmologist.

Nine widely used medications that can harm your eyes...

• ***Hydroxychloroquine* (Plaquenil).** This drug, which has been studied as a treatment for COVID-19, was originally used to treat malaria but now is widely prescribed for inflammatory diseases such as lupus and rheumatoid arthritis. When used for five or more years, hydroxychloroquine can cause damage to the macula, the central part of the retina where light-sensitive nerve cells are located in the back of your eye.

This side effect is insidious because symptoms usually don't occur until there's retinal damage. Even if the drug is discontinued, the impairment may be irreversible. In a recent study in *Arthritis & Rheumatology*, nearly eight percent of lupus patients who had the highest average blood levels of hydroxychloroquine developed maculopathy, an eye disease that can result in complete loss of central vision.

Self-defense: Get a baseline eye exam by an ophthalmologist followed by annual exams...and exams as needed after five years of hydroxychloroquine use. The goal is to remain on a weight-based dosage of less than 5 mg/kg per day.

• **Steroid nasal sprays.** Like oral and topical corticosteroids, steroid nasal sprays, such as *fluticasone* (Flonase) and *triamcinolone* (Nasacort), can increase your risk for cataracts and glaucoma. Widely used for allergies, these sprays can be problematic because they are available in prescription and over-the-counter (OTC) versions—and both types carry similar risks for eye damage.

Self-defense: Do not use an OTC steroid nasal spray unless you are advised to do so by your physician. If your doctor does recommend it, try to use the medication sparingly and ask about alternative treatments that do not contain steroids. Daily nasal salt rinses can be safer and cause fewer side effects.

• ***Digoxin* (Lanoxin).** This common heart medication can cause blurry vision and halos around bright objects. These drug-induced visual changes usually mean that you have too much in your system, called digoxin toxicity.

Self-defense: If you experience eye symptoms while taking digoxin, ask your doctor to reduce the dosage. Do not make changes to your medication without consulting your physician.

• **Blood pressure medications.** When taking these drugs, blood pressure can sometimes fall too low, making you feel light-headed or dizzy. If blood pressure is consistently too low, damage to the optic nerve, called optic neuropathy, can occur due to a decreased blood supply.

Self-defense: To decrease your chances of developing this serious side effect, ask your physician if it is OK to avoid taking your blood pressure medication at night, when blood pressure naturally drops during sleep. Do not make any medication changes without first consulting your doctor.

• **Bisphosphonate drugs.** *Alendronate* (Fosamax) and other drugs within this class are used to help prevent osteoporosis. In rare cases, a bisphosphonate can cause inflammation of the eye called uveitis. Symptoms include eye pain, redness and blurry vision. The inflammation stops when you discontinue the drug, but always check first with your doctor.

Self-defense: If you have eye symptoms while taking a bisphosphonate, ask your physician about the osteoporosis drug *denosumab* (Prolia, Xgeva), which may be safer for your eyes.

• ***Tamoxifen* (Nolvadex).** Many women with breast cancer are treated with this drug. It can be harmful to the retina, leading to distorted or blurry vision as well as cataracts. The effects are cumulative—risk for cataracts, for example, increases after using the medication for about five years.

Self-defense: If your doctor recommends this medication to reduce your risk for recurrent and/or worsening breast cancer, be sure to get yearly eye exams from an ophthalmologist.

• ***Topiramate* (Topamax).** Used to treat seizures and migraines, this drug can increase risk for a serious eye disease called angle-closure glaucoma. This condition results from a mainly inherited disorder, known as "narrow angle" eyes, that crowds the drainage structure of the eye, resulting in elevated eye pressure—a hallmark of glaucoma. Risk factors for narrow angle eyes include a family history of glaucoma and being farsighted. Only an eye exam, with a test called gonioscopy, can detect narrow angle eyes.

Symptoms of angle-closure glaucoma may include eye pain and headache, typically within a month of starting the drug. In severe cases, topiramate-induced angle-closure glaucoma triggers sudden blindness that is reversible if treated immediately.

Self-defense: If you develop eye symptoms while taking topiramate, see an ophthalmologist right away. If you are unable to be seen by your ophthalmologist, go to an emergency room with ophthalmologists on staff who can treat you urgently. Safer alternatives are available to treat migraines—consult your doctor for recommendations.

• ***Tamsulosin* (Flomax).** Commonly used by men with benign prostate enlargement, tamsulosin can weaken the iris, the colored part of the eye. When this occurs, a "floppy iris" can limit dilation during eye exams and eye surgery, which may prevent the pupil from staying open during cataract surgery. This can lead to complications, such as incomplete removal of the cataract and/or permanent damage to the iris with a permanent misshapen pupil. Women also may take tamsulosin for bladder problems and kidney stones.

Self-defense: If you have ever taken this drug, tell your eye doctor before having any eye surgery, including cataract removal. The effects of tamsulosin can linger for years. If the surgeon knows you've taken this drug, steps can be taken to greatly improve the odds of a successful eye surgery. There are alternatives to tamsulosin—discuss this with your doctor or urologist.

• **Erectile dysfunction (ED) drugs.** Because they divert blood flow away from the head and eye to the genital area, all ED medications, including *sildenafil* (Viagra), can cause blurry vision, light sensitivity, and a blue-green tinge to your vision. ED drugs also increase risk for optic nerve damage called ischemic optic neuropathy, which can, in rare cases, cause sudden blindness.

Self-defense: If you suffer a sudden loss of vision while taking an ED drug, see an ophthalmologist immediately.

TO KEEP YOUR EYES HEALTHY

The American Academy of Ophthalmology recommends a baseline eye exam for everyone at age 40—sooner if you have diabetes, high blood pressure, or a family history of eye disease. Your ophthalmologist will tell you how often to repeat your eye exams.

Important: If you have glaucoma or narrow angle eyes (described earlier), always read drug warning labels, and don't take any prescription or OTC medication without checking with your doctor. Glaucoma warnings are found on many drugs, including those that treat urinary incontinence, acid reflux or nausea, depression, and anxiety.

To find out if a drug you're taking has eye-related side effects, go to DailyMed.nlm.nih.gov, search the medication by name and click on "adverse reactions."

Drugs That Alter Your Gut Microbiome

Anita Gupta, DO, PharmD, MPP, a pharmacist, board-certified anesthesiologist, and former FDA adviser. She currently is a clinical professor at Rowan University School of Osteopathic Medicine in Stratford, New Jersey. AnitaGupta.com

New discoveries just keep coming about the importance of the gut microbiome—that trillions-strong trove of microorganisms, including both "good" and "bad" bacteria, that live all along the gastrointestinal (GI) tract. We know that this healthy balance of bacteria not only keeps your digestion humming but also promotes overall good health.

However, certain popular medications, such as antibiotics, heartburn drugs known as proton pump inhibitors (PPIs), and oral nonsteroidal anti-inflammatory drugs (NSAIDs), have been called out for upsetting the gut microbiome's delicate balance. Now, new research is making the list even longer.

Latest development: In a study presented at a recent United European Gastroenterology Week conference, researchers from the University Medical Center Groningen in Groningen, the Netherlands, detailed additional categories of drugs that can alter the balance of good and bad bacteria.

Disrupting this balance can not only lead to troublesome side effects, such as diarrhea but also increase the risk for other health problems, such as obesity, and set the stage for serious disorders, including inflammatory bowel disease, type 2 diabetes, and heart disease. Some of the same drugs have also been found to promote antibiotic resistance.

What you need to know to protect your gut microbiome...

DRUGS THAT CHANGE THE GUT MICROBIOME

In addition to antibiotics, most notably, *tetracycline*...PPIs, such as *esomeprazole* (Nexium)...and oral NSAIDs, including *ibuprofen* (Motrin), the following drugs have recently been found to alter the gut microbiome...

• ***Metformin.*** This often is the first medication prescribed after a person is diagnosed with diabetes—or, in some cases, prediabetes.

What the recent research revealed: Use of metformin was associated with higher levels of *Escherichia coli* (E. coli) in the gut. Some strains of E. coli normally live in the gut and help with digestion, but an imbalance can be harmful, potentially leading to such problems as diarrhea and urinary tract infections.

Important: When a drug is prescribed for a specific condition—in this case, managing blood sugar—researchers noted that it's hard to tell if the gut microbiome changes are from the disease or the medication. If you're taking metformin, be sure to note any new symptoms or if the drug isn't working and contact your doctor immediately.

Alternatives to consider: A lifestyle plan focused on diet and exercise and, if medication is necessary, possibly a sulfonylurea drug, such as *glyburide* (Glynase)...or a heart-friendly diabetes drug, such as the GLP 1 agonist *exenatide* (Byetta), based on a person's heart health.

• **Laxatives.** These are big gut disruptors, associated with higher, potentially harmful numbers of two types of bacteria—Alistipes and Bacteroides.

Alternatives to consider: Natural fiber products such as psyllium and, even better, eating more fiber-rich foods, such as fruit (including pears, figs, prunes, and apples), beans, peas, and lentils. Add them gradually to avoid bloating and gas as your GI tract adjusts to the change. Also, be sure to drink a lot of water.

• **Oral steroids.** People taking these drugs have high levels of the microbe *Methanobrevibacter smithii,* which has been associated with obesity, a known side effect of commonly used steroids such as *prednisone*, which is one of the steroids looked at in the study.

Alternatives to consider: There are few alternatives to oral steroids. Treatment could include IV infusions of anti-inflammatory medications, but this carries risks, such as bleeding.

• **Selective serotonin reuptake inhibitors (SSRIs).** Antidepressant medications, such as *sertraline* (Zoloft), *paroxetine* (Paxil), and *fluoxetine* (Prozac), led to increased numbers of the bacteria species *Eubacterium ramulus*, which lower the absorption of flavonoids, the powerful plant-based disease fighters.

Alternatives to consider: The SSRI *duloxetine* (Cymbalta)...a tricyclic antidepressant, such as *imipramine* (Tofranil)...or the herb St. John's wort—all of which may be less likely to increase harmful bacteria.

Worth noting: Gut microbiome changes were greater in people taking multiple medications, such as PPIs, laxatives, and antibiotics. Also, people with GI conditions, including an inflammatory bowel disease or irritable bowel syndrome, which directly affect gut bacteria, may experience even greater side effects from the medications that they take.

Important: When discussing with your doctor the risk/benefit of any drug you're taking, consider whether you're using the medication temporarily or need it long-term for a serious disease such as Parkinson's disease or multiple sclerosis. Some medications are helpful, and there may not always be an effective alternative. Never stop taking a medication without consulting your doctor.

DIET: A POWERFUL SOLUTION

Along with the findings on medications, the researchers reported on the effect of diet on the gut microbiome.

Using stool samples from healthy people and individuals with Crohn's disease, ulcerative colitis or irritable bowel syndrome, the researchers found that foods commonly included in a Mediterranean-style diet (such as vegetables, fruit, legumes, fish, and nuts) were associated with higher levels of friendly, anti-inflammatory bacteria.

Also: The findings confirmed that low-fat, fermented dairy foods, such as yogurt and kefir, increase good bacteria.

Key to Treating Chronic Digestive Conditions

Key to treating chronic digestive conditions such as Crohn's, celiac, and irritable bowel syndrome (IBS): Testing for small intestine bacterial overgrowth (SIBO). Research shows that 50 percent to 84 percent of IBS patients have SIBO. Treating the bacterial overgrowth can eliminate symptoms. Diagnosis is via a 10-minute breath test (cheaper and more accurate than endoscopy), where the patient takes the carbohydrate lactulose. Those with SIBO show premature metabolism in the small intestine.

Typical treatment: Antibiotics and repopulating the gut with probiotics.

Niket Sonpal, MD, board-certified gastroenterologist and an assistant professor at Touro College of Osteopathic Medicine, New York City.

3

Cures for Common Ailments

Calming Chronic Cough

From allergies to influenza, colds to coronavirus, a long list of irritants can spur a cough, the body's natural way of expelling everything from pollen to microorganisms.

It's not uncommon to have a nagging cough for a few days or even weeks, but once you pass the eight-week mark, your cough is considered chronic. For some people, the discomfort, sleep disruption, worry, and even stress incontinence can go on for many months, years, or even decades.

To learn more about managing this bothersome condition, we interviewed Rachel Taliercio, doctor of osteopathic medicine (DO), a pulmonologist and codirector of the Chronic Cough Clinic at the Cleveland Clinic.

Chronic cough is one of the most common reasons for people to visit the doctor. What causes a cough to linger for a long time?

Among nonsmokers, a chronic cough is most often caused by one or more of three conditions...

- **Cough variant-asthma.** While most people with asthma experience breathlessness, wheezing, and chest tightness, some have only a cough. Treatment with inhaled corticosteroids, with or without long-acting bronchodilators, or pills called leukotriene modifiers can provide relief from coughing and treat the inflammation caused by asthma.
- **Upper airway cough syndrome** consists of chronic sinus irritation or infection, postnasal drip, and allergies or non-allergens that irritate the upper airway. Treatment may include intranasal steroids, antihistamines, decongestants, or antibiotics.
- **Gastroesophageal reflux disease (GERD).** When people have GERD, acidic and nonacidic stomach contents leak into the

Rachel Taliercio, DO, a pulmonologist and the director of the Chronic Cough Clinic in the the Respiratory Institute at the Cleveland Clinic.

esophagus, the tube that runs from the throat to the stomach. It can then irritate the nerve that serves both the esophagus and the trachea, the tube that runs from the throat to the lungs. While GERD often causes heartburn symptoms, it can also be silent, causing nothing more than a cough.

What causes chronic cough in people who don't have any of these conditions?

A cough that is unexplained despite looking for and treating the most common causes is called a chronic refractory cough. When we meet such patients at the Cleveland Clinic, we take a thorough history, which can provide valuable clues. The story of the cough is incredibly important. What triggers it? What came before it? What is the character of the cough? What makes it better? Worse?

We also often repeat testing for asthma, upper-airway cough syndrome, and GERD. We have found that initially negative results can turn out to be positive, allowing our interdisciplinary team to treat those conditions.

If that doesn't explain or address the cough and we have ruled out all known triggers and causes, we think about cough hypersensitivity syndrome if the patient's history suggests this condition. Often, a chronic cough starts as part of an illness such as bronchitis, but when the illness resolves, the cough does not.

We think that this may be caused by a neural irritation or injury in the throat or larynx (the voice box). Changes in the peripheral and central nervous system may lead to hypersensitization of the cough reflex.

What treatments are available for patients with cough hypersensitivity syndrome?

The first approach for nerve-related coughing is called neuromodulation therapy. We use low doses of medications that are normally used for nerve pain to try to calm the nerves in the throat. These drugs, such as tricyclic antidepressants and *gabapentin*, are used off-label when treating chronic cough.

In a 2014 study, we found that neuromodulators helped 68 percent of patients. For about a third of them, however, the effects of the medication wore off over time. We call this tachyphylaxis. Ideally, if we find a medication that controls the cough, we continue it for six months, but in 27 percent of patients in our study, the cough returned when the medication dosage was lowered or stopped.

If neuromodulation therapy does not provide relief and we suspect that the person is experiencing laryngeal spasm as a component of the chronic cough, we can perform injection therapy with *onabotulinumtoxinA* (Botox) or a procedure known as a superior laryngeal nerve block. The nerve block uses a combination of numbing medication and a steroid injection.

Are there any approaches that do not require medication?

Behavioral cough suppression therapy is very promising. Speech language pathologists (SLP) can help patients regain control of the cough spasms without any need for medication. An SLP may start with strategies to interrupt or prevent the cough. For example, a patient can learn how to alter the sensation of an oncoming cough by using breathing techniques, distraction, forceful swallowing, and even voice therapy. The SLP will also educate the patient on how to reduce laryngeal irritation. That includes eliminating irritants (mouth breathing, smoking, and drinking excessive alcohol and caffeine) and increasing hydration. Chewing gum or sucking on hard candies can help some patients by encouraging more swallowing. Some patients can soothe the larynx by learning how to speak in slightly different ways.

What advice do you have for patients who are still looking for the cause of their chronic cough?

You know your body best. When you are reading articles like this and feel like you know what is causing your cough, share that information with your physician. Don't be afraid to get a second opinion if you're not finding answers.

How to Avoid Mask Mouth

Some dentists are reporting increases in what they call "mask mouth"—oral dryness, buildup of bacteria, more cavities, and gum disease, all thanks to the mouth-breathing we tend to do inside masks.

The fix: Drink more water to keep your mouth moist, reduce your consumption of caffeine, use a humidifier whenever possible, rinse with alcohol-free mouthwash, scrape your tongue regularly, and don't smoke.

Marc Sclafani, DDS, cofounder of One Manhattan Dental, New York City, quoted in the *Washington Examiner.*

Breathe Better: Four Easy Exercises to Strengthen Your Lungs and Restore Good Health

Belisa Vranich, PhD, a clinical psychologist, founder of The Breathing Class. Her books on breathing are *Breathe: The Simple, Revolutionary 14-Day Program to Improve Your Mental and Physical Health, Breathing for Warriors: Master Your Breath to Unlock More Strength, Greater Endurance, Sharper Precision, Faster Recovery,* and an *Unshakeable Inner Game.* TheBreathingClass.com

The main muscle that controls breathing is the diaphragm, a pizza-sized, parachute-shaped muscle at the bottom of your rib cage that flattens and spreads when you breathe properly. The intercostals—the muscles between the ribs—are also vital to breathing. Other muscles used during breathing include those on either side of your spine (erector spinae), the muscles that flank your abdomen (transverse abdominis), and your pelvic floor muscles, which form a kind of sling or hammock at the base of your torso.

When those muscles are weak, other muscles must step in to help: Shoulder muscles move up when you inhale and down when you exhale, and neck muscles tense during inhalation. But those muscles aren't built for the job, and they don't allow you to take full, deep breaths.

THE FOUR-EXERCISE FIX

While cardio exercises like brisk walking, biking, and jogging make you breathe more heavily, they don't actually help your breathing muscles (though they are wonderful for your heart). You can strengthen the breathing muscles only when your body is relatively motionless.

The following exercises, done for less than 20 minutes each day, will strengthen all of your breathing muscles so that you can take deeper, deeply oxygenated breaths.

- **Rock and roll.** Sit in a chair or cross-legged on the floor. If you're sitting on a chair, don't lean back. If you're on the floor, make sure you're seated on a blanket or pillow.

On the inhale, expand your belly as you lean forward. If you're very thin, you may have to push your belly out to get the right posture in the beginning. If you're heavier around the middle, think of releasing your belly or putting it in your lap.

On the exhale, lean back as if you were slumping on a couch. Contract your belly,

NATURAL RELIEF...

Teas That Relieve Asthma

Ginger—its compounds reduce airway inflammation. *Green*—the antioxidants lower inflammation and improve lung function. *Black*—contains caffeine, which relaxes the airway. *Eucalyptus*—reduces mucus production and expands the passageways inside the lungs. *Licorice*—one of its compounds relieves asthma symptoms, but don't exceed one cup per day. *Mullein*—relaxes the muscles in the respiratory tract. *Breathe Easy Tea*—a branded herbal formulation from Traditional Medicinals that contains ginger, licorice, and eucalyptus.

Note: Don't replace your asthma meds with tea—instead, use both.

Roundup of studies on tea and asthma, reported on Healthline.com.

narrowing your waist, and exhale until your lungs are completely empty. Every time you move your belly, you're actually teaching your diaphragm to activate when you breathe. Do 20 repetitions.

• **Diaphragm extensions.** Lie down on your back. Place a large book (or a small stack of small books) on your abdomen, right on top of your belly button.

Gaze toward the books: You should be able to see them at the very bottom of your field of vision. As you inhale, try to make the books rise. On the exhale, watch them lower. Do 20 repetitions.

• **Cat and cow.** Get on your hands and knees. Exhale audibly and round your back up. You should resemble a hissing cat at Halloween, with its back arched. Hollow out your belly and blow air out toward your belly button. Drop your head completely and stretch the back of your neck. Your tailbone should be tipped under.

On the inhale—the cow portion of the exercise—drop your body, relaxing your belly, and letting it expand downward toward the floor. Let gravity help. Your tailbone should now be tipped out. Swivel your head upward as if you're looking toward the sky. When doing cow, your belly should be relaxed and hanging low, and your head positioned up as if you're mooing.

Alternate the cat and cow 10 times, synchronizing the movement until it flows and you can easily rotate back and forth.

• **The perfect standing breath.** Change to a standing position and continue to inhale and exhale as you were doing in cat and cow. As you inhale, let your belly expand forward. Arch your back a bit and let your bottom pop back slightly. On the exhale, contract your belly, feel your lower abs tighten, and tuck in your bottom.

Your neck, chest, and shoulders shouldn't move: Only your belly and pelvis should be moving back and forth.

Do 20 repetitions.

DAILY ROUTINE

Practice the four exercises in a sequence twice per day. It should take three to 10 minutes. If you feel lightheaded, start with fewer repetitions and work your way up over time.

• **Do rock and roll 20 times.**

• **Roll over onto your back and do diaphragm extensions 20 times.**

• **Roll over and push up on all fours.** Do cat and cow 20 times.

• **Sit back on your feet momentarily (or come back onto a chair) and do 20 rock and roll breaths again.**

• **Stand up and do the perfect standing breath 20 times.**

For the first two weeks, breathe through your mouth while doing the exercises. This will help keep your attention on your breath so you don't default to your old way of breathing. After two weeks, start breathing through your nose, which is the best way to take full, deep breaths.

Case Study: Surprising Solution to Recurrent Nasal Infections

Andrew Rubman, ND, FABNE, medical director of Southbury Clinic for Traditional Medicines in Southbury, Connecticut. SouthburyClinic.com

The patient: "Anabel," a woman in her mid-60s who loves to spend her free time "exploring deep woods and trails."

Why she came to see me: Anabel simply could not escape her frequent nasal infections. She was referred to me by her friend whom I treated for ear infections.

How I evaluated her: I first sat and simply talked with Anabel about her ongoing problem. She shared that no matter what drugs and procedures had been tried, her nasal infections returned—sometime diagnosed as "viral," occasionally "bacterial," and often "allergic." She had tried dehumidifiers, HEPA filters, wheat- and dairy-avoidance diets, multiple antihistamines, allergy medications, and many, many, antibiotics. I did a physical examination of her nose and took a swab of the tissue relatively deep within. I applied the swab to a microscope slide and stained it with a small amount of iodine. I placed it under my microscope that had output into a laptop computer in my exam room. This stain would reveal if there were yeast organisms present in her nose.

Indeed, there were yeast organisms in the mucus sample. I explained that often these organisms can disrupt the physical and immunological strength of the underlying membrane and allow bacteria or viruses to take hold, and that common allergens found in the environment can further aggravate inflammation in the nose.

How we addressed his problem: While it is virtually impossible to eliminate yeast in the nose, it can be held at bay by simply deeply rinsing both nasal passages with a salt solution containing some aromatic alcohols like eucalyptol (from the eucalyptus tree bark), menthol (from a number of plants in the mint family), or thymol (from the cooking herb thyme). I made up a solution in my pharmacy and dispensed it to her. She performs the rinse at least twice a day and often when she returns from her woodland outings.

The patient's progress: Anabel reported feeling that her nose had "opened up" substantially and that she was breathing more freely. As of one month, she's had no reoccurrences of any of the past infections that had plagued her. Did we find a "cure"? Only time will tell but I believe that we found and limited a substantive trigger.

Sit Smarter and Prevent Pain

Shani Soloff, PT, CEO and founder of Stamford Physical Therapy in Stamford, Connecticut, and The Posture People, a national ergonomics consulting firm. ThePosturePeople.net

Having the perfect workstation on the job is essential to prevent issues such as back and neck strain and the resulting pain. How you sit at home is just as important, especially if home has become your new workplace. It is very easy to get lax about good positioning when you're working in the dining room, reclining on the couch, eating in the kitchen, or lounging in bed. *Here's how to sit smarter and comfortably to remain pain-free...*

- **Find your most supportive chair.** Whether you're sitting at a desk for most of the day or just to pay bills, sit in a chair that allows your knees to bend with feet supported on the ground. If your feet don't reach the ground, use a foot stool. Your thighs should be fully supported by the chair seat. The chair is too shallow if it ends at mid-thigh...too deep if your calves touch the edge. Better leg support means better back support.

- **Support your back—whether you're sitting on an upright chair, the couch, or a cushy chair.** If the seat is deeper than the length of your thighs, place a pillow behind your back to fill the space. For extra lumbar support, place a folded towel or lumbar back cushion in the small of your back.

Beware: Low-backed couches and chairs do not provide adequate back support.

When in bed reading or watching TV, put a small pillow beneath your knees to maintain a small bend—keeping your legs out straight strains the low back.

- **Get up and move before you feel discomfort.** Once an hour is typical, but if you know that you'll start feeling stiff sooner, move sooner. Adopt new habits that drive movement such as using an upstairs bathroom when you're downstairs and vice versa.

- **Change position whenever you change activity.** Rather than go from sitting to sitting—for example, from working at your computer to reading on the couch—spend at least a few minutes standing up and/or walking in between activities.

4 Common Moves That Lead to Injury...and What to Do Instead

Jonathan L. Chang, MD, orthopedic surgeon at Alhambra, California–based Pacific Orthopaedic Associates (PACOrtho.org).

We tend to associate injuries with car accidents and major falls, but the truth is our days are filled with chances to make small mistakes during very common movements that can lead to painful injuries. But with a few strategic changes, you can minimize your risk for injury—and the painful recovery that would accompany it.

EVERYDAY RISKY MOVE #1: LIFTING HEAVY OBJECTS

Nearly all adults will experience low-back pain at some point in their lifetime. One of the most common causes is lifting a heavy, unstable or unwieldy object. Most people know that they lift the wrong way, but they do it anyway thinking that they'll be fine.

How it happens: People overestimate how much they can lift or underestimate an object's weight, so they approach that bag of groceries or moving a box full of books with a false sense of confidence.

Next, they reach for the object by bending over, hinging from the waist, then attempt to lift it by simply straightening back up again. This leaves the lifting to the back muscles, which have evolved to hold the weight of your torso and head up when you are standing erect, not when bent over. Lifting in this position leaves the back vulnerable to injury.

If the object is unevenly weighted (such as a box stacked with books on just one side) or has moving parts (a wriggling child), your back muscles will automatically attempt to compensate for the instability, increasing injury risk.

Besides creating lower-back strain, improper lifting can exacerbate an existing herniated disk (also called a slipped disk) or create a new one.

Note: A strain results when muscles or tendons (the bands of tissue that connect muscles to bones) are overstretched or torn. A sprain occurs when the ligaments (the bands of tissue that connect two bones together in a joint) are torn or overstretched.

Do it safely: Preparation is key. Know the weight and weight distribution of what you're lifting. With your feet planted shoulder-width apart, squat halfway down until your thighs are approximately parallel with the ground, keeping your torso relatively upright, and then try lifting the object. Don't position your feet too narrowly, or you could lose your balance and topple over. And don't bend your knees more than 90 degrees or it will be difficult to stand back up.

Young children seeking to cuddle are a recipe for low-back strain. It may feel difficult to say no when they reach their arms up toward you, but if you're out of shape or have trouble lifting heavy objects, sit down and have them climb into your lap for that cuddle.

EVERYDAY RISKY MOVE #2: PUTTING ON A JACKET OR SHIRT

We tend to take an everyday activity such as getting dressed for granted. But the motions required to put on a coat, jacket, or a button-front shirt can trigger a rotator cuff injury.

How it happens: The rotator cuff is a collection of tendons and muscles surrounding and protecting each shoulder. It's what allows you to raise and rotate your arms. Dressing in the above items requires you to hold your arm up and out, often at a somewhat unnatural angle, which can strain a tendon in your rotator cuff. The tendon swells and becomes pinched by the shoulder joint, creating a sudden sharp, almost knifelike pain. Rotator-cuff injuries are more common with age.

Do it safely: Rotator cuff impingement pain intensifies when reaching behind your back or overhead—two positions involved in putting on a coat or a shirt. But there's no real need to put your arm into those positions. Instead, keep your arm below chest level and push your hand downward into the sleeve, using your other hand to pull the garment up.

EVERYDAY RISKY MOVE #3: OVERUSING YOUR NECK

If you have ever woken up with a "crick" or "kink" in your neck—pain accompanied by a limited ability to look from side to side or up and down—you likely attributed it to sleeping in an odd position. But a more likely culprit is neck muscle overuse the prior day.

How it happens: Gardening, housecleaning, too much time on your cell phone, and even reading all are common activities that require you to do a lot of looking down, taxing your neck and shoulders. Poor form when working on a computer can cause it, too. Then, when you finally rest, those muscles tighten up, creating a strain.

Do it safely: The neck usually assumes a natural curved position at rest unless strained or overused. Chin tucks are a safe and effective move to strengthen the neck and help prevent strain from overuse. Sit in a comfortable chair looking straight ahead. Move your head backward, tucking your chin in toward your neck in a slow and easy manner. Keep your gaze forward, and do not tilt your head. Hold the tuck for five seconds, then return to the starting (rest) position. Repeat five times twice daily.

EVERYDAY RISKY MOVE #4: NAVIGATING STAIRS

More than a million Americans hurt themselves on stairs every year. That's 3,000 injuries every day according to a study in *The American Journal of Emergency Medicine*. Injuries—usually sprains and strains, soft tissue injuries, and fractures—typically are worse when descending rather than walking up. A common mistake? Missing the last stair or two.

How it happens: When you trip while climbing up, you may be able to catch yourself with the railing or the stairs in front of you. But should you miss a step or two while walking down, gravity conspires against you and it is difficult to catch yourself.

Do it safely: The advice here will sound obvious, but people still don't follow it. Paying attention is paramount. Hold the handrail when going up and down. Avoid carrying objects that can obscure your vision, such as laundry baskets or large packages. Enlist aid from others if needed...otherwise proceed with great caution. Wear nonslip shoes, and avoid overly long pants. If you have vision issues, wear appropriate glasses or contact lenses.

As a preventive measure, consider enrolling in a tai chi class. This traditional Chinese practice involves slowly moving your body through a series of poses, benefiting core strength and balance in the process. Tai chi has been shown to help prevent falls in older individuals. And because it cultivates mindfulness, it improves your awareness of your surroundings, which could reduce falls.

Important: Certain medications, such as sedatives, pain medication, and antidepressants, can affect balance. Before taking any of these, talk to your doctor to make sure it is safe for you to navigate stairs.

For Knee Arthritis, PT Beats Steroid Injections

Osteoarthritis patients received either physical therapy (PT) or cortisone injections. One year later, the PT group's pain and disability level was significantly better. Steroid injections seem easier than PT, but risks include infection, cartilage loss, and bone fractures. And after the initial appointment, most PT patients walked better while injection patients had to rest for 72 hours.

Gail Deyle, DSc, professor of physical therapy at Brooke Army Medical Center, San Antonio, Texas, and leader of a study published in *The New England Journal of Medicine*.

How to Stretch and Roll Away Your Aches and Pains

Karl Knopf, EdD, director of fitness therapy and senior fitness for the International Sports Sciences Association and retired director of adaptive fitness at Foothill College in Los Altos Hills, California. He is author of many fitness books including *Stretching for 50+* and a board member of Sit and Be Fit, a nonprofit organization dedicated to healthy aging.

Overcoming the many aches and pains that come with living a long and active life can't be achieved simply by luck.

As we age, we lose muscle mass and our muscles become tighter and less flexible, especially if they're not exercised well. Add to that poor posture, injury, and diseases such as osteoarthritis, and muscles can fall prey to inflammation, spasms, and misalignments.

The secret to successful aging: Stay flexible.

Many older adults don't see the importance of flexibility work until they are hunched over and in constant pain, looking and feeling older than their years. The truth is that daily stretching is as important as regular aerobic exercise (five days a week) and weight training (two to three times a week).

STRETCHING TIPS

It's easy to sneak stretching into your life. Simply incorporate stretches into your normal routine or while working at your desk... watching TV...or between sips of tea while you read. *But stay safe...*

Warm up your muscles before you stretch by walking around for a few minutes first.

Don't bounce through stretches. Instead, hold steady, extending slightly on the outbreath, but push only as far as comfortable.

Hold stretches for at least 30 seconds or as tolerated, not to one minute unless otherwise noted for individual stretches below.

You're unlikely to notice immediate changes in your flexibility and range of motion, but if you keep up with daily stretching, you'll notice subtle changes. It will be easier to bend over and tie your shoelaces...you'll feel less stiff when you get out of bed in the morning...and you'll have an easier time getting in and out of the car.

The following are effective but simple exercises that can improve posture, prevent injuries, and target the most common sites of aches and pains...

NECK: THE TURTLE

This exercise reverses aches associated with sitting in front of a computer for hours a day and pushing your head forward. You can do it standing or sitting. Just be sure to keep your neck and back in alignment. The focus of the exercise is to pull the head back, which stretches the neck muscles.

1. Pretend you're holding an apple under your chin, or keep your chin parallel to the floor. Inhale deeply.

2. Exhale through your lips while pushing your chin forward.

3. Inhale through your nose, and slowly return your head to the neutral position you started with. Repeat as many times as you like to loosen up your neck.

SHOULDERS: THE ZIPPER

This exercise loosens the shoulder muscles. You can do it standing or sitting. As you become more flexible, you can eliminate the strap and try to grab your fingertips instead.

1. Hold a strap in your right hand, and raise your arm above your head. Bring your right hand down behind your head. Grab the end of the strap with your left hand.

2. Raise your right hand up as high as is comfortable, lifting the left hand along with it. Hold. Perform two times on each side.

3. Pull your left hand down to also bring your right hand down. Hold. Perform two times on each side.

4. Switch sides and repeat.

LOWER BACK: SEATED KNEE TO CHEST

This exercise stretches the lower back and gluteus maximus muscles and has been shown to improve blood flow and relieve muscle tension.

Sit with proper posture in a stable chair, and place your feet on the floor...or lie on the floor. Clasp both hands beneath your left leg.

Bring your left knee toward your chest. Hold, feeling the stretch in the gluteal region.

Release the knee, switch sides, and repeat.

STANDING HIP FLEXOR STRETCHING

Sitting for much of the day, as a lot of us do, can lead to tight hip flexors—the muscles that support the hip joints. To loosen them up, stand behind a sturdy chair with your hands on the back of it. Slide your right leg back a comfortable distance. Gently tuck your tailbone under and press your hips forward while keeping your rear heel down. When you can feel the stretch in your upper leg/hip region, hold.

Do two more times. Then do three repetitions on the other side.

LEGS: SEATED HAMSTRING MASSAGE

The hamstrings—the areas on the back side of the thighs that connect to both the hips and the knees—are prone to tightening up and are common areas of injury and pain. This exercise massages the area to boost blood flow and calm muscle tension.

Sit in a sturdy chair, and place a foam roller under one thigh...or, if you prefer, lie on the floor. Slowly and gently roll and press your leg along the roller. Hold the roller there for five to 30 seconds. If you notice a particularly tense area, return to it. Repeat with the other leg.

WRISTS: SEATED WRIST STRETCH

With all of the computer work and driving we do, our hands and wrists are prone to tightening up and cramping. This exercise targets both the wrists and the forearms.

1. Sit in a chair, and rest your forearms on your thighs with your wrists dangling just beyond your knees. Make loose fists with your hands, and slowly lift your knuckles toward the ceiling. Hold.

2. Lower your knuckles slowly toward the floor. Hold.

Repeat this exercise as many times as feels comfortable.

FEET: ARCH ROCKS

Many people have trouble with foot cramping, stiffness, and tightness as they age. This exercise helps to loosen the arches to relieve that discomfort.

1. Sit in a chair with both feet on a foam roller.

2. Slowly roll your feet forward and then back to massage the bottom of your feet. If you feel particular areas of tension, apply additional pressure and concentrate on those areas.

HANDS: V-W STRETCH

This exercise targets the hands and fingers and can be helpful for wrist strain. While the instructions are for sitting, it also can be done standing.

1. Sit with proper posture in a stable chair. Rest your hands on your thighs, palms facing down. Squeeze all your fingers together.

2. Separate one finger at a time, starting with the little finger, then the ring finger, until you've separated all your fingers. Squeeze your fingers together, and repeat.

To increase the challenge: Hold your arms straight out in front of you. Instead of just separating your fingers, try to make a V and W with them.

To make a V: Spread your little finger and ring finger away from your index finger and middle finger.

To make a W: Put your ring finger and middle finger together and separate the little finger and index finger from the group.

Ease Your Pain with These Soothing Self-Massage Tools

William G. Oswald, DPT, clinical instructor of rehabilitation medicine at NYU Grossman School of Medicine in New York City.

Are you relying on muscle relaxers to ease pain? A study from University of Pennsylvania found that prescriptions for these drugs—often handed out along with opioids—have skyrocketed in recent years... even though their benefits are largely unproven and their use has been linked to falls, accidents, and addiction.

Self-massage is a safe, soothing and convenient nondrug alternative to relieve muscle pain and return range of motion. It also is effective at dissolving trigger points, those localized nodules of tight muscle that develop as a result of trauma, stress, overuse, fatigue, or simply from failing to warm up properly before exercise. Applying pressure relaxes the compressed muscles and increases blood flow to the area, bringing relief.

Your hands alone can't always penetrate muscle fibers as deeply as you'd like, and it's hard to reach certain areas, such as the center of your back. That's where self-massage tools come in. In fact, it's great to have a toolbox of these aids for the large muscles of your legs and trunk as well as your neck, hands, feet, head, and even your fingers.

VIBRATING FOAM ROLLERS

Foam rollers usually are used for larger areas of tightness, such as the thighs, hips, and calves.

A new generation of these massage tools—with built-in vibration—has elevated the results you can get. The vibration allows you to go deeper without the added discomfort that actual deep-tissue massage can cause.

To use: Lie over the roller so that your own body weight creates pressure on the area you want to work. Roll back and forth in a slow, controlled way.

Product pick: The cordless and rechargeable Vyper 2.0 from Hyperice ($199*) is especially compact and can easily fit in a gym bag or suitcase.

MASSAGE STICKS

These batonlike massagers are much shorter, thinner and firmer than foam rollers and are made of very dense foam and rubber, usually with a line of nubby segments or beads

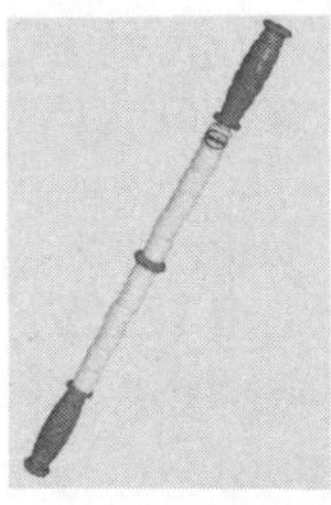

that roll. They're often about 18 inches long, so they're very portable, but they do require more elbow grease than a foam roller because the pressure is coming from the exertion of your hands and arms rather than the weight of your body. One benefit over a foam roller is that you can more easily vary the amount of pressure you exert. Massage sticks can be used on the neck, thighs, calves, and shins.

To use: Position the center of the stick on the area you want to ease, and use both hands to slowly roll the stick back and forth. For comfort, look for a massage stick that has contoured grips at the ends.

Product pick: The Stick muscle massager ($42).

PERCUSSIVE THERAPY DEVICES

These very popular handheld products, which look like an electric drill, are a favorite in professional sports locker rooms. They deliver short-duration pulses (about 40 per second) deep into soft tissue to relieve pain. One theory is that trigger points can stem from a lack of circulation, so increasing blood flow to these

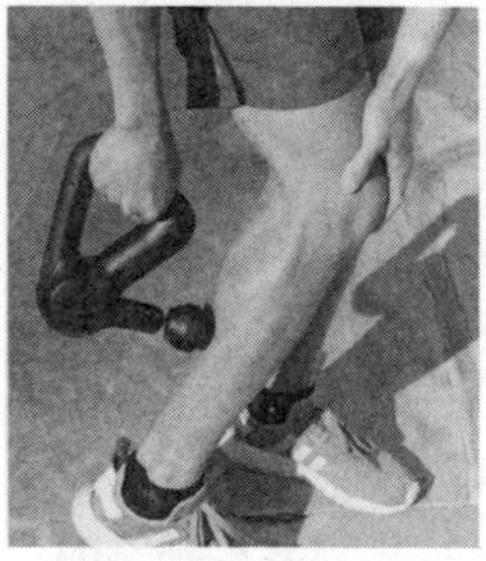

areas through the percussive action can help with recovery. On their own, percussive devices can reach deeper into the muscle than vibration devices, plus you can further increase the depth of penetration by exerting additional pressure with your hand. Speed and intensity are adjustable on the device, which has different heads for different parts of the body. The open-handle design lets you work just about anywhere on the body, although it will be more relaxing—and more fun—if you can snag a friend to help you with harder-to-reach spots such as your back or hamstrings.

To use: Apply the device head directly to a tight spot, and hold it in place for 30 or so seconds before moving to another area or

*All prices in this article reflect recent prices from major online sellers.

resting and then repeating on the same spot. You also can use a circular motion over a wider area for a massagelike effect. Just beware of applying too much pressure, which could damage capillaries and cause bruising. Do not use on your face, neck, or throat. Also avoid using percussive therapy devices if you are on blood thinners, at risk for blood clots, or have a condition that affects the blood vessels such as peripheral artery disease.

Product pick: Theragun ($299 and up).

MASSAGE BALLS

These handy hard rubber balls come in many designs—smooth, nubby (great for feet!) and even with built-in vibration. Some deliver heat, while others, such as T Spheres ($30 and up), offer the addition of aromatherapy, which can be relaxing when you're stressed and in a state of chronic pain. Massage balls can provide more specific direct pressure similar to that of a percussive therapy device but not as expensive.

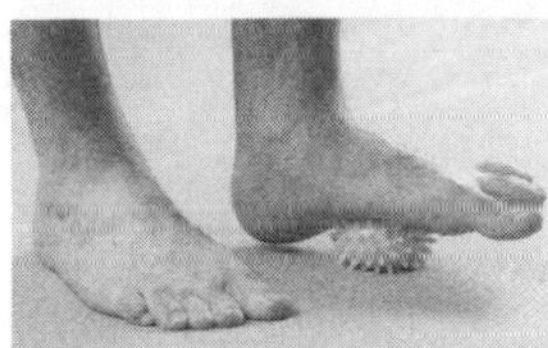

To use: A massage ball can apply pressure by rolling it with your hands on your neck, arms, and legs. You also can lean onto the massage ball against the wall for your shoulders and back. You can roll on the ball on the floor for your lower back, thighs, and feet.

ACUPRESSURE MASSAGERS

These mats and pillows have raised areas with hundreds to thousands of small plastic points in a set pattern. The acupressure points create pressure on trigger points and all over your body, stimulating circulation.

To use: Using one is as easy as lying down on the mat and putting the pillow under your neck or placing the mat over a chair and sitting on it for a few minutes at a time. The instruction booklet typically shows different positions to target different spots on the body.

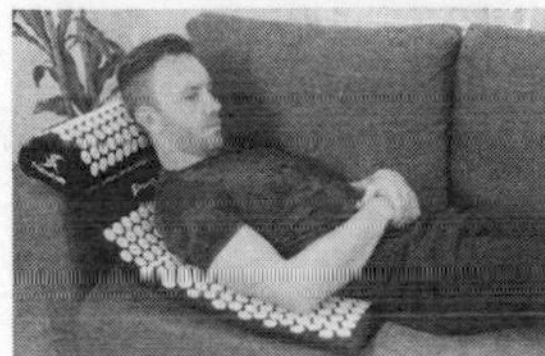

Product pick: ProsourceFit has a variety of acupressure mat and pillow sets that have a cotton or linen base ($21.99 and up).

SPECIALTY MASSAGERS

These inexpensive tools can be part of your full-body arsenal to relax and feel better faster.

For the back: The Thera Cane Massager ($29.95) looks like a coat hook with six treatment balls placed along its length. It's great for hard-to-reach areas of the back.

For the head: A head/scalp massager, widely available with 12 or 20 metal "fingers," or spindles, is a tool for relaxation, and some people find it also brings headache relief. Choose a model with a tiny rubber bead at the end of each spindle for smoother action and less hair tangling. Simply move it up and down over your skull for three or four minutes at a time (various manufacturers, about $8 and up).

For the fingers: For a fun way to relax, try acupressure rings (various manufacturers, about $7 for 12). Each finger has acupressure points that connect to different points on the body, which the rings stimulate when you twist them on your fingers.

More from William G. Oswald, DPT...

How to Relieve Muscular Pain Points

No matter what self-massage tool you use, the general principles for releasing trigger points are the same. Apply pressure directly to areas of pain—the trigger points—one at a time. This pressure will feel painful at first, but when you take off the pressure, the pain will start to subside. How long you maintain the pressure is unique to you. It can be a matter of seconds or up to a few minutes. You can rest and then reapply the pressure. Just keep in mind that a total of 10 to 15 minutes per spot per session is the limit, just as it is when applying ice or heat. You won't achieve more relief by doing it for any longer.

Surprising Migraine–Dry Eye Connection

Patients with migraines were 20 percent more likely than people without migraines to also have dry eye disease, according to a 10-year study of nearly 73,000 patients. The association was highest for older patients—men age 65 and older were nearly twice as likely to have chronic dry eye, and women in that age group were 2.5 times as likely. Inflammation, which plays a role in both conditions, may be the common link. While the study didn't prove that inflammation from dry eye causes migraine attacks, treating dry eye might improve migraine symptoms.

Richard M. Davis, MD, associate professor, Kittner Eye Center, University of North Carolina at Chapel Hill.

Green Light Reduces Migraines

When 22 chronic migraine patients were exposed to green light-emitting diodes (LEDs) for one to two hours daily for 10 weeks, the average number of headache days per month dropped from 22 to nine. Patients also reported significantly improved quality of life and no negative side effects. This appears to be a safe, drug-free way to reduce migraines. The green LEDs used in the study had 525 nanometer wavelengths, eight watts, and a 120-degree beam angle.

Laurent Martin, PhD, department of pharmacology, and Mohab Ibrahim, PhD, MD, department of anesthesiology, led a study published in *Cephalalgia*. Both are at University of Arizona, Tucson.

EASY TO DO...

Counting Down Can Keep Pain in Check

Recent study: Volunteers who were exposed to painful cold were asked to handle it in one of three ways—by counting down from 1,000 by sevens...thinking of something beautiful or pleasant...or persuading themselves that the feeling was not really too bad. Those who counted down reported feeling the least pain of all the groups—as much as a 50 percent reduction in perceived pain intensity. The high level of concentration required to count down by sevens was able to distract significantly from the experience of pain.

Study of 20 volunteers by researchers at Ludwig-Maximilians-Universität, Munich, Germany, and University of Oxford, UK, reported in *eLife*.

Simple Solutions for Hip Pain

Sanjeev Bhatia, MD, an orthopedic surgeon at Northwestern Medicine Central DuPage Hospital in Winfield, Illinois. He serves on the Northwestern Medicine Hip and Knee Joint Preservation Center Team.

If your normally active life is suddenly upended by hip pain, your response may depend on your age. A middle-aged runner may assume it's a severe injury, while a retiree might suspect arthritis and the need for hip replacement.

But there's good news for people of any age: The most common causes of hip pain are usually managed successfully with no surgery required.

PAIN LOCATION PROVIDES CLUES

Hip pain can arise from structures that are outside of the actual ball-and-socket joint (extra-articular) or from the cartilage inside the joint (intra-articular). The location of your pain can provide clues to what is occurring and guide treatment decisions.

- **Front of the hip.** If you have pain in the front of your hip, it's likely to be an intra-articular condition. If you feel a sharp pain after twisting, squatting, pivoting, or getting in and out of the car, you may have hip impingement. This condition strikes when the bones of the ball and socket don't fit together properly. The mismatch can lead to tears in the labrum, a ring of cartilage on the rim of the hip-joint socket. Hip impingement and labral tears can cause pain, but they can also hinder normal motion, destabilize the hip joint, and, in severe cases, lead to advanced arthritis.

• **Side of the hip.** If you feel pain when lying on your side, sitting with your legs crossed, walking, or climbing stairs, greater trochanteric pain syndrome (GTPS) may be to blame.

This extra-articular condition affects structures that surround the large bony prominence on the side of the hip (the trochanter). GTPS is one of the most common causes of side hip pain in adults and affects women more than men. One study in adults ages 50 to 75 found that 15 percent of women and 6.6 percent of men were affected.

In the past, it was called trochanteric bursitis, because it was generally accepted that it was caused by inflammation of the bursae—fluid-filled sacs that keep tendons and muscles from rubbing directly against the trochanter. Recent ultrasound and MRI studies, however, suggest that the pain is often caused by inflammation of the gluteal abductor tendons in addition to bursitis and tightness in the iliotibial band. The iliotibial band is a stretch of fibrous tissue that runs from the hip to under the knee.

• **Back of the hip.** Hip pain that is more posterior in nature often arises from extra-articular causes such as discomfort in the sacroiliac joint, which connects the hip bone to the sacrum, or conditions such as sciatica that stem from the lumbar spinal nerve roots (lumbar radicular pain).

Muscular causes of posterior hip pain can include tendinopathy of the muscles in the back of the thigh (hamstring). Tendinopathy can be caused by the inflammation of a tendon (tendinitis) or degeneration of a tendon's collagen (tendinosis).

NONSURGICAL TREATMENT

Nonsurgical treatment is almost always the first choice for hip pain, and the success rate is as high as 90 percent for extra-articular conditions and 50 percent for intra-articular causes. Although the intra-articular rate is lower, it still suggests that a nonsurgical approach may be beneficial.

Nonsurgical treatments include physical therapy, over-the-counter medications such as *acetaminophen* (Tylenol) and *ibuprofen* (Advil and Motrin), prescription antirheumatic drugs and biological response modifiers, and injections and infusions of medications such as corticosteroids. Dietary supplements such as glucosamine and chondroitin may help as well. Many people benefit from losing excess weight and participating in low-impact exercise.

Several studies have shown that mental and emotional factors, such as stress and anxiety, can affect the perception of hip pain, especially in the postoperative period. As such, stress reduction techniques may be beneficial.

This type of integrative approach to musculoskeletal pain may become the norm in the future as more research begins to support these efforts.

MINIMALLY INVASIVE PROCEDURES

If these efforts fail, it doesn't mean hip replacement is needed. Advances in minimally invasive procedures mean that surgeons can address issues such as hip impingement, labral tears, and gluteus medius tears with only tiny incisions in same-day procedures.

Another option, orthobiologic therapy, uses injections of substances like bone marrow or plasma that are already in your body to relieve pain and promote healing. Consider platelet-rich plasma therapy. A small amount of your blood is drawn and run through a centrifuge to concentrate the platelets. When those concentrated platelets are injected into the joint or tissue, they release growth factors and cytokines that boost healing and regenerate injured tissue. Similarly, stem cells may be taken from your bone marrow and injected into the site of injury to regrow tissue.

PREVENTING THE PAIN

One of the best things people can do to prevent pain is to help their cartilage remain healthy with a low-impact exercise program that preserves motion and strengthens the hip. That includes things like using elliptical machines, swimming, biking, yoga, and practicing Pilates. Additionally keeping one's core, gluteal, and lumbar back muscles strong helps decrease the incidence of extra-articular hip problems.

Suffering from Sciatica?

Start physical therapy (PT) right away. Patients whose lower-back pain extends into their legs often are told to remain active and monitor the condition. But when researchers randomly assigned 220 such patients to either take that wait-and-see approach or immediately begin PT, by week four the PT group reported less pain and that difference continued for the entire year of the study.

Julie Fritz, PT, PhD, associate dean for research at University of Utah College of Health, Salt Lake City, and leader of a study published in *Annals of Internal Medicine.*

The Four-Step Plantar Fasciitis Plan

Colin Dombroski, PhD, a Canadian certified pedorthist who has managed over 6,000 cases of plantar fasciitis since 2002. Dr. Dombroski runs SoleScience (SoleScience.ca) and is an adjunct research professor at Western University in London, Ontario, Canada. He is author of the book *The Plantar Fasciitis Plan*, available on Amazon.

If you wake up in the morning with pain in the bottom of your heel or the arch of your foot that goes away after walking, you might be tempted to think that warming up your foot is fixing the root problem. Not only is this assumption incorrect, but it can needlessly prolong your pain.

The plantar fascia is inelastic connective tissue that runs the length of the foot and supports your arch. If you stand or walk on hard floors all day, wear the wrong shoes, or simply have a body mass index over 30, the fascia can develop tiny tears that lead to inflammation and pain.

As you rest your foot in your sleep, or by sitting for a while, the fascia shortens. When you stand, it lengthens, which makes it prone to developing more tears. So while it feels like you can just push through that morning pain, you're actually reinjuring the fascia.

To get rid of plantar fasciitis pain for good, the first step begins before you even get out of bed.

STEP 1. Reduce morning pain.

To reduce both pain and the risk of reinjury, set your alarm a few minutes earlier so you can complete this series of simple exercises before your feet hit the floor...

- **Write the alphabet with your foot.** Sit at the edge of the bed with your knee extended. Pretend that you're holding a pen with your toes and trace each of the letters of the alphabet in the air. This will stretch the foot and ankle.

Next, cross your foot over the opposite knee and use your hand to gently pull your toes back toward your shins to relieve muscle tightness. You can also wrap a towel under your foot and pull on that. Hold the stretch for 10 seconds and repeat three times.

- **Sit on the edge of the bed and place a tennis ball, foam roller, or a similar object under the arch of your foot.** Roll it back and forth for about two minutes. Any time that you're sitting for more than 30 minutes, repeat these stretches.

Once your foot is stretched and before you get out of bed, put on your most comfortable, supportive shoes (not slippers). This will distribute your weight over the arch of the foot and help prevent additional tearing.

STEP 2. Evaluate your activity.

Plantar fasciitis can be deceiving. You may feel perfectly fine while you're being active, only to be struck with pain after you've finished exercising and are resting. The trick is to reduce your activity just enough to prevent the pain from kicking in. If you know that your plantar fasciitis acts up after the 18th hole on the golf course, try ending your game a few holes earlier and see how you feel. A good rule of thumb is to reduce activity by 20 percent to see if it makes a difference. If you can't find a comfortable level of activity for even short periods of time, try other types of exercise, such as bicycling and swimming. But don't stop moving. Inactivity can cause the plantar fascia to stiffen and then become painful again when you start to move around. You may have to experiment to find the right activity level.

STEP 3. Choose your shoes.

There is no single shoe that is the best choice for people with plantar fasciitis, but there is one type of shoe everyone should avoid—one that is worn out. I've met many patients who have been running in the same shoes for three years or who work on their feet all day in shoes that are no longer supportive.

If you see uneven wear on the soles of your shoes, it's a sure sign that it's time to get new ones. But you can't always see the whole story. Generally, shoes lose their support after a year. Athletic shoes can wear out much faster. If you're a long-distance runner, for example, you should replace your sneakers as often as every three months. Likewise, if you stand at work all day and wear the same shoes when you get home, you should probably replace your shoes more often than you have been.

When choosing new shoes, the first criterion is comfort. A good quality shoe feels different on different types of feet, so you need to find the one that feels best to you. It's a great idea to go to a running store or a traditional shoe store with professional employees who can assess your foot mechanics and suggest options that are made to work with your type of foot. When it's time to buy, you usually get what you pay for. A $35 pair of sneakers isn't the bargain it looks like—you'll end up paying in other ways down the road.

STEP 4. Try OTC solutions.

If you can't find just the right shoe, there are many over-the-counter products that may help. For example, if you're working all day in steel-toed boots and you can't find a comfortable fit, something like a gel heel cup or insole can reduce pressure, provide support, and make you more comfortable. The objective is to be as comfortable as possible so you don't compensate by walking differently. Turning your foot to the side to reduce plantar fasciitis pain can quickly turn into knee pain. Whatever cushioning device you use, be sure to put it in every pair of shoes you wear.

If orthotic therapy is not effective, you might want to try night splints to prevent shortening of the fascia while you sleep.

A nonsteroidal anti-inflammatory drug, such as aspirin, *ibuprofen*, or *naproxen*, can also help relieve pain and inflammation. These simple strategies can resolve pain in most patients, though it may take some time. If you still have pain after six months of following this plan, you may be a candidate for additional treatments, such as physiotherapy or custom orthotics.

Don't Let Arthritis Slow You Down: Reach Your Fitness Goals Without Pain

Brian Feeley, MD, chief of sports medicine and shoulder surgery at the University of California San Francisco.

Exercise is a fundamental tenet of good health, and that doesn't change with the onset of arthritis. With a few modifications, you can maintain your cardiovascular fitness and strength, and even reduce some of the pain and stiffness of arthritis.

Both resistance training and aerobic exercise are associated with less pain and disability from arthritis and better performance, but that's just the start of what exercise can do for you.

CARDIOVASCULAR EXERCISE

Cardiovascular (aerobic) exercise can strengthen the heart, lower blood pressure and LDL (bad) cholesterol, raise good HDL, regulate insulin levels, and lower blood sugar. It can improve body weight, fight insomnia, strengthen the immune system, improve cognitive performance, and boost mood.

For good health, you need about 150 minutes per week of moderate-intensity activity or 75 minutes per week of vigorous exercise.

• **Walking** is a safe way to relieve arthritis pain, strengthen muscles, and reduce stress for almost everyone. The workload can be easily adjusted by choosing flat or hilly ground or changing your speed. If you're outside, look for smooth, dirt trails, which are easier on your joints than sidewalks or the street. A treadmill in your home or at a gym can keep you moving even in inclement weather.

• **Water exercise.** Take your walk to the pool to halve the weight on your joints. Swimming and water aerobics classes deliver cardiovascular results with less strain on joints. Water-based exercise is ideal for people who are heavier or have advanced arthritis.

• **Cycling.** Riding a bicycle boosts cardiovascular fitness while also strengthening the muscles in your lower body. As with walking, you can adjust the intensity by choosing a flat or hilly trail and by changing your speed.

Make sure your seat is at the correct height: When your leg is extended on the down pedal, your knee should be slightly bent. If a traditional bicycle is uncomfortable, a recumbent bike provides more support. If you take an indoor cycling class and feel pain when you stand and pedal, remain seated.

• **Running.** While high-intensity exercise has traditionally been frowned upon for people with arthritis, the science is quite mixed. While running may be uncomfortable for some people, studies show it can be beneficial and safe for joints for others. The best approach is to listen to your body. If you are an avid runner and nothing is bothering you while you run, keep going. If you do start to experience pain, pay attention to when it happens. If you feel pain at mile three, try shortening your distance but increasing your pace. Instead of running every day, run three days a week and alternate with cycling, swimming, weight training, or yoga.

STRENGTH TRAINING

Weight training strengthens the muscles that help support and protect joints. Strong muscles help you more easily perform a wide variety of activities, from standing up from a chair to getting out of a car. It improves bone density and helps boost your metabolism too.

If you are starting a new weight training program or looking to get stronger, aim for three days per week. If you're looking to maintain your current strength and muscle mass, two days per week is sufficient. Don't work the same muscle group two days in a row. Arthritis can make some exercises you're used to doing uncomfortable, but simple modifications can get you the same results without the pain.

• **Knee pain.** If you have knee pain when doing squats or lunges, don't dip down as far. As you bend your knee, there is progressively more load on your joint and it is distributed less broadly, which can cause pain. By reducing the angle of your bent knee, you can decrease that load. You can also lower the weight that you're holding. To maintain the intensity of the exercise, increase the number of repetitions or speed them up.

There is one exercise that you should never do: Leg extensions. These are done in a chair or a machine where you sit with your leg bent over the edge of the seat and straighten it against resistance. This exercise puts excessive load on the kneecap.

• **Back pain.** If you suffer from low-back pain, the first thing you need to do is sit less. The most load that we put on the spine is by sitting. Get up and move around every 15 to 20 minutes to relieve it. To strengthen the back, focus on core stability with exercises like planks, side planks, and squats. Good form is imperative. Doing an exercise incorrectly can potentially cause more damage to your back.

• **Shoulder pain.** Shoulder exercises like military presses are safe—as long as your form is good. But many people, especially as they age, get in trouble when they take up activities like CrossFit and use maximal exertion to fatigue with heavy weight and high repetitions. This can put the shoulder at risk for dislocation. People who do heavy chest presses for years can also increase the risk of shoulder arthritis.

RHYTHM OF A WORKOUT

There's a pattern to every workout that helps prevent injury and reduce discomfort. Always start with a warm-up. Spend five to 10 minutes moving gently with range-of-motion exercises or easy cardiovascular work, and then transition into your work phase. Start slow and build up to harder work, whether that's heavier weights or a faster walking speed. At the end of the active portion of your workout, slow back down to let your heart rate and breathing return to normal. End the session with gentle stretches of any of the muscle groups that you used.

If you're continuing on an existing exercise program and these modifications ease your pain, you're all set to work out on your own. If you're trying to achieve new goals, however, a professional, such as a physical therapist or trainer, can help ensure that your form is good.

The Weather and Pain Connection

Robert Bolash, MD, a pain management specialist and assistant professor of anesthesiology at the Cleveland Clinic.

Do you feel more aches and pains when the weather changes? Can your joints predict when rain or snow is coming?

You can likely blame it on the barometric pressure. Before stormy, unsettled weather, the pressure of the atmosphere drops as the air rises and cools to form clouds. When there's less pressure, tendons, ligaments, muscles, and joints may swell, causing irritation. Coldness can also intensify symptoms by causing stiffness in muscles, ligaments, and joints. But it appears that the most significant effects come from rapid weather changes. A sudden change from a sunny, 80-degree day to a rainy, dreary day in the 50s may cause more discomfort than a shift from a 40-degree rainstorm to a 30-degree snowstorm.

THE PSYCHOLOGY ASPECT

Psychological and behavioral responses to the weather can affect pain, too. For example, some people feel depressed in gloomy weather, and those feelings can intensify pain. Conversely, when you're feeling happy and content, you may perceive less pain. People may be less active when the outdoors is uninviting and, as a result, spend less time moving and more time sitting indoors—leading to more stiffness and discomfort.

FIGHT BACK

If weather-related pain has you thinking about moving to a sunnier, drier climate, don't sell your home just yet. One study of four U.S. cities found that people with chronic pain reported weather-related changes in all of the locations, with higher levels of weather sensitivity in mild San Diego than in chilly Boston. Researchers concluded that people adjust to local conditions and react to day-to-day changes, and the weather changes just about everywhere.

Wherever you live, you can take steps to reduce weather-related pain flare-ups…

- **Stay flexible.** Exercise that involves stretching, such as yoga and tai chi, helps keep you limber and maintain joint health.
- **Use your muscles.** Joints surrounded by strong muscles are less prone to injury, strain, and pain. That's one reason that a walking routine can reduce knee and hip pain. Strength-training with weights and resistance bands also can be helpful.
- **Consider water exercise.** Exercising in water provides resistance without putting any weight on your joints, making it an excellent option for those with pain. Many community centers and health facilities have indoor pools—some are even heated to soothe aching joints and muscles. Even sloshing around in a warm bath at home might make you feel better.
- **Try an over-the-counter pain ointment** that contains a nonsteroidal anti-inflammato

ry drug (NSAID). These can be applied atop your painful joint and work directly at the site of inflammation. Topical NSAIDs avoid many of the side effects of systemic medications.

MIGRAINE AND WEATHER

Changes in the weather, especially dips in barometric pressure, can trigger or intensify headaches for some people. Falling air pressure may disrupt the fluid balance in your nasal and sinus cavities or affect pressure on the brain itself, changing your perception of pain, researchers speculate. It may even alter brain chemistry.

Some migraine sufferers get more headaches when there's a sudden drop or rise in temperatures, say experts at the Cleveland Clinic. But it's important to know that migraines can have multiple triggers that vary from person to person. So even if you are sure the weather is a trigger for you, it's crucial to work with your health-care providers to identify all of your personal triggers. These might include common dietary culprits such as too much or too little caffeine, aged cheeses, red wine, chocolate, and food containing monosodium glutamate (MSG). Other common triggers include loud noises, bright light, sleep deprivation, and stress. Some people also get rebound headaches when they overuse over-the-counter pain killers.

While weather variations can exacerbate pain wherever you live, there is anecdotal evidence that some migraine sufferers feel better in areas with lower barometric pressure variability. It's not the overall pressure, but rather the size of the changes that is to blame.

Prevent Gas, Pain, and Intestinal Bloat

Eat slowly so you swallow less air during a meal. Practice meditation or mindful breathing to reduce anxiety and stress, which are linked to increased gas. Exercise at least 30 minutes three to five times a week—workouts help move food through the gastrointestinal tract more quickly, reducing gas and bloating. Cut back on gluten—this can help even if you do not have celiac disease. Keep a food journal so you know if you become particularly uncomfortable after consuming specific foods or food combinations. Limit certain foods—some healthy, high-fiber foods can cause gas and bloating, such as beans, peas, cabbage, onions, broccoli, cauliflower, and prunes.

Roundup of experts on gastrointestinal discomfort, reported at Prevention.com.

Lysine to Help Prevent Fever Blisters

Alan M. Dattner, MD, a board-certified dermatologist and pioneer in integrating nutrition, holistic medicine, and dermatology. HolisticDermatology.com

The annoying appearance of fever blisters, those tiny, fluid-filled sores (often called cold sores) around the lip area, are usually caused by a viral infection...and are never a welcome sight.

Start with detective work with the help of a medical professional. Take a look at what could be causing the virus that causes fever blisters (herpes simplex) to flare up. When a fever blister goes away, the virus never leaves your body. It lies dormant in your nerves until something activates it. That activation could come from something as simple as eating too many arginine-rich foods, such as nuts, grains, seeds, or chocolate. If you overindulge in any of these, take extra lysine before, during, and after for a few days. One gram of lysine three times per day should work. Increase your dose if that is how much you take now. Since arginine promotes herpes reoccurrence but also supports the immune response, it is a good idea to take extra vitamins, herbs, and supplements that support the immune system. This might include vitamin A, D, and C, and astragalus.

Hormonal changes and decreased immune function can trigger the virus too. Even your posture can affect viral activity by putting excess pressure on the sensory nerve ganglia, where herpes resides. A physiatrist, chiropractor, or neurologist can test for such pressure and address it with exercise, posture correction, or manipulation of the cervical spine in the neck or in the lumbar region.

If you have recurring cold sores, you may benefit from a trial of *valacyclovir.* I don't recommend taking it all the time, just when you start to feel that tingle. I also recommend taking a daily vitamin B supplement and 1,000 micrograms of sublingual B12 to support your nervous system. For some people, lemon balm as a tea or tincture can also be helpful.

Rescue Dry, Chapped Hands

Kevin P. Cavanaugh, MD, dermatologist, Rush University Medical Center, Chicago.

With or without a pandemic, hand hygiene is one of the most important weapons in our fight against infection.

After multiple daily washings, however, it's not unusual for our hands to feel like sandpaper or even become raw and bleed. *But you can keep your hands clean—and soft and smooth...*

• **Opt for hand cream, not lotion.** Each time you wash your hands with soap or use a hand sanitizer (containing at least 60 percent alcohol), moisturize with hand cream. Lotions evaporate more quickly than creams, so they aren't as effective at repairing the skin's barrier.

Note: Let hand sanitizer air dry before applying hand cream.

• **Be prepared.** You'll want to wash or sanitize your hands after being in a public space. That's why it's smart to carry a small, travel-sized tube of moisturizer to use afterward.

• **Take care of cracks.** Frequent handwashing can cause the skin on your hands to crack and start to bleed. Apply a liquid bandage, which adheres to skin better than plastic or fabric bandages, up to twice daily to seal cracks and help them heal.

Good choice: New-Skin Liquid Bandage.

• **Go for some overnight TLC.** To penetrate the deeper layers of skin, apply an ointment, such as CeraVe Healing Ointment or Vaseline Petroleum Jelly, to your hands. Slip on a pair of cotton gloves, and wear them while you sleep. Your hands will thank you in the morning!

Cold vs. Heat Therapy: Smart Strategies to Relieve Backache, Headache, Gout, and More

Anne M. Rex, DO, FAOASM, staff physician in the Center for Sports Health in the department of orthopedics at the Cleveland Clinic. She is also a clinical assistant professor for sports medicine at the Ohio University Heritage College of Osteopathic Medicine in Athens.

Clinicians of all stripes agree that the direct application of cold or heat relieves a variety of aches and pains. Unfortunately, there's disagreement (and confusion) about which therapy to use for specific types of pain.

It's difficult to get a straight answer because there are few rigorous scientific studies on cold versus heat. On top of that, clinicians have their own favorite approaches. Despite the differing opinions, a few simple principles can help you get the best results from cold or heat therapy.

WHAT YOU NEED TO KNOW

It's helpful to have a basic understanding of the physiological effects of hot and cold treatments.

Cold therapy, which most often uses an ice pack, decreases the temperature of skin and muscle, which curbs blood flow and reduces swelling and bruising. Ice slows down the inflammation that follows an acute injury and numbs the area, reducing pain.

Heat therapy, using a heating pad or hot water bottle, for example, raises the temperature of skin and muscle, which increases blood flow, relaxing muscles and improving the elasticity of connective tissue, such as ligaments and tendons. That increased blood flow also brings more oxygen and nutrients to the site of an injury, which accelerates the healing process.

MAKING THE RIGHT CHOICE

Not all people respond in the same way to these therapies. *For the best odds of easing your pain with cold or heat, consider these points...*

• **Acute injury.** Ice is the go-to therapy for a new injury. In fact, for an acute injury such as a sprained ankle, heat can worsen swelling and bruising.

• **Chronic injury.** For chronic pain from an injury, try ice. Using an ice pack, for example, at bedtime is particularly helpful—it dulls the nerves, which helps promote sleep, the body's healing balm.

• **Back pain.** Chronic back pain is usually caused by deep inflammation within the structures of the back, which causes the muscles to spasm. Heat relieves the stress and anxiety caused by a chronic backache, relaxes the muscles, and reduces the spasm.

• **Neck pain.** A stiff neck, often caused by muscle spasms, is best treated with heat in moderation. A heating pad can be used, but only if you don't fall asleep and leave it on overnight. That increases inflammation, leading to more stiffness and pain, as well as the risk for serious burns.

If neck pain is due to a new injury, such as a motor vehicle accident versus generalized achiness, use ice for the first 48 to 72 hours to reduce new inflammation deeper within the neck. Gradually switch over to heat as needed.

• **Osteoarthritis.** Rheumatologists usually recommend heat for chronically stiff joints due to arthritis. If the knee is swollen, however, I favor using ice, which can be a soothing pain reliever before bedtime, when arthritis pain can be noticeable after a full day of activity.

Find out whether heat or ice works better for you. And whatever you do, move those joints with regular aerobic exercise, which is key to controlling arthritis pain.

HOW TO GET COMFORT FROM COLD

There are many ways to use cold, including crushed ice, ice packs (also called gel packs), cold compresses, and soaking in cold (but not freezing) water. My favorite method is an ice massage.

What to do: Freeze water in a paper cup filled half-full. Peel away the top one or two inches of the cup, exposing the ice. Apply the ice for three to five minutes, moving it around to gently massage the painful area. Keep a towel handy to absorb drips of melting ice.

If you use crushed ice, gel packs, or methods other than ice massage, always place something between the ice and the skin, such as a wet washcloth. (The ice massage doesn't need a barrier because you're moving the cold source and there's no constant application.)

With any type of icing other than a massage, a 10-minute application works well, particularly if you're icing your hands, wrists, ankles, feet, or knees. If you're icing an area with a lot of subcutaneous fat, such as your back or hips, consider icing for as long as 20 minutes. There is no benefit to icing for longer than 20 minutes.

After finishing, wait for as long as you iced before icing again: If you iced for 10 minutes, for example, wait 10 minutes until you ice again. With an acute injury, you can ice as many times a day as you like.

Caution: People with reduced skin sensitivity should be cautious about using ice. That includes individuals with peripheral vascular disease, Raynaud's syndrome, diabetes, and multiple sclerosis or other neurological issues.

HOW TO HARNESS HEAT

There are several ways to use heat, including heating pads, microwavable beanbags, hot water bottles, hot compresses, and hot baths. Hot water bottles are particularly effective for abdominal pain.

The length of time heat is applied varies. Heat can generally be effective when used for about 20 minutes, three times daily.

The same precautions that apply to cold therapy also apply to heat—be careful if you have reduced skin sensitivity due to diabetes or one of the other conditions listed above.

WHEN YOU NEED MORE HELP

Whether you're relying on heat or cold, the therapy can be used alone or with medication. If you don't get relief within a few weeks, consult your doctor. Immobilization with a splint or cast may be needed in addition to ice.

Looking for the Light

Paul H. Desan, MD, PhD, assistant professor of psychiatry, Yale University, Hew Haven, Connecticut.

Every year, from October to May, millions of Americans in the mid-Atlantic latitudes battle impaired function, depression, and low energy. Called seasonal affective disorder (SAD), this constellation of symptoms comes from reduced exposure to bright sunlight.

The treatment is simple: Exposure to bright light first thing in the morning works dramatically well for most people who have SAD. For people who can't get adequate exposure outdoors, there are light boxes, which studies have shown to be highly effective.

But beware: Most of the boxes you find on the Internet are a far cry from what's used in studies.

Light therapy isn't regulated by the U.S. Food and Drug Administration, which means that anybody can stick a light bulb in a box and say they've made a treatment device. When my colleagues and I put two dozen commercially available devices through rigorous testing, we discovered that only seven were supported by research. (See recommendations next column.)

DEVICE DIFFERENCES

Researchers use devices that emit 10,000 lux at a distance of about 20 inches. Lux is a measurement of how much light falls on a surface—in this case, your eyes. Because light disperses as you move away from it, lux decreases with distance. It also declines as you move away from the center of the light source. Researchers use large devices so the brightness is sufficient over a broad enough area to allow the user to sit at a comfortable distance and move around a bit.

To attain the benefits seen in research, consumers need light therapy devices that are comparable. The trouble with many commercially available devices is that they're dim, so you need to keep your eyes very close, and they're small, so you can't move side to side. The worst device in our study is advertised as a 10,000 lux light box, but it provides that level only if you keep your eyes a mere seven to eight inches away and barely move.

When you choose a device, follow the manufacturer's guidance on how close you need to be to obtain 10,000 lux. Use a measuring tape to ensure that you are in the correct range. Watch out for misleading product photos that show people using devices at much greater distances than the device is actually designed for.

PRODUCT RECOMMENDATIONS

In our analysis, we considered a light box to be effective if it produced at least 7,000 lux at the manufacturer's recommended distance (with a minimum distance of 12 inches) and at least 5,000 lux if the user moved six inches off-center. To make our recommended list, the device also had to be tolerable for the user by eliminating excessive glare and hot spots.

Three devices were very close to the quality used in clinical trials. These larger units are preferred as a first-line approach to bright-light therapy because they provide the most power, the least glare, and give you more freedom to do other things during the session to make it less burdensome.

- **SunRay II** (The SunBox Company)
- **NorthStar 10,000** (Alaska Northern Lights)
- **Day-Light Classic** (Carex Health Brands)

For people who prefer smaller devices, three met our standards if used closer and with less movement.

- **BOXelite** (Northern Light Technologies)

- **Day-Light Sky** (Carex Health Brands)
- **SunTouch Plus** (Nature Bright Company)

We also identified two promising visors that allow users to move around freely.

- **Feel Bright Light** (Physician Engineered Products)
- **SolarMax Light Visor** (BioBrite)

TIMING

Most people benefit from about 30 minutes of exposure to 10,000 lux. If the light exposure is lower, increase the duration. A 5,000 lux unit might take an hour to be as effective as a stronger unit used for 30 minutes.

The therapy is most effective when those 30 minutes are completed before 8 a.m. This allows the light to reset the internal body clock. The response may be even more powerful if you do it earlier, such as 6 a.m., but much earlier than that will just confuse the body. Conversely, as the morning wears on, the effect of light therapy decreases.

Use your light box at the same time each morning—even on weekends. If you struggle to wake up early enough—which is a common part of SAD—aim for 9 a.m. at first. While you won't get the full benefits of light therapy, you will get a body clock adjustment that will make it easier to wake up earlier.

You may come across dawn simulation devices that gradually brighten over time to help you wake up in the morning. The clinical trials are very interesting, and we've found that professional-grade devices, with a little fine-tuning, can benefit patients with SAD. Unfortunately, my experience is that a lot of the commercially available dawn simulators are just too dim to attain the positive results that the professional devices lead to.

A SPECTRUM OF SYMPTOMS

Until very recently, the medical community did not consider humans to be seasonal, but SAD, we now understand, is an exaggeration of a very normal seasonal response. Craving high-energy foods and feeling sleepier in the winter is the human form of hibernation. Light therapy can improve related symptoms that are mild but still bothersome, such as poor energy, difficulty waking up, or seasonal weight gain.

SAFETY RECOMMENDATIONS

While you can easily buy a light box without a prescription, I recommend working with a qualified clinician when you begin. There may be a risk of activating a manic state or increasing suicidal thoughts. (Some people with depression have a higher risk of suicide in the early period of recovery when their motivation and energy levels rise.)

Properly designed light boxes expose the eye to less light than being outside on a summer day and likely are safe for long-term use. Unfortunately, there is not as much research as we would like on this issue.

The beneficial effects can take some time to appear, so I recommend 30 minutes of light therapy at the same time every day for four weeks to see if it is beneficial for you. If you feel overstimulated, reduce treatment length by 50 percent for a few days.

Solve a Recurring Sleep Problem With a Journal

Write down what time you get into bed, when you awaken during the night, and when you wake up for the next day and get out of bed. Note how easily you wake up in the morning...the time and length of any daytime naps...sleep disruptions caused by pain, worry, noise, or other factors...how rested and tired you feel after awakening... what caffeinated beverages you consume... your tobacco and alcohol use...and any drugs you take. Share your sleep log with your doctor to discuss ways to make nighttime more restful and restorative.

University of California, Berkeley Wellness Letter.

4

Diet, Nutrition and Fitness

Eat for Life with the Anti-Inflammation Diet

More than a weight loss plan, an anti-inflammatory diet can help you add years to your life. You might have already given up some foods thought to increase levels of inflammation in your body, but new research has shown that while any one dietary or lifestyle factor on its own likely contributes only a little to inflammation, when you add up all of the dietary and lifestyle factors, the contributions to inflammation can be substantial. *Here's how to take your efforts to the next level...*

STUDY RESULTS

A study conducted at Emory University found that, in general, a diet that consists of diverse types of fruits and vegetables and foods rich in fiber, phytonutrients, omega-3 fatty acids, and various vitamins and minerals, such as calcium, tends to be associated with lower levels of inflammation. In contrast, processed foods and foods high in omega-6 fatty acids and saturated fats tend to be associated with higher levels of inflammation.

Among lifestyle factors, being physically active was associated with lower levels of inflammation and a greater ability to fight oxidative stress. Smoking tobacco, drinking more than two drinks per day for men or one drink per day for women, and, most notably, being overweight were all associated with higher levels of inflammation.

PERSONALIZE YOUR APPROACH

Removing any one component from the dietary or lifestyle scores did not change the overall conclusions of the study, demonstrat-

Doratha A. Byrd, PhD, MPH, a postdoctoral fellow in the metabolic epidemiology branch in the division of cancer epidemiology and genetics at the National Cancer Institute. She was the first author of the study "Development and Validation of Novel Dietary and Lifestyle Inflammation Scores" published in *The Journal of Nutrition*.

ing the importance of taking a broad approach and considering diet and lifestyle as a whole, rather than focusing on any one food or behavior.

The best approach may be to eat more anti-inflammatory foods while also reducing pro-inflammatory ones. For instance, if someone has a high intake of refined sweets, they may have a pro-inflammatory diet even if they consume high amounts of anti-inflammatory tomatoes.

You also need to make choices within the context of your own health profile. For instance, while the researchers did not find a strong association between red meat and inflammation, it is also important to bear in mind that red meat appears to be associated with a higher risk of heart disease and colorectal cancer. The same is true for low- vs. high-fat dairy—in terms of inflammation, both types of dairy contain calcium and fatty acids that could help regulate inflammation, but you might choose low-fat dairy if you are trying to reduce your overall fat intake.

HELPFUL TIPS

Here are some ideas to help you double up on dietary changes...

• **Get more creative with tomatoes.** Cook up a batch of tomato sauce from fresh or canned tomatoes, and use it to replace butter and oil-based sauces and to top whole-wheat pizza dough. Try adding cherry tomatoes to whole-wheat pasta and bean dishes.

• **Go for the gold with fruits and vegetables.** Put summer and winter squashes, yellow beets, and sweet potatoes on the menu. Add yellow or orange bell pepper rings to salads, and compose a fruit salad with papaya, mango, cantaloupe, peaches, and citrus.

• **Try alternatives to starches as side dishes.** Serve poultry or fish on a bed of greens rather than white rice. Mash carrots or cauliflower instead of white potatoes.

• **Make the switch from processed foods to home cooking.** Increase the amount of cooking you do not only to eat more healthful foods but also have better control over the proportion of inflammatory ones.

• **Measure portions.** It is possible to have too much of a good thing. To turn an anti-inflammation diet into a weight-loss diet, cut back on quantity as you improve the quality of your meals.

A Sample Day of Swaps to Lower Inflammation

MEAL	INSTEAD OF	SWITCH TO
Breakfast	Boxed cereal with added sugar	Oatmeal with plain yogurt and berries
Lunch	Deli cold-cut sandwich	Chicken breast, chopped walnuts, and diced beets on lettuce
Snack	Chips	Nuts
Dinner	Lasagna	Whole wheat pasta with fresh tomato sauce
Dessert	Cake	Apple crisp

THE INFLAMMATION SCALE

To study the inflammatory effects of different foods and activities, Doratha Byrd, PhD, MPH, and colleagues assigned scores to numerous foods and lifestyle behaviors based on how strongly they were associated with inflammation. A negative score means the item was associated with lower inflammation and a positive score means it was associated with higher inflammation. While the greatest associations with inflammation were seen when considering diet and lifestyle as a whole, the score weights can help you to understand how individual foods and behaviors were associated with inflammation.

Lower inflammation

Foods

Tomatoes .... -0.78
Apples and berries .... -0.65
Deep yellow/orange vegetables
and fruits .... -0.57
Poultry .... -0.45
Nuts .... -0.44
Coffee and tea .... -0.25
Other fruit and fruit juices .... -0.16
Other vegetables .... -0.16
Leafy greens and cruciferous vegetables... -0.14
Low-fat dairy .... -0.12
Fish .... -0.08
Legumes .... -0.04

Activities

Taking vitamin/mineral supplements ..... -0.80
Moderate alcohol consumption .... -0.66
Moderate physical activity........................ -0.18

Higher inflammation

Foods

Refined grains and starchy vegetables....+0.72
Processed meat .... +0.68
Added sugars... +0.56
Other fats such as mayonnaise, butter, and margarine......................................+0.31
Red and organ meats.............................. +0.02

Activities

Being obese.. +1.57
Being overweight.....................................+0.89
Smoking..+0.50
Heavy physical drinking .... +0.30

3 Food Myths That Could Hurt You

David L. Katz, MD, MPH, preventive medicine specialist and founder and president of True Health Initiative and coauthor with renowned food writer Mark Bittman of *How to Eat: All Your Food and Diet Questions Answered.* DavidKatzMD.com

Everyone knows that vegetables are good for you and French fries are not. But we still can't wrap our heads around some of the finer nuances of proper nutrition, such as how much protein to eat and whether we really need to cut our carbohydrate intake... and to even understand what a carb is.

To get a handle on persisting misperceptions about food and healthy eating, we spoke with diet expert and preventive-medicine specialist David L. Katz, MD.

3 BIGGEST FOOD MISPERCEPTIONS

***MISPERCEPTION #1:* You need to eat more protein as you get older.**

Truth: Most adults get more than enough protein to meet their nutritional needs. You would have to have a very unbalanced, quirky diet to be protein-deficient. Government recommendations advise getting 10 percent to 35 percent of calories from protein sources—roughly one-half gram per pound of body weight. Currently in the U.S., women eat, on average, about 90 grams per day and men eat about 100 grams—more than enough.

It's true that most people begin to lose muscle starting between ages 50 and 60. And it's also true that protein helps you maintain muscle. But it's a myth that eating more protein will help you build muscle. Only exercise enables you to maintain and build muscle. In fact, extra protein above that 35 percent of daily calories will turn into body fat, just as extra calories from fat or carbs do. Too much protein also can stress the kidneys and liver, leading to disease of those organs, as well as weaken your bones.

***MISPERCEPTION #2:* You need to eat animal products to get complete nutrition.**

Truth: A complete protein source delivers all of the essential amino acids (histidine, isoleucine, leucine, lysine, methionine, phenylalanine, threonine, tryptophan, and valine) that our bodies can't make but still need to function optimally. Yes, meat provides these essential amino acids in the ideal proportions all at once, but higher intake of meat is associated with higher overall risk for chronic disease and premature death.

Plant foods also deliver all of the essential amino acids, just at lower concentrations. The distribution of amino acids in nuts, grains, legumes, vegetables, fungi, and seeds is complementary—if you don't get all the amino acids that your body needs from one type of plant, you'll get it from another. Your body couldn't care less if you get these amino acids—so-called "complete protein"—all at once or from animals or plants. There's no need to worry about food combinations within one meal as long as you get a balance of foods in general.

***MISPERCEPTION #3:* Your diet can be healthy only if you limit carbs.**

Truth: Carbohydrates actually should be the predominant foods in your diet. Whether you are an omnivore, a vegetarian, or a vegan, 40 percent to 70 percent of your daily calories should come from complex carbs.

Important: Carbs don't just mean sugar, pasta, bread, grains and other starchy foods. All fruits, vegetables, and beans are carbs too. And all of the best diets around the world—"Blue Zone" diets that are associated with health and longevity—are predominantly plant-based and thus carb-based.

Beware: There are plenty of bad processed carbs out there—chips, pizza, candy, white bread, white pasta, cakes, sugary cereals, and sugar-sweetened drinks, etc.—all lacking in nutrition and designed to put your appetite into overdrive.

Coffee: Drink Up for Less Body Fat

The study "Regular Coffee Consumption Is Associated with Lower Regional Adiposity Measured by DXA Among U.S. Women," led by researchers at Anglia Ruskin University in East Anglia, UK, and published in *The Journal of Nutrition.*

Americans love their coffee. In fact, we drink about 400 million cups each day, making it one of the most popular beverages in the U.S. That's good news for those who love their cups of joe because there's increasing evidence showing that coffee has lots of health benefits, such as helping to protect against cirrhosis of the liver, to control Parkinson's disease symptoms, to promote heart health, and to slow the progress of dementia.

Now: A new study published in *The Journal of Nutrition* has found yet another benefit—coffee drinking is linked to having less body fat.

Study details: The finding was based on 5,000 Americans' responses to the National Health and Nutrition Examination Survey (NHANES), organized by the Centers for Disease Control and Prevention. NHANES asks respondents questions about their nutrition and health and includes measurements of body fat and its distribution using a dual-energy X-ray absorptiometry (DXA) scan. (The scan is also commonly used to measure bone density to diagnose osteoporosis.)

After analyzing the respondents' daily coffee intake and their DXA measurements over a two-year period, the researchers found a link between coffee consumption and body fat in women that varied by their age, while there was less overall effect among the men who were studied. *The specific findings...*

- **Compared with women who did not drink coffee,** women ages 20 to 44 who drank two to three cups per day had 3.4 percent less body fat.
- **Women ages 45 to 69 who drank four or more cups per day** had 4.1 percent less body fat than non-coffee drinkers.
- **Among men, the association between coffee drinking and body fat was less significant...**except for those ages 22 to 44 who drank two to three cups of coffee per day—they had 1.3 percent less body fat and 1.8 percent less trunk fat than men who did not drink coffee.

Interestingly, the benefits were present in those who drank caffeinated or decaffeinated coffee and were not affected by smoking or chronic disease.

"Our research suggests that there may be bioactive compounds in coffee other than caffeine that regulate weight and which could potentially be used as anti-obesity compounds," explained Lee Smith, PhD, senior author of the study and director of research at Anglia Ruskin University's Cambridge Centre for Sport and Exercise Sciences.

At some point, these bioactive compounds could be used as part of an anti-obesity treatment, according to the researchers. For now, however, coffee lovers can rest easy knowing that two to four cups a day could help reduce their overall body fat—and belly fat.

Mainly because of its caffeine content, people with high blood pressure may need to limit their intake of coffee—it can temporarily raise blood pressure in some people. Pregnant women and women who are breast-feeding should talk to their doctors about their consumption of coffee—high intake has been shown to increase risk for miscarriage. The

American College of Obstetricians and Gynecologists recommends that pregnant women drink no more than 200 mg of caffeine daily (approximately two cups of caffeinated coffee a day), while research recently published in the *BMJ Evidence-Based Medicine* recommends that they consider avoiding caffeine altogether.

Spices May Reduce Risks of a High-Fat, High-Carb Meal

The study "Spices in a High-Saturated-Fat, High-Carbohydrate Meal Reduce Postprandial Proinflammatory Cytokine Secretion in Men with Overweight or Obesity: A 3-Period, Crossover, Randomized Controlled Trial," led by researchers at Pennsylvania State University in University Park and published in *The Journal of Nutrition*.

If you wonder why 72 percent of the US population is overweight or obese, a good portion of the blame goes to a steady diet of foods that are high in saturated fat and/or refined carbohydrates. Not surprisingly, a regular diet of these same foods also has been linked to chronic inflammation, which increases risk for cardiovascular disease (CVD).

Switching to a diet that's low in saturated fat and refined carbs seems like an obvious solution. But as anyone who's ever tried to stick to such a diet will tell you, that's not always easy. So for those occasional lapses when a person indulges in a high-fat, high-carb meal, could there be a way to blunt the negative health effects?

To explore this question, researchers at Pennsylvania State University devised a study to test how spices might affect the body's response to one of those less-than-healthful meals. The researchers recruited 12 men ages 40 to 65 who were overweight or obese and had at least one CVD risk factor.

Study details: Over the course of three days, the men ate a series of high-fat, high-carb meals and received blood tests before and after the meals to measure their levels of proteins known as cytokines, which serve as markers for inflammation. In random order, participants were given meals that did not have any spices added…had 2 grams (g) of a spice blend added…or had 6 g of the same spice blend added. The spice blend contained basil, bay leaf, black pepper, cinnamon, coriander, cumin, ginger, oregano, parsley, red pepper, rosemary, thyme, and turmeric.

The result: After giving blood tests to the study participants hourly for four hours after each meal, the researchers found that the 6 g spice-blended meals significantly reduced cytokine levels compared with the other meals. The 6 g spice blend was roughly equivalent to one teaspoon to one tablespoon, depending on the spice's level of dehydration.

Although this study, which was published in *The Journal of Nutrition*, did not identify which spices work best to lower inflammation, numerous animal and human studies have shown that spices such as turmeric, ginger, and cinnamon have anti-inflammatory properties.

Earlier research has shown that meals that are high in fat, carbs, and/or sugar lead to spikes in inflammation, known as acute inflammation. It's not known whether these short bursts of inflammation result in chronic inflammation, but the researchers theorize that they do play a role, especially in people who are overweight or obese.

"Ultimately the gold standard would be to get people eating more healthfully and to lose weight and exercise, but those behavior changes are difficult and take time," said Connie J. Rogers, PhD, MPH, lead author of the study and an associate professor of nutritional sciences at Pennsylvania State University. In the interim, the study finding suggests that spices may be an effective and convenient way to at least help reduce the inflammation that results from a high-carb, high-fat meal. Even though this study was small, the researchers hope that larger studies with a more diverse population will support their findings.

Takeaway: The best way to avoid obesity and cardiovascular disease is to exercise, reduce calories, and eat a diet that includes lots of vegetables, fruits, and whole grains. For that occasional indulgence, adding some spice to your moussaka or lasagna could make your meal both tastier and healthier.

Foods to Wash—and Not Wash

Do not wash raw chicken, red meat, or fish—washing spreads bacteria around the sink and can cross-contaminate other foods. Kill bacteria by cooking poultry, meat, and fish to recommended internal temperatures. Do wash cantaloupe and other melons, whose skins can trap bacteria that can be moved into the flesh by cutting...and avocado, whose skin can also carry bacteria that can transfer inside. It is not necessary to wash foods that are dusty when they come out of the bag, such as dried beans, farro, and quinoa.

WebMD.com

Using Only Sea Salt or Gourmet Salt Can Lead to Iodine Deficiency

Iodized table salt is the most common source of iodine. Deficiencies can lead to fatigue, weight gain, hair loss, and goiter. One-half teaspoon of iodized salt per day meets the daily requirement for iodine. Sea vegetables such as nori, wakame, or dulse flakes are another potent source of iodine. Have a modest serving two or three times per week.

Neal D. Barnard, MD, adjunct associate professor of medicine at George Washington University School of Medicine and Health Sciences in Washington, DC, and president of Physicians Committee for Responsible Medicine. PCRM.org

Switch to Sourdough Bread

If commercially baked breads cause intestinal distress even though you do not have celiac disease, switching to sourdough bread made with a homemade starter could help.

Reason: Letting bread dough rise several times before it is baked breaks down hard-to-digest gluten proteins. Most commercial breads now are made using rapid-rise yeasts, and the shorter rising time leaves more gluten proteins intact. The long fermentation required for making sourdough, on the other hand, breaks down more of the gluten, making sourdough easier to digest.

Andrea Thompson, RDN, registered dietician nutritionist with Penn State Health St. Joseph Hospital, Reading, Pennsylvania.

EASY TO DO...

Trick to Eat Less

Cut your eight-slice pizza into 16 slices. People tend to eat in units, regardless of size. Works for brownies and other foods, too.

Lisa R. Young, PhD, RDN, author of *Finally Full, Finally Slim: 30 Days to Permanent Weight Loss One Portion at a Time.*

Get Creative With Super-Nutritious Quinoa

Janet Bond Brill, PhD, RDN, FAND, a registered dietitian nutritionist, a fellow of the Academy of Nutrition and Dietetics, and a nationally recognized nutrition, health, and fitness expert who specializes in cardiovascular disease prevention. Based in Hellertown, Pennsylvania, Dr. Brill is author of ***Blood Pressure DOWN, Cholesterol DOWN,*** and ***Prevent a Second Heart Attack.*** http://DrJanet.com

If you've never tried mega-popular and super-nutritious quinoa (pronounced KEEN-wah) or if you've tried it but the taste hasn't appealed to you, there are lots of delicious and creative new ways to enjoy it.

This superbly healthy protein- and fiber-rich seed has a unique nutty flavor and is incredibly versatile in the kitchen—it's a terrific alternative to brown rice or any other whole grain.

The fact that quinoa is a seed and not a grain (albeit it's considered by many to be a "pseudo-grain") makes it less starchy than grains. According to the Whole Grains Council, quinoa is a gluten-free, whole-grain, and fiber-rich carbohydrate. It's also a complete protein (meaning that it contains all nine of the essential amino acids). When compared with other whole grains, quinoa offers almost double the protein, fiber, iron, and calcium.

You can find white, red, black, or tricolor quinoa in grocery stores. These varieties all have the same amount of protein and fiber; however, the tri-colored, red, and black varieties have more antioxidant flavonoids, especially quercetin, than white quinoa. White quinoa is the most bland. Other varieties are chewier and nuttier.

Before cooking with quinoa, you will want to give it a quick rinse to remove any traces of its natural coating, called saponin. That's the component that can make quinoa taste bitter. To improve the taste of quinoa further, I sometimes add a dash of extra-virgin olive oil, chopped onions, and garlic, depending on the recipe. Other good additions include fresh chopped basil or thyme, dried oregano or rosemary, and/or a spritz of lemon juice.

Quinoa is frequently used in salads or simply served warm as a side dish, but there are many other ways to enjoy this nutritious powerhouse. For example, quinoa can be used as a crust for a quiche (mix up some cooked quinoa with egg and a bit of salt, press into the pan, and bake about 15 minutes), as an alternative to morning oatmeal (you can use milk instead of water—the quinoa gets deliciously creamy if slightly overcooked), and as "meatballs" in sauce and in soups. Find my recipe for quinoa salad on my website, DrJanet.com.

New Soy Alternative

Rapeseed may be a better source of plant protein than soy, according to nutrition scientists at the Martin Luther University Halle-Wittenberg. Rapeseed has a similar amino acid profile to soy, but it offers a more beneficial insulin response and a longer feeling of satiety. The downside, the researchers noted, is that it tastes like mustard, limiting its use to savory foods.

Christin Volk, PhD, Institute of Agricultural and Nutritional Sciences, Martin Luther University Halle-Wittenberg, Halle, Germany.

Try the New Green Mediterranean Diet for Optimal Health

Janet Bond Brill, PhD, RDN, FAND, a registered dietitian nutritionist, a fellow of the Academy of Nutrition and Dietetics, and a nationally recognized nutrition, health and fitness expert who specializes in cardiovascular disease prevention. Based in Hellertown, Pennsylvania, Dr. Brill is author of *Blood Pressure DOWN, Cholesterol DOWN,* and *Prevent a Second Heart Attack.* Dr. Brill's new book is *Intermittent Fasting for Dummies.* DrJanet.com

You've probably heard of the much-revered Mediterranean diet, the diet that consistently is rated the No. 1 "best overall diet" by the *U.S. News & World Report* annual review. Now, a new study just published in the journal *Heart* shows that making the conventional Mediterranean diet greener increases the health benefits even more.

Researchers randomly divided 300 overweight individuals at risk for heart disease into three groups: Healthy dietary guidance, traditional Mediterranean diet, and a "greener" Mediterranean diet—all with the same calories and exercise. The traditional Mediterranean diet includes fruit, vegetables, whole grains, legumes, and healthy fats like nuts and olive oil. It also includes fish and a reduced amount of meat and poultry.

The green Mediterranean diet participants added two things: They drank three to four cups of green tea a day, and they substituted plant protein for much of the animal protein consumed by the other two groups. Researchers found that after six months, the subjects following the modified "greener" version of the Mediterranean diet experienced greater weight loss and improved cardiovascular and metabolic risk factors compared with those following the other diets. The takeaway message is that if your goal is optimal health, a greener, more plant-based Mediterranean diet is best.

Translation: Replace fish, poultry, or meat with plant protein on most days of the week. Try sipping on green tea throughout the day as well.

Calcium: The Rest of the Story

Nicole Avena, PhD, a nutrition and diet expert and assistant professor of neuroscience at Mount Sinai Icahn School of Medicine in New York City. Dr. Avena is the author of *Why Diets Fail* and other nutrition-related books. Her research is focused on appetite and brain mechanisms that regulate food intake throughout the lifespan. DrNicoleAvena.com

It has been drilled into us for decades that calcium is crucial for the health of our bones and teeth. When we hit age 50, we hear the refrain even more loudly—don't slight your calcium intake, since bone-thinning osteoporosis affects one in four women and about one in 20 men in later life. Calcium even helps us keep our teeth as we grow older.

So you might have missed the rest of the story on calcium—that your muscles, heart, immune system...indeed, your very well-being ...are linked to this mineral, which comes from what we eat and drink rather than occurring naturally in our bodies.

And even though calcium is often pigeonholed as something mainly older women need to worry about, virtually every cell in every person's body, throughout one's lifespan, depends on this nutrient to work properly. *What you need to know about calcium—and the levels you need to stay healthy...*

TOO LITTLE CAN BE TOO LATE

At a fundamental level, calcium serves as a link between cells throughout the body. *Among the key body functions that involve calcium...*

- **Muscle contraction.** All the muscles in your body rely on calcium to trigger contraction by reacting with certain proteins in muscles that regulate movement. Without enough calcium, muscle contraction can be impaired, leading to muscle spasms.
- **Heart rate.** The heart is a muscle, of course, and its ability to pump relies heavily on calcium. Without it, a dangerously irregular heartbeat (arrhythmia) can develop.
- **Brain health.** For communication between our neurons to occur, we need calcium. Calcium is known as an intracellular messenger and plays many roles in the brain's ability to function properly.
- **Blood clotting.** Calcium contributes to the essential ability of blood to clot—for example, to stop the bleeding if you cut yourself. (This is different from life-threatening blood clots such as occur with atrial fibrillation, when the heart beats irregularly and/or quivers, causing blood to pool and form clots in the heart's chambers.)
- **Immune response.** Calcium is vital to the cell communication that helps regulate how well our immune system fights off germs and other invaders. Low levels of the mineral can lead to disruptions in the production of infection-fighting white blood cells.
- **Skin and other connective tissue.** Since our bodies are constantly creating new cells—a process that's key to the skin's elasticity—low calcium levels can contribute to sagging skin. The nutrient also helps support ligaments, tendons, and other connective tissues.

THE TESTING CONUNDRUM

Unfortunately, there is no good way to determine whether someone is running low on calcium. Technically, a simple blood test can measure your level of calcium. But because the body pulls calcium from the bones and teeth to make sure there is enough in the blood for critical body functions, the blood test isn't a reliable gauge.

Even if the blood level were consistent, this alone cannot reveal how well your body absorbs calcium. You may be consuming "enough," but what's most important is how well your body is using the mineral. Certain dietary habits, such as consuming a lot of salt, can interfere with calcium absorption.

Bone-density testing presents a catch-22. This type of test is able to deduce whether you're low on calcium by revealing problems such as osteopenia or osteoporosis after it's already developed...or worsened.

By then, the body has leached too much calcium from the bones—its calcium "bank"—and the only option is damage control to help prevent further bone loss since it's too late to completely shore up a weakened skeletal system.

Osteoporosis drugs can help slow further bone breakdown, but they can't reverse it. Some studies suggest that strength training can help to rebuild muscle strength and bone, which are related, but the mechanisms through which this occurs aren't well understood.

NUTRITIONAL TEAMWORK

Since our bodies don't produce calcium, our stores depend on what we consume in our diets. But the process is more complicated than simply downing calcium-rich foods.

Notice how a carton of milk might say, "Fortified with calcium and vitamin D"? Certain other nutrients (known as synergists) interact with calcium, boosting the mineral's ability to be more fully absorbed. This is why so many foods, such as dairy products, orange juice, and cereals, are fortified with calcium and vitamin D. Another significant synergist is vitamin K, which is rich in vegetables such as cabbage, watercress, broccoli, and asparagus.

Magnesium is also important to calcium functioning. It converts vitamin D into its active form so that it can help with calcium absorption. Other minerals, such as potassium, also play a role in calcium absorption.

It's not that difficult to fulfill your daily calcium requirements with a healthful diet. Ideally, look for fortified versions of dairy products such as yogurt, milk, and cheese...and eat plenty of dark-green, leafy vegetables such as kale, collard greens, and broccoli, which are also rich in vitamin K. Fish with edible, soft bones, such as sardines and canned salmon, are also calcium-rich and good sources of vitamin D.

The task gets more challenging for people who forgo dairy products. Fortunately, Lactaid, a lactose-free milk, and almond and other nondairy milk alternatives come in calcium-fortified versions. You can also double up on dark-green, leafy veggies and add other calcium-rich foods to your diet, including beans (such as kidney, navy, and Garbanzo) and fruit (such as oranges, figs, apricots, kiwi, and papayas).

To make sure you're getting enough calcium, aim for these daily levels through your diet and/or supplements (see below): For women age 19 to 50, the recommended dietary allowance (RDA) is 1,000 mg per day... and 1,200 mg daily after age 50. For men age 19 to 70, the RDA is 1,000 mg daily...and 1,200 mg thereafter.

Helpful: To make sure you are consuming enough calcium each day, you can use an app to log your food intake, which will show how much calcium you are getting.

Since excess caffeine intake, certain medications, renal disorders, or diets rich in foods that contain phytic acid or oxalic acid (such as whole grains, rhubarb, and spinach) may cause a decrease in calcium absorption, ask your doctor whether it's wise to consume a bit more, considering your age and any health conditions. This may be especially important if you have pancreatitis, celiac disease, or inflammatory bowel disease.

HOW TO USE SUPPLEMENTS SAFELY

Even though the foods described above—which offer multiple nutrients—are the preferred source of calcium, supplements can be used to ensure that you're getting enough of this vital mineral. While calcium supplements are available in many forms, calcium citrate is typically best absorbed. Look for a sublingual (under-the-tongue) version, which dissolves faster...and without sugar.

PROCEED WITH CAUTION

Of course, too much of anything is bad, and that's true for calcium as well. People who are predisposed to kidney stones face a greater risk for these nasty visitors if they consume more than the RDA of calcium, since the kidneys can't reliably filter out calcium that's not readily used by the body.

Some research also has linked the use of calcium supplements (without adequate levels of vitamin D) to cardiovascular disease. And calcium supplements may be associated with increased risk for dementia in older women who have had a stroke, according to research.

To help with bone health, research shows that it may require taking a vitamin D supplement (800 IU daily). Also, certain medications, such as H2 blockers and proton pump inhibitors for reflux or tetracycline antibiotics, can affect the efficacy of some calcium supplements. If you use one of these drugs, talk to your doctor before taking a calcium supplement.

The Vitamin Deficiency You Don't Know You Have

Sheldon B. Zablow, MD, assistant professor, department of psychiatry, UC San Diego School of Medicine, and author of *Your Vitamins Are Obsolete: The Vitamer Revolution.* SheldonZablowMD.com/author

---

Few vitamins are as misunderstood as B12. Considered by patients and doctors alike to be plentiful in the body and a concern only for vegetarians, deficiency in this crucial vitamin, along with its partner folate, is responsible for a vast array of seemingly unrelated—and often misdiagnosed—issues.

People with low levels of B12 and folate (B12/F) have been erroneously treated for multiple sclerosis, Alzheimer's disease, fibromyalgia, Parkinson's disease, dementia, and depression, while their B12/F deficiencies go unnoticed.

CONSEQUENCES OF DEFICIENCY

The most well-known sign of B12 deficiency is anemia, but it can also lead to memory problems, fatigue, depression, muscle weakness, poor balance, and permanent nerve damage. Low folate levels have been associated with a poor response to antidepressants, forgetfulness, difficulty concentrating, irritability, depression, behavioral changes, and memory loss.

If the body doesn't have enough B12/F, other vitamins and even medical interventions are less effective. For example, you could have plenty of vitamin D and calcium, but if you don't have enough B12/F, you can still develop osteoporosis. Having ample supplies of B12/F helps reduce inflammation and plays an essential role in DNA formation, reducing the damage caused by toxins. Studies show that low levels of B12/F are linked to various forms of cancer.

CAUSES OF DEFICIENCIES

Deficiencies in B12/F are common. Consider that only 30 to 40 percent of people have enough of the enzyme that efficiently converts the folic acid found in supplements and grain products into folate, the bioactive form used by the body. Similarly, there is plenty of B12 and folate in red meat, but 50 percent of people over the age of 50 can't manufacture enough stomach acid to break down the protein to release these vitamins. Vegetarians are commonly deficient.

A long list of medications can induce deficiency or block enzymatic reactions needed to convert common supplements into usable B12/F, including antacids, anti-inflammatories such as *prednisone,* nonsteroidal anti-inflammatory drugs like *ibuprofen*, antibiotics, anticonvulsants, estrogen and estrogen substitutes, nitrous oxide anesthesia, and drugs to treat diabetes, asthma, hypertension, and high cholesterol.

VITAMIN VS. VITAMER

In theory, supplementation should be a simple way to boost and maintain optimal levels of B12/F, but in reality, they often don't help. That's because vitamins come in many forms, and those found in supplements are not necessarily the kind the body uses. Most vitamins are made from inexpensive artificial compounds that are manipulated to improve their shelf life. But before the body can use these compounds, it has to convert them into biologically active structures called vitamers.

The B12 molecule exists in four configurations.—two are vitamers. *Adenosylcobalamin* (A-B12), found in the body's cells, plays a vital role in providing the energy for reproduction, cell maintenance, and fighting off infection. It also prevents the buildup of a molecule called methylmalonyl acid, which can damage the protective myelin sheath that covers the nerves.

Methylcobalamin (M-B12) circulates in the bloodstream until it's needed. When it's pulled into the cells, it works with folate to convert a waste product called homocysteine into S-adenosyl methionine (SAMe). When M-B12 is lacking, homocysteine accumulates in the bloodstream, where it has toxic effects on blood vessels in the heart and brain, increasing the risk of heart attacks, strokes, and dementia.

Taken orally, A-B12 and M-B12 are absorbed quickly and reach all cells in the body. (Your doctor may also give you B12 injections.) The two other forms of B12 have to be converted through a multistep process before the body can use them. *Hydroxocobalamin* (H-B12) is manufactured by bacteria and *cyanocobalamin* (C-B12) is made in a lab.

If you take a B12 supplement, you most likely take C-B12: It's found in 99 percent of all supplements in the United States. C-B12 requires a multistage conversion process to become usable—a process that can be disrupted by aging, infection, medications, toxins, or drinking alcohol. Because the vitamin is absorbed by passive diffusion, you use only about one percent of what the bottle advertises.

FOLATE

Folate (B9) is B12's partner vitamer. They rely on each other to complete a wide variety of cellular tasks. There are several causes of folate deficiency, including medications, alcohol consumption, celiac disease, and obesity. You may consume inadequate amounts via your diet, or your body might absorb the vitamin poorly. If you are fortunate, your body absorbs about 50 percent of the folate you eat, depending on the food (dark leafy greens, peanuts, and liver are good sources), its freshness, and how it is processed, stored, and prepared.

SUPPLEMENTATION: BUYER BEWARE

Supplementation can improve levels of both folate and B12—if you take the right product. Unfortunately, the labels on many supplement bottles do not accurately reflect what's inside the pills.

- **Folate.** While many supplements claim they contain folate, they actually contain folic acid, which is the synthetic form of folate used in food fortification and dietary supplements. As with C-B12, the body must convert the artificial folic acid into folate. The conversion process is genetically impaired in more than 50 percent of the population; therefore, many people don't use sufficient amounts of folate even though they're consuming large amounts of folic acid via fortified foods and vitamin pills.

The U.S. Food and Drug Administration notes that 1 milligram (mg) is the maximum recommended dose of over-the-counter folate, but it turns out that number is probably the minimal optimal daily dose of L-methylfolate for most people. The recommended dose of L-methylfolate is at least 1,000 mg per day, but the hard part is finding a good source. The best bet (for any supplement) is to buy a brand from a reputable manufacturer that you have researched. ConsumerLab.com is a reliable, independent source that tests supplements taken off the shelf in stores, rather than bottles provided by the manufacturer.

- **B12.** When it comes to B12, choose a supplement in the vitamer form, either as A-B12 and/or M-B12 in a total dose of at least 2 mg per day. Avoid C-B12. You often have to read labels and ingredient lists carefully to tease out what form of B12 the supplement contains.

TAKING YOUR VITAMER SUPPLEMENTS

Always make sure your physicians know about all supplementation used, to avoid any contraindications with other medications.

Once you get the go-ahead, take B12 and folate together on an empty stomach, with 4 ounces of water. The 4 ounces are necessary to fully dissolve the tablet and dilute the ingredients for efficient absorption. Vitamers are sensitive to the presence of other vitamins and minerals (iron), so take them without other supplements or food.

The first thing you may notice is thicker nails and hair as well as skin injuries that heal more quickly. You may have subtle positive changes in your mood, speech, and memory. If you don't notice any benefits after three months, stop taking the supplements for three to four weeks. Sometimes you don't realize how much a supplement has helped until you stop.

Miraculous Magnesium

Lina Velikova, MD, PhD, medical advisor for Supplements101.net. She is an assistant professor at Sofia University St. Kliment Ohridski, Sofia, Bulgaria, and is a member of the editorial board of the *World Journal of Immunology*.

An essential mineral, magnesium is involved in blood glucose control, blood pressure regulation, muscle and nerve function, and protein synthesis.

When a person is deficient—as an estimated 56 to 75 percent of Americans are—the effects can be widespread, causing symptoms as varied as fatigue, loss of appetite, seizures, abnormal heart rhythms, and even personality changes. Even if someone isn't deficient, low levels of magnesium can affect a variety of bodily systems.

• **Sleep.** Magnesium regulates the nervous system, particularly the neurotransmitters that pass information back and forth from the body to the brain. It promotes relaxation, which improves the ability to fall asleep faster and obtain better sleep quality.

• **Asthma.** By relaxing the bronchial muscles and widening the airways, magnesium can alleviate asthma symptoms. It is not a first-line treatment, but adding a magnesium supplement to traditional asthma medications can help prevent acute asthma attacks.

• **Anxiety and depression.** Magnesium has a vital role in the healthy functioning of the brain. There's a link between low magnesium levels and anxiety, which suggests that taking a supplement may ease anxiety. A cross-sectional study of close to 20,000 people published in 2019 reported that people who had more magnesium in their diets had lower rates of depression.

• **Type 2 diabetes.** Magnesium is essential for insulin metabolism and glucose control. Research has shown that most diabetics suffer from magnesium insufficiency and that magnesium helps manage the disease by improving insulin sensitivity. A meta-analysis published in the *Journal of Internal Medicine* in 2007 found that a 100 milligram (mg) per day increase in total magnesium intake decreased the risk of diabetes by 15 percent.

• **Blood pressure.** Adequate daily magnesium intake from food or supplements can decrease systolic and diastolic blood pressure in people who have both high blood pressure and magnesium deficiency. When blood vessels are narrowed or constricted, blood pressure rises, but magnesium reduces that constriction, allowing the blood to flow more freely. One meta-analysis of 22 studies concluded that magnesium supplementation decreased systolic blood pressure by 3 to 4 mmHg and diastolic blood pressure by 2 to 3 mmHg.

That may be why researchers found that people with serum magnesium levels in the highest quartile of normal (at least 0.88 millimoles per liter [mmol/L]) had a 38 percent lower risk of sudden cardiac death than people with levels in the lowest quartile (0.75 mmol/L or less).

• **Osteoporosis.** The National Institutes of Health reports that women with osteopenia and osteoporosis have lower serum magnesium levels than women without those conditions, suggesting that magnesium deficiency might be a risk factor for osteoporosis. Furthermore, several studies suggest a positive correlation between magnesium intake and bone mineral density in both men and women.

• **Migraine headaches.** A review of three placebo-controlled studies found that 600 mg per day of supplemental magnesium led to a small reduction in migraine frequency. The American Headache Society and the American Academy of Neurology note that magnesium supplementation should be considered for migraine prevention because evidence suggests that it is "probably effective."

The strongest evidence has been found in people who experience migraine auras and in women who have menstrual-related migraines.

BOOSTING MAGNESIUM

The recommended dietary allowance for magnesium depends on age and sex. Women need about 310 mg each day when they are between 19 and 30 years old, and 320 mg after age 31. Men should aim for 400 mg through age 30, then bump up to 420 mg. A wide variety of foods are excellent sources of magnesium. (See next column.)

You can also take a supplement. Magnesium supplements come in different forms, and absorption and bioavailability vary by type. Opt for magnesium citrate when available. If not, look for magnesium lactate and magnesium chloride, both of which are absorbed better than magnesium oxide and magnesium sulfate.

Prolonged soaking in Epsom salts may also increase magnesium levels in the blood.

SIDE EFFECTS

The most common side effect of magnesium supplementation is diarrhea. In fact, magnesium can also be used as a treatment for constipation. High doses can cause nausea and abdominal cramping. Very large doses (more than 5,000 mg/day) have been associated with magnesium toxicity, which can cause hypotension, nausea, vomiting, flushing, urine retention, depression, muscle weakness, difficulty breathing, irregular heartbeat, and cardiac arrest.

MEDICATION COMPLICATIONS

Before taking a magnesium supplement, talk to your doctor about potential medication interactions. Magnesium can decrease the absorption of oral bisphosphonates, such as *alendronate* (Fosamax), so they should be taken at least two hours apart. Similarly, if you're taking a tetracycline antibiotic, such as *demeclocycline* (Declomycin) and *doxycycline* (Vibramycin), or a quinolone antibiotic, such as *ciprofloxacin* (Cipro) and *levofloxacin* (Levaquin), take the magnesium two hours before the antibiotic.

EAT YOUR MAGNESIUM

Many common foods are excellent sources of the mineral...

Nuts

Almonds, 1 oz, 80 mg
Peanut butter, 2 Tbsp, 49 mg
Cashews, 1 oz, 74 mg

Seeds

Pumpkin seed, 1 oz, 168 mg
Flaxseed, 2 Tbsp, 78 mg
Chia seeds, 1 oz, 111 mg

Whole grains

Brown rice, ½ cup, 42 mg
Dry buckwheat, 1 oz, 65 mg
Shredded wheat, 2 biscuits, 61 mg
Oatmeal, instant, 1 packet, 36 mg
Bread, whole wheat, 1 slice, 23 mg

Beans

Black beans, cooked, ½ cup, 60 mg
Kidney beans, ½ cup, 35 mg
Edamame, ⅓ cup, 50 mg

Fruits and vegetables

Spinach, cooked, 157 mg
Potato with skin, 3.5 oz, 43 mg
Banana, 32 mg
Raisins, ½ cup, 23 mg
Avocado, ½ cup, 22 mg
Broccoli, ½ cup, 12 mg
Apple, 1 medium, 9 mg
Carrot, raw, 1 medium, 7 mg

Meats

Salmon, 3 oz, 26 mg
Chicken breast, 3 oz, 22 mg
Beef, 3 oz, 22 mg
Halibut, 3 oz, 24 mg

Dairy and dairy replacements

Milk, 1 percent, 1 cup, 39 mg
Yogurt, 1 cup, 30 mg
Soy milk, 1 cup, 61 mg

Vitamin C Is Associated With Higher Muscle Mass

Men with sufficient levels of vitamin C in their blood had about 2 percent more fat-free muscle mass than men with insufficient levels...women, nearly 4 percent more. After age 50, we lose 0.5 percent to one percent of muscle mass per year, contributing to health problems and earlier death.

Best: Obtain vitamin C from a range of vegetables and fruits.

Ailsa Welch, PhD, professor of nutritional epidemiology at University of East Anglia, Norwich, UK, and leader of a study of 13,000 adults ages 42 to 82, published in *The Journal of Nutrition.*

Strength Training After 50

Brad Schoenfeld, PhD, associate professor of exercise science at Lehman College in Bronx, New York, and a certified strength and conditioning specialist (CSCS). He is author of numerous fitness books including *Women's Home Workout Bible.*

Have you been shying away from weights? You're not alone. Less than 15 percent of older adults regularly do strength training, according to a study published in *Clinical Interventions in Aging.*

Yes, cardio is a must for heart health, and those tai chi classes are terrific for mind-body wellness and balance. But when it comes to building up the muscles that will help you be independent and flexible, strength training is the ticket.

Unexpected bonuses: In addition to improving key biomarkers, such as blood sugar and blood fats, research shows that strength training even improves executive functioning and memory.

With all those benefits, what's stopping you? While it's easy to lace up your walking shoes, many people just don't know how to get started with a strength-training regimen.

The good news is, it's never too late to start—and strength training can be easy to do. However, if you're new to strength training, it's wise to book an appointment with a personal trainer, who can assess your abilities, show you proper form, and customize a routine for you with body-weight, free-weight, and/or machine exercises.

It takes only about 10 to 15 minutes two or three times a week to obtain benefits in health and functional capacity with a strength-training workout. To gain muscle strength, you need to do as many repetitions (reps) as it takes to reach exhaustion. One set (eight to 12 reps) of each exercise usually does the trick if the weight is heavy enough. To continually challenge your muscles, add weight and/or reps as you progress.

To get started, here's a simple strength-training program...*

GET STRONG WITH THESE 6 SIMPLE EXERCISES

- **Squat.**

Target: Quads (front of thighs), glutes (buttocks), and hamstrings (back of thighs).

What to do: While standing with your feet shoulder-width apart and slightly turned out, contract your core (abdominal and back) muscles and slowly lower your body as though sitting down in a chair until your thighs are parallel to the floor. Once you reach the "seated" position (or as low as you can safely go with proper form), straighten your legs to return to start.

Goal: When you're just beginning, do the exercise without hand weights and work up to using weights that challenge your muscles.

Good rule of thumb: If you aren't struggling on the last repetition, then the weight is too light.

- **Front plank.**

Target: Core.

What to do: Lie on your stomach with your forearms on the floor and feet together. While keeping your spine straight, lift your body off the floor, balancing on your forearms and toes

*As with any new exercise program, consult your doctor before starting.

and contracting your core muscles. Hold for up to 60 seconds.

Goal: To make the exercise more challenging, work up to balancing on your hands instead of your forearms.

- **Chest press.**

Target: Pectorals (upper chest).

What to do: Lie face up on a bench with your legs on either side, feet flat on the floor and holding a hand weight in each hand. Bring the weights to your shoulders, palms facing away and upper arms pressed to your sides. Then extend your arms straight up, bringing both weights together until they touch when your arms are fully extended.

Alternative: If you don't have a bench, you can lie on the floor when performing this exercise—but it will limit your range of motion and somewhat lessen the results.

- **Lateral raise.**

Target: Deltoids (shoulder).

What to do: While standing with your feet shoulder-width apart, grasp a hand weight in each hand, palms facing your body and arms at your sides. Keeping your elbows slightly bent, raise your arms out to the sides and lift the weights to shoulder level. Be sure not to raise your shoulders as you lift the weights.

- **Single-arm row.**

Target: Back.

What to do: Place your left hand and left knee on a flat bench with your right foot firmly on floor. Grasp a hand weight in your right hand, palm facing your body and arm at your side. Raise the weight straight up until it's just below your armpit. Contract the muscles in your upper back as you lower the arm back down. Complete reps on one side, then repeat on the other side.

Alternative: If you don't have a bench, you can grasp any secure object. If it's a chair, be sure that it's very sturdy to avoid injury.

- **Calf raise.**

Target: Calves.

What to do: While steadying yourself with a handrail, stand on a stair tread with your weight on the balls of your feet, heels hanging off and below the stair. Rise up as high as you can onto your toes until your ankles are fully extended. Contract your calves, and then slowly return to starting position.

Stay Motivated to Stay Fit

Jillian Michaels, fitness expert, owner of Empowered Media LLC, and star of the reality television shows *The Biggest Loser* and *Losing It With Jillian*. She is certified as a nutrition and wellness consultant with the American Fitness Professionals and Associates. Her diet and exercise app, The Fitness App, is available on Apple and Android platforms.

It can be difficult to stick with a fitness routine in the best of times, but dealing with the pandemic has been unlike any other. Lockdowns, gym closures, and the stress of coronavirus have disrupted many people's exercise schedules and healthy eating habits.

To get tips on how to stay fit in the face of any challenge, we talked to Jillian Michaels, personal trainer, producer of more than 20 exercise videos, star of the television show *The Biggest Loser* and developer of a new app called The Fitness App.

Can you share a personal story of a time when you had to overcome obstacles to your own fitness routine?

To be honest, at least half the time, I struggle to make myself train. So, arguably, the answer would be daily. When I'm tired, work is stressing me out, my kids are wearing me down, the day has been particularly crappy, I think to myself that I would rather stick needles in my eyes than exercise. I just want to order a pizza.

But I don't, because I then think about how I would feel after I did that, and, conversely, how I will feel if I do some physical activity instead.

I remind myself of all the reasons I work out and how it brings me all the things I care most about—being a good role model to my kids, feeling confident in my own skin, having the peace of mind that my health is good. That said, sometimes I play little tricks with myself.

I'll say, "Okay. Just do 15 minutes. Then if you want to stop you can stop." But 99 times out of 100, I end up doing at least 20 minutes, and I never regret it.

What makes a routine—whether it's exercise or healthy eating—resilient?

Resolve. It starts with your state of mind. If you want it and you have a reason to work for it, then you will do it. That said, there are certain elements that help someone stick with healthy eating and fitness.

Take a balanced approach that is rooted in passionate purpose. Don't be too strict. There's no need to cut out carbs. Don't dramatically reduce calories or starve yourself. The key is simply to not eat more than you burn in a day.

Practice the 80/20 rule. Make 80 percent of your food choices healthy and limit treats to 20 percent. For example, if you eat 1,800 calories a day, allot roughly 400 calories to whatever you like (a slice of pizza, a brownie, a serving of ice cream) and then spend the other 1,400 calories on healthier choices. Go with sashimi and sushi instead of fattening rolls with tons of sauce. Choose the side salad instead of the fries. Order water instead of a soda.

What do you recommend people do if they can't or won't go to the gym and, in many parts of the country, it's too cold to exercise outdoors?

There are so many solutions. You can get an incredible workout at your home with inexpensive equipment or none at all. You can take classes online if you still pay for a gym membership, as many gyms are doing this to keep patrons signed up. If you have a trainer, you can do FaceTime training sessions with him or her. For far more affordable solutions, you can use apps and streaming platforms.

I recently launched my own app, The Fitness App (available on Apple and Android devices), that has my entire DVD library, as well as completely customizable programs including yoga, kickboxing, free weights, body-weight training, calisthenics, jump rope, kettlebells, slides, and booty-band workouts.

What advice do you have for someone who just dislikes exercise?

If you truly have no physical activity you are passionate about, that's fine. Instead, ask yourself what fitness results you are excited for? Do you want to walk without feeling breathless? Live to meet your great-grandkids? Feel comfortable in a two-piece instead of a one-piece?

It doesn't matter how superficial or how profound your reasons are, as long as you're passionate about them. If you have that why, you can tolerate the how (the work associated with the goal). Then from there, remind yourself that four 30-minute sessions a week are a reasonable price to pay for those bigger things you are passionate about attaining.

Challenges arise. What is your advice on how to get back up when we fall off the wagon?

I like to play devil's advocate. What if you just kept up the downward spiral? What if you thought, "Hey I had a piece of pie last night and a couple of glasses of wine. That's it. My health is shot. I'm just going to quit exercising forever and eat terribly." Honestly, think about that. How is that rational?

It's like getting a flat tire and then getting out of your car, slashing all three other tires, and tossing a Molotov cocktail into the driver's side window all because you had a bad meal, day, week, and, yes, even a bad year. It happens. It's never too late. And honestly, there is no other rational alternative than to get back on the horse at some point.

Plus, if you are practicing a more balanced approach, you realize that some days you eat more, and then other days, you can balance it by eating less. You can exercise a bit longer the next day. If you've incorporated treat foods into your regimen, a slip won't trigger you, making you feel a massive pendulum swing that happens when you restrict yourself too intensely.

The Best Home Gym Equipment for Any Budget

Carol Ewing Garber, PhD, professor of movement sciences and director of the graduate program in applied physiology at Teachers College, Columbia University, New York City. She is a registered clinical exercise physiologist and past president of the American College of Sports Medicine. TC.Columbia.edu

There are so many makes and models of home exercise equipment that you could work up a sweat trying to choose which are right for you.

Among the questions you need to consider: Do I really need to spend big bucks to have an effective workout? Which items are built to last? And which will make me want to work out?

Here are some of the best pieces of exercise equipment for different needs and budgets*...

TREADMILLS

Construction quality and warranty length are especially important with motorized treadmills, which take a pounding.

Best overall treadmill: Precor TRM 445 is an extremely durable, gym-quality product backed by an excellent warranty. It features an effective shock-absorption system that reduces stress on knees, hips and feet, and it's capable of creating inclines as steep as 15 percent and declines up to 2 percent. It's very quiet, has a 22-x-56-inch running surface and can reach speeds up to 12 miles per hour (mph)—a five-minute mile. $4,999. PrecorAtHome.com

Best folding/budget treadmill: Sole F80 doesn't sacrifice durability or running surface area for the sake of compact size the way some folding treadmills do. Its running surface is a big 22-x-60 inches and provides effective shock absorption—it's capable of speeds up to 12 mph and inclines up to 15 percent, though it does not decline. $1,600. SoleTreadmills.com

*Some products listed here were temporarily out of stock at press time because of increased demand and production delays. Prices are the lowest recently available.

STATIONARY BIKES

It's important that you choose a stationary bike that makes you feel comfortable. The best ones have seats and handlebars that can be adjusted in multiple ways. A "recumbent" stationary bike allows you to sit at a relaxed angle on a truly supportive seat rather than perch leaning forward on a small bike seat. Some high-end bikes offer live spin-class workouts or sessions with trainers on video screens, though that generally requires paying a membership fee. You could skip that and just mount a tablet computer in front of a lower-priced no-membership-fee bike, then use free fitness apps or stream spin-class videos and first-person-perspective rides available for free on YouTube. (See page 204 in chapter 12, "Consumer Savvy," for more information.)

Best overall upright stationary bike: Diamondback 510ic Indoor Cycle Magnetic Trainer, which has an extremely adjustable seat and handlebars, can fit riders from 5' 2" to 6' 5". This sturdy bike's chain drive and 32-pound flywheel provide an admirably smooth ride, while its 16 resistance levels and many preset workout programs help keep those rides challenging and interesting. Its video screen displays data such as speed, distance and heart rate, but if you want a video distraction, you'll have to place it near a TV or attach a tablet. $720. DiamondbackFitness.com

Warning: Fit and comfort are crucial, as noted above, and not even the impressively adjustable 510ic feels right to everyone. Other well-made stationary bikes worth a test ride include the Assault AirBike Classic ($699, AssaultFitness.com)...Concept 2 BikeErg ($990, Concept2.com)...and Peloton Indoor Exercise Bike, which has grown tremendously popular because of its subscription-based live-video spin classes (Starting at $1,895, OnePeloton.com).

Best budget/folding stationary bike: Xterra Fitness FB150 Folding Exercise Bike is solidly built for its price range, yet also capable of folding down to an impressive small amount of floorspace when not in use—18.1"

x 18.1". It features eight resistance settings and, unlike many low-cost models, a useful display screen that provides feedback such as speed, time, distance, pulse rate, and calories burned. It's not designed for people heavier than 225 pounds or taller than 5' 10", however, though it does fit riders as short as 4' 10". $160. XterraFitness.com

Best recumbent stationary bike: Schwinn 270 Recumbent Bike is quiet and extremely versatile—with 25 levels of resistance and 29 workout programs, nine of them controlled by the rider's heart rate. There are heart-rate monitors in the handlebar grips, or an optional heart-rate–monitoring chest strap can be added. Its comfortable seat has ventilation and lumbar support, while its "step-through" frame design makes it easy to get on and off, even for riders who have limited mobility. It can support riders up to 300 pounds, though people significantly taller than six feet or shorter than 5' 3" might find it a poor fit. $649. SchwinnFitness.com

Best budget recumbent stationary bike: Marcy Recumbent Exercise Bike ME-709 has impressively solid construction quality considering its low price. Like the Schwinn, it has a step-through design and can handle riders up to 300 pounds, but the ME-709 also can handle riders with inseams of 27 to 36 inches. It has eight resistance settings and—unlike some in this price range—it includes a screen that reports time, distance, speed, and calories burned. $210. MarcyPro.com

ELLIPTICAL TRAINERS

High-end ellipticals are more likely than cheaper ones to have adjustable stride length, making them appropriate for a greater range of heights and gaits. Better units also offer a greater range of resistance levels and exercise routines.

Best overall elliptical trainer: Sole E95S lets users set stride length from 18 inches up to 24 inches with the push of a button, a range wide enough to accommodate almost everyone. Users also can choose among 20 resistance levels and 10 workout programs, including two controlled by the user's heart rate—pulse sensors are built into the grips, or you can wear the wireless chest strap. The E95S is impressively sturdy—it's capable of handling users up to 400 pounds—and is backed by an excellent warranty. It has moving arms for a full-body workout, and its big 30-pound flywheel provides smooth, quiet operation.

The main downside: It's so solidly built that it can be a challenge to reposition—it weighs 265 pounds. $2,199.99. SoleTreadmills.com

Best budget elliptical trainer: ProForm Endurance 620 E is sturdy and backed by a

solid warranty. Its stride length is fixed at 19 inches, but it has moving arms, 18 different resistance levels and a zero percent-to-20 percent adjustable "ramp" angle that mimics an incline. Like many ellipticals, it's heavy—over 300 pounds. $999. ProForm.com

ROWING MACHINES

Different rowing machines produce resistance in different ways. Some use hydraulic pistons, but those provide poor durability and unpleasant, inconsistent resistance. Others use magnetic resistance, which is reliable and very quiet. For a more authentic rowing feel, a few use water resistance where paddles pull through a water tank, or air resistance, where rowing spins a flywheel.

Best overall rowing machine: Concept2 RowErg is an air-resistance rower that's durable enough to be used in professional gyms. It separates easily into two sections, making it simple to store away if, for example, you need

to convert your workout room to a guest room for the holidays. The RowErg is sturdy enough to handle rowers up to 500 pounds even though the unit itself weighs a modest 57 pounds. Users with inseams greater than 38 inches might require an optional extra-long monorail. $900. Concept2.com

Alternative: The Concept2 Model E, costing $1,100, is similar to the model D but with a higher seat that's easier to get on and off.

Best for simulating the feel of rowing on water: WaterRower Classic Rowing Machine does this as well as any rowing machine on the market—resistance results from rotating a flywheel that's inside a small, sealed water tank. With its black walnut frame the WaterRower is more attractive than most exercise equipment, but it doesn't put style ahead of substance. It's so sturdy that its maximum user weight is listed at 1,000 pounds, though users with inseams greater than 37 inches might benefit from the XL Rail Option, which adds $100 to the price. $1,495. WaterRower.com

Best budget rowing machine: Sunny Health & Fitness SF-RW5515 uses magnetic resistance rather than the less desirable hydraulic resistance provided by many rowing machines in its price range. Build quality is good for home use, and users with inseams up to 44 inches should find it a good fit, though maximum user weight is 250 pounds. $249.98. SunnyHealthFitness.com

---

Raising the Barre

Kristen Gasnick, PT, a doctor of physical therapy at Excel Orthopedic Physical Therapy, Livingston, New Jersey.

Don't let the dance origin of barre exercise scare you off. This popular workout focuses on simple movements that people of any ability can do to build strength, increase flexibility, improve balance, and optimize posture and core stability.

Barre is low impact, so it puts less pressure on the body's joints than activities like running. It employs a combination of bodyweight movements and light weights for resistance training as well as high repetitions of very small movements called isometric exercises.

Barre exercises incorporate movement in all three body planes—frontal, sagittal, and transverse. The frontal plane divides the body into front and back. The sagittal plane divides it into left and right, and the transverse plane divides it into top and bottom halves. Multiplanar movement engages muscles and joints through their full ranges and helps to maintain optimal mobility.

WHAT A WORKOUT LOOKS LIKE

A barre workout should incorporate both upper and lower body movements as well as exercises that target balance and core strength. If you take a class, you'll use a ballet barre for balance. At home, you can use a sturdy chair. *Here are four exercises to try...*

• **Backward lunge.** Stand upright and take a large step back with one foot. Lower your body until the opposite thigh is parallel with the floor. Keep your front knee over your front ankle. Return to a full standing position and switch sides. Do three sets of 10 repetitions. When you are in the lowered position, try adding in a set of pulses where you move up an inch up and down an inch 10 times.

This movement targets the gluteus muscles unilaterally, ensuring that both sides of the body are being worked equally, and improves balance when transitioning between starting and ending positions.

• **Lateral leg lifts.** Lift your leg to the side and slowly raise it to hip height or as far as is comfortable, and lower it back down. Do three sets of 10 repetitions. You can also add in pulses when your leg is lifted.

This movement targets the gluteus medius, a hip muscle that is key for providing stability to the pelvis and maintaining balance.

• **Arm sweeps.** Sweep your arms out to the side while rotating your palms toward the front of the room. You can do this exercise with or without hand weights. The lifting motion targets the shoulder muscles (deltoids), while rotating the palms forward encourages external rotation and activation of the rotator cuff musculature that stabilizes the shoulder. Bring the arms all the way back down and complete three sets of 15 repetitions. A set of pulses can be added at the top of the movement.

• **Seated core.** Sit on the ground with your knees bent and your feet flat in front of you. Lean back so that your torso is at about a 45-degree angle. Holding this position for five to 30 seconds without using your hands to touch the ground or hold onto your legs for support will get the core muscles firing. When holding this position becomes easy, increase the challenge by adding dynamic arm movements, such as alternating arm lifts, or by rotating the arms and trunk from side to side.

CHALLENGES

While anyone can benefit from barre exercises, people with poor balance need to be careful. Dynamic movements such as lunges and single-leg exercises that alternate from one leg to the other can be challenging if performed without a barre or chair. Many instructors, whether in a studio or through an online video, provide modifications for different fitness levels.

Barre exercise does not offer cardiovascular benefits, so it should be part of a broader program. A fitness regimen should include both strength training and cardiovascular exercise to keep muscles, joints, and the heart and lungs functioning optimally. Walking is a simple and effective cardiovascular exercise that helps keep the heart healthy and is low impact on the body. Adults should aim for 30 to 60 minutes of walking at least three to five times a week in addition to some form of strengthening workout, such as barre, for a comprehensive exercise routine.

How to Spot-Train Your Butt

The idea of targeting one specific body part to shed fat is a myth. But you can certainly target a specific area for muscle growth and toning.

Here's how to train your glutes: First, learn to activate your glutes through resistance-band or body-weight exercises such as kickbacks, air squats, and unweighted lunges. Once you have successfully mastered contracting one butt-cheek at a time, you're ready for weighted lifts. Deadlifts, sumo squats, barbell glute bridges, reverse lunges, curtsy lunges and weighted step-ups work the glutes from all angles and make your butt perkier, rounder, fuller and firmer. (YouTube is a good resource for how to perform each one properly or to find a premade booty workout.)

Roundup of personal trainers reported at Health.com.

5

Natural Cures

Fight Back Against Winter Illness: Super Immune-Boosters Your Doctor Doesn't Know About

Tis the season for watching the snow fall...drinking hot cocoa and reading by the fireplace...and getting hit with viruses, which thrive in colder weather.

You most likely already know about the immune-enhancing powers of zinc, vitamins C and D, and medicinal plants such as echinacea and elderberry. But several other powerful supplements exist that may decrease your chances of getting sick and help you recover faster if you do get sick.

Note: These supplements are generally safe in the amounts mentioned here, but discuss taking them with your doctor, especially if you are immune-compromised or taking medication.

IMMUNE-BOOSTERS FOR EVERYONE

N-acetylcysteine (NAC) is an amino acid that supports immunity directly. Also, the body easily converts NAC into the antioxidant glutathione—more on glutathione later. NAC is well-tolerated, inexpensive, and so effective against influenza that in one Italian study, only 25 percent of elderly people taking 600 mg twice daily throughout flu season exhibited flu symptoms, versus nearly 80 percent of those in the placebo group. Of those who did show symptoms, NAC significantly decreased the severity and intensity.

Mark A. Stengler, NMD, naturopathic medical doctor and founder of the Stengler Center for Integrative Medicine in Encinitas, California. He has served on a medical advisory committee for the Yale University Complementary Medicine Outcomes Research Project and is author of *The Natural Physician's Healing Therapies* and coauthor of *Outside the Box Cancer Therapies: Alternative Therapies That Treat and Prevent Cancer* and *Prescription for Drug Alternatives.* His newest book is *Healing the Prostate.* MarkStengler.com

Daily dose: 1,200 mg daily, divided into two 600-mg doses. At the first sign of influenza or cold symptoms, increase to 3,600 mg to 4,000 mg daily for adults, divided into two doses a day, and continue until symptoms subside.

• **Probiotics.** For decades, naturopathic doctors have been saying a healthy gut, populated by beneficial bacteria, is necessary for a healthy immune system. This immune booster might not be as surprising as the others, but probiotics are so powerful and vital for a healthy immune system (the word probiotic itself means "beneficial for life") that they cannot go unmentioned.

Good bugs: While the cold virus and influenza are most certainly bad bugs, probiotics are the kind that are good for you. These bacteria, which come in several strains, including Lactobacillus, Bifidobacteria, and Saccharomyces, live in your gut and have many jobs, including regulating the immune system. In fact, about 70 percent to 80 percent of your immune system resides in your gut!

Supplemental probiotics taken regularly for preventive defense have been shown to decrease duration of the common cold in the elderly, adults and children.

New: "A clear decrease" has been seen in numbers of Lactobacillus and Bifidobacterium strains in the guts of patients with COVID-19, according to an August 2020 *Frontiers in Microbiology* study.

Daily dose: Probiotics are measured in CFUs—colony-forming units, which represent the bacteria's potential to divide and reproduce. Aim for 20 billion CFUs a day. *You can get there via a combination of food and supplementation...*

• **Food.** When you consume probiotic-rich foods and beverages, such as kefir, yogurt, kimchee, sauerkraut, miso soup, and other fermented foods, you bathe your gut in helpful bacteria. Kefir is especially good, as it has multiple strains of bacteria, whereas yogurt typically offers only one or two.

Try: Lifeway Kefir, with 12 strains and 25 billion to 30 billion beneficial probiotic CFUs per cup ($2.99 to $4.99 for 32 ounces). There also are dairy-free yogurts such as those with an almond, soy, or coconut base that contain healthful bacteria.

• **Supplements.** When choosing a daily probiotic, look for one containing strains used in published human studies, such as *Lactobacillus paracasei* and *Lactobacillus plantarum.*

Try: Metagenics UltraFlora Immune Booster ($44 for 30 capsules).

Note: Some probiotics are stable at room temperature, but if a product's label says that it needs to be refrigerated, buy it only if it has been refrigerated at the store. This could help prevent some of the bacteria from dying on the shelf before you get the product home.

FOR AN EVEN BIGGER BOOST

If you are immune-compromised with a chronic health condition or want to be more proactive, you also can add these supplements...

• **Glutathione.** Known as "the mother of all antioxidants," glutathione is one of the body's most powerful weapons against immune-damaging compounds. When viruses, bacteria, or even toxins such as pesticides and heavy metals enter the body, the liver begins secreting glutathione to help neutralize them. Besides being worthwhile for those who are immune-compromised, taking glutathione preventively is beneficial to those who are exposed to a lot of toxins in the workplace, such as someone working in a hair salon or as a welder or painter, etc.

Powerful research: In a study published in *European Journal of Nutrition,* 54 healthy nonsmoking adults were given either 250 mg or 1,000 mg of glutathione every day for six months or a placebo. By three months, those receiving the larger supplement dose showed double the natural killer-cell activity, meaning that they were producing twice as many of these cells known for scavenging the bloodstream for bacteria, viruses, and even cancer cells.

Created by a combination of three amino acids (cysteine, glutamic acid, and glycine), glutathione also binds to free radicals—naturally occurring yet damaging by-products of daily living that contribute to cellular damage and premature aging.

Production of this important immune-system protector decreases with age and is compromised in individuals with chronic conditions such as obesity and type 2 diabetes, as well as in those who smoke. When levels drop, white blood cells are diminished, allowing viral and bacterial infections to thrive.

LINK WITH COVID-19?

A number of new studies have identified glutathione deficiency as a possible contributing factor to COVID-19 deaths in the elderly and people with chronic diseases. Higher levels of glutathione may protect against acute respiratory distress syndrome and cytokine storm—the massive flood of inflammatory cells into the body that can lead to death in COVID-19 patients—by inhibiting replication of the virus.

Daily dose: Glutathione is made by the body and also is found in small amounts in certain foods, including cruciferous veggies such as cauliflower and broccoli, asparagus, avocado, cucumber, green beans, apples, and spinach. Most Americans consume only about 150 mg of glutathione per day through the foods they eat, just half of the minimum daily amount recommended by most experts, making supplementation an excellent strategy. Try 200 mg/day to 250 mg/day for general immune support, or 250 mg twice daily if you're sick.

I like Setria, the brand used in the *European Journal of Nutrition* study ($15 for 60 250-mg capsules).

Note: Although the label says to take this supplement with a meal, I think it is best to take it on an empty stomach so that it does not compete with other amino acids.

• **Beta glucan.** Derived from yeast or mushroom extracts, beta glucans are naturally occurring polysaccharides—chains of sugar molecules linked together—that activate the soldiers of your immune system known as macrophages. Once activated, macrophages gobble up viruses and signal the rest of the immune system to stand at attention. Various studies have shown that beta glucan supplementation reduces the number of symptomatic cold episodes...reduces upper-respiratory symptoms in colds and other infections...and reduces sleep difficulties caused by colds. In one study, 75 marathon runners between the ages of 18 and 53 took either 250 mg or 500 mg of a commercial form of beta glucan called Wellmune WGP, which is yeast-derived, or a placebo every day for four weeks post-marathon, a time when the immune system can become run down from overexertion. Those in the beta glucan groups reported significantly fewer upper-respiratory symptoms, increased energy and better overall health compared with the placebo recipients. Beta glucan supplements also can help combat the immunosuppressive effects of daily stress.

Daily dose: Aim for 250 mg to 500 mg for prevention and treatment.

Try: California Gold Nutrition Immune Defense with Wellmune Beta Glucan Supplement, 250 mg ($26 for 90 capsules).

More from Mark A. Stengler, NMD...

If You Catch a Cold...Pelargonium

Should you catch a cold, you can give Pelargonium sidoides a try. This South African plant, known as umckaloabo, effectively relieves cold symptoms, sinusitis, sore throat, and bronchitis. It is available in syrup, drops, powder, and chewable tablets.

Try: Nature's Way Umcka ColdCare Soothing Hot Drink Packets in Lemon flavor ($10.99 for 10 packets)...Nature's Way Umcka ColdCare Cherry syrup ($10.99 for four ounces)...or Integrative Therapeutics V Clear EPs 7630 Original Flavor syrup ($16 for four ounces). Follow package directions for dosing.

4 Natural Ways to Prevent Dementia

Michael Edson, MS, LAc, a licensed acupuncturist, certified herbalist and qi gong teacher based in Yonkers, New York. He is author of *Natural Brain Support* and *Natural Parkinson's Support.* EdsonAcupuncture.com

Much of the research on Alzheimer's and other forms of dementia focuses on pharmaceuticals, which often fail to reduce risk for dementia or improve symptoms.

Problem: About one-third of people who live to age 80 or older suffer from dementia.

Good news: Licensed acupuncturist and certified herbalist Michael Edson says there are safe, gentle, nondrug therapies that help delay the onset of symptoms and slow their progression...approaches that are supported by a growing body of evidence. *His four favorites**...

JUICING

Every minute of the day, you are exposed to environmental toxins, such as smoke and pollution. Your body also produces toxins as it goes about the very important job of keeping you alive. These toxins, known as free radicals, essentially "rust" your brain's wiring. Antioxidants—which are abundant in fruits and vegetables—neutralize free radicals, preventing them from causing damage.

Finding: Studies of centenarians have linked a high-antioxidant diet with reduced free radical damage and lower incidence of dementia.

Juicing or smoothie making concentrates a high amount of neuroprotective antioxidants into a tasty beverage. Start with green leafy vegetables such as spinach or kale. Then add a handful or two of berries. Berries and pomegranate are high in polyphenolic compounds, most prominently anthocyanins, which have powerful antioxidant and anti-inflammatory effects.

Other brain-healthy vegetables to include are broccoli, avocado, and red beets. Other healthful fruits include apples, black currant, citrus (especially lemon), kiwi, and grapes. For even more brain-healthy nutrients, add some garlic, ginger, chia seeds, parsley, ginseng, walnuts, yogurt, coconut oil, and/or honey. Experiment to find your favorite combinations.

ANTIOXIDANT SUPPLEMENTS

In addition to an antioxidant-rich diet, those with a family history of dementia also should consider taking these supplements...

*Combine these with a healthy, whole-foods–based diet and plenty of aerobic exercise. Stop smoking if you currently smoke. Discuss any supplements and dietary changes with your doctor, particularly if you are on blood-thinning medications or have low blood pressure.

- **Acetyl-L-carnitine.** Several Alzheimer's medications work by increasing this neurotransmitter. It is vital for processing memory, learning, and focus but is decreased in people with Alzheimer's. Acetyl-L-carnitine fuels the production of acetylcholine. It also reduces the buildup of dementia-predisposing waste products in the brain. Acetyl-L-carnitine is found in meat, fish, poultry, milk, nuts, seeds, cheese, asparagus, and broccoli. Taking a 500-milligram (mg) supplement daily on an empty stomach will ensure that you get enough.

- **Curcumin.** This spice increases the production of new brain cells. It also may slow age-related cognitive decline by inhibiting the buildup of beta-amyloid plaques, clumps of proteins that accumulate between neurons and, over time, can interrupt cell function and pave the way for Alzheimer's. Curcumin gives curry powder its golden hue. This may help explain why the rate of Alzheimer's is so low in India—just one percent of those age 65 and over have it. Try a daily 500-mg to 1,200-mg supplement.

- **Ashwagandha root extract, also known as Indian ginseng.** Chemical changes in the brain caused by chronic stress reduce brain plasticity. This, in turn, can kick-start an irreversible cascade of neuronal death, a characteristic of many brain diseases including dementia. Ashwagandha may reduce neuronal death and beta-amyloid buildup.

Ashwagandha leaves are thought to enhance cognitive performance.

Scientific evidence: In one study, subjects either took 300 mg of ashwagandha twice daily or a placebo for eight weeks. At the end of the study, those in the ashwagandha group showed greater improvements in both immediate and general memory as well as improved executive function, attention, and information-processing speed. Try 300 mg twice per day, taken with meals.

- **Vitamin D, zinc, and magnesium.** Low levels of the first two may result in cognitive difficulty and learning impairment and even may mimic symptoms of dementia. Most seniors have been found to be significantly deficient in vitamin D—a blood test can determine your level. Higher magnesium levels have been associated with a lower risk for dementia.

Recommended: 5,000 IU/day of vitamin D...40 mg/day of zinc...and 500 mg/day of magnesium.

ESSENTIAL OILS

Certain essential oils have been shown to support memory and cognition...boost circulation...reduce inflammation...reduce anxiety...and support healthy sleep, all critical for avoiding dementia.

- **Lemon balm.** This bright, sunny scent has been shown to improve cognitive function in patients with mild-to-moderate Alzheimer's. Lemon balm also has been used for centuries as a calming agent. Used at night, it can help promote sleep.

Why sleep matters: In the short term, inadequate sleep (less than seven hours a night) can lead to forgetfulness and other cognitive impairment. During sleep, the events of the day are consolidated and turned into memories...and accumulated waste products in the brain are flushed away. It's believed that this cleaning process is linked with a lower dementia risk because clumps of these same waste products typically are found in the brains of people with Alzheimer's.

- **Frankincense.** This iconic Christmastime scent has been shown to increase communication between neurons in the hippocampus, one of the brain's memory hubs. It also may help enhance concentration and focus and even promote sleep.

- **Rosemary.** This essential oil contains several compounds shown to enhance long-term memory.

Scientific evidence: In a British study, 150 healthy individuals over age 65 were divided among three rooms—one scented with rosemary, one with lavender, one unscented—where they were presented with a series of memory challenges. Those smelling rosemary experienced significantly improved memory compared with the others.

How to use oils: Dilute one drop of a quality essential oil brand such as Rocky Mountain Oils, dōTERRA, or Aura Cacia in one teaspoon of a carrier oil such as coconut oil or jojoba oil. Apply to the skin of your neck, above the eyebrows, temples, behind the earlobes, chest and abdomen, arms, legs, and/or bottoms of feet. Alternatively, use a diffuser to disperse the scent in your room.

Important: Before full application, apply a small amount of diluted oil to the skin and check for an allergic reaction after at least 24 hours.

SOCIALIZE

Poor social engagement was linked with significantly increased dementia rates in a recent review of 33 studies encompassing nearly 2.4 million people.

Socializing—even via a video or phone call—provides mental stimulation. It also reduces feelings of loneliness, which are stressful and inflammatory. In fact, loneliness is associated with a two-fold increase in incidence of dementia.

Stop Inflammation: 9 Ways to Reverse Chronic Illness, Prevent Infection, and More

Jacob Teitelbaum, MD, board-certified internist, holistic physician, and nationally known expert in the fields of chronic fatigue syndrome, fibromyalgia, sleep, and pain. Based in Hawaii, he is author of numerous books, including *Real Cause, Real Cure, The Complete Guide to Beating Sugar Addiction* and *The Fatigue and Fibromyalgia Solution*, as well as the phone app Cures A–Z. Vitality101.com

Medical experts have known for years that many serious medical conditions tie back to chronic inflammation. That includes the most significant and dangerous conditions in modern life, such as cardiovascular disease, cancer, asthma, diabetes, and autoimmune diseases including rheumatoid arthritis, lupus, and inflammatory bowel disease. Chronic inflammation also makes you more vulnerable to acute viruses, such as the common cold, flu, and the new COVID-19 that recently took over the globe.

Isn't it time that you actually do something to bring your body back into balance? You don't need medication to do that! *Here are the most important lifestyle changes you can make to help you feel great for years to come…*

• **It's all about the food.** Nutrient-filled foods help your body work at its best while "junk" foods make your body angry and inflamed, just as bad fuel gums up the engine of your car. Start by increasing your intake of colorful produce, seafood, and nuts, which contain antioxidants and other nutrients that keep inflammation in check. Even a handful of blueberries on your morning cereal and three to four servings of salmon or tuna each week can have a dramatic effect. The Mediterranean diet, which focuses on colorful fresh vegetables and fruit, healthy oils, and nuts, is an ideal model for reducing inflammation.

On the other hand, get rid of refined carbs including sugar and white flour. Having sweets, fruit juices, and soft drinks, with their high levels of sugar (even natural sugar) and high-fructose corn syrup, are like throwing gas on a fire when it comes to creating inflammation in your body. Also nix trans fats such as those found in Crisco, margarine, and processed foods, all of which can contribute to inflammation.

Vegan and vegetarian diets are great choices for reducing inflammation, but if you're having meat, opt for grass-fed beef, which is higher in omega-3s, instead of inflammation-fueling grain-fed beef.

Warning: Preparation methods are also important. Fast-food fried fish has lost most of its omega-3s. Some good news? Certain dairy products, such as yogurt, are associated with decreased inflammation. (See page 75 in chapter 4 for more information on an anti-inflammation diet.)

• **Watch the alcohol.** A landmark *Lancet* study found that both nondrinkers and heavy drinkers had higher levels of C-reactive protein, an inflammation marker associated with cardiovascular disease, than people who drank moderately. (Moderate drinking is no more than one drink per day for women and no more than two drinks per day for men.) Red wine offers the most potential benefits. Although people who have one or two drinks a day live longer than teetotalers, there are numerous other ways to get these benefits without the alcohol. So have it if you can enjoy it in moderation.

• **Increase your omega-3 intake.** Most people don't get enough omega-3 fatty acids, the anti-inflammatory polyunsaturated fats that have been shown to help prevent or treat cardiovascular disease, Alzheimer's disease, arthritis, cancer, and more. Your body cannot produce its own omega-3 fatty acids, so it all must come from your diet. Oily fish such as salmon, tuna, sardines, herring, and mackerel all are good choices—or consider taking a daily fish oil supplement.

Tip: When you're choosing a fish oil supplement, look for one that is all omega-3. Most fish oils contain other oils that you don't need.

One I like:* Vectomega from Terry Naturally. Algae-sourced omega-3s can be effective if one is vegetarian.

• **Take some curcumin.** A chemical found in the golden-hued curry spice turmeric, curcumin is a noted anti-inflammatory. However, unless you eat curry a few times a day, you likely won't get enough of the compound, and it is notoriously hard for your body to absorb and reap the benefits of curcumin if it's not taken in combination with a fat. Curcumin supplements that add back some of the turmeric oil are much easier for your body to use and digest.

One I like: CuraMed from Terry Naturally.

• **Nutritionally optimize your own immune function.** The key nutrients for your immune system are zinc (15 mg a day), vitamin A (2,500 international units/IU a day), vitamin D (1,000 IU a day) and vitamin C (200 mg to 500 mg a day). But don't subscribe to a "more is better" approach. For example, doses of vitamin A over 8,000 IU a day can trigger birth defects.

Note: Use the retinol version of vitamin A (the type found in fish oil) for optimal results.

*Dr. Teitelbaum receives consulting fees for some of the supplements mentioned in this article and donates the money to charity.

Two multivitamin supplements I like: ViraPro from Terry Naturally, and the Energy Revitalization System vitamin powder from Enzymatic Therapy—both offer optimal amounts of zinc, selenium, and vitamins A, C, D, and E.

• **Reduce your body's chemical load.** Chemicals in your environment can trigger your immune system and cause inflammation. When you have the option, choose natural household products that can do the job—or at least reduce your use of chemicals.

Examples: If you need to use insecticide to deal with a bug problem in your home, try to spray it just on the outside of your home or buy a natural one. Choose natural cleaners instead of chemical-laden ones. Skip the air freshener, dryer sheets, and scented candles.

• **Get out in the sunshine.** The vitamin D your body produces from a little time in the sun also has been shown to help boost immunity. Pair it with a little moderate exercise—such as a walk or a bike ride in the park—and you'll get even more benefits.

• **Get good sleep.** We all know we should be getting seven to nine hours of sleep every night, but how many of us actually do? People who consistently get too little sleep have increased inflammation activity in their bodies. This is no surprise—even in short-term studies, researchers found higher levels of inflammation markers such as white blood cells. Try to get the amount of sleep that leaves you feeling your best.

• **Tune out the stressors.** Stress plays an important role in developing chronic inflammation. When you feel safe, your immune system is at ease, and that eases inflammation. But if your body is feeling threatened constantly, your immune system goes into overdrive. Try to tune out things that make you feel fearful—such as the news, for instance—and focus on the things that make you feel happy and safe.

Helpful: Meditation, yoga, and breathing exercises all can help you feel less stressed.

Natural Ways to Fight Diabetes

Flax and Pumpkin Seeds...

Recent study: When rats with induced diabetes were fed a mixture of flax and powdered pumpkin seed, their blood chemistry normalized, becoming more like that of rats without diabetes.

Study by researchers at Institut Supérieur de Biotechnologie de Sfax, Tunisia, published in *Journal of Diabetes and Its Complications.*

Cinnamon Improves Blood Sugar Control

Taking a 500-milligram cinnamon capsule three times per day for 12 weeks lowered abnormal fasting glucose levels in people with prediabetes and improved their response to eating a meal with carbohydrates. The study from Joslin Diabetes Center, Boston, suggests that cinnamon could be used to reduce the risk of developing type 2 diabetes over time.

Romeo GR, Lee J, Mulla CM, et al. Influence of cinnamon on glycemic control in subjects with prediabetes: a randomized controlled trial. *Journal of the Endocrine Society,* July 2020.

Natural Therapies That Ease Parkinson's Symptoms

Michael Edson, MS, LAc, a licensed acupuncturist, certified herbalist and qi gong teacher based in Yonkers, New York. He is author of *Natural Parkinson's Support: Your Guide to Preventing & Managing Parkinson's.* NaturalEyeCare.com

If you or a loved one has Parkinson's disease (PD), you want to do everything possible to control the brutal symptoms, such as tremors, stiff muscles, and anxiety.

Until recently, the standard treatment regimen mainly paired powerful medications, such as *carbidopa/levodopa* (Sinemet) and *pramipexole* (Mirapex), with exercises to ease symptoms.

Now: More people with PD are adding gentle, nondrug therapies to the mix. Essential oils and acupuncture are two safe options with a growing body of evidence—and clinical success—to support their use alone or in combination as a complement to PD treatment. *For example...**

ESSENTIAL OILS FOR TREMORS, ANXIETY

When using essential oils, nonmotor symptoms, such as anxiety, often improve within a few days. Tremors may require a few weeks of regular use before showing improvement.

- **Frankincense.**

Scent: Spicy, woodsy.

Helps with: Tremors.

In PD, nerve cells in the brain that produce dopamine, a neurotransmitter that regulates many motor and cognitive functions, progressively die off, leading to tremors. In a 2019 animal study published in *Avicenna Journal of Phytomedicine,* frankincense was shown to have anti-inflammatory and antioxidant properties that protected dopamine-producing neurons, improving the motor impairments of PD.

- **Bergamot.**

Scent: Citrus.

Helps with: Anxiety and agitation.

Perhaps due to its nonsedating, analgesic effects, bergamot essential oil is used to relieve anxiety and agitation in people with PD. Researchers also are investigating bergamot's ability to control agitation in patients with dementia.

HOW TO USE ESSENTIAL OILS FOR PD

To get the most benefit from essential oils, they are best applied to the skin of the person with PD. This combines the calming, therapeutic qualities of touch with the benefit of inhaling the healing scent. Even though up to 96 percent of newly diagnosed patients with PD have lost some degree of their sense of smell, essential oil is still beneficial because the oil's healing compounds not only penetrate the skin but also are still inhaled, even if the scent is not as strong as it would be to a healthy person.

What to do: Add a few drops of your essential oil to one ounce of a carrier oil (such as almond, olive, or coconut oil), and massage it two to three times a day into your or your loved one's neck, temples (being sure to avoid the eyes), arms, legs, and/or soles of the feet...use a diffuser...or, with agitated or aggressive patients, add the drops to a cotton ball and discreetly pin it to the upper half of his/her shirt so that it's inhaled.

Important: Do an allergy test before full application. Apply a small amount of the diluted oil to an area of skin, and check for an allergic reaction after 24 hours. (Allergic reactions can, in rare cases, occur several days later.) Never ingest an essential oil. If you want to use more than one essential oil, wait at least three minutes between oil applications.

Good essential oil brands: Rocky Mountain Oils...dōTERRA...and Plant Therapy.

ACUPUNCTURE

Acupuncture is based on a system of energy pathways, called meridians, through which life force, or qi, flows. When these pathways become blocked, pain, illness, and degeneration can develop, according to traditional Chinese medicine (TCM). By inserting ultra-thin, stainless-steel needles along various meridians, acupuncturists strive to rebalance the flow of energy to restore health—or, in the case of PD, improve symptoms.

Scientific evidence: In a study published in *CNS Neuroscience & Therapeutics* involving 519 patients with PD, acupuncture improved motor symptoms, such as tremor, rigidity, and slowed movement, and "markedly improved" nonmotor symptoms, including sleep problems and depression, according to research. When acupuncture was used with levodopa, the medication was more effective.

With acupuncture, nonmotor symptoms often improve within one to six treatments, while tremors and other motor symptoms may require about a dozen treatments.

To find a licensed acupuncturist, consult the National Certification Commission for Acupuncture and Oriental Medicine, NCCAOM.org.

*Consult with your physician before trying these therapies—especially if you have a chronic condition, such as high blood pressure.

Restorative Yoga Is the New Power Yoga

Caren Baginski, author of *Restorative Yoga: Relax. Restore. Re-energize.* She has been teaching yoga and meditation since 2009 and is trained in yoga nidra as well as restorative and vinyasa yoga and soon will complete her certification in yoga therapy. You can subscribe to her YouTube channel, which offers free restorative yoga videos. CarenBaginski.com

If you've ever taken a yoga class, you know the routine. You move through a series of postures, stretching and twisting and building strength and flexibility. At the end of each session, you lie in Savasana (Corpse Pose), tired but feeling good.

Restorative yoga is different. It doesn't involve moving. You don't even stretch. Instead, you get into each pose and stay still for five minutes or so, focusing on your breath in a mindful way. As your body gradually realigns itself during the pose, your breathing and heart rate slow. You calm down and experience the same deep well-being, only with a lot less effort. Restorative yoga may feel passive, but it's more like active relaxation—and the perfect antidote to your busy, super-scheduled life.

RESTORATIVE YOGA BASICS

There are four essentials to restorative yoga…

• **Stillness.** Rather than push yourself to the edge, you settle into a pose and let your body open up, taking all of the tension out of the muscles so that they are free to relax. To help in the process, props are used to gently hold your body in that particular pose. You can buy yoga-specific ones or simply use items that you already have.

• **A dimly lit practice space.** When you withdraw from sensory overload, it's easier to rediscover your body's natural rhythm. Create this environment by turning down the lights, drawing the shades and/or using an eye covering during practice.

• **A quiet space.** Noisy environments can increase the body's stress-hormone levels. Opt for silence, which relaxes the brain even better than soothing music or nature sounds.

• **Staying comfortably warm.** Your body will naturally cool down as you stay still. You may want to keep your socks on and cover up with a blanket as you practice.

3 RESTORATIVE POSES

Practicing for 20 minutes a day will help train your body and your brain to become calm more easily. Some poses may compress the abdominal region, so make sure you have not eaten for at least two hours before you get on your mat to allow food to digest. To practice these poses, you'll need a yoga mat, two to three blankets, a yoga strap (or belt or scarf), two yoga bolsters or regular bed pillows, and an eye covering (such as an eye pillow or washcloth). Many people choose to practice in the evening to wind down before bed, but experiment and see what works best for your routine.

Legs Up the Wall: This pose helps ease tired leg muscles, reduce swelling in the legs, lower blood pressure, and decrease stress.

1. Preparation. Fold one blanket into a large square, and place it on a mat that is set perpendicular against the wall. That will cushion your hips. Take another blanket, fold it into a slightly smaller square and place it in the middle of the mat to provide support for your head. Have your eye covering nearby. Set a timer for 10 minutes.

2. Sit on your left hip with your back against the wall and legs tucked away from your mat. Plant your hands on the mat in front of your body, thread the left arm under the right one to help you tuck and roll until your legs are up against the wall. Your goal is to lie on the floor with your legs up the wall and your back/pelvis area flat on the floor (shown above).

3. As you look upward, set your ankles, knees, and hips in a line. Relax your feet with toes neither pointed nor flexed. If your legs are splaying outward, take your strap or scarf, tie it around your calves and corral your legs so that they are hips' width apart but in a straight line.

4. Put on your eye covering, or simply close your eyes. Open your arms in a V-shape by your sides, palms up. Breathe fully into your abdomen and lungs for three rounds of breath, using your exhalations to relax your face, lips and finally your whole body.

5. Rest in silence, breathing naturally. If your legs tingle or feel numb, bring the soles of your feet together in a butterfly shape and lower your legs until the feeling returns. Then place them against the wall again.

6. When you're ready to get out of the pose, wiggle your toes. Bend each knee one at a time, and slowly walk your feet down the wall. Once you can reach your legs comfortably, slip off the strap if you're using one.

7. Rest with your knees bent and feet against the wall. Slide your legs down from the wall, lift one arm over the head, slip off the eye covering, and slowly roll to that side. Rest on your side in a fetal position for as long as necessary.

8. Roll into a seated position on the blanket, and take a moment to reflect on how you feel.

Mountain Brook: This gentle backbend opens up your chest and shoulders, improves breathing, and eases tension in the throat while boosting a low mood.

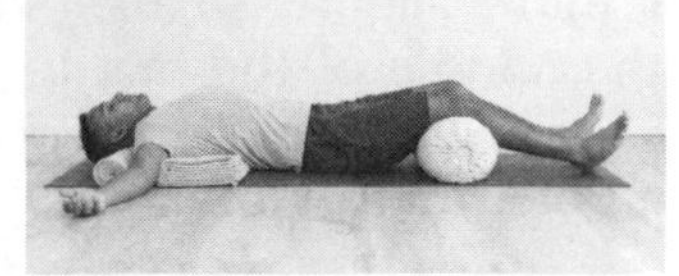

1. Preparation. Fold two blankets into skinny rectangles as wide as your yoga mat, and stack them on top of each other on one-third of the mat. Take the third blanket, place it four inches away from the blanket stack and toward the top of your mat. Roll it up halfway or all the way to support your neck. Place the bolster near the bottom of your mat. Set a timer for five minutes.

2. Sit in between the bolster and the blanket stack, and drape your legs so that your knees are over the bolster and your legs are flat on the mat.

3. Lie back, placing your shoulder blades on top of the blanket stack but making sure your lower back isn't touching the stack at all. Rest your neck on top of the roll.

4. Extend your arms, palms up, into a T-shape in the space between the blankets. Your chin should be slightly higher than your forehead, but if that's uncomfortable, change the roll so that your chin and forehead are level. Make any adjustments necessary to become fully comfortable. Your hips will be grounded on the floor.

5. Close your eyes and visualize your body as a mountain brook, flowing over the props. Breathe in fully through your nostrils, counting to four. Breathe out slowly through your nose, counting to eight. Keep breathing at a comfortable pace, with the exhales longer than the inhales.

6. Begin to breathe naturally and just be still in the pose.

7. Guide yourself back by breathing deeply in and out. Bending one knee at a time, anchor your feet on the bolster. Roll the bolster away from your body until your feet touch the mat. Gently slide the blanket roll to one side so that your head rests upon the mat.

8. Pull your knees inward and roll onto one side, using one arm as a pillow to cradle your head. Rest for a few seconds. Inhaling, use your hands to push yourself up slowly to a comfortable seat. Observe how you feel after this pose.

Supported Side Lying Stretch: Like all restorative yoga poses, this two-sided stretch calms the nervous system, reducing stress and inflammation. And because this pose affects the digestive organs—the liver, gall bladder, spleen, and stomach—it's particularly good for improving gut health. After all, when you're angry or anxious, you definitely feel it in your stomach!

1. Preparation. Fold the blankets into two thick double squares, and stack them on top of each other to support your head at the top of your mat. Place the round bolster in the middle of the mat and the flat bolster at the bottom. Set a timer for three minutes.

Photos of yoga poses: © DK: Jimena Peck

2. Sit in between the round and flat bolsters. Lay with your left hip on the floor, your right leg on top of the flat bolster, and place your left leg in front of the bolster at the edge of your mat.

3. Hold onto the round bolster with your right hand as you inhale, wedging the bolster into your waist. Exhale, sliding your left arm forward, palm up, as you lie on your side. The blankets should be supporting your neck and head. Make sure the top of your head lines up with your shoulder, hip, and right foot.

4. Your right arm can rest against your hip. Or for more opening, send your right arm over your head so that your right bicep rests against your ear and your hand touches the floor. (If your hand can't reach, place a blanket or block under it for support.)

5. Close your eyes. Inhale fully. As you exhale, release all effort in your body. Breathe naturally, and rest in silence.

6. When you are ready to switch sides, return your right hand to the space next to your left hand. Press against the floor, inhale and lift up slowly sideways. Turn away from the round bolster, and keep turning to come to the other side. Repeat the pose on this side, again setting the timer for three minutes.

7. Once complete, sit up slowly into a comfortable seated position. Place your hands to your heart, with your right hand stacking on top of your left hand. Close your eyes, and connect with your heartbeat. As you take deeper breaths, feel the expansiveness in your waist, ribs, and chest. Thank yourself for taking this time to support yourself in self-care so that you may continue to be a support for others.

Face Rash Cured from the Inside Out

Andrew L. Rubman, ND, a naturopathic doctor who specializes in gastroenterology. Dr. Rubman is founder and director of the Southbury Clinic for Traditional Medicines in Southbury, Connecticut. SouthburyClinic.com

The patient: "Loretta," a nationally known TV anchor.

Why she came to see me: I was delighted to have an office visit from a media personality I watched regularly on television. I was aware of the fact that for many months a persistent rash on her right cheek had been concealed during her broadcasts quite effectively by the station's makeup artist—still noticeable to my trained eye. A colleague of hers at the Manhattan-based network who has been a patient of mine urged her to come up to my clinic in Southbury, Connecticut, as her rash, while not getting worse, was not getting better despite the treatments from some of "New York's finest" dermatologists.

How I evaluated her: After exchanging pleasantries, we carefully reviewed the history of Loretta's rash as well as her diet, lifestyle, and challenging events like relationship or employment changes. Her prior diagnoses and treatments ran the gamut from psoriasis to atopy (a kind of immune-related dermatitis) and topical corticosteroids to "biologics" typically used for autoimmune diseases, the latter she had ardently refused to take.

I explained how quite often the skin mirrored internal issues and treating chronic conditions required both external and internal interventions. What I saw during our first visit presented like a chronic "zymotic" condition (characterized by an overgrowth of yeast and/or fungus) with a minimal contribution of normal surface bacteria.

How we addressed her problem: Since Loretta's job was inherently stressful and she was a "young" 58-year-old woman, I convinced her to take a digestive enzyme formula to not only enhance her system's ability to extract nutrients from her meals, but also to help her liver bind and remove substances that may not have been sufficiently exported via the stool and instead were ending up being "excreted" into her skin.

I also explained that improving the function of her large intestine and its resident microbiome quite often will have a direct impact on the health and resilience of the skin. We discussed and agreed upon an improved diet that included cutting down on hurried commissary fast food, giving up French fries, and basing her meals around a large, fresh garden salad with healthy protein and carb "toppings"...a regimen of digestive enzymes and immune-enhancing supplements...and naturally derived topical applications for her skin, all of which would gradually improve the outward appearance while addressing the underlying causes of her skin rash.

The patient's progress: Two weeks after our initial appointment, Loretta and I had a video check-in. She reported improvement in both digestion and the appearance of her skin, confirmed by her makeup artist and clearly visible to me as well. Within a month's time the chronic problem on her face was virtually gone. We do stay in touch with periodic consults, but I reminded her that as I see her frequently on television, she can't hide from my scrutiny!

Acupuncture Before Surgery Lessens Pain

When 106 veterans underwent surgery for hip replacement, gallbladder removal and other common problems, researchers gave one group "battlefield acupuncture," in which tiny needles are inserted at trigger points on the ear, before their procedures. After surgery, those patients required one-third to one-half as many opioids and reported significantly less pain and much higher satisfaction compared with the control group.

Brinda Krish, DO, an anesthesiology resident at Detroit Medical Center. Her research was presented to the American Society of Anesthesiologists.

Focus on Natural Heart Health

Jamison Starbuck, ND, a naturopathic physician in family practice in Missoula, Montana, and producer of *Dr. Starbuck's Health Tips for Kids,* a weekly program on Montana Public Radio, MTPR.org. DrJamisonStarbuck.com.

The heart often conjures up images of love: Candy hearts, chocolate hearts, broken hearts, and hearts bursting with happiness. There are so many things we can do to benefit our physical hearts and reduce the risk of cardiovascular disease, but I have room for only a few of my favorites. Happily, some involve chocolate and flowers.

• **Move.** First, for excellent heart health, you have to move. Studies show that vigorous endurance exercise (running, swimming, biking, hiking, running stairs, or rowing), done in intervals of 30 to 50 minutes a day for a total of 150 minutes a week, will significantly reduce your risk of cardiovascular disease.

Don't be discouraged if you're not an athlete and won't ever log in that sort of aerobic burn. Recent research in the *Journal of the American Heart Association* also tells us that low-intensity physical activity (walking, biking to work, the bending and stooping of gardening, and walking up and down the stairs in your home) done for at least 60 minutes a day is also associated with a reduced risk for cardiovascular illness. In other words, a healthy heart needs movement, circulation, oxygen from breathing, and your making your muscles, including your heart, work.

• **Lower stress.** Stress is another significant factor in heart disease, and here's where flowers come in. Putting flowers in your home or office, growing them in your yard, or visiting botanical gardens are known to reduce stress and lower blood pressure. Lowering stress decreases your blood cortisol levels, and that diminishes plaque accumulation in your blood-vessel walls.

You can also take heart-healthy medicine made from plants. My two favorites are Linden flowers and Hawthorne flowers and berries. Linden flowers make a pleasant, gently calming tea. Use 2 teaspoons of dried flowers per 10 ounces of boiling water. Steep for five to seven minutes before drinking. Linden is very helpful at bedtime as it can help you relax and fall asleep. Hawthorne flowers and berries are best taken in a tincture or extract form, often dosed at one-quarter teaspoon per day as a cardiovascular tonic. Herbal teas and tinctures should be taken at least 30 minutes away from food for the best benefit.

• **Healthy diet.** As most folks know, food choices affect heart health. Make sure that vegetables—raw, steamed, or roasted, not fried—occupy the majority of your plate at both lunch and dinner. Eat purple and red fruit, whole grains, nuts, seeds, olive oil, and plain dark chocolate.

• **Supplements.** My favorite daily heart supplements include magnesium (300 milligrams [mg]), potassium (99 mg), B12 (800 micrograms in sublingual form), and CoQ10 (100 mg). If you take blood pressure medications or heart medications, talk with your doctor before starting a supplement program. If you are on a statin drug, supplementing with CoQ10 is especially important, as statin drugs can cause your body to become deficient in CoQ10.

GOOD TO KNOW...

Eat to Beat Hypertension

A flavanol-rich diet lowers blood pressure. Researchers objectively measured indicators of dietary intake among more than 25,000 adults and found that those who consumed the most flavanols—compounds that promote circulatory health—had lower blood pressure. Flavanols are found mainly in some fruits (such as berries and apples) as well as in green and black teas.

Gunter Kuhnle, PhD, professor of food and nutritional sciences at University of Reading, UK, and leader of a study published in *Scientific Reports*.

No-Hassle Natural Therapies for Varicose Veins

Jamison Starbuck, ND, a naturopathic physician in family practice in Missoula, Montana, and producer of *Dr. Starbuck's Health Tips for Kids*, a weekly program on Montana Public Radio, MTPR.org. DrJamisonStarbuck.com

Purple, blue, and red. The more veins I see, the more I say, "This aging I do dread." Writing medical poetry amuses me and helps me cope. In this case, with my varicose and spider veins. I'm not alone, though. It's estimated that about half of adult women have these unsightly veins. Men can have them, too, but develop them much less often.

Some veins are closer to the surface of the skin than arteries, so when they become stretched or damaged, they can look like reddish-purple spider webs (spider veins)...or bluish-purple bulging cords (varicose veins). Spider veins are small, dilated blood vessels that are painless. They most often show up on the face, chest, or legs or in places where one has suffered an injury or had a surgery. Fortunately, spider veins don't cause symptoms.

Varicose veins are wider and longer than spider veins and most often appear in the lower legs and ankles. The primary cause is a malfunction of the valves inside the veins, which leads to a buildup of blood. When the pressure is more than the thin vein wall can handle, bulging occurs. Varicose veins can be painless, or they may ache and cause a painful heaviness that's fatiguing. Varicose veins don't cause blood clots, but people who have a lot of them may have a higher incidence of clots due to an unhealthy vascular system.

These vein issues often are blamed on pregnancy, obesity, and jobs that involve a lot of standing, but the latest research finds that inflammation, poor circulation, and genetic vulnerability are the most common causes of spider veins and varicose veins. Even if you undergo surgery, laser treatment, or saline injections, called sclerotherapy, you need to improve blood vessel health, enhance circulation, and reduce inflammation or problematic veins will return. *What I advise to help prevent and treat varicose veins and spider veins...*

- **Walk, ride a bike, or swim every day.** Gentle exercise that uses the leg muscles helps move blood out of veins in the lower legs. Exercise doesn't reduce existing vein problems, but it does prevent more from developing. If your varicose veins hurt, elevate your legs above your abdomen for five minutes after exercise and/or consider wearing compression stockings.

- **Take supplements that support healthy blood vessels.** I recommend 100 mg of CoQ10...400 IU of vitamin E...1,000 mg of vitamin C...and 300 mg of magnesium citrate daily. Take these nutrients with food.

Note: Always check with your doctor before starting a new supplement.

- **Eat an anti-inflammatory, blood vessel–beneficial diet.** This means one-half cup of dark-colored fresh or frozen berries daily and plenty of foods rich in vitamin K, such as kale, chard, brussels sprouts, and broccoli.

Important: If you take a blood thinner such as *warfarin* (Coumadin), be careful about consuming vitamin K–rich foods. Check with your doctor.

- **Take botanical medicines that promote circulation and blood vessel health.** I usually prescribe a tincture containing equal parts of horse chestnut, hawthorn, linden, and ginkgo. A typical dose is one-quarter teaspoon of the mixture daily, taken in two ounces of water, away from meals.

Caution: If you are taking prescription heart medications, check with your doctor before using these herbs.

A Vegan Diet Balances Haywire Hormones

Neal Barnard, MD, president of the Physicians Committee for Responsible Medicine, founder of the Barnard Medical Center, adjunct professor of medicine at the George Washington University School of Medicine, and a fellow of the American College of Cardiology. He has written more than 19 books on nutrition and health, including *Your Body in Balance.* Follow Dr. Barnard on Twitter @DrNealBarnard and Facebook@NealBarnardMD.

A switch to plant-based eating can lower hormone-related cancer risk, menopause symptoms, even erectile dysfunction.

Estrogen and testosterone do more than subject you to the vagaries of puberty. Throughout your life, hormones control everything from your metabolism to your moods, your fertility to your body fat. When they go haywire, they can also increase your risk of cancer.

The good news is that simply adjusting your diet can tune down the risk of everything from menopausal hot flashes to prostate cancer. Even erectile dysfunction may be a simple matter of what's on the menu.

DIET AND BREAST CANCER

Breast cancer strikes one in eight American women every year. For 5 to 10 percent of them, there is a genetic factor, but for many others, it is a hormone-related disease. Postmenopausal women with high levels of estradiol, a form of estrogen, have more than double the risk of developing breast cancer. Estradiol, particularly when it's not bound to a protein, can easily enter the nucleus of breast cells and damage the DNA inside, creating a cancer cell. It can then act as a fertilizer, stimulating the growth of tumors.

In the mid 20th century, researchers discovered a stunning trend: Women in Japan rarely developed breast cancer. When they did, it was less aggressive than the cancer in American women. The difference? Diet. Japanese women at the time ate mostly rice and vegetables with very little meat or fish. But as more Western foods entered the Japanese diet in the 1970s, researchers saw a clear pattern. Women who ate meat- and cheese-laden meals showed an 83 percent higher risk of developing breast cancer than women who maintained a traditional diet.

Here's why: Fatty foods, like meat and cheese, increase estrogen levels. Fiber-rich fruits, vegetables, and grains do the opposite. The fiber binds to excess hormones and escorts them out of the body. Further, women who eat vegan diets have higher levels of a protein that inactivates hormones until they are needed, the sex hormone-binding globulin.

DIET AND PROSTATE CANCER

The hormone and cancer link affects men too. Prostate cancer is common in the United States and Europe but rare in Asian countries. In this case, the culprit appears to be dairy.

Our bodies respond to dairy products by producing insulin-like growth factor-1 (IGF-1). When we're young, we produce our own IGF-1 to help us grow. In adulthood, the body produces much less—we simply don't need it anymore. Dairy consumption, however, floods the body with IGF-1 long after we have any use for it. The Harvard Physicians' Health Study found that men who developed prostate cancer had 10 percent more IGF in their blood than those without cancer, suggesting that it plays a role in the disease.

Looking beyond IGF-1, a 2016 review reported that men who drink the most milk and milk products have a 43 percent higher risk of dying from prostate cancer than men who avoid dairy.

ERECTILE DYSFUNCTION

A plant-based diet can have more immediate benefits as well. Many men who make the switch experience an unexpected side effect—the end of erectile dysfunction (ED). While ED can be caused by prostate surgery or certain medications, like antidepressants, it is most often the result of narrowed arteries that reduce normal blood flow. Narrowed arteries aren't limited to just one part of the body. A man with ED likely has impaired blood flow to the brain and heart as well, putting him at high risk of heart attack and stroke. Dumping dairy and meat can actually undo that arterial damage.

MENOPAUSE

Many women get a pleasant surprise as well: Plant-based eating is linked to the cessation of bothersome menopause symptoms. For women in the United States and other countries where a Western diet is prevalent, menopause often comes with hot flashes, night sweats, irritability, depression, and insomnia.

It turns out that this is a uniquely Western experience: Women who eat traditional Asian diets with little to no meat and dairy report no such symptoms—unless they switch to a Western diet. Long before menopause begins, a vegan diet can even lessen menstrual cramps.

THE GAME PLAN

Balancing sex hormones is just one example of the many proven benefits of a plant-based diet, so why isn't everyone doing it? Changing dietary patterns can be difficult, especially when it involves giving up something you enjoy. Start your journey by adding foods, not removing them.

For the next seven days, try as many new plant-based foods as you can to determine what you like. Don't give up meat and dairy yet, just enjoy a week of discovering new flavors.

Once you've identified foods that you enjoy, start making some simple swaps. Try soy milk in your cereal. For lunch, try a burrito stuffed with beans, veggies, and rice. Dinner might be pasta with a hearty marinara sauce. You can stick with your proven winners from week one or experiment with new recipes and flavors. Skip cooking oil—even vegetable oil—and try steaming, roasting, cooking with broths, or using an air fryer instead.

Once you fully eliminate animal foods, give it a three-week trial run. You don't have to give up skepticism. You don't have to commit long term. Just try it and see how you feel.

THERE IS VEGAN JUNK FOOD

Some plant-based foods are high in fat, and they should be reserved for only occasional consumption. If you're running errands and have to stop for fast food, you could grab an Impossible Whopper from Burger King, for example. While it's better than a beef burger, it's a far cry from healthy. Meat replacements are loaded with fat and salt to make them meat-like. Vegan cheeses are also an occasional treat and not a daily food group.

KNOW YOUR WHY

To make it easier to make healthy food choices when temptation strikes, remember your reason for trying a plant-based diet. Whatever you set out to do, you're likely to get even more benefits. A healthy plant-based diet is like a box of Cracker Jacks—you get it for the popcorn but always get an extra prize in the box. Will your prize be fewer mood swings? Lower cholesterol? Better sex? Try it for three weeks to find out.

Yoga for Migraines

Rohit Bhatia, MD, DM, DNB, professor, department of neurology, All India Institute of Medical Sciences, New Delhi, India.

A yoga practice may reduce the severity, duration, and frequency of migraine pain, researchers reported in *Neurology,* the medical journal of the American Academy of Neurology.

A total of 114 study participants who had four to 14 migraine headaches per month were randomly assigned to either a medication-only group or a yoga-plus-medication group. Both groups were counseled about lifestyle changes, such as exercising, getting adequate sleep, and eating regular meals, that can help with migraine, and given a log book to record daily headache information.

For the first month, the yoga group practiced breathing and relaxation exercises and postures with an instructor for one hour three days per week. Then they practiced on their own at home for five days a week over the next two months.

Participants in both groups improved, but those in the yoga group had greater improvement in headache frequency (48 percent reduction vs. 12 percent in the medication group). After three months, yoga practitioners also took 47 percent fewer pain-relieving medications.

More research needs to be conducted to evaluate the benefits of yoga on migraine over longer periods of time.

Foods for Immunity

Janet Bond Brill, PhD, RDN, FAND, a registered dietitian nutritionist, a fellow of the Academy of Nutrition and Dietetics, and a nationally recognized nutrition, health and fitness expert who specializes in cardiovascular disease prevention. Based in Hellertown, Pennsylvania, Dr. Brill is author of *Blood Pressure DOWN, Cholesterol DOWN,* and *Prevent a Second Heart Attack.* DrJanet.com

Our immune system acts like a security team that destroys invaders, such as viruses and bacteria, before they can settle into the body and start a full-blown infection. We can support that process by eating a diet filled with plant foods that are rich in immune-boosting, disease-fighting antioxidant nutrients. *Here are five foods to load up on...*

1. Garlic. This member of the allium family has been used for millennia for its anti-infection properties. Garlic has been shown to boost the number of virus-fighting T-cells in the bloodstream. The sulfur in garlic also helps the body absorb the trace element zinc, which is an immunity booster.

2. Onions. Another member of the allium family, onions are loaded with immune-boosting nutrients like selenium, sulfur compounds, zinc, and vitamin C. In addition, they are one of the best sources of quercetin, a potent flavonoid and antioxidant that has antiviral properties as well.

3. Ginger. This natural blood thinner contains a phenolic anti-inflammatory compound called gingerol that may relax blood vessels. It's also an antibacterial with strong anti-inflammatory and antioxidant effects.

4. Carrots. Carrots contain vitamin C as well as antioxidants that help fight free radicals, cell damage, and inflammation.

5. Spinach. This power food is rich in vitamin C and myriad antioxidants that increase our infection-fighting ability.

Try the following recipe for a warm and comforting immune-boosting chicken soup that contains all five foods and is perfect for cold and flu season. Eating healthy, nutrient-dense plant foods is a great start, but there are plenty of other things you can do to protect yourself and your family from illness. Wash your hands often, don't touch your face, get your flu vaccine, and wear a mask when around groups of people.

Dr. Janet's Chicken Soup

2 Tbsp extra virgin olive oil
2 Tbsp fresh garlic, minced
2 Tbsp fresh ginger, minced
1 sweet onion, diced
½ cup sliced carrots
32 oz. chicken broth
6 oz. water
2 lbs. boneless skinless chicken breasts, cut into pieces
2 cups fresh organic baby spinach leaves

In a large soup pot, heat the olive oil over medium heat. Add garlic, ginger, onions, and carrots, and cook until softened and golden, 10 minutes.

Add the chicken broth, water, and chicken. Bring to a boil. Reduce heat and simmer for 30 minutes. (Feel free to cook on low for up to an hour.)

Add spinach and let cook for five minutes just before serving.

Optional: You can also add mushrooms to include another powerful immune-boosting food into your soup.

Makes 9 servings.

Nutrition information per one-cup serving: *Calories:* 200, Fat: 5 g, *Saturated Fat:* 0 g, *Cholesterol:* 60 mg, *Sodium:* 260 mg, *Carbohydrate:* 13 g, *Dietary Fiber:* 0 g, *Sugars:* 2 g, *Protein:* 26 g.

Prebiotics Improve Sleep

Stressed animals given high doses of bacteria-nourishing (prebiotic) fibers, including those found in lentils and cabbage, spent more time in restorative (non-REM) sleep and had a greater diversity of intestinal organisms.

Journal of Feline Medicine and Surgery

Charcoal: A Versatile Treatment

Jamison Starbuck, ND, is a naturopathic physician in family practice in Missoula, Montana, and producer of *Dr. Starbuck's Health Tips for Kids*, a weekly program on Montana Public Radio, MTPR.org. She is a past president of the American Association of Naturopathic Physicians and a contributing editor to *The Alternative Advisor: The Complete Guide to Natural Therapies and Alternative Treatments.* DrJamisonStarbuck.com.

Medicinal-grade activated charcoal (AC) is a versatile, effective, and safe treatment for a variety of conditions. AC is made from wood, coconut shells, or other natural fibers that have been burned at a very high temperature and then "activated" by creating holes and crevices to increase the surface area.

It works as a medicine because it is adsorptive, which means it draws things to itself, such as chemicals, drugs, viruses, and bacteria. It is also inert, which means that it will not enter your bloodstream but will pass through your intestines and leave via stool—taking attached substances with it.

AC is commonly used in emergency rooms (ER) as a treatment for many types of poisoning and overdose. But while it's very effective, it should never be used for poisoning at home. The necessary dosage is extremely high, and there is no guarantee that a product purchased for home use has the same strength as that used in the ER.

There are some home uses, however, that are quite safe as long as you use medicinal-grade AC purchased over-the-counter from a pharmacy or vitamin store. Never ingest charcoal briquettes or charcoal sold for fish tanks, water filters, and other commercial purposes. They can be toxic.

• **Intestinal gas and diarrhea.** Several studies show that AC reduces excessive intestestinal gas accumulation, according to the European Food and Safety Authority, which gives a green light to its use. It also appears to have an anti-diarrheal effect. In 2018, researchers reported in *Current Medical Research and Opinion* that it is a suitable treatment that offers fewer side effects than other anti-diarrheal medications.

For an acute bout of painful gas or diarrhea, I recommend taking three to four 250-milligram (mg) charcoal capsules with an 8-ounce glass of water. Repeat in 30 minutes or after every bowel movement as needed for up to 24 hours. Do not use charcoal on a daily basis because it can interfere with the absorption of nutrients and medications. Don't take it within two hours of taking medication, as it may make some medications ineffective.

- **Insect bites.** Relieve the pain, swelling, or itch from bee stings, spider, and fly bites with a charcoal poultice. Open a charcoal capsule into a bowl and add a few drops of water to make a paste. Apply the paste to the bite or sting. Cover with a bandage and leave it on for a few hours. Wash away the charcoal with cool water and repeat if needed. Because it is inert, it will not be absorbed by the skin.
- **Splinters.** Charcoal can help bring a stubborn splinter up and into view where you can remove it with tweezers. Make a poultice as you would with insect bites.
- **Poison ivy.** Mix a tablespoon of charcoal into 8 ounces of water. Soak the affected area in the slurry or pour the slurry over the poison-ivy lesions and cover with plastic wrap for 30 minutes. Repeat as needed.

Calming the Pain of Chronic Tendonitis

Jamison Starbuck, ND, a naturopathic physician in family practice in Missoula, Montana, and producer of *Dr. Starbuck's Health Tips for Kids*, a weekly program on Montana Public Radio, MTPR.org. DrJamisonStarbuck.com

"Ouch! I can't believe this still hurts. It's been so long!" Those were my patient's words as I asked her to flex and turn the wrist she had sprained three months ago, words common in patients suffering with tendonitis.

Tendonitis is inflammation in a tendon, the fibrous cords that attach muscles to bones and other body structures and move the bone or the structure. Tendonitis is generally caused by either acute injury, such as a sprain or strain, or chronic inflammation, such as arthritis, fibromyalgia, or failing to heal well from an acute injury. An injured tendon usually takes four to eight weeks to heal. That healing can be helped along nicely with rest, ice, limited gentle movement, Arnica topical applications three times a day, and large doses of vitamin C (1,000 milligrams [mg]) and bioflavonoids (500 mg), each three times a day with food. (If you experience loose stools or diarrhea from the vitamin C, cut back your dose.)

It's trickier to effectively care for chronic tendonitis or acute tendonitis that isn't getting better. Conventional medicine offers daily nonsteroidal anti-inflammatory drugs like *ibuprofen* (Advil, Motrin) and sometimes steroid injections. These medicines help with pain, but they are rarely curative, so I prefer a different approach.

- **Reduce inflammatory foods from your diet.** That means that coffee, alcohol, sugar, processed preservative- and dye-rich foods, and fried foods need to go. You don't have to become a vegan, but if you want to reduce inflammation and pain, limit meat intake to no more than six ounces a day.
- **Drink 70 to 90 ounces of water each day.** Water delivers nutrients to tendons, and it helps remove pain-inducing waste. Try to drink most of your water away from meals for optimal benefit.
- **Eat lots of beta-carotene-rich foods.** Beta-carotene converts to vitamin A inside the body. Vitamin A is known for its ability to reduce inflammation and promote elasticity in blood vessels and muscle tissue. But unless you like eating liver, it can be hard to get vitamin A directly from food. Instead, eat lots of carrots, sweet potatoes, dark leafy greens, cantaloupe, and squash.
- **People with chronic tendonitis often have calcium deposits on the tendon fibers**

that cause pain and limit mobility. With chronic tendonitis, limit calcium supplementation to no more than 300 mg per day. Take 1,000 micrograms of B12, 2,000 mg of vitamin C, and 1,000 mg of bioflavonoids daily. Research indicates that supplementation with these nutrients may reduce calcium deposition on tendons, decrease inflammation, and increase flexibility.

• **My favorite botanical medicine for chronic tendonitis is Boswellia serrata,** which you can find in tablets and capsules. It's often combined with another popular and effective anti-inflammatory botanical, turmeric. Because formulations vary, your best bet is to follow the manufacturer's recommendations for dosing.

Excellent Health Benefits of Chamomile

Laurie Steelsmith, ND, LAc, licensed naturopathic physician and acupuncturist in private practice in Honolulu. She is coauthor of three books—*Natural Choices for Women's Health, Great Sex, Naturally* and *Growing Younger Every Day.* DrSteelsmith.com

---

Mother Earth doesn't just supply us with the air we breathe and the stunning settings we see. The plants she produces provide us with heaps of health benefits, from turmeric's brain-boosting properties to echinacea's immunity-enhancing qualities.

Chamomile doesn't just fall under this category of healing plants. The herb epitomizes it. There are two different types of chamomile—German and Roman, with the former being the more potent of the two and the one used most often for therapeutic applications. Thanks to the flavonoids, sesquiterpenes, and antioxidants it contains, it's traditionally been used to treat everything from rheumatic pain to ulcers. Now, chamomile is gaining even more ground as a large body of research shows its varied benefits. *Whether you choose to drink chamomile tea, take a chamomile supplement, use chamomile essential oil, or invest in a topical treatment, here are nine ways the herb may bolster your wellness...*

1. Improves sleep. Savoring a cup of chamomile tea before bed is a common habit for many—and not just for the earthy, apple taste it offers (indeed, "chamomile" goes back to the Greek word, khamaimëlon, or "earth apple"). Chamomile contains apigenin, an antioxidant that binds to certain receptors in your brain that help decrease restlessness and induce sleep.

2. Reduces premenstrual symptoms. Bloating, cramping, mood swings—we women are well-aware that PMS can do a number on us. Fewer of us, however, may know that chamomile can be used to mitigate its symptoms. A systematic review of chamomile's benefits, published by the *Journal of Pharmacopuncture,* demonstrates that chamomile's anti-inflammatory, anti-spasmodic, and anti-anxiety effects renders it a stellar remedy for alleviating abdominal and pelvic pain, as well as period-related anxiety and irritability. Drink as a tea, one cup twice a day from mid cycle until the period starts. One of my favorites is Organic Chamomile with Lavender tea by Traditional Medicinals containing not only chamomile but two herbs that soothe the nervous system, lavender and lemon balm.

3. Relieves eczema. Atopic eczema—a dermatological condition that causes the skin to become red, itchy, and inflamed—is often treated with hydrocortisone cream. Data published by the National Institutes of Health show that chamomile is roughly 60 percent as effective as 0.25 percent of the over-the-counter remedy. While additional research is needed to evaluate the true efficacy of chamomile's effect on eczema, present findings show that it may be a promising alternative option. You can reap its skin-soothing benefits in a topical treatment or use chamomile essential oil. How? Dilute with a carrier oil, such as coconut and jojoba, and add to warm bath water or your favorite body lotion. Alternatively, you can make a hot compress by soaking a towel or cloth in warm water, adding one to two drops of diluted chamomile oil, and then applying it to your skin.

4. Helps inflammatory conditions. While acute inflammation helps keep you alive—the process is your body's first line of defense against injuries, toxins, and infections—chronic inflammation tells a different story, and may result in tissue damage, gastrointestinal distress, and skin issues. Chamomile may aid in these consequences. Studies have shown that chamomile inhibits Helicobacter pylori, the bacteria that causes stomach ulcers, while its anti-spasmodic effects can help relax the abdominal aches frequently associated with gastrointestinal inflammatory disorders. The herb can also help with inflammation of the skin. Approved by the German Commission E for wound and burn therapy, one of chamomile's active constituents, levomenol, has anti-inflammatory and naturally-moisturizing properties that can diminish the signs of photoaging, reduce pruritis (itchy skin), and improve skin texture and elasticity.

For gastrointestinal issues, drink the tea (a few cups a day) or take chamomile as a supplement (900 mg/pill, two pills three times a day). For topical issues, the tea can be applied topically by soaking a wash cloth in a warm cup of tea and then apply the compress to affected tissue. Or have a lovely chamomile soak by adding six bags of chamomile tea to a bath. You could also use the bulk herb—which is less expensive—by pouring two cups of chamomile flowers into your bath. A bath provides a special experience with chamomile flowers keeping you company.

5. ...and osteoporosis. While further studies are needed before chamomile can be considered for clinical use in the treatment of osteoporosis, research on the topic demonstrates great potential. In one study, chamomile extract was shown to stimulate osteoblastic cell differentiation, the NIH reports. Translation? It may help protect bones that are prone to depletion due to age and the loss of estrogen. Take chamomile as a tea and drink a few cups a day.

6. Aids in digestion. Chamomile is chock-full of health-boosting properties, including compounds, called sesquiterpene lactones, that urge the pancreas to produce the digestive enzymes your body needs to break down food. What's more, stress-related gastrointestinal issues that thwart proper digestion can be helped by chamomile's naturally calming effects. Drink a cup of chamomile tea after meals to support your digestion.

7. Lowers anxiety. That soothing effect isn't reserved just for sleep or your stomach. Chamomile can help diminish anxiety, period. One study, published in the journal *Phytomedicine,* found that chamomile extract lessens symptoms of General Anxiety Disorder (GAD). Harvard Health seconds this and suggests it can be a safe and effective alternative remedy for anxiety. (Do note that chamomile is not recommended if you're taking *warfarin, clopidogrel,* and other blood thinners.) Drinking a few cups a day of chamomile tea on a daily basis can soothe your nerves.

8. Boosts oral health. Chamomile's antiseptic properties make it a boon for your oral health by heading off infections, protecting your teeth and gums, and warding off gingivitis. It can also help relieve the discomfort of toothaches. "Administering" it is simple too. All you have to do is swish chamomile tea around in your mouth before drinking it.

9. Bolsters immunity. Immune health is your health—and chamomile can be used to encourage it. Why? Because the herb boasts a number of phenolic compounds—acids with tremendous antioxidant activities that can help rouse the action of leukocytes and T-cells (cells responsible for safeguarding you against infections and toxins). You can use chamomile tea on a daily basis to support your immunity, or you can take it as a supplement. Most supplement products contain 900 mg of German chamomile extract. Take 900 mg twice a day.

Sip a cup of soothing tea and protect your health while you're at it? Now there's a(nother) reason to start stocking chamomile in your pantry!

Aging Well

The Secret to Successful Aging: Habits for Health and Happiness

Successful aging is the ability to take pleasure from things that you enjoy, to discover new things, and to live your life in a way that is meaningful—at any age. It requires discipline and commitment throughout your lifetime. Although it is never too late to begin, the earlier you commit to the habits that promote successful aging the better.

In my book *Successful Aging: A Neuroscientist Explores the Power and Potential of Our Lives,* I use the acronym COACH to describe the key habits necessary to age successfully and lead a happier life—conscientiousness, openness, associations, curiosity, and healthy lifestyle.

Conscientious people are dependable, reliable, and proactive. They seek medical attention when they are sick. They listen to a doctor's advice and take their medications. They live within their means and put money aside for future needs and retirement.

Being open to new experiences is crucial to successful aging and can even help prevent cognitive decline. Try a new sport, join a book club, or take piano lessons. You will feel better physically and mentally.

Associations with others, through friendships and hobbies, keep you engaged and not isolated. Maintaining these associations and adding new ones gives you new perspectives and can lead to new relationships as well as shared interests.

Curiosity. People who are curious are more apt to challenge themselves intellectually and socially. They are also more likely to be inter-

Daniel L. Levitin, PhD, an award-winning neuroscientist, musician, and best-selling author. Dr. Levitin is the founding dean of Arts & Humanities at the Minerva Schools at the Keck Graduate Institute, San Francisco, and James McGill Professor Emeritus of Psychology, Neuroscience and Music at McGill University in Montreal, Quebec, Canada.

ested and engaged. Curiosity helps to make us mentally agile and alert and helps to boost the immune system.

FOLLOW A HEALTHY LIFESTYLE

Exercise is key to both physical and emotional health, but there is too much emphasis on aerobic exercise and lifting weights. Although going to the gym is helpful, being in nature is better. Taking walks in natural surroundings, going on hikes, or riding a bike keep our minds active. An extra 20 minutes on an elliptical machine is good for the heart, but it does not stimulate your mind.

I have learned that there is no one right diet for everyone. Maintaining a healthy weight is key to successful aging, but it's fine to eat dessert occasionally.

A good night's sleep is essential for health and cognitive function. Restorative sleep allows the body to engage in cellular repair processes and for the brain to digest all of the experiences of the previous day. Disruptions in sleep can lead to depression and anxiety and raises your risk of high blood pressure, cardiovascular disease, diabetes, and obesity. It also weakens your immune system. The National Sleep Foundation recommends seven to nine hours of sleep each night for adults ages 26 to 64, and older adults (65+) should get seven to eight hours.

It's not always easy to sleep, and it gets harder as we age. I recommend that you have a ritual before you go to bed. Take a bath, or read, or listen to relaxing music. Go to bed at the same time each night, and get up at the same time each day. Don't drink alcohol before bedtime. Sleep in a darkened room, and use earplugs if necessary. I don't recommend sleeping pills such as *zolpidem* (Ambien) or *eszopiclone* (Lunesta), especially in seniors, as they can cause confusion and double the risk of falls and hip fractures. Additionally, they disrupt the normal rhythms of sleep. I do not generally recommend natural sleep aids such as melatonin either. Supplements are not regulated by the U.S. Food & Drug Administration, so their quality is not guaranteed.

KEEP WORKING

Working keeps your mind engaged. It gives you a routine and keeps you from being isolated.

If you must retire, retire to something else: Volunteer, teach a class, tutor, or become a mentor.

The easiest way to be happy is to help others. Helping others gives our lives purpose. It even helps with the minor aches and pains we have, as they recede when we are focused on others.

BE GRATEFUL

Being grateful allows you to feel more positive emotions and to deal with adversity. There is also evidence that it can lower stress levels and give people an optimistic approach to life. Studies have shown that genes can make some people more grateful and others less so. To help boost your gratitude, try making a list of even simple things that you are thankful for, such as "I'm grateful I can still read," or "I'm happy my friend called me today."

OTHER FACTORS

High blood pressure, diabetes, cancer, and Alzheimer's disease often run in families, but genes are not destiny. Research has shown that diet, exercise, and sleep can lessen the risk or delay the onset of chronic illnesses.

Many studies show that (happily) married people live longer, but a bad relationship can actually shorten your life. Many single people live long, happy lives. The key is to connect with people in other ways.

WE GET HAPPIER AS WE AGE

Numerous studies have shown that after age 50 people tend to get happier. A study by the Office for National Statistics in England found that 65 to 79 is the happiest age group for adults. A different study found that happiness peaks in the 80s. Older people have fewer arguments and come up with better solutions to conflict. They are also better at controlling their emotions, accepting misfortune, and coping with the ups and downs of life.

While we tend to grow happier, depression can still strike at any age. If you lose interest in things you previously enjoyed or feel sad, hopeless, or empty over an extended period, talk to your doctor.

BUSTING BRAIN MYTHS

Your body and brain age. This is natural. We cannot run as fast as we could in our 20s at age 60. But when it comes to brain health, decline is not inevitable. Failing memory is one of the biggest misconceptions about aging. If you are over 60 and forgot where you put your keys or glasses, you might fear that it is the beginning of dementia, but teenagers forget their cell phones, and middle-aged people lose their car keys all the time. No one suggests that those lapses are a sign of Alzheimer's disease. While people are quick to draw that conclusion for seniors, those little memory lapses are normal at every age.

The more we use our brain, the better we will succeed both mentally and physically. Being mentally engaged, whether it's through work or play, keeps us interested, present, and sharp. These habits are the foundation of successful aging.

It's Never Too Late to Get Fit

James P. Owen, author of *Just Move: A New Approach to Fitness After 50* and producer of *The Art of Aging Well,* available at TheArtOfAgingWell.com.

I always wanted to be an athlete, but it took me until I was 75 to succeed. I went from being wracked with pain to feeling better than I did in my 30s, and you can, too.

My first attempt to get fit didn't go as planned. In my 50s, I became a "weekend warrior," alternating long weekdays sitting at a desk with an intense workout schedule. I ran up hills on the weekends and hired a personal trainer to help me push my limits.

But instead of feeling better, I felt pain: Everything in my body protested. Dispirited, I put away my plans for exercise and didn't think about it again for decades.

A PASSION PROJECT

In the early 2000s, I began traveling extensively, giving more than a dozen lectures each month, living in hotels, and eating late-night restaurant meals. I was mentally fulfilled but physically depleted. When I turned 70, I saw a video of myself and thought, "I'm an old man!" My knees were shot, my rotator cuff was frozen, and I had excruciating back pain. I couldn't stand up straight, and I was overweight.

I came across a statistic that changed my life: It said that if you make it to age 70, you're likely to live another 15 years. I thought, "If I'm in this bad of shape now, imagine how I'll feel in 15 years." I knew I had to do something.

GETTING STARTED

I began by thinking through my goal. I wasn't after big biceps, but I wanted to be able to carry my suitcase without throwing out my back. I wanted to complete normal activities without pain—climbing the stairs, squatting down to pick something up, staying mobile, active, and energetic.

So I set a goal for myself: In five years, I wanted to be pain-free—what I call "geezer-fit." I knew there were no quick fixes and that I was bound to have setbacks, but I persisted.

On day one, I couldn't do a single push-up. It took me two weeks to do even one. Once I could do that, I thought, "In time, I might be able to do two or even three." I took it slow and steady. I knew that when people try to do too much too fast, they are liable to get hurt. But small steps, taken consistently, lead to success over time.

GOAL ACHIEVED

When I turned 75, I could do 50 push-ups. My pain was gone and I had finally found my inner athlete. So then I set a new goal. I wanted to be "80 years young," which to me meant having a wellness age younger than my chronological age. I kept up my fitness routine and increased my focus on healthy eating. A week before my 80th birthday, I underwent a battery of tests and was happy to learn that I'd met my goal. My doctor said I have the vitals of someone 10 years younger.

I'm now working toward being what I call a "super-ager." That means living life to the fullest and making the most of whatever gifts I have for as many years as I can. To do that, I work out for an hour a day five to six days a week. It might sound like a lot of work, but it's much easier than dealing with the infirmities of old age.

INTRINSIC MOTIVATION

So many people, when they turn 70 or 75, they look at the world and say, "My best days are behind me." But I don't agree with that at all. You can't give in and say, "I'm old. I'm feeble. There's no hope." In my heart, I know that my best days still lie ahead.

Ready, set, go!

Getting fit is a journey at any age. *Here are some practical tips to get started…*

1. Set a goal and know what you're working for. Fitness affects more than appearance.

2. Plan for setbacks so they don't derail you.

3. Include all of the dimensions of fitness—strength training at least twice a week, cardiovascular work for 30 minutes on most days of the week, stretching, and balance training.

4. Look ahead. No matter how old you are, your best days can lie ahead if you're willing to work at it.

Living Alone? Stay Safe and Secure When You Are Far from Family

Kristina Butler, RN, founder of Comfort Keepers, an international care service for seniors and adults who need assistance with everything from errands to long-term planning and personal care so that they can remain at home for as long and as safely as possible. ComfortKeepers.com

Being able to stay in your own home as you age is the gold standard for many of us, but that ideal can be challenging to pull off when you live on your own and don't have family nearby to help.

The secret to doing it successfully: Preparing for a potential emergency, whether it's a natural disaster such as a hurricane…an injury such as a fall…or an acute illness.

Here are the steps to take now to help keep yourself safe and secure in any event in the future…

1. Get all your legal documents in order, and store them in one place in your home. This includes your health insurance cards and policy information, will, trusts, power of attorney, and an advance health-care directive that states your wishes in the event that you become incapacitated. Also give a set of copies to someone you trust. I can't tell you how common it is for a scavenger hunt to ensue because no one knows where these documents are when an emergency occurs and first responders and medical staff don't know your wishes.

2. Wear a medical-alert pendant or bracelet. Even if you are active and healthy, wearing one of these devices gives peace of mind in case of emergency. You shouldn't just rely on a cell phone—you may not be able to reach it. And digital assistants, such as Alexa, currently can't call 911. Consider a plan that offers a mobile network with GPS technology that you also can use when you are away from home if you were to get lost or, say, suffer cardiac symptoms or an injury on a hike or bike ride. Buy a waterproof model that can be worn in the shower. The Apple Watch is another option, although it can be difficult to set up for those who are not tech-savvy.

These devices aren't just for injuries and illness. You can use them to call 911 in the event of fire or flood or if someone is trying to break into your home.

3. Make a plan for responders to get into your home. What happens if you need emergency help and can't get to the door to unlock it? Besides a delay in your treatment, first responders are going to knock down your door or break a window to get inside, and the repair costs will be up to you. Giving a neighbor a key—and including him/her on the contact list for your medical-alert provider—is one way to avoid that. Add an extra level of security by getting a lockbox to hold your keys on your front or back doorknob. (This is the gadget that realtors use in order to enter a house that is for sale.) Or install a keypad lock that requires only a numerical code. Give the access code to a neighbor and to your local police and fire departments. This way, it's in the dispatcher's instructions to first responders if you call 911.

4. Make your kitchen emergency central. One of the first places responders look for info is the refrigerator door. Post a list there of what responders should do in an emergency. Include the people to contact and their phone numbers, the location of those important legal documents you've stored in one place, preferred doctor and hospital information, and the medications you take and where they are located.

Also helpful: Keep all those meds (prescription and over-the-counter) in a visible container on your kitchen counter.

5. Stock up on provisions. Make sure you have at least one week's worth of medications on hand at all times—set up auto refills and delivery service with your local pharmacy. Keep about two weeks of nonperishable foods (canned soups and vegetables, pasta, cereal, peanut butter, etc.) on hand, as well as personal-care items, a supply of batteries, and a working fire extinguisher.

6. Get involved in your community. Social support and companionship have been shown to improve physical and mental health, and there's another plus for those who live alone—it extends your care network. Attending a regularly scheduled event might raise a red flag if you don't show up one week, for example. You also can develop a buddy system with other people in the same situation and check in on one another daily with a call or text—just as you should be doing with faraway family members. YWCAs/YMCAs typically offer many programs, as do many church and religious organizations and local community centers. Seek out local clubs for your personal interests.

7. Interview home care agencies well before you need them. Most people call for professional assistance only in an emergency —after an injury, returning home after rehab, or when they suddenly realize that they need help. If you investigate care providers when you're well, you can decide which one you prefer and have your information in its system so that it is ready to go when you are.

Home care isn't just for the immobile or cognitively impaired. Services such as grocery shopping, transportation to the doctor, light housekeeping, and companionship also come in handy.

8. Stay on your feet. One out of every four adults age 65+ suffers a fall annually. It is the leading cause of injury and death in this age group, according to the Centers for Disease Control and Prevention (CDC). Prevent falls by having your bathroom outfitted with grab bars, shower benches, nonslip mats, and elevated toilet seats—these items can be useful for anyone, not just for seniors. As a precaution, always wear your medical-alert device while in the bathroom.

You'll also want to remove any area rugs with corners you can trip over...make sure that you have plenty of lighting (including nightlights)...eliminate clutter on floors and steps...and arrange furniture so that you have plenty of room to maneuver. Eldercare and home-safety companies often will have safety pros available who can come to your home, usually for an hourly rate, and do an assessment of what you need. You also can find checklists online, such as from the CDC at https://bit.ly/2AaGPQp.

And, of course, stay physically active. Exercise helps prevent injury by maintaining strength and balance.

9. Consider working with a geriatric-care manager if you become infirm. These professionals are typically licensed nurses or social workers who specialize in geriatrics—though they can help people of any age. They are sometimes referred to as "professional relatives" because they can take over a lot of what family members might help manage—assessing your assistance needs, helping develop a care plan, hiring help, and acting as your advocate. They usually charge by the hour and typically aren't covered by insurance. The cost may be worth it, however, because they can ensure a more positive outcome and reduce medical costs down the road, lessen the need for distant family members (if you even have them) to engage in emergency travel and save the time spent trying to coordinate care. Ask about nearby care managers at your doctor's office, elder-care companies that probably have them on staff and local senior programs... or go to Eldercare Locator at Eldercare.acl.gov.

Aging in Place

Steve Cunningham, a certified aging-in-place specialist (CAPS) and owner of Cunningham Contracting, Williamsburg, Virginia.

Brandy Archie, OTD, OTRL, CLIPP, doctor of occupational therapy, certified living-in-place professional (CLIPP), and owner of AccessAble Living, Kansas City, Missouri.

Most people want to stay in their own homes as they age, but often don't think about the kinds of modifications they may later need to make that possible.

The best time to prepare your home to age in place is when you're still healthy and financially able to make the modifications that will become vital in the future. *Here's a room-by-room look at essential home improvements, both large and small...*

THE STAIRS

Mobility problems that often occur later in life can make climbing stairs difficult, if not impossible. If finances allow, consider adding a first-floor bedroom and full bath. If the layout can't accommodate these changes, a stairlift or, in some cases, an elevator can be a valuable addition.

THE BATHROOM

Bathroom renovations increase safety and independence and, as a result, dignity. One of the best design advances is the curbless shower. It has a wide entry that's either completely level with the bathroom floor or has a very low step-up instead of a step-over. This makes getting in and out easy, whether the user is still mobile or needs a walker or shower chair.

A handheld showerhead and a built-in tile bench or teak seat make showering easier for those who have a hard time standing or are unsteady. Despite the availability of walk-in bathtubs, many people don't like having to sit in them naked and feel cold while they fill up with water and while they drain. They also have a high step to get in, which can be problematic as we age.

Some lower-cost modifications also have a great impact. Switching to a taller toilet means less difficulty getting up and down. Buying one with a built-in bidet or retrofitting it with a bidet feature is extremely helpful for personal hygiene, though many people are too embarrassed to bring up this subject. But the ease of cleansing that a bidet offers can help with avoiding urinary tract infections, which can be particularly dangerous during the senior years.

Strategically placed and professionally installed grab bars are essential to avoid slips and falls, especially for people with balance problems. Falls are one of the most common reasons that people can no longer live safely at home. Newer designs can blend seamlessly into the décor by doubling as towel racks and shampoo shelves.

THE KITCHEN

A top tweak for increasing accessibility and safety in the kitchen is moving the microwave, which many seniors use more often than the oven, from the traditional spot above the oven or cooktop to a microwave drawer. This reduces the risk of spills when reaching up to retrieve a hot cup of soup with unsteady hands, for example. Speaking of cooktops, replace yours if the knobs are at the back and require reaching across burners to get to them.

When upgrading appliances, a refrigerator with the freezer on the bottom is easier than one with the freezer on top for finding and taking out items. A touch faucet at the kitchen sink is ideal for people with hand arthritis. Install pullout shelves in deep cabinets to eliminate having to hunt around for kitchen items or food staples. Upgrade overhead and task (under-cabinet) lighting, elements that are particularly important in a workroom like a kitchen to make it easier to see as vision becomes less sharp.

THE BEDROOM

While you often hear the advice to anchor bookcases, dressers, and wardrobes to walls as part of childproofing, this is also smart advice for seniors, who might grab onto furniture for support when feeling unsteady. Place nonskid pads under the legs of nightstands and other moveable furniture to prevent them from sliding in such a situation. If a walker is needed, the bed should be positioned with enough clearance to maneuver it easily. In addition, a bed rail can be added for a secure handhold, making it easier to get in and out of the bed.

ALL AROUND THE HOUSE

Simple fixes can make everyday tasks easier, even ones that you might not think twice about, such as switching door handles to levers and changing light switches from toggles to paddles.

• **Review the lighting in each room.**

Have an electrician install overhead lights to get rid of lamps: The cords can be a tripping hazard. Consider motion-sensor lighting at floor level along the hallways that run from the bedroom to the bathroom to light a path in the middle of the night.

• **Do a walk-through to evaluate the transitions from one room to the next.** Measure doorways to see if any would need to be widened to accommodate a walker or wheelchair. Remove area rugs and clutter on the floor to eliminate these tripping hazards. A more expensive project is replacing carpeting with wood or wood-like flooring, which is easier for maneuvering a walker or wheelchair and easier on the lungs of anyone with respiratory issues.

With people of all ages relying on electronic gadgets, make sure charging stations are easily accessible in the bedroom and living room. Remember, outlets don't have to be near the floor. Have some installed higher up the wall.

Many people forget to update closets, but it's important to adjust shelving for better access to commonly used items. The closet doors themselves should be wide enough to accommodate a walker if needed. Inexpensive items like grabbers are handy for reaching items on high shelves.

Professionals such as occupational therapists and contractors who are trained in aging-in-place projects can help you make smart choices.

Feeling Dizzy? This Question Helps Diagnose the Cause

Study titled "Asking About Dizziness When Turning in Bed Predicts Examination Findings for Benign Paroxysmal Positional Vertigo," by researchers at University of Gothenburg, Sweden, published in *Journal of Vestibular Research.*

Benign paroxysmal positional vertigo (BPPV) is a medical mouthful but an important condition to know about—especially because it's often challenging to get a proper diagnosis for this common type of dizziness.

When you break down the medical terms of BPPV, each one describes a key element of the condition—benign means it's not life-threatening...paroxysmal means it starts and stops suddenly...positional means symptoms are triggered by position changes...and vertigo, which is the main symptom, refers to the unpleasant sensation of feeling like you or the room is spinning.

Because dizziness, a general term used to describe vertigo, light-headedness and/or impaired balance, is estimated to affect three of out every 10 people age 70 and older, it's crucial to correctly diagnose the problem so it can be treated appropriately. With BPPV, X-rays and other diagnostic tests don't identify the condition. Instead, a special type of physical exam that many health care providers may not be familiar with must be used for a proper diagnosis. The good news is that once BPPV is diagnosed, it's fairly easy to treat (see below), and you don't need to take medication.

To help physicians home in on BPPV and the dangers of its related fall risk in older adults, researchers at the University of Gothenburg asked 149 older adults being treated for dizziness to answer a 15-question survey about their symptoms in addition to receiving a physical exam.

The key question: "Do you get dizzy when you lie down or roll over in bed?" was most often associated with the correct diagnosis of BPPV. Patients who answered "yes" to this question were about 60 percent more likely to be diagnosed with BPPV than those who answered "no."

Patients who said they had "continuous dizziness" were less likely to be diagnosed with BPPV than those who had dizziness "lasting seconds," according to the research, which was published in *Journal of Vestibular Research*. Short periods of dizziness are linked to BPPV.

Effective treatment for BPPV: While the exact cause of BPPV has not yet been determined, doctors know that the condition occurs when calcium crystals, known as otoconia, break loose from sensory hair cells inside the inner ear. Until the crystals settle back into position, sudden movement causes them to float in the inner-ear fluid, triggering vertigo. BPPV usually goes away on its own within a few weeks, but you can eliminate it sooner by doing simple exercises called the Epley maneuver.

This treatment involves positioning your head and body in ways that help the otoconia settle inside the inner ear. The maneuvers can be done by a health-care provider (such as an ear, nose and throat doctor, or otololaryngologist, or an audiologist). They take only a few minutes to complete, and they usually relieve BPPV after a few sessions.

Important: If you have sudden episodes of spinning vertigo triggered by movement, especially while lying down or turning over, you may have BPPV and should consult your health-care provider for a diagnosis. Other causes of vertigo include Meniere's disease, which is believed to result from a buildup of fluid in the inner ear and may lead to hearing loss, and labyrinthitis, which often results from an infection in the inner ear. Treatment depends on the cause.

To get a diagnosis and appropriate treatment for vertigo, start with your primary care provider. He/she may refer you to an otolaryngologist, who specializes in these conditions. To find an otolaryngologist near you, consult the American Academy of Otolaryngology-Head and Neck Surgery at ENTnet.org and click on "Find an ENT."

Vertigo: Not Just Dizziness

Oliver Adunka, MD, director of the division of otology/neurotology and cranial base surgery, and clinical professor of otolaryngology at the Ohio State University Wexner Medical Center in Columbus.

One of the hallmarks of Alfred Hitchcock's masterpiece *Vertigo* is the camera work that captured the overwhelming sensation of the world spinning out of control. That feeling is all too real for the one in three people who experience vertigo at some time in their lives.

WHAT IS VERTIGO?

Vertigo is the uncomfortable sensation of feeling like the room you're in is spinning around you, or that you are spinning within the room. It can be mild or severe and frequent enough to keep you from even the simplest activities of daily life. Vertigo is not as simple as feeling dizzy when standing too quickly or being off balance from poor muscle tone. Rather, it is a symptom of a problem within your vestibular system, a circuit linking parts of the brain and inner ear that works to control balance, eye movements, and even posture.

The vestibular system may be impaired by a variety of factors, from a temporary injury to a progressive disease. Here are the most common vestibular disorders that can cause episodes of vertigo. Note that how long an episode lasts provides a great clue to the underlying cause.

BENIGN PAROXYSMAL POSITIONAL VERTIGO (BPPV)

This is, by far, the most common cause of vertigo. With BPPV, vertigo episodes usually last for a matter of seconds up to one minute, often when you're lying in bed or when you lean over.

Typically, BPPV occurs when microscopic calcium deposits within the ear called otoliths come loose and float in one of the canals of the vestibular system. This can be caused by ear or head surgery (the vibration from surgical drills can cause otoliths to break free), trauma to the head, or dental work. It may occur as an after-effect of an ear infection or even the remnants of an upper respiratory infection. Often, no cause can be identified.

One way to manage BPPV is to use the Epley maneuver, a set sequence of head motions that is designed to change the balance in the canal and help put the otoliths back into place. You should learn how to do them and how often to do them from a trained physical therapist or occupational therapist, but once you know them, you can do them on your own to manage symptoms. The movements can feel somewhat awkward, but people do respond very well to them.

MÉNIÈRE DISEASE

This inner ear disorder stems from an imbalance of fluids in the inner ear and affects both balance and hearing.

While it is a common cause of vertigo, it is relatively rare and is often overdiagnosed: Eight out of 10 people referred to me for Ménière disease don't actually have it. Who develops it and why are still enigmas, and it seems to come out of the blue. Fluids in a tube in the inner ear that are not normally under pressure suddenly become pressurized.

There are four defining symptoms of Ménière disease—episodes of vertigo that last between 20 minutes and two hours, ringing in the ear (tinnitus), hearing loss, and the sensation of pressure or fullness in the ear—almost always on one side only. Vertigo episodes with Ménière disease can happen infrequently or they can be daily, getting in the way of your normal life. The more frequent the attacks, the greater the chance of permanent hearing loss, so treatment is important.

Though Ménière disease isn't caused by salt intake, salt can bring on an attack—people often get one right after eating a fast food meal, for instance, so a low-salt diet is part of the plan. Taking medications, such as a diuretic, can help reduce pressure, while a two- or three-day course of steroids can help prevent hearing loss during an attack. Pressure devices and surgical interventions can also reduce the frequency and severity of life-altering vertigo episodes.

VESTIBULAR MIGRAINES

Many people misdiagnosed with Ménière disease instead have silent migraines. Vestibular migraines are characterized by daylong attacks of vertigo without actual migraine head pain. They can occur frequently or months apart. Some other signs are a lack of balance, problems with motion, like not being able to read a book in a moving car, and/or a personal or family history of migraine. Hearing is not typically affected.

Vestibular migraines can be hard to diagnose because there's no single test to identify them. It may first be necessary to rule out other causes with imaging tests. Some people find relief by taking a migraine-prevention medication, an antihypertensive, a beta blocker, or a low-dose anti-seizure drug. Finding the right medication can be trial and error, but it's reassuring just to know that this is a functional problem—it's not subtle, but it's also not dangerous.

FINDING HELP

Getting the right diagnosis can be a challenge, but there are many specialists who can help. Otolaryngologists, also called ENTs for ear, nose, and throat, are skilled at treating problems with those structures. Some specialize in vestibular disorders. An otologist/neurotologist, for example, has additional training in how the ears and brain work together. Seek out a neurologist with a headache subspecialty if you have vertigo and other possible signs

TAKE NOTE...

Low Blood Sugar and Dementia Linked

Diabetes-associated episodes of low blood sugar may increase the risk of developing dementia, researchers reported in *JAMA Internal Medicine,* and having dementia or mild cognitive impairment may increase the risk of experiencing low blood sugar. "Individuals with dementia or even those with milder forms of cognitive impairment may be less able to effectively manage complex treatment regimens for diabetes and less able to recognize the symptoms of hypoglycemia and to respond appropriately, increasing their risk of severe hypoglycemia," explained senior author Kristine Yaffe, MD.

JAMA Internal Medicine

of vestibular migraine, such as double vision or seeing flashing lights. Depending on your diagnosis, you might be referred to a physical or occupational therapist as part of your treatment plan.

MEDICATION MAY BE TO BLAME

It's important to distinguish between a drug that causes standard dizziness and one that causes vertigo because it's toxic to ear structures. A careful evaluation of all medications you're taking by your doctor or pharmacist can help pinpoint a possible culprit, and switching to a different drug could stop your symptoms. Exposure to environmental chemicals, like lead and mercury, can also damage the ear.

Can Dehydration Cause Dementia?

Betsy Mills, PhD, senior program manager, aging and Alzheimer's prevention, Alzheimer's Drug Discovery Foundation, New York.

What is the link between dehydration and dementia?

The human body is made up of over 50 percent water, and it requires this water to carry out all of its essential day-to-day functions, including cognitive function. When the brain cells don't have enough water, they have to work harder, so they end up operating at a slower pace, which results in mental fog.

The cognitive symptoms of dehydration differ depending on the age, sex, and overall health of the person. Young, healthy people tend to experience fatigue and irritability, while older individuals are more likely to experience a reduced ability to focus and a slowing of processing speed, which is the time it takes to complete a mental task.

Although both men and women can experience cognitive symptoms of dehydration, they tend to be more pronounced in women. Women and the elderly may be more vulnerable to the negative effects of dehydration due to decreased muscle mass. Muscle tissue is composed of nearly 80 percent water and can buffer against dehydration by releasing its stored water when fluid levels get low. Therefore, in addition to eating a well-balanced diet containing many water-rich fruits and vegetables, engaging in muscle strength-building exercises is a good way to protect against dehydration.

The effects of dehydration on cognitive function are usually temporary and should resolve once the body is adequately hydrated. However, dehydration is a state of stress for the brain, and if it persists, then the brain cells could sustain long-lasting damage, which can pave the way for permanent cognitive dysfunction. Temporary cognitive dysfunction in response to dehydration is generally not considered a sign of dementia, but dehydration may exacerbate cognitive symptoms in people with dementia.

Additionally, dehydration can accelerate cognitive decline in individuals with dementia. The sensitivity to thirst declines with age, so elderly individuals, especially those with dementia, may not recognize that they are dehydrated. Since individuals with dementia are more prone to becoming dehydrated, it may be necessary to keep track of their fluid intake. Importantly, the brain can also be harmed by excessive water consumption, because it can lead to a dangerous drop in sodium levels. For more information on brain health and avoiding risks, visit CognitiveVitality.org.

Protect Your Aging Brain

Ginger Schechter, MD, chief medical officer of AffirmativHealth, in Sonoma, California, where she helps implement the RE:mind Program, which educates and empowers individuals and families to take control of their cognitive health. She is co-author of *Outsmart Your Brain: The Insider's Guide to Life-Long Memory.* AffirmativHealth.com

What is the most feared illness? It's not heart disease, cancer, stroke, or diabetes, according to a survey by the Marist Institute for Public Opinion. It's Alzheimer's disease.

Feared because Alzheimer's robs you of your ability to care for yourself, your memory, and even your identity. Feared because no one feels prepared to care for a loved one with Alzheimer's. Feared because many other deadly diseases can be treated—even reversed. Alzheimer's can't.

PROTECTING COGNITION

The good news is that the mental decline that leads to Alzheimer's and other forms of dementia is not inevitable. When my colleagues and I treated seniors with a customized, multifactorial program, we saw no decline in memory, executive function, and attention, as measured by the Montreal Cognitive Assessment test. Further, we reported in the *Journal of Alzheimer's Disease Reports*, we often saw improvement. The key to fighting cognitive decline, we found, is to follow a treatment program that addresses multiple risk factors.

TREATING A MULTIFACTORIAL DISEASE

Mild cognitive impairment (MCI) and early-stage Alzheimer's disease (AD) are diseases and, like heart disease, diabetes, and cancer, they rarely have a single cause.

One of the reasons why modern medicine fails to control cognitive decline: It typically targets only a single factor of a disease, usually with a drug. And it often does that with a "one-size-fits-all" approach. Health problems, however, are always unique to the individual.

Our custom program fine-tuned treatment to address those differences, but you don't need a customized program to start reducing your risk right now. There are many simple steps you can take to minimize the risk factors of cognitive decline and prevent, stop, or reverse the problem.

Now is the best time to start. Cognitive decline occurs over decades, so the sooner you start, the better.

But it's also never too late: The brain can form new neuronal connections throughout your lifetime, so you can see benefits even if you're just getting started in your 80s, 90s, or beyond. Changing just two or three risk factors can make a big difference.

EAT A GLUCOSE-BALANCING DIET

Our study found that cognitive improvement was directly linked to lowering levels of glucose (blood sugar) and insulin (the hormone that regulates glucose). High glucose and insulin create neuroinflammation, a risk factor in cognitive decline.

The best way to control blood sugar levels and nourish the brain is to follow a healthy diet. *Here are my recommendations for daily eating...*

- **Eat plenty of lean protein,** focusing on plant-based proteins, such as beans, legumes, nuts, and seeds. Other good sources of lean protein include eggs, poultry, and fish, particularly fatty fish rich in brain-nourishing omega-3 fatty acids, such as salmon, sardines, and anchovies.
- **Eat several daily servings of non-starchy vegetables,** which are low in carbohydrates and high in fiber. That's any vegetable other than corn, potatoes, peas, and winter squash.
- **Eat several servings of fruit,** particularly berries, which have been shown to be especially important for memory and brain health.
- **Eat more foods rich in probiotics,** the friendly gut bacteria that support the "gut-brain axis"—the connection between healthy digestion and a healthy brain. Probiotic-rich foods include yogurt, kimchi, sauerkraut, kombucha, and miso.
- **Eat more foods rich in prebiotics,** the undigested fiber that provides intestinal fuel

for probiotics. Prebiotic-rich foods include flax, leeks, garlic, and dandelion greens.

• **Eat plenty of monounsaturated fats,** which are found in olive oil, avocados, and nuts.

Focus on gluten-free grains, such as oats, millet, brown rice, wild rice, quinoa, and amaranth.

EXERCISE SEVERAL TIMES A WEEK

Regular exercise preserves brain tissue, stimulates brain areas involved in cognition, and improves neural plasticity, the ability of neurons to generate new connections that improve memory and learning. It also reduces stress, which inhibits memory and concentration. And, like a good diet, regular exercise balances blood sugar.

I recommend a weekly mix of three types of exercise…

• **Aerobic,** such as brisk walking or bicycling, three to five days per week;

• **Strength-training** using weights or other resistance devices such as resistance bands on nonconsecutive days each week; and

• **Balance training exercises,** such as yoga, three days per week. These exercises strengthen the muscles that keep you upright, including your legs and core, and they improve stability and reduce the risk of falls. Falls and head injuries can lead to cognitive problems, and cognitive problems increase the risk of falls.

GET SEVEN TO EIGHT HOURS OF SLEEP

Sleep is a must for cognitive health: Memory, language, reasoning, and focus all depend on it. That's because sleep allows the body, including the brain, to repair and reorganize. It also helps the body clear the brain of toxins. Poor sleep is linked to faster cognitive decline and to a higher risk of developing AD.

Sleep apnea, a sleep disorder in which breathing repeatedly stops and starts throughout the night, is also linked to cognitive decline. If you snore, a possible symptom of sleep apnea, talk to your doctor about being tested for the condition.

MANAGE CHRONIC STRESS

Chronic stress and the inflammatory stress hormones that accompany it damage cognitive health. Stress is tension, and the best way to manage it is with a tension-relieving relaxation technique, such as deep breathing, mindfulness meditation, progressive muscle relaxation, yoga, tai chi, or listening to calming music. Choose one that makes you feel relaxed and practice it daily for 10 to 20 minutes.

SOCIALIZE MORE

Making and keeping good social connections with your family and friends improves cognitive health. One study showed that socializing when you're older reduces the risk of dementia by 70 percent. *Here are some ideas…*

• **Join a group** or organization.

• **Participate in a book club.** This provides a double benefit because mental activity, such as reading and having discussions, stimulates and protects your cognition.

• **Take a class** at a local community college or through your township.

• **Volunteer** at your local hospital, school district, or local nonprofit.

• **Care for an animal.** Spending time with people isn't the only way to socialize. Caring for an animal provides a sense of companionship and purpose, and stimulates your mind.

TYPES OF EARLY COGNITIVE DECLINE

1. Subjective cognitive decline. This is when you sense something is wrong with your memory and mental clarity, but it's unlikely a doctor or psychologist could detect the problem.

2. Mild cognitive impairment. Memory problems are far more obvious. In fact, your memory is poorer than most other people your age. You often forget names or other new information. You also might have difficulty writing your name or experience other movement problems.

3. Early Alzheimer's disease. In early-stage or mild AD, mental decline has become noticeable—and probably very troublesome. You might not remember a sentence someone just said to you. You could have trouble handling money and paying bills. Maybe you're taking longer to do daily tasks. This is the stage at which cognitive decline is usually diagnosed.

Dementia Patients Often Get Ineffective Drugs

Among more than 700,000 people with dementia, nearly three-quarters had been prescribed an antidepressant, opioid painkiller, epilepsy drug, anxiety medication, or antipsychotic drug—which have limited evidence that they ease dementia-related behavior problems and which all carry significant risks.

If your loved one has dementia: Ask the doctor what symptoms the proposed drug is supposed to alleviate and about its proven effectiveness.

Donovan Maust, MD, geriatric psychiatrist at University of Michigan, Ann Arbor, and leader of a study published in *JAMA*.

GOOD NEWS...

Parkinson's Drug May Also Fight Alzheimer's

Pimavanserin, sold as Nuplazid, was FDA-approved in 2016 for reducing delusions in people with Parkinson's disease. A new study in patients with Alzheimer's disease found that it also improves Alzheimer's-induced symptoms of dementia-related psychosis—which causes hallucinations that can lead to anxiety, aggression, and verbal and physical abuse of caregivers. In fact, the drug's success for Alzheimer's was so evident that independent monitors stopped the study early. The manufacturer plans to ask the FDA this year to expand approved uses of the drug—which would become the first new medicine for Alzheimer's in nearly two decades. Doctors already can prescribe the medicine off-label.

Jeffrey Cummings, MD, ScD, founding director, Lou Ruvo Center for Brain Health, Las Vegas, and leader of a study presented at a recent Clinical Trials on Alzheimer's Disease meeting.

Treating Hypertension Could Reduce Dementia Risk

A meta-analysis of 12 trials with more than 92,000 patients shows that taking medication to lower your high blood pressure can reduce your risk for cognitive impairment and dementia by 7 percent.

Michelle Canavan, PhD, research fellow, National University of Ireland, Galway, and leader of a study published in *Journal of the American Medical Association*.

More TV Viewing, Greater Cognitive Decline

People who regularly watched television for more than 3.5 hours a day had poorer verbal memory six years later than those who watched three hours daily or less. And the greater the amount of TV watched above the 3.5-hour level, the larger the decline in this form of cognition.

Analysis of data on 3,662 adults, ages 50 and older, by researchers at University College London, UK, published in *Scientific Reports*.

Poor Vision Linked to Dementia Risk

Postmenopausal women who wore glasses or contact lenses that corrected their vision to 20/40 or worse were from two to six times as likely to develop dementia within seven years as women whose corrected vision was 20/20. The vision problems were in at least one eye and could not be fully corrected due to various eye diseases. The highest dementia incidence was in women who scored 20/100 or poorer. Impaired corrected vision also was linked to risk for mild cognitive impairment, which sometimes turns into dementia. The association does not mean poor corrected vision causes dementia—both conditions may result from the same underlying factors.

Study of 1,061 women, average age 74, led by researchers at Stanford University, published in *JAMA Ophthalmology.*

This Eye Surgery Improves Driving Safety

When researchers used a driving simulator to test the driving skills of 44 patients before and after cataract surgery, near misses and crashes dropped by 35 percent after surgery on one eye...and by 48 percent after surgery on the second eye.

Explanation: Cataract surgery not only improves visual acuity (how well one sees an eye chart) but also contrast sensitivity (the ability to distinguish increments of light versus dark) and night vision.

Jonathon Ng, MD, clinical senior lecturer, School of Population Health and Global Health, The University of Western Australia, Nedlands, Australia.

Coping with Eye Floaters

Margaret Liu, MD, medical director of the Pacific Vision Surgery Center, Pacific Vision Foundation, San Francisco Eye Institute.

Eye floaters, the spots and strings that drift across your visual field, can range from an annoyance to a downright problem if they interfere with the ability to drive or read. They are more common in people who are over age 50 and those who are nearsighted.

Let's take a look at what is happening in the eye when these appear. Most of the eye is filled with vitreous, a gel-like substance that is about 99 percent water and one percent solid materials that include collagen. As we age, bits of collagen can cluster into masses that cast shadows on the retina, causing most floaters.

A large, ring-like floater, called a Weiss ring, appears when the condensed vitreous gel separates from the retina at the optic nerve.

THE RISKS

While floaters are most often a harmless result of aging, they can sometimes be a sign of something more serious, such as a sight-threatening retinal tear or detachment, inflammation in the back of the eye, or bleeding in the eye from diabetes, hypertension, blocked blood vessels, or injury.

If you experience a sudden onset or increase in the number of floaters, flashes of light, or darkness in your peripheral vision, make an appointment with an eye doctor as soon as possible. Even if you don't have signs of a serious complication, it's a good idea to have an eye checkup whenever floaters appear. Once potentially serious conditions are ruled out, it's perfectly safe to leave floaters alone. Over time, many people no longer notice them.

COPING STRATEGIES

Not everyone adapts, however, and floaters can be maddening for some people. *Here are some tips to help manage the annoyance...*

- **Distract yourself.** If you are sitting idle, you are more prone to focus on the floaters. Distract yourself with an enjoyable activity, like riding a bike or going out with friends.

- **Wear brown, polarized sunglasses.** They can make the floaters less obvious, particularly in bright light.

- **Go dark.** Use dark mode and reduce the brightness on your electronic devices to make the floaters less visible.

- **Consider interior design.** White walls and bright lights accentuate floaters. If you can't repaint light walls, use art to create visual distraction.

- **Meditation** can help reduce your stress levels and allow you to gain control over your emotional response to floaters.

- **Change your diet.** Some people report that cutting out sugar and fatty foods can reduce the appearance of smaller floaters.

• **Rest your eyes.** Get enough sleep and take regular breaks from computer screens.

TREATMENT

For people who can't tolerate floaters or are debilitated by them, there are treatment options, but they're not to be taken lightly. Vitrectomy, a surgery to remove the vitreous, has risks including infection, retinal detachment, or bleeding.

Laser treatment (vitreolysis) is a less invasive option. An ophthalmologist focuses laser energy onto the clusters that are causing the shadows and administers a burst of energy for a tiny fraction of a second about 150 to 300 times. This energy pulverizes some of the floaters into a gas that completely vaporizes them and breaks apart others into smaller pieces that are less bothersome.

The effectiveness of laser therapy varies. Studies show that some patients have complete resolution, some only partial, and some report worse symptoms. The risks of vitreolysis include retinal or lens damage due to the laser hitting these structures, inflammation, high eye pressure, and retinal tear or detachment. Because the treatment options are risky, eye doctors consider them only for very severe cases.

Many people have the hardest time with floaters during the first year after they appear. Often with time, the floaters will naturally settle down and become less noticeable as the brain learns to adapt.

A Potential Glaucoma Treatment Could Replace Daily Eye Drops and Surgery

The treatment uses an injection of a polymer preparation into a structure just below the surface of the eye called the suprachoroidal space. The material creates a channel for blocked aqueous humor from within the eye to drain out, reducing excess pressure. In the study, the pressure reduction was sustained for four months.

Ross Ethier, PhD, professor and Georgia Research Alliance Lawrence L. Gellerstedt Jr. Eminent Scholar in Bioengineering in the Wallace H. Coulter Department of Biomedical Engineering at Georgia Tech and Emory University, Atlanta, Georgia.

You're Never Too Old For Cavities

Louis Siegelman, DDS, board-certified dentist anesthesiologist in New York City. Dr. Siegelman is assistant director of the dental anesthesiology residency program at NYU Langone Medical Center and clinical assistant professor at NYU College of Dentistry. He specializes in patients with dental phobias and special needs. DentalPhobia.com

Most people think one's "cavity-prone years" end in your teens. But guess what…that's not true.

Growing risk: Compared with earlier generations, older adults today are at greater risk for cavities because more are keeping their teeth. In the early 1970s, about 55 percent of adults ages 65 to 74 had at least some of their teeth. Now, 87 percent do. What about those over age 75? About three-quarters still have some of their teeth. The scary part is that about one in every five adults over age 65 has at least one untreated cavity, which can lead to tooth loss and other harms.

5 CAVITY TRAPS—AND SOLUTIONS

There's a lot you can do to prevent cavities as you grow older.

Here's a no-brainer: If you're a smoker, your dental health gives you just one more reason to quit—tobacco increases risk for tooth decay. *Other cavity promoters…*

• **Dry mouth.** A steady supply of saliva helps fight cavities by washing away food particles and coating your teeth with minerals such as calcium and phosphate. Hundreds of medications, however, contribute to inadequate saliva, also known as dry mouth.

Common culprits: Drugs used for pain, high blood pressure, depression, and bladder control. Dry mouth also is common in people with diabetes and those undergoing chemotherapy or radiation treatments for cancer.

Self-defense: If you are taking a medication that causes dry mouth, ask your doctor about alternatives, including nondrug approaches.

Also: Be sure to drink plenty of water. Sugar-free dry-mouth lozenges, such as TheraBreath, Biotène and Act Dry, can help but aren't a cure. (Lozenges with sugar increase your risk for cavities.)

- **Acid reflux.** When stomach acid backs up into your mouth, it can erode tooth enamel, setting the stage for decay.

Self-defense: If you have heartburn or bad breath or notice a sour taste in your mouth after eating, ask your doctor whether you could have acid reflux and, if so, get it treated.

- **Receding gums.** Tooth decay at the gum line is common with age because so many older adults have gum disease. As gum tissue gradually pulls away from teeth, pockets can form, creating a breeding ground for the bacteria that damage teeth. Even people who took excellent care of their teeth in younger years may brush and floss less often or less thoroughly because of physical challenges, such as arthritis.

Self-defense: Be sure to brush twice daily and floss at least once daily. Consider using an electric toothbrush to assist with effective brushing.

Also: Consider using a toothpaste that contains "remineralizing" agents, such as stannous fluoride, sodium fluoride, and calcium phosphate. These ingredients can bond to weakened enamel, strengthening teeth and creating an extra shield against decay. If your gums have receded, these products help prevent cavities on vulnerable surfaces.

- **Sugary and acidic drinks.** Sweet drinks, such as soda, bottled tea, and juice, are among the greatest threats to your teeth. In addition to large doses of sugar, many such drinks also contain high levels of corrosive acid. Even many unsweetened drinks, such as flavored mineral waters and teas, are acidic.

Self-defense: Make water your go-to beverage. When you do indulge in a favorite sweet drink, have it with a meal, then swish with plain water.

- **Processed foods.** A diet heavy on processed foods is, by default, heavy on sugars and acid and low in nutrients that support a healthy mouth.

Self-defense: Avoid processed foods, and opt for whole, nutrient-packed foods. Emphasize crunchy fruits and vegetables, such as apples, carrots, and celery, that help remove food particles and promote saliva production.

Important: Some adults may cut back on dental visits when they retire, lose employer-paid dental insurance, and learn that routine dental care is not covered by Medicare. Don't do that. Get cleanings and exams at least twice yearly. If you have periodontal disease, you may need four visits. Stand-alone private dental plans and some Medicare Advantage plans cover such services.

GOOD FOR YOU...

Heart-Healthy Diet Good for Hearing

A heart-healthy diet may also save your hearing, based on a review of 22 studies on nutrition and hearing loss. Key vitamins and minerals reduce inflammation and support the health of the small blood vessels crucial for hearing. Aim to fill half your plate with nonstarchy vegetables (such as greens, broccoli, onions, and peppers) and/or fruit and half with whole grains, plant proteins, and/or fish.

Hugo Olmedillas, PhD, professor of functional biology at University of Oviedo, Oviedo, Spain, and leader of a study published in *Journal of the Formosan Medical Association.*

Surprising Danger of Earwax

Jackie L. Clark, PhD, clinical professor of audiology at The University of Texas at Dallas and past-president of the American Academy of Audiology.

If you have had trouble with your memory lately, there may be a simple answer…and it's not in your brain.

More than 30 percent of elderly people have excessive or impacted cerumen, the technical term for earwax, that can block hearing and accelerate cognitive decline because of associated disconnection from community and loneliness. If you can't hear, you can't make memories or exercise your brain through communication. Unfortunately, few people—and even some doctors—think to check the ears when investigating a failing memory. Hearing loss also can worsen behaviors associated with dementia, such as distress and depression.

Normally, earwax moves up and out on its own. It's best not to interfere with this natural self-cleaning function. Even cotton swabs such as Q-tips can force the cerumen migrating out of the ear back into the canal. And the FDA has warned against ear candles due to risk for injury, such as burns, ear-canal blockages, and perforations.

Instead: Simply let new earwax form and push out the old on its own. If your ears feel full and sounds are muffled, place a few drops of mineral oil or commercially made drops into the ear to loosen wax. Or see an ear, nose, and throat (ENT) doctor or an audiologist to have the wax removed. It is an extremely common ENT procedure.

Note: People who wear hearing aids are especially likely to accumulate earwax because the devices push wax down into the ear canal. Every day, use the pick and brush provided by your hearing professional to gently remove wax from the hearing aids. Wipe aids with a dry or slightly moistened cloth (with water only), and air-dry them overnight.

Taming Tinnitus

Chris Iliades, MD, a retired ear, nose, throat, head, and neck surgeon. He is now a full-time medical writer and regular contributor to *Bottom Line Health*.

The word tinnitus means the tinkling of bells, but for the 50 million Americans who experience it, tinnitus is far less pleasant.

The low- or high-pitched roar or ringing that comes from inside your own head can be a maddening ailment that can interfere with daily activities and lead to high rates of depression and anxiety. Fortunately, you can do something about it.

WHAT IS THIS RINGING?

For most people, tinnitus is not caused by a serious disease that needs to be treated: It is most often a symptom of a problem with your hearing system called sensorineural hearing loss. The cause is nerve damage from aging or noise exposure.

If you have tinnitus that bothers you, makes you anxious, keeps you awake at night, or lasts longer than six months, you need to talk to your primary care doctor, who can start by looking for treatable causes of tinnitus, such as wax near your eardrum or fluid in your middle ear.

Since tinnitus is usually associated with hearing loss, your doctor may send you to a hearing specialist called an audiologist for a detailed hearing test (audiogram). If your tinnitus is associated with sensorineural hearing loss, you may be diagnosed with primary tinnitus.

If your hearing test doesn't suggest sensorineural hearing loss, you may need to see an ear, nose, and throat (ENT) specialist to see if you have secondary tinnitus, which may be caused by a treatable condition such as stiffening of the little bones inside your middle ear or arthritis of your jaw joint. People with secondary tinnitus may experience ringing in just one ear, a pulsating ring, dizziness, and jaw pain. If your hearing test or ENT exam suggests secondary tinnitus, your ENT doctor may order imaging studies of your hearing system.

CAN TINNITUS BE TREATED?

Secondary tinnitus can often be treated by addressing the underlying cause. In some cases, a simple medication change can make a difference. Aspirin, *acetaminophen*, diuretics, and antibiotics are just some of the drugs that can cause the disorder.

Primary tinnitus has no cure, but there are management strategies to make it less bothersome. Many people get used to the sound and stop noticing it, but there is hope if you're not one of them.

• **Using a hearing aid can improve your ability to hear regular sounds,** which can drown out the tinnitus.

• **Sound therapies may also help.** Using a masking sound device, like a white noise machine, listening to pleasant sounds can cover the bothersome noise of tinnitus. Sound therapies may be especially helpful at night when tinnitus may seem loudest and interfere with sleep.

• **Medications or talk therapy (psychotherapy)** can help treat anxiety or depression that can either accentuate or result from tinnitus.

• **Some people find that a healthy lifestyle that includes a healthy diet, exercise, and stress reduction improves symptoms.**

• **Don't waste your money on supplements and other over-the-counter medications that claim to treat tinnitus.** Treatments like ginkgo biloba, melatonin, vitamins, zinc, and lipo-flavonoid have no evidence to support their use.

• **Avoid loud noise exposure that can make tinnitus worse.**

FUTURE OPTIONS

In the future, tinnitus sufferers may find relief with painless electromagnetic stimulation given through electrodes placed on the scalp. Early research shows that about 40 percent of people benefit from this therapy.

In deep brain electromagnetic stimulation, a more invasive option, the electrodes are placed in the brain. Some patients with Parkinson's disease who coincidently had tinnitus were found to have a reduction in the tinnitus after treatment with deep brain electromagnetic stimulation.

No one solution works for everyone, so you need to partner with your health-care providers to find what works best for you.

Tired of Looking Tired? How to Erase Undereye Dark Circles and Bags

Doris Day, MD, renowned cosmetic dermatologist in New York City and clinical associate professor of dermatology at NYU Langone Health. She is a member of the medical advisory board for the *Dr. Oz Show* and coauthor of *Beyond Beautiful: Using the Power of Your Mind and Aesthetic Breakthroughs to Look Naturally Young and Radiant.* DorisDayMD.com

Do you long to have smooth skin around your eyes—no puffiness or hollows, no dark circles, no lines or wrinkles? Getting more sleep and drinking more water are important, but there are some less obvious causes and do-it-yourself solutions.

• **Drinking too much alcohol.** Alcohol depletes your skin of water, and the sugar increases skin inflammation. Also, when people drink, they typically eat foods high in salt and low in nutritional value, further increasing dehydration and inflammation. Cut back on alcohol, and you'll see the difference within a day. Alcohol also can disrupt sleep. An occasional drink is fine, but always have extra water when drinking alcohol.

• **Allergies cause increased redness, and rubbing will further darken and irritate the skin under your eyes.** If you have seasonal allergies, start taking allergy medication a week before they tend to start. Speak with an allergist if over-the-counter treatments are not enough.

Rubbing can create a response in the skin, which leads to inflammation, wrinkling, and dark circles. When you're tired from staring at your computer or phone screen, suffer from sleep deprivation, or are having an allergy attack, resist the urge to rub out your discomfort. Instead, gently pat on eye cream or try the home remedies below.

• **Vascular inflammation.** Blood vessels under the skin can be prominent if there is irritation in the area, causing dark circles. Use a firming eye cream or one that reduces inflammation such as ISDIN K-Ox Eyes. Products that have white and green tea extracts also work well. My product, CE HPR Eye Cream, has a high-potency retinol and vitamins C and E to firm and reduce puffiness, redness, and dark circles.

FAST HOME REMEDIES

Tea-and-honey-soaked cucumbers ease eye bags and lighten dark circles within minutes. Cucumbers are cooling and astringent, honey is anti-inflammatory, and tea has antioxidant properties. Green tea has the most healing benefits, but black or white tea also will work. This brew can last up to a week in the refrigerator. The best time to do this is morning and evening.

Brew four cups of strong tea. Add three tablespoons of honey. Let the tea cool to room temperature. Add one cucumber, cut into about 16 thin slices. Refrigerate for at least four hours.

To use, lie down, close your eyes and put one cucumber slice on each eye for about two minutes.

If you don't want to wait hours for a remedy, you can simply place moist tea bags on your eyes. Again, green tea has the most benefits, but black and white tea also will work.

Dip two tea bags in a cup of room-temperature water for 60 seconds. Take them out, and squeeze out the water. Lie down and close your eyes. Place a damp tea bag on each eye for three to five minutes.

EASY TO DO...

DIY Honey-and-Lemon Face Mask

To prevent acne and slow aging, make this simple concoction. Mix one tablespoon organic honey with the juice from one-half lemon. Apply the mask to your face and neck, avoiding your eyes. Leave it on for 20 minutes. Rinse with warm water, then cold. Honey is antibacterial and full of antioxidants, while the vitamin C in lemon juice helps form collagen, the protein that gives skin its elasticity.

Sejal Shah, MD, dermatologist in New York City, quoted on TheHealthy.com.

How to Live to 100

Charles B. Inlander, a consumer advocate and health-care consultant based in Fogelsville, Pennsylvania. He was the founding president of the nonprofit People's Medical Society, a consumer-advocacy organization credited with key improvements in the quality of U.S. health care, and is author or coauthor of more than 20 consumer-health books.

As of 2021, more than 100,000 Americans will be at least 100 years old. That number has doubled in the last decade, and experts predict that by 2060, just 39 years from now, more than 550,000 Americans will be centenarians.

As the coauthor of a book on living to 100, I've studied the medical literature and interviewed dozens of centenarians. *Here are some of the most helpful tips on how to live a century...*

- **Medical screening.** Most of the people I spoke with had experienced major medical problems at some point. Many had bouts with cancer or heart disease. But by diligently getting screening tests, such as mammograms, prostate exams, colonoscopies, and regular checkups with a primary care doctor, these elders identified problems early and effectively treated them.

- **Vaccinate.** Make sure you are up to date on your immunizations, including an annual flu shot, tetanus booster, pneumonia, shingles, and COVID-19 vaccines. The older we get, the more vulnerable we are to these conditions, so taking a preventive approach pays off.

- **Get second opinions.** If you are confronting a serious diagnosis, seek out one or more second opinions from top-rated doctors or hospitals. Places like the Cleveland Clinic or Mayo Clinic are excellent places to turn to for the latest thinking on your condition and its treatment options.

- **Safety.** Preventable deaths due to accidents are common. Falls account for almost 40,000 deaths, primarily among older people, many in their own homes. So throw away those slippery throw rugs (or secure them to the floor with double-sided rug tape), install grab bars in your bathtubs and shower, have railings installed on both sides of the staircase, and keep the walkways leading in and out of your house clear of ice, snow and debris. If you have balance issues, use a cane or walker. Be careful driving, particularly if you are on medication that causes drowsiness, and wear your seatbelt.

• **Reduce stress.** Stress can exacerbate heart issues and cause depression, anxiety, and other mental health issues. There are many ways to reduce stress, including exercise, socialization with family or friends, getting adequate sleep, and finding activities or hobbies that help keep your mind active. In addition, most health insurance covers psychological therapies.

• **Nutrition.** Healthy eating can help prevent many deadly conditions, and it's never too late to change your diet. Eating a well-balanced diet of fruits, vegetables, and healthy proteins (such as lentils or skinless chicken), cutting back on salt and animal fats, and choosing low-fat dairy products all help to prolong your life.

• **Exercise,** even as little as 15 minutes per day, boosts heart health, lowers blood pressure, burns body fat, and lowers blood sugar levels. It keeps blood vessels healthy and helps reduce the risk of stroke. It might also help ward off Alzheimer's disease, dementia, and even cancer.

REASON TO BE HAPPY...

A Positive Disposition May Protect Your Memory

Researchers assessed disposition and memory in 991 middle-aged and older adults three times between 1995 and 2014. They discovered that positive emotions over the years were linked to better word recall, a measure of memory, as the participants aged.

Association for Psychological Science

Very Personal

How to Sweat Less and Stop the Stink

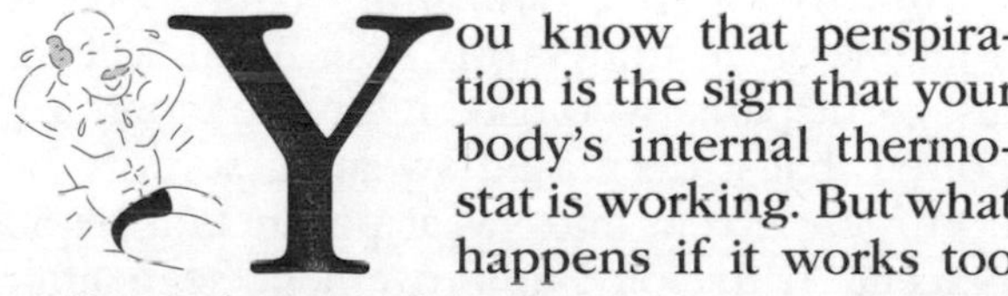

You know that perspiration is the sign that your body's internal thermostat is working. But what happens if it works too well...and you're faced with constant telltale sweat marks on clothes, not to mention the odor? *Here are strategies you can use, depending on how bad the problem is...*

SWEAT GLANDS 101

You have two main types of sweat glands. The eccrine glands are over most of your body. This type of sweat is what gives your skin that moist glow when you exercise, but most people don't notice the loss of moisture during low-exertion times. As your temperature goes up, these glands release fluid, mostly water, that cools you off as it evaporates. The sweat from the eccrine glands has no odor.

The apocrine glands are more problematic. They're found mostly in areas where hair grows—underarms, scalp, groin. When you're stressed, they release a milky fluid that's odorless on its own, but once it mixes with the bacteria on your skin, that's when the stink starts.

WHY AM I SWEATING SO MUCH?

You expect to sweat when you work out, start feeling nervous in social and business situations, or have a fever that breaks. But there are health conditions—and it's not just menopause—that ramp up the level of sweating.

Heavy sweating can be traced to infections...the nervous system, heart, lung, and thyroid diseases...and diabetes (often from low blood sugar), among others. Hyperthyroidism and other hormone-related problems that stem from the hypothalamus, the part of the brain that regulates temperature, can

Ahmad Shatil Amin, MD, medical practice director at Northwestern Medicine Dermatology in Chicago and assistant professor of dermatology at Feinberg School of Medicine at Northwestern University.

cause excessive sweating during sleep. Managing those conditions should get your sweating under control, so check with your doctor to rule out these causes.

Some medications, such as antidepressants and heart and blood pressure medications, also can cause night sweats. Ask if a change in prescription is possible.

Being overweight can make you sweat more—you might notice it even with just a few pounds of weight fluctuation. Losing weight can help.

Important: Because changes in your perspiration pattern can be a warning of an undiagnosed medical condition, such as diabetes, leukemia, or non-Hodgkin's lymphoma, see your doctor if...

- **You suddenly begin to sweat much more or less than usual.**
- **You experience night sweats for no apparent reason.**
- **You notice a change in your body odor.**

There also are millions of people who experience excessive sweating with no underlying cause. Called primary hyperhidrosis, there's no rhyme or reason to when the sweating happens. B*ut there are ways to resolve it...*

SIMPLE AT-HOME SOLUTIONS TO SWEAT LESS

Slight changes to your daily routine can have a big impact...

- **Double up on deodorant/antiperspirant.** Most people apply a combination deodorant/antiperspirant each morning to their underarms to block sweat and fight odor.

Better: Also apply it each night before bed. This gives your sweat glands the time needed to absorb the aluminum, which is the active ingredient in antiperspirants. Choose a higher-strength product, which often will say "clinical grade" on the label.

Note: Many people have switched to deodorant-only underarm products, because of skin irritation or because they believe that the aluminum in antiperspirants can increase the risk for breast cancer, dementia, kidney disease, and other health problems. There is no substantial scientific evidence to support these fears. And deodorant-only products do nothing to stop the sweat.

- **Dry off.** Before getting dressed or putting on your pajamas, carefully dry yourself—especially between your toes and under your arms—to reduce bacteria growth on skin, which is the foundation for odor. Skin also must be thoroughly dry before you apply antiperspirant for optimal absorption.
- **Relax.** If your emotions bring on perspiration, practice relaxation techniques such as yoga, meditation, and biofeedback. These can help you learn to control the stress that triggers sweating.
- **Change your pajamas and your bedding.** If you sweat in your sleep, whether or not it's related to hot flashes, try cooling, moisture-wicking sleepwear, underwear, and sheets—it is easy to find these using an Internet search. Certain fabrics, such as cotton flannel, can make sweating worse.

SERIOUS REMEDIES FOR HYPERHIDROSIS

If you're sweating through your clothes during the day and the amount is bothering you, see a dermatologist to discuss treatment options, starting with prescription-strength antiperspirants. *If that's not enough, here are other medical options to try...*

Topical: *Glycopyrronium* (Qbrexza) is available as an underarm wipe. In clinical trials, participants who used it for one month reported that it decreased sweating severity by up to 30 percent and sweat production by 50 percent, with some improvement seen after the first week. While glycopyrronium can be used in other areas of the body, it is approved only for underarms and may not be as effective elsewhere.

Glycopyrronium is an anticholinergic, meaning that it blocks the neurotransmitter acetylcholine, responsible for activating the sweat process. As with other anticholinergics, it's not for anyone with glaucoma, severe ulcerative colitis, myasthenia gravis, or Sjögren's syndrome because it can make those conditions worse.

Injection: *Botulinum toxin* (Botox) is the most effective treatment we have for excessive underarm sweating. It also can be used on the palms of the hands and soles of the feet. For most people, it reduces sweating by 75 percent to 90 percent, bringing it down to a normal level. The treatment needs to be repeated every six months. Some health insurers will cover the injections because they're for a medical reason although Botox is not covered for cosmetic purposes. Check with your dermatologist's billing office—some may need repeated requests to do the paperwork and follow-up phone calls required for insurance approval.

Oral: *Glycopyrrolate* (Robinul). For people who aren't helped by Botox, off-label use of glycopyrrolate may help. This is another form of the active ingredient in Qbrexza but is given in pill form. It was developed to reduce other types of body secretions and a decrease in sweating is one of its side effects. It works for some people, but not everyone finds its other side effects—dizziness, drowsiness, nervousness, loss of taste, and headache—worth the benefit.

Noninvasive procedure: miraDry. The noninvasive, FDA-approved procedure uses a handheld device to target thermal (heat) energy at sweat glands in the underarms while keeping skin at the surface cool. One to two treatments are all that's needed to destroy underarm sweat glands. You will continue to sweat normally in other parts of the body.

HOW TO STOP THE STINK

Sweat by itself doesn't cause body odor. That happens when it meets bacteria on your skin. Washing off sweat after a workout will help. So will washing workout clothes every time you wear them—something that a surprising number of people don't do. But if you've ever felt that these clothes weren't becoming truly stink-free, your nose isn't deceiving you. High-performance fabrics tend to hold on to odors. Try specialty detergents developed for these fibers.

You can wash your hands or dab on sanitizer when your palms get sweaty, but it's harder to keep your feet odor-free when they're in shoes and unable to breathe all day. One of the best things you can do is not wear the same pair of shoes two days in a row. This gives the shoes a chance to completely dry out. *Try any or all of these additional tips to conquer foot odor...*

- **Wash feet nightly with an antibacterial soap, and dry them completely.**
- **Use a spray underarm deodorant or antiperspirant on your feet.**
- **Place deodorizing insoles in every pair of shoes, and change them as needed.**
- **Buy socks and hosiery made from breathable, moisture-wicking fabrics and shoes made from natural materials such as canvas,** especially important for closed-toe shoes that limit air circulation around your feet.

Plagued by Bad Breath

Isabel Suastegui-Mursuli, DDS, Winston Dental, Palatine, Illinois; Chris Lewandowski, DDS, president, Princess Center Dentistry, Scottsdale, Arizona; Elizabeth Kampschnieder, DDS, Kennedy Dental, Bellevue, Nebaska; Eugene Gamble, BDS, MFD RCSI, MClinDent, MPerio RCSEd, FFD RCSI, Rosedale Dental Centre, St. Michaels, Barbados; and Leann Poston, MD, BeWell Medical Clinic, North Vancouver, Canada.

Patients often believe that bad breath is only related to the care and maintenance of their teeth, but halitosis can have numerous causes.

1. Gingivitis. Brushing and flossing regularly are indeed important, but you need to be sure you are brushing and flossing properly.

Don't just pass your toothbrush and or floss over your teeth: You really need to clean them. If not, biofilm settles on your teeth and creates plaque, which builds up along the gum line, causing gingivitis.

2. Tonsil stones. Food and mucus can become trapped in the crevices of your tonsils and emit a foul odor. A dentist may be able to manually remove the stones. In some cases, lasers or surgery may be necessary.

3. The ketogenic diet. The popular "keto" diet is notorious for causing bad breath, as are foods like garlic and onions. Unexpected culprits include citrus, dairy, cheese, and peanut butter.

4. Old broken fillings and crowns. If you have a broken filling or crown, you may not be able to clean the areas sufficiently. This will allow odor-creating bacteria to fester unhindered.

5. Health conditions. Gastric reflux conditions, sinus infection, tonsilitis, diabetes, and throat and other cancers can cause bad breath.

6. Medications such as antihistamines can decrease saliva production, while others have halitosis as a side effect.

7. Your tongue. One of the biggest reservoirs of bacteria in the mouth is the tongue. Clean it with the roughened back of your toothbtush (this is designed precisely to clean the tongue) or a specialized tongue scraper.

Visit your dentist at least twice a year for thorough cleanings and check-ups. If your problem persists, make an appointment with your primary care provider to check for any underlying health conditions.

Put an End to UTIs

Amin Herati, MD, an assistant professor of urology and assistant professor of gynecology and obstetrics at Johns Hopkins School of Medicine, Baltimore.

The first time you experience a urinary tract infection (UTI), it takes a doctor's visit and urinalysis to determine that microscopic bacteria are the cause of so much discomfort. But for people who experience recurring infections, the first signs of urgency, frequency, and pain are unmistakable.

If you experience so many UTIs that you've memorized your physician's phone number and only have to utter the words, "I have another..." to have an antibiotic prescription called in to the pharmacy, you're in good company. More than 25 percent of women will have a second UTI within six months and up to 70 percent will within a year. Men also experience UTIs, but not as often.

Women have an anatomical disadvantage: A short urethra (about 4 centimeters long) gives bacteria a quick trip to the bladder, where infection can cause inflammation that leads to those telltale feelings of urgency and frequency. The bacteria can increase the acidity of urine, too, which can cause painful urination.

Sufferers may also experience discomfort or pressure in the pelvic and lower abdominal areas, and strong-smelling or cloudy urine.

Men's longer urethras keep more bacteria at bay, but past age 50, men are more prone to prostate gland enlargement and infection (prostatitis), which can block the flow of urine and increase the risk of bacterial build-up, boosting UTI rates.

Infection in the bladder is called cystitis. If the infection affects the kidneys (pyelonephritis), there may be pain in the back and sides, fever, chills, nausea, and vomiting. Infection can also affect the urethra (urethritis), which can cause burning when urinating. Untreated UTIs can lead to permanent kidney damage and life-threatening sepsis.

CAUSES OF CHRONIC INFECTION

While simple anatomy raises the risk for women overall, some people have receptors on the bladder cells that make it easier for the bacteria to connect, leading to more frequent UTIs.

Women with pelvic floor dysfunction also have a higher risk as they may not be able to fully empty the bladder, creating a breeding ground for bacteria similar to that seen in men with prostate enlargement. Kidney stones can also increase the risk.

ANTIBIOTIC RESISTANCE

The standard treatment for a UTI is a course of antibiotics, which should provide relief in one to three days. But for a growing number of people, antibiotics aren't working as well as they used to—if they work at all.

One-third of uncomplicated UTIs no longer improve with the combination medication *trimethoprim/sulfamethoxazole* (Bactrim), which used to be the standard of care. Furthermore, 20 percent of UTIs are resistant to five other antibiotics.

That means longer periods of discomfort and a higher risk of complications like kidney infections and sepsis, as physicians fight to find a drug that will work. Physicians are afraid that, one day, oral antibiotics won't work at all.

PREVENTION

A shrinking list of effective antibiotics makes it even more important to reduce the risk of developing a UTI in the first place. *Here are some science-supported strategie...*

- **Hydration.** Drinking more water is the simplest and cheapest preventive strategy. A study in *JAMA Internal Medicine* showed that women who drank 11 eight-ounce glasses of water per day had half as many UTIs over one year as women who drank an average of five glasses of water.

- **D-mannose,** an over-the-counter product, may prevent bacteria from latching onto cells. Some studies have found that it can be as effective as the antibiotic *nitrofurantoin* (Macrobid; which is generally no longer used) for preventing UTIs and trimethoprim/sulfamethoxazole for treating and preventing them. Research suggests that dissolving 1 gram (g) in water and drinking it twice a day can help prevent UTIs. For treatment, bump that up to 1.5 g twice daily for three days, and then once daily for 10 days. Alternately, you can double the dose and take it once daily.

- **Vaginal estrogen.** Menopause changes the vaginal pH, which can kill protective bacteria and encourage the growth of harmful bacteria. A topical estrogen cream can realign pH to support healthy bacteria. While there are no apparent side effects, vaginal estrogen is contraindicated in women with thrombotic or cancer risk.

- **Prophylactic antibiotics.** At low doses, antibiotics stop bacterial replication, while at high doses, they kill the bacteria. People who are prone to chronic infections may benefit from daily low-dose antibiotics, such as trimethoprim/sulfamethoxazole.

- **Cranberry juice** has long been a staple in UTI prevention and care, but a recent study reported that it offered no significant protection over placebo. That's not the final word, though, and clinical trials taht look at the potential benefits of much higher doses continue.

While there are no definite answers yet, pure cranberry juice is a low-risk intervention that's certainly worth a try. To avoid the high levels of sugar in juice, consider cranberry pills. Research suggests that cranberry supplements need to contain at least 36 milligrams of proanthocyanidins per daily dose to be effective.

- **Reduce the risk from sex.** Sexual activity makes it easier for bacteria to enter the urethra and cause UTIs for many women. To lower the risk, empty your bladder and gently wash the genital area before sex. Thoroughly rinse away any potentially irritating soap. Avoid diaphragms, spermicide, and non-lubricated condoms, all of which are linked to a higher risk of infection. Empty your bladder again after sex to help wash bacteria out of the urethra.

If you are prone to developing UTIs, your doctor may prescribe a single dose of an antibiotic to take after intercourse.

PHAGE THERAPY: AN ANTIBIOTIC ALTERNATIVE

As antibiotic resistance increases, there is renewed interest in an old treatment for bacterial infections, including UTIs—bacteriophage therapy. A bacteriophage (or simply phage) is a virus that injects its DNA or RNA into a specific strain of bacteria. The DNA or RNA repeatedly replicates itself until the bacterium bursts and dies. Because each phage is matched with a specific bacteria, it doesn't cause collateral damage to beneficial bacteria or cells. The specificity of each phage can make it challenging for scientists to find just the right one, but researchers are finding success with cocktails that include multiple strains. While phage therapy is not currently approved by the U.S. Food & Drug Administration, physicians can submit a special request to the FDA's emergency investigational new drug program.

Demystifying Incontinence

Jill Maura Rabin, MD, a professor of obstetrics and gynecology at Zucker School of Medicine at Hofstra Northwell in Hempstead, New York. Dr. Rabin is coauthor of *Mind Over Bladder: A Step-By-Step Guide to Achieving Continence.*

It's an alarming moment: You sneeze, cough, laugh, or pick up a heavy package, and a bit of urine leaks out.

Urinary incontinence is incredibly common—affecting about 25 million American adults, three-quarters of them women—but it isn't inevitable. No one needs to endure the distress and disruption of what is often a closeted problem, since 80 percent of those with incontinence can now be helped or cured using a tailored treatment menu that may combine several leading-edge therapies.

UNWANTED INTRUDER

Always unwelcome, incontinence comes in two main forms. By far, the most prevalent is stress incontinence—urine leakage when the bladder feels pressure from a sudden movement. Urge incontinence, dubbed overactive bladder, occurs when the bladder squeezes down without "warning" the urethra—allowing even larger amounts of urine to escape. Some people can even be dealt a double whammy, suffering from a combination of stress and urge incontinence. But why does incontinence happen?

Stress incontinence stems from weakness in the muscles and connective tissue supporting the bladder, uterus, and rectum. Age is a predisposing factor, with the loss of estrogen from menopause thinning these vital structures. More famously, pregnancy and childbirth take a toll, as do smoking, obesity, and chronic coughing.

The incidence of urge incontinence ticks up with age, but it can also coexist with a variety of other conditions, such as spinal cord injury or irritable bowel syndrome. Simply put, overactive bladder happens when there's a disconnect between the nerves that relax and contract the bladder. Notably, 300 different medications, from sleep aids to high blood pressure pills, can contribute to this disconnect.

Men are more often spared from incontinence not only because they can skip childbirth and menopause, but because their urethras are much longer than women's, making it easier for this "gatekeeper" against urine loss to close off against bladder pressure.

THOROUGH DIAGNOSTIC PROCESS

As with many medical problems, accurately diagnosing incontinence and its causes begins with your doctor asking a bevy of questions about your symptoms, medical and surgical history, and number of pregnancies and births. He or she should also review a full list of your medications and supplements.

Next is a thorough physical exam to understand the size, shape, consistency, and placement of the pelvic organs. This crucial exam can reveal if organs have prolapsed, slipping from their normal positions and placing pressure on the bladder or other organs. The answers will help point to type of incontinence—whether stress, urge, or another form. *A variety of tests may also be done, including...*

- **Urine sample** to detect infection
- **Ultrasound** to reveal any fluid remaining in the bladder after urination
- **Urodynamic testing,** which fills the bladder with sterile water through a catheter placed into the urethra. This tube and another placed in the rectum monitor pressure in both organs. Then you're asked to cough, showing stress incontinence if fluid leaks from the bladder. You're also asked to urinate to check for any blockages and ensure the bladder muscle works properly.

TAILORED TREATMENT MENU

While there's no one-size-fits-all approach to treating incontinence, several tactics tend to provide at least some relief. Losing five to 10 pounds lowers pressure on the bladder by 10 to 15 percent, for example, while changing medications can zap urine leakage for a surprising number of those affected. Even avoiding food triggers such as alcohol, chocolate, spicy foods, or aspartame, which can prompt bladder contractions, spells drier days for some with overactive bladder.

After zeroing in on the type of incontinence and learning about your day-to-day lifestyle, your doctor should be able to offer a menu of treatment options tailored to your individual situation and severity. And just like any menu, you get to pick and choose—in this case, typically two or three approaches to try simultaneously or sequentially.

NEW OPTIONS

The latest treatment options include techniques to quiet an overactive bladder—in many cases without medication. *Nonsurgical interventions include…*

- **Behavioral therapy** that "retrains" the brain to suppress unwanted bladder contractions,
- **Keeping a diary of fluid intake and trips to the bathroom,**
- **Bladder training** that gradually increases the amount of urine you can hold in your bladder,
- **Kegel exercises** and physical therapy to strengthen pelvic floor muscles,
- **Mechanical devices** such as a pessary, inserted to support prolapsed pelvic organs,
- **Tibial nerve stimulation,** wherein a small electrode sends pulsating signals to calm bladder muscles.

SURGICAL TREATMENTS

There are also several minimally invasive surgeries that boast a quick recovery…

- **Bladder neck injection,** which injects synthetic "bulking agents" into the urethra wall to hamper urine leakage
- **Sling procedure,** which places a sling under the urethra that's attached to the abdominal wall to support the bladder and block leakage
- **InterStim,** a "pacemaker" for the bladder that implants a device sending mild electrical signals to the sacral nerve at the bottom of the spine, calming overactive bladder.

If you're hesitant to get help, ask yourself: "How important is my quality of life?" Ultimately, it takes getting out of your emotional comfort zone to achieve physical comfort.

BE YOUR OWN ADVOCATE

Astoundingly, more than two-thirds of women don't consider urine leakage while coughing or sneezing a health problem, and one-third think a loss of bladder control is a natural part of aging. Yet the typical incontinence sufferer spends between $1,000 and $3,000 each year on absorbent products whose chirpy names are the polar opposite of how these women feel while buying them. Serene and poised on the checkout line? Probably not. So it's somewhat perplexing that only one of 12 people affected by incontinence seeks medical help, waiting an average of nearly seven years after first experiencing bladder control issues.

TAKE NOTE…

Floating Poop Could Be a Sign of Trouble

An occasional bowel movement that floats is not cause for alarm—it probably just means that you ate something that made you extra gassy, and some of that gas got lodged in the waste. But if you get floaters more than a few times a week over the course of a month, you may be suffering from malabsorption, an inability to absorb nutrients during digestion. Malabsorption can be caused by celiac disease, lactose intolerance, and pancreatitis. All three conditions come with other symptoms such as diarrhea, nausea, and abdominal pain. If you experience such symptoms along with frequent buoyant bowel movements, see your doctor.

Roundup of gastroenterologists reported at Health.com.

Watch Out for a Strong Rotten Egg Smell When You Pass Gas

A strong rotten egg smell when you pass gas, particularly if accompanied by bloating and diarrhea, suggests small intestinal bacterial overgrowth (SIBO). It's commonly treated with the antibiotic rifaximin (about $1,400 for 14 days). Instead, the herbal supplement Ultra MFP Forte (about $56 for one month) often is as effective. It contains olive leaf, berberine, and burdock. Gassiness without much sulfur smell suggests Candida overgrowth.

Helpful: Take a good probiotic and an antifungal, and avoid sugar. See an integrative doctor for comprehensive treatment.

Jacob Teitelbaum, MD, fibromyalgia specialist and author of *Real Cause, Real Cure.* Vitality101.com

Causes of an Itchy Butt

Wiping technique—not wiping cleanly, or being overzealous, can cause butt itch. Premoistened wipes or scented soaps can also cause irritation. Eczema, psoriasis, or lichen sclerosis—these skin conditions should be treated by a doctor, usually with a topical steroid. Pinworms—these tiny white intestinal parasites leave visible eggs in your stool. They can be eradicated with oral medication. Anal cancer—while it's rare, an anal itch can be caused by certain forms of cancer. Anemia, liver, or kidney disease—these conditions can entail generalized itchiness. Yeast infections—although most people think of the vagina when they think of these fungal infections, they cause about 10 percent to 15 percent of cases of anal itching.

Roundup of studies and health experts, reported at Health.com.

Drug-free Constipation Cure: A Vibrating Pill

Satish S.C. Rao, MD, PhD, director of neurogastroenterology, Medical College of Georgia, Augusta University, and coauthor of study titled "Brain Fogginess, Gas and Bloating: A Link between SIBO, Probiotics and Metabolic Acidosis," published in *Clinical and Translational Gastroenterology.*

Constipation is often the butt (sorry!) of crude humor, but for sufferers it's no joking matter. And when the condition is chronic, the desire for relief is chronic, too. Now, a new high-tech cure may change that. It doesn't use drugs, has virtually no side effects, is amazingly effective—and works by literally shaking the you-know-what out of you. *Here are the details...*

Laxative drugs are the common go-to solution for chronic constipation. These laxatives work chemically by stimulating or irritating the colon, or by attracting fluid to flush out stool. But they may become less effective if used regularly and may lead to dependency.

An Israeli company called Vibrant came up with a remedy that works mechanically. The remedy is a small capsule that is swallowed and programed to vibrate when it reaches the large intestine. The vibrations both relieve the constipation practically immediately...and also induce natural peristaltic activity, stimulating additional spontaneous bowel movements. The capsule is then excreted with bowel movements.

In early clinical trials, the Vibrant capsule almost doubled the number of bowel movements and achieved effective relief of constipation in close to 90 percent of patients with chronic constipation within eight weeks.

Researchers at Augusta University in Georgia and other institutions also recently tested the new device. They conducted two studies with a total of 245 patients with chronic constipation. For eight weeks, some of the patients took five Vibrant capsules (programmed to vibrate either one or two times a day) for five days per week...while others (the control group) took the same number of sham capsules.

Results: Compared to the control group, the patients who took vibrating capsules had twice as many spontaneous complete bowel movements. (The study did not track what happened to the patients after they stopped taking the vibrating capsule, so they don't know if the beneficial effect persisted.)

The capsule is about the size of a fish oil pill, and the mechanism inside the pill that vibrates uses novel technology similar to the vibrating device you get at a restaurant when you wait for a table. The device is activated (the pill starts flashing) using a small magnet just before swallowing and is preprogrammed to start vibrating in eight to 12 hours.

The vibrations are not felt by most people. (One out of 10 patients did sense some vibration but did not find the sensation unpleasant—and none dropped out of the study.) There were no other side effects—including no diarrhea or stool leakage, as can be the case with drug laxatives—and the device was found to be safe, according to the researchers.

Note: The researchers don't know whether the magnetic component within the pill will cause problems for people with implantable electronic medical devices, such as pacemakers. Safety studies are currently ongoing. In the meantime, it is not recommended that people with such devices use the vibrating pill.

The Vibrant company continues to test their vibrating pill in 10 to 12 research centers using larger numbers of patients. If the pill continues to perform well and gets FDA approval, they hope to have it available in about three years. While cost has not yet been determined, most likely it will be competitive with other prescription medications for chronic constipation. The researchers also are planning long-term studies to determine whether constipation relief persists without continuing to take the pill…and if so, for how long. If you are interested in getting onto a clinical trial, check Vibrant's website (VibrantGastro.com) and/or ClinicalTrials.gov for upcoming trials and when they start recruiting.

Bee Venom Kills Breast Cancer Cells

In laboratory experiments, melittin, a peptide in honeybee venom, destroyed triple-negative breast cancer cells. It reduced the chemical messages that are essential to cancer cell growth and division and destroyed the cancer cell membranes.

Harry Perkins Institute of Medical Research

3-D Mammography Is Best for Breast Cancer Screening

Study titled "False-Negative Rates of Breast Cancer Screening with and without Digital Breast Tomosynthesis," led by researchers at Yale School of Medicine, New Haven, Connecticut, published in *Radiology*.

Women have a few choices when it comes to screening for breast cancer. They can test with mammograms printed on X-ray film, digital mammography, or with a newer imaging technology called digital breast tomosynthesis (DBT). In many screening centers, digital mammography, or two-dimensional (2-D) mammography, has actually replaced X-ray film mammograms.

Recent development: A growing body of research suggests that DBT, also known as three-dimensional (3-D) mammography, may provide better results than standard digital mammography. Now, a new study comparing digital mammography against DBT supports DBT as the better screening method for breast cancer.

Digital mammography allows the radiologist to make X-ray images darker or lighter—this helps find breast cancer, especially in dense breasts. These images can be viewed on a computer and the images can be made larger to focus on specific areas. DBT also uses computer imaging, but the images are taken as a camera arcs over the breasts taking pictures from different angles. This allows for a 3-D image and eliminates overlapping breast tissue that can hide a cancerous tumor.

Studies show that DBT misses fewer cancers than digital mammography. If a screening exam does not find a cancer (a negative exam), but a cancer is found within the following year, the exam is called a false negative. It's been shown that DBT provides a lower rate of false-negative exams, which may mean screening with DBT can find cancers earlier and increase survival because these cancers are less advanced and easier to cure.

Research details: To compare false negative results from digital mammography versus DBT, researchers from 10 academic and community screening centers reviewed more than 380,000 screening exams. The exams were divided almost equally between digital mammography and DBT. *These were the key findings...*

• **DBT had a false negative rate of 0.6 per 1,000 exams compared with a rate of 0.7 for digital mammography.**

• **DBT had a higher sensitivity rate (89.8 percent) than digital mammography (85.6 percent).** Sensitivity indicates how likely a test is to detect a condition when it is actually present in a patient.

• **DBT had a higher specificity rate (90.7 percent) than digital mammography (89.1 percent).** Specificity is the ability of a test to rule out the presence of a disease in someone who does not have it.

• **DBT had lower odds of missing an advanced cancer than digital mammography.**

Takeaway: Based on its improved sensitivity, specificity, and ability to detect invasive cancers before they spread, screening with DBT is superior to digital mammography, according to this study. The researchers anticipate that DBT will eventually become the standard of care for breast cancer screening

A Breast Cancer Drug Could Revolutionize Prostate Cancer Treatment

In a study of 387 men with advanced prostate cancer, *olaparib* (Lynparza), used to treat breast and ovarian cancers, significantly improved survival.

Study by researchers at Institute of Cancer Research, London, UK, published in *New England Journal of Medicine.*

GOOD TO KNOW...

Breast-feeding Reduces Ovarian Cancer Risk

Women who have breast-fed have a 24 percent lower risk for invasive epithelial ovarian cancer, compared with women who have never breast-fed.

Analysis of 13 studies by researchers at Brigham and Women's Hospital, Boston, published in *JAMA Oncology.*

Prostate Cancer Surgery Can Safely Be Delayed for Six Months

Analysis of 32,184 patient records showed that outcomes and survival rates were similar whether surgery was performed at 30 days or 180 days. Surgery may be delayed for a variety of reasons, including treatment toxicity and time to get a second opinion.

Leilei Xia, MD, urology resident, department of surgery, Perelman School of Medicine, Philadelphia.

What Your Doctor Won't Tell You About Your Prostate

Mark Stengler, NMD, naturopathic physician and founder of The Stengler Center for Integrative Medicine in Encinitas, California, and author of numerous books including most recently *Healing the Prostate* and the best-seller *Outside the Box Cancer Therapies.* MarkStengler.com

The health of your prostate gland is a reflection of many factors, from your diet and weight to your stress level and medications. Your prostate also is intertwined with your urinary system...and many men with an enlarged prostate, or benign prostatic hyperplasia (BPH), also have bladder problems. If you treat only the prostate—the conventional medicine approach, and often with only conventional medications—you won't get the best results. *Here's a better way...*

THE BLADDER-PROSTATE CONNECTION

Over the years, a man's prostate can grow from the size of a walnut to as big as a tennis ball. The upper portion of the prostate rests against the lower section of the bladder. When the prostate enlarges—a condition that most older men have at least mildly—it can pinch the urethra (the tube that drains the bladder), causing urinary symptoms.

Lower urinary tract symptoms (LUTS) is the name for a constellation of bladder-related issues including waking multiple times at night to urinate...frequent or urgent need to urinate...waiting for urine to flow while at the toilet...a slow stream...dribbling at the end of urination...and not being able to empty your bladder completely. Another problem is overactive bladder, caused by an impaired bladder muscle. An enlarged prostate can worsen these symptoms. Healing the prostate and the bladder involves a multiprong approach.

WHAT TO EAT...WHAT TO AVOID

As with all body systems, the right diet is important to a healthy prostate. The Mediterranean diet's anti-inflammatory nutrients—particularly vitamins D-3 and E and zinc—are associated with improved BPH and LUTS symptoms. Vitamin E is in nuts, seeds, fruits and vegetables. Take daily supplements with a meal to get adequate D-3 (2,500 international units to 5,000 IU) and zinc (25 mg). Since obesity is associated with BPH and LUTS, losing weight also is important.

Avoid the following foods because of their association with a higher risk of getting or aggravating BPH and LUTS: Too much animal protein...high-glycemic grain-based foods, such as refined bread, pasta, and rice... too much caffeine, including coffee, tea, soft drinks, and chocolate...carbonated beverages, excess alcohol, artificial sweeteners, citrus fruits, tomato-based products, and spicy foods.

SUPPLEMENTS FOR BPH AND LUTS

Conventional drugs prescribed for BPH and LUTS often don't help enough. I almost always recommend prostate formulas that contain two or more of these ingredients, such as Life Extension Ultra Prostate Formula or Now Foods Prostate Health.

- **Pycnogenol,** a patented form of French maritime pine bark extract, contains many therapeutic plant compounds.

Daily dosage: 150 mg. *Caution:* If you are on anticoagulant therapy, check with your doctor before using.

- ***Pygeum africanum***, also known as *Prunus africana*, appears to lower cholesterol within the prostate, inhibit prostate growth and reduce inflammation.

Daily dosage: 100 mg to 200 mg of a standardized extract (usually 14 percent triterpenes).

- **Rye pollen extract,** known as rye grass flower pollen, rye grass, flower pollen extract, or Cernilton, can significantly improve LUTS, according to a study published in *Clinical Therapeutics* and, for some men, decrease prostate volume when taken along with saw palmetto, beta-sitosterol, and vitamin E.

Daily dosage: 126 mg three times daily.

- **Saw palmetto.** A study found that 90 percent of men noticed an improvement in mild-to-moderate urinary symptoms of BPH within four to six weeks of starting saw palmetto in a formulation containing 80 percent or higher fatty acids and sterols.

Daily dosage: 320 mg.

- **Stinging nettle** (*Urtica dioica*) is helpful in treating BPH and urinary tract infections.

Daily dosage: 120 mg to 600 mg.

For overall bladder health: I like Urox, which is a combination of concentrated ex-

GOOD NEWS...

Good News for Men

An at-home urine test may reveal aggressive prostate cancer more effectively than blood tests or uncomfortable rectal exams performed during doctor visits. The test, in development, may predict which patients require further monitoring and treatment.

Norfolk and Norwich University Hospital

tracts of Crateva nurvala stem bark, *Equisetum arvense* (horsetail) stem and Lindera aggregata root. It improves urinary symptoms in up to 85 percent of users, with 60 percent experiencing a reduction in urinary incontinence. It can be life-changing for any man who has more than mild urinary problems.

Important: Do not self-treat. See your doctor to diagnose urination problems. Then review these options with him/her to determine your best protocol.

RELIEVE CHRONIC PELVIC PAIN SYNDROME (CPPS)

Men with CPPS have long-standing pain throughout the pelvic area, including in the groin, lower abdomen, genitals (especially the tip and the testicles), perineum, rectum, and lower back, as well as pain or burning during ejaculation and/or urination—without any obvious underlying cause. CPPS often goes with prostate problems, such as prostatitis (inflammation of the prostate).

Treating CPPS includes the same diet changes suggested on page 145.

Helpful: Psyllium fiber and water promote bowel movements so there's less bladder and pelvic pressure from the intestines and colon...and chamomile tea is anti-inflammatory. Keep a food diary to track which foods worsen your symptoms...drink 50 ounces or more of purified water daily.

Some supplements that help BPH also can relieve pelvic pain, such as rye pollen and saw palmetto, especially in combination with selenium, lycopene, and quercetin (a flavonoid found in onions, kale, broccoli, apples, berries, and scallions). In one study, men who took 500-mg quercetin supplements twice a day had significant symptom improvement compared with those given a placebo. A follow-up study found that the enzymes bromelain and papain enhance the body's absorption of quercetin—combination supplements are available.

Working with an osteopathic physician, chiropractor, acupuncturist, and/or physical therapist may help, too. Tight muscles and nerve inflammation can be root causes of CPPS. Pelvic floor–strengthening exercises, in particular, may ease pelvic pain.

More from Mark Stengler, NMD...

Testosterone and Your Prostate

Many men with prostate problems also have deficiencies or imbalances in testosterone and other male-related hormones. Levels of hormones such as estrogen and dihydrotestosterone may be too high, contributing to BPH and even prostate cancer.

Symptoms of low testosterone, such as fatigue and loss of muscle mass, can be related to several medical conditions, so make sure you're not missing a serious underlying cause. Ask your doctor for comprehensive hormone testing, including free testosterone, luteinizing hormone (LH), prolactin, estradiol, cortisol, DHEA, pregnenolone, IGF-1 (a marker that reflects growth hormone activity), and sex hormone–binding globulin (SHBG). Also important is testing for key nutritional deficiencies—ferritin to measure iron stores, zinc, magnesium, and vitamins D and B-12. These all are blood tests.

A low-testosterone diagnosis is made when results from two separate tests show total or free testosterone levels below the reference range for your age. Though some men may require testosterone replacement, it's possible to get levels into the normal range with other treatments.

A healthy diet, good sleep, and regular exercise all help to balance hormone levels without supplemental testosterone. If these aren't effective after three months, then consider using the supplements below or testosterone replacement with a knowledgeable doctor.

Two herbal extracts are particularly helpful. Younger men up to age 55 may use these for three months along with diet and exercise and then may not need to continue. Men over age 55 often need to use these indefinitely.

Ashwagandha (*Withania somnifera*) helps rebalance hormones, increasing testosterone and decreasing the stress hormone cortisol.

Daily dosage: 600 mg to 675 mg of a standardized extract.

Eurycoma longifolia, also known as tongkat ali or Malaysian ginseng, can increase libido and stimulate testosterone production.

Daily dosage: 200 mg to 400 mg in extract form.

Be sure to get enough zinc (25 mg to 50 mg daily), vitamin D (2,000 IU to 5,000 IU daily), and magnesium (250 mg to 500 mg daily) as well.

8

Investment Insider's Guide

Value Investing Makes a Comeback

Stocks that trade at bargain prices have struggled for years as shares of fast-growing companies raced ahead. But many analysts say that is changing as the economy recovers from 2020's pandemic-induced recession.

Reason: The performance of many undervalued companies is closely tied to how well the economy fares, and a robust economic recovery is occurring as of mid-year 2021 as COVID-19 vaccines help unleash pent-up consumer demand.

HOW TO PICK VALUE STOCKS

To help you find the most attractive value stocks for your portfolio, we spoke with stock picker Chuck Bath, CFA.

CHUCK BATH, CFA
Diamond Hill Large Cap Fund

Reallocating assets in your portfolio is important if the portfolio is heavily weighted toward growth, given how much leading growth stocks, especially stocks such as Amazon and Facebook, have gained already. Growth stocks will underperform their value competitors if they fall short of Wall Street's high expectations, a possibility as life returns to normal and consumers get out of their homes. In contrast, even a small improvement in the corporate earnings of undervalued companies will give their shares a big boost. *My advice on how to find the best value stocks without getting hurt...*

Chuck Bath, CFA, manager of the Diamond Hill Large Cap Fund (DHLAX) whose 10-year annualized returns of 12.6 percent rank in the top 9 percent of its category. Diamond-Hill.com

Tony Thomas, PhD, associate director of equity strategies at Morningstar, Inc., Chicago, which tracks 620,000 investment offerings. Morningstar.com

• **Look for stocks in the market's most beaten-down sectors,** which could rebound strongly in the near future.

Often when a sector has been very out of favor, stocks of the most promising companies get dragged down along with those with less potential.

• **Beware value traps.** Many stocks are cheap because the companies face long-term problems...have limited growth potential... and/or suffer from changes in their industries.

Example: Energy was the stock market's worst-performing sector in 2020, down 37 percent. But even though major oil stocks have rebounded in 2021, they made up only about 2 percent of my portfolio recently.

Reason: With a global oil glut and subdued demand, oil prices are likely to stay flat. Alternative energy sources are gaining market share, and the long-term viability of fossil fuels is being questioned. To avoid value traps, I focus on businesses that can grow earnings steadily for years...have strong cash flow and solid balance sheets...have lasting advantages over competitors...and are run by strong management teams.

MY FAVORITES NOW

Here are three attractive sectors and my favorite stocks in each...

• **Financial services**—the second-worst-performing sector of the S&P 500 in 2020, behind energy. Banks and insurance companies are my portfolio's biggest sector weighting because in strong economies they typically make more loans or sell more policies and improve earnings and profit margins. *My favorite financial-services stocks now...*

• American International Group (AIG) is one of the world's largest insurers. Its stock was down about 24 percent in 2020 but up over 30 percent as of June 2021. Investors were worried that AIG would face more commercial insurance claims due to the pandemic. In fact, AIG losses have been manageable and the company has benefited from reduced claims as activities decreased. Post-pandemic, AIG should be able to increase premiums on insurance products as it has done after disaster-related events in the past.

• Truist Financial (TFC) became the sixth-largest US bank, serving more than 10 million households, as a result of a December 2019 merger between two regional powerhouses, BB&T and SunTrust Banks Inc. The stock fell 12 percent in 2020 as the merged banks suffered, but is up 27 percent as of June 2021. Earnings should continue to improve significantly, and Truist expects to save more than $1.6 billion annually in operating costs from the merger.

• **Travel-related businesses.** COVID-19 slammed travel and leisure companies in 2020, creating some great opportunities as the country opens up. However, investors must be cautious. For example, even though airlines should see higher revenues in 2021 and beyond, many have borrowed heavily to survive and are burdened with massive debt. *My favorite travel-related stock now...*

• Booking Holdings (BKNG), the world's largest online travel service by sales, operates Priceline, OpenTable, and Kayak. The company's revenues were crushed in 2020, and it was forced to close global offices and lay off a quarter of its workforce. But with $14 billion in cash, it had a solid balance sheet to help weather the crisis. It will benefit from a resurgence in travel demand as the economy normalizes and consumers look to take long-delayed vacations. In addition, its strong competitive advantages should allow it to gain market share from weaker competitors that have been affected more severely by the economic impact of the pandemic.

• **Commodities.** Increasing demand for construction and manufacturing materials is a reliable indicator of an economic upturn. In the last six months of 2020 and beginning of 2021, prices of silver, copper, and timber rose sharply. *My favorite commodity stock now...*

• Weyerhaeuser Co. (WY) is one of the world's largest timber companies, manufacturing products such as plywood and lumber. The stock struggled in 2020 because of wildfires in the West that affected some of Weyerhaeuser's timberland, a slowdown in production at its mills and its decision in May 2020 to temporarily suspend its dividend to preserve cash. Weyerhaeuser has since reinstated the dividend, and it will benefit from strong new-home and home-renovation markets, which are keeping lumber prices high.

TONY THOMAS, PHD
Morningstar, Inc., Chicago

BEST VALUE FUNDS

If you don't want to pick individual stocks and are looking for broadly diversified exposure to undervalued companies, Tony Thomas, PhD, says there are several top-rated mutual funds that specialize in value investing and are in a strong position to outperform the market in 2021 and beyond if value stocks surge…

• **AMG Yacktman (YACKX)** focuses on about 50 beaten-down large-, mid-, and small-cap stocks, including consumer-goods businesses with well-known brands. The fund is best-suited for patient, more conservative investors because it's willing to hold large amounts of cash until it finds compelling opportunities.

10-year annualized returns: 11.7 percent.*

• **Dodge & Cox (DODGX)** has used the same disciplined, contrarian approach since its launch 56 years ago. It invests in about 70 large companies with solid prospects but bargain-priced shares because of temporary problems. The fund's performance ranks in the top 2 percent of its category over the past decade, although its bets on big turnarounds make it more volatile than its peers and better for aggressive investors.

10-year annualized returns: 13.6 percent.

• **Vanguard Equity Income (VEIPX)** picks about 175 large, undervalued companies able to grow dividends quickly. It keeps a total of 38 percent of its portfolio in the health-care and financial-services sectors. With a 2.19 percent recent yield, its best for income-seeking investors willing to endure moderate volatility.

10-year annualized returns: 12.3 percent.

*All performance figures are through June 7, 2021.

Can You Trust the Financial Markets Anymore?

Pam Krueger, CEO of Wealthramp.com, an SEC-registered referral service that matches consumers with financial advisers, Osterville, Massachusetts. She also is executive producer of the PBS TV show *MoneyTrack*.

Scott B. Tiras, CPA, CFP, president of Tiras Wealth Management, a financial advisory firm with $2.2 billion in assets under management, Houston. AmeripriseAdvisors.com/scott.b.tiras

Marguerita Cheng, CFP, CEO of the investment advisory Blue Ocean Global Wealth, Gaithersburg, Maryland. BlueOceanGlobalWealth.com

Frank F. Murtha, PhD, a managing partner at MarketPsych, a behavioral-finance consulting firm, New York City. He is coauthor of *MarketPsych: How to Manage Fear and Build Your Investor Identity*. MarketPsych.com

Harry Newton, an investor, entrepreneur, and editor of the blog InSearchOfThePerfectInvestment.com.

Day traders and hedge funds bid up dubious investments to astronomical levels. Online brokerage firms turn investing into a high-stakes, multiplayer game rather than a sensible way to grow your nest egg.

All this recent turmoil has tempted some investors to join the hunt for big returns. Others feel the markets are rigged and want to sell everything, wondering if they can ever trust the markets again. Many feel overwhelmed and don't want to even look at their 401(k) statements.

Here are somewhat comforting perspectives from the experts…

• **Short-term trading is particularly dangerous now and will continue to be plagued by transitory frenzies** that could affect the broad markets and especially niche areas such as heavily shorted stocks, options, cryptocurrencies (such as Bitcoin), and small-tech stocks. If you need your money back in fewer than three years, you should have little or no exposure to these assets.

• **For longer-term investors willing to ride out the current volatility,** the financial markets still are structurally safe. The pandemic created a highly unusual and temporary environment for financial markets—millions of amateur investors, trapped at home and bored, turned to the stock market for thrills. Their interest in, and influence on, the market are likely to dissipate in coming years.

• **Tougher regulations for Wall Street that will rein in day traders and help control volatility are likely after years of deregulation.** These may include new taxes on stock transactions, penalties for brokerages such as Robinhood that provoke their customers into heavy and aggressive trading, and also cracking down on short-selling with hedge funds.

Here are the panel's ideas on how long-term investors can tweak their portfolios to feel safer now…take smarter risks…and avoid mistakes that can sabotage retirement goals…

If you're panicked and feel like selling your stock portfolio and getting out…

PAM KRUEGER
Wealthramp.com

• **Ensure that you never suffer a major loss.** Professional investors are willing to suffer moderate losses if they make a mistake or the market irrationally turns against them, but never a catastrophic one. They exit losing positions quickly rather than hang on to a losing stock or exchange-traded fund and hope it recovers.

What to do: Set up stop-loss orders on investments you expect to be volatile. It's a free service offered by most brokerage firms that triggers a sale when an investment's price falls to a predetermined threshold.

Example: You might set up a stop-loss order for 10 percent below the current price of a large-company stock you own but 20 percent below for volatile small-company stocks. As your investment appreciates, consider placing a "trailing stop-loss order," which constantly adjusts to remain at the same percentage level below the fluctuating market price.

SCOTT B. TIRAS, CPA, CFP
Tiras Wealth Management

• **Micro-rebalance your portfolio.** If you've established a sensible long-term investment plan and your life circumstances haven't changed, rethinking your overall asset allocation isn't necessary and could be detrimental.

Instead: Regain some control and relative safety in volatile markets by rebalancing more frequently, either monthly or whenever your portfolio strays by more than five percentage points above or below your long-term allocation levels. Don't just rebalance between stocks and bonds. Restore your desired level of exposure between pricey, fast-growing stocks and slower-growing undervalued ones.

Important: Micro-rebalancing works best in tax-deferred portfolios where you don't have to worry about the tax consequence of capital gains and losses.

If you feel paralyzed…

MARGUERITA CHENG, CFP
Blue Ocean Global Wealth

• **Remember why you are investing.** When you're nervous about making investment decisions, go back to your financial priorities and how you can earn the return that you need to maintain the standard of living you want without the risk for substantial loss. When you do that, your next move becomes clear.

Example: One client came into a half-a-million-dollar windfall from the sale of his primary residence after a divorce. He couldn't decide if he should invest aggressively or stay in cash and wait for a pullback. His number-one priority was making sure he had adequate cash reserves and enough funds for a down payment on another property. To sleep better at night, I advised him to keep $250,000 of the windfall in a stable-value fund, a portfolio of bonds that are insured to protect against a decline in yield or a loss of capital. He didn't need the remaining $250,000 for a long time, so it was earmarked for long-term retirement planning with a diversified portfolio of both value and growth stocks.

FRANK F. MURTHA, PHD
MarketPsych

• **Take small bites.** I know investors who got out at the bottom of the bear market in 2020 and then couldn't decide when to get back in, missing the entire rally the rest of the year. When you reach this level of paralysis, making small, automatic, and regular moves usually is the right solution to get unstuck. Add or remove a set amount of stock each month from your portfolio for the next six months to a year. After that period, you can reevaluate.

If you are afraid of missing out and are itching to make speculative bets...

HARRY NEWTON
InSearchOfThePerfectInvestment.com

• **Start a "too-hard" pile.** Investing means taking the time and learning the skills to understand why a company will keep growing and, hence, become more valuable. If I'm not 100 percent confident that I understand an investment, I avoid it no matter how much enthusiasm and hype it's receiving. I pride myself on being too stupid to understand many "hot" opportunities—and I pride myself in saying "no" to investing in them. Missing losses is my primary rule.

Recent hot investments in my too-hard pile: Cannabis growers...biotechs with miracle cures...special purpose acquisition companies (SPACs)...gold miners...energy producers... and Bitcoin. If my friends are striking it rich with investments that I don't understand, I wish them well. I'm not jealous. I stick to what I understand.

• **Quarantine your high-risk investments.** Many investors set aside a small portion of their assets as play money. But the intense rush you get from risky trading can easily infect and endanger the rest of your portfolio. If a high-risk gamble fails, you're tempted to replenish your play money. If it soars, you're inclined to double down on your own brilliance.

What to do: Set up and reinforce strict barriers with play money. Establish an entirely separate account for it (ideally at a separate brokerage firm). Once you fund the account, you cannot add additional money. You can further strengthen the quarantine by making it less convenient to access, check on, and trade your play money. Don't keep the brokerage firm app on your smartphone, and set up two-step security verification when you sign in to it.

• **Find your Charlie Munger.** Munger is the 97-year-old vice chairman of Berkshire Hathaway, the conglomerate controlled by Warren Buffett. Buffett affectionately calls Munger "the abominable no-man" because he's often skeptical about potential investments. You need a similar sounding board if you're considering a speculative investment. It could be a friend, spouse, or financial adviser—someone to provide objectivity and force you to rationalize/defend your decisions. If your idea seems like a good one after speaking with your sounding board, it's probably worth trying.

Stocks for the Biden Presidency

Charles Lewis Sizemore, CFA, chief investment officer of Sizemore Capital Management, Dallas, and coauthor of *Boom or Bust: Understanding and Profiting from a Changing Consumer Economy.* SizemoreCapital.com

When the same political party controls the White House and both houses of Congress, as the Democrats now do, it can set the stage for dramatic action and legislation that can boost the stock prices of certain industries and companies but hurt others.

All presidents can influence stock sectors through executive orders and actions that he/she issues to manage operations of the federal government, none of which require Congressional approval. In his first three weeks in office, President Biden delivered 49 such directives that reversed many of former President Trump's policies.

To help you figure out how the Blue Wave in Washington, DC, could affect your investments, we asked top stock picker and analyst Charles Lewis Sizemore, CFA, which areas of the market could be big winners and losers and which stocks are his favorites.

RENEWABLE ENERGY

This is the sector in which the president and the Democrats could have the strongest influence. Renewable energy was already on an upswing before the 2020 elections, thanks to falling costs, improving technology, and shifting consumer demand. The president plans to make U.S. climate policy an engine for employment and economic growth. Biden's "New Green Deal" calls for a nationwide emissions-free electricity grid in just 15 years through energy legislation, executive orders, incentives, and subsidies that will benefit solar, wind, and hydroelectric companies. *My favorite renewable-energy stocks now...*

• **Brookfield Renewable Partners (BEP)** owns a portfolio of more than 5,000 renewable power–generating properties including wind, solar, and hydroelectric facilities across four continents. The company has projects in development that should nearly double its power-generating capacity.

Recent share price: $39.32.*

• **NextEra Energy (NEE)** provides electricity for 5.5 million customers in Florida. But it is best known as the world's largest producer of wind and solar energy. NextEra, which has increased its annual dividend for 26 consecutive years, is so far ahead of its peers in converting fossil fuel–powered plants to cleaner energy sources that it should continue to deliver a double-digit compound annual growth rate in a sector known for low single-digit growth.

Recent share price: $72.14.

• **Invesco Solar ETF (TAN).** Many solar stocks have exhibited huge volatility in the past year. So I'd rather use an exchange-traded fund (ETF) to diversify and bet on a wide swath of them—all of which could benefit from renewable-energy legislation and wider consumer adoption of solar energy. Invesco Solar, launched in 2008, is the largest and oldest solar-focused ETF with about $3 billion in assets. It holds 30 of the top companies including First Solar, the leading US solar-panel manufacturer, and Enphase Energy, which provides solar-energy software and systems for homeowners.

Recent share price: $76.96.

HEALTH INSURERS

President Biden was a champion of the Affordable Care Act (ACA) as vice president. He intends to protect and expand the ACA by increasing tax credits to lower premiums and creating an option to buy a public health-insurance plan, similar to Medicare. That could dramatically increase the customer base of big health-care insurers. Just as important, the president has opposed extreme health-care reform such as a single-payer health-care system, which could eliminate private health insurance and replace it with a government-run program to provide insurance for all Americans. *My favorite health-insurer stock now...*

• **UnitedHealth Group (UNH)** is the country's largest private health insurer with nearly 50 million members in all 50 states. Selling Medicare Advantage plans has been a vital source of growth for the company. It has estimated that it enrolled about 700,000 new Medicare customers in 2020.

Recent share price: $401.74.

MARIJUANA

Although the federal law preventing the use or possession of marijuana for medical or recreational purposes is unlikely to fall anytime soon, incremental changes under the Democrats are likely to lead to a surge in cannabis stocks. President Biden has pledged to decriminalize marijuana, which will help legitimize it. That could lead to increased institutional ownership in these companies, which is currently quite limited. *My favorite marijuana-related stock now...*

• **Innovative Industrial Properties (IIPR)** invests in infrastructure supporting the cannabis economy. This real estate investment trust, which trades on the New York Stock Exchange, rents marijuana growing, distribution, and manufacturing facilities to state-licensed medical cannabis operations. With about 67 properties across 18 states, the company plays an essential role in the industry.

Recent share price: $188.88.

INFRASTRUCTURE

One of Biden's top campaign promises was a plan to spend $1.3 trillion over a 10-year period on infrastructure projects such as repairing highways and upgrading airports,

*Recent share prices as of market close on June 8, 2021.

railways, and ports. Infrastructure improvement enjoys bipartisan support in Congress as a way to continue to help get the U.S. economy back on its feet, and much of that spending would flow to U.S. heavy-construction and materials companies. *My favorite infrastructure stock now...*

• **Martin Marietta Materials (MLM)** sells $4 billion a year worth of aggregates—crushed stone, gravel, and sand—widely used in construction work. It's a primary beneficiary of new federal funding to rebuild the nation's roads and bridges. The company's geographic diversity, with operations in 27 states, gives it pricing advantages because shipping aggregate is expensive and shortening distances saves money.

Recent share price: $361.91.

AREAS TO AVOID

• **Big Tech.** The pandemic helped bring stocks of many of the world's technology giants to new heights in 2020. But these companies are in Washington's crosshairs. President Biden supports modifying or revoking Section 230 of the Communications Decency Act, which provides Internet sites with legal immunity from liability even if users post illegal or false content. That has allowed companies such as Facebook, Twitter, and YouTube to flourish.

Democratic senators are likely to press for legislative restrictions on issues such as privacy, data collection, and mergers, all of which could hurt Big Tech profits. And last year, the U.S. Justice Department and Federal Trade Commission filed antitrust lawsuits against Google and Facebook, threatening to break up these companies.

• **Fossil-fuel companies.** While oil and gas prices are rebounding from their pandemic lows and energy is, by far, the cheapest major sector in the stock market, Democrats are no friend of the industry. President Biden placed a temporary moratorium on oil and gas leasing in the Arctic and revoked approval for the Keystone XL pipeline, meant to carry crude oil to the US from Canada's oil sands—among the most greenhouse-gas intensive energy in the world. Investors should expect more legislation and directives that will hurt fossil-fuel company profits, including stricter standards for carbon emissions.

US Home-Construction Stocks Should Continue to Rise

The Dow Jones U.S. Select Home Construction Index is up 26.9 percent year-to-date through June 2021, versus 13 percent for the S&P 500. Catalysts include strong housing prices, record-low mortgage rates, and greater demand in suburban and rural markets.

Two ways to invest: iShares US Home Construction ETF (ITB)...SPDR S&P Homebuilders ETF (XHB), with stocks ranging from building products to home furnishings and appliances.

Tom Lydon, president of Global Trends Investments, Irvine, California, and editor of ETFTrends.com.

3 Ways to De-Risk Your Investments

Ric Edelman, founder of Edelman Financial Engines, Santa Clara, California, which manages more than $200 billion in client assets and was ranked by *Barron's* as the top registered independent financial advisory firm in the country in 2020 for the third year in a row. EdelmanFinancialEngines.com

Many investors are anxious over how the stock market can maintain such euphoric growth. Today's sky-high stock valuations may be justified by the recovery of both the economy and corporate earnings as the pandemic wanes. But if you're worried that this growth may not continue and can't stomach market drops, it's time to "de-risk" your portfolio. *Top financial adviser Ric Edelman told us how...*

De-risking means reevaluating how much volatility you can handle in the short term—anywhere from six months to two years—then reducing your stock exposure and raising your cash holdings appropriately. How much should you de-risk? It depends on your particular situation, but enough so that you have the fortitude to avoid panicking and selling stocks during a scary pullback…and feel confident that you won't be forced to liquidate stocks when they're down just so that you can pay your bills.

Three options I suggest to clients who plan to own stocks long-term (at least five years) but want extra protection for their portfolios now…

• **Trim the stock portion of your portfolio by at least 10 percent.** While 10 percent doesn't sound like it will make much of a difference in a stock market correction, if your portfolio is composed of 50 percent stocks/50 percent bonds, reducing your stock exposure to 40 percent lowers your overall risk by 20 percent.

Steps to take: Sell some shares of your biggest winners or shares of your most aggressive stocks. In taxable accounts, you'll need to keep capital gains taxes in mind, perhaps by selling losing stocks that you're no longer enthusiastic about in order to offset some of your gains with capital losses. You can buy back positions of stocks you like when you feel the economy is on stronger footing or when their valuations look attractive again.

• **Cash out a large portion—or even all—of your stock portfolio.** Then dollar-cost average back in over the course of the next year. This is for investors who simply cannot stomach the stock market now. The strategy reduces your chances of big losses, but you'll also miss big gains and potentially have a high tax bill, which is why it is best for tax-deferred retirement accounts.

Steps to take: After you cash out, don't try to time the market to get back in. Automatically reinvest one-twelfth of the money each month until you reach your original long-term asset allocation and have re-created the portfolio you sold off.

• **Increase your emergency savings to cover at least two years of living expenses.** I recommend this to many of my clients, but especially those in retirement. Retired investors find great resolve knowing that they won't have to compromise their lifestyle or sell assets in the midst of a down market. Beef up your emergency savings by trimming winners and selling losers that you no longer want to own.

"Alternatives" Offer a Better Balance

Janet M. Brown, president of the FundX Investment Group and managing editor of the *NoLoad FundX* newsletter, San Francisco. FundX.com

When stocks are plunging, bonds typically rise, helping to offset volatility in your portfolio. That's why advisers recommend that you maintain a balanced portfolio. But from the start of 2020 through March 18, 2020, when the total stock market lost 26 percent, the total bond market fell 5 percent—softening but not completely offsetting the harm. So where can you turn for help to better balance your portfolio?

Consider "alternative" funds, specifically ones that use strategies designed to reduce volatility and possibly provide some growth in topsy-turvy markets. Alternative funds can short-sell (bet against) stocks and/or invest in non-traditional investments that move differently from stocks and bonds. Although alternative funds lagged behind stocks during the 11-year bull market, they could be helpful in the coming years when bonds likely will offer very low returns and stocks are likely to continue their jarring volatility.

Studies have shown that converting a portfolio of 60 percent stocks and 40 percent bonds to one with 50 percent stocks, 30 percent bonds and 20 percent alternative investments can produce similar long-term returns while reducing volatility.

Two attractive alternative funds…

• **Core Alternative ETF (CCOR)** mixes high-quality dividend-paying stocks and stock options, which offer protection by giving the fund manager the right to buy or sell a stock for a predetermined price at a future date regardless of the actual price on that date. The fund gained 5.99 percent this year through June 8, 2021. It has returned an annualized 6.07 percent since its 2017 launch.

Recent yield: 1.45 percent. CoreAltFunds.com

• **Alger Dynamic Opportunities (SPEDX)** seeks long term low volatility capital appreciation, primarily in long equity positions. Fund is up 7.84 percent for 2021 through June 9 and up 9.65 percent since inception. Alger.com

CHECK IT OUT...

Perks Your Broker Might Offer

If you have a brokerage account, there's a good chance the broker is offering goodies that you're missing out on.

Partial-share trading: If you find it hard to cough up enough for a full share of stock, some brokers let you buy into a piece for as little as $5 or $1.

Income-estimator tools: These can be great for planning cash flow from income investments.

Sign-on bonuses: Some brokers reimburse transfer fees when you join. Others have referral awards and sign-on bonuses.

Credit card rewards: If your broker offers an account-linked credit card, you could be getting cash back on purchases, and that cash gets directed into your brokerage account.

ATM fee reimbursement: Brokers that are parts of banks can waive ATM fees for you, but even some nonbank brokerages offer debit cards linked to your account that have fee-waiving perks attached.

Kiplinger.com

These 2021 Trends Could Drive Stocks for Years

Alex Ely, CIO for U.S. growth equity at Macquarie Investment Management, Philadelphia, and manager of the Delaware Smid Cap Growth Fund (DFDIX) since 2016. The fund has had annualized returns of 17.9 percent over the past 10 years, ranking in the top one percent of its category...and 26.24 percent over the past five years, ranking in the top 5 percent. MacquarieIM.com

As the economy recovers from the effects of the coronavirus pandemic, many investors are taking a cautious approach to investing. Not Alex Ely. The fund manager is comfortable taking investment risks as he seeks stocks that are shaking things up. And his approach is paying off big. His stock portfolio of fast-growing small and medium-size companies gained 55 percent for one year ending June 9, 2021 versus 40 percent for the S&P 500. The companies he hunts for are tapping into consumer trends that have gotten a boost from this year's shifts in consumer behavior and spending. Their businesses should thrive over the next few years—but these stocks tend to be much more volatile than those of large companies and the overall market. The companies include such gems as a maker of camping and outdoor gear... a service that simplifies shopping for health insurance...and an all-natural pet-food maker.

We asked Ely to describe today's most promising trends and the stocks likely to benefit from them...

HOW TO FIND THE NEW STOCK WINNERS

I start by looking for disruptions. These are changes from the normal or traditional ways of doing things—usually aided by technology or some form of innovation—that allow consumers and businesses to live, work, and spend in better, cheaper, and/or faster ways. Recently, the forces driving these changes have not only been maintained but have been accelerated by the health crisis. The most obvious disruption in 2020 through 2021 has been led by giant tech companies whose services make staying home more enjoyable and/or productive, such as Amazon.com, Netflix, and Zoom Video. Not surprisingly, their stocks have become very expensive. *Here are examples of three disruptive trends that Wall Street is less focused on and that have benefited various stocks that are still relative bargains...*

• **Great outdoors.** As the pandemic continues to suspend people's long-distance travel plans, consumers are turning to local outdoor experiences and they are spending to improve their own backyards. Even before the pandemic, the outdoor-recreation industry was projected to continue growing by an annual average of 7 percent through 2023, according to the accounting firm Moss Adams.

• **Digitalization of financial services.** Both consumers and small businesses want simpler, safer, and more efficient ways to bank, send money, pay bills, purchase insurance, and perform financial transactions remotely without having to handle cash or paper documents. In a survey this year by the financial-services research firm Novantas, only 40 percent of respondents said they expect to do their banking in person at brick-and-mortar branches in the future.

• **Premiumization of food.** The dramatic decline in restaurant visits in 2020 and 2021 has put new emphasis on higher-quality food and drink for home consumption. That has dovetailed with a larger societal shift toward all-natural and locally sourced foods. Nearly 70 percent of millennials are willing to pay more for high-quality foods, according to a survey by Whole Foods.

7 ATTRACTIVE STOCKS

Once I have identified a disruptive trend, I look for the companies best positioned to tap into it. Each of the following companies reflects one of the trends described above. They range from $2 billion to $7 billion in stock market capitalization. And each should continue to benefit from annual revenue growth of at least 10 percent...annual earnings growth of at least 20 percent...strong, experienced management...and a leading position in its market niche.

Adding one or more of these stocks to your portfolio could help boost your long-term returns...

TREND: **Great outdoors...**

• **SiteOne Landscape Supply (SITE)** is the U.S. landscaping supply industry's largest wholesaler, offering more than 120,000 products ranging from fertilizers and trees to natural stone and outdoor lighting. SiteOne is four times as large as the nearest competitor and has been consolidating a highly fragmented industry of regional mom-and-pop companies. It made 10 acquisitions last year but has plenty of room for growth because its annual sales amount to just 12 percent of the $20 billion landscape-supply market.

Recent share price: $162.36.*

• **Trex Co. (TREX)** makes plastic-composite boards for residential decks that are resistant to fading, scratches and stains, and they cost less over time than pressure-treated lumber. The company controls nearly half the nonwood decking market in the US. Its proprietary manufacturing process combines sawdust with more than 500 million pounds of recycled plastics each year.

Recent share price: $97.42

• **Yeti Holdings (YETI)** manufactures high-quality gear and rugged products for the amateur outdoor recreational market. The items are sold at about 4,700 retailers around the country as well as seven of Yeti's own stores. The brand has developed a cult following thanks to its emphasis on innovative design of products including signature Tundra coolers with two-inch thick insulation as well as steel drinkware and waterproof blankets, duffel bags, and totes.

Recent share price: $91.15.

TREND: **Digitalization of financial services...**

• **Bill.com Holdings (BILL).** More than 90 percent of small and medium-size businesses still rely on paper checks to make and receive payments. Bill.com provides an alternative—a suite of cloud-based software and services that

*Prices as of June 10, 2021 (unless otherwise noted).

offer low-cost bill-paying and invoicing. That makes it easier for businesses to accept payments from major banks and card companies while preventing errors caused by manual processes. The company, which went public in December 2019, has more than 100,000 customers and processes more than $100 billion in transactions annually. The stock is up more than 100 percent as of the first half of 2021 and has room for further growth.

Recent share price: $154.72.

• **eHealth (EHTH).** This 20-year-old company operates eHealth.com, the nation's largest private online health insurance exchange. In an industry filled with small independent brokers with minimal online presence, eHealth can offer individuals and various small businesses better pricing and more than 10,000 plans from major insurers. The big catalyst for the company is the 10,000 baby boomers who turn 65 each day and become eligible for Medicare and supplemental plans. First quarter of 2021 showed an increase of 65 percent over first quarter of 2020 for approved members of Medicare Advantage products.

Recent share price: $61.70.

TREND: **Premiumization of food...**

• **Boston Beer Co. (SAM).** The craft brewer is best known for its Samuel Adams beers. But Boston Beer's non-beer products such as Angry Orchard Hard Cider and Truly Hard Seltzer make up about two-thirds of the total volume it produces—its beers make up only about one-third. These alternative alcoholic beverages have had explosive growth as consumers turn to lower-calorie and gluten-free alcoholic drinks.

Recent share price: $597 (August 2021).

• **Freshpet (FRPT).** This company has pioneered the concept of refrigerated food for cats and dogs made from farm-raised chicken, beef and fish and all-natural vegetables and fruit. It is sold in branded fridges at more than 20,000 supermarkets, pet stores, and big-box chains around the country.

Recent share price: $168.07.

Ready to Rebound—Big Opportunity in Small-Cap Stocks

Robert Male, CFA, and Jamie Cuellar, CFA, comanagers of the Buffalo Small Cap Fund (BUFSX), which has a 10-year annualized performance of 17 percent vs. 12.2 percent for the Russell 2000 index, and ranks in the top 8 percent of its category, Mission, Kansas. BuffaloFunds.com

Battered by the pandemic, the stocks of small companies are ready to shine. For most of 2020, the stock market was dominated by giant technology firms that seemed impervious to the coronavirus.

But for the first six months of 2021, the Russell 2000 index, the benchmark for small-cap stocks, has bounced back with a 18.21 percent surge versus 13.15 percent for the S&P 500 index.

Reason: Small-cap stocks typically outperform after recessions because their earnings are more sensitive to economic changes than large-cap stocks. The nonpartisan Congressional Budget Office forecasts that U.S. gross domestic product (GDP) is expected to reach pre-pandemic levels by the end of 2021 as the country opens up again.

To help you get the most out of this stock market shift, we asked two top small-cap specialists—Robert Male, CFA, and Jamie Cuellar, CFA, of the Buffalo Small Cap Fund—to explain their focused strategy for finding winners for 2021 and beyond.

FOCUS ON LONG-TERM TRENDS

All of the stocks we invest in tap into long-term secular trends, which are quantifiable changes in culture, demographics, technology, and/or major industries that influence our lives and affect consumer and business buying habits. The trends, which accelerated in the pandemic during 2020 and will benefit from an economic recovery, range from the voracious hunger for Internet bandwidth to the digitalization of health care to e-commerce as it matures and expands its base.

Once we identify a secular trend, we look for small companies that gain the most from these trends and have the following characteristics…

• **$500 million to $4 billion in market capitalization.** However, we are willing to hold on to these companies as they become larger if they maintain the potential for fast growth, generally 15 percent annual earnings growth or more.

• **Significant competitive advantages,** which allow them to weather downturns and take market share from rivals.

• **Manageable debt and strong free cash flow to sustain growth without having to raise additional capital.**

Four long-term secular trends and the stocks we own in our fund that tap into them…

TREND: **Precision Medicine**

Advances in scientific understanding of the activity of genes in the body, including their role in certain diseases, have revolutionized the diagnostic-testing industry. Non-invasive tests give doctors the ability to quickly and cost-efficiently screen for diabetes, cancers, and, most recently, COVID-19. Diagnostic testing is expected to grow 9 percent annually through 2027 and become a nearly $300-billion-a-year market. *A precision-medicine stock that we own…*

• **OraSure Technologies Inc. (OSUR)** is best known for DNA testing kits. But the 33-year-old company also has pioneered an over-the-counter HIV test kit, urine testing to detect urological cancers, and the first emergency-use authorizations from the FDA for an at-home COVID-19 sample collection kit.

Recent share price: $9.65.

TREND: **Hunger for Bandwidth**

By 2023, monthly U.S. Internet traffic is forecast to be nearly double the current usage as Internet providers race to offer faster, more powerful, and reliable broadband equipment, services, and software. *A communication bandwidth stock that we own…*

• **Calix (CALX)** manufactures broadband-access equipment and software that allows small U.S. telecom providers to deliver the latest Internet and cloud services to residences without expensive upgrades. Calix also is a prime beneficiary of a new $20 billion program from the FCC to finance the construction of high-speed broadband networks for more than six million homes and businesses in rural communities.

Recent share price: $46.36.

TREND: **Maturation of E-commerce**

The shift to online retailing seems to have taken over the world, but it's still a new phenomenon. In the first quarter of 2021, e-commerce sales in the U.S. accounted for just 13.6 percent of total retail sales. *E-commerce–related stocks that we own…*

• **Air Transport Services Group (ATSG)** purchases used Boeing airplanes, refurbishes them and leases them out to shipping companies such as UPS and DHL. The company's largest partner is Amazon.com's "Amazon Air" delivery. It operates 73 Boeing 767s on behalf ov various shippers.

Recent share price: $24.89.

• **The Lovesac Co.** (LOVE) is best known for selling oversize beanbag chairs at showrooms around the country. Unlike most furniture companies, management optimized the business for e-commerce during the pandemic, vastly expanding future growth opportunities. For the quarter ending April 30, 2021, Lovesac increased total revenue and gross profits year over year by 54 percent and 57 percent, respectively, largely due to sales of its sectional couches, which are designed to come apart for personalized configuration, allowing the components to be shipped to consumers inexpensively.

Recent share price: $87.76.

TREND: **Digital Transformation of Healthcare**

New technology is helping to streamline physicians' work, optimize billing systems, and lower costs. *A health-care digital-transformation stock that we own…*

• **Phreesia (PHR)** makes software that allows about 50,000 physician offices, hospitals, and clinics to manage their patient intake and coordinate patient billing. The company, which has partnered with dozens

*Prices as of June 10, 2021.

of major electronic-health record and payment networks, facilitates more than 50 million patient visits a year and $1.4 billion in payments.

Recent share price: $57.68.

Ride the Rebound with Small-Cap Funds

Janet Brown is president of FundX Investment Group and managing editor of the NoLoad FundX newsletter, San Francisco. FundX.com

If you don't want to pick individual stocks, there are veteran fund managers who have achieved good long-term returns with less volatility. *Here are two of my favorite small-cap funds now…*

- **Carillon Scout Small Cap I (UMBHX)** invests in companies with market values under $2 billion that are poised for growth and is 97% U.S. based.

10-year annualized performance: 14.95 percent versus 12.91 percent for the Russell 2000 index (as of early June 2021).

- **Royce Pennsylvania Mutual Service Fund (RYPFX)** avoids risky, fast-growing companies and focuses on high-quality, profitable businesses with low debt. The fund's cautious approach has caused performance to lag in recent years, but it should do well as the economy strengthens.

10-year performance: 10.76 percent.

Traps in Trading ETFs

Ben Johnson, CFA, director of global ETF research at Morningstar Inc., Chicago, which tracks more than 620,000 investment offerings. Morningstar.com

With exchange-traded fund (ETF) trades now commission-free at most brokerage firms, they make even more sense than investing in traditional mutual funds.

ETFs tend to cost less than traditional funds, are more tax-efficient and are more transparent about their holdings. But if you're not careful with your choices, ETFs can wind up costing you a lot more.

One potential drawback: Since ETFs trade like stocks, the difference in their intraday price and the underlying value of their individual holdings (known as the net asset value) can vary throughout the course of the day, meaning that the price you get when you buy or sell shares can be dramatically different depending on when you trade. *To get the best prices…*

- **Avoid trading in the first and last 30 minutes of market hours,** when the spread between an ETF's price and its net asset value tends to be greatest.

- **Use limit orders.** When you trade ETFs, your brokerage firm gets you the "market" price—the best price available at that moment. If you want more control over the share price, specify the price you want with a limit order.

For buy limit orders, the trade will be executed only at your limit price or lower. You also can set up a sell limit order, which means that a holding will be sold at your limit price or higher.

- **Trade ETFs that invest in foreign securities only when the underlying markets are open** and the holdings are actively changing hands.

Example: For the best price, trade Vanguard FTSE Europe ETF (VGK) during the morning while European markets are still open…though, as above, avoid the first and last 30 minutes of market hours.

ETF Versions of Mutual Funds Offer Attractive Choices

Ben Johnson, CFA, director of global ETF research at Morningstar Inc., Chicago. Morningstar.com

If you're a fan of actively managed mutual funds but wish they had the lower fees, tax efficiency, and convenience of increasingly popular exchange-traded funds (ETFs), the big brokerages may have a solution. Brokerages including Fidelity and T. Rowe Price have begun offering ETFs with portfolios similar to or the same as those of attractive existing mutual funds.

How these new ETFs work: Most traditional ETFs use a passive strategy, closely tracking indexes such as the S&P 500. That's because the Securities and Exchange Commission (SEC) had required ETFs to provide portfolio transparency, revealing their holdings to the public on a daily basis. That meant managers of actively managed stock mutual funds rarely launched new ETFs or offered ETF versions of their funds because they didn't want to reveal what moves they were making each day. However, the SEC has approved a new type of ETF that can use actively managed strategies but has to disclose portfolio holdings only monthly or quarterly. It's called a "non-transparent" ETF.

What that means for investors: You now can get access to some of the top stock-picking managers through an ETF. As of April 2021, there were about 40 non-transparent ETFs, and many of them are near clones of attractive mutual funds but with lower fees.

Examples: American Century Focused Dynamic Growth ETF (FDG), with an expense ratio of 0.45 percent vs. 0.85 percent...Fidelity Blue Chip Growth ETF (FBCG), 0.59 percent vs. 0.8 percent...T. Rowe Price Blue Chip Growth ETF (TCHP), 0.57 percent vs. 0.69 percent...and T. Rowe Price Dividend Growth ETF (TDVG), 0.5 percent vs. 0.62 percent.

Important: The SEC doesn't allow non-transparent ETFs, which focus mostly on large-cap stocks, to invest in riskier investments such as foreign stocks or private equity, so their holdings may not exactly match their mutual fund counterparts.

Private Equity: Proceed with Caution

Ric Lager, president of Lager & Company, which advises 401(k) plan participants, Golden Valley, Minnesota. He is author of *Forget the Pie: Recipe for a Healthier 401(k).* LagerCo.com

You might be tempted by an opportunity to invest in young, fast-growing companies long before they go public. In 2020, the Labor Department approved the inclusion of such "private equity" investments in 401(k) and retirement plans. Investors can invest in them indirectly through target-date, balanced, or similar funds offered by the plans, and no more than 15 percent of total assets held by any of those funds can be in private equity. Over the past two decades through the second quarter of 2020, U.S. private-equity funds averaged a 10.48 percent annual return after fees versus 5.9 percent for the S&P 500 Index, according to Cambridge Associates. And the super-performing stocks Facebook, Netflix and Tesla all were funded in part with private-equity money before they issued stock to the public.

As tempting as private equity might seem, most small investors should steer clear. *Here's why...*

- **Uncertain performance figures.** Unlike stocks traded on a major exchange, there is no simple way to determine the value of an investment in a private company until the company goes public or is sold.
- **Money lock-ups.** Private-equity funds often have strict limitations on when investors can cash out shares. Lock-up periods typically last five years or more.
- **Exorbitant expenses.** Private-equity funds typically take 20 percent of any profits each year in addition to a 2 percent annual expense ratio, which can hurt the performance of a target-date or balanced fund holding private equity.

What to do: If you are investing in a target-date or balanced fund, ask your plan sponsor whether the fund has exposure to private equity, which could significantly increase volatility and uncertainty about the fund's performance. Consider shifting to a fund that does not invest in private equity or a more conservative target-date fund, such as one with an earlier target date.

A Smart Way to Invest in Electric Vehicles

Shawn Kim, equity analyst specializing in the EV and automotive industry for Gabelli Funds, part of GAMCO, which oversees more than $30 billion in assets, Rye, New York. Gabelli.com

Tesla's stock performance—skyrocketing from under $200 to nearly $900 within a year—has tempted investors to bet on other start-ups in the electric vehicle (EV) industry, such as truck maker Nikola... Chinese electric-car company Nio...and pickup and delivery-vehicle producer Workhorse Group, all of which saw their stock prices soar even though they have little or no revenue, let alone profits.

But be careful. Although the global EV industry is expected to grow 20 percent a year and hit $1.3 trillion by 2030 as it moves from a fringe technology to become competitive with conventional automobiles in price, style and performance, the battles will be fierce and chaotic. In recent months, Nikola lost 75 percent of its value as its founder resigned amid corporate fraud allegations. Even Tesla will find it challenging to grow fast enough to justify its sky-high market capitalization.

Smarter way to play the EV boom: Invest in companies that make electrical systems for traditional autos and have the technology and vast global supply chains to capture that market for the EV industry. They aren't glamorous or high-profile, but they benefit no matter which company thrives among EV makers. Even better, shares of these suppliers are bargains at recent prices because their existing sales to gas-powered and hybrid-car makers have slumped during the pandemic. *Two of my favorite electrical-system suppliers...*

- **Aptiv (APTV)** is a global leader in electrical distribution systems, high-voltage connectors and engineered components, all of which represent critical systems in next-generation EVs.
- **Lear Corporation (LEA)** makes power electronics and electrical wiring that powers parts of vehicles and runs wireless sensors that interact with vehicle computers as well as audio systems and external LED lighting systems.

You Can Buy Slices of a Stock

Kimberly Foss, CFP, president of Empyrion Wealth Management in Roseville, California, and author of *Wealthy by Design: A 5-Step Plan for Financial Security.* EmpyrionWealth.com

Want to get your kids and/or grandkids interested in investing or tip-toe into the stock market yourself? Buy a slice...a slice of stock. You can trade "fractional" shares of stocks and, in some cases, exchange-traded funds (ETFs) at more than a half-dozen brokerages including Charles Schwab, Fidelity, and Robinhood. Fractional shares can be useful because many popular stocks are pricier than what you want to spend as a gift or what investors with limited assets can afford. A single share of Amazon.com recently cost $3,300...Google parent Alphabet $2,500...Netflix $500...Tesla $600... McDonald's $225...Disney $175.

How it works: Fractional shares can be bought and sold online without commission in taxable accounts and IRAs and even workplace retirement plans if your employer's plan has a brokerage option. You can choose from several hundred or even several thousand stocks, depending on which brokerage you use, and can invest as little as a few dollars—for instance, $5 at Schwab or $1 at Fidelity and Robinhood. Dividends are passed on to you in proportion to your fractional stake.

Best brokerages for fractional shares now...

If you want lots of investment choices: Fidelity offers fractional shares in more than

7,000 stocks and ETFs, including all those on the New York Stock Exchange and Nasdaq, compared with only stocks in the S&P 500 at Schwab and most stocks that have a market value of at least $25 million at Robinhood.

If you want to give gifts to minors: At Fidelity and Schwab, you can open a custodial account for a child. At Schwab, you can print a Schwab Stock Slices certificate to give to the child.

If you want to make recurring purchases automatically: Robinhood lets you buy fractional stock and ETF shares on a monthly basis or other schedule.

The Best and Worst Bond Funds 2021

Robert M. Brinker, CFS, editor of Brinker Fixed Income Advisor, Littleton, Colorado. BrinkerAdvisor.com

Can bonds continue to perform well after two years of strong gains and amid a robust economic recovery? An index of the overall U.S. investment-grade bond market gained 7.43 percent in 2020 and 8.7 percent in 2019. That's due in great part to sinking interest rates, which took a further dive as the Federal Reserve fought to combat the pandemic-induced recession and pledged to keep short-term rates near zero for years. But record-low interest rates leave little room for further gains in the bond market, whose prices move in the opposite direction to interest rates, and make it harder to use bonds to offset stock volatility in your portfolio.

THE OUTLOOK

In 2021, for the overall bond market I expect flat or slightly negative total returns, which reflect both the yield and changes in price. That means you should steer clear of certain types of bond funds that are most likely to do poorly in 2021. However, there are pockets of opportunity for yield and/or capital appreciation in areas that include mortgage-backed securities, intermediate-term corporate bonds and junk bonds with short maturities.

Major factors that will affect bonds in 2021…

- **Short-term interest rates are likely to remain unchanged,** in the zero percent to 0.25 percent range.
- **Long-term interest rates could rise if the economy continues to improve and commodity prices rise,** triggering higher inflation. The yield on 10-year U.S. Treasuries, recently at 1.44 percent, should remain in the 1.5 percent range by year-end 2021.
- **The U.S. economy is likely to grow 3 percent in 2021** as new vaccines and treatments help harness the pandemic and the federal government provides additional stimulus.
- **Inflation, as measured by the Consumer Price Index, could tick up to the 2 percent to level range for 2021,** from a recent 1.2 percent, driven by stronger consumer spending, rising employment, and higher commodity prices.

BOND FUNDS TO SHUN

If you hold individual bonds to maturity, fluctuations in interest rates and bond prices won't affect you directly. But if you invest in bond funds, the following categories are unattractive. *Consider trimming or selling existing holdings, and avoid new purchases…*

- **Short-term government and short-term corporate bonds.** This category, which focuses on bonds with maturities of five years or less, had total returns of 4.6 percent in 2020 and a recent average yield of 0.35 percent. If you want reliable income with no risk of losing principal, you can find yields almost double that in FDIC-insured online savings and money-market accounts.
- **Long-term government bonds.** This type of fund, which typically holds bonds with maturities ranging from 10 to 30 years, benefited greatly as nervous global investors flocked to the security of U.S. Treasuries. This bond category outperformed every other bond category over the past two years. But its average yield dropped to just 1.8 percent. Also, for the benchmark index of long-term government bonds, the average "duration"—a measure of how sensitive a bond or portfolio of bonds is to changes in interest rates—is 18.5 years. That duration indicates that if long-term rates

rise just one-half percentage point, the funds would suffer a 9.25 percent drop in price.

• **Municipal bonds.** These bonds, which pay interest that is exempt from federal tax and sometimes state and local taxes, are popular with high-income individuals because they provide higher after-tax yields than comparable U.S. Treasuries. But the economic fallout from the pandemic has wreaked havoc on many state and local government balance sheets, making muni bonds unusually volatile.

Note: The average yield on intermediate-term munis was recently 0.06 percent (the equivalent of a 0.78 percent after-tax yield on Treasuries in the 24 percent tax bracket). If you want to own munis, favor "general-obligation" bonds from fiscally strong states such as Texas and Virginia, not munis focused on such things as airports or transportation projects that can't raise taxes to boost revenue.

Foreign government bonds are often attractive to more aggressive fixed-income investors because they typically offer higher yields but also greater risk than U.S. Treasuries. But 10-year government bonds in Japan had a recent yield of just 0.035 percent. And 10-year bonds in France, Switzerland, and Germany all paid negative yields recently, meaning that you could lose money if you hold the bonds to maturity. Bonds issued by countries with developing economies yielded a recent average of 3.6 percent, which is not enough to compensate for the considerable volatility they entail.

BOND FUNDS TO FAVOR

While avoiding the bond funds described above in 2021, consider investing in the following funds, which are less vulnerable to rising interest rates...have greater potential for capital appreciation...or pay relatively high yields.

• **Dodge & Cox Income (DODIX).** Many investors invest in intermediate-term, investment-grade corporate bond funds with maturities between five and 10 years as core portfolio holdings.

Reason: They often provide the best tradeoff among yield, interest rate risk, and total return. This bond category returned 6.9 percent in 2020 and can do well in 2021 even if interest rates rise a bit. The Dodge & Cox fund uses a simple but effective strategy that's attractive for fixed-income investors who can stand moderate risks. Specifically, it holds more than 1,100 bonds considered undervalued, with an average credit rating of A and a duration of 5.4 years.

Recent yield: 1.68 percent.

10-year performance: 4.14 percent.*

• **Vanguard Wellesley Income (VWINX).** With interest rates on high-quality bonds so low, more aggressive investors may want to take a calculated risk by adding exposure to dividend-paying stocks. This venerable hybrid fund has maintained the same strategy for the past 50 years. It keeps about 40 percent of its portfolio in blue-chip stocks that seem undervalued and pay a dividend...and the rest in intermediate-term corporate bonds. With the economy likely to grow 3 percent in 2021, the fund's stock holdings should do well and push up its total return.

Recent yield: 1.85 percent.

10-year performance: 7.59 percent.

• **Osterweis Strategic Income (OSTIX).** High-yield (junk) bonds returned just 3.7 percent in 2020. I am mostly avoiding them because their yields in the 4 percent to 5 percent range may seem attractive but aren't nearly high enough to justify the risk for heavy losses that would occur if the economy stalls...if issuers default on interest payments...and/or if the stock market sinks, since junk bonds correlate closely with stocks. However, the Osterweis fund offers a unique and cautious strategy that tends to excel in volatile markets. It holds about 135 bonds, with an average duration of just 1.9 years. So even if interest rates jump in 2021, the fund is unlikely to be hurt much. Also, manager Carl Kaufman excels at evaluating credit risk. Since the fund's 2002 launch, none of its bond holdings has experienced a default.

Recent yield: 4.15 percent.

10-year performance: 4.84 percent.

• **Vanguard GNMA (VFIIX)** invests in more than 15,000 government-guaranteed

*All performance figures, unless otherwise specified, are through June 14, 2021.

mortgage-backed securities (GNMAs), which are large groups of high-quality residential home mortgages that are bundled together and sold as investments. Its holdings are rated AAA and backed by the federal government against default, but they offer higher yields than comparable intermediate-term U.S. Treasuries. That's because the major uncertainty with GNMAs, which returned 3 percent in 2020, is that fast-rising interest rates would lower the value of the securities it owns. That's unlikely to happen in 2021.

Recent yield: 0.76 percent.

10-year performance: 2.56 percent.

GOOD TO KNOW...

Specialized ETFs Are Not a Great Investment

Exchange-traded funds are investment vehicles that typically track the stocks in an index such as the S&P 500. But in recent years, firms have created specialized ETFs that focus on a basket of stocks within a hot theme—cannabis retailers, video game companies, etc. A new analysis shows that, between 1993 and 2019, earnings of traditional index-based ETFs were relatively flat, while specialized ETFs lost about 4 percent of their value per year. The reason? Specialized ETFs tend to be launched right when hype is causing their underlying stocks to be overvalued, so they start underperforming almost immediately.

Study led by researchers at The Ohio State University, Columbus, presented at the American Economic Association 2021 Annual Meeting.

"Real" Growth Stocks Are Rare

Michael Kantrowitz, CFA, chief investment strategist at Cornerstone Macro, which provides equity research for institutional investors, New York City. CornerstoneMacro.com

Companies that continue to grow their revenue and profits significantly are highly prized by investors. But real fast-growth stocks are relatively rare. Although about 280 stocks in the S&P 500 are classified as "growth," as opposed to bargain-priced "value" stocks, only 66 are truly worthy of that designation, having increased revenue by an average of 15 percent or more over the past five years.

Preeminent among them are some of the biggest tech names—Amazon.com, Facebook, Google parent Alphabet, and Microsoft, which drove much of the stock market gains in 2020.

The cumulative gain for the real growth stocks through October 12, 2020, was 195 percent versus 118 percent for the overall S&P 500 Growth Index and 75 percent for the overall S&P 500 Index.

Over a recent five-year period, these companies have significantly higher valuations and volatility than the S&P 500, but their share prices are likely to keep rising because investors looking for robust growth have so few choices.

In addition to the big tech names, the real growth stocks, whose performance has trounced the S&P 500's returns recently, include less prominent companies such as semiconductor manufacturer Broadcom...cable-TV and Internet giant Charter Communications...diabetes-testing company DexCom...software service providers Paycom Software and ServiceNow...and cystic-fibrosis drugmaker Vertex Pharmaceuticals.

9

Money Management

How to Become the CEO of Your Household Finances

The financial challenges confronting the head of a household are often comparable to those faced by a corporate CEO. Both must keep an eye on long-term goals while navigating day-to-day challenges and setbacks—ranging from small ones to sometimes colossal ones. *To incorporate CEO strategies into your family finances...*

• **Create a family finance mission statement.** Whether you're running a company or a family, it's easy to get so caught up in the *Here's what I have to do today* that you lose sight of the *Here's what I'm trying to do long-term.*

Examples: LinkedIn's mission statement is, "Connect the world's professionals to make them more productive and successful." Nordstrom's is, "Provide outstanding service every day, one customer at a time."

Household financial mission statements should similarly encapsulate financial plans or goals.

Examples: Spend wisely to allow a comfortable retirement at 65...protect the financial futures of current and future generations of our family.

Repeat the mission statements often, especially when times of crisis threaten to throw those goals off track.

• **Tune out the noise, but respond dynamically to fundamental change.** Even the best-laid plans inevitably come under threat, some relatively minor and some potentially catastrophic. For a CEO, that threat might be a new competitor or changing customer preferences. For a head of household, it might

Lauren Wybar, CFP, a financial advisor with Vanguard Personal Advisor Services, Silver Spring, Maryland. Vanguard.com be unexpected medical bills or a stock market crash....or job loss due to a global pandemic. For either the CEO or the head of household, the question is the same—*Should I try to stick with my existing plan as much as possible or quickly come up with a drastically new one?* Both options carry risk—change course too drastically based on every new development, and you'll never complete any long-term plan...but ignore new developments for too long, and you might be sticking with a plan that's now obsolete.

Savvy CEOs confront this dilemma with a pair of weapons—time and teams. They know that events that are developing rarely require an immediate response—for one thing, to respond immediately often means responding before all the relevant facts are known. That means they may reflect on possible changes for days or weeks before responding...waiting for the initial, emotional impulse for a knee-jerk reaction to pass while watching to see how events unfold...gathering information... and soliciting input from a team of trusted underlings, analysts, and/or consultants.

A head of household also should delay reacting to unexpected news until the initial emotional response of hearing the news passes. And he/she, too, should confer with a "team" before acting. If the change is financial, this team might include a financial adviser, tax adviser, estate-planning attorney, and/or a friend or relative who is very good with money. If the change is health-related, the team might include a primary care physician and medical specialists. *General questions to ask include the following...*

• **Do I need to change anything about my current plan to reach my goals, and if so, what?**

• **Are there any tools or resources available specifically for people facing this situation?"**

For example, if you or your spouse has just been diagnosed with an expensive-to-treat medical condition that is not well-covered by your insurance, there might be nonprofit organizations that make grants to people who have this condition.

To create more detailed questions, read about the responses other people have made to this change, describe these and then ask, *Would a similar response make sense for me?*

• **Pursue expense-trimming with the same vigor as earning.** Successful CEOs know that belt-tightening isn't just something to do in difficult times—every dollar saved at any time is a dollar that can be put to productive use. Households should consider cost-cutting a continuous process too. Unfortunately, most don't bother cutting costs until a financial emergency occurs...and many don't even have a firm grasp on where their money is going.

Helpful: Mint.com offers useful free tools for tracking spending. Many credit cards provide spending breakdowns as well. Once you have a handle on where your money is going, divide your expenses into necessities and discretionary expenses. Rank the discretionary expenses in order of importance to you. Then eliminate most or all of the entries at the bottom of the list, and redirect the money previously spent there to achieving your most important financial goals.

MONEY SMARTS...

Before You Take on More Debt...

Cut your budget to necessities, and stop contributions to retirement and education accounts. Take advantage of free financial guidance from organizations such as the National Association of Personal Financial Advisors (NAPFA.org) and the Association for Financial Counseling & Planning Education (AFCPE.org). Look at loan options, not only from banks but also from family members who may be willing to lend at no or low interest. Use a credit card to cover expenses only as a last resort. Make a plan to repay it and handle your finances in the future—plot a repayment timeline showing how long you will rely on debt and how you will pay it off.

The Wall Street Journal

Smart Ways to Raise Emergency Cash Quickly

Daniel Duca, CFP, managing adviser at Altfest Personal Wealth Management, which oversees more than $1 billion in client assets, New York City. Altfest.com

Even before the pandemic crisis hit, the Federal Reserve found that 60 percent of U.S. households couldn't quickly gather enough cash to cover three months of living expenses. That became an even greater challenge amid millions of job cuts and deflated interest rates. *But there are various steps you can take to bolster your cash cushion while limiting damage to your long-term financial plans...*

STRATEGY #1: **Reduce your contributions to long-term savings, including 401(k)s, IRAs, and/or 529 college savings plans.** Although this could leave you in a weaker financial position when you retire or your children attend college, you may be able to make up for the reduction later in the year or next year. *How to do this...*

- **Consider cutting contributions to 529 education savings plans first.** Your children or grandchildren can help pay for college by taking out federal loans and/or going to less expensive schools. However, when deciding whether to reduce your 529 contributions, keep in mind that in many states you can take a state tax deduction for at least part of your contribution to that state's 529 plan.

- **Weigh various factors when deciding whether to cut contributions to Roth accounts versus traditional retirement accounts.** Keep in mind that, unlike with a traditional 401(k) or IRA, you don't get a tax deduction on Roth contributions that you make...and if you are in a cash crunch, you may need those deductions to lower your tax burden. However, also consider that in the long run, Roth contributions may make sense for some people because future tax rates may be higher than current tax rates. That benefits a Roth account because, unlike with traditional retirement accounts, the money in a Roth account is not taxed when you eventually withdraw it.

- **Cut your 401(k) "match" amount last.** Many companies match a certain percentage of what an employee contributes to a 401(k), typically 50 percent of every dollar up to 6 percent of salary. Maximize getting this free money.

STRATEGY #2: **Withdraw from existing taxable investments.** This allows your retirement account investments to continue to benefit from tax-advantaged growth. However, you must choose which investments to sell strategically or else you could lock in steep losses and/or face a big tax bill on investment gains. *How to do this...*

- **You can gain access to more cash by suspending automatic reinvestment of dividends generated from stocks and funds... and capital gains from funds.** Keep in mind that you must pay tax on this income whether you reinvest or not.

- **If you need more emergency cash, sell bonds or bond funds that have appreciated.** This allows your hard-hit stocks and stock funds time to recover.

- **Sell stocks and stock funds last.**

Use this litmus test for each holding: At the current price, would you be willing to buy and hold it as a long-term investment? If not, it becomes a candidate for sale. Keep in mind that if you sell a stock whose current market value is below its cost basis, you may be able to take a capital loss to offset gains from profitable investment sales, as well as up to $3,000 in income, this year or in the future.

STRATEGY #3: **Borrow against your taxable investments.** Many brokerage firms offer an investment line of credit, allowing you to borrow up to 40 percent to 80 percent of the current value of your taxable portfolio assets, which serve as collateral for the loan. You pay a variable interest rate, recently ranging from 3 percent to 6.575 percent.

Downside: If financial markets fall and lower the value of your pledged assets, you may get a "maintenance call" in which your brokerage firm requires that you post additional collateral or pay down part of your outstanding balance.

What to do: Be sure your broker explains how large a decline might trigger a call. Each firm has proprietary standards based on the type and amount of assets pledged and your loan balance.

STRATEGY #4: **Take Social Security earlier than planned.** You can claim benefits as early as age 62 and start receiving a guaranteed monthly stream of income for the rest of your life. However, the amount of the monthly payments will be significantly lower than if you wait until full retirement age—66 to 67 depending on when you were born—or until 70, the longest the eventual amounts will keep rising. For every year you delay, eventual payments increase by about 8 percent.

Helpful twist: There are ways to access some Social Security income early and still get higher benefits later on. *How to do this...*

•If you're between 62 and full retirement age, start taking benefits—then withdraw your claim within 12 months. As long as you repay the total amount of benefits you received, Social Security will treat your claim as if it never happened. This is effective if you just need cash for a few months to tide you over and you don't expect your total monthly earned income in 2021 to exceed $1,580—otherwise your benefits are reduced by one dollar for each two dollars over this amount.

•**If you already have reached full retirement age,** take benefits as long as you need the money, then suspend them. You don't have to pay any cash back, and for every month you suspend payments, up to age 70, you earn delayed retirement credits, which will ultimately result in a higher monthly benefit payment amount.

Example: If your full retirement age is 66 and you start taking payments at that time, then suspend them at age 67 and delay resuming benefits for three years, the payments you get each month starting at age 70 will be about 24 percent higher than those at 67.

STRATEGY #5: **Tap the equity in your home.** Use your home as collateral to get a new loan with a relatively attractive interest rate. Your loan and rate are contingent on factors such as your credit score, your income and the amount of equity in your home, which is the difference between the current value of your home and what you owe on your existing mortgage. Keep in mind that if you default, your lender could foreclose on your home. *How to do this...*

•**Do a cash-out refinance.** It allows you to refinance your mortgage at today's low interest rates and borrow extra money. Keep in mind that although your monthly payments may be lower, the balance you owe on the new mortgage will be the same as the old one plus any additional money you borrow. Recent rates averaged 2.45 percent for a 15-year refinance and 3.15 percent for a 30-year.

•**Get a home-equity line of credit (HELOC).** This is best for people who don't need the money immediately but may need it soon. You draw only on the money you need when you need it. Interest rates on HELOCs are variable and recently averaged 3.75 percent. Closing costs often are minimal.

•**Avoid home-equity loans.** If the value of your home declines, which is not unusual in a recession, you could owe more than the home is worth. Closing costs can be as high as a refinance, but the rates are not as low.

•**Avoid reverse mortgages**—the entire loan may become due shortly after you move out of the home for more than a year, sell it, pass away, or become delinquent on your property taxes and/or insurance.

STRATEGY #6: **Withdraw cash from your retirement accounts.** I rarely recommend digging into these accounts because the long-term tax-advantaged growth they offer is so valuable.

Important: The money you repay on loans and hardship withdrawals does not count toward the annual contribution caps for retirement accounts. Also, check to make sure your company actually offers these new loan and hardship options since it is not obligated to do so.

Ways to Raise Your Credit Score

Credit-builder loans are put into a CD by the lender, usually for one year—you pay part of the loan amount, plus interest, monthly, then take out the cash and interest at year's end. (These loans typically are for up to $1,000.) The high interest rates of 10 percent to 15 percent may be worthwhile if you need to build your payment history. *Have rent payments reported to credit bureaus*—ask your landlord to do this if it is not happening already. *Become an authorized credit card user on someone else's account*—payments will track for both of you. *Get a secured credit card*—you make a deposit that becomes your credit limit, then pay off all charges monthly. Set up automatic payments so that you never forget to pay bills on time.

ThePennyHoarder.com

The Best Credit Cards for Groceries, Gasoline, Online Shopping, and More

Sara Rathner, credit card expert for NerdWallet.com, a website that provides information and reviews about credit cards and other financial products and topics.

Here are the best credit cards for 2021 and beyond to maximize your rewards.* (Unless otherwise noted, there is no annual fee and bonuses have no limits.)

ONLINE SHOPPING

Three online retailers have dominated during the pandemic—Amazon.com, Target.com, and Walmart.com. Each has a credit card offering a big 5 percent cash back.

• **Amazon Prime Rewards Visa Signature** offers 5 percent back at Amazon.com and Whole Foods—but only if you have an Amazon Prime membership, which typically costs $119 per year. The card also offers 2 percent back at restaurants, gas stations, and drugstores...and one percent on everything else. You can claim your rewards as cash back or redeem them for Amazon.com purchases. New applicants receive a $100 Amazon gift card upon approval.

• **Target RedCard** offers 5 percent back on almost all Target purchases in-store and on Target.com. It also provides free shipping for most Target.com purchases (excluded are optical and nonreturnable items and contract mobile phones) and extends the window for returns/exchanges by 30 days, which for most items means 120 days rather than 90.

• **Capital One Walmart Rewards Mastercard** offers 5 percent back on purchases made at Walmart.com. You get 5 percent back on in-store Walmart purchases during your first 12 months as a cardholder if those purchases are made through the Walmart Pay app that is linked to the card. Other Walmart in-store purchases earn 2 percent back, as do restaurants, gas and travel purchases. Everything else gets one percent.

Helpful: Many Chase and MasterCard credit cards offer complementary one-year memberships for ShopRunner, a service that offers free two-day shipping and free returns at more than 100 retailers. Membership normally costs $79 per year. American Express offers ShopRunner membership free for as long as you remain an eligible card member.

BEST FOR HOME IMPROVEMENT

People are spending more time at home—and more money on their homes as a result.

• **Lowe's Advantage Card** offers cardholders a choice when they make purchases at Lowe's or Lowes.com—5 percent cash back...or special financing terms, such as zero percent interest if paid in full within six months on purchases of $299 or more.

• **The Home Depot Credit Card** offers zero percent interest if paid in full within six months on purchases of $299 or more.

New applicants also can get up to $100 off qualifying purchases through the end of January 2022 (at press).

*Offers are current at press time, but are subject to change.

Warning: If you accept this Lowe's or Home Depot financing offer but don't pay off the purchase in full by the end of the zero percent period, you will be charged retroactive interest on the entire purchase price.

SUPERMARKET SPENDING

Rising prices for certain grocery items such as meats have pushed supermarket bills higher, which makes cards that offer bonuses for purchases at markets extra valuable.

•**Blue Cash Everyday** from American Express offers 3 percent cash back on up to $6,000 in U.S. supermarket purchases each year (at select stores, including ALDI, FreshDirect, ShopRite, Stop & Shop, Trader Joe's and Whole Foods)...2 percent at gas stations and some department stores...and one percent on everything else. New cardholders also receive $100 back if they spend $2,000 in the first six months...and 20 percent back (up to $150) on Amazon.com purchases during those initial six months.

•**Blue Cash Preferred** from American Express offers 6 percent cash back on up to $6,000 in annual U.S. supermarket spending at select stores. It also offers 6 percent back on many streaming subscription services...3 percent at gas stations and on certain transit expenses... and one percent on everything else. New cardholders can receive $350 back by spending $3,000 in the first six months. The card has no fee the first year, then costs $95 annually.

Rule of thumb: If you spend more than $3,167 on groceries each year, it's worth paying this card's annual fee...if not, the no-annual-fee Blue Cash Everyday is probably better.

FOOD TAKEOUT AND DELIVERY

Restaurant dining is recovering, and these cards offer savings whether you eat in restaurants or order food to-go or for delivery.

•**US Bank Altitude Go Visa Signature** card offers the equivalent of 4 percent back on restaurant spending including to-go and delivery. Technically, you earn four points per dollar spent, but those points don't expire and can be exchanged for cash back at the rate of one cent apiece. This card also provides the equivalent of 2 percent back on grocery store, gas station and streaming-service spending, and one percent on everything else. New cardholders receive 20,000 bonus points—the equivalent of $200—for spending $1,000 in the first 90 days.

•**Capital One SavorOne Rewards** offers 3 percent cash back at restaurants, including take-out and delivery, as well as entertainment, streaming services and grocery stores and one percent on other purchases. New cardholders earn a $200 bonus by spending $500 in the first three months.

GAS

Driving is recovering quickly as more people are returning to offices and getting out and about. A card that offers cash back on gas could also be attractive if you expect to do lots of long-distance driving this year rather than flying.

•**Sam's Club Mastercard** offers 5 percent back on up to $6,000 in gas purchases annually—even gas not purchased at Sam's Club—plus 3 percent back on restaurant and Sam's Club purchases and one percent on everything else. There's no annual fee, but you must be a member of Sam's Club, a warehouse club with an annual $45 membership fee (currently offering a $45 gift card for purchases in Sam's Club when you sign up).

•**Costco Anywhere Visa** by Citi offers 4 percent cash back on up to $7,000 in gas-eligible purchases annually—even gas not bought at Costco—plus 3 percent back on eligible restaurant and travel spending, 2 percent on Costco and Costco.com purchases and one percent on everything else. Costco membership ($60 per year) is required.

OTHER SPENDING

These cards are among the best options for purchases that don't fit the spending categories above.

•**Citi Double Cash Mastercard** offers 2 percent cash back on all purchases without limit.

Alternative: Alliant Cashback Signature Visa offers 2.5 percent cash back on virtually all purchases up to $10,000 in spending per month. But it has a $99 annual fee (waived the first year), and when that's factored in, it tops Citi Double Cash's 2 percent only if you charge more than $19,800 on it per year. You must be a member of Alliant Credit Union to qualify, but anyone can join by becoming a member of Alliant's partner charity, Foster Care to Success—the credit union will pay this charity's membership fee for you.

•**Discover it Cash Back** offers 5 percent cash back on up to $1,500 in spending per quarter in "bonus categories" that change each quarter, plus one percent on other purchases. Those bonus categories often are well-suited to today's shopping.

Example: In the first three months of 2021, you got 5 percent cash back on purchases made at grocery stores, Walgreens, and CVS....and during the final three months of 2021, you can get 5 percent cash back on Amazon.com, Walmart.com, and Target.com purchases. If you're a new cardholder, Discover will match all the rewards you earned during your first year, essentially increasing your cash back on these purchases to 10 percent.

•**Chase Freedom Flex** offers 5 percent cash back on up to $1,500 in spending each quarter in rotating categories, much like the Discover it card above. It also offers 3 percent back at drugstores and restaurants, including takeout and delivery...and 1.5 percent on everything else. Chase doesn't announce all of the upcoming year's categories in advance, however. New cardholders also can receive $200 for spending $500 in the first three months.

BEST FOR LOW INTEREST RATES

Recent challenges have left some Americans struggling to pay their bills. If you carry a balance on your credit cards, a low interest rate is much more important than a credit card's rewards program.

•**US Bank Platinum Visa** offers zero percent APR on new purchases and balance transfers for the first 20 months with the card, plus no annual fee. After that, the variable interest rate is 14.49 percent to 24.99% depending on your credit rating.

•**Citi Diamond Preferred Mastercard** and **Citi Double Cash Mastercard**, mentioned above, both offer a zero percent APR on balance transfers for 18 months. After that the variable APR for Citi Diamond Preferred is 14.74 percent to 24.74 percent...and for Citi Double Cash, it's 13.99 percent to 23.99 percent. These cards have a 3 percent balance transfer fee, which is relatively low by industry standards.

CAUTION...

Credit and Debit Card Fraud Has Risen

Credit and debit card fraud has risen since the coronavirus pandemic shut down the U.S. economy. The dollar volume of attempted fraudulent transactions rose 35 percent in April 2020 from one year earlier. Most attempts were caught before they hit cardholders' accounts—but the sheer volume of attempts means that more thieves may succeed, which could lead to higher losses for card issuers and, eventually, higher costs for consumers. Thieves are using multiple techniques to steal—they generate random card numbers until they happen to hit real ones...they use phone calls, e-mails, and text messages to trick consumers into handing over information...and they take advantage of the very long wait times at card issuers' contact numbers, which make it hard for fraud victims to report crimes quickly.

The Wall Street Journal

BEST CARD FOR FUTURE TRAVEL

Travel rewards credit cards that charge big annual fees might not make much sense now, but if you're looking forward to the day when traveling the world fully returns, a travel card that helps you save up for a future trip could be a smart choice.

•**Capital One Venture** has a $95 annual fee and provides two miles for every dollar spent, plus a onetime bonus of 50,000 miles if you spend $3,000 in the first three months (100,000 miles if you spend $20,000 in the first 12 months). Miles can be redeemed for travel expenses at one cent apiece, so if you reach the bonus level, you'll have at least $560 in credit. Unlike most travel cards, its miles can be easily redeemed for virtually any travel expenses—you're not restricted to certain airlines or hotel chains, you don't need to chase down elusive awards tickets, and there are no blackout dates.

How to Keep a Late Payment from Damaging Your Credit Score

If you're accidentally late on a credit card payment, there's a chance you can keep it off your credit report. To do so, make the payment and then either call the card issuer or write a "goodwill letter" apologizing for missing the due date, explaining why your payment was late, promising not to be late in the future, and requesting that the issuer not pass along the information to the credit-reporting agencies. The issuer is not required to honor your request, but many will. If you decide to do it by phone, understand that you may have to work your way up to a manager. Unfortunately, if your card is with Bank of America or Chase, they have policies prohibiting them from honoring goodwill adjustment requests.

ThePointsGuy.com

Ask Credit Card Issuers to Waive Annual Fees

If you signed up for a card for its travel benefits but haven't been able to travel, point this out, note that you've been a good customer, and ask that the fee be waived for a year. Issuers agreed to waive or lower annual fees upon request 70 percent of the time prior to the pandemic, and they're even more likely to do so now...or they might offer rewards points or miles as compensation.

Ted Rossman, an analyst at CreditCards.com.

Beware Credit Score Damage from Incorrectly Reported "Missed Payments"

Federal law requires lenders to report accounts as "current" if program terms are followed and payments weren't in arrears prior to modification, but many borrowers have reported that lenders have inappropriately reported a "missed payment," which can lower a score by up to 100 points. Monitor your score, and if it drops sharply, request free credit reports at AnnualCreditReport.com and challenge any "missed payment" with the credit-monitoring agencies.

Herb Weisbaum, contributing editor for nonprofit consumer organization Checkbook.org and founder of the website ConsumerMan.com.

MONEY HELP...

Financial Self-Defense Against Job Loss

If you have been laid off or worry that you may be, first analyze all of your spending and break it into fixed and discretionary. Find your rock-bottom cost of living, and figure out how you must cut to get to it. *Negotiate with lenders, cable and phone companies, Internet providers, and anyone else you pay regularly. Pause retirement contributions and college savings. Consider changing your tax withholding. Check health insurance options*—depending on your income and family size, you may be eligible for Medicaid. *Talk to your children* so they understand what is happening, and ask for their ideas on cost-cutting. *Consolidate credit card debt,* and ask card issuers for a rate adjustment or other relief.

Roundup of financial advisors reported in *The Wall Street Journal.*

Flexible Spending Accounts Now More Flexible

Stephen Miller, certified employee benefit specialist and online manager/editor of compensation and benefits for the Society for Human Resource Management, Alexandria, Virginia. SHRM.com

Has the pandemic thrown off your expectations for health-care costs in 2021? Many consumers are spending less than they anticipated because they continue postponing elective surgery and/or avoiding routine visits to doctors and dentists. Or they are spending more because of an unanticipated jump in costs related to COVID-19.

If you're enrolled in a health-care Flexible Spending Account (FSA), miscalculations could mean that you end up forfeiting the unspent amount of the pretax FSA payroll deductions you designated for this calendar year or getting less of a tax break than you could have.

Fortunately, new IRS rules could allow FSA account holders to adjust the amounts that they have designated to be taken out of their paychecks for the remainder of the year. The new rules also apply to amounts you may have taken out of your paycheck for a dependent-care FSA, which you may have overestimated if, for instance, you are skipping summer camp or have not had daycare expenses while staying at home. *What you need to know…*

The IRS rules enable—but don't require—your employer to let you adjust the amount you're contributing to your FSA in 2021. That could include lowering your contributions, ending them entirely, increasing them, or even opening an FSA if you didn't sign up for one during open enrollment.

The employer can allow you to "carryover" as much as $550 of the money you contributed to an FSA in 2020 to anytime in 2021, up from the $500 carryover allowed in earlier years. This new increase is permanent and indexed to keep up with inflation.

If you contributed an amount to an FSA in 2020 and didn't spend it all, you can spend the remaining money on qualifying expenses until the end of 2022 if your employer offers a "grace period." Ordinarily, such FSA grace periods extend only two and a half months after the end of the plan year—until March 15 for a plan with a December 31 plan-year end date. At press, this rollover has been extended through 2022 only.

Important: As in earlier years, FSAs cannot offer both carryovers and grace periods—employers must choose one, the other, or neither.

If you participate in an FSA, contact your employer's benefits department to check whether it is allowing changes—most employers are expected to do so—and to what extent.

If changes are allowed, determine whether it makes sense for you to adjust the amount you are contributing based on the health-care or dependent-care costs you expect to incur. Consider doing this as soon as possible if you expect to reduce the designated amount—you can't reduce it below what has already been deducted from your paychecks.

If you contributed to an FSA in 2020 but did not use all the money, ask the benefits department whether you now have a grace period that extends to the end of 2022.

Double Your Money Safely

Daniel Pederson, CFP, president of Savings Bond Informer. He previously was supervisor of the savings bond division of the Federal Reserve Bank's Chicago-Detroit branch. DanielPederson.com

At a time when stock prices and bond yields are volatile, there's a way to double your money without taking risks.

It's the old-fashioned series EE U.S. savings bond. Keep it for 20 years, and it guarantees that you will get back at least double your investment. That's the equivalent of a 3.53 percent annual yield, far better than what other low-risk investments have been yielding. Income from EE savings bonds is state and local tax-exempt…and federal taxes are deferred until you redeem the bonds (or after 30 years when the bonds reach final maturity). It also may be federal tax–exempt if you use it to pay qualified higher education expenses.

But there's a catch—redeem these bonds before 20 years, and the annual yield is just 0.1 percent. The Treasury makes a onetime adjustment on the 20th anniversary of the purchase month, increasing redemption value to twice the purchase price. (These bonds cannot be redeemed for the first year following purchase, and modest penalties apply if they're held for less than five years.)

There's also a cap—you can't buy more than $10,000 of EE savings bonds per year. A couple can double that by buying bonds under each partner's name. A family could buy bonds under minor children's names, too, but the bonds will become property of those children and are not eligible for the education tax break.

What to do: Purchase EE savings bonds through TreasuryDirect.gov only if you're confident that you won't need the money for 20 years. Redeem as soon as the redemption value is adjusted at the 20-year mark—the annual yield is just 0.1 percent after that. Include instructions in your estate plan noting when these bonds should be sold and why that sale date makes sense.

Prepare Your Finances for an Emergency Handoff

Amanda DesBarres, owner of Help Unlimited, which provides personal money-management advice, with offices in the Washington, DC, metro area and Charlottesville, Virginia. DailyMoneyManager.com

Could someone step in and successfully manage your financial affairs if you are unable to do so yourself? Of course, you could execute a "financial power of attorney" designating someone as a "financial agent" to act on your behalf in financial matters if you're incapacitated. But just drafting that document with an attorney, which you should do, doesn't guarantee that this relative, friend, or adviser will know what to do. The issue isn't so much whether he/she lacks financial savvy—it's that figuring out someone else's finances on the fly is a massive challenge.

Having a financial plan in place for health emergencies is especially on many people's minds now because of the coronavirus pandemic, but an incapacitating emergency could come up at any time. *Here's how to prepare finances for an emergency handoff...*

SIMPLIFY IN ADVANCE

• **Consolidate credit cards and bank accounts.** Missed credit card payments are among the most common missteps when someone takes over your finances. The more cards you use, the greater the odds that there will be a problem. Cut back to only two, if possible.

If you have multiple checking or savings accounts, consider consolidating to one of each, preferably at the same bank—more accounts mean higher odds of overdrafts. Especially troublesome are accounts with automated withdrawals or payments—easily overdrawn if no one is paying close attention. If there are lots of CDs, savings accounts, and/or money-market accounts at different institutions, some could be easily overlooked.

• **Stick with paper statements.** It's perfectly fine for you to access your accounts online, but it's easy for someone else to overlook or be shut out of your online-only accounts, which may be difficult to access. Bills and statements that arrive in the mail provide a wonderful fail-safe. That's true even if the financial agent doesn't live near you—your mail can be forwarded to that person by the post office or a trusted neighbor.

DRAFT A ROAD MAP

• **Create a concise guide to your finances.** Having all of your financial information in one place will save your designated agent a lot of time and greatly reduce the odds that something will be missed. Handwrite this list, or type and print it. But don't save it on your computer or send it via e-mail—that would increase the risk that this sensitive info could be stolen. *Among the details to include...*

• Income sources. Note how each of your income streams arrives—pensions and Social Security payments often are direct-deposited into bank accounts, for example. If you have income that arrives by check, explain where it comes from, when it should arrive, and what to do if it doesn't arrive.

Example: If you have a rental property, your tenants or property-management company might send you paper checks each month.

• Recurring payments—including mortgage/rent, utilities, taxes (estimated income taxes and property taxes), insurance premiums... payments made to personal or household assistance providers...and other bills that recur on a regular basis. Search your checking account and credit card transaction histories to make sure you haven't missed any of these. For each listing, provide your account number, password/PIN, and the company's contact phone number or website, as well as a brief description of when and how it is paid. Indicate whether you write a check or have set up automatic payments from an account.

• Any payments made annually or semiannually deserve special attention—the less often a recurring bill is paid, the greater the odds that your financial agent will overlook it when reviewing your finances. This is common with long-term-care insurance, home/auto insurance, and property taxes. Highlight the dates these are due, and add a warning that this date is important.

Example: A woman was in a rehab facility when her long-term-care policy's bill arrived. The deadline passed before she or her loved ones realized anything was amiss. The insurer refused to reinstate the policy.

Helpful: Many insurers allow you to name a third party, such as a friend or family member, to be notified if the policy is behind in payments.

• Bank, investment, and credit card accounts. Include each institution's name and contact phone number, account number, and passwords/PINs.

• Financial professionals you work with. This could include a tax preparer, estate attorney, financial planner, investment adviser, and/or trust officer. Provide phone numbers and e-mail addresses. These pros might be able to help the agent answer questions about your finances—though likely only questions related to their specialties. In addition to keeping this list with your plan, give it to loved ones so if all else fails, these people can piece together your financial activity.

• Your personal information. Provide your full name, mailing address, e-mail address and phone number(s), date of birth, Social Security number, and mother's maiden name. If you were widowed within the past five years, include your late spouse's personal info, too. Photocopy your driver's license and health insurance/Medicare card and attach these to your financial guide.

PROVIDE FURTHER GUIDANCE

• Confirm that your financial guide is understood and properly stored. When you hand your guide to your financial agent, ask him to read it in your presence so that he can ask about anything that isn't clear. Ask him to store it where he stores his important documents—storing it anywhere else increases the odds that it will be lost. Review the guide annually together and make necessary updates—this is also a good way to confirm that he remembers where your guide is stored.

• Offer guidance about paying big bills. If your agent is one day forced to take charge of your finances, it probably will be because you've had a medical emergency—which means that he might have to pay sizable health-care–related bills on your behalf. Provide advice—either in your written guide or verbally when you discuss it—about what to do if there isn't enough money in your bank account and emergency fund to pay big bills. You could recommend that the agent contact the billers to ask whether payments can be spread out over many months...and/or explain which of your investments should be tapped first if needed to help pay bills.

• Explain required minimum distributions (RMDs). Tax penalties can apply if insufficient withdrawals are made from tax-deferred retirement accounts each year. Unfortunately, RMDs often are overlooked when people take over older relatives' finances—many preretirees have never even heard of RMDs. If you must make RMDs (or will have to in the years ahead), make sure your loved one is aware of this. Provide details about how much must be withdrawn...from which account(s) to withdraw money...what to do with withdrawn money...and how to tell if the withdrawal already has been made for a particular calendar year.

GOOD TO KNOW...

Safe-Deposit-Box Dos and Don'ts

Locking away certain items in a bank safe-deposit box can be a good idea. Others, not so much. Cash? No—it may be hard to get to in an emergency. Social Security card? Yes. Passport? No—you might need it when the bank isn't open. Vital records (birth certificates, etc.)? Yes. Living will, power of attorney, etc.? No—copies are OK, but leave originals with your attorney so they're accessible to loved ones. Property records and car titles? Yes. Spare house key? No—you could get locked out when the bank isn't open. Home inventory? Yes—a list of the belongings in your home will help with insurance claims in case of disaster.

Kiplinger.com

Best Ways to Help a Grandchild Pay for College

Mark Kantrowitz, publisher of PrivateStudentLoans.guru.

More than half of the grandparents in the U.S. are saving or plan to save for their grandchildren's college expenses, according to a Fidelity Investments survey called "Generation Generosity." If you're one of them, how you decide to save and gift money for postsecondary education, including trade schools, should be determined by several factors. These include your grandchild's eligibility for need-based financial aid...your personal estate plan...income tax breaks you can get in the state where you live...and how much control you'd like to retain over when and how the money is distributed.

Four popular options and how to decide which is best for you...

- **Write a check directly to the college.** *Advantages...*
  - You ensure that your money will be used for tuition.
  - Because the IRS doesn't consider the payment to be a gift, it doesn't count against the $15,000 a year that you can give directly to a grandchild without triggering gift taxes. This may be useful for reducing the size of your taxable estate for estate-planning purposes. (*Note:* Payments for nontuition expenses such as books, travel, and/or room and board do count toward the $15,000 annual gift-tax exclusion.)

Drawback: Colleges often treat payments that are made directly to the college as "cash support" on the student's federal financial aid form, known as the Free Application for Federal Student Aid (FAFSA). Cash support is counted as untaxed student income, reducing aid by as much as 50 cents for every dollar of income. Some colleges even treat direct tuition payment as a "resource," which can have an even greater negative impact because every dollar contributed reduces the financial aid that the student qualifies for by a full dollar.

Best for: Grandparents whose grandchildren likely will not qualify for or need financial aid.

- **Open a 529 state-sponsored college-savings plan with your grandchild as the beneficiary.** *Advantages...*
  - You ensure that your money will be used for college expenses.
  - The investments in the plan grow tax-free, and eventual distributions are tax-free when used for qualified educational purposes including many nontuition expenses.
  - You can contribute as much as $15,000 a year ($30,000 if you are married) without triggering the gift tax. In a given year, you also are

allowed to contribute up to five years' worth of the annual gift-tax limit to the plan (as much as $75,000 or $150,000 if married). You won't, however, be able to give your grandchild any more money for five years without gift-tax consequences.

• Money held in a grandparent's 529 plan isn't counted as a parental or student asset when determining a student's aid eligibility.

• You receive a state income tax deduction or tax credit in 34 states on contributions for using a 529 plan offered by the state in which you reside. (Arizona, Arkansas, Kansas, Minnesota, Missouri, Montana, and Pennsylvania give you the break for contributing to any state's plan). *Drawbacks...*

• A 529 plan may have a very limited menu of investment options.

• Although assets in a grandparent-owned 529 plan are not counted in the financial aid formula, distributions are. They hurt your grandchild's aid eligibility because they're treated as his/her income, which is weighed more heavily than parental income and assets in the financial aid formula. You can work around this by delaying distributions until after the final tax year that counts toward the financial aid application for your grandchild's college years is filed (typically after January 1 of the student's sophomore year of college).

Best for: Grandparents who want to receive tax advantages on their contributions and maintain some control over the money if, for instance, the grandchild drops out of school, wins a scholarship, or goes to a school that's cheaper than expected.

• **Contribute to a 529 plan owned by the parents for the benefit of your grandchild.** *Advantages...*

• Like most 529 plans, the investments grow tax-free, distributions are tax-free for qualified educational purposes, and you still can contribute as much as $15,000 a year ($30,000 if you're married) without worrying about gift taxes...or you can "super-fund" the plan with up to five years' worth of contributions in a single year.

• Unlike grandparent-owned plans, distributions aren't counted as income in the financial aid formula. The money is considered a parental asset, which has less impact on financial aid. *Drawbacks...*

• A 529 plan may have a very limited menu of investment options.

• A parent controls the assets, not you, which creates a potential for family conflict.

Example: The parent can change the beneficiary from your grandchild to any qualifying family member, which includes siblings, aunts, uncles, nieces, nephews, first cousins—even themselves. The parent also has the option of withdrawing the money for non-education purposes, which could mean paying income tax and a 10 percent penalty on the earnings portion of the distribution.

Best for: Grandparents who don't want the responsibility of setting up and maintaining a 529 and who feel comfortable letting the parents make decisions.

• **Wait until after your grandchild graduates from college, and then help pay off his/her student loan.** *Advantages...*

• You can write the check directly to the lender to make sure the money is used for paying down debt, up to $15,000 ($30,000 if married) annually without triggering gift taxes.

• The prospect of getting help with post-graduation debt can give your grandchild an added incentive to graduate. *Drawbacks...*

• If you suffer unforeseen circumstances such as death or illness before your grandchild graduates, it may prevent you from being able to keep your promise.

Best for: Grandparents who are in good health and whose grandchildren are likely to finish school with a significant amount of student-loan debt.

Two options I would avoid...

• **Setting up an education trust for the grandchild.** In addition to the fact that setting up a trust can be costly, trust funds are considered to be part of the grandchild's assets on FAFSA. That hurts aid eligibility because colleges typically expect that 20 percent of the assets owned by a dependent student will be used for educational expenses each year.

• **Loaning money to your grandchild during college years,** then forgiving the debt after the child graduates. Colleges consider such loans during college years to be "cash support," which compromises your grandchild's financial aid chances.

New Financial and Health Protections for People with Chronic Disabilities

Martin M. Shenkman, CPA, JD, an estate- and tax-planning attorney with the New York City and Fort Lee, New Jersey, law firm Shenkman Law. His books include *Estate Planning for People with a Chronic Condition or Disability.* ShenkmanLaw.com

Living with a chronic health condition—such as Parkinson's disease, early-stage dementia, multiple sclerosis, or a history of strokes—might require that someone else makes health-care and financial decisions at some point. New options can help with this difficult process.

You might already know that an estate-planning attorney can prepare documents that detail your health-care preferences when you cannot make them yourself...and safeguard your assets during your life, not just after your death. However, the standard documents—living wills and powers of attorney—are not always effective.

The newer options offer potential solutions. These options are especially important if you suffer from a health condition that might leave you incapacitated for extended stretches. Because a major health issue could arise without warning, these documents are worthwhile for everyone.

A SUPPLEMENT TO A LIVING WILL

You may already have a living will—a document that lays out your health-care treatment preferences when you become unable to make decisions for yourself. This document might, for example, explain whether you would want mechanical ventilation and/or a feeding tube if there is no chance that you ever again would be able to live without these.

Problem: Living wills often focus on end of life, and they are not always properly enforced. Health-care providers sometimes fail to realize that a patient has a living will until the patient's family brings the document to their attention—by which point unwanted treatment already might have been provided. A health-care proxy, also called a medical power of attorney, could help here—it authorizes someone to make decisions for you when you can't. But what if you have no one to name...or if the person you do name is not available when you require treatment?

Better option: A Physician Orders for Life-Sustaining Treatment (POLST) details the health-care treatments that you would and would not want, much like a living will. But unlike a living will, a POLST is included in your digital medical records, which can be accessed by all health-care providers. It doesn't require the physicians to contact a family member to make decisions—your wishes are stated in the POLST. That greatly improves the odds that health-care providers know about it and avoids the delays and possible issues of contacting a family member to make a difficult decision. There's no harm in also carrying a copy of your POLST form and/or providing copies to your health-care providers and medical facilities where you receive treatment, though this is not necessary.

This form is not drafted by an estate-planning attorney—you fill it out with the assistance of your doctor or possibly your nurse practitioner or physician's assistant. Keep a copy with your estate-planning documents so that it is readily available.

POLSTs have been around for several years but only now are becoming widely available. Nearly every state currently has or is developing a POLST program. Visit POLST.org/programs-in-your-state for details...or ask your primary care physician or other health-care professional for details.

A POLST does not necessarily replace a living will. POLSTs generally have been used to detail the patient's treatment preferences for a specific illness or late-life condition. A living will, despite its flaws, might offer greater flexibility to address additional, unforeseen health conditions as well. Some in the estate-planning community do believe that POLST forms can be used more broadly, so it is possible that these might replace living wills entirely for some people in the future. For now, however, the safest solution for people who suffer from serious health problems or chronic conditions is to have both.

IN ADDITION TO A POWER OF ATTORNEY

Many people have drafted a power of attorney with the help of an estate-planning attorney. This document designates someone who will manage your personal business in the event that you are not able to. Typically, this person is a close relative, such as a spouse or descendant. Having this document in place is considered especially important for people who have potentially debilitating chronic health conditions. For these people, the odds that someone will have to act on their behalf is high.

Problem: Not everyone has a close relative qualified to serve in this crucial role. This person must be financially savvy, willing, and able to find the time to manage your affairs and honest enough to be trusted with your assets. Unfortunately, it's not uncommon for powers of attorney to be used to commit financial elder abuse.

Even if the person you select to manage your affairs is capable, willing, and honest, powers of attorney can be difficult to use. Financial institutions are wary of being sued for transferring control improperly, so they might insist on legal department reviews and other steps before allowing your agent to act on your behalf, inhibiting his/her ability to act promptly.

Better option: Instead of a power of attorney, use a revocable living trust, which allows you to better safeguard against financial abuse using several methods, such as appointing an institution as trustee. With a revocable living trust, some of your financial assets—but not retirement assets, annuities, or other restricted assets—are transferred to a trust. Then the trustee you name manages the assets when you cannot. Depending on your condition, this trustee might be a co-trustee who works with you when you are able to manage your own affairs...or a successor trustee who takes over only as needed, based on criteria that you and your estate-planning attorney have written into the trust. In addition to the trust, you can use a power of attorney for assets you cannot transfer to the trust, such as an IRA.

Revocable living trusts are not an entirely new planning tool, but historically they have been used mainly to avoid the costs and hassles of probate for multimillion-dollar estates. A new approach by financial institutions makes them a suitable option for managing assets should you not have an appropriate friend or family member to designate as your trustee. Several large, reliable, low-cost financial institutions now provide professional trustee services with fees low enough that they are accessible for estates of relatively modest size.

Examples: Fidelity Personal Trust Company (0.45 percent fees on the first $2 million* in the trust with a $4,500 minimum annual fee)...Charles Schwab Personal Trust Services (0.5 percent on the first $5 million* with a $5,000 annual minimum fee)...Vanguard National Trust Company (0.55 percent fees on assets below $5 million* with a minimum annual fee of $3,500 but also a minimum account balance of $1 million).

That still may seem like a lot of money, but having a professional available may be well worth the cost, especially for someone with a chronic condition.

Other advantages of having a revocable living trust...

- **You can obtain a tax ID number for a trust rather than list it under your Social Security number.** This tax ID number won't be in dozens of files and databases the way your Social Security number is, reducing the odds that an identity thief will be able to gain access.

- **You can name a "trust protector" for a revocable living trust.** This trust protector can be given the power to replace a trustee who is not doing a good job—an added level of checks and balances not possible with a power of attorney. An accountant you've worked

*Lower fee rates apply above these thresholds.

with for years or a family member who is not a beneficiary could be ideal for this role.

Speak with your estate-planning attorney about whether a revocable living trust or a power of attorney makes more sense for you. When you do, be honest with yourself and your attorney about the level of faith you have in the loved one you have named to act on your behalf in your power of attorney. Costs could be a factor, too—in addition to the fees charged by institutional trustees, expect to pay at least a few thousand dollars to set up a trust and several hundred dollars to a tax preparer to file a return for the trust each year.

---

6 Tricky Financial Traps of Divorce...and How to Avoid Them

Shawn Leamon, MBA, certified divorce financial analyst based in Dallas. He is host of the "Divorce and Your Money" podcast and author of *Divorce and Your Money: The No-Nonsense Guide.* DivorceAndYourMoney.com

---

Few divorces approach the recent $36 billion settlement between Amazon founder Jeff Bezos and his wife, MacKenzie. But divorce can have a big financial impact no matter what your assets look like.

Here's what you need to do to avoid being surprised—and hurt financially more than you have to be—if you contemplate divorce...

• **Take into account future taxes when splitting up assets.** Say one spouse opts for a 401(k) or an IRA worth $250,000 in the divorce...while the other takes the house or a nonretirement account worth $250,000. That might sound fair, but the spouse who gets the retirement-plan assets may be getting a bad deal if it's a traditional 401(k) or IRA—he/she likely will end up having to pay taxes on distributions. (This generally doesn't apply to Roth 401(k)s and Roth IRAs if the account has been held at least five years and the account holder is at least 59½.) If this spouse hasn't reached age 59½, the spouse also might face a 10 percent IRS penalty on a portion of the assets if he takes an early withdrawal.

What to do: Before accepting a divorce proposal that involves keeping most or all of a traditional 401(k)/IRA, confirm with your divorce attorney that the settlement takes the potential future tax bite into account.

• **Beware spending lots of money to search for hidden assets.** Some spouses attempt to conceal assets before their marriages end so that they don't have to split them with their soon-to-be exes. Money might be withdrawn from a bank account and hidden away...valuables might disappear from the home...or the spouse might say he has had big gambling losses. Unfortunately, hiring a forensic accountant to track down missing assets and/or engaging in a protracted legal battle over them could easily cost tens of thousands of dollars or more, with no guarantee of success. Unless the soon-to-be-ex is believed to have hidden a small fortune, tracking down these assets likely will cost more than it recovers.

What to do: Rather than launch a big investigation into hidden assets, people going through divorces should express their concerns to their attorneys and provide any evidence—for example, account statements showing mysterious withdrawals...or insurance inventories listing valuables that no longer are in their usual spots in your home. Also provide the attorney with copies of recent joint tax returns, which sometimes provide clues about hidden assets. The attorney could ask the suspected spouse pointed questions about these issues during a deposition or interrogatory. Spouses who have hidden assets often admit to what they have done when confronted directly because they fear getting caught lying under oath.

• **Decide whether or not it makes sense to hang on to the home.** Keeping the home is a common goal for divorced people, but family homes often are unnecessarily large for single people or single-parent families with children who will soon strike out on their own. Home maintenance can be difficult and expensive for a single person. And if there's a mortgage on the home, it likely will have to be refinanced in only the remaining homeowner's name—which might not be possible if this spouse doesn't have sufficient income to qualify for the loan…or the new loan might come with a higher interest rate.

What to do: Set aside any emotional connection to the home, and think objectively about whether keeping it is the best use of assets after divorce. Estimate how much the mortgage, taxes, insurance, and home upkeep will cost, then see how all this fits into a realistic post-divorce budget. Speak with a mortgage lender before finalizing divorce terms to see if it even will be possible to qualify for a new loan as a single homeowner—and if so, at what rate.

• **Don't assume your ex will do what your divorce agreement says he will do.** Divorce might not mark the end of fighting about money with a spouse. Some former spouses don't make required alimony or child-support payments. Also, an ex might fail to pay the premiums on a life insurance policy that names his former spouse as beneficiary even if it is required by the agreement.

What to do: If payments from an ex are a crucial component of your post-divorce income, create an emergency fund—or some other contingency plan, such as getting a home-equity line of credit (HELOC)—in case payments are missed. It could take many months to resolve the dispute through the courts. If any special payments are required down the road, create a calendar that lists these or arrange e-mail reminders from a calendar program such as Calender.Google.com to ensure that they are not missed. If you are the beneficiary of a life insurance policy under the divorce agreement, make sure the agreement requires your ex-spouse to regularly provide proof that the premiums are being paid and the policy remains in effect.

• **Separate any joint financial obligations.** Perhaps the divorce agreement assigns the ex-husband the responsibility for paying off the credit card that he usually used…and the ex-wife responsibility for paying off the one she usually used. That may seem like a fair agreement—until debt collectors start calling both former spouses because one hasn't made his/her payments.

Lenders are not obliged to honor the terms of a divorce. If a loan or credit card account was opened in both ex-spouses' names—or you live in a community-property state—the lender will consider both people responsible for payments no matter what the settlement says. The ex who wasn't supposed to be responsible for the debt could sue his former spouse for not living up to the terms of the divorce agreement, but that could take months to sort out and cost thousands of dollars in legal bills.

What to do: Seek a divorce agreement that requires as much debt as possible to be paid off before the divorce is finalized. Debts that cannot be paid off should be transferred to new loans/accounts that are opened in just one spouse's name, and the joint loans/accounts should be closed. If one spouse is keeping the house, the mortgage could be refinanced with a loan taken out in only that spouse's name, with the other spouse agreeing to transfer the title to that spouse.

If the spouses are not able to pay off all joint debts before the divorce, the ex who is not responsible for paying off a debt should insist on receiving account statements proving that debt payments are being made as directed by the divorce agreement.

• **Be aware of the possible ways that alimony could end.** It's common for divorce agreements to include clauses terminating alimony if the ex on the receiving end remarries or even if she cohabitates for a specified period of time. Also, an ex who pays alimony might return to court to ask that the payments be reduced if his income declines…or if the recipient's income increases. And alimony payments end if the payer dies. The surviving ex can make a claim on the estate for any payments owed at the time of death, but unless there are life insurance proceeds for unpaid alimony, no further payments are required.

What to do: Spouses who will receive alimony should review the terms of their divorce agreement before moving in with a new partner to make sure that they understand the potential financial implications. And they should resist the urge to brag about salary increases to their former spouses.

Also, a divorced person who will depend on alimony should confirm with his/her attorney that the divorce agreement will include a life insurance policy on the other former spouse's life, naming the alimony-dependent spouse as beneficiary.

One more alimony twist to keep in mind when constructing a post-divorce budget: Under new tax rules that affect divorces finalized in or after 2019, former spouses who pay alimony no longer can deduct those payments from their income taxes...and spouses who receive alimony no longer have to pay taxes on this money. (These new rules do not affect you if your divorce was finalized prior to 2019.)

A New 0.5 Percent Fee Will Increase Mortgage Refinancing Cost by $1,400, on Average

To help offset anticipated pandemic-related losses, Fannie Mae and Freddie Mac are imposing the fee on refinance loans that they back. To avoid the extra up-front fee, a homeowner likely could instead pay a rate one-eighth-percentage-point higher, although that means slightly higher monthly payments totaling more than the added fee over the life of the loan. The fee doesn't apply to refinanced mortgages not sold to Fannie or Freddie, such as FHA loans or private loans.

Keith Gumbinger, vice president of New Jersey–based HSH Associates, which publishes consumer-loan information. HSH.com

Points or No Points? The Mortgage Dilemma

Keith Gumbinger, vice president of New Jersey–based HSH Associates, which publishes consumer-loan information. HSH.com

Mortgage lenders typically offer borrowers the option of lowering their interest rates by paying "discount points" at closing. If you're in the market for a "jumbo" mortgage these days, paying discount points, which are sometimes simply called points, could be a great deal.

Each point typically costs one percent of the mortgage amount—$3,000 for a $300,000 mortgage, for example. How much each point lowers your interest rate varies, but for standard mortgages, it usually is about 0.25 percentage points, such as from 3.5 percent to 3.25 percent. But as of early 2021, paying a discount point with a jumbo mortgage could reduce your rate by more—often 0.5 to 1.0 percentage point, depending on the lender—which could reduce monthly payments by about $150 to more than $400 on a $600,000 30-year loan.

Reason for the different policy: Jumbo mortgages are those too large for lenders to easily resell on the secondary market—in 2021, that meant larger than $548,250...or in certain high-cost areas, larger than $822,375. Lenders often keep these mortgages on their books for the duration of the loans, dramatically increasing their risk. Offering attractive deals on jumbo mortgage points encourages borrowers to pay more up front, which reduces lenders' risk during these uncertain economic times. The up-front payments also help lenders cope with their pandemic-related cash-flow problems.

What to do: When you request jumbo mortgage quotes from lenders, ask what your rate would be if you paid one or two discount points. Anything much above a 0.25-percentage-point reduction per discount point is a better-than-normal deal worth strongly considering, assuming that you can afford the added up-front expense. Obtain multiple quotes—

the lender that offers the lowest mortgage rate might not offer the lowest rate when you pay points.

One caveat: Pay discount points only if you expect to stay in the home and not refinance for at least three to five years.

How to Save Thousands on Real Estate Commissions

Stephen Brobeck, PhD, senior fellow and former executive director of the nonprofit Consumer Federation of America, Washington, DC. He is author of several Consumer Federation studies on real estate brokerage. ConsumerFed.org

Home sellers in the U.S. typically pay a 5 percent or 6 percent commission—usually split between the home seller's real estate agent and the buyer's agent. That's a staggering payment of $25,000 or $30,000 to sell a $500,000 home—as much as buying a car.

If you want to save some money when selling your home, the best strategy is to attempt to negotiate a lower rate. These attempts won't always work, but it's worth trying—you could save thousands of dollars with just a few minutes of effort.

HOW—AND WITH WHOM—TO NEGOTIATE

The key to negotiating real estate commissions is to ask multiple agents for a lower rate before signing a listing agreement with anyone. Only about 27 percent of agents are willing to negotiate down from the standard commissions, according to a 2019 study by the nonprofit Consumer Federation of America, so if you ask only one, your odds aren't great. But ask four or more, and your odds improve dramatically.

It's up to you to raise the subject of commissions—agents almost never mention this if they can avoid it. If your home is more valuable than most in the area and/or you can sell and buy through the same agent, raise these topics before discussing commissions to make sure that the agent has as much incentive as possible to agree to a lower commission. If an agent says he won't accept less than the standard rate, say you'll keep him in mind but that you have several other agents who you're going to contact before making your decision.

If an agent is willing to lower his commission, it is most likely to be by one-half to one percentage point, which would be $2,500 or $5,000 for selling a $500,000 home. Larger reductions are unlikely because listing agents don't actually pocket all of that money—half of the commission typically goes to the buyer's agent.

Finding four or more real estate agents who are worth calling can be challenging. Start by asking people you trust who live in your area whether they had a good experience with a local agent. But don't stop when you get one appealing recommendation, as most people do. Keep asking around until you have at least four. Look up each recommended agent on Zillow.com before making contact. The Consumer Federation studied the agent reviews and information provided by five real estate–related websites and concluded that Zillow's are the most useful. As with other online customer reviews, some could be fake, so put the greatest weight in long reviews—positive or negative—that provide specific details, which are more likely to be legitimate rather than brief reviews that are glowing but lacking in specifics.

Use Zillow to confirm that each agent has sold multiple homes within the past year...that these homes sold for close to their listing prices...and that the agents have been working in the area for at least a decade. Examine the photos and video included on each agent's current listings. Are these visually attractive compared with the ones on other listings...or do they seem amateurish? The quality of photos and videos truly does influence buyers—especially if buyers prefer to tour homes online, rather than in person.

Warning: Never use online real estate agent recommendation/rating websites such as TopAgentsRanked.com and EffectiveAgents.com to choose an agent. Most sites like these actually just recommend whichever agents agree to pay the referral site a slice of their commission. The best agents in an area are almost never willing to pay these sites.

If a discount real estate brokerage is active in your area, proceed with caution. While it may offer rates as low as one percent, discount brokerages often hire relatively inexperienced agents and those agents might put limited time and effort into marketing homes than other agents. Still, if a discount broker's agent seems appealing after investigating him on Zillow as described above, this could be a viable option, especially in a hot real estate market.

WHEN AN AGENT AGREES TO TAKE LESS

Before committing to work with an agent who agrees to take less than the standard commission...

- **Confirm that the reduction will be entirely from the listing agent's share of the commission.** As noted above, sellers' agents traditionally split commissions down the middle with buyers' agents. But when a seller's agent agrees to take less than the standard commission, it's best for you if the buyer's agent still receives his/her standard amount. Buyer's agents tend to steer clients away from homes that offer less than the standard buyer's agent commission.

Example: If the standard commission in your area is 6 percent percent but you find an agent willing to work for 5 percent, confirm that this means your agent will take 2 percent and offer buyers' agents 3 percent.

- **Confirm that the agent will not spend less marketing your home because of the lower commission.** If his other listings feature open houses, slick professional photos, and online virtual tours, yours should, too.

- **Ask, "What commission would you accept if in the end you represent the buyer as well as me?"** It's reasonable to request especially attractive terms if the agent does not have to split his commission with a buyer's agent. Representing both seller and buyer, called "dual agency," is not permitted in Alaska, Colorado, Florida, Kansas, Maryland, Oklahoma, Texas, and Vermont, however.

Example: An agent might agree to reduce his commission from 6 percent to 5.5 percent and drop it again to 5 percent if he also represents the eventual buyer.

More from Stephen Brobeck, PHD...

Commissions for Buyers

Commissions can affect home buyers even though they don't directly compensate their agents. How? Buyer's agents sometimes nudge clients toward properties being sold by their own firms so that the company can double-dip on commissions...and/or steer them away from properties that offer less than the standard commission. Before contacting buyer's agents, skim through home listings on a real estate website such as Zillow or Trulia to find a few properties that seem to meet your needs. Jot these down, then call an agent you're considering. During the conversation, ask about these specific properties. If the agent steers you away from these listings and toward other properties, look up the properties that he mentions on Zillow or Trulia—if they're offered only by this agent's firm, find a different agent.

In some areas, buyers will come across "discount buyer's agents." These discounters refund a portion of the commissions they receive, often called a "commission rebate," back to their clients. This can be a viable money saver for buyers who are very confident in their ability to evaluate real estate, but less experienced buyers should proceed with great caution—many discounters have limited experience and/or provide less hand-holding when it comes to deciding how much to offer for properties...spotting problems with properties...and closing real estate deals. These discounters are not in every market and are not legal in Alabama, Alaska, Kansas, Louisiana, Mississippi, Missouri, Oklahoma, Oregon, and Tennessee...and Iowa prohibits rebates if two or more brokers are used for the transaction.

10

Tax Savvy

How to Use Losses to Cut Your Taxes

By selling stocks and/or funds that have suffered losses, you can offset gains on investments that have registered profits...and possibly lower taxes on regular income, too. *But to take the greatest advantage of your so-called capital losses, you need to use the strategies that are described below and avoid making various mistakes...*

• **Don't abandon investments that you still believe in just to generate tax savings.** Investors often sell an investment at a loss just before it rebounds. Consider selling an investment that has losses only if you don't believe that it has good future prospects...it no longer fits into your strategy or your target mix of allocations...and/or you would not buy the investment at its current price. Alternatively, if you are selling a fund that you still like, consider investing in a similar fund at the same time, but don't violate the "wash sale rule." (See below.)

• **Within 30 days before or after you sell an investment at a loss, don't invest in one that is "substantially identical."** This could violate what's known as the IRS "wash sale rule" and invalidate your loss for tax purposes. The rule applies even if the selling is in a taxable account and the buying is in a tax-advantaged account such as an IRA. It also applies if the investments are from different sources but virtually identical, such as the Vanguard S&P 500 exchange-traded fund (VOO)...Vanguard 500 Index fund (VFINX)... and SPDR S&P 500 ETF (SPY), which all track the same market index.

Work-around strategy: Quickly buy a fund with similar characteristics but not substantially identical to the one you sell. For example, you could sell your S&P 500 ETF and

David Rae, CFP, president of DRM Wealth Management in Los Angeles. DavidRaeFP.com buy a fund with the nearly identical top 10 holdings, such as the iShares Russell 1000 ETF (IWB). After 30 days, if you would rather sell your new investment and shift back to your original one, you can do so without running afoul of the wash-sale rule.

Important: This strategy does not work well for individual stocks because it typically is difficult to find a stock that is similar enough to the one you might be selling.

• **Understand how short-term and long-term capital losses work.** For instance, the IRS requires that short-term losses—those on investments held for up to one year—are used first to offset short-term gains...and long-term losses are used first to offset long-term gains. However, whatever losses of either type remain can then be used to offset losses of the other type. If you have lots of short-term capital gains, the use of losses to offset those gains can be especially valuable because short-term gains are taxed at your ordinary income tax rate while long-term gains have a lower tax rate (20 percent, 15 percent or zero percent, depending on your income level).

• **Remember to use *leftover* capital losses.** Once you have run out of capital gains to be offset by capital losses, the IRS allows you to deduct your capital losses from other kinds of income, including wages and interest, up to an annual limit of $3,000—or $1,500 if married and filing a separate return. Any amount remaining beyond that annual cap can be carried over to subsequent years to offset new capital gains first, then income, so it's important to keep accurate records.

New Benefits for Taxpayers and Retirement Savers for 2021 and Beyond...

Bob Carlson, editor of the *Retirement Watch* newsletter. He is a managing member of Carlson Wealth Advisors and chairman of the board of trustees of the Fairfax County (Virginia) Employees' Retirement System. RetirementWatch.com

The massive Consolidated Appropriations Act 2021, signed into law in December 2020, had many benefits that you may have missed...

• **Medical expense deductions.** Since 2017, taxpayers who chose to itemize deductions on their income taxes could deduct qualified medical expenses that exceeded 7.5 percent of their adjusted gross income (AGI). For 2021 and beyond, that percentage was set to increase to 10 percent. But the new law establishes the threshold at 7.5 percent indefinitely.

What to do: If you are near the threshold in 2021 and plan to itemize, consider moving up elective procedures instead of waiting so that you can meet the threshold.

• **Charitable contribution deductions for those taking the standard deduction.** In 2020, in an effort to stimulate philanthropy during the pandemic, individuals who opted for the standard deduction still were allowed to claim a federal income tax write-off for up to $300 in cash contributions to IRS-approved charities. The same $300 limit applied to married couples filing jointly. That tax break has been extended through the end of 2021, plus the deduction limit for married couples filing jointly this year has been raised to $600.

Important: Stocks or other noncash assets are not eligible.

• **Higher charitable-tax-deduction limits for generous donors.** The 2020 CARES Act allowed individuals who itemized deductions to deduct cash contributions to charities up to

TAKE NOTE...

New IRS Life-Expectancy Tables

New IRS life-expectancy tables will run to age 120+ instead of the current 115+, to take increasing life spans into account. This will mean new calculations for required minimum distributions. (RMDs) from retirement accounts—owners will be able to take out a smaller amount each year. The new tables were finalized in November 2020 and they will go into effect for RMDs beginning in 2022.

Federal Register.

100 percent of their AGIs. The new law extends this deduction through 2021, after which the threshold reverts back to 60 percent of your AGI.

What to do: Check with your accountant to make sure the amount that you choose to donate this year makes sense in maximizing your deductions.

• **Tax- and penalty-free distributions from your retirement accounts.** The CARES Act act of 2020 allowed individuals experiencing coronavirus-related job loss or illness to take a total of up to $100,000 in early distributions from IRAs and traditional 401(k) accounts, plus avoid the 10 percent penalty for those under age 59½. For income tax purposes, you were allowed to spread the distribution over three years...or return any or all distributions back to your retirement accounts within that period and file amended returns to recoup any taxes paid.

Update: In response to recent wildfires and hurricanes, Congress now applies these same provisions to anyone who lives in a federally declared disaster area or has suffered sustained economic loss due to a disaster declared between January 1, 2020, and February 25, 2021. (At press the declaration time span has been extended to include summer 2021 wildfires. Speak to your tax adviser.)

You Should Keep Tax Returns Indefinitely If You Can

If you ever fail to file, or the IRS thinks you haven't filed, there is no statute of limitations for coming after you. At minimum, returns should be kept for three years from the filing date—that is the general statute of limitations for an IRS audit although there are a number of exceptions.

Roundup of tax experts, reported in *USA Today.*

Scholarships and Grants Often Are Taxable

Students who get financial aid frequently do not realize this and are hit with unexpected tax bills. Students are required to calculate what taxes they owe—and the taxable percentage of aid varies based on a variety of factors. Form 1098-T, Tuition Statement, which shows students how much they paid and how much financial aid they received, does not indicate how much of the aid is taxable. A worksheet is available directly from the IRS, but it may be better to consult a tax adviser if the family can afford one.

The Wall Street Journal.

States That Do Not Tax Pension Income

States that do not tax pension income may be good retirement destinations for the few people who still have defined-benefit plans.

There are 14 states that do not tax pensions: Alabama, Alaska, Florida, Hawaii, Illinois, Mississippi, Nevada, New Hampshire,

Pennsylvania, South Dakota, Tennessee, Texas, Washington, and Wyoming.

Caution: Some of the states tax other forms of retirement-related income.

Example: Alabama taxes 401(k) distributions.

Also: The federal government taxes payments from pensions no matter where you live.

Kiplinger.com

A Roth IRA Could Cost You More

Anqi Chen, assistant director of savings research at Center for Retirement Research, Boston College, Chestnut Hill, Massachusetts. She is coauthor of the new study "How Much Taxes Will Retirees Owe on Their Retirement Income?" CRR.bc.edu

Traditional IRAs commonly allow pretax contributions and tax your withdrawals, while Roth contributions are made with after-tax dollars and all withdrawals are tax-free. As tempting as tax-free withdrawals are, most people benefit more from taking the tax break up front with a traditional IRA during their working years.

Reason: Four-fifths of retired households grouped by annual income pay an effective tax rate of zero percent or nearly zero. So who should have Roth IRAs?

• **People with large nest eggs and who expect high annual incomes.** Serious tax liabilities arise only for the top fifth of retired households by income that paid an average effective tax rate of 11 percent on federal and state income taxes (23 percent for the top one percent). Effective tax rates (based on taxable income after the standard deduction or itemized deductions are taken out) are generally much lower than your marginal rate (the highest tax bracket and rate that applies to your annual income).

• **People who plan to leave their Roth as an inheritance.** There are no required minimum distributions with a Roth, so investments can grow untouched for many years. After your death, all distributions taken by your beneficiaries typically are tax-free but must be taken over set periods to avoid a 50 percent penalty.

• **People with a large part of retirement savings in traditional IRAs and 401(k)s and who are seeking more tax flexibility as a retiree.**

Example: If you have both types of IRAs, you can tap the Roth in years in which you need more income but are close to triggering Social Security taxes, since Roth distributions aren't counted as part of your taxable income.

TAKE NOTE...

Required Withdrawals from IRAs Decrease in 2022

At age 72, retirees must begin making minimum withdrawals from their IRAs each year or face a significant penalty. Fortunately, seniors are living longer now, and the 2022 minimum withdrawals will reflect that need for the income to last longer. According to the new formula, for example, a 72-year-old with a $300,000 IRA will need to withdraw $10,948, down from $11,719, a reduction of about 7 percent. The amount that must be withdrawn is based in part on life-expectancy statistics (see box on previous page).

Kiplinger.com

Little-Known Tax Trap in Roth IRAs

You must not take money out until five years after your first contribution...and that applies even if you reach age 59½ less than five years after you first contribute. The five-year period starts on the first day of the tax year of the first contribution.

Example: If you put money into a Roth IRA in 2020 but designated that for the 2019 tax year, the five years end on January 1, 2024.

Also: If you convert a traditional IRA to a Roth, each conversion has its own five-year countdown—starting in the tax year in which it is completed. So withdrawing before age 59½ from a converted IRA less than five years after the conversion triggers a 10 percent early-withdrawal penalty. Details of these rules are complex—consult a knowledgeable tax adviser.

Roundup of experts on Roth IRAs, reported at Fool.com.

Electric Cars: Tax Credits and Fees to Consider

Karl Brauer, executive analyst at automotive research firm iSeeCars and executive publisher of Car Expert, an automotive news and reviews website. CarExpert.com

If you're thinking about making the leap to an electric vehicle (EV), there's some news you should know...

• **The federal tax credit ran out for some of the most popular EVs.** The $7,500 tax credit that has helped make EVs affordable phases out for cars made by an automaker after that automaker sells 200,000 eligible vehicles. GM and Tesla now have passed that sales threshold, so they no longer qualify for federal tax credits. Fortunately, a number of excellent EVs available from other automakers are still eligible for the tax credit.

Example: The Hyundai Kona EV is a superb EV crossover—reliable, fun to drive, and well-equipped—with a starting price of $38,045. That's $30,545 after the tax credit.

• **Some states are imposing fees on EVs.** Many states have imposed, or are considering imposing, EV fees to make up for the fact that EV drivers don't pay gas taxes. Sometimes these fees are higher than car owners pay in gas taxes, according to Consumer Reports.

Examples: Alabama, California, Georgia, Idaho, Mississippi, North Dakota, Ohio, Washington State, West Virginia, and Wyoming have annual EV fees of $120 to $225, which is in excess of the typical car owner's gas taxes, according to a recent analysis.

• **The latest generation of EVs offer more than 200 miles per charge.** That helps eliminate the "range anxiety" felt by the owners of earlier-generation EVs, which often provided little more than 100 miles of range.

Examples: Kia Niro EV offers 239 miles of range...Kia Soul EV, 243 miles...Tesla Model 3, 263 miles...Porsche Taycan, 225 miles ...Kona EV, 260 miles...Tesla Model X, 340 miles...Tesla Model S, 405 miles. Ford claims its new electric SUV, the Mustang Mach-E, offers 305 miles per charge...and Rivian, a new U.S. automaker, says its R1T pickup will have 300 miles of range.

Save on Taxes for Gold and Silver Profits

Robert Carlson, editor of the monthly newsletter *Retirement Watch*. He is a managing member of Carlson Wealth Advisors and chairman of the board of trustees of the Fairfax County (Virginia) Employees' Retirement System. RetirementWatch.com

As bond yields and the U.S. dollar have sunk in 2020 and 2021, and inflation is starting to appear, many investors have taken refuge in gold and silver. These alternative investments have proven to be attractive as gold prices soared more than 30 percent as of August 2020, topping $2,000 an ounce before pulling back...and were still around $1,900 as of June 2021...and silver gained more than 55 percent, to $29, where it still hovers mid 2021. The method you choose for investing in these precious metals can have a big effect on the taxes you pay on profits.

Here's how to factor taxes into your investment choices...

• **American Eagles, Canadian Gold Maple Leafs, and other coins.** Their value closely mirrors the daily price of gold or silver. The IRS considers them "collectibles," which means that any gains when they are sold are taxed at your marginal income tax rate but no higher than the 28 percent bracket if held more than one year.

• **Exchange-traded funds (ETFs) trade like stocks and track the daily price of gold and silver,** with each ETF share typically reflecting the price of one-tenth of an ounce of the metal. These precious metal ETFs are more convenient to own than physical forms but, like coins and unlike stocks and most other kinds of ETFs, are considered collectibles for tax purposes.

• **Mining-company stocks get the same tax treatment as most stocks.** If they are held for one year or less, their gains are taxed at ordinary income tax rates...more than one year, at zero percent, 15 percent, or 20 percent, depending on your income tax bracket. That means you get more favorable tax treatment than with the coins or ETFs. Mining-stock shares fluctuate based on various factors in addition to precious-metal prices, including company performance.

SMART TAX MOVES

In taxable accounts, use any investment losses, including losses on gold and silver, to offset gains on collectibles, stocks, and bonds. If you have no capital gains, you can use the losses to offset ordinary income up to $3,000. Any leftover losses can be rolled over for use in subsequent years.

In tax-advantaged accounts, favor gold and silver ETFs or mining stocks.

Reason: Most 401(k) plans don't allow you to invest in physical metal, and the IRS makes it difficult and expensive to do so in IRAs. Gold and silver investments in tax-advantaged accounts grow tax-free, and you pay ordinary income tax rates on any distributions from a traditional IRA or 401(k) and no taxes on Roth distributions.

11

Retire Right

5 Social Security Surprises That Could Cost You Big—and How to Avoid Them

In some ways, Social Security is the simplest part of the retirement income equation. There's no need to choose investments or even decide how much to set aside. But the closer you look, the more complex the Social Security system is. *Among the surprises...*

The best age to claim your Social Security benefits might depend on the ages of your children...receiving Social Security benefits could undermine your Health Savings Account (HSA)...you could miss out on benefits if you fail to keep tabs on the spouse you divorced decades ago.

Five Social Security situations with easy-to-overlook twists...

• **Waiting to claim could be costly if you have young or disabled kids.** The standard Social Security advice is to delay the start of benefits—potentially all the way to age 70—because by delaying you increase the size of future monthly benefits. But there's an often-missed exception—if you have minor or disabled children, there's a good chance it's better to claim as soon as possible. Why? These children likely can receive dependent child benefits based on your earnings history, but they can't do that until you start receiving benefits yourself. To be eligible, a child must be younger than 18...a full-time student (no higher than grade 12) and 19 or younger...or any age if disabled before age 22. The child also cannot be married.

Cindy Lundquist, author of *Answers to Your Social Security Questions That You Didn't Even Know to Ask*. She currently is an Atlanta-based Social Security consultant who works with financial advisers, corporations, and government agencies. She previously spent 27 years working for the Social Security Administration. CindyLundquist.com

Example: Sam retires at age 63 but intends to wait to start his benefits until 66. Based on Sam's earnings history, this delay would increase his monthly benefit from $2,080 to $2,600. But Sam has children ages 15 and 16. If he starts his benefits at 63, each of those kids will be eligible for benefits of $1,040 per month until the older child reaches 18. When that child's benefits stop, the younger child will receive an increase to $1,300 per month until age 18. If, however, Sam waits until age 66 to start collecting his benefit, both children will be too old to qualify for benefits. If Sam lives the typical life span of a 63-year-old man—that's another 20½ years—waiting to age 66 to claim will have cost the family $48,480.

• **If you receive Social Security disability benefits, you are (or soon will be) eligible for Medicare, too.** If you are deemed eligible for Social Security disability benefits, you will become eligible for Medicare as well, once you have received 24 months of Social Security benefits. That's true even if you have not yet reached age 65, the usual age for Medicare eligibility. Similarly, if one of your children receives Social Security disability benefits based on your earnings, this child will be Medicare-eligible after 24 months of benefits. Medicare does not inform people that they are eligible, however, so many fail to apply.

• **Receiving Social Security benefits might mean that you can't make HSA contributions.** If your only health insurance is a "high-deductible health plan," you typically can make contributions to an HSA—a savings account that lets you put aside pretax dollars to pay health-related expenses. But you cannot make these contributions if you're 65 or older and receiving Social Security benefits. Why? Social Security recipients 65 and older are automatically enrolled in Medicare Part A, even if they have employer-provided health insurance and don't yet need Medicare. Medicare Part A counts as health insurance but doesn't qualify as a high-deductible health plan, so if you have Medicare Part A, you can't make HSA contributions.

Not only is there no way to decline this Part A automatic enrollment, it's retroactive for up to six months prior to the Social Security application, dating back as far as your 65th birthday, the age at which you become eligible for Medicare. Unfortunately, many people don't realize this and later face both income taxes and a 6 percent penalty on these ineligible contributions.

• **Young families can be eligible for surprisingly generous benefits when wage earners die.** The death of a young parent is a tragedy, but Social Security survivor benefits can at least help survivors pay their bills—if the survivors know to apply. Unfortunately, many widows and widowers don't apply because they believe they won't be eligible for Social Security until they reach retirement age. They're only partially correct—a widowed spouse isn't eligible for survivor benefits until age 60, but there still might be benefits available for the household.

Children in these households typically are eligible for survivor benefits if they are under age 18 (or up to 19 if still a full-time student… or any age if disabled before age 22) in grade 12 or lower. And although a young widow/widower won't qualify for survivor benefits, he/she could be eligible for a caregiver benefit if raising one or more children younger than 16 and/or disabled. Each of these benefits can be up to 75 percent of what the wage earner's estimated benefit would have reached had he worked until full retirement age.

Example: Joe and Mary are married with two young children, ages two and four, when Joe dies at age 30. Joe had only eight years in the work force, and his final salary was $50,000, but Mary and the children together are eligible for approximately $3,200 per month after Joe's death. That's more than three quarters of the income Joe earned in his final year.

• **An ex-spouse's death could boost your benefits—even if you married someone else more recently.** You already might know some of the basics of eligibility for spousal benefits. For instance, if you divorce after at least 10 years of marriage and currently are not remarried, you likely will be eligible for a spousal benefit based on that ex's earnings starting as early as age 62. If you're widowed, you likely will be eligible for a survivor benefit based on that late spouse's earnings starting as early as age 60, as long as the marriage lasted at least nine months (under certain circumstances, even shorter marriages qualify) and you are not currently remarried to someone you wed before age 60. But many people don't realize that if they were married multiple times, they could have the option of choosing which ex's earnings record is used to calculate their benefit—and fewer still know that the death of an ex could affect which of these options is best.

Example: Rachel was married to Bennett for 12 years before the marriage ended in divorce. She later married Eric and remained with him until his death. When Eric died, Rachel began receiving a widow's benefit based on Eric's earnings in the amount of $1,800 per month. That was more than the benefit she could receive based on her marriage to Bennett even though Bennett earned significantly more during his career than Eric did during his. Why? Eric's death meant Rachel was entitled to a survivor benefit equal to 100 percent of Eric's $1,800 monthly benefit...but Bennett was alive, so Rachel was entitled to a spousal benefit of just 50 percent of Bennett's $2,800 benefit, which comes to $1,400. (It's one or the other—Rachel can't claim both.) When Bennett died last year, Rachel became entitled to a survivor benefit equal to 100 percent of his $2,800 per month. Unfortunately, she was not in contact with Bennett and did not realize that he died. Had she periodically asked the Social Security Administration to check if she was eligible for a survivor benefit based on Bennett's earnings, she could have received $1,000 more per month—but the Social Security Administration won't tell her that if she doesn't ask.

Caution: If you are not yet at full retirement age and still are working, survivor benefits may be reduced so much that it doesn't make sense to claim the benefits until you do reach full retirement age or are no longer working.

GOOD TO KNOW...

Social Security Tasks You Can Do Online

There is no need to trek to a Social Security office to take care of a variety of tasks. Here are some things you can handle once you set up a "My Social Security" account at SSA.gov...

- **Estimate your future benefits**
- **Apply for new benefits (Social Security, disability, and Medicare)**
- **Appeal a benefits decision**
- **View past earnings**
- **Set up or change direct deposit**
- **Print your Form 1099 for reporting Social Security income at tax time.**

Social Security Administration. SSA.gov

Avoid These Mistakes When Investing in Target-Date Funds

Leo Acheson, CFA, director of multiasset ratings, including target-date funds, at Morningstar Inc., Chicago, which tracks 620,000 investment offerings. Morningstar.com

Target-date funds are supposed to make investing easier and less risky. That's why they have become enormously popular as a way to automatically make your investments more conservative as you grow older.

So how have target-date funds performed in this tumultuous period for the stock market? They've done what they're supposed to do, says fund expert Leo Acheson, CFA. That means they didn't completely avoid the volatility, but they did help protect investors and smooth the ride. For instance, target-date funds designed for people who were retiring in 2020 dropped by an average of 17 percent during a 30-day "coronavirus sell-off period" ending March 20, 2020, compared with a 32 percent plunge for the S&P 500 Index of U.S. stocks. However, the losses among various 2020 target-date funds ranged widely during that period—from 13 percent to 23 percent—reflecting big differences in how they invest their assets. Looking further out, target-date funds designed for investors retiring in 2035—who have more time to make up for setbacks—lost an average of 24 percent.

Acheson says that 2020's chaos has highlighted the importance of knowing your target-date fund's risk profile in order to avoid mistakes you might make in how you invest, as all target-date funds are not created equal. Potential mistakes include believing that your fund is less risky and less volatile than it actually is at any given point...assuming that it will offer adequate protection when nearing retirement...and failing to figure out what to do with money you have invested in the fund as you approach and enter retirement.

Acheson's strategies for avoiding these mistakes...

DON'T JUST SET IT AND FORGET IT

Simplicity and one-stop shopping are central to the appeal of target-date funds. Typically, you invest in a single fund with a date closest to your retirement date, currently ranging in five-year intervals from 2005 to 2060. Then you let the fund managers worry about which investments to buy and how to rebalance the mix each year. The idea is that the fund will adjust the mix of stocks, bonds, and other assets to make the fund more conservative as you approach and pass the retirement date.

But you still need to understand what you own and make some strategic decisions about your fund investments if you want to avoid costly mistakes...

MISTAKE: **Thinking that all target-date funds are the same.** Some of the fund providers take more aggressive approaches than others, meaning that different funds with the same target date offer very different levels of volatility. Typically, the higher the percentage of stocks, the greater the short-term volatility but also the higher the long-term returns. Among the various series of target-date funds from the leading providers, Fidelity Freedom and T. Rowe Price Retirement take relatively aggressive approaches...American Funds Target Date Retirement Series, BlackRock LifePath Index, J.P. Morgan SmartRetirement, and Vanguard Target Retirement take more moderate approaches...Charles Schwab Target Date, John Hancock Multi-Index Preservation, and Wells Fargo Target Date are more conservative. *What to do...*

- **Understand your fund's risk level.** Go to the fund family's website or Morningstar.com, and examine portfolio allocations to stocks and bonds.

Example: T. Rowe Price Retirement 2030 recently had 71 percent* of its assets in stocks, 20 percent in bonds and the rest in cash. Its 10-year annualized performance of 9.96 percent ranks in the top 2 percent in its category. In contrast, Wells Fargo Target 2030 had just 58 percent in stocks and 37 percent in bonds. Its 10-year performance was just 6.89 percent, but the fund was also 30% less volatile than the T. Rowe Price fund over that period.

- **Select a target date that suits your risk tolerance, not just your expected retirement date.** Choose a fund dated slightly earlier than your planned retirement for less volatility or a later one if you will be comfortable with the extra volatility.

Example: If you are retiring in 10 years and have your investments in the T. Rowe Price Retirement 2030 fund, gradually switch to the 2025 fund if you are more risk-averse since it has a lower allocation to stocks (62 percent instead of 71 percent) and less volatility.

- **Go to a different fund family if you feel your current one's approach is too risky.** Although your 401(k) plan typically offers target-date funds from just one provider, you can roll over some of the assets into a self-directed IRA, which gives you many more choices while maintaining your 401(k) for new contributions.

*Figures as of June 11, 2021.

Careful: Some fund providers may charge individual investors with IRAs an upfront load or high annual fees. If you want to keep your assets in your 401(k), ask your plan sponsor if you have an option to use a "self-directed brokerage account" or "brokerage window." More than 40 percent of large employers now allow you to venture beyond the 401(k) plan's core menu of investments and use target-date funds from other families.

MISTAKE: **Glossing over the risks when you're on the cusp of retirement.** The average target-date fund holds 40 percent in stocks when it reaches its target date. Two of the largest target-date fund providers—Fidelity and T. Rowe Price—are more aggressive, holding about 50 percent in stocks.

Reason: With increasing life expectancy, investors need to take risks now to generate the growth they'll need in the next few decades to keep from running out of money. But steep portfolio losses near retirement could compromise your long term financial plans, especially if you must soon start drawing on the assets, locking in your losses. In addition, some people find that they retire a few years earlier than planned because of ill health, layoffs, or buyouts. *What to do…*

- **Sell some stock shares in the five years leading up to retirement to build up cash savings.** This can be an effective way to reduce risk, especially if you don't have savings outside of your 401(k). You need enough emergency cash that if your fund suffers big losses, you won't have to tap the assets right away, allowing your portfolio time to recover. You also can raise cash by continuing to make contributions to your retirement plan but not investing the money.

- **Invest some or all of your retirement savings in the most conservative target-date fund your provider offers.** This can lower your volatility significantly but still give you a chance for growth.

Example: The Fidelity Flex Freedom Blend 2005 fund recently had 26 percent in stocks, 53 percent in bonds, and 21 percent in cash. It has been 70 percent less volatile than the S&P 500, and during the coronavirus sell-off period, it lost just 10 percent. By the end of 2020 it was up 9.80 percent and is up over 2 percent as of June 2021, year to date.

MISTAKE: **Not determining how your fund fits into your plans once you have retired.** Target-date funds continue on after they hit the target date. A few fund families such as BlackRock maintain a static portfolio allocation (40 percent stocks/60 percent bonds and cash) from that point on. But most providers continue to gradually lower the allocation to stocks and increase bond holdings each year.

Examples: T. Rowe Price continues this process for 30 years after the target date is reached until its final allocation of 30 percent stocks/70 percent bonds and cash is reached. Fidelity continues for 20 years (*final allocation*: 20% percent stocks/80 percent bonds and cash). Vanguard, seven years (*final allocation*: 30 percent stocks/70 percent bonds and cash). The problem is that after you factor in income such as pensions and Social Security benefits, your need for additional income and the ability to draw down your portfolio may be more nuanced than what your target-date fund can provide. *What to do…*

- **Gradually liquidate enough of your target-date fund over several years** to ensure that your short- and medium-term income needs are covered in retirement. To do that, you'll need to put the money in relatively safe places including savings accounts, certificates of deposit (CDs), and/or bonds or bond funds.

Another possibility: Many fund providers have rolled out "retirement income" funds such as Fidelity Freedom Income and Vanguard Target Retirement Income, which use a combination of mostly bonds and some dividend-paying stocks to throw off steady income. Dividend-paying stock funds may look more attractive than bond funds now because yields are so low.

Use what remains in your target-date fund as the long-term growth portion of your portfolio.

MONEY SMARTS...

Easy Ways to Save More for Your Retirement

Invest your "third paycheck." If you get paid every other week, then two months out of the year you'll get a third paycheck. Invest that paycheck directly into your retirement account. *Use credit card rewards.* Some cards let you deposit rewards directly into an investment account. Making everyday purchases on such a card is a great, easy way to build your nest egg. *Bank your raises.* If you get a pay increase, devote it to retirement rather than getting used to the new level of income. *Leverage employee matches.* If your company offers to match funds invested into your retirement account, maximize the opportunity, since it's free money for your future. *Turn coupons into retirement.* Any time you save money by using a coupon, put what you've saved into your retirement account—every cent helps!

Christie Bieber, personal finance writer for *The Motley Fool,* writing at USAToday.com.

Retirement Rule Drops to 3 Percent

David M. Blanchett, PhD, CFP, CFA, head of retirement research for Morningstar Investment Management, Chicago. Morningstar.com

Thanks to historically low interest rates that are unlikely to rise any time soon, following the popular "4 percent rule" for retirement account withdrawals may deplete your savings. In the past, a 65-year-old who withdrew 4 percent in Year One plus an inflation adjustment thereafter had a 95 percent chance of sustaining a portfolio for 30 years. However, this is based on a historical average yield of 4 percent for five-year Treasuries. Their recent yield of just 0.78 percent cuts the probability of a 4 percent initial withdrawal rate lasting 30 years down to roughly 55 percent. That could force you to rely on guaranteed income alone (e.g., Social Security retirement benefits and/or a pension), which may not be enough to maintain your lifestyle.

What to do instead: Follow a 3 percent rule. First, create a portfolio split evenly between large-cap stocks, which have historically returned about 10 percent per year, and five-year Treasuries. The first year that you start to make retirement withdrawals, take out 3 percent of the total value of your portfolio. From Year Two forward, withdraw the same amount as Year One plus an adjustment for inflation. Even using recent ultra-low Treasury yields, a 65-year-old following this strategy for 30 years has a 90 percent chance of not running out of money.

Example: With a $1 million 50/50 stock-and-Treasury portfolio, you withdraw $30,000 in Year One. In Year Two, if the inflation rate is 2 percent, you withdraw $30,000 plus $600 and so on.

For investors still saving for retirement, you'll need a nest egg 25% larger than you might have planned if interest rates stay low. For those already retired, consider replacing some or all of the bond investments with an immediate annuity, which may guarantee more annual income than you could get using bonds.

10 Cheapest States to Retire In

Average annual expenditures: Mississippi, $43,129. Oklahoma, $43,994. Arkansas, $44,299. New Mexico, $44,859. Kansas, 45,011. Missouri, $45,011. Tennessee, $45,062. Alabama, $45,367. Georgia, $45,367. Michigan, $45,672. These results are based on the average household cost of groceries, housing, utilities, transportation, health care, and other factors in each state.

GoBankingRates.com

Your 401(K) Balance Could Automatically Follow You When You Change Jobs

The Labor Department has greenlit a program allowing employers to transfer sub-$5,000 balances to employees' new 401(k)s when they change jobs if the employees don't opt out of the transfer. This helps employees whose former employers close sub-$5,000 accounts, often resulting in taxes and 10 percent penalties for the departing employees who don't transfer the accounts to a new 401(k) or IRA. Employees are charged up to $59 per automatic transfer.

Stephen Miller, a certified employee-benefit specialist in Alexandria, Virginia, and online manager/editor of compensation and benefits for Society for Human Resource Management. SHRM.com

The Pandemic and Your Retirement Account

Researchers from MassMutual recently found that 55 percent of Americans surveyed have adjusted their accounts thanks to developments related to the coronavirus pandemic. Of those making changes, 54 percent reduced their contributions...22 percent increased them to take advantage of market pullbacks...and 24 percent said they plan to contribute the same amount but change their risk exposure. Reduce contributions if you need cash to pay bills, to avoid running up credit card debt, or to build up a three-to-six-month emergency fund. Increase contributions if you have job security, an emergency fund, and sustainable levels of debt.

Roundup of personal finance experts quoted at GoBankingRates.com

Retirement Benefits Should Be Safe

Retirement benefits should be safe even if a company declares Chapter 11 (reorganization) or Chapter 7 (liquidation). Federal law requires plan benefits to be kept separate from a company's assets, so they cannot be taken by creditors.

Robert S. Ellerbrock III of FisherBroyles, Washington, DC. FisherBroyles.com

Best Workplace Retirement Plans

If your 401(k) or other retirement plan is managed by one of these providers, congratulations—in a 2020 survey of more than 10,000 workers, employees gave them the highest satisfaction ratings based on features, fees, information resources, and other factors.

Large plans: Bank of America, Charles Schwab, Principal Financial Group.

Medium plans: Bank of America, Charles Schwab, OneAmerica.

Small plans: Fidelity, AIG, Nationwide.

JDPower.com

Reduced or Ended 401(K) Matches

Companies may reduce or end 401(k) matches because of the serious financial losses they have incurred from the coronavirus pandemic. Amtrak, La-Z-Boy, Macy's, Marriott, Mattress Firm, Sabre Corporation, and other firms have announced plans to suspend or reduce their contributions to employees' 401(k) plans. Those contributions have been rising in recent years as companies used them to attract and retain workers. But the firms say they must now cut costs and are trying to minimize layoffs. Some companies also are considering matching employee contributions with company stock rather than cash, so the cash can be used to keep the business going.

The Wall Street Journal.

Saving for Retirement Easier for Grad Students

Saving for retirement is now easier for grad students because of a new federal law. It means money that graduate students and postdoctoral researchers receive from taxable fellowships is recognized for determining eligibility to make IRA contributions. In the past, this type of income wasn't treated as taxable compensation unless reported on a Form W-2. That made it hard to fund an IRA because contributions cannot exceed earnings, wages, tips, and/or other taxable employee compensation.

Emily Roberts, PhD, founder of the website and podcast "Personal Finance for PhDs." She is based in Seattle. PFforPhDs.com

MONEY SAVERS...

States with the Cheapest Houses

Considering everything from closing costs to property taxes to price per square foot, these were the seven most affordable states for buying a home (with median list prices indicated). West Virginia ($169,000), Arkansas ($179,900), Mississippi ($189,000), Oklahoma ($193,000) Indiana ($195,000), Kentucky ($199,000) and Alabama ($220,000).

SmartAsset.com

The Key to a Happy Retirement? Keep a Schedule

With nothing but time on their hands, some retirees fall into a kind of low-end chaos, no longer guided by the job that used to provide their lives with structure. While the freedom to spend your time as you wish can be exhilarating, some degree of predictability can help you avoid stress, restlessness, and boredom. Having a plan for each day can, paradoxically, save you time, because, when you know what you're going to do, you can move directly into it instead of dithering. It also helps ensure that you do all the things you've been looking forward to. Of course, an overly rigid schedule will feel restricting, so just create a general routine that allows you to live life at a pace that's comfortable for you.

MoneyTalksNews.com

12

Consumer Savvy Secrets

Take Control of Your Medical Bills

If you're worried about financial ruin from big medical bills, you're not alone.

Consider these startling statistics: In a survey of 1,000 Americans, 64 percent said they delayed or neglected seeking medical care in the past year because of concern about high medical bills.

In another survey, one-in-four people had trouble paying a recent medical bill. And—because of high deductibles, co-pays, co-insurance rates, and surprise out-of-network charges—that includes many people with health insurance.

MEDICAL DEBT

All told, one in three Americans has debt from medical expenses. Often that debt is delinquent. About 20 percent of consumer credit reports include one or more medical collections, which means the consumer has one or more medical bills that are unpaid and overdue, with creditors in pursuit.

The pandemic complicated issues. An estimated 5.4 million Americans lost their health insurance since the virus struck in early 2020. Furthermore, a study shows that the hospital treatment for COVID-19 patients without insurance (or receiving out-of-network care that isn't covered by insurance) typically ranges from $35,000 to $46,000, with some bills as high as $93,000.

Even insured patients paying so-called "allowed amounts" are typically charged about $24,000, which translates into plenty of fiscal stress if you have a plan with a high deductible. (The number of people with high-deductible health insurance plans has doubled in the last decade.)

Cynthia A. Fisher, MBA, founder and chairman of PatientRightsAdvocate.org, an advocacy organization that seeks to reduce the cost of health care through systemwide price transparency and the creation of a functional, competitive marketplace.

The first emergency coronavirus bill passed by Congress was supposed to provide money for hospitals and health-care providers to forgive all COVID-19 related medical bills—but lack of insurance, loopholes in funding for those who are insured, and the expiration of benefits left many people with a high tab. And possibly poorer health as a result.

A recent article published in the *Journal of the American Medical Association*, one of the leading medical journals in the United States, stated that financial harm from medical care is every bit as dangerous to health and well-being as harmful side effects from drugs or complications from surgery. The authors asserted that patients can and should demand "transparency and honesty in pricing and in billing for medical services."

WHAT YOU CAN DO

If you're dealing with a medical bill that seems confusing, wrong, or unfair, or if you're faced with a bill you can't pay, here are ways to deal effectively with insurers, doctors, hospitals, and creditors to prevent or reduce your financial harm.

• **Know your coverage before you receive care.** Before seeing any new doctor or specialist, check with your insurance company to make sure they are in your network.

Call the insurance company to confirm: Online directories are not always updated and if a physician drops off the list, the extra cost is on you.

If your doctor or hospital orders tests and services, call your insurer's customer service line and ask to review the Summary of Benefits and Coverage (SBC) section of your policy to make sure they're covered. If the services aren't covered, call the customer service department and find out why. Your doctor may be able to appeal the decision or request a "peer-to-peer" consultation with the insurance company's medical director. Or your doctor may be able to order a different and generally comparable test or treatment that is covered.

• **Shop around for medical tests and procedures—and negotiate a fair price.** Prices for the exact same service vary widely—if you can find out the price at all. For example, in a survey of 101 hospitals, prices for coronary artery bypass surgery ranged from $44,000 to $448,000, and only 53 of the 101 hospitals were willing to provide a price. Further, the varying prices reflected no difference in the quality of care, according to a quality score from the Society of Thoracic Surgeons.

Fortunately, there are ways to discover the fair prices of medical tests and procedures, which is particularly important if you don't have insurance, or you have a policy that is not compliant with the Affordable Care Act (Obamacare).

• **Check what Medicare** (Medicare.gov/coverage) and commercial insurance companies (FairHealthConsumer.org) pay for the medical service you need.

• **Explore price-checking websites,** such as Healthcare Bluebook (HealthCareBluebook.com) and Clear Health Costs (ClearHealthCosts.com).

• **For surgical procedures, look up the price at surgical centers that provide price transparency,** such as The Surgery Center of Oklahoma (SurgeryCenterOK.com) and Texas Free Market Surgery (TexasFreeMarketSurgery.com).

Once you know the fair price, you can negotiate with your doctor, hospital, or insurance company. First, ask for the cash price. If your doctor or hospital accepts the Medicare "allowable amount," offer to pay it in cash before your visit or procedure. In many cases, the doctor or institution will offer significantly discounted rates for upfront, cash payments—sometimes as much as 40 percent lower than the insurance-negotiated rate.

• **Don't sign any paperwork in the emergency room.** If you go to the emergency room and the hospital insists you sign a form for financial paperwork, refuse, or write "Did Not Read," instead of your signature.

This is your legal right: The Emergency Medical Treatment and Active Labor Act (EMTALA) requires hospital emergency rooms to stabilize anyone needing emergency care—and ensures public access to emergency services regardless of a patient's ability to pay.

• Watch out for balance bills. Many consumers with health insurance are blindsided by balance bills—charges from out-of-network providers (anesthesiologists, radiologists, and pathologists) who work at an in-network hospital. Up to 57 percent of all medical bills now include unexpected, out-of-network charges. (You don't have to worry if you live in California or Florida—both states have outlawed balance billing.)

To help avoid this problem, make it clear to your doctor that you want to stay in-network and avoid all out-of-network charges. You can also contact your insurance company and ask them to help you find nearby in-network labs and facilities. (Quest and LabCorp are on most plans.)

• Ask for an itemized bill from your doctor or hospital, and dispute inaccuracies. It's your legal right to know what you're being charged for, but you'll likely need to ask for an itemized bill. Don't expect it to be accurate. About 80 percent of medical bills contain an error, such as duplicate or incorrect charges.

If there are any discrepancies—for example, you're being billed for a test you didn't get, a medication you didn't take, or an incorrect number of days in the hospital—dispute them without delay. Some insurance companies have a statute of limitations for appeals, such as 60 days.

• Don't pay for complications. You should never pay for treatment for complications that resulted from an adverse event, such as a hospital-acquired infection or surgery on the wrong part of the body. If you're pressured to pay, tell the hospital that the price for the treatment was not disclosed and that you would like an itemized listing of the charges in discovery (or litigation). Hospitals are so averse to revealing their prices in court—where they would be revealed to the general public—that they often forgive the entire bill.

If your insurance company refuses to pay, complain. If the service should be covered by your insurance according to the Summary of Benefits of Coverage in your policy, but the company is refusing to pay—don't give up. File an appeal. You can find ways to do that at https://advocacy.consumerreports.org/research/insurance-complaint-tool/.

If a debt collector calls, ask to see the contract. If a debt collector insists that you pay for an unfair bill, demand they provide you with the contractual agreement that obligates you to pay. If there's no written agreement, you have no legal obligation.

• Let your voice be heard. Lack of fair and transparent pricing is the key problem plaguing our health-care system. Health care should be regulated by the competitive, free market, where you know the price before the purchase and can shop accordingly. My organization is devoted to advocating for patients, families, and caregivers to receive real-time, free access to prices before undergoing medical services.

7 Ways to Save Money on Prescriptions

Richard Sagall, MD, who specializes in family medicine and occupational medicine, Gloucester, Massachusetts. He is founder of NeedyMeds, Inc., a nonprofit that tracks money-saving pharmaceutical programs such as the ones listed above. NeedyMeds.org

Americans have an expensive drug habit—prescription drugs. Drug costs now average around $1,200 a year per person in this country, and prices are continuing to rise. Health-care costs play a role in more than half a million bankruptcies each year, sometimes because of new cancer drugs that can cost hundreds of thousands of dollars for a course of treatment.

"Everyday drugs" also take a greater chunk out of consumers' pockets even if they have health insurance or Medicare Part D prescription drug coverage thanks to high deductibles and copays.

You may already know some common ways to save money on prescription drugs—among them, asking for generic versions of drugs... splitting pills in half if the doctor or pharmacist says that's allowable...and asking a doctor for free samples of a drug. But there are additional ways to cut your costs that you may not know about.

Here are seven strategies that can help lower the cost of your prescriptions...

SHOPPING STRATEGIES

• **Comparison-shop multiple pharmacies.** The price of a prescription can vary dramatically from pharmacy to pharmacy—sometimes by hundreds of dollars. Drug-price comparison apps and websites offer the best way to find the lowest prices available in your area.

Examples: NeedyMed's Drug Pricing Calculator (NeedyMeds.org/drug-pricing)...GoodRx (GoodRx.com, a free app available for Apple or Android).

Traditional pharmacies are not the only sellers. Warehouse clubs such as Costco and Sam's Club often allow even nonmembers to fill prescriptions at their pharmacies (rules vary by both warehouse club and state). And online pharmacies are an option if you plan ahead or can safely wait for the drugs to be delivered. Just confirm that the online pharmacy has "Verified Internet Pharmacy Practice Site" (VIPPS) accreditation, which ensures that it meets its state's licensing and inspection requirements as well as National Association of Boards of Pharmacy standards.

Warning: Avoid any online pharmacy that says it can provide prescription drugs without a prescription—they are especially likely to provide counterfeit drugs that could be ineffective or dangerous.

• **Obtain a prescription drug discount card.** Dozens of nonprofit organizations, pharmacy chains and other health-care–related companies offer drug discount cards that can provide savings on certain drugs at certain pharmacies. The size of these discounts will vary dramatically depending on the drug, the pharmacy and the card—anywhere from no savings to 80 percent savings. It depends on how much of a savings the card issuer managed to negotiate on behalf of its cardholders. Or in the case of the pharmacy chain–issued cards, how much of a discount the pharmacy was willing to offer.

These cards cannot be used in conjunction with health insurance/Medicare—you have to use one or the other—but sometimes the total price with the discount card is less than the copay imposed by an insurance or Medicare plan. Before paying for any prescription, ask your pharmacy to compare the price you would pay with your discount card to the amount you would pay out of pocket with your insurance/Medicare.

Downside: If you use a discount card to buy a drug, the money you spend will not count toward your annual insurance/Medicare out-of-pocket maximum.

There are many discount cards available. Which ones are best depends on which drugs and pharmacies you use, but pick only those that do not charge any fees.

Examples of widely accepted free discount cards: GoodRx (GoodRx.com), NeedyMeds Drug Discount Card (offered by my nonprofit organization, NeedyMeds.org), ScriptSave WellRx (WellRx.com), and SingleCare (SingleCare.com).

• **Seek a lower-priced drug if there is no way to affordably obtain a drug that you have been prescribed.** Ask your pharmacist whether he/she can contact your doctor's office to check whether a lower-cost drug would be a suitable replacement. For example, there might be an older version of the exact same drug available that's just as effective but less expensive because it is in a form that is less convenient to take.

ADDITIONAL MONEY-SAVING STRATEGIES

• **Request assistance from drugmakers.** Perhaps you've seen a drug commercial that says that if you can't afford your medication, the drugmaker might be able to help. Most pharmaceutical companies have "Patient Assistance Programs" that provide free or deeply discounted drugs to patients who could not otherwise afford them. These programs typically are designed to help limited-income patients obtain high-cost drugs, but program rules vary and income limits can be surprisingly high—in many cases $40,000 to $65,000. Details and application forms are available on drug-company websites. They also can be found at www.NeedyMeds.org/pap. If you appear to fall just short of eligibility for the program for a drug you need, file an application anyway—sometimes drugmakers are willing to stretch eligibility rules a little.

• **Look for drug-company copay rebates/ coupons.** Drugmakers offer "copay assistance" rebates and coupons for certain drugs—often drugs that have high out-of-pocket costs. The savings can be substantial, in many cases lowering the out-of-pocket price all the way to $0. Unfortunately, these rebates and coupons tend to be available only to people who have commercial insurance, not people who have government-provided health coverage such as Medicare or Tricare. On the plus side, these programs do not have income caps or other need-based eligibility restrictions such as the patient-assistance programs discussed above. These coupons and rebates can be found on pharmaceutical-company websites…or check the list available at NeedyMeds.org/coupons. The offers change frequently, so check back every few months.

Examples: Recently the list of drug copay coupon and rebate programs featured thousands of medications, including the chemotherapy drug Abraxane, which has a program that provides access and reimbursement support (BMS Access Support, 800-861-0048), and the hypertension treatment Azor, with a coupon that reduces copays to as little as $5 (Azor.com/savings).

• **Apply to nonprofits associated with your diagnosis for assistance.** There are thousands of nonprofit organizations in the U.S. devoted to specific medical problems and topics. Many of these nonprofits offer financial support to people struggling to afford prescription drugs or other treatments. Each program has its own eligibility rules, application forms, deadlines, and limits. NeedyMeds maintains a list of nonprofits that have such programs at NeedyMeds.org/copay-diseases.

• **Retry the strategies above every few months.** Drug prices, assistance programs, and discount-card savings can change. So if you're taking a drug long-term, it's worth rechecking whether there are ways to save that were not available when you initially looked.

Beware Websites Offering Online Prescriptions

Adriane Fugh-Berman, MD, professor of pharmacology and physiology at Georgetown University Medical Center, Washington, DC.

You've seen the commercials on TV, promising to fix all your intimate problems with a quick prescription—and without ever having to step foot in a doctor's office. But while skipping doctor's appointments might seem like a time- and money-saver, it also can be dangerous for your health.

These web-based companies work by promoting certain prescription drugs directly to consumers. Consumers can order those drugs without first obtaining prescriptions from their regular doctors. In some cases, the sites even push medications for uses for which they have not been approved, such as blood pressure medication to control anxiety.

These companies, which include Cove (for migraine medication), Hers (for women's health issues), Hims (for men's health issues), Kick (for anxiety drugs), and Roman (for hair loss, erectile dysfunction, and other conditions), comply with health-care laws by offering an "online medical consultation," which consists of a simple online questionnaire that is reviewed by a doctor. These online doctor "visits" might be free or have a modest surcharge—often $5 to $15, but sometimes as much as $50—but their real business is selling prescription medications. And, no, they generally do not accept health insurance.

Dangers: There are many risks to the use of prescription medications without proper oversight, including serious side effects that may go unmonitored, improper dosing, and dangerous interactions with other drugs or supplements that the patient is taking. Some of the conditions "fixed" by these sites actually are symptoms of more serious medical issues. If you don't see a doctor in person about your health problems, you won't learn about possible underlying causes.

It would be almost impossible for the doctors signing off on these prescriptions to un cover underlying conditions—they cannot physically examine patients...often have access only to patients' questionnaire answers, not their full medical histories...and frequently do not ask patients any follow-up questions.

What to do: Don't cut corners. See your regular doctor for diagnosis and treatment. If costs are a concern, save money not by skipping the doctor's appointment but by shopping around to find the drug for a low price at a website such as GoodRx.com or find out about patient assistance programs at NeedyMeds.org.

Create a "Peloton" Experience for Less

Louis Mazzante, test director for Hearst Enthusiast Group, which includes *Bicycling* magazine, Center Valley, Pennsylvania. Bicycling.com

The popular Peloton indoor exercise bikes provide remote access to fitness-club spin classes from the safety of home. But the $1,895 price (down from $2,245) plus the $39 monthly subscription fee is a lot to pay to pedal a stationary bike. The newest model, the Bike+, will cost even more—$2,495. But it's possible to create an engrossing indoor riding experience and stay in shape for a lot less, especially if you already own a stationary bike or a conventional outdoor bike. *Here's how...*

SUBSCRIBE TO AN APP

There are a number of indoor-cycling apps that offer benefits similar to the Peloton membership for a lot less—simply position a digital device running one of these apps in front of a stationary bike. You can use the screen-mirroring function available on some phones and tablets or a screen-casting device such as Google Chromecast to display the phone or laptop screen on a smart-TV screen.

Zwift lets you pedal your indoor bike on a wide array of virtual outdoor rides—cross deserts, climb volcanos, explore a futuristic version of New York City, and much more. You can ride with friends, compete in races, or join classes with coaches and—if you have compatible equipment (see below)—Zwift will track performance data such as your speed, distance, and heart rate. You also can use Zwift while running on a treadmill. $14.99/month. Zwift.com

The Sufferfest uses licensed footage from past events such as the Tour de France to put you right in the middle of world-class races. With compatible equipment, it will track your performance, including basics such as heart rate and speed plus advanced measurements such as neuromuscular power and anaerobic capacity. It also offers on-screen coaching tips. Strength-training and yoga classes are available on the app as well. $14.99/month. TheSufferfest.com

Peloton Digital offers access to the exact same celebrity-instructor–led spin classes and vibrant virtual biking community that Peloton owners receive through their memberships—but for less than one-third of the monthly membership price. In addition to spin classes, there are yoga and strength-training classes and more. But unlike with full Peloton membership—or with either of the previous apps—the Peloton Digital app won't communicate with your exercise equipment to provide on-screen performance stats such as your speed and distance covered, and the instructor won't be able to monitor your performance. $12.99/month. OnePeloton.com/app

CONVERT A BIKE TO INDOOR USE

A "trainer" converts an outdoor bicycle into an indoor stationary bike by holding the rear end of the bike off the ground and providing resistance. If your goal is to create a Peloton-like experience, purchase a "smart" trainer, which connects wirelessly to a bike-training app on your phone, tablet, or other digital device. *Two types worth considering, both are compatible with apps including Zwift and The Sufferfest...*

With a "direct drive" smart trainer, the bike's rear wheel is removed. By pedaling, you spin a flywheel that's part of the trainer. These systems usually are quiet and can adjust resistance levels automatically when a rider pedals up or down virtual hills in a compatible indoor-cycling app or when your workout calls

Wahoo Fitness KICKR Core Bike Trainer

for more effort. They cost much less than the Peloton, but they're not inexpensive.

Recommended: Wahoo Fitness KICKR Core Bike Trainer, $900.

With a "friction" smart trainer, the rear wheel remains on the bike and turns a resistance-providing cylinder. These tend to be affordable but loud. The rider must shift gears to adjust resistance levels—this won't happen automatically when there's a virtual hill in a biking app.

Recommended: Kinetic Road Machine Smart 2 Bike Trainer, $299.

A FEW MORE DETAILS

To complete the experience...

- **Point a fan at the bike.** Aim it so the airflow is directed at your torso as you ride. It keeps you from overheating.
- **Put a yoga mat under the bike.** This will absorb some of the bike's noise and keep sweat off the floor.
- **Wear a heart-rate monitor.** These wirelessly track your heart rate through a biking app.

Recommended: Wahoo Tickr, $50, is comfortable and compatible with Zwift, The Sufferfest, and Peloton apps. Or if you own a watch or other wearable device that tracks your heart rate, use that instead.

Free Ways to Do Workouts at Home

Download the free FitOn app, specify your fitness goals and stream videos on your TV, computer or smartphone. Go to Orange theory's YouTube channel for a new workout every day—you do not have to be a member. If you have exercise bands, use them—perform exercises as you usually would, but keep tension on the band at all times for a better workout. For weight-based training, use common household items, such as canned food or drinks for bicep curls. Do interval training with the stairs in your home by moving up them as quickly as possible, then walking slowly back down to catch your breath, and repeating several times.

MoneyTalksNews.com.

Free Ways to Learn New Things

Music: HoffmanAcademy.com offers free online tutorials for children who want to learn to play the piano. MusicTheory.net offers free lessons on music theory. *University-level classes:* There are hundreds of course offerings at Saylor.org, Coursera.org and Class Central.com. *Computer instruction:* Try Khan Academy.org, CodecAdemy.com, and Coursera.org—premium classes may have costs, but many classes are free. *Languages:* Duolingo.com uses a game-based teaching model. Open Culture.com offers a list of lessons available around the web.

Kiplinger.com

Great Sites to Save on Online Shopping

Kiplinger.com and Lifewire.com.

FreeShipping.org checks all retailer sites and provides terms, conditions and codes for free-shipping offers. RetailMeNot has coupons for tens of thousands of stores—you can search for specific ones, browse by department, find codes for free shipping, and more. Slickdeals is community-driven and posts numerous deals and coupons throughout the day, including ones that don't require a coupon code. The browser extension Pop-cart sends a pop-up notice whenever a product you are looking at costs less at a competitor's site. DealsPlus has a wide list of supported stores and offers e-mail alerts so you do not miss newly issued coupons. CouponCabin has a huge selection of promo codes and printable coupons so you can find deals both online and at brick-and-mortar stores. The Honey browser extension searches for all relevant program codes for an item you are buying and applies the one with the biggest savings. DealNews has a selection of product deals updated daily.

CardCash and GiftCardGranny are exchange sites where you can buy gift cards for less than face value.

Pay-for-Opinion Websites Worth Trying

Swagbucks.com gives points redeemable for gift cards or through PayPal for answering surveys about advertising, brand recognition, services, and more, and for various online tasks. *PointClub.com* gives points for various surveys and sometimes offers a signup bonus. The points can be redeemed for cash or gift cards. *PineconeResearch.com* offers points redeemable for cash or at its own rewards site. *OneOpinion.com* has especially good customer service, and the points you earn can be redeemed for cash or gift cards. *SurveyPolice.com* is a good resource for checking out more survey opportunities and avoiding scam sites.

MoneyTalksNews.com

Ways to Avoid the 11.9 Percent Coinstar Fee

Cashing in $100 of change at a Coinstar machine will cost you $11.90. But there is no processing charge if you accept a Coinstar eGift card instead of cash. The cards are good at 25 participating companies, including Amazon, Home Depot, Lowe's, and several restaurant chains and movie-theater groups. If you want to turn in your coins for cash without a fee, find out if your bank will take them—some have coin-counting machines that are free for customers, and some will provide paper coin sleeves that you can use to wrap coins yourself before turning them in.

GoBankingRates.com

MONEY SMARTS...

Easy Ways to Cut the Cost of Buying Products

Sign up for newsletters—Companies including Betty Crocker, Pillsbury, and Procter & Gamble regularly offer samples and full-sized products for free to new subscribers. Try following your favorite brands and companies on Facebook and Twitter for additional rewards. *For freebees for dogs*—BringFido.com sends weekly e-mails through which you can get samples. *E-books*—Gutenberg.org offers thousands of books for free download. And you can search for free e-books at Amazon.com and BarnesandNoble.com. *Audiobooks*—try DigitalBook.io and LoyalBooks.com...both sites also offer some free e-books. *Beauty products*—Sephora.com and Ulta.com offer a free gift for your birthday month. *Shipping*—go to FreeShipping.org for online retailers that offer free shipping and discount codes.

Kiplinger.com

Great Sources for Free Audiobooks

The free books offered on these sites range from biography to fiction and nonfiction, but each site has a fairly limited selection. Audible Stories are free from Audible.com, whose main business is selling audiobooks.

OverDrive.com and HooplaDigital.com are free services associated with your local library. OpenCulture.com and LibriVox.org feature many public-domain titles. Etc.USF.edu/lit2go offers MP3 downloads and lets users search by readability level. LoyalBooks.com not only makes free audiobooks available but also lets users rate and review them. Storynory.com specializes in children's audiobooks—but its site is particularly ad-heavy, so be careful to click on stories, not ads.

MoneyTalksNews.com

Where to Get Free Air for Your Tires

Costco inflates tires with nitrogen, which may keep them inflated longer, and fills tires even if you don't have a membership. Discount Tire inflates tires with air, no matter where you bought them, at its 1,000 stores. Getgo, owned by supermarket Giant Eagle, offers free air. Regional chains where you can get air for free include Hy-Vee in eight Midwestern states...Kum & Go in 11 states...Kwik Trip in Iowa, Minnesota, and Wyoming...QuickChek in New York and New Jersey...QuikTrip in 11 states in the Midwest and South...Sheetz in six states...Stewart's Shops in New York and Vermont...Wawa in six states and Washington, DC.

Clark.com

How to Buy a New Car from Home

Philip Reed, who writes a syndicated column about cars for NerdWallet.com that has appeared in newspapers including *USA Today* and *The Washington Post*.

Buying a new car from home not only helps you avoid crowds and aggressive salespeople—it also can save you lots of time and hundreds or even thousands of dollars. *Here's what you need to know to help you succeed...*

WHY IT WORKS

The in-person car-buying process is grueling on purpose—dealerships know that the more time a buyer spends discussing a purchase, the greater the odds that he/she eventually will make that purchase, even if the price isn't great. It's psychologically difficult for would-be buyers to walk away empty-handed, especially when face-to-face with a salesperson. That would mean admitting those hours were wasted...and dealing with the fact that the process will have to be launched all over again at a different dealership.

In contrast, dealerships tend to offer significantly better deals to buyers who contact them online—without prolonged negotiations or dealership tricks—rather than shop in person. They have learned that at-home shoppers tend to be savvy consumers who solicit quotes from multiple dealers and won't overpay. Online shopping also forces dealers to compete with other dealers because shoppers can contact many dealers in the time it takes to visit one dealership in person.

Not every dealership is anxious to sell cars this way, and certain aspects of the buying process remain tricky to handle from home. But in this sketchy economic and health environment, dealerships are more likely than ever to work with buyers who decline to drop by.

9 KEY STRATEGIES

1. Test drive cars from home. Call the closest dealerships that sell makes and models that interest you, and ask whether the cars can be brought to you for test drives. If you are concerned about visiting a showroom for health-safety reasons, explain that you intend to buy a car soon but you don't want to visit the dealership. Many dealerships began offering no-cost, no-commitment drop-off test drives to local shoppers this year, and some were willing to do this even before this year. You might want to confirm that the employees who bring the cars wear masks and wipe down the cars with disinfectant—or you might want to do so yourself.

Alternatively, you could test drive at the dealership but then quickly leave to maintain your negotiating edge—do not let yourself get roped into negotiating the price of the car while you're on the dealership lot.

2. Request quotes from dealers through car-shopping websites. Sites including Cars Direct.com, Edmunds.com, Kelley Blue Book (KBB.com), Rydeshopper.com, and TrueCar.com allow you to request online quotes from multiple dealerships in your area. Edmunds, Kelley Blue Book, and TrueCar also have tools that show shoppers how much other buyers in their area have paid, on average, for the same vehicle. Try several sites—different dealers may use different ones. You typically will have to provide contact info including an e-mail address and phone number, so you might receive sales calls and/or e-mails, at least until you have bought a vehicle.

There's nothing unethical about test driving with one dealership and buying from another—and if this does bother you, you can always give the test-drive dealership business by bringing your car there for servicing.

Some dealerships might suggest that you stop by to discuss the purchase rather than provide a quote. Respond that you are interested in receiving quotes only via e-mail or phone.

3. Call area dealerships that sell the type of car you want but that did not provide online quotes through the websites above. Not every dealership works through the third-party websites, but virtually every dealership has an "Internet Department" these days that handles customers who make contact through the website. When calling, ask for this department or the "Internet Sales Manager"—or e-mail this person—and then request a quote on the car and option packages you want. The Internet specialists are more likely to offer a fair price right off the bat with relatively little sales pressure—their mandate tends to be to sell cars in high volume, not necessarily with the highest possible profit margins.

Gather quotes from at least five dealerships, either directly or through the third-party websites. Using price-comparison tools on the third-party sites, confirm that the lowest of the quotes is less than what the average buyer paid—or whatever price you consider appropriate based on your research.

In rural areas (or with uncommon makes or models), you might have to include relatively distant dealerships to obtain five or more quotes.

Reminder: You don't have to bring a car back to the dealership where you purchased it when it needs warranty or recall work. Any of the make's dealerships can do these repairs.

4. Call your bank or credit union to prequalify for a car loan if you intend to finance the car. Many automakers have been offering extremely attractive financing deals these days—in some cases, zero percent interest. But the best of these deals often are not available to buyers who have less-than-excellent credit. If your credit score is below the mid-to-high 700s, call bank/credit unions and ask to be prequalified for an auto loan. If the dealership later says that you don't qualify for an attractive financing deal, use this bank/credit union loan offer instead.

5. Obtain quotes on your trade-in from online car-buying companies. Dealerships often make low-ball quotes on trade-ins because they know many car buyers don't want to deal with the hassles of selling their used car on their own. That's especially true given this year's health concerns—selling a used car can mean interacting with multiple strangers.

Instead, obtain offers on your current car from CarMax.com, Carvana.com, Shift.com, and/or Vroom.com. These used-car dealers often offer more than a new-car dealership would for a trade-in—though likely less than you could get if you sold your car on your own. Some even will pick up your vehicle from your home. If nothing else, having a quote in hand from one of these companies could help you negotiate a better price on a trade-in with a dealership.

6. Check for automaker incentives and rebates on the vehicle you intend to buy. Look for these on the automaker's website and on Edmunds' Car Deals and Incentives page (Edmunds.com/car-incentives). Note any that seem to apply to you.

7. Pin down the best price. Reach out to the dealership that quoted you the lowest price, and ask it to confirm that this is your "out-the-door" price, including all fees, taxes, and registrations. Ask the dealer to e-mail you a breakdown of the quote, detailing all fees, taxes, and other costs, if it hasn't done so already. If you found any incentives or rebates for the vehicle, ask if these are included in the quoted price and, if not, whether they can be applied to the quote.

If you want to try to negotiate, contact dealerships that did not offer the lowest quote and give them a chance to beat the lowest quote... and/or make a counteroffer to the dealership with the best price. But don't expect to lower your price very much—if you've obtained five or more quotes online, the best of them is likely within $200 to $500 of the lowest feasible price.

8. If you're financing the purchase, run the numbers through a car-payment calculator. Occasionally, dealerships agree to a price and interest rate but then use a higher price or rate when calculating the buyer's monthly payments. They know that most buyers won't spot the discrepancy. You can easily check for this trick if you're buying a car from home—enter the agreed-upon price, interest rate, loan length, down payment, and trade-in value, if applicable, into NerdWallet's Car Payment Calculator (Nerdwallet.com/blog/loans/car-loan-calculator). If the monthly payment displayed doesn't match the one quoted by the dealership, ask the dealership to explain the discrepancy—and work with a different dealership if you're not satisfied with the explanation.

9. Ask the dealership if it can deliver the car to you along with the paperwork that needs to be signed. Some, though not all, dealerships will agree to do this if that's what is needed to close the sale. Depending on state law, it even might be possible to sign the necessary paperwork online.

If delivery is not possible, ask whether the paperwork can at least be handled with as little in-person contact as possible.

Best Wall Chargers for Electric Vehicles

If you have an electric car or plug-in hybrid, consider installing a wall charger, which may be able to charge your car in hours instead of overnight or over days when plugging the cable into a regular 120-volt outlet in your garage.

Three top picks: JuiceBox 40 comes with a 25-foot cord, a dedicated app, and Wi-Fi connectivity that allows you to schedule charging at off-peak times. It charges at 40 amps. $569. ChargePoint Home Flex has a compact, sleek design with a 23-foot cord. The current can be ramped up to 50 amps. $699. Blink HQ 100 is inexpensive, and easy to use. Comes with an 18-foot cable that features a convenient hook for storage. Charges at 30 amps. $450. The cost to install one of these chargers averages $750 nationally.

ConsumerReports.org

Save Money on Golf

Your favorite game doesn't have to cripple your wallet. Shop around for greens fees. The more flexible you are with the place and time, the more money you can save. Use GolfNow.com or TeeOff.com to find little-used time slots. Play later in the day. "Twilight" tee times (which are defined differently at different courses) can save you up to 50 percent. Google "golf discount card" in your area. A "passport" or "season pass" at a local course can quickly pay for itself in discounts. Let YouTube be your pro. If you're looking for tips, don't underestimate the value of free online videos to help you improve your golf game.

Reviewed.com, a product testing and review site.

Zappos Is Selling Single Sneakers

In response to customer feedback, the shoe company Zappos has begun offering sneakers in singles, or pairs in two different sizes, to amputees and other people with physical needs that make a traditional pair a poor fit. The program involves such big names as Converse, Nike, and New Balance, and there will be no price bump for a single sneaker. "One half of the pair is half of the price," according to the retailer.

Shape.com

GOOD TO KNOW...

You Can Have Confidence in Vitamin C Supplements

All 17 common brands tested by ConsumerLab.com contained the amount of C advertised, were free of contaminants and broke down correctly—so don't stress about brands. Pills or powders are better than gummies, which cost more, stick to teeth, add calories and are too easy to consume like candy.

Tod Cooperman, MD, president and editor-in-chief of ConsumerLab.com.

Hidden Dangers in Food from China

Tony Corbo, senior government affairs representative at Food & Water Watch, Washington, DC, responsible for food-related legislative and regulatory issues that come before Congress and the Executive Branch. FoodAndWaterWatch.org

Regulations that the Chinese government instituted to food-safety laws in December 2019 don't address key problems—heavy metals such as lead, mercury and arsenic in their soil...and the overuse of pesticides, animal antibiotics, and additives in food processing. The riskiest foods are fish, shellfish, vegetables, and fruits.

Adding to the problem is lack of U.S. oversight. Our agencies don't have the manpower to inspect enough food plants in China or check more than one percent or 2 percent of shipments that arrive in the U.S.

High percentages of the apple juice, processed mushrooms, frozen spinach, and tilapia we consume are from China. The USDA has not permitted China to export poultry products from birds raised there to the U.S. until recently. Poultry products have to be cooked, but a hidden provision in the trade act opens the door for fresh poultry to come here in the future.

Our "Country of Origin Labeling" law requires most markets to post where foods, including fresh and frozen chicken, some meats, seafood, fruits, and vegetables, come from. So buying whole, fresh foods is safest.

Once a product has been prepared or processed, country-of-origin labeling isn't mandatory. For example, breaded chicken products and dried spices do not have to be labeled. Country of origin usually is marked on the box in which spice containers come to the store, so ask at the customer-service desk.

Note: Other countries that have a high number of food shipments refused by the FDA for contamination are Mexico, primarily for vegetables, and India, notably for spices and farm-raised shrimp. An organic label is not a guarantee that a product is safe to buy.

Don't Waste Your Money on These Mosquito-Repellent Products

Consumer Reports and *Reader's Digest.*

Makers of mosquito repellents have responded to consumers' reluctance to use DEET-based sprays by introducing a host of alternatives. Unfortunately, many are ineffective, unproven, or unsafe.

Wristbands: When testers plunged their arms into cages full of mosquitoes, they were immediately bitten despite the wristbands.

Vitamin B mosquito patches: Studies still are underway, but the U.S. National Library of Medicine's National Center for Biotechnology Information has cast doubt on the efficacy of taking the vitamin orally as a mosquito repellent.

Clip-on fans: This product uses a personal fan to circulate the chemical metofluthrin about your person. Not only does it provide less protection than spray-on repellents, metofluthrin is classified by the EPA as a neurotoxin and potential carcinogen.

TAKE NOTE...

Hummus and Beans Often Are Contaminated

Hummus and beans often are contaminated with glyphosate, the weed killer in Roundup linked to cancer, warns toxicologist Alexis Temkin, PhD. Investigators tested conventional and organic hummus, beans, and lentils purchased online and from major food retailers. Ninety percent of chickpea-based samples had detectable glyphosate, many with quite high levels. Lowest were canned chickpeas from Goya, Hanover and Simple Truth Organic. There also were low, hummus samples such as O Organics, The Perfect Pita, and Asmar's.

Best: Make your own hummus from organic chickpeas.

Alexis Temkin, PhD, a toxicologist with the Environmental Working Group, Washington, DC. See the full study results at EWG.org.

This Form of Identity Theft Slips Through Traditional Protections

A scammer applies for credit using your Social Security number but different name and address so the fraud won't appear on credit reports and avoids a credit freeze. Watch for unfamiliar "aliases" on your credit reports. If your credit score drops 50 points or more despite no new problems or major activity, ask the credit bureaus for any "sub files"—associated with your Social Security number but not your name. If they exist, follow procedures for reporting identity theft.

Steven J.J. Weisman, Esq., an attorney in private practice and founder of the scam-information website Scamicide.com.

Five Signs of a Furniture-Moving Scam

The company is not authorized by the Federal Motor Carrier Safety Administration. Check at Safer.FMCSA.dot.gov. *Quotes are misleadingly low.* The company waits until moving day to tell you that there are extra fees for stairs, heavy items, and so forth—charges that may be legitimate but should be disclosed in advance. *A company has no reviews online.* It could be new or small—but check the FMCSA site to be sure it is legitimate. Check each firm's online customer reviews before getting a quote. *The company charges by the cubic foot.* Many scammers charge this way instead of by weight. But so do a few legitimate companies, so check customer reviews and comments. *The estimate is nonbinding.* A binding estimate locks in your price as long as you do not add anything to the move. Avoid companies that ask you to sign with them before an appraisal and binding estimate are completed.

MoneyTalksNews.com

Costly Scams Targeting Seniors Now

Steven J.J. Weisman, Esq., founder of the scam-information website Scamicide.com. He is an attorney in private practice and senior lecturer at Bentley University in Waltham, Massachusetts. He is author of *Identity Theft Alert.*

Grandparents love their grandkids—and that's just one of the weaknesses that scammers have learned to exploit. Scammers use various specific tactics to target older victims, according to a recent report by the Federal Trade Commission (FTC). When the FTC analyzed the 1.5 million fraud reports it had received from consumers for a recent 12-month period, it was not surprising that some key differences emerged between the scams that victimized people age 60 and older and those that targeted younger people. Knowing the details of these senior-focused frauds can help older people protect themselves...and help younger people provide support to their older loved ones.

Among the report's highlights...

• **Older victims are most often contacted over the phone.** People tend to assume that the Internet is where scammers are lurking these days, and certainly there are plenty of dangers online. But based on reports to the FTC, scammers actually contact victims age 60 and up via phone more than four times as often as by all other forms of contact combined.

Scammers like the phone because calling allows them to keep the pressure dialed up—if they contact a would-be victim via e-mail or text, that victim is more likely to take a moment to pause and think before responding. Scammers probably would prefer to call younger victims, too, but younger generations rarely answer calls from people they don't know, preferring to text their friends and let callers leave voicemails.

What to do: If you don't recognize a caller on caller-ID, don't answer—if it's important, the caller will leave a message. A scammer might leave a message, too, but at least you would have time to consider whether it's a scam before calling back. Be suspicious if your phone's caller-ID names a government agency or well-known corporation. Scammers often show up on caller-ID with fake government and big-company IDs. Consider signing up for a robocall-blocking service offered by your cell-phone service provider. If you're not satisfied with your provider's service, you could try a third-party robocall-blocking app such as Nomorobo (free for landlines, $1.99 per month for smartphones, Nomorobo.com). This can reduce the number of automated calls you receive, including scam calls, though it won't stop them entirely.

• **Scammers take advantage of grandparents' love for their grandchildren.** People age 60 and older are more than three times more likely than younger people to lose money to the so-called family/friend imposter scam. Even if you have heard about this scam before, it's easy to get caught off guard and fall for it, so it's wise to review what to do. *There are several versions, but when it's perpetrated on an older victim it usually works like this...*

A grandparent receives a call explaining that one of his/her grandkids is in a very difficult situation and desperately needs money. Sometimes the grandchild is said to be in the hospital too badly injured to speak on the phone...other times the grandchild is said to be in jail, perhaps a foreign jail during a spring-break trip to Cancun gone wrong. The parents can't be reached—the grandparent is the grandchild's last hope. In fact, the grandchild is just fine, but concerned grandparents sometimes are convinced to send money before they learn this. The scammer's presumption is that grandparents feel responsible for their grandkids but often don't know enough about their grandkids' whereabouts to spot the lie.

What to do: If someone claims your grandchild needs cash, refuse to be rushed—demand a callback name and phone number, then hang up and try to reach the grandchild and/or his parents to determine whether the call is legitimate. If the caller refuses to provide a callback number, assume it's a scam. If the caller claims to represent a particular hospital or police department, look up that organization's actual phone number, call that number, and ask to speak with the name you were given.

Don't be swayed by the fact that a caller knows a few details about your grandchild, such as her name or where she is spending spring break. A scammer might have gleaned that information from social-media websites or elsewhere.

• **Scammers increasingly ask for gift cards.** Historically, scammers have tried to get victims to send money via wire transfer, credit card, check, or cash. That still happens—but these days, gift cards are the preferred plunder in 23 percent of all scams reported by victims who are 60 or older. Gift cards are easy for scammers to convert to cash but very difficult for victims to cancel once the card or its identifying numbers have been provided.

What to do: If anyone other than a retailer tells you that gift cards are an acceptable method of payment, there's a good chance that you're being scammed—hang up.

• **Time-share scams often are incredibly costly.** Time-shares can be difficult to resell, and some scammers take advantage of this challenge by offering to help time-share owners sell these properties. In reality, these scammers pocket payments from time-share owners, then do little or nothing to help them. Older people are far more likely to be targeted with this scam than younger people, because they're often the ones with time-shares to sell.

What to do: Never work with any time-share–resale service that demands payment from you before the sale is finalized.

• **Tech-support scams are especially likely to snare seniors.** A victim receives a phone call from someone claiming to be with a well-known tech company—the victim's caller-ID likely lists a big-name tech company, such as Microsoft or Apple (as noted previously, caller-ID can be faked). This ersatz phone rep claims he has identified a problem with the victim's computer, but says he can help. Or in a different version of this scam, a message pops up on a victim's computer screen claiming that the computer has a problem and its owner should call the provided phone number for help. In either version of this scam, the victim might be asked to pay for tech support…to provide personal information that could be used for ID theft…and/or to take steps that provide this "tech support" worker with remote access to the victim's computer—which hands total control of the machine to this stranger.

What to do: Ignore calls and pop-up ads claiming to be from tech support. Legitimate tech support does not call unprompted or send pop-up messages asking you to call. If this pop-up message cannot easily be closed, try closing the Internet browser and/or turning off the computer. Install a well-regarded security program on your computer, such as Malware Bytes (Free, MalwareBytes.com)…or Kaspersky Total Security (from $44.99/year, USA.Kaspersky.com), and keep this up to date.

If you believe that there might be an actual problem with your computer, ask a tech-savvy loved one for help or bring it to a local computer repair shop.

TAKE NOTE…

Scammers Are Sending Bogus Invoices through the Real Paypal System

These invoices usually purport to be from well-known companies or charities and often are for modest amounts—$50 or less. All that scammers need to send a bogus invoice is the e-mail address associated with the victim's PayPal account. If you receive a PayPal invoice for a purchase or donation that you didn't make, delete it—the scammer can't take your money if you don't click "pay."

Robert Siciliano, cofounder of Protect Now LLC, a security training company, Boston, and author of *Identity Theft Privacy.* ProtectNowLLC.com

Rising Cybercrime Threat

Pixel tracking. When you open an e-mail—even without responding or clicking on any links—pixel trackers show the operating system you use, when you opened the message and with what device, your IP address, and other data. Advertisers and marketers have used pixel tracking for some time to target their messages. Now thieves are using it, too—to increase their ability to steal money and identities.

Self-defense: Block images from displaying in e-mail—the images contain the tracker. In Gmail, go to Settings and click on "Ask before displaying external images," then save changes. Similar blocking is available for other e-mail programs—check their settings. To find out which e-mails contain tracking code, use a browser extension such as PixelBlock or Ugly Mail.

Kim Komando, technology expert writing at Komando.com.

Useful Google Maps Features

Change the time window based on when you plan to travel—tap the "depart at" button near the top of the screen. Bookmark places you like by tapping the save button after searching for a location. Use the explore section, near the bottom of the screen, for recommendations on places to go. Find parking at your destination when searching for driving directions—look for the circled P icon next to the estimated trip time. If you are using public transportation and concerned about crowding, type your destination in the search box, select public transit as the mode of travel, and tap the route suggestion—you will see route details, including how crowded the train likely will be when you go.

BusinessInsider.com

Free Cloud Storage

Apple device users automatically get 5 GB of free iCloud space—enough to store perhaps 1,000 photos...Windows users get 5 GB free on OneDrive...buyers of Microsoft Office 365 get a terabyte (1,000 GB)...Amazon Prime members get unlimited photo storage and 5 GB of video storage included with membership. Independent companies offering free storage include Box and MediaFire, each of which gives 10 GB free...and iDrive, which offers 5 GB free. All the firms sell additional cloud storage—amounts and pricing vary widely, so shop around.

MoneyTalksNews.com

Easy Ways to Get Money for Old Cell Phone

You can get cash for old cell phones and other electronics that are in good condition. Decluttr.com, accepts phones, gaming consoles, video games, tablets, Apple and Samsung wearables, and MacBooks, as well as CDs and DVDs. Gazelle.com buys and sells cell phones, tablets, iPods, and Apple computers. Amazon.com has a trade-in program that offers gift cards for cell phones, Kindles, gaming devices, Bluetooth and smart speakers, streaming media players, and tablets. Best Buy takes trade-ins by mail and at some stores—it accepts cell phones, tablets, MP3 players, video games, gaming consoles, computers, cameras, wearables and TVs. Staples accepts cell phones, tablets, and laptops in return for its eCash cards. Target takes cell phones, tablets, gaming consoles, wearables, and voice speakers. Walmart accepts cell phones, tablets, E-readers, gaming consoles, smart speakers, and MP3 players. Visit websites for details.

MoneyTalksNews.com

MONEY SAVERS...

Save On Your Cell-Phone Bill

Save on your cell-phone bill by leaving the major carriers and moving to smaller, independent companies. Mint charges $15/month if you commit to a full year of service with 4 GB of mobile data...Unreal Mobile charges $15/month if you commit for a full year of service with 3 GB of mobile data. Plans offering 12 GB start at $25/month. Straight Talk from Walmart, with 5 GB of mobile data, costs $35/month. If you consume a lot of data away from Wi-Fi, you may be better off choosing a major carrier. The best way to keep costs low is by using Wi-Fi as much as possible—preferably all the time. Then your mobile-data usage will be zero or close to it.

Roundup of experts on cell phones and plans, reported in *USA Today.*

Check Your Laptop Battery's Health

Check your laptop battery's health so you know when it is losing the ability to hold a charge and you can replace it.

PC laptops: Click the Start menu, search for PowerShell, click on it, and type "powercfg/batteryreport." Press Enter to generate a report with battery-health information. Then search for the folder with the name C:\Users[YourUsername] to locate it. Scroll down to Battery Information—the subsection called Battery Life Estimates will indicate how long your battery will currently last on a full charge, compared with how long it lasted when new.

Mac laptops: Hold the Option key and click on the Apple menu. Click System Information. Scroll down to Hardware > Power > Cycle Count. This will indicate how many times the battery has completed a cycle—battery cycles before necessary replacement vary with each Macbook model. For example, Macbook Pros released from 2009 rated for 1,000 cycles on their batteries.

Komando.com

Wi-Fi Systems to Boost Internet

Ry Crist, senior editor at CNET, the consumer electronics review and information source. He specializes in smarthome-electronics products and systems. CNET.com

Your home Wi-Fi connection has become even more of a lifeline this year, whether it's for work, shopping, entertainment, or chats. *Here are some of the best devices to improve your Wi-Fi performance and extend its range...*

• **For houses and apartments up to 1,800 square feet.** If your router is more than a few years old, consider replacing it with one that has the most recent version of Wi-Fi technology—Wi-Fi 5, the standard nowadays.

My favorite economically priced router: D-Link DIR-867 offers one of the fastest download/upload speeds of any Wi-Fi 5 router—better than many higher-priced models—and reduces lag time even when multiple devices are streaming. $169

Alternative: Next-generation Wi-Fi 6 routers offer faster speeds than Wi-Fi 5 and maintain more stable connections in densely furnished spaces and between rooms with thick walls. A growing number of devices, such as iPhone 11 and 12 and Samsung Galaxy S10 and S20 phones, can take advantage of Wi-Fi 6 enhancements. Meanwhile, most devices will function at Wi-Fi 5 level performance with Wi-Fi 6 routers.

My favorite: TP-Link Archer AX6000 has eight antennas and surpasses the speed of typical Wi-Fi 5 routers by as much as 40 percent. $329.

• **For larger homes up to two stories and/or if you have a dead zone.** Expand the range of your Wi-Fi in a particular room or area by adding an extender. It's a small, low-cost device with an internal antenna that plugs into any electrical socket and functions like a bridge, capturing the signal from your router and rebroadcasting it.

My favorite extender: TP-Link RE220 takes less than a minute to set up and wirelessly connects with almost any router, extending the range to as much as 3,200 square feet. $34.

• **For homes with more than two stories and/or multiple dead zones.** Consider a mesh network, which replaces your router and extender with a set of small devices that include powerful internal antennas. You hook up one to your modem and place the others around your home. Unlike multiple extenders, whose Wi-Fi signals weaken as you add more, each mesh network device boosts the signal, so you get the same signal strength and speed everywhere.

My favorite: eero Wi-Fi mesh system includes three devices and provides an ultra-reliable Internet connection. $279 for a basic three-pack that reaches up to 5,000 square feet plus $89 for each additional unit.

through the web or can be downloaded as an app for Roku, Apple TV, Google Play, Amazon and Xbox. Vimeo is a website and an Android and iOS app—plans range from free for Vimeo Basic to $7 to $20 per month. Internet Archive offers public-domain films, mostly from the 1920s and 1930s. Sony Crackle features action and thriller movies and some old TV shows. Vudu has free content in addition to its paid offerings. IMDb TV, owned by Amazon, is free with ads or ad-free on Fire TV devices and within the Prime Video App. Hoopla offers DVDs, CDs, and audiobooks to libraries—ask if yours participates. The Roku Channel has free movie and TV content for Roku owners. YouTube offers some licensed films for free—search Movies & Shows and click on "Free to Watch" category.

Komando.com

Indoor HDTV Antennas

Indoor HDTV antennas give TV viewers free access to local channels, which cord-cutters often miss after they cancel their cable subscriptions. Good HDTV antennas can also produce picture quality better than what cable provides.

Antennas that performed best when placed near a window: Mohu ReLeaf, $47…Winegard FlatWave FL5500A, $60…Clearstream 2Max, $80.

Best performers when placement near a window is not possible: 1byone Digital Amplified, $30…AmazonBasics Ultra Thin Indoor TV Antenna, $20.

Consumer Reports.

Great Ways to Watch Movies for Free

Kanopy offers art-house and classic films—your local library, university, or college must be connected to it. Popcornflix streams

Save on Utility Bills

Shop around: Call your power company, and ask for a list of energy providers—then call them directly to compare prices. *Use a smart thermostat* to set the temperature higher (or lower during the winter) during the day if you are not home and during the night while you are asleep—also try programming it to use less energy at peak hours. *Cool your hot water* by turning the water heater down to 120°F. Water heaters can be nearly 20% of your electricity bill, so setting your heater a little lower—the default setting is usually 140°—can save a lot over time. *Run appliances late at night,* when energy costs are lower. *Keep up with filter changes*—if filters get dirty, your heating and air-conditioning system will use more power. *Use timers on lights* so they turn off when not in use. *Switch to LEDs,* which use 80 percent less power than incandescent bulbs and last more than 40 times longer. *Use ceiling fans*—each costs about a penny an hour to run versus 36 cents an hour for air-conditioning.

Roundup of experts on energy use, reported in *USA Today.*

13

Insurance Alerts

Tricky Medicare Rules Lead to Costly Mistakes

There are times when you might think that your health-care expenses are covered by Medicare—but they're not. Or you think you're not covered—but you are.

That's because Medicare is an enormously complex system of rules and exceptions that lead many people astray. *Tricky Medicare situations that can confuse even savvy participants...*

• **Employee, retiree, or Cobra coverage may be secondary to Medicare once you turn 65—even if you don't have Medicare.** Some people do not sign up for Medicare when they turn 65 because they still have health-care coverage through an employer, former employer, or union. Some of these people will learn the hard way that their employer-based plan may no longer provide adequate coverage once they turn 65.

If you have retiree coverage or Cobra coverage—which is primarily for employees who recently lost their jobs—that coverage becomes "secondary" on your 65th birthday. The same is true if you have active-employee coverage through an employer that has fewer than 20 employees—though not if you have active employee coverage from a larger employer. "Secondary" means this insurance will pay only the portion of medical bills that is covered by this insurance after Medicare pays. If you signed up for Medicare Part A and Part B, you can draw on both plans to get full coverage. But if you have not signed up for Medicare, you'll have to pay the portion that Medicare would have paid.

Tatiana Fassieux, training specialist and past board chair for California Health Advocates, a Sacramento-based nonprofit that provides Medicare advocacy and education. She has more than 20 years of experience as a Medicare educator and trainer and has testified before the US Senate's Special Aging Committee. CAHealthAdvocates.org

Unfortunately, people unaware of this quirk often fail to sign up for Medicare at age 65 and don't realize there's a problem until big, uncovered medical bills arrive. In fact, insurance companies sometimes initially cover these bills, then demand repayment months later—at which point the patient might have missed his/her Medicare initial enrollment window.

Example: A California woman who failed to sign up for Medicare when she stopped working owed her Cobra coverage provider $150,000 after the provider realized that its coverage should have been secondary to Medicare and demanded repayment.

What to do: Consider signing up for Medicare Part A and Part B during the open-enrollment period that falls before your 65th birthday even if you have active-employee coverage from a small employer...or retiree or Cobra coverage.

However, if you are employed with a company that has 20 or more employees when you turn 65, it might not be worth signing up for Medicare Part B or prescription drug Part D—it may add little or nothing to your existing benefits for the premium you pay. Confirm with your employer's benefits coordinator that the company has 20 or more employees. Large-company employees typically should sign up for Part A as age 65 nears, however. Part A does not have a monthly premium for most participants, so there usually is no downside to doing this.

Potential exception: If the coverage you receive through a large employer is a high-deductible health plan and you wish to contribute to a Health Savings Account (HSA), it might be worth delaying enrollment in Part A. If you are enrolled in Medicare Part A and/or B, you are not eligible to make contributions to an HSA, though you still can spend money that you already have in an HSA.

• **At-home custodial care isn't covered—unless it is.** You might have heard that Medicare does not pay for "custodial care"—in-home assistance with basic life activities such as bathing, dressing and cooking. But buried in Medicare's rules is an exception that many people miss—if you require skilled nursing service and/or skilled therapy care, such as physical therapy or speech therapy, and you cannot easily travel to medical facilities to obtain this care, then your custodial care could be covered as well. There are limits on this coverage, however, and hoops you would have to jump through to obtain it.

What to do: If your doctor says you require skilled nursing care or skilled therapy care, explain that you are unable to travel to receive this care and ask the doctor if he/she can order home health care. If your doctor agrees to order this and that skilled care is required no more than once each day and for a finite period of time, then the part-time custodial-care services you also require could become covered as well—though only if you obtain this custodial care from a Medicare-certified home health agency. You can find these by entering your location into the "Find a Home Health Agency" tool on Medicare.gov (Medicare.gov/HomeHealthCompare/Search.html).

• **You might be billed for vaccinations—even though they're covered by Medicare.** Many vaccines are covered under Part D, the Medicare component that covers prescription drugs. But patients generally receive vaccinations at their doctor's offices—and doctor's office administrators are used to sending bills to Part B, the Medicare component that provides medical insurance.

Result: Many vaccination bills are submitted for the wrong part of Medicare. When Medicare denies payment because of this mistake, these doctor's offices often fail to notice that the problem was a billing error and bill the patient for the vaccination. Most patients pay, assuming that the vaccine must not have been covered.

What to do: If you receive a bill from your doctor's office and/or an "explanation of benefits" notice from Medicare informing you that a vaccination was not covered, read the notice and/or contact the doctor's billing department to confirm that the proper Medicare component was billed. With many vaccines—including shingles, Tdap (for tetanus, diphtheria and pertussis), chicken pox and hepatitis A—Medicare Part D should have been billed.

Other vaccines, including those for influenza, pneumonia and hepatitis B, are covered by Part B. If you discover that a vaccination was misbilled, instruct the billing department to resubmit its request for payment to the proper Medicare component. If the billing department drags its heels, contact your Part D plan and ask how to submit a claim for reimbursement if you must pay the bill out of pocket.

You also could remind your doctor's office that Part D should be billed when you receive a Part D–covered vaccine, but don't be surprised if this fails to prevent the problem. The person who does the billing for the office might not be the person you spoke with.

• **A hidden hospital decision might mean that your stay in a skilled nursing facility is not covered.** Medicare typically fully covers the cost of a stay in a skilled nursing facility for up to 20 days (and partially covers up to an additional 80 days) as long as this stay follows a hospital stay of three days or longer. But perplexingly, not every stay in a hospital counts as a hospital stay. Sometimes hospitals assign patients rooms but give them "observation" status rather than officially admitting them. This generally happens to patients who initially receive treatment in the emergency room but then are advised to remain in the hospital. Hospitals often fail to make it clear to these patients that they have not officially been admitted—and even when they do, patients rarely realize the financial consequences of this decision. If a patient is not officially admitted, Medicare will not pay for a subsequent stay in a skilled nursing facility. The same is true if a patient was initially given observation status and later switched to inpatient status, if that changing status means that total inpatient time was less than the required three days. Additionally, observation status can lead to higher out-of-pocket costs for the hospital stay itself, because it means bills are paid by Medicare Part B, which typically has higher coinsurance payments than Part A.

What to do: If you are advised to stay overnight in the hospital after initially visiting the emergency room, ask the doctor providing treatment (or another hospital employee) whether you are being admitted or instead you are under observation status. If the answer is observation, ask how you can appeal this decision—the hospital should have a process for doing so.

MEDICARE PLANS DEFINED

Medicare Part A covers hospital stays, hospice care and some skilled nursing. Medicare Part B covers doctor and outpatient services such as diagnostic screenings, lab tests and medical equipment. Medicare Part D pays for some prescription drugs.

You May Be Overpaying for Medicare

Danielle Roberts, founding partner of Boomer Benefits, a Fort Worth–based insurance agency specializing in Medicare-related coverage. She is a Medicare Supplement Accredited Advisor. BoomerBenefits.com

Most Medicare beneficiaries pay part B premiums of $148.50 per month in 2021, but some are charged an amount between $207.90 and $504.90—for exactly the same coverage.

The inflated premiums are imposed on a sliding scale on Medicare recipients whose modified adjusted gross income (MAGI) plus any tax-exempt interest income tops $88,000 ($176,000 for married couples filing jointly). But there's a twist—your premiums are calculated based on your income from two years prior.

Example: Your 2021 premiums are based on your 2019 MAGI. So if your income is lower now than it was two years ago, there's a chance you're paying more than you should. This is especially likely if you or your spouse were working in 2019 but now are retired.

What to do: If you are paying more than $148.50 per month for Medicare Part B, you might be able to appeal the inflated premiums. To successfully appeal, you must have experienced a "qualifying life event" that lowered your income during the prior two years. The most common qualifying life event is that you and/or your spouse stopped working or are working fewer hours. Other qualifying events include marriage...divorce...death of a spouse...loss/sale of an income-producing property...changes in or termination of a pension...or receipt of a settlement from an employer due to its bankruptcy or closure. You also can appeal if you believe that the IRS misreported your income to the Social Security Administration.

Download and complete Social Security form SSA-44, Medicare Income-Related Monthly Adjustment Amount—Life-Changing Event (SSA.gov/forms/ssa-44-ext.pdf) if you think you might qualify. Include any documentation you have.

Example: If your qualifying event is retirement, include a letter from your former employer noting your retirement date. Also include your most recent tax return.

It's certainly worth investigating if you or your spouse recently retired and your MAGI prior to retirement topped $88,000 ($176,000 if married and filing jointly). Go to Medicare.gov for more details and for 2022 rate adjustments. (Click on Get Medicare costs.)

GOOD TO KNOW...

Storm Damage That Your Insurance Will and Won't Cover

Most homeowner's policies will cover damage from tornados, hurricanes, severe storms, rain, wind, and fire. But check your policy to be sure, since some policies exclude weather that is common in your area, such as windstorms in coastal states. Most states have special programs for you to purchase insurance covering such exclusions. What homeowner's policies almost never cover are flooding or "earth movement"—earthquakes, mudslides, and sinkholes. That coverage must be bought separately. You can get flood insurance from the National Flood Insurance Program or a private insurer, and you can buy earthquake insurance from private companies or, if your home is in California, from the California Earthquake Authority.

USAToday.com

How to Find Better Rates on Insurance

MoneyTalksNews.com

Car: At Gabi, you upload your existing policy and the company searches for a better deal. The Zebra has a real-time comparison engine to search more than 200 insurance companies.

Life: In all states except New York, Bestow sells term policies at prices determined by algorithms, for as little as $10/month. Policygenius compares quotes from dozens of companies based on your age and health.

Homeowner: In 24 states and the District of Columbia, Lemonade offers coverage for as little as $25/month. Clearsurance does not sell policies, but lets you compare companies based on community reviews.

Health: Many people will do best with Healthcare.gov, the official federal health-insurance marketplace. Also try eHealthInsurance, whose online tools search thousands of options from hundreds of companies. In limited areas, you may be able to use Oscar, which offers classic plans and lower-cost ones...or, for Medicare beneficiaries, Clover, which bundles multiple services.

New Developments with Long-Care Insurance

Charles B. Inlander, a consumer advocate and health-care consultant based in Fogelsville, Pennsylvania. He was the founding president of the nonprofit People's Medical Society, a consumer-advocacy organization credited with key improvements in the quality of U.S. health care, and is author or coauthor of more than 20 consumer-health books.

Long-term-care (LTC) insurance has been around for more than 30 years, and many people have already decided whether or not they want this coverage. But LTC policies keep changing each year, so it's worth staying on top of these developments to make sure that you're still satisfied with having—or not having—this type of coverage.

You already know the basic pitch for LTC policies—with most people living longer these days, many more will need some form of assisted-living support. None of this is cheap. The national average cost for a nursing home is about $90,000 per year, while a spot in an assisted-living facility averages nearly $48,000 a year. What about Medicare? It covers only 100 days of skilled nursing-home care—and only if a doctor certifies that you can undergo rehabilitation so that you can be released following treatment. To be eligible for Medicaid, you must spend basically all of your assets before it pays for a nursing home. Assisted living is not covered by Medicaid.

Most of the changes taking place around LTC coverage are not consumer-friendly, and fewer people are purchasing it each year. Is LTC insurance right for you? *What to consider...*

• **Do you have large assets to protect?** Unless your estate exceeds $300,000 and you want to save a good portion of that for your heirs, many financial advisers say that LTC insurance isn't worth the cost.

Here's why: Premiums are hefty. For a healthy 55-year-old, annual LTC premiums start at around $1,000 per year for a limited coverage policy (one that caps the coverage by dollar amount). For someone over age 65, the numbers can be double that. And premiums can go up as you get older.

A newer option to consider: Many life insurance companies now sell life policies with a LTC rider, allowing you to start receiving benefits up to the policy's limits if used for approved long-term care. For details, check with a reputable independent insurance broker who represents a number of companies.

• **Will I get coverage?** With fewer companies selling policies (about 15 in 2019 versus 125 in 2000), insurers are getting stricter on who qualifies. Unlike health insurance, LTC insurers can reject purchases due to preexisting conditions, age, or previous denials. Even if you have a LTC policy, denials of claims are quite common.

• **Should you keep LTC insurance?** If you already have this coverage, ask yourself whether you can still afford the premiums. Last year, for example, a Florida insurer won state insurance department approval to double its premiums. If you are unable to cover your normal cost of living, it may be time to simply ditch your LTC policy. Unfortunately, you will lose the premiums you've already paid.

• **Is there a better option than LTC insurance?** If you need assisted-living services, such as adult day care or other caregiver-type assistance, check with your county's Area Agency on Aging. Those offered by state or federal programs often charge on a sliding scale based on need. For-profit and nonprofit groups also offer services such as help with bathing and medication monitoring.

Recent trend worth considering: A group of friends hires house cleaners or health aides, sharing the services between them each week. Having a consistent stable of caregivers/providers gives peace of mind—and sharing makes it less expensive.

New Rules for Amyotrophic Lateral Sclerosis (ALS) Disability

Bottom Line Health

People with ALS, also called Lou Gehrig's disease, experience a rapid decline in health that can quickly create a financial crisis that traditional disability insurance is too slow to address. The recently passed ALS Disability Insurance Access Act speeds up the process to get money to patients faster.

Normally, the Social Security Administration (SSA) takes more than three months to verify an applicant's eligibility for benefits. In 2018, the Compassionate Allowance Initiative shortened that process to about 29 days for 242 urgent medical issues, but there is still a five-month waiting period to start receiving the benefits. This new law waives that five-month wait for people with ALS.

In the weeks leading up to passage of the bill in December, 2020, Senator Mike Lee, R-Utah, sought to broaden the scope of the legislation to include other conditions. In Senate floor remarks, he mentioned Creutzfeldt-Jakob disease, cardiac amyloidosis, and peritoneal mesothelioma as just a few examples, and noted, "It should not matter which fatal, rapidly progressing, debilitating disease an American is suffering—all fatal diseases with no known cure should have access to disability benefits after their SSA determination." He vowed to continue to fight for those benefits.

At the time of the law's passage, the SSA had not yet set up procedures to implement the new policy.

MONEY SAVER...

Lower-Cost Car Insurance for Seniors

Insurers raise rates for older drivers because eyesight, hearing, and reflexes tend to diminish with age...and seniors' accident injuries tend to be more serious and cost more to treat.

How to keep premiums down: Maintain a clean driving record...take a defensive-driving course intended for seniors, such as the one offered by AARP...drive less if your insurer offers low-mileage discounts...consider insuring your car and home with the same company to get bundled rates...raise your deductible for collision and comprehensive coverage...decrease or drop unneeded coverage...drive a safer car—you may get a discount if your car has collision-avoidance technology or other features.

Insure.com

Some Insurers Are Cutting Telehealth Benefits

Virtual medical visits were made free to patients during the earlier part of the pandemic, but some insurers now require copayments for telehealth or have established deductibles to be met before they will pay. Rules vary and can be complex, using factors such as the type of plan you have and the purpose of the virtual medical visit. Even if your telehealth benefits have been free, do not assume they still are—check with your plan, preferably online, since phone representatives can be hard to reach and delays when calling can be substantial.

Kiplinger's Personal Finance.

If You're Still Driving Less, Make Sure You're Paying Less

When the pandemic hit, many wise consumers asked their auto insurers to "re-rate" them because they were no longer commuting or running errands. Some companies did so immediately for a limited time, and some promised to adjust at the next renewal.

Important: Call now to make sure you're still being billed at a fair rate, given your reduced risk to the insurer. Expect a double-digit discount off the original rate.

Doug Heller, an insurance expert with Consumer Federation of America, an association of nonprofit consumer organizations, Washington, DC.

14

Emotional Rescue

Physical and Emotional Trauma Linger in Your Body: How to Free Yourself

Trauma—whether emotional or physical—is a painful, horrifying experience that overwhelms your capacity to cope, and its effects often last for decades. Victims are more likely to be irritable, anxious and depressed...have difficulty focusing...miss work...have financial problems...sleep poorly...abuse alcohol or drugs...suffer from a major health problem... and/or feel suicidal.

There are many ways to be traumatized. Experts estimate that an astounding 75 percent of us have experienced one or more traumatic events of varying degrees.

Examples: You suffered through a childhood of abuse. Your parents had a bad divorce, or one or both were mentally ill, alcoholic, or addicted to drugs. You were raped or sexually assaulted. You were mugged. You killed people in combat and watched friends die. You lived through a natural disaster. You were in a serious accident. You're a cancer survivor. Now, the COVID-19 pandemic has the potential to leave traumatic scarring on some.

What often gets overlooked: Beyond physical injury caused by the event, trauma leaves an imprint on your body, not just your brain, in the form of heartbreaking and gut-wrenching physical sensations.

For real healing to take place, your body needs to learn that the danger has passed and that it's possible to live in the safety of the

Bessel van der Kolk, MD, founder and medical director of the Trauma Research Foundation in Brookline, Massachusetts. He is professor of psychiatry at Boston University School of Medicine and author of *The Body Keeps the Score: Brain, Mind and Body in the Healing of Trauma.* BesselvanderKolk.com present. *Here's what you need to know to lay the residues of trauma to rest—and recover...*

GOALS OF RECOVERY

The challenge of recovering from trauma is to know what you know and feel what you feel without becoming overwhelmed, enraged, ashamed, or collapsed. *For most, this involves four goals...*

GOAL #1: **Finding a way to become calm and focused.**

GOAL #2: **Learning to maintain that calm in response to images, thoughts, sounds, and physical sensations that remind you of the past.**

GOAL #3: **Finding a way to be fully alive in the present and engaged with the people around you.**

GOAL #4: **Not keeping secrets from yourself,** including secrets about the ways you have managed to survive (for example, by abusing alcohol or drugs).

There are several body-based methods that I have used extensively to help my patients, and I've also experienced their effectiveness personally. *In addition to those body-based techniques, there are several other approaches that research shows can be very helpful...*

• **Eye movement desensitization and reprocessing (EMDR).** In this well-researched technique, you recall a traumatic event while a therapist moves his/her fingers back and forth in front of you, and you follow them with your eyes. EMDR rebalances brain circuits, allowing you to experience the "true" present without interferences from trauma-related perceptions. It is most effective for trauma caused by a single event in adulthood, such as a car accident, but it can be useful as an adjunctive treatment for people struggling with the legacy of childhood trauma.

Scientific evidence: In a National Institute of Mental Health–funded study conducted by myself and my colleagues, 88 people with post-traumatic stress disorder (PTSD) were treated for eight weeks with EMDR...an antidepressant drug...or a placebo. At a six-month follow-up, 75 percent of those with adult-onset trauma who received EMDR had complete relief of symptoms, compared with zero percent in the antidepressant group. (We did not keep people on a placebo for the entire study.)

Resource: To find an EMDR practitioner, check the EMDR International Association (EMDRIA.org).

• **Yoga.** Traumatized individuals tend to become overwhelmed by their physical sensations and spend a lot of energy trying to block out what is going on in their bodies. Some do this naturally...others turn to drugs, alcohol, or eating disorders. The memory of helplessness during trauma tends to be stored as muscle tension in the affected areas—for example, head, back, and limbs in accident victims... vagina and rectum in victims of sexual abuse. Also, trauma victims often are chronically angry or scared, which leads to muscle tension that produces back pain, migraine headaches, fibromyalgia, and other forms of chronic pain. Yoga, which typically combines breath practices, stretches, and meditation, can help people develop a harmonious relationship with their physical sensations, relax those muscles, and normalize rage- and fear-causing circuits between the body and the brain.

Scientific evidence: We studied women with chronic, treatment-resistant PTSD, enrolling them in 20 weeks of trauma-sensitive yoga sessions. Participants experienced significant reductions in PTSD, which was amplified in two subsequent long-term follow-up studies.

Resource: Find a teacher certified in trauma-sensitive yoga at TraumaSensitiveYoga.com.

• **Neurofeedback.** When neurons (brain cells) communicate with each other, they generate electrical pulses—brain waves—that can be detected with sensors on the scalp. One study showed that people with PTSD can have brain waves that lack coherent patterns and don't generate brain wave patterns that filter out irrelevant information and help you pay attention to the task at hand, which is why lack of focus is a hallmark of PTSD. Neurofeedback helps correct these dysfunctional brain wave patterns.

The method "harvests" a person's brain waves and projects them onto a computer screen, allowing him/her to play therapeutic computer games with his own brain waves—reducing the brain waves that create fearfulness, shame, and rage...and increasing the brain waves that create calm and focus.

Scientific evidence: My colleagues and I first studied 52 people with chronic PTSD from multiple events, dividing them into two groups. One group received neurofeedback, and one didn't. By the end of the 40-session study, only 27 percent of those receiving neurofeedback still met the criteria for a diagnosis of PTSD, compared with 68 percent of those who didn't get neurofeedback. Most dramatic was the improvement in executive functioning—being able to plan, be mentally flexible, being able to look at a problem from a variety of points of view and inhibiting their impulses. Another neurofeedback study of foster children with histories of abuse and neglect had similar positive results.

Resources: To find a neurofeedback provider trained in overcoming trauma near you, visit the website of the International Society for Neuroregulation & Research (ISNR.org).

• **Talk therapy.** As you use body-based methods to relieve the physical burdens generated by trauma, you can make better use of talk therapy. You need to acknowledge and name what happened to restore feelings of control. Feeling listened to and understood also changes your body—being able to articulate a complex feeling and having your feeling recognized creates an "aha moment." Modern-day therapy for PTSD has focused on treatment through prescription drugs such as antidepressants. These aren't a solution. They dampen the physical systems that create symptoms of trauma but don't resolve them.

Another effective way to access your inner world of feelings is through writing. When you write to yourself, you don't have to worry about other people's judgment—you just listen to your own thoughts and let their flow take over.

Scientific evidence: In a study published in *British Journal of Clinical Psychology,* 88 trauma survivors received trauma-focused psychotherapy. After four months, the participants had better verbal memory, information processing, and executive functioning (the ability to plan and make decisions). And in a six-month study on Afghanistan and Iraq war veterans, those who wrote expressively about their feelings had greater reductions in PTSD, physical complaints, anger, and distress compared with veterans who didn't write at all.

Look for a therapist who has mastered a variety of techniques—EMDR, psychodrama, expressive writing, neurofeedback, and trauma-focused talk therapy. Feeling safe and comfortable with the therapist is necessary for you to confront your fears and anxieties. If you don't feel that connection or that he/she is curious to find out who you are and what you need, look for another therapist.

Recovery from Anxiety Disorder

A key element to full recovery from anxiety disorder is having people in your life who provide a sense of emotional security. Religious or spiritual beliefs also are integral to helping cope with difficulties. Top detriments to recovery are poor physical health, insomnia or a history of depression—addressing them should be part of a comprehensive treatment strategy.

Esme Fuller-Thomson, PhD, director of the Institute for Life Course and Aging, a professor at University of Toronto, and lead author of a study published in *Journal of Affective Disorders.*

Overcoming Loneliness

Vivek Murthy, MD, former Surgeon General of the United States and author of *Together: The Healing Power of Human Connection in a Sometimes Lonely World.*

Loneliness is part of the human condition. When our ancient ancestors found themselves separated from their tribes, they had plenty to fear—wild animals, enemy peoples, cold nights alone—and they felt overwhelming stress. Today, when we feel lonely, we feel the same kind of stress, even if we face no immediate danger. On top of that, in a world where social media, advertisements, and TV shows can make it appear that everyone else is happily socializing all the time, lonely people can feel like they are unlikable, unlovable misfits, far removed from the mainstream. But that's an illusion. Loneliness, the subjective feeling that you lack the social connections you need, is a common part of modern life. One AARP study found one in three adults over age 45 were lonely.

Loneliness is common, but it's not harmless. It's linked to coronary heart disease, high blood pressure, stroke, dementia, depression, anxiety, poor sleep, immune system dysfunction, and even premature death. When you lack sufficient human connection you lack something vital to your survival. So, how do you find your own tribe? *Here are a few things to consider...*

• **Know thyself.** Are you an extrovert, an introvert, or somewhere in between? Extroverts feel energized by crowds and crave frequent social contact. Introverts enjoy more time alone, prefer to socialize in smaller groups, and feel drained by too much interaction. An introvert might feel lonely at a party with strangers, while an extrovert may feel lonely after an evening home alone. It helps to recognize where you fall on this continuum and to know that there's no right number of friends or social outings.

• **Embrace solitude.** To build better connections with other people, you first need to connect with and accept yourself. Lonely people who focus on feelings of hurt, shame, and rejection can fall into a vicious cycle: They feel unlovable and defensive and end up pushing others away. Consider taking up meditation, especially a form known as "loving kindness meditation," in which you focus on good wishes for yourself and others. Or just take a few minutes to get outside and appreciate nature.

• **Connect through service.** Most lonely people have heard the advice that they should join a group of people with shared interests. While book clubs and quilting groups are fine, you will reap even greater benefits if you join others in service activities—taking the focus off yourself to pursue a greater, shared purpose.

• **Connect through song and movement.** While many group activities can build bonds, some research suggests that synchronized activities—such as singing or dancing with others—can be especially powerful. When we sing, dance, or exercise in groups, we tune into one another in a way that's often missing in our everyday lives.

• **Recognize technology as a mixed blessing.** Many people have recently discovered the joy of connecting with friends and family through newer technologies, but technology also can make loneliness worse. Social media, in particular, can have a corrosive effect by creating the illusion that everyone is having a better life than you are. One study found that heavy social media users were twice as likely to feel lonely as less frequent users.

• **Reach out everywhere.** To stave off loneliness, we need intimate relationships, but we also need wider circles of connection and support. Ask a coworker how she's doing and really listen to the answer. Wave to neighbors and smile at familiar faces at the store. Even strangers can build brief, meaningful bonds.

EASY TO DO...

Better Way to Beat Loneliness

Say yes if someone invites you to an event—do not think of all the reasons to avoid going. Get out of your home for religious services, volunteer activities, or hobbies. Find your comfort area—some people like one-on-one conversation, while others prefer noisy group activities.

HealthLetter.MayoClinic.com

Boost Your Spirits by Helping Others

Discover rewarding opportunities for volunteering from home. *Examples:* CreatetheGood.AARP.org...VolunteerMatch.org.

Specialized opportunities: Counsel people in crisis—CrisisTextLine.org/become-a-volunteer. Record audiobooks—Librivox.org. Write letters to seniors—LoveForTheElderly.org. Transcribe historical documents for the Smithsonian—Transcription.si.edu.

Bottom Line Personal.

Spread the Love!

Studies show that people who have frequent "micro-moments" of connection—even those as fleeting as a kind interaction with a neighbor—tend to have better psychological well-being than those who have fewer.

Helpful: Smartphone reminders may lead to greater awareness of such positive interactions.

Personality and Individual Differences.

Focus on Fun for a Happy Life

Researchers at the University of Zurich found that people who can fully enjoy relaxing activities, like watching a movie, without thinking about what they should be doing instead, like working out, have a higher sense of well-being as well as less depression and anxiety than people who can't fully immerse themselves in pleasurable activities.

Bernecker K. and Becker D. "Beyond self-control: Mechanisms of hedonic goal pursuit and Its relevance for well-being." *Personality and Social Psychology Bulletin.*

EASY TO DO...

Trick Yourself into a Better Mood

Forcing a smile stimulates the amygdala, the emotional center of the brain that releases neurotransmitters to encourage an emotionally positive state. Even if you're faking it, the muscle movements alone can boost your mood.

University of South Australia

Better Use of Social Media

Limit the apps you use by deleting the ones you do not genuinely enjoy. Comment and reply nicely instead of passively liking posts—taking the time to comment increases your involvement with people. Use the Twitter "lists" feature to reduce randomness and mental wheel-spinning—for example, create feel-good lists that contain only uplifting stories or videos of cute animals. Turn off push notifications so that you are less tied up in comments and likes when you post something. Stop following anxiety-provoking politicians, celebrities, and influencers whose seemingly perfect lives make you unhappy with your own. Set time limits for how long you spend on social media each day. Make certain places off-limits to social media, such as your bed or dinner table.

Self.com

Use Instagram to Lift Your Spirits

Use Instagram to lift your spirits by following feel-good accounts from celebrities and influencers and about animals. Jennifer Garner's feed often features celebrities reading children's books and acting them out. Golden Retrievers is nothing but cute photos and videos of those specific dogs. My Therapist Says is sarcastic and filled with puns, memes, and jokes. Chunk the Groundhog shows footage of a real groundhog that walks up to a backyard camera, stares at it, and keeps eating from the homeowner's vegetable garden. Kristin Bell offers a mixture of humor and thoughtfulness. Upworthy shows ways in which people are helping each other, fighting climate change, and contributing to the common good. Tank's Good News offers similar content.

Better Homes & Gardens. BHG.com

GOOD TO KNOW...

Art Relieves the Stress of Caregiving

Spending 45 minutes filling in a coloring book or creating original art brought feelings of greater pleasure and enjoyment—and less anxiety and tension—to professional caregivers and to family members who are taking care of loved ones.

Girija Kaimal, EdD, associate professor, College of Nursing and Health Professions, Drexel University, Philadelphia, and leader of a study of caregivers, published in *European Journal of Oncology Nursing.*

The 3 Steps to Worry Less...and Enjoy More

Mark Goulston, MD, host of the "My Wakeup Call" podcast. Dr. Goulston speaks globally on teaching people throughout the world to listen to one another. His books include *Why Cope When You Can Heal? How Healthcare Heroes of COVID-19 Can Recover from PTSD...Just Listen: Discover the Secret to Getting Through to Absolutely Anyone...Talking to "Crazy": How to Deal with the Irrational and Impossible People in Your Life*...and *Get Out of Your Own Way: Overcoming Self-Defeating Behavior.* MarkGoulston.com

The word "neurotic" might conjure up images of lovable worrywarts such as *Seinfeld* character George Costanza or comic strip icon Charlie Brown, who famously lamented, "My anxieties have anxieties." But true neuroticism—a personality trait that describes people who are prone to anxiety, self-consciousness, irritability, emotional instability, and depression—is no laughing matter. Neurotic individuals worry excessively, often about things that they have no control over, and they are more likely to develop a variety of psychological conditions, from mood disorders to substance abuse.

Now, a new study published in *Journal of the American Geriatrics Society* has linked neuroticism with an increased risk for a specific type of predementia called non-amnestic mild cognitive impairment (MCI), in which one's memory remains relatively unscathed but language, visual-spatial skills, decision-making, planning, and/or other cognitive abilities become impaired.

WHAT IS NEUROTICISM?

People tend to use the word "neurotic" loosely. In order to be clinically neurotic, one tends to ruminate constantly. These people often have trouble leaving anything to chance and live life with a perpetually pessimistic point of view.

If a neurotic person was, say, waiting for his/her doctor to call with important test results, each passing moment without the phone ringing would be interpreted as, *I must have cancer...that's why the doctor is taking so long.* In contrast, someone who tends toward openness or agreeableness (two of the other Big Five personality traits) might think, *The doctor is calling other patients who do have cancer, and that's not me.* Interestingly, unlike neuroticism, openness is believed to be protective against dementia.

Chronic worry bathes the body and brain in the stress hormone cortisol. In short bursts, cortisol can help motivate people through challenging times and even keep them safe from danger—it's one of the key focus-sharpening hormones released when your brain senses a threat, such as a dog running toward you or a car cutting you off in traffic. But with chronic worrying, elevated cortisol levels damage brain cells and shrink the hippocampus, the brain's memory center.

TRAIN YOURSELF TO BE LESS NEUROTIC

Just because you're a natural worrier doesn't mean that you're destined for cognitive trouble. There are ways to temper your neuroticism. The payoff may come not only in the form of healthier brain functioning but also as reduced anxiety, less pessimism, improved memory, and/or focus. And this can lead to an overall improved quality of life.

***STRATEGY #1:* Boost the bonding hormone.** During times of bonding, such as cuddling, breast-feeding, or orgasm, the brain secretes the hormone oxytocin. Besides promoting attachment between two individuals, this so-called "love hormone" also helps reduce cortisol levels. That's one reason cuddling feels so relaxing and enjoyable. New research also suggests that oxytocin may have a preservative effect on brain functioning. It's a win-win!

When it comes to oxytocin, snuggling and sex get all the attention, but there's another way to get your love hormones flowing—by talking with someone you trust and who makes you feel heard. When you allow yourself to open up to a friend, family member, or even a therapist and that person treats you with kindness and empathy, you experience a surge of oxytocin. As a result, you feel less alone and you help rewire your brain in a way that promotes openness, trust, and optimism.

***STRATEGY #2:* Try this spin on cognitive behavioral therapy (CBT).** CBT is a type of talk therapy that helps individuals change their distorted thought patterns and damaging behaviors. One popular CBT strategy involves catching yourself in harmful thinking in the moment and then reframing it in a more logical way. *Here's how you can do this without a therapist...*

Buy a journal, and paste a photo of a loved one—someone who cares about you or someone you look up to—inside the front cover. This person can be living or deceased. When your neurotic worrying starts to ramp up, grab your journal, look at the photo, and imagine the person saying, *You can get through this.* Or, if it suits his/her personality, imagine him saying, with love, *Stop it! You're fine!!*

Now, picture that person asking you about your worrying and write down your answers. Questions can include, *What happened that got you worried?...How did you feel when it happened?...What does it make you want to do?...What would happen if you did that?...How likely is your worry going to come true?...* and *Look at me, take a deep breath, and tell me what would be a better thing to do?* Writing your responses acts as a neuroticism-release tool...and because you've invoked the image of a caring, empathetic person, you feel seen and heard, which sparks oxytocin.

***STRATEGY #3:* Stop, look, listen, smell.** Long practiced by the military, this technique encourages you to pause and focus on your surroundings. The stop-look-listen aspect is widely known, and in the context of anxiety, these action items help force you to focus on something else.

The addition of smell makes it a game-changer when it comes to calming the nervous system. Smelling your environment requires inhaling deeply through the nose. Doing this also stimulates the vagus nerve, which connects the brain to almost every organ in the body. When stimulated, the vagus nerve initiates the body's natural relaxation response, eases anxiety, and enhances mood. While you're smelling what you smell, make an internal association that is pleasurable—for instance, the smell of gasoline may remind you of pleasant road trips with your family or the smell of perfume or lotion may remind you of a scent you associated with a loving grandmother.

The next time you get caught up in a cycle of neurotic worrying, try the SLLS protocol...

Stop: Stop what you're doing...recognize your worrying is unproductive and spinning out of control.

Look: Look around you, and identify something you've never noticed or paid attention to. It could be the fabric on your couch, a tree, a button on an appliance. *After observing the object for 30 seconds or so...*

Listen: What do you hear? A neighbor's lawnmower? A bird chirping? Your freezer humming? Can you associate that noise with something positive, such as the backyard of your childhood home or tasty ice cream?

Smell: Smell something—coffee, perfume, a flower. Inhale slowly through your nose, expanding your belly to fill your lungs with air, then exhale through your mouth.

A note on medication: Sometimes neurotic worrying can grow so out of control that no amount of journaling or talking or professional counseling can tame it. In these cases, antianxiety medication may be an appropriate next step. For short-term help, your doctor may prescribe a fast-acting antianxiety drug called a benzodiazepine, such as Xanax (*alprazolam*) or Ativan (*lorazepam*). They work quickly to punch a hole in your anxiety, but last only a few hours. In the longer term, selective serotonin reuptake inhibitors (SSRIs) such as Prozac (*fluoxetine*), Zoloft (*sertraline*), and Lexapro (*escitalopram*) can offer relief. I'm not advocating that you rush to medication—that can start you down the road of physical or psychological dependence and possible addiction. What I do suggest is, with your physician's agreement, perhaps using medicine that may calm your mind enough to begin to learn new and effective psychological coping mechanisms that you eventually are able to turn to without medication.

Ways to Keep Anxiety from Spiraling

Deep diaphragmatic breathing: Hold one hand on your belly and the other on your chest. Expand your belly but not your chest when you inhale.

Dip your face in cold water: A 15-second dip can calm the body.

Touch something cold: It distracts you and interrupts your body's stress response.

Get moving: Outside is best, but any physical activity works—mow your lawn, clean your shower, or do some sit-ups.

"5-4-3-2-1" method: Focus on five things you can see, four things you can touch, three things you can hear, two things you can smell, and one thing you can taste. This can help you create some distance from the feeling of anxiety.

Progressive muscle relaxation: Clench then relax your toes, then calves, then thighs, etc., working your way up your whole body.

Roundup of experts quoted on Self.com.

Ways to Get Through the Tough Spots

Bruce Feiler, who interviewed hundreds of people in all 50 states and a range of fields—from politics to business to the performing arts—about their life transitions for his book, *Life Is in the Transitions: Mastering Change at Any Age.* BruceFeiler.com

The typical American will experience three to five life-altering disruptions, according to author Bruce Feiler's research, and each will leave him/her unsettled for an average of nearly five years.

Waiting until things "get back to normal" isn't the answer—life rarely returns to the way it was previously. Instead, we must improve our ability to manage life transitions. *The following tools can be employed in any order. It's best to draw upon as many as possible...*

- **Accept that the transition is happening—and that it will be emotional.** It's natural to resist transitions, even those that are voluntary. We cling to our former lives because that feels safe and comfortable while transitions seem daunting and uncertain.

EASY TO DO...

Step Outside Yourself

Recalling troublesome events as an observer instead of from our own point of view helps us keep psychological distance. Also, it changes the interaction between different parts of the brain, helping us to view the past from a new perspective.

Peggy St. Jacques, PhD, assistant professor of psychology at University of Alberta, Canada, and leader of a study published in *Cortex.*

To accept a transition, we must accept the emotions that it stirs up—even if our natural response to challenges is to push feelings aside—and roll up our sleeves and get to work. Such emotions typically include fear, sadness, and/or shame. Guilt and anger also are common.

• **Some people find that journaling about their emotions helps.** Follow-up research from a landmark study done in 1986 at University of Texas at Austin found that 27 percent of people laid off from their jobs who wrote about their thoughts and feelings found new jobs within three months, compared with 5 percent of those who didn't journal.

Whether you journal or not, you should acknowledge what you're feeling and use hard work as a way to overcome these emotions, not as an excuse to ignore them.

Example: Army interrogator Eric Maddox felt fear when he was sent to Iraq—he was trained in Mandarin, not Farsi, and felt ill-equipped for the assignment. Rather than ignore his fear, he told himself, I can turn away because I am scared, or *I can go to work and learn how to develop trust in this part of the world through an interpreter.* Maddox's interrogations helped track down Saddam Hussein.

• **Create a ritual or tribute to mark the transition.** When people experience a major transition, they often stage some sort of event or activity to commemorate the change. Negative events need closure, while positive events, such as a child's marriage or a new job or relocation, need celebration and acknowledgment to mark the new beginning. These "rituals" take many forms—a memorial service where friends and family members mourn the past or a party to celebrate the future...a good-bye letter written to a deceased partner or former life...a name change, such as a return to a maiden name...cleaning out a home...shaving off a beard or switching to a new hair style...a once-in-a-lifetime activity, such as skydiving... or something else entirely.

A ritual is something you can take control over at a time when much of life feels outside of your control. It also reinforces to you—and to your friends and family—that you are not going back to your old life.

• **Shed old mind-sets, routines, possessions...and even dreams.** A heart problem might mean that we must give up some favorite foods. A layoff might mean that we have to give up the dream house we were planning. A divorce might mean that we must give up some of the comfortable daily habits we've developed.

It helps to remember that this is a great opportunity to clear away parts of yourself that were not serving you well—decluttering your life to make room for the rewarding life you will create.

Example: When Loretta Parham's daughter died in a car crash, Parham was left to raise her two granddaughters. She discovered that to be a good parent, she had to give up being an indulgent grandparent, a role that she loved. It turned out that, despite the loss of her daughter, the role of parent was tremendously rewarding.

• **Find a creative outlet.** People who find time for a new creative endeavor, such as painting, cooking, dancing, or writing, often discover that this helps with their transition. It's more than just a diversion from the long slog and mental strain of a life transition—new creative activities also encourage us to believe that we have it within us to be more than we previously were. If we can begin baking delicious bread or painting beautiful landscapes, it seems much more plausible that we also can find a new job or new relationship.

Example: Evan Walker-Wells was a student at Yale when he was diagnosed with stage 4 non-Hodgkin's lymphoma. The diagnosis forced him to leave school for six months of chemotherapy and leave behind his youthful sense that he was free to do whatever he wanted. He taught himself to cook and play guitar during this time—he was someone who had the capacity and drive to continue learning and growing under any circumstances. He was recently in his second year at Yale Law School.

• **Seek support from others.** It's probably no surprise that aid from other people is among the most powerful tools to help us through challenging transitions. What is surprising is that different people tend to crave very different types of support—and most of us are not very good at obtaining the type we prefer.

Many people crave comfort during times of transition and so welcome supportive feedback such as, "I love you" or "You can do it." But others want a nudge in the right direction—"I love you, but maybe you should try this." And a smaller percentage want a proverbial kick in the backside—they yearn for someone to say, "Get over yourself—you've had your pity party, now get back to work."

The trouble is, the people we go to for support often fail to give us the type we prefer—they give us what they think we need... or what they would want if they were in our position, leaving us frustrated and perhaps deterring us from seeking outside support again.

Solution: Tell people which type of support you hope to obtain and which you don't want...and/or seek support from people who show a tendency to provide specifically what you need.

• **Publicly unveil your new self.** At some point during your transition, a sense of normalcy will return to your life. That's when it's time to make a public statement that you've made a life transition. Tell your friends you're ready to date again...throw a housewarming party for your new home...or update your LinkedIn page to show that you've launched a new career. If the "ritual" described earlier commemorated the end of your old life, this unveiling celebrates your new normal.

Helpful: One way to launch a "new self" is to provide assistance to someone else. Volunteer with a nonprofit, or help a friend in need.

• **Rewrite the story you tell yourself about your life.** When people are in the midst of transitions, they usually think of themselves in terms of what they used to be—*I was happily married* or *I was a successful professional.* Rewrite this into a story of overcoming obstacles or of rebirth—*I used to be that. I went through a life change. Now I am this.*

Example: Chris Waddell, a medal-winning Paralympian, set out to be the first paraplegic to climb 19,000-foot Mount Kilimanjaro—but just 100 feet from the summit, the boulders were too large for his arm-powered four-wheel mountain bike to pass. The other members of the expedition carried him to the summit. Waddell was initially crushed by what he viewed as a failure until he rewrote the story from *I set out to climb a mountain unassisted but failed*...to *Nobody climbs a mountain alone.*

Treatment-Resistant Depression: New Hope

Dan V. Iosifescu, MD, MSc, associate professor of psychiatry, NYU School of Medicine, New York City, and director of the clinical research division at the Nathan Kline Institute for Psychiatric Research, Orangeburg, New York.

If you've been diagnosed with major depressive disorder (MDD), the good news is that, along with psychotherapy, there are several classes of drugs that can treat it. If one particular drug doesn't work for you, there are other choices to try that are often effective.

The bad news is that up to one-third of patients don't get relief from any of those antidepressants.

People with depression who don't improve after taking at least two different FDA-approved antidepressants at adequate doses for at least six weeks (for each drug) are considered to have treatment-resistant depression (TRD).

PROVEN THERAPIES FOR TRD

The order in which these treatments are tried depends on the doctor's opinion and patient's preference. These treatments may be used along with psychotherapy, antidepressants, and some of the other natural treatments mentioned below.

• ***Ketamine.*** Ketamine, a common anesthetic that is also, tragically, used as an illicit street drug, is now being used off-label for treatment of TRD. Over the past decade, research has demonstrated that low doses of ketamine, administered via intravenous or intranasal infusion, can help two-thirds of TRD patients experience significant improvement.

Ketamine works much faster than conventional antidepressants—within days rather than weeks—which can be lifesaving for a patient with suicidal impulses. The effect wears off about one week after treatment, requiring repeated administrations.

At the time of administration, patients can experience an increase in blood pressure or distorted perception of reality, so they need to be monitored in the doctor's office for two hours after treatment. Ketamine may impair your driving. Additional research is needed on the long-term side effects of multiple therapeutic doses.

In March 2019, the U.S. Food and Drug Administration (FDA) approved a new ketamine formulation called *esketamine* (Spravato), which comes in the form of a nasal spray, for patients with TRD. Spravato can cost more than $4,700 for the first month of treatment and is covered by only some insurers.

As with standard ketamine, patients' vital signs need to be monitored in the doctor's office for several hours after administration, which means additional cost.

• **Repetitive transcranial magnetic stimulation.** With rTMS, brief, magnetic pulses are noninvasively administered via an insulated coil placed over the patient's scalp near the area of the brain thought to regulate mood.

Treatment sessions vary in length, depending on the type of coil used and the number of pulses delivered, but usually last around 30 to 40 minutes. Patients typically receive rTMS five days a week for four to six weeks. A trained physician needs to determine the dose of rTMS for each patient, but other sessions are generally done by TMS operators. If the initial round is successful, patients may get maintenance treatments for months. The effects wear off when the treatments stop. Side effects can include headaches, hearing loss if there is inadequate ear protection and, very rarely, seizures.

• **Electroconvulsive therapy (ECT).** Although ECT has been used for decades and has about a 75 percent to 80 percent success rate, most people view it negatively due to films such as *One Flew Over the Cuckoo's Nest*. ECT has been refined over the years and is much safer today, but because ECT works by inducing a seizure and carries a risk of adverse cognitive effects, such as memory gaps, it is used only after multiple other treatments have been unsuccessful.

ECT requires anesthesia and is performed by a trained psychiatrist. It is typically given two to three times weekly for three to four weeks, so that the patient gets a total of six to 12 treatments. After a course of treatment, the patient may need either maintenance treatments or another therapy to prevent recurrence of depression.

ADD-ON TREATMENTS FOR TRD

The following treatments make sense for some patients with mild forms of depression, but for TRD and MDD, I would use them only in conjunction with more proven treatments for a possible minor boost in symptom relief.

• **Acupuncture.** There are a few studies that show that acupuncture can help people with mild depression. For these patients, there are no downsides to trying it, but acupuncture has not been shown to be effective for TRD by itself and should not delay the use of more effective treatments.

• **Supplements.** Research has shown that the supplements S-adenosyl-L-methionine (SAMe), L-methylfolate, and omega-3 fatty acids can be effective for mild depression, with few side effects. However, for TRD, these supplements should be used only as an addition to other treatments.

• **At-home electrical stimulation.** The Fisher Wallace Stimulator is a portable, battery-powered micro-electric pulse generator. It was cleared by the FDA with respect to safety, and data suggest that it may be helpful for milder forms of depression as well as insomnia, anxiety, and chronic pain. It is safe to use and can be used at home without medical supervision. There is no data on its effectiveness for TRD.

A PROBLEMATIC TREATMENT

- **Vagus nerve stimulation (VNS)** involves the use of an implantable, pacemaker-like device to stimulate the vagus nerve, one of the cranial nerves that connects the brain to the body, with electrical impulses. The FDA approved VNS for TRD in 2005, but VNS requires the patient to undergo a very expensive neurosurgical procedure for implantation of the device. It works in only a minority of patients, and most insurers don't cover the procedure. For now, VNS is not a practical option for most people.

GOOD TO KNOW...

Happiness Lies in Change

When 20,000 people were allowed a coin toss to determine whether to make a change in their lives (leaving a job, ending a relationship, etc.), those who were instructed by the coin to quit the status quo were happier six months later. If you're on the fence about a choice, opting for change may be wiser than maintaining the status quo.

Steven Levitt, PhD, professor of economics at The University of Chicago and leader of a study published in *The Review of Economic Studies.*

Depression After Surgery

Although it's seldom talked about, depression after surgery is quite common even when the operation is small and successful. Postsurgery depression—feelings of hopelessness extending two weeks or more after the operation—can interfere with recovery and continue for months if left untreated. Experts say it may be caused by feelings of vulnerability and trauma.

What to do: After surgery, be sure you have a good support system. Spend as much time as possible outdoors, and eat and sleep well. If depression does find you, talk to a therapist promptly.

Amy Vigliotti, PhD, founder of SelfWorks: Therapy Professionals, quoted on Health.com.

Magic Mushrooms Can Relieve Depression

Just two doses of psilocybin—the psychedelic compound found in so-called magic mushrooms—brought rapid reductions in depressive symptoms in a study of people with major depression. And half the patients were in remission after four weeks. Psilocybin produces visual and auditory hallucinations and significant changes in consciousness over a period of several hours. It was used along with supportive psychotherapy. The magnitude of the effect was four times larger than the effect of traditional antidepressants, which can take weeks or months to work and may have undesirable side effects. The side effects of using psilocybin were more limited, and its benefits appeared after only one or two uses.

Study of 24 patients with a long-term history of depression by researchers at Johns Hopkins School of Medicine, Baltimore, published in *JAMA Psychiatry.*

Make a Big Change in Small Increments

Small shifts in behavior can lead to big changes over time. Instead of worrying about your ultimate goal, ask yourself, *Can I do 5 percent more? Do 5 percent more exercise? Relax 5 percent more? Be 5 percent more open-minded?*

Shauna Shapiro, PhD, clinical psychologist and professor of counseling psychology at Santa Clara University, California, and author of *Good Morning, I Love You.* DrShaunaShapiro.com

Finding Meaning After the Death of a Loved One

David Kessler, grief specialist based in Los Angeles and founder of the website Grief.com. He was a protégé of the famed grief and death researcher Elisabeth Kübler-Ross and coauthor with her of *On Grief and Grieving*. His most recent book is *Finding Meaning: The Sixth Stage of Grief.*

Candy Lightner, whose daughter was killed by a drunk driver, launched Mothers Against Drunk Driving to save other lives. John Walsh, whose son was murdered, created and hosted the TV series *America's Most Wanted* to help catch killers.

Not everyone who suffers the loss of a loved one finds meaning through such dramatic actions. *But finding meaning in some form is an essential step in the grieving process and dealing with the pain of the loss…*

THE SIXTH STAGE

When I coauthored *On Grief and Grieving* —published in 2005—with my mentor, Elisabeth Kübler-Ross, we discussed the five stages that she had originally identified in her 1969 classic *On Death and Dying*. They are denial, anger, bargaining, depression, and acceptance. However, those stages of the healing process do not represent the entire journey for most people.

To find a path forward from their grief, even after they have experienced the five stages, survivors often need to identify some kind of greater meaning in the lives and/or deaths of their loved ones. Their pain doesn't disappear when this happens, but it is cushioned. They find that thinking about the deceased no longer brings only pain—it now brings a mixture of pain and love.

The meaning that survivors find does not fit a single form or framework. While Lightner and Walsh launched crusades, other people find meaning by reflecting on the positive influence that the deceased had during life… by using the death as inspiration for positive changes in their own lives…through belief in an afterlife…and in various other ways. The pursuit of meaning doesn't have a predictable time frame, either—some survivors find meaning almost as soon as the death occurs, while for others it takes months or years.

Six ways to find meaning…

CHANGED BEHAVIORS

- **Create stronger bonds with fellow survivors.** The death of a loved one can draw survivors together, presenting an opportunity to tighten weak relationships and overcome longstanding differences. These improved relationships can serve as a legacy for the deceased.

Example: A pair of siblings who have been estranged for years reconnect at their mother's funeral "because that's what mom would have wanted."

- **Treat the death as a wake-up call in your life.** Are you living the life you want to be living? If not, the death of a loved one could serve as a reminder that our time on Earth is short and that, whatever we want to achieve, we'd better get started achieving it.

Example: A woman quits smoking after her mother dies of lung cancer.

Using the Healing Power of Gratitude

Making a "gratitude jar" to acknowledge the things and people we're grateful for can bring contentment and healing.

For individuals: Each day, jot down something that you're thankful for on a slip of paper and drop it into the jar. This practice will increase your happiness and make you more satisfied with life.

For families: Make a gratitude jar accessible for everyone in the family. At intervals—perhaps during a holiday—pull out the slips of paper, and celebrate the things you're thankful for together.

For couples: Telling your beloved what you appreciate about him/her can strengthen your bond. If you feel like you have been growing apart, this can remind you of what you see in the other person. Reviewing the notes can put you in a good mind-set before you face difficult discussions.

Ruth Williams, business psychologist and former director of Department Store for the Mind, where people can explore ideas and emotions, and author of *The Mind Remedy: Discover, Make and Use Simple Objects to Nourish Your Soul.*

TRIBUTES

• **Become the legacy.** Grieving people often lament that "a part of me died when he did." Maybe so, but consider the flip side as well—part of him lives on in you. Think about what made this person wonderful—what were his very best qualities? One way to find meaning is to make a conscious effort to expand this part of yourself in his honor.

Example: A man always respected his brother for pulling over to offer assistance whenever he saw a motorist stranded by the side of the road. After his brother died, this man began doing the same thing.

• **Find a physical touchstone that shifts your focus to a positive legacy.** Our brains have a negativity bias—they're much better at recalling bad things than good ones. That's one reason why it can be difficult to escape negative emotional triggers when a loved one dies—our brains recall the negative of the death much more readily than the positives of the life. A lasting physical memorial can serve as an enduring reminder of the good of the life. If your mother enjoyed watching the sun set in a local park, finance a park bench with a plaque bearing her name in her favorite spot. If you have a photo of your husband that always makes you smile and recall a happy time, have this photo enlarged, framed, and hung in your home.

The memorial even can be something that no one but you will notice or understand.

Example: A woman purchased many sheets of postage stamps featuring a picture of comedian Danny Thomas and put these on all of her mail. Each time she used one, she smiled at the pleasant memory of her deceased father's sense of humor and his story about the day he met Thomas.

DONATIONS

• **Contribute to good works in the deceased's name.** Wealthy families sometimes create nonprofit foundations in the name of the deceased. It's an effective way to create a meaningful legacy—and it's possible on a more modest scale, too. Make donations in honor of your loved one to a cause that he/she cared about...or to a nonprofit working to solve the problem that led to his death. The recipient doesn't even have to be a nonprofit—you might help out local families in need or young people struggling to pay college tuition, if you believe your loved one would have wanted to help these people. The amounts you give don't have to be large if your budget is tight—you could periodically contribute $5 or $10 to charity drives and think, *That's for you, mom.* Helping is healing even in small denominations.

Another option is to do good works rather than donate money. Volunteer your time to a cause that the deceased gave his time to during his life...or participate in a project connected to the loved one or his death.

Examples: A man in India whose son died in an auto accident caused by a pothole started filling potholes in his spare time.

• **Reflect on the lives that might have been saved by the loved one's donated organs.** A woman who was devastated by the death of her 17-year-old son hired a house painter a few years later—and made the remarkable discovery that her son's kidney had saved this man's life. (This unlikely fact was confirmed through the transplant center.) Without her son's death, the painter's sons might have grown up without their father—and that was only one of the organs that her son donated.

Most people never get to meet the people saved by a loved one's organ donations, but knowing that these people are out there can bring meaning to the loss. More than half of Americans have signed up to be organ donors. It sometimes is possible to exchange messages with organ recipients through organ-donation programs if both the recipient and the donors' family are interested in doing so.

Best Ways to Regulate Your Emotions

"Regulating" emotions requires experiencing them head on, not ignoring or avoiding them, which is unhealthy and counterproductive. Getting better at regulating your emotions can mean that you will be less likely to indulge bad habits. Plus, you'll just feel better about yourself in the long run.

Identify your "numbing" behaviors: Do you retreat into video games? TV? After a binge, you may only feel worse.

Name what you're feeling: Identifying a negative emotion—without judgment—is the first step toward regulating it.

Ask what the feeling is telling you: What action should you take?

Mindfully express the emotion: Do it however works for you—talk to a friend, write in a journal, or have a good cry.

Focus on physical sensations: Take a shower, exercise, or get outdoors.

Roundup of therapists quoted at Self.com.

Thriving When There Is No Cure

Craig K. Svensson, PharmD, PhD, dean emeritus and professor of medicinal chemistry & molecular pharmacology in the Purdue University College of Pharmacy, as well as adjunct professor of pharmacology & toxicology in the Indiana University School of Medicine. Dr. Svensson is author of *When There Is No Cure.* https://craigsvensson.com

I am just one of the millions of people who live with chronic medical conditions. I have lived through the uncertainty of not knowing what was causing my symptoms, the frustration of not being able to find relief, and the fear of losing mobility and independence. Diseases such as systemic lupus erythematosus, fibromyalgia, multiple sclerosis, rheumatoid arthritis, ulcerative colitis, and chronic pain have no cure (yet), but those of us who have them can still thrive and experience fulfillment and joy.

LEARN ABOUT YOURSELF

When you live with a chronic condition, you need to arm yourself with information. Keep a health diary to become familiar with how the ailment affects your body. What worsens your symptoms? What lessens them? What patterns can you discern?

Next, think about what behaviors you can change to be more comfortable. Do you need to limit the time you sit to avoid aggravating underlying pain? Do you need to limit the number of evening activities in a given week to avoid cumulative fatigue? Do vacation plans need to account for your heightened sensitivity to heat or cold?

Consider how your illness affects others. Studies have found that the quality of life for spouses and partners is sometimes poorer than the quality of life for a patient with chronic illness. Family and friends want to ease our burden, but don't always know how. Careful reflection and open communication can ease the way.

LEARN ABOUT THE DISEASE

Once you have a diagnosis for your symptoms, the second educational focus is about the disease. How does it manifest in most people? What does normal progression look like? Should you expect a decline in your functioning? What options exist for treatment or symptom relief?

While your primary care physician is a valuable source of information, you may need to dig deeper. A single physician may not have ample experience with your specific condition and may not have all of the answers you need. In many cases, chronic illnesses are misdiagnosed by busy doctors. Furthermore, studies show that patients who understand diseases such as diabetes, high blood pressure, and asthma have better health outcomes. We have every reason to believe the same to be true for other ailments as well.

While researching, be aware that websites often post bad health information. The Access to Credible Genetics Resource Network has created a helpful tool patients can use to assess the credibility of posted health information. You can find it at Trustortrash.org.

Disease-specific patient advocacy groups are often valuable for both information and support. The best groups include an expert advisory panel to assess the accuracy of the information provided.

LEARN ABOUT DISEASE PROGRESSION

People living with a chronic disease often make two opposing errors. The first is seeing any change in health as a sign of disease progression. The second is ignoring signs that merit attention. It is imperative to learn how to strike the right balance between these two extremes.

Many chronic ailments, even those associated with a progressive decline, wax and wane over time. You need to identify benchmarks to identify when it's time to self-manage and when it's time to seek a medical expert.

Speak frankly with your health-care providers about how they will assess progression over the years to come. Are there symptoms that suggest a more rapid progression? How will the disease affect functional and cognitive abilities? How might these impact your professional or personal plans?

HOW TO LIVE WITH PAIN

For many people with chronic pain, there comes a point when you must recognize that eradicating pain is an unrealistic near-term goal. That doesn't mean giving in to suffering, but it does mean that you need to establish new goals to enable you to live life to the fullest extent possible.

• **Identify the most important areas of your life that are disrupted by pain and look for adaptation strategies.** For example, I suffer extreme back pain when driving, but I'm not willing to accept drowsiness or dulled cognitive ability to obtain this goal through medication. Ultimately, I purchased an SUV of substantial height that did not require lowering myself into the seat of a car. That purchase did more to improve my pain while driving than any form of physical therapy or medication.

• **See a pain-management specialist.** Unlike a general physician, pain-management specialists have focused their training on the effective management of chronic pain. The growing trend toward telemedicine can make the limited number of pain-management specialists available to people no matter where they live.

• **Avoid idleness and isolation.** When the mind is idle, pain is more noticeable, and we are more prone to brood on thoughts of despair about our plight. Keeping your mind busy with activities and social interaction provides distraction, which actually alters sensory pain signals in the spinal cord, and it gives life more meaning and joy.

• **Manage stress.** People living with chronic pain will often experience increased pain during times of stress. Learning how to reduce stress or to better cope with its presence in our lives can reduce pain. Similarly, anxiety can provoke pain in patients with ailments like trigeminal neuralgia (painful attacks arising from a misfiring of the trigeminal nerve in the jaw). Addressing the underlying causes of anxiety can reduce the episodes of painful attacks in such patients.

LIVE YOUR LIFE

The foolish but oft-repeated mantra, "If you don't have your health, you don't have anything," represents a depressing and narrow view of life. The truth is, many who suffer from chronic illness have found their life journey to be fulfilling and marked by abundant joy. I am convinced this path is open to all who live with an incurable ailment that leads to chronic suffering. Yes, life is different from before chronic illness. Nevertheless, different can be fulfilling.

15

Love, Family, and Friends

Four Hidden Marriage Killers

You're still angry about that? It isn't always a big, obvious misstep such as infidelity or dishonesty that derails a marriage. Some relationships are undone by an event so small or distant that one partner is befuddled about why the other considers it a big deal. Other marriages fail because of misunderstandings or miscommunications that slowly and steadily undermine the partnership. In 2020 and 2021, an added element has exposed how vulnerable many marriages are to stressful irritations. Lawyers say there has been a spike in divorce requests because couples have spent much more time together as they have sheltered in place and because they have faced greater financial challenges.

Here are four seemingly small things that can bring a relationship crashing down…

THE LONG-AGO MISSTEP

A wife asked her husband to skip a business trip and stay home to care for her when she felt very sick. He went anyway. Decades later that decision still haunted the relationship. The wife couldn't get past it because, to her, the long-ago business trip was just one example of a larger pattern—she felt her husband was never there for her when she needed him. The event triggered in her a need to constantly monitor her husband's behavior for further evidence that he would disappoint her.

Although there were times throughout their marriage when he took her feelings into consideration, the wife failed to notice these exceptions.

Michele Weiner-Davis, LCSW, founder of The Divorce Busting Center in Boulder, Colorado. She is a TEDx speaker and best-selling author of eight books including *Healing from Infidelity…The Sex-Starved Marriage…*and *Divorce Busting*. DivorceBusting.com

This wife wasn't intentionally being unfair to her husband—she truly believed he kept letting her down. But her belief had less to do with her husband's behavior than it did with human psychology—people tend to seize on evidence that supports their existing beliefs and ignore evidence that refutes it.

What to do: If your partner continually accuses you of a pattern of misbehavior that you do not believe exists, set aside your defensiveness for the sake of the relationship and apologize. Whether or not the accusation is warranted, your partner believes it is. Your relationship will not escape the cycle of blame and defensiveness unless you express contrition and genuine empathy for the pain your partner is feeling. It helps to remember that your partner's pain is real even if the pattern you're being accused of is not. Promise to work hard at correcting the pattern, then go above and beyond to do so. Your promise of change followed by clear evidence of new behavior could convince your partner that a new and positive pattern has begun.

You might be thinking, *That's not fair—why should I apologize for something I didn't do?* No, it isn't fair. But you have to make a choice—would you rather be right or be happy?

If you are the one who sees a problematic pattern that your partner denies, watch carefully for counterexamples that suggest the pattern is less clear-cut than you believe. Keep a list of these counterexamples to balance the mental list you likely already keep of examples that support the pattern, and then be open to letting go of your negative belief.

GIVING LOVE THE WAY YOU WANT IT

You probably learned the golden rule as a child—treat others as you would want to be treated yourself. Turns out, that's not always good advice for couples.

When people show love for their partners, they tend to express their love in the way that they like to receive love. But the things that make your partner feel loved probably are very different from the things that make you feel loved. Sometimes this is because of gender differences—many women feel most loved when they have deep, meaningful conversations with their partners...while many men feel most loved when they are physically intimate with their partners. But not everyone falls into these gender roles.

There are five broad ways in which people give and receive love to partners, sometimes called "love languages." Some people feel most loved when their partner spends quality one-on-one time with them, doing things together or just listening closely to what they say...or when the couple has sex. Other people feel closest when the partner does things to lighten their load...or provides encouraging words...or gives thoughtful gifts.

When partners speak different love languages, it can leave both of them feeling unloved even when both are genuinely trying to express their love.

What to do: If you have been with your partner for many years, you probably already know which of the five love languages he/she most values. If you don't, it's time to ask. Then express love to your partner this way, no matter your personal preference. Meanwhile, confirm that your partner understands what makes you feel truly loved. Don't get angry if your partner occasionally reverts to showing you love the way that he likes to receive love—it takes time to break habits. When you receive your partner's preferred type of love, remind yourself that your partner is showing you love but in his preferred way.

SEEKING AGREEMENT

Many people believe it must be a positive thing for partners to always seek to be on the same page on any given topic. Actually, that thinking can devastate a relationship.

It's not realistic to expect two people to be in agreement on everything, and when couples treat total agreement as a goal, they tend to see their inevitable disagreements as a serious problem—a sign that they're not really right for each other. These problems are exacerbated when one partner squelches disagreements by insisting that the other partner must fall into line and agree.

Example: A man refused to accept that his wife could have different opinions than his own regarding virtually anything, including the state of their marriage. When she suggested that they had begun to drift apart following a relocation to Chicago, he said, "You don't really believe that, right?"

What to do: Remain open to the possibility that two people can have completely different opinions without either of them being wrong. Make it your goal to listen to and understand your partner and to treat her point of view with respect, even if you do not fully agree. Consider differences of opinion as opportunities for engaging in debate or for learning something about your partner—not as arguments or signs of incompatibility.

FEELING OUT OF FOCUS

"I love you...but I'm no longer in love with you." When someone says these words, it means that he no longer feels close to his partner but can't point to any big, dramatic reason why. His partner hasn't made any major missteps...the spark is simply gone.

The partner's focus usually is at the root of these feelings. At the beginning of the relationship, you felt like you were your partner's primary focus...but over the years, the focus has shifted to career, kids, or other interests. That has left one or both feeling disconnected from the other and wondering, *Is this how I want to spend the rest of my life?*

What to do: Think back to the beginning of your relationship, when you felt passion for each other. What, specifically, did you and your partner do together that made you feel like you were each other's focus? Maybe you had special meals together...or took long walks where you discussed art and movies.

Do those things again, at least once a week. The activities that made a couple feel focused on each other in the past often will do so again in the present. Schedule this together time in advance if life has become too busy to depend on it happening naturally.

Meanwhile, stop keeping score. A partner who feels he is no longer the other's focus probably has been blaming that partner for the lack of closeness for some time. Your feelings of distance are not something that your partner did to you—it's perfectly normal for the passion and focus that existed early in a relationship to be replaced by routine and responsibility as the years pass. If you want that passion and focus back, don't allow your sense of having been hurt or rejected prevent you from doing something positive such as scheduling meaningful time together.

Many Americans Commit Financial Infidelity

About 44 percent of U.S. adults admit hiding a bank account or debt, or spending more money than a partner would be comfortable spending. Millennials are more likely than baby boomers or members of Generation X to commit financial infidelity.

Ted Rossman, industry analyst, CreditCards.com, which surveyed 1,378 adults who are married, in a civil partnership, or living with a partner.

How to End a Romantic Relationship with Grace

Guy Winch, PhD, clinical psychologist in private practice in New York City. He is author of *How to Fix a Broken Heart* and cohost of the podcast "Dear Therapists." GuyWinch.com

Breakups can be painful whether you've been on just a few dates or have been together as a couple for many years. No matter the reason nor the length of the relationship, handling a breakup poorly can create undue pain. *Clinical psychologist Guy Winch, PhD, explains how to make this difficult process easier...*

UP TO THREE DATES

If you've gone out with someone no more than a few times, he/she is unlikely to be permanently devastated by the dissolution of the relationship, although the two of you may have drastically different opinions of whether you were a good match...and rejection always hurts.

What to do: Often the best thing to do is nothing—don't call or text, and simply allow the relationship to end. This approach sometimes is portrayed as cowardly or cruel, but there's a good chance that the other person also would rather let your nascent relationship drift away than endure the unpleasantness of an official breakup. Sometimes, though, the other person doesn't get the hint. If you receive a message from the partner suggesting that he doesn't realize it's over or wants a clear-cut conclusion, then it's your responsibility to respond.

Even if the other person phoned you, a text message or an e-mail is acceptable here—it spares both partners from an emotionally difficult conversation that really isn't necessary after only a few dates.

This message should include a positive statement about the other person or the time you spent together plus the explanation that the match just wasn't working for you. There's no need to add greater detail about what went wrong—pointing to shortcomings or missteps is more likely to add pain than reduce it.

Examples: "I really enjoyed getting to know you, but I don't think that it was a good romantic match for me"... or "I don't think that the chemistry was working, but you're great and I hope you find the right person."

FOUR OR MORE DATES BUT STILL NOT "EXCLUSIVE"

By date four, your partner has invested substantial time and emotional energy in the relationship and has reason to believe that you think the match might work. You owe this person an explanation if you end the relationship.

What to do: A conversation is required, either in person, by phone or via video chat. You might want to send a text or an e-mail to set up this conversation—"Do you have time to talk tonight? There's something I need to discuss." Most daters understand what could be coming when they receive a text like this, which gives them a chance to mentally prepare for the coming conversation.

Explain that your feelings "haven't been progressing"...or that you don't see a future together because you "want different things" or "have different interests." As above, add something positive, such as how much you've enjoyed the time you've spent together.

If this partner wants greater detail about what went wrong, point to areas of incompatibility.

Example: "I like to go out a lot more than you do. That worked during the pandemic because we couldn't get out much, but eventually either you would get tired of going out or I would get bored staying in."

Don't say, "Let's be friends"—it's extremely rare for romantic relationships to transition into nonromantic relationships...and suggesting this might send mixed messages or prolong an uncomfortable situation.

It's usually best not to be swayed if the partner asks for another chance. Your carefully thought-out decision is much more likely than your partner's emotional response to be the better choice.

Alternative: If your partner responds to the preconversation warning text above by texting back that she would rather that you told her now than wait for a later conversation, she's likely signaling that she would prefer to avoid the unpleasantness of a breakup chat. In this situation, it's acceptable to end the relationship via a follow-up text. Mention in this text that you're available for a phone call if she does want to talk about the breakup, although this offer is unlikely to be accepted.

LONG-TERM COMMITTED RELATIONSHIPS

If you've been together more than a few months, breaking it off is going to take more than a few minutes—and possibly more than a few tears. Your partner likely will feel blindsided by the breakup even if it seems obvious to you that the relationship isn't working. Long-term relationships usually end because of a slow accumulation of issues, not a single massive misstep. Often, one partner considers this slow accumulation of issues to provide proof that the relationship isn't working... while the other believes that these issues are in the past and assumes the couple has overcome them or underestimates the problems.

What to do: Long-term relationships must be ended in person. Have this conversation in a private place that isn't your home—private so that your partner can express his feelings and emotions freely...and not your home so that you can leave afterward. Your partner's home often is the best choice.

Exception: A public setting is justified if you fear that your partner might become violent.

Leave no doubt that the relationship is 100 percent over. Opening the door even a crack for a potential future reunion only makes it harder for your partner to move on. Provide a clear explanation that doesn't assign most of the blame to your partner or yourself.

Examples: "I don't feel in love anymore"... "I think we want different things"..."We fight too much"...or "I can't adapt to your lifestyle."

Don't back down if your partner claims he can change and the relationship can improve. The issues leading to the breakup of a long relationship inevitably have been discussed before. If the situation was going to improve, that should have happened already.

Be patient and understanding if your ex has questions or a strong emotional response. You've been processing the impending demise of the relationship for some time, but it's new and perhaps unexpected for your partner. Try not to take it personally or get drawn into an argument if your partner says mean things to you—that's just a reaction to the pain and embarrassment of being rejected. But, if in your opinion, your partner steps over the line from anger to verbal abuse, it's perfectly valid to draw a line.

Example: You might say, "We can continue to talk, but I won't be yelled at" or "I know I've hurt you, but if you want to keep talking, you have to stop insulting me."

If you and your partner have possessions in each other's homes, suggest that you arrange the exchange later, perhaps through the mail. Or if the breakup conversation occurs in your partner's home, bring a few collapsible bags and say, "I'm going to pack up my things...let me know later how you'd like me to get yours to you."

Suggest that you and your partner coordinate what you tell shared friends to minimize the breakup fallout. Recommend that you both update your Facebook relationship status at the same time, for example...and note that when asked about the breakup, you'll say something positive such as, "It just didn't work out. She's wonderful, and we had a good run." Criticism of an ex makes both partners look bad.

Take physical cues from your partner during the breakup conversation. It's fine if she reaches for your hand or wants to cry on your shoulder, but inappropriate for the person initiating the breakup to initiate physical contact, even if it's a well-intentioned attempt to provide comfort.

For the first month following the breakup, try to avoid social situations where you might bump into your ex, if feasible.

How Not to Be Annoyed by People Who Annoy You

Michele Weiner-Davis, LCSW, founder of The Divorce Busting Center in Boulder, Colorado. She is a TEDx speaker and best-selling author of eight books, including *Healing from Infidelity, The Sex-Starved Marriage* and *Divorce Busting.* DivorceBusting.com

---

My mother was an amazingly wise, renowned therapist who taught me many important life lessons but none more important than the one encapsulated in the words of a button she gave me: "Never try to teach a cow to sing. It doesn't work, and it annoys the cow."

We all know that cows won't sing. They moo. And because we know this, we allow cows to be cows, which, in turn, avoids irritating them and disappointing ourselves.

Yet, when it comes to our human counterparts, we are not nearly as realistic. No matter how consistently our loved ones moo, we're surprised, disappointed, and critical when they aren't singing instead. It makes us miserable. And therein lies the magic formula for happiness in life—let cows be cows.

NOT SURPRISED, YET DISAPPOINTED

In many ways, the people in our lives are fairly predictable. They are who they are. Their behaviors—both desirable and undesirable—show up like clockwork. Your husband's voracious sexual appetite rarely seems to coincide with your interest in being connected physically. Except for wishing you a happy birthday each year, your sister typically relies on you to initiate contact with her. Your best friend consistently shows up 30 minutes late for everything you plan together. Your relatives get into heated arguments at all family gatherings.

In short, we are well aware of our loved ones' quirks and idiosyncrasies. We know what to expect. Nevertheless, we are oddly taken aback each time a friend or family member moos. We're put off. We're annoyed. We're disappointed.

That's when our little inner voices—the ones that narrate our lives—go on overload. Even after years of experiencing predictable patterns in behavior in the people we love, we find ourselves thinking, I can't believe that _____ (fill in the blank), or I just wish my (friend, family member) would _______ (behave a particular way) rather than _____ (the way they usually act.) *Examples…*

- **I can't believe my sister isn't able to pick up the phone and call me once in a while to say hello!** She has such a sense of entitlement. She takes me for granted.
- **It is so rude that my friend can't meet me at the agreed-upon time.** Obviously, she doesn't care about my feelings. I would never do that to her.
- **It's hard to believe that my family has to ruin every holiday with their obnoxiously heated conversations.** They're so self-centered. They think the world revolves around them.

I think you get the point.

BELIEVE WHAT IS

If you want to find peace in your life and relationships, every time you tell yourself (or those within earshot), *I just wish that… I just can't believe that…* or *Why can't he/she* (do this rather than that?), do yourself a favor and start believing what is and stop wishing for what isn't!

If you're thinking, *That's depressing! It means that people can't change or that I have to live with totally unacceptable behavior*, I totally disagree. People can change. They do it all the time—when change becomes important to them. And you shouldn't accept behaviors that violate your own important personal values.

But—and this is a big but—there's probably a good reason the people in your life are in your life. It's not because of their annoying behaviors…it's because of what's good about them. All people are package deals—your family members…friends…your partner. There are lovable, wonderful qualities in all of us, and there are ones that…well…let's just say, aren't so easy to live with.

And we have a choice. We can focus on the exasperating qualities in our loved ones and try to turn moos into songs, or we can shine a light on their endearing qualities instead and allow these qualities to define our relationships.

ACCEPTANCE WORKS!

Here's an example of how I practice acceptance in my own life. I have many fabulous girlfriends. They sustain me. When I stand back and think about how different they are from one another, it truly is remarkable.

One friend—I'll call her Susie—is an artist. She appreciates art and nature on a very profound level. She's deep and very serious. She has a need for structure and likes to make plans well in advance of the actual event. She marks it in her calendar in blood. Taking hikes to remote mountainous areas and watching the spectacular way the light hits the leaves or the snow glistens on the rocks is one of our favorite pastimes.

Another friend—I'll call her Jamie—is what I call my "yes friend." She's light-hearted, spontaneous, filled with laughter, and always up for the next adventure. She loves last-minute plans and is totally understanding if, for any reason, plans fall through.

Although I find Susie's need for structure and seriousness a bit restrictive at times, I choose to focus on the uplifting, rich time I know we will have together communing with nature. And although Jamie's spontaneity and lust for life has meant that she hasn't always been available, even at times when I've "needed" her—a value that is very important to me—I choose to focus on the laughter and joy I feel when we play together.

I never try to make Susie or Jamie sing when they moo. I'm not surprised or disappointed when they don't. I like—no, I love—their moos.

I can honestly say that I practice this art of acceptance with everyone in my life—my husband, kids, parents, siblings, friends, colleagues. And because I do, my loved ones are "lifers." I'm still friends with my bestie from third grade!

PAY THE RIGHT ATTENTION

Ask yourself whether you spend too much time trying to change things that are unchangeable rather than paying more attention to what's good in your life and the people around you.

If it's challenging to find work-arounds for behaviors that bother you, here's one more suggestion—stop making up negative stories about why people behave the way they do. She's spiteful...he's stingy...she doesn't care about my feelings...he's controlling. These stories are just that—stories. They add fuel to the already everlasting fire.

Instead, consider a simple lesson I've learned over the years—people do the best they can with the tools they have. When they know better, they do better. And that goes for all of us.

Playing Hard-to-Get Pays Off

A study of dating behaviors shows that when people present themselves as needing to be won over, prospective partners find them more appealing and invest more effort in the relationship.

Daters: Show initial interest so as not to alienate a potential partner, but keep some cards to yourself. People are less likely to desire what they already have. Building a connection gradually creates a sense of anticipation and a desire to learn more about a potential partner.

Gurit Birnbaum, PhD, associate professor of psychology at Interdisciplinary Center Herzliya, Israel, and leader of a study published in *Journal of Social and Personal Relationships.*

How to Track Down Old Friends Online

Dan Ribacoff, founder and CEO of International Investigative Group, Ltd., a private investigation firm with offices in New York, Los Angeles, Boca Raton, and London. He is author of *I, Spy: How to Be Your Own Private Investigator.* IIGPI.com

Locating long-lost friends and family used to be a challenge even for experienced private investigators. These days anyone can track people down in just minutes with the help of the Internet—but you need to know where to look online and some tricks for how best to use various websites. In fact, some of these same online resources can be useful if your goal is not to find someone you've lost track of but to check the background of someone you've met, such as a prospective tenant or employee...your child's new boyfriend or girlfriend...or your own new beau.

You probably can guess where to start these searches. Enter the name into popular social-media sites such as Facebook, LinkedIn, Instagram, and Twitter...and into search engines such as Google and Yahoo. There's a good chance you'll find the person you're looking for. Enclose his/her name in quotation marks when using search engines, as in "Harold Greene." Try nicknames if searching the proper name fails, such as "Harry Greene."

If these initial searches come up empty, here are some lesser known websites worth trying...

PEOPLE-SEARCH WEBSITES

Enter a name into AnyWho.com...Intelius.com...and/or Whitepages.com, and these sites will provide lists of potential matches from across the US. Often many people share the same name, so these sites also supply details to help identify the right individual, perhaps including age...prior hometowns...names of relatives...colleges attended...and/or employers.

While these sites are free to use at a basic level, they charge for providing certain details. Contact information such as phone numbers and e-mail addresses usually are among the facts hidden behind the paywall.

Exception: Whitepages sometimes provides home phone numbers for free.

Their prices vary dramatically based on the site and the amount of info provided—anywhere from $1 for a few details to $40 or more for a monthly subscription that allows you to conduct criminal background checks.

If all you want is someone's contact info, there's usually no need to pay—the free information supplied by these sites often is sufficient to track someone down with just a little more online digging. Each of these people-search sites provides slightly different information for free, but they sometimes supply out-of-date or inaccurate info, so it's worth using all three.

Here's how to put their free information to use...

- **All three sites typically list the person's hometown and some prior hometowns for free.**

What to do: Enter the person's name (in quotation marks) and this hometown together into a search engine. This search might turn up a phone number, e-mail address, and/or physical address.

Example: Enter "John Doe" Phoenix into Google.

- **AnyWho and Intelius often provide partial phone numbers for free, with the final four digits Xed out.**

What to do: Enter the name plus this partial phone number (in quotation marks) into a search engine. The full phone number might appear among the results.

Example: Enter "Jane Doe" "212-555" into Google.

- **Intelius and Whitepages often list the names of relatives for free.** (Be aware that these lists are not 100 percent accurate and might contain the names of some unrelated people, too.)

What to do: Search these relatives' names on social-media sites, on Google and with the other search tools listed here. If you can reach a relative, he/she might be able to put you in contact with the person you are looking for.

- **AnyWho and Whitepages often provide a complete physical address for free.**

What to do: If you can't track down a phone number or e-mail address for your friend, you could use this to mail a letter.

USING EXTRA INFO IN YOUR SEARCH

Don't give up on search engines such as Google.com or Yahoo.com if just entering a name doesn't work. Try combining this name (in quotation marks) with other details you have about this individual. That could be information gleaned from people-search sites, as explained above, or it could be this person's hometown/high school...profession...his/her spouse's name...his college...or an activity that he was passionate about, such as "marathon" or "quilt."

Example: Searching "Jane Doe" and "stained glass" might turn up workshops that your old friend Jane taught about making stained glass...or a website where she displays or sells examples of her stained glass.

NICHE PEOPLE-FINDING SITES

These sites can be useful if you have a few specific details about the person you're looking for...

The alumni site Classmates.com can be helpful if you know where the person went to high school. This site has contact info only for people who have registered with it—but even if your friend hasn't registered, it could provide contact info for another classmate who remains in touch with your friend.

Although you can register with Classmates.com for free, a "Classmates+" membership is required for certain searches and if you want to send e-mails through the site to other members. The introductory price of Classmates+ is $9 for three months.

Similar: If you and your friend attended the same college or you know which college he/she attended, look for an alumni directory on that school's website or enter the name of that college and the phrase "alumni directory" into a search engine. You might be able to access your friend's contact info by completing an online registration. Or try calling or e-mailing the alumni-relations department and ask it to pass on your contact info to your friend. Some high schools have alumni associations, too.

Databases that list members of a particular profession are a good resource if you know what the person does for a living. Enter the profession and "association" into a search engine to locate relevant databases.

If the profession is one that requires a license and you know or suspect which state this person might live in, also search the name of the profession together with the state. Look in the results for a webpage with a ".gov" ending...then look on that page for a licensee search tool.

Example: Searching the terms "barber," "license" and "Maine" turns up the State of Maine Barbering and Cosmetology Licensing page, which has the option "Find a licensee or a list of licensees" in its menu.

County public records are worth searching if you know or suspect which county the person might live in. If he owns property, the deed and mortgage should be in that county's public records and likely will include a mailing address. Many counties now make these records available for free online. Enter the county, state, and phrase "public records" into a search engine to find these.

Obituary databases such as Tributes.com and Legacy.com's newspaper obituary search tool are worth searching if you can recall the names and hometowns of your friend's parents or siblings, especially if these relatives would be old enough that there's a good chance they have died. Entering the names of family members along with their hometowns and the word "obituary" into a search engine also might steer you directly to the obit. If you can find the obituary of a family member, it often list the names and current hometowns of surviving relatives.

Helpful: If you locate a death listing for your friend's parent or sibling but it doesn't include details about surviving relatives, make note of the date of death. Check the obituary section of local newspapers for the days following that date in search of a more detailed obituary.

More from Dan Ribacoff...

Common-Name Challenges

Two situations when online people searches are especially likely to fail: When the person has such a common name that it's difficult to locate him/her among all the other people who share that name...and when the person has changed his/her name. This most often occurs when a woman weds and takes her husband's name...or she divorces and reverts to her maiden name.

What to do: Use the websites listed on pages 245 and 246 again, this time searching the name of a relative or close friend of the person you're trying to find—ideally one with an uncommon name. This person likely will be easier to find, and he/she might be able to put you in touch with the individual you hope to reach. If this friend or relative is hesitant to give out your friend's contact info, provide your contact info and ask if it could be forwarded to your friend.

Choose Your Words of Support Thoughtfully

Choose your words of support thoughtfully the next time you offer a shoulder to lean on. No matter how well-intentioned, support messages can worsen a loved one's stress if they are critical or dismissive of the person's feelings. Support messages that convey care and concern, validate their feelings, and encourage them to reach their own conclusions are particularly helpful. It's as simple as saying "You have every right to feel upset" rather than "You're making too much of this."

Xi Tian, a graduate assistant in communication arts and sciences at Pennsylvania State University, University Park, and an author of the study published in *Journal of Communication.*

How to Write a Heartfelt Sympathy Note

Florence Isaacs, author of numerous books on writing, including *Just a Note to Say: The Perfect Words for Every Occasion* and *Business Notes: Writing Personal Notes that Build Professional Relationships.* Her newest book is *Do I Have to Wear Black to a Funeral? 112 Etiquette Guidelines for the New Rules of Death.* FlorenceIsaacs.com

---

Writing a sympathy note has never been easy. It's a reminder of our own mortality and the possibility of loss. We also feel helpless in the face of someone else's grief.

It's fine to send an e-mail—I think a text is intrusive—when you first learn of the death, as in, "We just heard the terrible news. You are in our hearts." A call is also OK if you know the person well. But don't stop there.

Whether you use a blank notecard or a preprinted condolence card, it's your personal handwritten message that gives meaningful comfort to the bereaved. People pull out sympathy notes to reread even 10 or 15 years after the death of a loved one. Online condolences are unlikely to be saved.

Start with a simple message such as, "Please accept my sincere sympathy on the death of your parent/spouse/loved one." *Then…*

- **Share a memory or inspiration.** If the bereaved is a relative or close friend, mention a memory you have of the deceased, as in, "He gave me such good advice" and share an anecdote or "She always made me laugh. I'll miss that smile."

When writing to your boss or a client/customer, your handwritten message can simply read "I'm thinking of you at this very sad time."

- **Keep it short, unless you know the bereaved or knew the deceased well.** Survivors appreciate just being in your thoughts, and you don't want to accidentally say something inappropriate.

- **Offer specific help.** Do not write, "Please let me know if there is anything I can do." People who are bereaved have enough on their plates in the weeks and months after the loss of a loved one. If you really wish to help, suggest something specific, such as grocery shopping, preparing a meal, or mowing the lawn.

What not to say: It's so common to write, "I'm sorry for your loss," but times have changed. These days, younger people may resent those words and feel, *What are you sorry for? It's not your fault.* Think twice before mentioning God or religion, too, unless you're certain the recipient is a believer. Americans are less religious today than ever before. And never say, "I know how you feel." Survivors tend to believe their loss is singular.

Do try to write promptly after hearing of the death. Remember, too, that simplicity is key, especially in the saddest or most turbulent times.

How to Help Someone Downsize

Mary Kay Buysse, executive director of the National Association of Senior Move Managers. NASMM.org

---

Even when you know "it's the right thing to do," helping parents or loved ones downsize from the large family home can be emotionally difficult. *To make it easier for everyone…*

- **Take your time.** If possible, give the process a few weeks—even months. Older adults typically don't have the physical or emotional energy to do this for more than a few hours at a time, so tackle it in small doses. Let your loved ones share their stories as you sort through their possessions.

Important: Unless asked to do so, don't just throw out belongings or make other decisions on their behalf. That will feel disrespectful and demeaning.

- **Start in emotionally neutral rooms.** Tender memories are stored in different rooms for different people.

Example: Many people keep old letters and photographs in their bedroom closet, so leave that area for last. Instead, start with less challenging rooms such as bathrooms, kids' bedrooms, or the garage.

- **Distribute precious mementos now.** Encourage loved ones to give away jewelry, china, and other valuables they may be inclined to hold onto. Doing so will allow them to see the next generation enjoy them.

Important: Prepare your parents that their 30-year-old granddaughter is unlikely to want their dining room set even if it's a "valuable" antique. Suggest they give each person one keepsake—a vase, a necklace, a book, a figurine.

- **Eliminate maybes.** The "maybe" pile typically ends up in a storage unit that costs thousands of dollars before the stuff is thrown out or given away anyway.

- **Figure out what stays.** Map out the new residence to help determine what furniture and other items can fit.

Tip: If your loved ones are going from 12 kitchen cabinets to two, try putting essentials into two cabinets in the current home. Give away the rest.

- **Hire a senior move manager who specializes in downsizing for older adults.** If you live far away, you may not be able to spend a lot of time on this. Senior move managers help with going through belongings...distributing, donating, and discarding unwanted items...moving clients...and setting up new residences. They also can find homes for quality collections or donations, but they will be honest with you if something is best thrown away rather than donated. He/she works closely with all of the donation sites in your area and online sites for specific collections, so he will know who will take your donations and who won't.

Rates range widely from about $40 to $125 per hour depending on location. Find a senior move manager in your area at the National Association of Senior & Specialty Move Managers website, NASMM.org.

Navigating Family Caregiving

Aaron Blight, EdD, adjunct professor at Shenandoah University, advisory board member of the Shenandoah Area Agency on Aging, and founder of Caregiving Kinetics. He is author of the book *When Caregiving Calls: Guidance as You Care for a Parent, Spouse, or Aging Relative.*

Caring for a loved one is a noble calling that teaches you much about yourself. You will reevaluate the roles you play in life, test your limits, and likely find an inner strength you didn't know was there. But you'll also feel intense stress, difficult emotions, and even physical repercussions.

MY JOURNEY

Twenty years ago, I was writing national health-care policy for the Centers for Medicare & Medicaid Services when my own caregiving journey began. After surgery to remove a malignant brain tumor, my mother-in-law stayed with my family to recuperate. What we thought would be two weeks stretched into two years. Even after she returned to her own apartment, she required constant, extensive care as the state of her cognition and body steadily declined. When the cancer returned in the fifth year, we hired a home care agency to help us care for her in her final days.

That experience changed everything—even my career. I went on to open my own home care company to provide others with the kind of support we found so valuable, and I then began studying caregiving as a phenomenon of social science for my doctoral degree. Throughout this journey, I've garnered a wealth of knowledge that I'd like to share with you.

CHANGING ROLES

Dealing with conflicting roles is among the first and biggest challenges that caregivers have to face. When you are caring for a loved one who needs an outsized amount of your attention, care, and time, you may struggle to maintain the standards you're accustomed to in your other roles. You may be less effective at work, unable to attend your children's school activities, or too busy to socialize with friends. Your loved one needs your attention and care, but so do your boss, your children, and other people in your life.

TIME CONSTRAINTS

As the needs of your loved one grow, you will have to spend more of your time in caregiving, while still trying to fulfill all of your other roles. It can feel like a marathon without a finish line. *To ease the way, try these strategies...*

1. Carve out time in your existing schedule to address your loved one's needs. What can you swap?

2. Choose the timing that works best for you. For example, if your mother needs you to accompany her to a doctor's visit, get involved in the scheduling so you can select an appointment time that's most convenient—or least disruptive—for you.

3. Determine how much time you will spend in a caregiving task. When you stop by for a visit, for example, decide in advance how long you will stay.

4. Evaluate how often you must perform care-related tasks to be more efficient. For instance, if you're picking up prescription medications, try to plan one pharmacy trip per month for all refills.

5. Consider the order of all the other things you're doing, and perform your caregiving tasks at the most convenient place in the order.

6. Make sure your schedule allows you to do things that you find personally rewarding. You have to give yourself permission to do this. It can feel indulgent to take time for yourself, but you have to restore the energy and the motivation that you need to keep going.

MANAGING EMOTIONS

As you experience a new role, juggle obligations, and adjust to caregiving, you will likely face a range of "negative" emotions. Of all the emotions that family caregivers confront, guilt is one of the most pervasive. You're also likely to feel grief as you watch a loved one decline, and anticipatory grief for the loss of a future relationship or time together. You may feel resentment, anger, anguish, or countless other emotions that are completely normal. The stress of caregiving can leave you feeling exhausted, fatigued, irritable, compulsive, and depressed.

SKILLS

Because your loved one's health will change over time, the skills you need to care for them must continually evolve. A person who can walk now may need to be lifted in a year. You may have to learn to give injections, clean wounds, or use home medical equipment. If you know a Certified Nursing Assistant, invite him/her to come with you to see your loved one so they can show you some tips. You can also request a demonstration by a provider who's working with your loved one, or watch training videos on YouTube.

OUTSOURCE

If there comes a time that you can't provide the level of care that your loved one needs, you can turn to professional help. There is nothing wrong with outsourcing caregiving, whether it's as simple as hiring a nursing assistant to bathe a parent or as complex as finding a memory care facility for a spouse with Alzheimer's disease. Seeking help is not abandoning your loved one, but rather taking steps to make sure they get what they need to have the best quality of life possible.

BEWARE BURNOUT

As stress grows, you're at risk of burnout or compassion fatigue. That can be characterized by bottled-up emotions, isolation from others, substance abuse used to mask feelings, poor

DID YOU KNOW?...

One-Third of Adults Give Their Parents Money

One-third of adults give their parents money even when that causes financial strain in their own lives. Half of those who have helped support their parents said they gave them at least $1,000 in the past year, and 20 percent gave $5,000 or more. More than one-quarter of those who helped parents said doing so caused a high level of strain on their own finances.

Results of a survey by *AARP The Magazine*.

self-care (related to hygiene or appearance, for example), debt, and even chronic physical ailments such as gastrointestinal problems or recurrent colds.

It's important for caregivers to practice self-care to avoid burnout and continue helping those who depend on them. *Here are 10 tips you may want to consider to reduce caregiving-induced stress...*

- **Seek help from a counselor.**
- **Exercise.**
- **Arrange for respite care by another caregiver.**
- **See your physician.**
- **Engage with a caregiver support group.**
- **Connect with online caregiver communities.**
- **Set realistic expectations about what you can and cannot do.**
- **Go outdoors.**
- **Start keeping a journal and write about things you're grateful for.**

While caregiving for your loved one is never going to be easy, it will be easier when you address your emotional needs rather than suppressing or ignoring them.

8 Questions That Will Unearth Your Family History

Perri Chinalai, managing director of learning and engagement and of the Legacy Initiative at StoryCorps, a nonprofit organization. StoryCorps has helped orchestrate the recording of more than 600,000 people's stories since 2003, and preserves those recordings in the Library of Congress. StoryCorps.org

In most families, a few well-worn anecdotes are told and retold, but much of the family history has not been passed down. If your parents—or aunts or uncles or other relatives—are still alive, a link to your family history still exists. By interviewing or having informal conversations with these older relatives and possibly recording their stories, you can deepen what it means to belong to your family.

We asked Perri Chinalai of StoryCorps, a nonprofit dedicated to preserving personal stories, to share questions to ask during conversations with older relatives...

Could you paint a picture of your childhood home and hometown for me? Phrases such as "paint a picture of..." and "what do you see when you recall..." are very useful during these interviews. When you ask people to describe memories visually, you greatly increase the odds that their responses will be rich and detailed.

Example: A man who grew up in Coney Island described an idyllic wonderland with iconic amusement parks and grand movie houses where waiters took orders for treats like pie and hot dogs. "It was just the greatest place to be."

Could you tell me about your parents? What comes to mind when you think of them? Do you remember any stories they used to tell about their lives? A conversation with a parent, aunt, or uncle isn't just an opportunity to learn about his/her life—it's a chance to learn what we can about the generation that came before, people we might barely remember or have never met.

Example: A man described his long-deceased father as a tough man but a good father. This father was proud to work in a local wire mill—he often would boast that he had helped make the cables when the family drove over a bridge. But when his son said he wanted to quit school to work in the mill, this father pushed him against a wall, got in his face and told him he was staying in school and getting a college degree—which he did. Yet even when his son was in his late teens, this tough father never failed to visit the young man's room before turning in to say, "Good night, son. I love you."

What were the proudest moments and achievements of your childhood? Of your adult life? The moments mentioned likely are things this person would love to have descendants remember.

Example: A 93-year-old retired nurse from Tennessee told her grandson that nursing was "the most rewarding profession you could have." She noted with evident pride that people still stopped her to say, "Oh, you took care of my boy. I will never forget you."

What traditions or beliefs did your parents pass down to you or try to pass down to you? Family and cultural traditions can become lost in modern times. Learning these traditions—and perhaps even rekindling them—could reconnect the family to a heritage that might date back generations or centuries.

Example: A mother who grew up in the Philippines but moved to Texas as an adult described her family's tradition of eating the big holiday meal together at midnight on Christmas Eve.

What's your best memory of childhood? Your worst? How would you describe a perfect day when you were young? What's the worst thing you ever did as a child? Stories from a parent's childhood date from an era when the world—and this parent—were very different from what younger generations know.

Example: A man who grew up in Kansas in the 1940s told his nephew about the time he and three friends hopped a freight train headed west, in hopes of seeing California. When the train stopped, they imagined they must be around halfway to their destination. But they discovered they were still in Kansas. They gave up and got a ride home.

How did you meet your husband/wife? When did you know he/she was "the one"? What was married life like before you had kids—what are your favorite stories or memories of those early years together? The early years of a relationship before children arrive can be very different from what follows—and these times often are virtually unknown to the children.

Possible follow-up questions might include, "When did you first find out you were going to be a parent?" and "What went through your mind when you found out?"

What are the biggest challenges you faced in your life, and how did you overcome them? Stories about tough times often go unmentioned—they can be difficult to relive. But these can be the stories that shape people, and descendants can draw strength from the knowledge that their ancestors were resilient.

Example: A mother told her son that she had become pregnant at 17—something she had never mentioned to him before. Her father responded to her out-of-wedlock pregnancy by kicking her out of the house. She gave her baby up for adoption, but when she did, she vowed that one day she would adopt a child who needed a home. She did—the son conducting the interview had been adopted.

Similar: Ask how this person and his/her family survived specific global events that occurred during his lifetime or his parents' lifetimes. This might include, "How did your family get through the Great Depression?"... "Did anyone in the family catch the Spanish Flu?"..."How did your life change during World War II?"

How did you get into your line of work? Is that what you always wanted to do—and, if not, what did you want to do? Plenty of parents have never shared much about their professional lives with their kids—they kept their work and home lives separate.

Similar: Related questions include, "What was your first job like?" and, "Do you have any favorite stories from your career?"

Full House: How to Make It Work When Your Adult Child Moves Back Home

Jane Adams, PhD, a social psychologist based in Seattle who specializes in parent/adult child relationships. She is author of *I'm Still Your Mother: How to Get Along with Your Grown-Up Children for the Rest of Your Life.* JaneAdams.com

Whether kids are returning home for economic reasons or simply because they are having a hard time cutting the cord, the key is to make the situation successful for all involved. Having a history of getting along is no guarantee that things will go smoothly when adult children move back in. Parent/child relationships change when children become adults (and adults get used to living in their "empty nest"), and it's important to set new ground rules that respect the needs of all involved.

There are five topics that need to be discussed and agreed to when parents and their adult children work through the details of the child's return...

• **Money.** If the child is moving in to save money...pay down student debt...or survive a spell of unemployment, it might not be practical to request market-rate rent. Still, adult children who live at home should contribute to the household, even if it's a token amount such as $25 a week.

Exception: If money is extremely tight for the child, you could give him the option of contributing a certain number of hours each week toward household chores in lieu of rent.

Money is especially likely to become a point of contention if an adult child pays very low (or no) rent but splurges on vacations, dinners out with friends, and/or excessive clothes. Parents can offer assistance with setting budgets. As time goes on, parents can request an increase in rent if it appears the child is capable of paying more without hardship. It is not appropriate to criticize his spending or demand that it stop. He is an adult who has a right to make his own financial decisions—even if you don't agree with those decisions. But the parents have a right to tell the child he must move out if their goodwill is being abused.

• **Guests.** It is perfectly reasonable for an adult child to have friends over—including romantic friends. But it's also perfectly reasonable for parents to feel a bit uncomfortable about having adult strangers in their house. The best compromise often is to allow guests but set limits. These might include constraining the hours when guests can visit...the days when they can visit (not on weeknights, for example)...the number of days per week/month when guests can visit...and/or that advance notice be provided when guests will visit. It's certainly reasonable to set a limit on how often romantic friends can sleep over—or even if they can sleep in the same room if it runs counter to your religious or moral beliefs. It's one thing to let your child move back in, but another thing entirely to have his partner virtually living in your home.

• **Curfews.** It is not appropriate to set a curfew for an adult child. If your adult child were living somewhere else, you wouldn't even know she was out late. Some parents struggle with this, lying awake at night worried about the adult child's safety until they finally hear the door open in the wee hours.

It's reasonable to request a text message on nights that she'll be out later than expected. Try presenting this request as a courtesy the adult child could do for you, not an obligation.

Example: "You have every right to stay out late. It's just hard for a parent to get out of that worrying mode, even when their kids are grown. A quick text would really help me."

• **Personal spaces.** Your adult child's room must be treated as his private space. Do not enter the room without permission unless there's some emergency. Do not insist that the child keep his room tidy—that's not your business (within reason, of course...you don't want old food attracting bugs). But you can insist that shared spaces such as bathrooms be kept to your standard of cleanliness. The adult child also should understand that he will be expected to clean up after himself and do his own laundry.

• **Move-out date.** Consider establishing a tentative end date for the child's stay before she moves in.

Examples: Is the child moving in to save money while in grad school? Perhaps the move-out date could be within a few months of graduation. Are you expecting to retire, sell the home, and relocate? Share the anticipated sale date with the adult child.

Having a move-out date can decrease the odds of misunderstandings...improve the adult child's motivation to search for a job or pay down debt...and help parents reassure themselves that this is a temporary situation.

CONSIDER THE UPSIDE

Having an adult child move back in might feel like a setback—but for many families, it actually turns out very well. This is a chance to build a new relationship with a loved one who previously was your responsibility but who now is something much closer to a peer. You might enjoy having a drink together or trying a new hobby.

Moving back might mean that the adult child will be partially dependent on you longer than expected...but it also means that you can be dependent on this adult child in ways that otherwise might not be possible.

Examples: If you go out of town, he can water the plants and take care of your dog. If you need a ride to the airport, she might drive you.

Remind yourself—and your adult child—that it's perfectly normal for families to be interdependent on each other. Right now, that means you're providing your child with a place to live...but later it might mean that the child is there to help you.

How to Find Work as a Recent Grad

The pandemic tanked the job market for the class of 2020, with a 70 percent drop in "entry level" or "recent grad" employment listings. *Here are a few ways to stay in the fight...*

• **Rethink location.** Given the new acceptance of remote work, you can open your search to places thousands of miles away.

• **Be open to a new plan.** Since the pandemic hit, up to 30 percent of internship applicants have said they're considering changing fields. Tech, sales, and health care are still hiring.

• **Leverage volunteerism.** Donating some time to charitable organizations, such as food banks, looks good on résumés and could open some doors.

• **Be your own boss.** It won't work for everyone, but people with in-demand skills can outmaneuver the competition by going into business for themselves instead of waiting for a company to hire them.

Money.com

Could Foster-Parenting a Teen Be for You?

Bob Herne, MSW, national project director for AdoptUSKids.org, which helps connect families interested in adoption and foster care with the appropriate resources and agencies.

There's a special way to make a profound contribution in the world—one you surely know about but maybe haven't actually thought about. It is adopting or foster-parenting a teenager. Those who do it find it unbelievably rewarding to share and help guide these deeply appreciative young people through many of life's milestones, including learning to drive, first dates, graduating from high school, and getting their first job. Even more rewarding is the knowledge that you're making a difference—perhaps the biggest, best difference possible—in a child's life. The teenage years are an especially critical period during which children need guidance and stability.

Sadly, although approximately 19 percent of kids in foster care waiting to be adopted are teens, last year only 10 percent of adoptions from foster care were teenagers. Those who age out of the system without finding adoptive families face a world where they are more likely to be unemployed and homeless versus their peers who are adopted.

Bob Herne, MSW, national project director for AdoptUSKids.org, explains the joys, concerns, and details about bringing a foster or adoptive teen into your home...

What are some common misconceptions about fostering?

A lot of people hear "foster youth" and think that the child is in the system because of something he/she did. Not so. It's because his/her parent was unable to keep that child safe. These children are not at fault. Most are scared, don't know what's happening to them, and crave guidance and care.

Another misconception? Lots of interested parents don't think they're good enough to be foster or adoptive parents. All families have quirks, and those quirks are our greatest strengths. These are the qualities that allow us to relate to each other. So long as you can provide love, safety, and unconditional commitment, you can do this. We have empty nesters who still want to actively help a younger person and older professionals who spent years focusing on career, never had kids and now, in their 50s, feel ready.

In most states there is no age limit to adopt. Being older offers unique advantages—you have a lifetime of experience to draw on, and older parents tend to be more patient. Both can be tremendously beneficial to a teenager. You just need to show that you can parent the child. You can be single or partnered... straight, gay, or anywhere else on the LGBTQ+ spectrum...and own or rent your home.

Screening includes...

- **Standard background check,** including fingerprinting, to show that you have not been convicted of any major crimes.
- **Attending a training curriculum,** where you will learn more about the children and youth who are living in foster care and how to best meet their needs.
- **Providing information to show you can sufficiently support yourself financially.**
- **Home study,** where a social worker will assist in understanding you and your support system and assist in determining the child/youth whose needs you can best meet (see below).

Can I really handle helping a child through whatever difficulties got him to this point?

When beginning the fostering process, a social worker will conduct a home study, designed to find the right match between you and a youth. The social worker will ask about your family, career, and community...if you're open to children of different ethnicities...what types of experiences you've overcome in your life...and more.

All children removed from their families have experienced some form of trauma. At a minimum, they've lost their primary caregivers, friends, maybe their teachers and classmates. Many also have been abused or neglected or witnessed violence or drug use. There are straight-A students, children who struggle academically, kids with emotional issues, ones who are incredibly well-adjusted. There is a family out there for every one of them.

No family will be put into a situation where they don't feel comfortable or able to help the child feel safe, loved, and unconditionally accepted. The child-welfare professional works with the family and the youth to meet the needs of both.

What kind of support does one receive when fostering or adopting a teen?

You and the child will receive 24/7 emotional and informational support from your foster agency and access to a social worker. There also are support groups for foster and adoptive parents that can help guide you and share resources and ideas. Families will work with social workers to determine the services and supports that a child needs to thrive.

On the financial side, there usually are no (or at most, minimal and reimbursable) fees involved. Foster families receive a monthly state and federal subsidy based on the child's age and needs to help cover expenses, but the subsidies do not cover all the expenses of raising a child/youth.

The majority of families adopt after a child has been placed in their home for foster care. However, there are families that are interested only in adoption. Support includes a monthly adoption-assistance payment that is set by the county or state. Adoption and foster payments last until the child reaches age 18 to 21, depending on the state.

Will I need to interact with the child's biological family? Is that safe?

When a child first enters foster care, the main goal generally is reunification with the biological family, so there usually are supervised visits. Sometimes those visits are supervised by a social worker, who will bring the child to the family, or you may be asked to partner with the family directly. The family and social worker will determine what is safe for the foster family. Honestly, most biological parents are not scary. While they may have issues they are dealing with, such as drug addiction or mental illness, they love their children and are grateful that families are opening up their homes for their children. I operated a large agency for 18 years and never once has a biological family threatened or harmed a foster family assisting in visits.

I'm not ready to commit just yet. How else can I get involved?

If you're not able or ready to bring a child into your home, you still can help. Volunteer to mentor a college-bound foster youth (fc2 success.org)...or become a court-appointed special advocate (CASA) volunteer, which means you're empowered by the courts to advocate on behalf of a child in foster care (NationalCASAgal.org). A CASA spends time with and gets to know the child and informs the court about the child's needs. You could become a respite-care provider—short-term child-care relief for parents and caregivers—or fundraise or donate supplies to foster care organizations.

These children need to hear over and over that someone cares about them. These options allow you to do just that.

To learn more, AdoptUSKids.org can refer you to a local agency to help start the process.

Smartphones Lower Students' Grades

When students use smartphones to look up homework answers, they often fail to retain the information and then do worse on their tests than they did on their homework. In 2008, only 14 percent of students scored lower on exams than on their homework, but with the increasing prevalence of smartphones, the number jumped to 55 percent in 2017.

Strategy: When doing homework, students should generate and commit to their own answers, solidifying the information in their minds, and then use the smartphone only to check their work.

Study by researchers at Rutgers University, New Brunswick, New Jersey, published in *Educational Psychology.*

Kid-Friendly Podcasts

Sesame Street Podcast: Mini-episodes of the popular show. *Noodle Loaf Show:* Singing, learning, active listening. *Cool Facts About Animals:* One species per week—genuinely interesting. *Dad & Me Love History:* A father and son explore historical events. *But Why? A Podcast for Curious Kids:* Questions and answers about anything and everything. *Smash Boom Best:* Structured debates intermingling scientific and historical facts. *Short & Curly:*

Discussions of actual interest to kids (which singers use autotune, getting ears pierced, why certain games are popular). *Good Game: Spawn Point:* Wholesome gaming content.

Lifewire.com

Kids Know When Parents Suppress Stress

When parents hold negative emotions in, parents and children become less engaged with each other. The children realize that the parent is less available and reciprocate by becoming less available themselves. Researchers say they know this finding can itself become something else causing stress to parents. They urge parents to open up to their children more about how they are feeling, giving kids the opportunity to work through their responses and allowing parents and children to problem-solve together.

Study by researchers at Washington State University, Pullman, published in *Journal of Family Psychology.*

DID YOU KNOW?...

When Kids Play with Dad, They Learn Self-Control

Evidence from the past 40 years on how children from birth to age three play with their parents suggests that those who get regular father-child play will later do better when it comes to controlling their feelings and regulating their behavior. Fathers tend to play more physically with kids than do mothers, which may help them understand boundaries and consequences, teaching them to self-regulate in a fun and exciting setting.

Study by researchers at University of Cambridge, UK, published in *Developmental Review.*

Playfulness Can Be Taught

Research has shown that people who are playful also have a good eye for detail, easily adopt new perspectives, are good at making monotonous tasks interesting, and generally are more satisfied with their lives. But what if you're not lucky enough to have been born that way? A new study of 533 people suggests that the trait can be induced through training. When participants engaged in playfulness exercises for 12 weeks, their personalities actually changed, as did their self-reported well-being.

Study by researchers at Pennsylvania State University, University Park, and University of Zurich, Switzerland, published in *Applied Psychology: Health and Well-Being.*

The Quietest Dogs

Basenjis actually are called barkless dogs—but they do make other sounds, including something that resembles yodeling. Great Danes are generally calm, and so are other large breeds that tend not to bark much, including Bernese Mountain Dogs and Newfoundlands. The Scottish Deerhound, which looks like a Greyhound with coarse hair, tends to be quiet and gentle. Wrinkly-faced bulldogs, French bulldogs, and Shar Peis usually are calm nonbarkers. The Irish Setter needs a lot of exercise—and rarely barks as long as it gets enough. The Cavalier King Charles Spaniel loves to stay quietly around people but may bark if left alone for extended periods.

Roundup of experts on dogs, reported at RD.com.

Ways to De-Stress Your Dog or Cat

Separation ***anxiety***: Use conditioning training. Slowly leave the house for longer and longer periods of time, so when you have to run an errand or leave for work, your pet is used to you leaving. Start by leaving the house for a few seconds, then a few minutes, then a few hours. Build up the time slowly so your pet has time to adjust.

Noise sensitivity: Play movies that contain the sounds of thunderstorms or fireworks—but stop if they cause additional distress. You'll need to do this consistently to desensitize the pet to the sounds.

Products that can help ease mild anxiety: Species-specific pheromones mimic the chemical signals that puppies and kittens receive when nursing...a compression shirt can make an animal feel swaddled and safe. And ask your vet whether supplements or medications might be appropriate.

Roundup of experts on reducing canine and feline stress, reported at Health.com.

Train Your Dog Not to Bark at the Doorbell

Have someone you know ring the bell or knock on the door at an agreed-upon time. When your dog starts to bark and rushes for the door, give a one-word command to stop, such as, "Shush." Then you and the other person wait patiently. Stay relaxed and still until the barking stops. The instant it does, give your dog a food treat and loads of praise for being good. Repeat patiently and calmly as many times as necessary, until your dog associates being quiet with getting a treat and being praised.

TuftsYourDog.com

TAKE NOTE...

Human Foods You Can—and Shouldn't—Share With Your Dog

Foods that you can safely share as treats include coconut, unsalted cashews, low-fat cheese, corn (off the cob), honey, cooked eggs, cooked and deboned fish, ham, milk, peanut butter (as long as it doesn't contain the sugar substitute xylitol), unsalted peanuts, unsalted popcorn, pork, quinoa, cooked and shelled shrimp, turkey, wheat and grains, and yogurt. Foods that may be toxic, irritating or dangerous for your dog are almonds, bread (small amounts are OK, but it can be fattening), chocolate, cinnamon, garlic, ice cream, onions, and macadamia nuts.

AKC.org

Podcasts and Playlists for Pets

Podcasts and playlists for pets are tailored to provide human voices, relaxing music, and ambient sounds for animals left alone while owners do their daily tasks away from home. Spotify offers the pet-focused material for both free and premium accounts. Log in at Spotify.com/Pets, indicate the type of pet, describe its personality, enter its name, and Spotify produces a playlist of about 50 songs. To find the podcasts, search in Spotify for "My Dog's Favourite Podcast," where there are episodes designed to relieve canine stress. A couple of the episodes are five hours long each.

Better Homes & Gardens. BHG.com

16

House and Garden Help

Annoying Home Problems You Can Fix without Spending a Lot

You don't have to live with annoying home problems ranging from holes in screens and rusted dishwasher racks to squeaky floors and stuck drawers. And you don't have to spend much to solve the problems yourself. *The following fixes are well within the ability of most homeowners...*

• **Fix small holes in window screens.** Home centers sell patch kits to cover holes in screens, but these patches are obvious and ugly. If the hole is small—a half inch in size or less—there's a better solution.

Push the broken screen strands back in place as best you can, using your fingers, tweezers, or needle-nose pliers.

With the screen lying flat, apply a coating of clear nail polish. Let this dry for a few minutes, then flip the screen over and apply a second coat on the other side. The unobtrusive clear nail polish blocks bugs from entering and also holds damaged screen strands in place so holes don't expand.

• **Repair rusty dishwasher racks.** The vinyl coating on dishwasher racks eventually cracks and splits, allowing the metal beneath to rust. Replacement racks can cost $40 to $100—depending on the dishwasher model. Fortunately, rusty racks can be repaired rather than replaced.

Use sandpaper to remove any corrosion and wire cutters to snip off the ends of rack tines that have rusted through. Buy a bottle of dishwasher-rack coating, available in appliance stores or online.

Danny Lipford, host of *Today's Homeowner with Danny Lipford,* a syndicated program that has been on national television for more than 20 years. He has more than 30 years of experience as a remodeling contractor based in Mobile, Alabama. TodaysHomeowner.com

Example: Performix ReRack, around $7 for a one-ounce bottle.

Use the small brush inside the bottle's cap to apply the coating to the rack's exposed metal...or, if the exposed spots are tine ends, dip them by turning the rack upside down and then lifting the coating bottle up onto the troubled tines. Let the new coating cure for at least 24 hours before running the dishwasher. Applying a second coat can improve durability.

• **Remove stripped screws.** It happens to every homeowner at some point—the metal head of a screw gets so rusted or torn up by a screwdriver that it will no longer turn.

Position a piece of rubber band—a flat, wide rubber band, not the narrow kind—over the stripped screw head, press your screwdriver into the screwhead through this rubber band, then try to turn the screw again while applying significant force. The rubber often provides enough added grip that the screwdriver can do its job.

If this fails, you could use a small rotary cutting tool, such as a Dremel (prices start at around $40), to cut a new notch into the damaged head of the screw, then use a flathead screwdriver to remove the screw. Or you can buy a damaged-screw extractor kit, which costs around $10 and includes drill bits designed to drill into all kinds of damaged screws and pull them out.

• **Eliminate floor squeaks.** Floor squeaks usually are caused by pieces of wood rubbing together or rubbing against nails that are intended to hold the floor in place. There are several options for solving annoying floor squeaks, depending on the flooring and the floor's location in the home.

If the floor is wood, sprinkle talcum powder in the vicinity of the squeak and sweep it around until there's powder in all the cracks between boards in that area. The powder can prevent the boards from rubbing together, a common source of squeaks.

If that fails (or there are no gaps in the flooring) and the squeak is above a basement with an unfinished ceiling, locate the spot beneath the squeak by having someone walk on the squeaky spot while you search for it below... and insert wood shims between the subfloor (that's the plywood beneath the flooring) and nearby joists (these are the wood or metal beams supporting the floor).

If that also fails or if you don't have access to the underside of the squeaky floor, use a stud finder on the squeaky floor to locate the nearest joist, then drive a trim screw—a type of screw with a head so small it's hard to even notice once it's in place—through the floor and into that joist below. Continue driving this trim screw until its head is slightly below the floor surface. Then cover the screw head with a tiny amount of a putty or wax filler that matches the floor's color.

• **Help sticky cabinet drawers slide freely.** The solution to this problem depends on the drawer's construction.

If the drawer has wood runners—that is, the wood of the drawer slides directly on the wood of the cabinet—remove the drawer and apply a coat of "paste wax" to any surfaces of the drawer and cabinet that rub when the drawer is opened or shut. Make sure the paste you choose is designed for use on wood, not for auto body.

Example: SC Johnson Paste Wax (around $7 for 16 ounces).

If the drawer has metal drawer slides, wipe away any accumulated dust and debris, then spray a "dry lubricant" onto the slides. Dry lubricants are a better choice than oil or grease-based ones, because unlike greasy lubes, lubricating powders won't attract dirt and dust that eventually would gum up the drawer slide and they're less likely to drip off onto items stored in the drawers.

Examples: Blaster Advanced Dry Lube with Teflon (around $5 for 9.3-ounce can at home centers)...WD-40 Specialist Dry Lube (around $7 for a 10-ounce can).

• **Prevent picture frames from going out of level.** It's one of life's little annoyances—every time you walk by a picture, it's hanging at a slight angle.

Apply a tiny amount of adhesive putty or mounting putty to the back of the frame near its lower corners. These putties are sticky enough to prevent frames from slipping, but not so sticky that they'll damage the wall when pictures are removed.

Example: Loctite Fun-Tak Mounting Putty (around $3 for two ounces).

• **Stop doors from squeaking, rattling, or drifting.** Doors have several ways to annoy homeowners.

If door hinges squeak, tap a hinge pin out from below, apply a very modest amount of graphite lubricant to it, return the pin to the hinge, then repeat with the door's other hinge pins. Unlike oil-based lubes such as WD-40, graphite doesn't attract debris that eventually causes problems for the hinge. You could spray on a dry lubricant like those mentioned above, but graphite from a tube applied to the hinge pin will stay in place longer. Expect to pay $5 to $10 for a three-ounce tube of graphite in a hardware store or home center. Brand name is unimportant.

Exception: If the hinge is above carpeting, use a silicone spray lubricant instead, such as Blaster Silicone Lubricant (around $5 for 11 ounces)—graphite powder is black and could stain the carpet if any worked its way out of the hinge over time.

If a closed door makes annoying rattling noises when someone walks past or the HVAC system operates, open the door to access the strike plate—that's the metal piece on the door frame that has an opening for the latch bolt to enter when the door is shut. Inside the strike plate's hole, there's a small metal tab that's angled inward, away from the door opening. Use pliers to pull this tab slightly, or a flat-head screwdriver to pry it outward, so that it's no longer angled quite as dramatically away from the door opening. (If you have trouble bending this tab, you could unscrew the strike plate from the door jamb so you can access the tab from behind.) To see how it's done, go to TodaysHomeowner.com/video/how-to-stop-a-door-from-rattling. This will increase the contact between the strike plate and the latch bolt when the door is shut, which usually eliminates rattling.

If a door drifts open or shut on its own rather than remaining right where it's left, the door is likely hanging slightly out of plumb. Remove the pin from one of the hinges, lie the pin on a workbench (or some other flat, hard surface), strike it once near the middle of the pin's length with a hammer using only modest force to put a very slight bend in the pin, then reinsert the pin into the hinge. You might have to use the hammer to tap the slightly bent pin back into the hinge. The slight bend in the pin can increase hinge friction enough to eliminate ghost-door syndrome without causing any problems for the door. (To see how it's done, go to Youtu.be/cE8XcWAzxrc.) If this doesn't do the trick, do the same with the door's other hinge pin(s).

House Hunting?

Check the flood risk of homes that interest you by looking them up at Realtor.com. It is the only major real estate website that discloses current flood risk and how climate change may affect it in coming decades. Realtor.com includes information from both the official flood-zone maps of the Federal Emergency Management Association and from private corporations that have assembled data beyond the FEMA maps. Other websites, including Redfin, Trulia, and Zillow, say they do not plan to include flood information with listings—their representatives say flood-risk data could decrease the value of homes.

NPR.org

Easy Ways to Declutter for a Profit

Sell unwanted items via smartphone-app–based sites. Try Decluttr and Nextworth for electronics...Mercari, ThredUp, Poshmark and The RealReal for clothing. Check out what is being sold at each site—look for a place where an item you want to sell, or something similar, is featured. Research shipping fees, return policies, and what percentage of the sale the site keeps. Try out the site to see how easy it is to list and sell. Be sure to test a customer service phone number or chat feature to find out how good the site's support is.

Kiplinger.com

GOOD TO KNOW...

Home-Inspection Red Flags That Are Not Deal-Breakers

Failed window seals can cause fogged glass and condensation but are not hard to fix or you can have the windows replaced. Basement floor cracks are normal in homes with unfinished concrete floors. Faulty light switches are easy to replace. Outdoor shed or garage issues may be easy to handle—or you can replace a shed altogether. Inadequate insulation may not matter much, since it can be easy to add more. Minor wall cracks are rarely a safety hazard. Leaking faucets usually are easy to fix or replace. Noisy toilets and slow-draining tubs are the types of plumbing problems that may not indicate anything serious and usually can be repaired fairly simply.

Roundup of experts on home inspections, reported at RD.com.

Home Improvements That May Need a Permit

Check with your local building department before you put up a fence, which may be regulated as to height, materials, or aesthetics—this varies by community. Other projects that may require a permit include constructing a retaining wall over a certain size...basic wiring, an area where many municipalities are strict—some even make it illegal to add an outlet without a permit...window and door replacement, not just an addition where there was not one before...roofing, even for patches above a certain size, may require a permit... sheds and outbuildings—they may be OK up to a certain size, but check with your municipality, especially if you plan to run electricity and/or water to it.

FamilyHandyman.com

9 Low-Cost Ways to Slash Your Home Heating Bills

Danny Lipford, host of *Today's Homeowner with Danny Lipford*, a syndicated series that can be streamed on Amazon Prime Video or Crackle. Based in Mobile, Alabama, he has more than 30 years of experience as a remodeling contractor. TodaysHomeowner.com

Steamed over high heating bills? Many homeowners pay hundreds or thousands of dollars just to stay warm each winter. Unfortunately, many heating-bill–busting strategies come with massive price tags of their own—upgrading to triple-paned windows or a furnace with a high Seasonal Energy Efficiency Ratio (SEER) rating costs thousands of dollars.

Here are nine often-overlooked heating-bill–lowering projects that don't come with big bills themselves...

• **Improve the insulation over your attic ladder or scuttle hole.** You probably already know that adding insulation in an attic can lower heating bills. But even in homes that have abundant attic insulation, there's often a big gap in the spot where the attic is accessed from below. Maybe there's supposed to be insulation here, but it slides out of place whenever the attic is accessed...or maybe there's no insulation at all to allow room for a folding ladder.

To fix this problem, buy an "attic tent," which stands over the attic access area to create an insulating air cushion, much like the insulation provided by the air between the panes of glass in a double-paned window.

Example: Duck Brand Attic Stairway Cover, available in several sizes for around $40.

• **Hang insulated curtains.** Even if your home has modern, energy-efficient windows, some heat will inevitably escape through them—glass doesn't insulate as well as insulated walls. But it is possible to insulate windows, at least at night. Hang "thermal insulated" curtains, which typically include one or more layers of cotton batting, flannel, felt, or foam sandwiched between a decorative fabric and an inner liner. These create an insulating air pocket between the curtain and the window, reducing the amount of heat that escapes and preventing drafts from getting in. These curtains are most effective when they reach from ceiling to floor.

• **Put aluminum foil behind radiators.** If your home has radiators, cut pieces of cardboard to approximately the size of those radiators...cover the cardboard with aluminum foil on one side...and position the cardboard between the radiators and exterior walls, with the foil facing the radiator. The foil reflects heat back into the room that otherwise would have been lost into the exterior walls.

• **Use HVAC air filters that tell you when to change them.** You may already know that changing your HVAC system's filter regularly helps the system function efficiently—a filter full of dirt and pet hair can inhibit air flow. Rather than trust a preset filter-change schedule, use Bluetooth-enabled filters that monitor air pressure and send an alert to your smartphone when they actually need to be changed.

Example: 3M Filtrete Smart Filters, available in multiple sizes, $44 for a package of two.

• **Move obstructions away from HVAC vents, registers and radiators.** Furniture or curtains within 12 inches of these can inhibit air flow or, in the case of radiators, block heat from radiating throughout the space. The result can be decreased heating efficiency and/or cold spots in rooms.

• **Run ceiling fans in the winter.** The temperature at ceiling height often is 10 degrees or more warmer than it is lower in a room, because hot air rises. A ceiling fan can circulate that hot air back down through the living space. Run fans clockwise at their lowest speed to accomplish this—a ceiling fan turning clockwise pulls cold air up from below rather than pushing hot air down from above. Either direction should circulate hot air back down from ceiling height, but pulling cold air up at low speed does so without generating a cooling breeze that would be unwelcome in winter.

• **Run a humidifier.** We feel warmer when air is more humid—that's why humid summer days feel oppressive even when the temperature isn't tremendously high. Similarly, operating a humidifier can make you feel warmer in winter without cranking up your thermostat. Humidifiers cost just pennies per day to run, so you'll almost certainly save money compared with cranking up the heat. But don't increase the relative humidity in your home above 40 percent in the winter—too much humidity feels uncomfortable and promotes mold and mildew growth. Digital hygrometers that track indoor relative humidity are available for around $10 to $15 in home centers and online.

• **Find and fix duct leaks.** Much of the hot air produced by your furnace might never reach its destination—according to the Department of Energy, 20 percent to 30 percent of the air that moves through duct systems escapes through leaks, holes, and disconnected ductwork. Homeowners can't easily examine ducts inside walls, but they can turn on their heat or air-conditioning—it doesn't matter which—then follow along accessible ductwork in attics, basements and crawl spaces, holding their hands near all ductwork joints to feel for drafts. Pay particular attention to spots where duct lines branch off—gaps are especially common here. Wherever you feel air escaping, cover the leak with aluminum foil tape, then use a paintbrush to apply a generous coating of duct mastic, a sticky material that dries to form a strong airtight seal.

• **Fly a "chimney balloon."** The damper in your chimney probably doesn't do a particularly good job of preventing hot air from escaping up the chimney. A chimney balloon is a reusable, durable bladder that's inserted in a chimney then inflated, preventing air from getting past.

Caution: Installing the balloon can be a little tricky and messy...and you will need a large garbage bag to store it. The balloon must be removed, of course, before starting a fire.

Example: Chimney Balloon, available in a range of sizes, $45 to $60.

Best Space Heater for Your Home

Cameron Pitts, a member of the editorial and product review team with *Best Reviews*, which tests and reviews consumer products. BestReviews.com

A space heater can keep you comfortable without cranking up the heat throughout your home...or provide warmth when you're working in an unheated spot such as a garage. *Among the best space heaters...*

Best overall: Dr. Infrared Original Heater provides both conventional convection heating, which circulates warm air, and infrared heating, which efficiently and almost instantly warms nearby objects and people via invisible infrared light. This 13-x-12.5-x-17-inch unit is solidly built, attractively designed and includes safety features such as tip-over automatic shutoff. It is designed to heat areas up to 1,000 square feet. Like most electric space heaters, it consumes 1,500 watts of power, so it costs around 20 cents per hour to operate at full power at typical 13-cent-per-kilowatt-hour rates. But it's so efficient at delivering warmth—60 percent more efficient than 1,500-watt heaters that heat only the air, according to the manufacturer—that it won't have to operate at full power for as long to maintain a desired temperature. $110.

Best for extended operation: De'Longhi Portable Radiator Heater looks like an old-fashioned cast-iron radiator and generates warmth by heating up oil that's contained inside its metal framework. This 14-x-9-x-25-inch unit is most appropriate for small rooms—perhaps 250 square feet or smaller—that you want to keep warm for several hours or longer. Radiator-style heaters warm up slowly but maintain warmth efficiently. Like most space heaters, it consumes 1,500 watts at full power, but once warm its 700- or 800-watt setting often is sufficient, roughly halving energy costs. De'Longhi is perhaps the most reliable space-heater brand, and this is a particularly safe design—never scalding hot to the touch. $80.

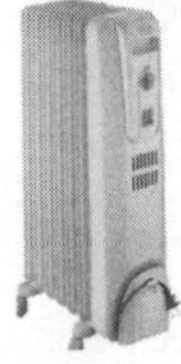

Best for circulating hot air throughout a room: Vornado AVH2 features a powerful fan that is extremely effective at distributing the hot air it generates throughout a room up to perhaps 250 square feet in size. However, the fan makes it a bit louder than many heaters. This 12-x-12-x-9-inch unit consumes 1,500 watts on high power or 750 on low. $89.

Best low-price tabletop heater: Lasko 754200 Ceramic Heater with Adjustable Thermostat is tiny—just 9-x-6-x-4-inches—but this 1,500-watt unit is powerful enough to heat small rooms up to 300 square feet. *Price:* $26.

Even smaller: If you want a portable, affordable heater that will warm you as you sit in a chair nearby but not the entire room, the 6-x-6-x-3-inch Brightown Mini Desk Heater can do the job for an even lower price. It consumes just 400 watts of electricity per hour. $20.

Best Humidifiers

Paige Szmodis, editor and reviewer for Hearst publications, including *Popular Mechanics.* PopularMechanics.com

Did you know that the dry indoor air of winter might make it easier for airborne viruses to spread? Researchers have conducted experiments indicating that's possible.

One possible weapon: A humidifier.

Humidifiers add moisture to indoor air, weighing down virus particles and speeding their descent to the ground. Of course, humidifiers also provide relief for dry throats, noses, skin, and lips.

However, buying a humidifier can be confusing. "Evaporative" humidifiers use a replaceable filter to wick water up from a tank while a fan blows the moist air through that filter out into the room. "Ultrasonic" humidifiers use high-frequency vibrations to convert water into a mist that a fan then distributes.

Ultrasonic humidifiers run the risk of overhumidifying and may create a "white dust" residue around the room if you fill the tank with unfiltered tap water.

Evaporative humidifiers require replacement filters, which adds to the cost. Another decision is whether you want a warm-mist option, which is available on some ultrasonic models.

Warning: Whatever humidifier you choose, clean it at least once a week and do not boost relative humidity in a room above 40 percent to 50 percent, or you could promote growth of mold and mildew.

Product reviewer Paige Szmodis to recommens some of the best humidifiers...

Best for a bedroom up to 400 square feet: Honeywell HCM-350 Cool Moisture Germ Free Humidifier is among the most reliable and easy-to-use evaporative humidifiers. Its 1.1-gallon tank has a handle for easy carrying and an opening wide enough for you to reach a hand inside for cleaning. It has parts that are dishwasher-safe...and it's large enough that it can run for up to 24 hours between refills. But like most evaporative humidifiers, it requires filters that should be replaced every month or two. $75. Replacement filters $13.95 each.

Best for large spaces: Levoit LV600HH Hybrid Ultrasonic Humidifier can humidify up to 750 square feet for up to 36 hours with its 1.6-gallon tank. This ultrasonic humidifier has an "auto mode" that uses a built-in sensor to automatically adjust humidity levels and avoid overhumidification. It has both cool- and warm-mist settings and a remote control. $89.99.

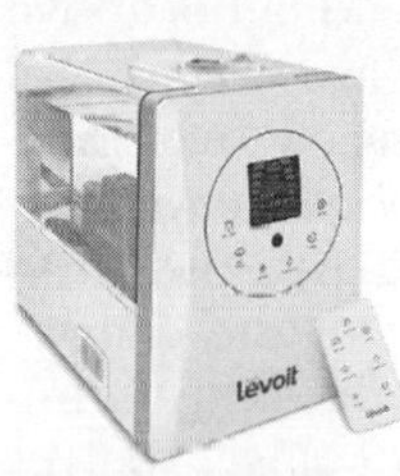

Best value: TaoTronics 4L Ultrasonic Cool Mist Humidifier is bargain priced and includes a humidity sensor to avoid over-humidifying, unlike many other low-cost ultrasonic humidifiers. It can humidify up to 320 square feet for as long as 30 hours on a 1.1-gallon tank of water. It has a filter, but that filter is reusable—soak it in a vinegar-water mix every month. $49.99.

Best for quiet in small rooms: Pure Enrichment MistAire Ultrasonic Cool Mist Humidifier is nearly silent—most other humidifiers create noticeable fan noise or humming. Its 0.4-gallon tank can humidify up to 175 square feet for up to 16 hours. Cleaning its tank is challenging, however—you have to reach inside with a special brush, which is included. $39.99.

Best when you have a cold: Vicks VWM845 Warm Mist Humidifier doesn't just distribute warm, moist air. If you put Vicks VapoSteam cough-relief medicine in its "medicine cup," this ultrasonic humidifier will distribute that as well, providing additional relief for sore throats and coughs without the messiness of the well-known Vicks VapoRub balm. Its one-gallon tank can run for up to 24 hours and is easy to clean. $45.

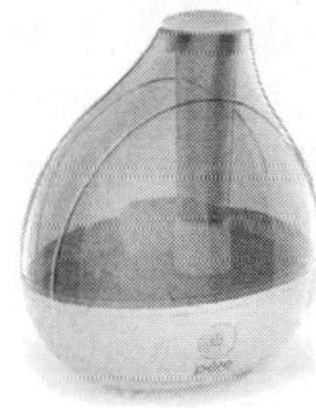

Indoor Lighting Mistakes and How to Fix Them

Gary Gordon of Gary Gordon Architectural Lighting, a New York City–based architectural lighting company. He is author of *Interior Lighting for Designers,* now in its fifth edition. GaryGordon.com

As we get older, indoor lighting is especially important. Aging eyes often struggle to read and work in low light, and they cope poorly with excessive glare. After you've maximized natural light—the kind that comes streaming in through your windows and skylights—pay attention to how your home is lit when you draw the blinds and when nighttime falls.

Five lighting mistakes to avoid...

***MISTAKE:* All the lights in a room shine down from above.** When the only lighting in a room is from overhead, the room seems emotionally cold and impersonal—the lights can cast harsh shadows on faces and make homes feel like offices or retail spaces.

Solution: Add lighting at head level, and the room will instantly feel homier and more comfortable. What constitutes "head level"? That depends on the room. In spaces where people tend to stand, such as in entryways and hallways and at bathroom counters, sconces mounted approximately five to six feet up the wall work well. Near seating areas in living rooms and family rooms, opt for table or floor lamps that shine light approximately from seated head height.

***MISTAKE:* Skipping the sparkle.** Nature has three types of lighting. There's ambient light, the general brightness of the daytime sky...focal light, the direct light of the sun... and sparkle, the glimmering light that reflects from bodies of water. Sparkle is the most beautiful and enchanting. But while all people already have the first two types of light inside their homes (ambient from wall reflection and focal direct from fixtures), most people do not have sparkle in their homes. The glimmering light from sunlight striking water isn't just pretty to look at, it also stimulates our appetites (a good thing in your dining room) and fosters a sense of well-being. One hypothesis is that we have evolved to associate glimmering light with being safe—sunlight sparkles off water only when the skies are clear and the water is fairly calm.

Solution: Sparkle is attractive almost anywhere, but it is an especially good lighting addition in dining rooms and kitchen eating areas, where fostering appetite and a sense of well-being encourages great family meals. Sparkle also is good in entranceways, living rooms, family rooms and bedrooms. A crystal chandelier is an effective way to create sparkle, but if that's too showy for your tastes, any lighting fixture that features faceted glass or a shiny, pebbled metal finish is likely to produce sparkle, too.

Caveat: Don't use sparkly lighting in a home office...it's too distracting.

***MISTAKE:* Banishing shadows.** Many home owners assume that shadowy areas are an interior design problem that they need to fix by adding more or brighter lights. That's not true—shadows can be beneficial.

It's counterintuitive, but shadowy areas in rooms tend to boost the moods of people who spend time there. We tend to think of shadows as gloomy, but the absence of shadows is more likely to elicit negative moods.

Consider: Which kind of day makes you feel more energetic and upbeat—a sunny day of bright light peppered with areas of crisp shadow...or an overcast day where everything is the same even brightness?

Solution: In most homes, it is hallways, family rooms and living rooms that are most likely to be "over fixtured"—these spaces do not need to be brightly lit throughout. In a hallway, we need only enough brightly lit areas to see where we're going. In a family room or living room, we need bright lighting only in the seating and play areas.

Of course, not all shadows are beneficial. You don't want shadows on faces where people often sit or stand...or in spots where people cook, read or work.

***MISTAKE:* Overlooking useful spots for lighting.** Some rooms in your home already may appear to have the lighting they need. But adding a new fixture often can solve problems. *Examples*...

Bedrooms often have focal lights above the head of the bed for reading. But very few have a focal light positioned above the foot of the bed, where suitcases often are packed and laundry sometimes is sorted.

Bathrooms often lack overhead lights above the shower or tub, where they are very useful for shaving and other grooming. A "wet location" lighting fixture is appropriate here.

Walk-in closets generally have overhead lights positioned in the center of the ceiling. That not only creates glare if the bulb is uncovered, it leaves items on lower closet shelves hidden in shadow. The ideal spot? Often it's directly above the inside of the closet door. That's where people are least likely to look directly at the light, so it cuts down on glare…and it's where the light will illuminate deepest onto closet shelves along the far wall.

Kitchens benefit from under-cabinet lights. But when under-cabinet lighting is located at the back and pointing forward, it may shine in your face when you're seated. Instead, locate lights at the front, pointing toward the back.

More from Gary Gordon…

Choosing the Right Bulb

Even the best lighting design can be ruined by poor bulb choices. *Here are two common mistakes…*

- **Too-high color temperature.** The overall color emitted by a light bulb is described as its "color temperature" and expressed in terms of degrees Kelvin (K). If you like the warm tone of a traditional incandescent bulb, choose a bulb (of any kind) with a color temperature of 2700K. If you prefer the whiter tone of a traditional halogen bulb, a Kelvin temperature of 3000K will serve you well. A color temperature above 3000K leans toward blue and will not seem warm and welcoming.

Note: Color temperature is particularly important for bulbs where you sleep, such as nightlights and illuminated displays on bedside clocks, because blue light at night tends to disturb our sleep/wake cycle.

- **Too low on the "color-rendering index."** The lower a bulb's color rendering index (CRI), the less accurately colors will appear in its light—reds start to look gray and faces seem sallow. Incandescent or halogen bulbs always have a perfect CRI score of 100. But when buying LED or fluorescent bulbs, choose those with CRIs of 90 or higher. While CRI isn't always listed on bulb packaging, manufacturers almost always tout on their packaging when bulbs provide 90-plus CRIs. Two bulb makers known for high-CRI bulbs are Hyperikon (about $18 for a six-pack of 60-watt-equivalent 3000K LED bulbs with a 95 CRI) and Cree (about $34 for an eight-pack of 40-watt-equivalent 2700K LED bulbs with a "90+" CRI).

Prevent and Treat Mold on Your Houseplant Soil

Mold is a fungus that thrives when there's too much moisture in your soil. That fuzzy, white mold is not harmful to your plants, but the conditions that cause it are.

Prevention: Don't overwater your plants…keep them in appropriately sized pots with drainage holes…use soil that is not too dense for water to pass through…remove any dead leaves that have fallen onto the soil…keep your plants where they can get adequate natural light and air flow.

Treatment: Scrape the mold away and then try sprinkling cinnamon—which has antifungal properties—onto the soil, or use a houseplant fungicide spray.

FamilyHandyman.com

Keep Your Houseplants Alive When You Are Away

Teri Dunn Chace, author of more than 35 gardening books, including *The Anxious Gardener's Book of Answers*. She lives in central New York. TeriChaceWriter.com

It's wonderful to travel during the holiday season to celebrate with family or in faraway places, but who wants to come home to dead houseplants? *Here's how to keep your plants happy while you are gone—without hiring a plant sitter…*

FOR A LONG WEEKEND

In case you haven't noticed, even houseplants slow down in the cooler months. To give them their natural rest period, water less and less often—let the soil mix go dry between waterings—and don't fertilize. The soil mix should be lightly moist, not soggy (plunge in a finger to confirm that there's dampness an inch or more deep).

Everything from spider plants to bay trees to pothos will survive a long weekend without attention during the colder months. Do move everything but cacti away from the window prior to a long weekend, but plants don't need any extra watering.

Exception: Plants that bloom in winter, such as amaryllis, poinsettia and Christmas cactus. Water these until you see water coming out the bottom of the pot, then stop.

FOR LONGER TRIPS

The options here will help your plants retain moisture for up to one month.

Bathtub/sink method: Place recently watered plants—watered normally, not extra—in the sink or bathtub, then stretch clear plastic wrap over the top of the tub and duct tape in place (scotch tape is too frail). If the tops of any plants are hitting the plastic, peel it back and insert a few tall stakes in the pots so the plastic will rest on the stakes. Do not fill the tub with water or plug the drain. Standing water will lead to rot.

Bag method: First, water well and let plants drain. Next, cover each plant with a clear plastic bag. To keep the plastic from touching the foliage, insert small sticks—I use chopsticks. If a plant is too large to bag up entirely, just pull a bag up from below to enclose the pot, then tie it gently around the base of the plant at the soil line with string or yarn. This helps keep in moisture but lets in a bit of air, too. Finally, move the plants out of direct sunlight.

Thirsty plants: Rig a temporary wick-watering system for thirstier plants, such as ferns and spiderworts, including Tradescantia zebrina ("Wandering Jew") and Tradescantia pallida ("Purple Heart"). Set up a jar or bowl of water adjacent to the plant(s). For each, dunk one end of a thin strip of absorbent fabric—strips of an old cotton t-shirt serve well—in the water, dangling it to the jar's bottom. Securely tuck the other end an inch or more down into the pot's soil.

Prized plants in clay pots, such as African violets: Water normally. Line a cardboard box with a plastic trash bag or use a plastic storage tub. Pack it half-full with damp sphagnum moss or wet sand. Nest the pots in, and tuck the moss or sand all around them. They will be set for the duration of your trip. Do not do this for succulents, which can go up to a month without water.

BACK HOME AGAIN

Once you return home, liberate your houseplants from their temporary quarters and check them over. Remove any dead or dying growth. Give them water if their soil mix is dry an inch or so down, and return them to their usual locations.

Transform Your Dining Room into a Warm and Welcoming Space

Joanna Thornhill, a London-based interior stylist and author of several decorating books, including *Home for Now* and *My Bedroom Is an Office & Other Interior Design Dilemmas.* JoannaThornhill.co.uk

Creating a cozy and comfortable atmosphere in your dining room can make a big difference in sparking conversation and making dining together as a family—or with friends—an entertaining and enjoyable experience.

• **Make sure your chairs are comfortable.** The top of the seat pad should fall around 12 inches below the bottom of your tabletop for comfortable legroom for most guests. If space in your dining area is tight, remove chairs that have armrests to allow for more space around the table.

Upholstered chairs are the most comfortable. If yours are not upholstered, add seat cushions.

Tip: If you have young children or frequently host your grandchildren, choose easy, wipe-clean material for your seat cushions such as vegan leather. For a more luxe yet still practical look, choose synthetic, machine-washable velvet or micro suede seat cushions.

• **Give your dining area its own personality.** If space is tight, tuck the table into a corner with bench seating on one side for a more intimate feel. Consider using a strip of drop pendant lights over the center of the table to help frame the space.

Why this matters: By separating the dining space from the rest of your home, you are creating an area that is associated with that one activity over others. When diners enter that space, their mind-set changes. This is especially important in open-concept homes where "rooms" are undefined.

• **Choose a round or oval table.** If you are in the market for a new table, a round or oval dining room table is more conducive to group conversation. Opting for a curved edge also creates a softer space visually, which can help put everyone at ease.

Note: If you have limited space, a pedestal table—one with a single central support—allows you to squeeze more chairs around it because you don't have anyone straddling a table leg. Visually, it appears to be a lot less cluttered. An uncluttered dining space is important for the creation of a relaxed zone and a better conversational experience.

• **Set up a sideboard.** No one should have to get up from the table to run to the kitchen for more water or napkins. Include an extra pitcher of cold water, additional seasonings, extra bread or other items, so you don't have to interrupt the conversation—and your good time—to keep the meal flowing.

• **Use color to your advantage in the dining room.** Red is often said to be a great color for dining rooms, as its vibrant hues can evoke hunger and even passion—which can mean better appetites and more animated and interesting conversations. That energy is why red is often a dominant color in fast-food restaurant decor. But because red is an intense color, not everyone wants red walls. You might prefer to use red more sparingly—just for accessories, for example. To get the best of both worlds, you could choose natural, calming tones such as blues and grays for the walls, but add touches of red in the table linens, artwork, rugs and other room accessories.

• **Keep your table decor casual, even for fancy occasions.** Overly fussy and structured centerpieces at a big family holiday can give your table a stiff feel. Instead, arrange a less formal, even mismatched, collection of candles, vases and other tabletop accessories down the center of a table to create a more homey, authentic look than what can be achieved with perfectly coordinated and perfectly placed pieces. Group decorative items in odd numbers, and play with their heights for a less imposing look.

• **Mismatched dishes and table linens can help diners feel more at ease.** No one is intimidated by the prospect of breaking great-grandma's best china in a mismatched set. If over the years, you have lost pieces of a set to breakage, don't think you can't continue to use those dishes. Pair them with pieces from other sets, especially if they are in the same color family.

Note: If you don't already have a large dinner service, this theory allows you to buy single elements at a time and mix them in slowly. This can be an economical way to build a service, rather than investing in the full set all at once.

• **Create a flexible lighting scheme.** Lighting helps set the mood, so creating a scheme that allows you to dim the lights for a more intimate party—or brighten it up for a bigger celebration—is essential. Over the table, use a low-hanging pendant or chandelier instead of one big central light to create a more relaxed ambiance. If your table is very large, hang multiple lights but try to ensure that they are not too spread out or they could end up looking too small. Keep them confined to the central third of the table. Hang light fixtures about three feet above tabletop height, so they don't get in the way of conversation. Wall sconces, a table lamp on the side bar or a floor lamp in the corner of the room (even if the room is small) give you the option to illuminate other areas of the room or even to turn the main ceiling lights off altogether.

Note: Plants can help create a soothing atmosphere for your dining room. You might consider adding a few potted herbs to your space. The scent of potted herbs can make the room smell wonderful without overpowering the aroma of the dishes you've cooked. In a small dining room, small potted plants can be a permanent centerpiece.

TAKE NOTE...

Never Store These Items in Your Garage or Basement

Propane tanks should never be kept in an enclosed space, where they could leak or, in case of a fire, explode. *Natural fabrics*—cotton, linen, wool, and silk—can grow mold if the humidity gets too high, as it often does in a garage or unfinished basement. *Furniture*—wood furniture can warp, and upholstered furniture can develop mold. A second refrigerator—the appliance is not designed for extreme heat or cold and can break down unless it is specifically designed for use in a garage or basement. *Important papers and photos* could suffer water damage and are best kept in a safe or other secure location. *Leftover paint and cleaning products* can be fire hazards. *Extra firewood*—pests are likely to come inside with wood, and the wood itself can absorb moisture and be hard to dry out for later use. *Candles, wine, and electronics*—temperature fluctuations can damage them.

Roundup of experts on storage of items at home, reported at RealEstate.USNews.com.

This Type of Dehumidifier Is All Wet

Jeffrey C. May, principal scientist with May Indoor Air Investigations, LLC, an air-quality assessment company in Tyngsborough, Massachusetts. He is author of *My House Is Killing Me!* MayIndoorAir.com

Have a moisture problem in a basement or crawl space? A contractor might recommend an "exhaust-only dehumidifier," claiming that its low electricity use relative to conventional dehumidifiers will save you money in the long run despite up-front costs that can top $1,000. In fact, those energy savings are an illusion—and these "dehumidifiers" don't actually do any dehumidifying.

This product, also called a "basement ventilation system," is essentially just an expensive exhaust fan that sucks air out of damp basements or other spaces and expels it outdoors, similar to a window fan or attic fan. (Brands include EZ Breathe and Humidex.) This causes drier air from upstairs to be drawn down into the basement, which in some cases can eliminate musty odors and humidity problems as promised. However, although these fans consume much less electricity than conventional dehumidifiers, they do so by forcing your HVAC system to work harder. The air that's drawn down to the basement is replaced by outdoor air pulled into upstairs rooms through cracks and door gaps—additional air that your HVAC system must heat or cool. The extra HVAC effort required to do that will greatly reduce or eliminate any energy savings, and it could shorten the life of your HVAC system.

What's more, if the air upstairs is humid—perhaps because you don't have a whole-home air-conditioning system...or you sometimes open windows rather than run your air conditioner—a ventilation fan can't solve your basement humidity problem. It will simply replace humid air with different humid air.

What to do: If your basement is damp, use a condensing dehumidifier. Therma-Stor's Santa Fe line of dehumidifiers is extremely energy-efficient and is the only major brand that provides effective air filtration. They're expensive—typically $1,200 to $2,500 depending on size—but that's not much more than many exhaust-only dehumidifiers.

If you don't want to spend that much, a standard freestanding $200 to $300 condensing dehumidifier from any well-known appliance brand is likely to be a more effective choice than an exhaust-only dehumidifier. Choose one that's Energy Star–certified to minimize electricity bills. Wash the bucket, clean the filter screen, and wipe down its coils regularly to avoid mold and mildew growth.

Deck Out Your Deck (or Patio) for Cold-Weather Fun

Lawrence Winterburn, president of GardenStructure.com, which builds decks in southern Ontario and sells plans for decks and other outdoor structures to do-it-yourselfers worldwide. He has more than 30 years of experience as a master carpenter.

Who doesn't love sitting in front of a warm fire on a cold winter's night? How about doing it under the stars? A few upgrades could transform your deck or patio into a warm, welcoming place to relax in the cold of winter. *There are many options to consider, including some that are very affordable...*

ENCLOSE YOUR DECK/PATIO

Adding a roof and retractable see-through plastic or glass walls around your patio or deck will shield you from the worst of the winter weather while still allowing you to feel like you're outdoors. The cost of having such an enclosure constructed will vary dramatically depending on deck/patio size, materials selected, and building costs in your area, but it's usually possible to have a basic structure and roof erected for $5,000 to $15,000. The roof of this structure will be permanent and should be strong enough to support snow in the winter, but the walls will be uninsulated plastic or glass—enough to block the wind but not to make this a true sunroom. With the addition of a heater, the space can stay warm enough for winter use.

Helpful: Opt for a roof made from clear polycarbonate panels, which are manufactured primarily for greenhouses. Not only will these clear panels add warmth to the space, they also allow light to reach the windows of the room behind the patio or deck—other deck roofs can make adjacent rooms feel dark and claustrophobic.

If you would prefer a more upscale look, the Finnish company Lumon makes glass wall systems for balconies and terraces that can be folded out of the way when not needed. The windows create a solarium on your deck or patio to capture the warmth of the sun. Prices can reach well into five figures depending on the size of the space you're enclosing.

Budget option: It won't look as nice as the glass panels above, but for around $2,000 to $3,000 you can add clear plastic screens around the perimeter of a roofed or awninged deck or patio. It doesn't insulate, but it does block wind and rain.

Example: MosquitoCurtains.com custom-makes durable clear vinyl deck curtains. The plastic can be swapped for netting to keep out bugs in the summer.

In most areas it's necessary to obtain building permits to enclose a deck or patio, just as if you were having an addition put on the home. If this permitting proves problematic, ask your local zoning department whether permits are required to build a freestanding covered gazebo in your yard. In many places, little or no permitting is needed for these, although you won't be able to step directly from your home into a free-standing gazebo. A contractor typically can construct a 12-by-12-foot covered roof made from pressure-treated or red cedar for perhaps $8,000 to $15,000, though prices can climb depending on size and materials. Avoid the prefab gazebos sold at discounters such as Costco. These tend to feature wood such as Chinese cedar, which could rapidly discolor or decay in the elements.

HEAT YOUR DECK/PATIO

Adding a heater to your deck can make it toasty even on cold evenings. *Among the best options...*

- **Radiant patio heaters deliver warmth almost instantly at the flip of a switch,** even when the outdoor air is very cold or there's a breeze. Radiant heaters use infrared technology that travels through the air (without heating it directly) and casts heat to floors and people.

Radiant-heater options include free-standing units that look a bit like floor lamps...and units that mount unobtrusively to ceilings or high on walls. The mounted units usually are

the best choice because they don't take up deck/patio space and are made for enclosed spaces, they don't have to be dragged to a garage in the summer and there's no risk that they'll blow over and get damaged.

Some radiant heaters run on electricity...others on propane or natural gas. Electric units require no ventilation and don't produce any odors.

Natural gas heaters tend to be slightly less expensive to operate than electric but typically require ventilation. Propane units generally are the most expensive to operate and also require ventilation, which could be through an open window or a duct pipe, but many of these use the same portable propane tanks used by gas grills so you can avoid paying the $500 or more it might cost to have electrical or natural gas lines installed.

Expect to pay perhaps $500 to $2,000 for one or two units sufficient to heat a typical outdoor seating area—roughly 300 to 400 square feet. There are radiant patio heaters on the market for as little as a few hundred dollars—but low-end units tend to fail quickly, heat poorly, and even can be fire risks. Infratech and Sunglo are among the top brands.

• **A fire pit or fire table offers the warmth and visual appeal of sitting around a fire.** Their warmth isn't immediate, as with radiant heat, and they require ventilation—it isn't safe to have a fire on a patio that's enclosed by both ceilings and walls.

Fire pit options include movable metal fire pits and more permanent masonry fire pits that are constructed into patios.

Fire tables are outdoor tables that have a fire pit built into the table top, allowing a group to sit around the table for a meal while also sitting around a fire. Wood-burning, propane, and natural gas fire pits and fire tables all are available.

As a rule of thumb, well-made fire pits and fire tables tend to be manufactured in the U.S. or Canada and cost several hundred to several thousand dollars depending on style and materials. Companies that make high-quality fire pits and fire tables in North America include American Fyre Designs...Cooke Contemporary Furniture...Fire Pit Art...Impact Fire Tables...and Ohio Flame. You can find thin metal fire pits for less than $100, but don't be surprised if these corrode through in a few years.

• **An outdoor fireplace can be a dramatic centerpiece of a winter patio.** Unlike fire pits and fire tables, a wood- or natural gas–burning fireplace can be used even on a deck/patio that's enclosed by a ceiling and walls, because the chimney lets the smoke escape. It typically costs at least $5,000 to have even a simple

fireplace and chimney constructed—and yes, you can build a fireplace on a deck! An architecturally designed, artisan-built fireplace could cost as much as $35,000. Adding a well-designed fireplace insert can greatly improve heating performance.

Example: Napoleon outdoor fireplace inserts are durable and effective at heating outdoor open spaces. Prices start at around $2,300.

FURNISH YOUR DECK/PATIO FOR WINTER WEATHER

If your patio furniture is going to spend the snowy months outside, it's a good idea to choose furniture that's made from cast aluminum, which won't rust. If you prefer wood furniture, teak red cedar and redwood last well if the wood is properly sealed.

Also seek out furniture that has Sunbrella-brand outdoor upholstery on its cushions. Sunbrella makes extremely durable fabric that's mold-, mildew-, and weather-resistant—it barely fades even when left in direct sunlight for years.

Examples: Cast-aluminum patio furniture with Sunbrella cushions include Macy's Vintage II Outdoor Cast-Aluminum 11-Piece Dining Set with Sunbrella Cushions, $6,389...

Ridge Falls Dark Brown Aluminum Outdoor Patio Dining Set with Sunbrella Cushions, $2,049.

Photos: GettyImages

Driveway Resealing Is Rarely Worth the Price

Tim Carter, former contractor based in Meredith, New Hampshire, who has written the syndicated "Ask the Builder" newspaper column for more than 25 years. He offers a free weekly newsletter through his website. AskTheBuilder.com

Asphalt resealing services often warn homeowners that driveways quickly degenerate if sealer isn't applied every few years. The resealing process applies a new coating to the driveway's surface, replacing asphalt that has become brittle and worn. However, resealing usually is not necessary, and for most homeowners it is not worth the price, which averages around $500 but varies greatly depending on the size of the driveway and other factors. Also, once you have resealed a driveway, you must reseal it every few years or it will look even worse than if you had never sealed it in the first place.

Resealing is not completely without benefits—it makes driveways that have begun to fade to gray look darker and newer...and it fills hairline cracks, preventing water from seeping in. Contractors are correct when they say that water seeping into hairline cracks could over time lead to larger cracks or potholes. What they're failing to mention is that there's a way to cope with cracks that won't cost you hundreds of dollars.

What to do: Scan your driveway each year for cracks that have grown to one-eighth inch in width or larger, and fill these cracks with a blacktop caulk or epoxy, which should prevent them from growing any further. These products cost around $8 to $20 in home centers or hardware stores, and this job typically can be done in just a few minutes per crack.

If cracks and gaps continue to expand after you've used caulk or epoxy, the problem almost certainly is with the gravel base beneath the driveway, not with the asphalt itself. If so, the only way to fix the problem is to have that section of driveway dug up and reconstructed—resealing would not solve the problem.

Helpful: If you ever have your driveway completely redone or a new driveway constructed, confirm that the contractor is creating a gravel base that is at least eight inches deep and that extends at least one foot beyond each edge of the paved surface. That will significantly reduce the odds of future problems.

Exception: It's worth having your driveway resealed only if you expect to sell the home in the next few years and want an aging driveway to look its very best for potential buyers...or you like the look of a fresh-looking driveway despite the cost or time required.

How to Care for a Rarely Driven Car

Russ Evans, an ASE Master Certified Automotive Technician and cohost of the syndicated automotive radio show *Under the Hood.* UnderTheHoodShow.com

Your car needs you even when you don't need it. Maintenance issues arise when cars sit unused or barely used for weeks or months at a time. As a rule of thumb, you should at least take one 20-minute drive every two weeks, but even then a car could suffer from underuse. *If a car is underused for an extended period, here's how to make sure it won't suffer badly...*

•Attach the battery to a battery maintainer. When a car sits unused, its battery will slowly go dead. If your car was built within the past 10 years, that could happen in as little as two weeks—modern cars are packed full of electronics that drain power even when the car sits idle. Driving only on short trips can make things worse—each start taxes the battery... and drives lasting less than 20 to 30 minutes don't give the alternator sufficient time to recharge it. A battery maintainer plugs into an electrical outlet and keeps the battery charged without overcharging it.

Examples: Diehard Battery Charger/ Maintainer, $26...NOCO Genius 6V/12V 1.1 Amp Battery Charger and Maintainer, $50.

• **Keep tires inflated.** When cars are driven regularly, drivers tend to notice low tire pressure and add air. Most modern cars even have a dashboard light that warns of low tire pressure. But when a car sits for an extended period, pressure can become dangerously low. If pressure falls to around 10 psi or below—way below the proper psi, which can be found inside the car's driver door—driving even a short distance to a gas station for air could permanently damage the tires. That damage could cause an accident if the tire later fails at high speed. Instead, buy an air compressor so you can reinflate tires at home.

Example: Rugged Geek RG1000 Safety Plus Gen2 features a portable jump starter and portable air compressor, $140.

Also: If the car is sitting unused for multiple months, occasionally drive or roll it a foot or so to prevent the tires from developing flat spots, which could make the ride less smooth in the future.

• **Add fuel stabilizer to the fuel tank if the car will sit for six months or longer.** Fuel degrades over time and after around half a year can gum up carburetors and fuel injectors, causing hesitation and stalls. Fuel stabilizer keeps gas fresh for a year or two.

Example: Sta-Bil Storage Fuel Stabilizer, $4 for an eight-ounce bottle sufficient to treat up to 20 gallons of fuel.

• **Change your oil based on the calendar.** Car owners are used to getting their oil changed each time they travel a certain number of miles—as much as 5,000—but check your owner's manual. It likely recommends changing the oil every six or 12 months even if that mileage hasn't been reached.

• **Thoroughly clean the car's interior.** Rodents often are emboldened to enter cars that sit unused for extended stretches—especially if they can smell food inside. Carefully vacuum out all crumbs, and remove food packaging. Also, rodents can get under the hood and chew wires and hoses. Placing mousetraps around the garage can reduce the odds of this if the traps are monitored and reset as needed.

• **Leave the parking brake disengaged.** Parking brakes sometimes fail to release after they've been engaged for months. Instead, park on level ground, and of course, leave the transmission in park...or in gear if the car has a manual transmission. Use wheel chocks, too, if there is no perfectly level parking spot available.

EASY TO DO...

Banish Bird Poop

Use WD-40 to clean dried bugs and bird droppings from cars and trucks. Then rinse and wipe with a soft cloth.

Danny Lipford, host of *Today's Homeowner with Danny Lipford.* TodaysHomeowner.com

---

Fixing Car Dents and Scratches: A Master Technician's Secrets

Russ Evans, ASE Master Certified Automotive Technician who manages Nordstrom's Installation and Diagnostic Center in Garretson, South Dakota. He is cohost of the syndicated radio show *Under the Hood.* UnderTheHoodShow.com

A small scratch or dent can be all it takes to make a car look old and worn—and make it harder to sell at a good price if you are looking to do so. Even seemingly minor cosmetic flaws can be expensive to repair if you bring the car to a body shop—repairing a small scratch typically costs $350 to $700, and dent repairs usually climb into four figures.

If you're not willing to pay such steep prices, there are do-it-yourself solutions that can make some flaws much less apparent for far more palatable prices. *DIY options for two common car cosmetic issues...*

SCRATCHED PAINT

There's a layer of protective clear coat over your car's paint. If a scratch has penetrated only this clear coat, not the paint below, then a product called rubbing compound, available in auto-parts stores, could make the scratch much less apparent.

Rule of thumb: If you can see primer or metal, the scratch is too deep for this strategy. But if you don't and your fingernail doesn't catch when you gently run it across the scratch, the scratch likely is shallow enough to try this.

Rubbing compound gently smooths out these sharp edges. It also can remove paint left behind by a vehicle that made contact with yours. Choose a highly regarded brand, because a bad rubbing compound could make the car look worse.

Examples: Meguiar's Ultimate Compound ($10.99 for 16 ounces) is made by the most respected name in this field. Turtle Wax Premium Grade Rubbing Compound ($8 for 18 ounces) also is well-respected.

After applying a rubbing compound according to directions on the package, apply polish and then wax to restore the shine and protect the paint.

Examples: Meguiar's Ultimate Polish ($9.99 for 16 ounces) and Meguiar's Ultimate Liquid Wax ($20 for 16 ounces).

If the scratch removed some of the paint below the clear coat, you'll have to add new paint to make it less apparent. Small bottles of touch-up paint are available in auto-parts stores, from dealership parts departments, or on Amazon.com and elsewhere online, typically costing $15 to $30. Use the touch-up paint sold by the automaker itself...or a highly regarded paint company's brand, such as Sherwin-Williams Dupli-Color, which offers a wide range of colors. A lesser paint might not match your car's color as well. The "paint code" identifying the proper paint for your car typically is listed on a sticker inside the driver's-side door or doorjamb (sometimes it's under the hood or under the trunk lid). If you can't find it, give your vehicle identification number (VIN) to one of the make's dealers and ask what your color code is. If your paint is badly faded, it might no longer match perfectly.

Expert tip: Don't use the nail polish–like paintbrush that often is included in the paint bottle—this tends to spread paint over too wide an area. Instead use the tip of a toothpick to slowly and cautiously apply a very thin coat of paint into the scratch...or ask at an art-supply store for a paintbrush appropriate for painting extremely narrow lines. Apply the paint only inside the scratch, not over the surrounding area. Too much touch up paint can look almost as bad as missing paint.

DENTS

Shallow dents in metal body panels sometimes can be pulled out using a suction-cup dent-puller, available at auto-parts stores for $10 to $20. Most brands of suction tools are pretty much the same. They are most effective when there's a relatively flat section inside the dented area large enough for a four-to-five-inch suction cup to stick to. If the metal inside the dent has a sharp crease, the odds of success are far lower.

Clean the dented area well before using the suction cup—dirt makes it harder to form a seal. Spraying a light water mist on the cleaned dented area can help improve suction, too. It might take several tries and a bit of arm strength to pull out a dent. These tools don't work every time, and even when they do, the result might not be perfect—some waviness could be visible in the metal surrounding the spot where the dent used to be. Still, it's an inexpensive option worth trying.

If the dent is in a plastic body part, such as the caved-in corner of a bumper cover, it's often possible to push the dent out from behind. The secret is heat—use a heat gun or even a hair dryer on its maximum setting to heat up the dented area, rendering the plastic more pliable, then use your hand to push out the dent from the inside. Wear work gloves to shield your hand from the heated plastic.

Try to maneuver the plastic back into place every few minutes, and heat it some more if it still won't budge. If there's no obvious way to get your hand behind the dent, you still might be able to reach thin tools such as metal pry bars into the area and use them to push from behind...you can sometimes remove a part or two to improve your access to the area behind the dent....and/or you could try using a suction tool to pull out the dent, as above.

If you cannot repair a metal or plastic dent on your own, seek out a "paintless dent removal" specialist. These body-repair pros tend to be much more affordable than traditional body shops because they use dent-removal techniques that don't require repainting the dented area—they typically charge only $100 to $200 per body panel repaired. This isn't a viable option with every dent, however, particularly if the paint in the dented area has cracked. Search for someone who has been doing paintless dent removal in your area for years, not someone who suddenly pops up offering these services after a hailstorm rolls through.

Helpful: Call the service departments at local auto dealerships, and ask if someone can recommend an independent paintless dent-removal pro. Some dealerships do this work in house, but others hire outside pros and know which ones can be trusted.

Best Outdoor Home-Security Cameras

Arlo Ultra—super-clear 4K Ultra HD video and 180-degree view. $330. *Blink XT2*—incredibly small (less than three-by-three inches), so this camera is easy to hide. Wireless, runs on special AA batteries that are designed to last up to two years. $100. *Ring Stick Up Cam Battery* features night vision, HD video, advanced motion detection and the popular Ring app. $100. *Arlo Pro 3 Floodlight Camera* puts out 2,000 lumens of brightness and features a blaring siren, color night vision and 12x zoom. $239. *Ring Solar Floodlight* is easy to install and use. Comes with two-way talk, a siren, and motion detection. $90. *Nest Cam IQ*—even at a distance of 50 feet, its facial recognition can tell strangers from regular visitors, and its tracking system follows a person's movements. $399.

FamilyHandyman.com

Best DIY Home Security Systems

Mike Prospero, managing editor specializing in smart-home devices for *Tom's Guide*, which reviews new technology products. TomsGuide.com

---

People want to feel secure in their homes. But the lofty price of home security systems is a big reason why only one-quarter of U.S. homes have any home security setup. Now the latest generation of do-it-yourself systems provide many features of professionally installed setups at a more attractive price.

A starter kit that you install and monitor starts at $200 to $300, although adding features or outfitting a larger home could add a few hundred dollars. In comparison, a basic professional system could cost about $1,300 for equipment and installation...and a monitoring contract for two years will add about $35 a month.

DIY kits include a wireless base station that connects to your home Internet and a built-in alarm...a battery-powered door/window and interior-motion sensor...a wall-mounted keypad or key fob and smartphone app that controls everything...and cellular and battery backup in case your electricity or Wi-Fi fails. Some DIY systems offer professional monitoring with flexible contracts ranging from $10 to $25 per month if you'd rather have the security company alert the police and/or fire department when your alarm is triggered.

Best DIY systems, all of which feature cellular and battery backup if you purchase a monitoring plan...

Best overall: Abode Smart Security. This is the easiest to set up and use. It integrates with Amazon Alexa, Apple HomeKit, and Google

Assistant, so you can control the system with voice commands.

Professional monitoring: $20 per month. Or order three- or seven-day monitoring for when you are away for $8 or $15, respectively.

Included: One entry sensor for a door or window, one motion detector. $229. GoAbode.com

For low-cost professional monitoring: Ring Alarm Security costs $10 a month for the service of alerting the police if your alarm sounds. Ring's Neighbors app lets you get crime and safety alerts from neighbors if they have Ring installed. Includes one entry sensor and one motion detector.

Smart-home capabilities: Works with Alexa but only a limited amount of third-party smart-home devices. $199. Ring.com

For extra security features: SimpliSafe Essentials has a wider range of add-ons than many competitors, including smart locks…panic buttons to activate your alarm silently…a 105-decibel alarm, about 15 percent louder than typical alarms…and sensors that detect water, smoke, low temperatures, and breaking glass. The advanced motion sensor can distinguish between people and pets.

Professional monitoring: $25 monthly. Includes three entry sensors, one motion detector.

Smart-home capability: Works with Alexa and Google Assistant, but only a limited amount of third-party smart-home devices. $259. SimpliSafe.com

---

HANDY HOME HELP…

Handy Uses for Chopsticks

Use as a trivet—if you do not have enough hot pads, put a pan on three chopsticks placed two inches apart. *Dry plastic or silicone bags*—put two crisscrossed chopsticks in a cup, and hang the just-washed bag over them. *Take toast out of a toaster*—unlike metal, dry wood does not conduct electricity.

Roundup of experts reported in *Real Simple*.

How to Green Your Kitchen

Lisa McManus, executive tasting and testing editor at America's Test Kitchen. AmericasTestKitchen.com

Tired of making so much waste in the kitchen—and ready to stop feeling guilty about it? *Swap out these common disposable products for something you can keep on using…*

• **Plastic wrap.** As much as we all would love to be plastic-free, there's no one catchall replacement for plastic wrap. You'll need to invest in a few different options for different applications. Bees Wrap ($11 to $42), made of cotton coated with beeswax, jojoba oil, and tree resin, works well for bread and baked goods, but you can't use it for meat or fish and it can leave waxy (though harmless) residue on dishes and hands.

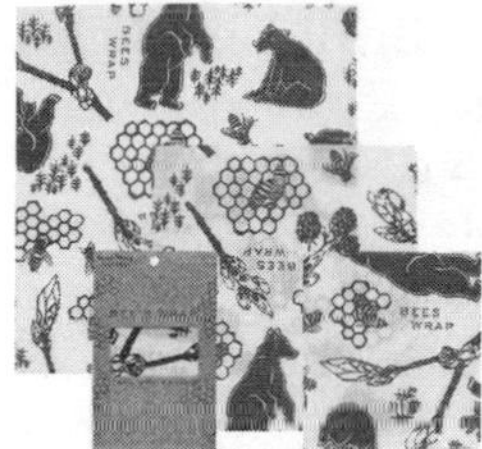

Silicone bowl covers make it easy to seal bowls or pots of all sizes. The Charles Viancin Lilypad Silicone Lids ($34 for a set of four) create an airtight seal when you push down on the center of the bloom, and because they're made of silicone, you can use them in the microwave, oven, refrigerator and on the stovetop. Another advantage to these flat lids is that they stay put during microwaving, preventing splatters, while stretchable silicone lids inflate from the expanding, warming air and pop off, making a mess.

• **Waxed paper.** Instead of using waxed paper to cover food that you warm in the microwave, use the silicone Marna Piggy Steamer (about $15), which lets excess steam out of the adorable snout. It also can be used to open jars.

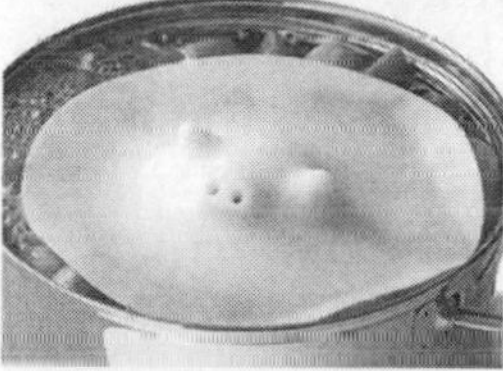

• **Parchment paper.** Parchment paper can be added to your compost pile, so it is a better environmental choice than plastic wrap or waxed paper. But for something more durable for lining a cake or cookie pan, a silicone mat reinforced with fiberglass mesh works wonders. The Silpat Premium Half-Sized Nonstick Silicone Baking Mat ($25) cleans up easily in the dishwasher, so it won't get sticky or stained or retain odors.

• **Plastic freezer bags.** Instead of using zip-top plastic bags for freezer storage, reusable containers are an easy option. Rubbermaid's Brilliance line is BPA-free, goes from freezer to microwave to dishwasher, and doesn't leak—and it comes in different size options to store whatever you need.

• **Paper towels.** Cotton dish towels can get the job done just as well as—or better than—their paper counterparts. The classic WilliamsSonoma Striped Towels ($19.95 or $24.95 for eight, depending on color) are very absorbent, just the right weight for use in the kitchen, and they get softer over time without losing strength.

• **Food waste.** More than 200 pounds of food is sent to landfills per person, per year. Composting can help cut back on that by taking everything from coffee grounds to orange peels and converting it to rich soil (perfect for your kitchen garden). The Exaco Trading Company ECO-2000 2.4 Gallon Kitchen Compost Waste Collector ($19.95) features a carbon filter that helps control odor, works with or without bio bags and can hold 2.4 gallons of kitchen scraps before you have to take it out to your composter.

Easy Way to Revitalize Old Cookware

If you have a stock pot or saucepan that's seen better days—especially if it has burnt-on residue—try this trick before tossing it. Put some water into the pot along with a dishwasher tablet, and bring it to a boil. Let it boil for 10 minutes, as the tablet releases its full concentration on the surface of the pot. If the pot isn't completely clean in 10 minutes, boil for longer. Scrub lightly if needed.

RD.com

Cook a Delicious Steak with the Reverse-Sear Technique

Meathead Goldwyn, who shares the science of barbecue grilling and outdoor-cooking techniques at AmazingRibs.com. Based west of Chicago, he is known as the "Barbecue Whisperer" and is author of *The New York Times* best-seller *Meathead: The Science of Great Barbecue and Grilling.*

Most home cooks assume that a steak should be cooked at a high temperature. That works fine for a steak less than an inch thick, but for a steak of about one-and-a-half inches, the way to get a tender, juicy-on-the-inside steak with a nice dark brown, even crust at home is different—it's called the reverse-sear technique. *What to do...*

• **Choose the right cut.** A rib eye or strip steak is a good choice. Also, for steakhouse quality, ask your butcher for "USDA top choice," which is more flavorful because it contains more marbling (fat throughout the steak) than regular USDA Choice or lower grades. USDA Prime choice is even better, but most groceries don't carry prime cuts.

• **Use a digital thermometer.** Controlling the temperature is the key to a tender steak—and unless you are a world-famous chef, you cannot tell when meat is properly cooked by poking it with a finger.

CHARCOAL OR GAS GRILL

• **Set up two cooking areas on your gas or charcoal grill.** Turn the gas on high on one side of the grill. Or if using a charcoal grill, move all the charcoal to one side and light it, then wait until the coals turn white. Season both sides of the steaks with salt and pepper. Place the steaks on the side of the grill that is not over the flame (the indirect heat). Cover the grill. The warm airflow will heat the steak evenly on all sides, with no need to flip it. Continue cooking until a digital thermometer inserted near the center reads 120°F.

• **Move the steak to the hot-flame side of the grill (direct heat), and keep the lid open.** Flip the steak after one minute. Continue to flip approximately every minute or two, browning the surface of the steak evenly on both sides until the crust is a nice dark brown and the thermometer reads 130°F to 135°F.

OVEN AND STOVE METHOD

• **Heat the oven to 200°F.** Place the seasoned steaks on a wire rack in a baking pan in the oven. Cook until the meat thermometer reads 120°F to 125°F.

• **Heat a cast-iron pan on the stovetop on high (while the steak is in the oven).** After the meat has reached 120°F in the oven, brush it on both sides with vegetable oil. Place the steak in the pan, keeping the stove on high. Flip the steak every minute for an even, brown crust and until the thermometer reads 130°F to 135°F.

WORKS FOR OTHER MEATS, TOO

The reverse-sear technique is extremely effective for other meats, too.

Examples: Cook pork chops on indirect heat to 130°F, transfer to direct heat and cook to 140°F to 145°F. Chicken can be cooked to 150°F on indirect heat and then brought to 160°F to 165°F over direct heat. You will never burn the skin again with the reverse sear.

BETTER WAY...

To Make the Best Baked Sweet Potato, Freeze It First

A popular winter street snack in China is a baked sweet potato. The secret to its deliciousness is that it's been out in the cold before being cooked—ice crystals macerate the potato's flesh, giving it a mashed-potato texture when it comes out of the oven.

To get the same effect: Select a few small sweet potatoes, freeze them for an hour or two, then roast them on parchment paper or foil for at least one hour at 450°F. You can scrub them beforehand, but don't pierce the skin. Once the caramelized sugar is seeping from them and the steam has separated the skin from the flesh, they're ready to eat. Top with whipped cream, spiced honey, chopped nuts, or salt.

Lucas Sin, lead chef, Junzi, New York City, quoted at Eater.com.

How to Freeze Every Type of Food...and Not Lose the Fresh Taste

Julie Garden-Robinson, PhD, RD, LRD, professor in North Dakota State University's department of health, nutrition, and exercise sciences. She is author of the university's online food-freezing guides, available at NDSU.edu (search Food Freezing Guide).

Can't eat all the green beans growing in your garden? No time to fry the fish in your fridge? Lunch leftovers languishing? There's no need to let excess food go to waste, as long as there's room in your freezer. Most foods still taste good if they're frozen, then thawed even a few months later—if you freeze and thaw properly.

THE GUIDELINES

Certain strategies apply to freezing almost any type of food...

• **Freeze food while it's fresh.** People often wait until food has nearly expired to freeze it—which guarantees it will taste like it's past its prime when thawed.

• **Freeze food in freezer bags, freezer paper, or reusable rigid containers designed specifically for the freezer.** These do a better job than other packaging at keeping out air. Zip-top bags specifically designed for the freezer are made from thicker plastic than other zip-top bags, for example, which makes them much less likely to crack, tear, or otherwise allow air to leak in. Air is the enemy of frozen food, causing dehydration and "freezer burn." Press excess air out of freezer bags before sealing, and pack rigid freezer containers completely full. Better yet, use a vacuum sealer to enclose foods before freezing.

Exception: When freezing food that has high water content, such as fruit or a sauce, leave some open space in the package so that the bag or container doesn't burst when it expands as the water inside turns into ice.

• **Label and date frozen foods.** Unmarked frozen food packages can be a challenge to identify...and you don't want to waste food simply because you can't tell what it is.

• **Set your freezer temperature no higher than 0°F.** Food freezes slower at higher temperatures, leading to larger ice crystals that can rupture cells and damage texture.

• **Don't load lots of not-yet-frozen food into a freezer at the same time.** This can cause freezer temperatures to temporarily climb, causing food to freeze slowly.

• **Defrost food in the refrigerator.** Food defrosts very slowly in the fridge—and that increases the odds that moisture from melting ice crystals will be reabsorbed into food, reviving its former flavor and texture. If you don't have time for refrigerator defrosting, alternatives include defrosting in the microwave and/or defrosting in cold water. If you defrost in cold water, change the water as often as necessary to ensure that it remains cold. For safety reasons, never defrost at room temperature.

FREEZING MEAT, FISH, POULTRY, AND DAIRY

When possible, freeze meat, fish, and poultry raw rather than cooking it first, which may result in an off-putting "warmed over" flavor. Keep in mind that refreezing previously frozen and thawed food can harm quality—that is, flavor and texture. Food remains safe as long as it stays solidly frozen, but the quality can suffer over long periods.

Fish: If fresh fish will be consumed within a few months, wrap well and freeze. If possible, wrap tightly in a clinging plastic, then overwrap with freezer wrap. Assuming your freezer is set to 0°F, frozen fish ranging from fatty fish such as salmon and tuna to leaner, flakier fish such as flounder and cod should taste fine for up to three months. Some shellfish, such as shrimp and king crab, can last longer than three months, but lobster tail meat lasts just two to four weeks.

Poultry: Don't stuff whole birds before freezing. Wrap giblets separately from the rest of the bird. For best flavor and texture, whole frozen birds should be consumed within one year...pieces within nine months...giblets and ground poultry within four months.

Red meat: Whole cuts of frozen red meat should be consumed within 12 months... ground meat within four months...sliced deli meat within two to three months. If the meat is packed in wrapping from the market, leave it in this, but put the package in a tightly sealed freezer bag as well—the plastic wrap used by markets does not keep out air very well, and the meat might become freezer-burned in as little as a month.

Less freezer friendly: Ham and bacon should not be frozen for more than one to two months—their high salt content and fat can lead to rancidity if they're frozen longer. Sour cream, yogurt, and buttermilk lose their smooth texture when frozen. Eggs in the shell freeze poorly but freezing often is not necessary—eggs can last a month in the fridge.

FREEZING VEGETABLES

The secret to successfully freezing most veggies is to blanch them first. Blanching—briefly boiling or steaming—inactivates enzymes in vegetables that otherwise would cause them to become tough, discolored, and/or oddly flavored over time. Let vegetables dry after blanching but before freezing. *Some common vegetables...*

Asparagus: Blanch two to four minutes, depending on stalk size. Consume within five months.

Beets: Rather than blanch these, boil until tender before freezing. Consume within eight months.

Brussels sprouts: Remove the coarse outer leaves, then blanch for three to five minutes, depending on size. Consume within 12 months.

Carrots: Blanch small whole carrots for five minutes. Large carrots should be diced, sliced, or stripped, then blanched for two minutes. Consume within 12 months

Cauliflower: Break into one-inch pieces, then blanch for three minutes. Consume within 12 months.

Corn on the cob: Blanch for seven to 11 minutes depending on size. Consume within eight months.

Green beans, snap beans, and wax beans: Blanch for three minutes. Consume within eight months.

Green peas: Shell, then blanch for one-and-a-half minutes. Consume within 12 months.

Zucchini: Cut into half-inch slices then blanch for three minutes. Consume within 12 months. Zucchinis contain a lot of water, so they tend to be too mushy for grilling once thawed but still good in soup or muffins.

Don't bother thawing most vegetables—simply cook from frozen. Take care not to overcook—remember that the veggies were partially cooked by the blanching process.

Exception: Corn on the cob should be partially thawed before cooking so the thick cob isn't still cold after cooking.

Less freezer friendly: High-water content vegetables such as lettuce, cucumbers, tomatoes, celery, and radishes become limp and watery when thawed.

FREEZING FRUIT

Fruits that freeze particularly well without sugar or syrup include blueberries, cranberries, currants, gooseberries, raspberries, and rhubarb.

However, the best way to preserve the texture and flavor of most fruit is to freeze it in sugar or syrup. In general, syrup is better if the fruit will be consumed raw...sugar if it will be used in recipes. Syrup can significantly affect recipes.

If you opt for syrup, dissolve two-and-three-quarter cups of sugar in four cups of boiling water, creating a 40 percent syrup...cool this syrup...then use just enough to cover the fruit to be frozen. If packing in sugar, sprinkle sugar over the fruit and mix gently until the sugar dissolves. Consume fruit within 12 months if frozen in syrup or sugar...within three to six months if frozen without these.

Some common fruits...

Apples: Dissolve one-half teaspoon of ascorbic acid in three tablespoons of water, and sprinkle over sliced apples, then pack and freeze. If desired, before packing sprinkle with one-half cup of sugar per quart of apple slices. If packing in syrup, slice apples into cold syrup and add one-half teaspoon of crystalline ascorbic acid per quart of syrup.

Bananas: These can be frozen whole ... or peel them and mash thoroughly, mixing in one teaspoon of lemon juice per cup of mashed banana, then pack and freeze—no sugar or syrup required.

Berries: With firm berries, such as blueberries, elderberries, and huckleberries, steam for one minute, immediately cool in cold water, then pack and freeze either in syrup or unsweetened. With soft berries, such as blackberries, raspberries, boysenberries, and loganberries, remove any underripe berries, then pack and freeze in syrup, sugar, or unsweetened. Strawberries also can be frozen separately on a tray, then quickly transferred to a freezer bag or container when frozen. This will lead to more air in the package and somewhat quicker deterioration, but some people consider it worthwhile so the strawberries are not frozen into a block.

Melon: Remove seeds, then slice, cube, or ball. Pack in 30 percent syrup—one-and-three-quarter cups of sugar dissolved in four cups of water. Melon also can be frozen unsweetened, but this will be best if it is served before completely thawed.

Serve fruit promptly after thawing in the fridge, or it could become soft and dark. Thawing in the microwave is also fine if the fruit will be used in a recipe. Sugar-packed fruit thaws faster than syrup-packed fruit.

BETTER WAY...

Keep Refrigerated Food Fresher Longer

Be sure the refrigerator temperature is between 35°F and 40°F. Store high-ethylene produce, which can speed the ripening of other fruits and vegetables, separately—apples, tomatoes, potatoes, melons and peaches are all high-ethylene foods. Remove the leafy tops of root vegetables, such as carrots and turnips, to keep the vegetables fresher longer. Put cut leafy herbs, such as cilantro and parsley, in a jar of water with a plastic bag placed loosely over the top—and change the water regularly.

Roundup of experts on food storage, reported at RD.com.

Beyond the Cucumber: Pickled Vegetables Are a Tangy Treat

Kirsten K. Shockey, coauthor of *Fermented Vegetables* and *Fiery Ferments*, from which these recipes are excerpted, and most recently *Miso, Tempeh, Natto & Other Tasty Ferments*. Ferment.Works

---

Do you love the taste of a dill pickle...the tang of sauerkraut...or the spicy burn of kimchi? If so, you might be intrigued to know that creating those incredible flavors at home is much easier than you would imagine. All of these tasty treats—and so many more—are fermented, or pickled, foods. Plenty of folks think fermentation is a complicated, mysterious science experiment that requires an advanced degree, but this couldn't be further from the truth.

Making your own pickled vegetables is easy once you know the basics, and the incredible tastes that you'll unlock will keep you pickling for years to come. Plus, it's a great way to use up veggies that you might otherwise be tempted to throw away, which helps reduce waste and can be a good excuse to go a little crazy at the supermarket when your favorite veggies are on sale or in season.

A WORD OF CAUTION

Every now and then, things go wrong, so trust your nose if you're not quite sure about a batch. Pungent and pickle-y, even a little funky scents and tastes are good. Anything that smells like rotting potatoes or compost is not. Also on the throwaway list—veggies that taste slimy or are overly soft.

TWO EASY RECIPES

These two recipes are ideal for beginners—they're easy but yield delicious results.

Lemon Dill Kraut

3 pounds (1 head) green cabbage
3 cloves garlic, finely grated
1 lemon, juice and zest
1½ teaspoons dried dill weed
1 Tablespoon salt*

Remove any coarse outer leaves of the cabbage. Rinse a few unblemished leaves, and set them aside. Rinse the rest of the cabbage in cold water. Quarter and core the cabbage. Thinly slice, then transfer the cabbage to a large bowl. Add the garlic, lemon juice and zest, and dill. Add the salt, then use your hands to massage the salt into the shreds, then taste. You should taste the salt without it being overwhelming. Add more salt if necessary. The cabbage should quickly start to look wet and limp, and liquid will begin to pool. If not, make sure that there's enough salt, and let it stand, covered, for 45 minutes and then massage.

Transfer the mixture, bit by bit, to a two-quart glass container with a lid or a wide-mouthed jar. Press down on each portion. Make sure that the brine is covering all the

**Best salt:* Mineral-rich salt, free from additives, such as Redmond Real Salt or Himalayan Crystal Salt. Do not use table salt with added iodine or, ironically, pickling salt—both contain additives and often produce ferments that have a too-salty taste.

cabbage. Even a small amount of brine is fine as long as it is at the top of the cabbage. If you think you need more liquid, check back in an hour. Often the salt will have pulled more liquid from the cabbage. If not, you can add more lemon juice. Allow two to three inches of headspace. Top the cabbage with one or two of the reserved outer leaves (they should be submerged as well), then top that with a water-filled, sealable plastic bag to keep everything below the level of the brine. Next, tighten the lid. Set aside for five to 10 days. Check daily to ensure that the vegetables are submerged. Using a utensil, you can taste-test the kraut on day five.

You'll know it's ready when it's pleasingly sour, pickle-y tasting without the strong acidity of vinegar...the veggies have softened a bit but retain some crunch...the cabbage is more yellow than green and slightly translucent. When it's finished, toss the top leaves.

Spicy Carrot and Lime Salad

1¾ pounds carrots (sliced very thin on a grater or mandolin)

3 to 4 Fresno or other hot red peppers, seeded (if you want less heat) and sliced thin, or 1 Tablespoon dried chile flakes

Zest and juice of 2 limes

1 (1-to-2-inch) piece fresh ginger, sliced thin

2 teaspoons salt

Combine all the ingredients except the salt in a bowl. Massage the salt into mixture. Pack the mixture into a jar using the method above. Set aside for seven to 10 days. You can taste-test on day seven. When ready, it will have a pleasing acidic smell and taste pickle-y. It also may have a bit of an effervescent zing. A slight cloudiness in the brine is normal.

GOOD TO KNOW...

Best Footwear for Cooks

Serious chefs wear clogs while standing for long stretches to protect their feet from drops and spills and support their arches and spines. Here are the best brands according to the pros. *Dansko:* Snug-fitting with great traction. *Crocs:* Skid-free, easy to wash. *Birkenstock:* Comfortable cork footbed and adjustable buckles. *Sanita:* Great support without a break-in period. *Klogs:* Cushioned insoles, lots of colors and styles. *Zuzii:* Stylish leather and wood. *Calzuro:* Ventilated rubber in numerous colors.

AmericasTestKitchen.com

Simple Household Hacks

Wrinkle-free clothes—toss a few ice cubes into your dryer (with dry, wrinkled clothes), and run the machine for 10 minutes. ***Milk-jug watering can***—just drill some holes in the plastic cap, fill with water, and turn upside down. ***Recipe hanger***—get your recipe or a light cookbook off the counter and up to a more accessible height by hooking a coat hanger (the kind with pants clips) to a cabinet handle and clipping the recipe to it. ***Makeshift dusting pad***—wrap used dryer sheets around the business end of a floor sweeper. They do the job as well as name-brand refills. ***Homemade dry-erase board***—place a sheet of attractive stationery inside a tasteful picture frame, and write on the glass with a dry-erase marker.

FamilyHandyman.com

Donate Your Garden Surplus

If your neighbors hide when they see you carrying bags of zucchini up their walkways, you still can make good use of your surplus garden produce by donating to a local food pantry. The nonprofit Ample Harvest (AmpleHarvest.org) hosts a database of 8,700 such organizations that accept garden produce.

Better Homes & Gardens.

Be Careful When Using Potting Mix

Though rare, there have been cases over the years of people dying from diseases, such as Legionnaire's, contracted from potting mix. Potting mix is a combination of organic and inorganic materials, and the bacteria and fungi in the mix can thrive in the moist and warm conditions where it's stored.

Self-defense: Wear gloves when working with potting mix, and if you don't have gloves, thoroughly wash your hands immediately after. Wearing a mask while handling it also can help protect you, as some diseases, such as Legionnaire's, are airborne.

CNN.com

Planting Shrubs and Perennials in the Fall

Teri Dunn Chace, author of more than 35 gardening books, including *The Anxious Gardener's Book of Answers.* She lives in central New York. TeriChaceWriter.com

Spring and summer planters may be missing out on the best time of year for gardening—the fall. Beyond planting spring-blooming daffodils, tulips, and other bulbs, the fall offers both great weather and great bargains for beautifying your yard.

• **Capitalize on fall's assessing opportunities.** Now is the perfect time to make calm and prudent planting decisions. In springtime, the abundance of choices, enticing displays, and/or seductive catalog photos, not to mention the end of winter's cabin fever, can impel you to buy the wrong plants for your garden's soil or daily sunlight situation, or bring home more plants than you can wedge in.

By early autumn, you've watched and spent time in your yard and are aware of where the sunniest spots are and where the rains puddle. This time of year, you're also best able to identify where the gaps are—where you'd like another plant to fill in or flower color to diversify.

• **Choose fall's more mature plants.** Many plants offered now are leftovers or overstock from the season gone by, which actually works to your advantage. The garden center or nursery nurtured them all summer, and now they are more mature, larger, and have bigger root systems. Thus they begin life in your yard bigger and stronger. Don't worry if their foliage is no longer fresh and beautiful or their flowering period has come and gone. Get those roots in the ground, and let them get established this fall.

• **Take advantage of fall's gentler conditions.** In contrast to spring, fall soil is warm, a welcoming situation for the root systems of shrubs and perennials. Sunlight is less intense now, too. No flowering plant likes to be popped out of a pot and into the ground when conditions are hot and dry. It's too stressful—they'll wilt as their roots struggle to access moisture and deliver it up to the plant above. And weeds are essentially done growing and expanding their numbers for the year. Unlike spring-planted shrubs and perennials, fall garden additions won't have to compete with them for space, moisture, and nutrients.

• **Plant as fall begins, not when it's well under way.** This gives your fall-planted selections maximum time to start growing in place before winter dormancy. If your new plants have only two or three weeks before a frost hits, they may struggle or die. Ideally, get them in the ground a good six to eight weeks before any frost is expected. Make a quick call to your nearest Cooperative Extension office, or look for predictions from your local weather sources.

• **Plant properly for best results.** Planting this time of year is otherwise similar to spring planting. You should still dig a hole that is wider and deeper—by a few inches on all sides—than the pot the plant arrived in. You should still amend the planting hole with organic matter. Use half compost and half native soil, well-mixed.

In fall, however, take time with the roots—they are the stars of this project. Tease a dense root system apart with your fingers to loosen it up. If this is not possible, score the sides of the roots vertically with a sharp knife every few inches, approximately one-quarter-inch deep. This does not harm the roots. On the contrary, it inspires them to regenerate.

Lastly, as with spring planting, create a basin where water can collect and go down directly where needed instead of running off. Line up the perimeter with the outer edge of the plant's current width. Pour water in or deliver it with the hose until it stops sinking in.

• **Water right up to the brink of winter.** In fall's milder, cooler days, plants are less prone to wilting or drying out. Still, give them a good soaking, as described above, every few days their first week, then taper off to once a week. Continue this practice until the ground freezes. Skip when there are good soaking rains.

• **Do not feed.** Plant food would only inspire new leaves, stems, or even flower buds. Should any buds appear, snip them off with clippers. The plants' focus must be on root development, so they are strong heading into winter.

• **Last-minute winter prep.** Local weather reports will alert you when the first frost is expected. Several days beforehand, swing into action. If fall rains don't do this for you, give each newcomer one last good soaking.

• **Do not cut back the plants.** It is better for a perennial or shrub's survival to leave tidying until spring.

Lastly, using your hands or a shovel, place three or four inches of compost and/or chopped-up fall leaves over each planting basin. This protective layer helps prevent "frost-heaving," where temperature fluctuations push root systems up out of the ground.

• **Enjoy next spring's payoff.** Your fall-planted perennials and shrubs will have a significant head start on their spring-planted counterparts. The root growth they made in your yard before winter came will fuel robust growth. What a joy it will be to see them burst forth!

SAVVY FALL PLANT SHOPPING

Health: Always check for signs of trouble. Insect pests can hide under leaves, along stems, and where side stems meet main ones. Diseased leaves may be mottled, spotted, or have distorted shapes.

Proportion: A shrub or perennial's top growth ought to be no higher than two-to-three times the depth of the container it comes in. This indicates a good ratio of roots to stems.

Roots: When you pop a plant out of its pot (you may do this before buying at local nurseries), the roots should be white and crisp. Avoid those with black, wiry, or mushy roots and those with very thick or tangled root systems, which don't transplant as well.

Perennials and shrubs that I've had great success with fall planting...

Perennials: Astilbe, bee balm, black-eyed Susan, catmint, daylily, hardy ("cranesbill") geranium, iris, peony, phlox, Russian sage, sedum, yarrow.

Shrubs: Chokeberry, camellia, cotoneaster, fothergilla, heavenly bamboo (nandina), hydrangea, rhododendron, roses, shrubby dogwood, spirea, witch hazel.

Good mail-order sources: Avant Gardens, Bluestone Perennials, Fieldstone Gardens, Forestfarm, High Country Gardens, Plant Delights Nursery, Spring Hill Nurseries, Wayside Gardens and White Flower Farm.

Attract Dragonflies with These Plants

Dragonflies eat up to 100 mosquitoes per day, and they have an appetite for midges, gnats, and other little flying creatures you don't want around, plus they're pretty to look at. So are the perennial flowers that attract them. Black-Eyed Susan—a classic, easy-to-care-for type of daisy...Dwarf Sagittaria—an aquatic plant that needs fertile soil and can tolerate hard water...Blue Hill Meadow Sage—ideal for dry areas…Yarrow White Wildflower—which needs lots of sunlight.

Prevention.com

Beyond the Bird Feeder: Attract More Feathered Guests to Your Yard

David Mizejewski, a naturalist with The National Wildlife Federation. He has hosted television series on Animal Planet and NatGeo WILD and is author of *Attracting Birds, Butterflies, and Other Backyard Wildlife,* now in its second edition. NWF.org/garden

If you'd like more—and more varied—birds to flock to your yard, provide what the feathered set searches for. It's not as simple as scattering some seed and building a birdhouse because birds have subtle preferences that people often fail to understand. *Here's a look at the four ways to attract more birds—and a greater variety of birds…*

BIRD FOOD

Many people figure that the best way to feed wild birds is to provide lots of store-bought seed, but they're wrong. Birds would far prefer to eat food from native plants in your landscaping. The plants that are native to your area co-evolved with local bird populations and inevitably supply those birds' favorite foods. *Among the native plants most likely to attract birds…*

• **Berry-producing shrubs.** Visit a nursery or garden center in your area, and ask which berry-producing shrubs are native to your area. In addition to being big draws, native shrubs usually are easy to grow.

Examples: Depending on where you live in the U.S., options might include blueberry, chokeberry, chokecherry, dogwood, elderberry, holly, huckleberry, juniper, Oregon grape, serviceberry, sumac, viburnum, wax myrtle, and/or winterberry, among many others.

• **Native wildflowers and grasses.** Many birds are seed eaters. Your neatly mowed lawn might appeal to your homeowner's association or neighbors, but it's less popular with birds. They prefer it when grasses and flowers are allowed to grow naturally until they produce seed. Even if you don't allow your entire lawn to grow unchecked until it "goes to seed," you could devote a section of your property to unmowed native grasses and wildflowers.

Examples: If sunflowers and purple coneflower are native to your area, their seeds likely will be popular with birds.

• **Oak trees.** Oak leaves are a popular meal for a wide range of caterpillars—and caterpillars are a favorite meal of virtually all birds likely to touch down in U.S. yards.

Warning: If you want to attract birds to your property, don't spray pesticides on your lawn and trees. That will kill off the caterpillars and other insects that virtually all backyard birds hope to find.

• **Red tubular flowers.** If your goal is to attract hummingbirds, red flowers shaped to hold nectar, which allow the birds to insert their long beaks, will be especially popular.

Examples: Coral honeysuckle, trumpet creeper, or red columbine.

• **Providing store-bought seed in a bird feeder can attract birds, too**—just not the wide variety of birds you could attract with the food options above. Chickadees, woodpeckers, goldfinches, cardinals, titmice, nuthatches, and certain sparrows are attracted to bird feeders…but many other birds including bluebirds, robins, warblers, and wood thrushes typically are not.

• **Black oil sunflower seed is popular with birds that frequent feeders and is good for them.** Avoid seed mixtures, which usually are full of fillers such as millet and cracked corn that birds generally consider undesirable. In fact, birds often kick this filler out of the feeder and onto the ground, where it could attract rodents.

Exception: Wild-bird supply stores, such as the chain Wild Birds Unlimited (WBU.com), often sell high-quality bird seed mixtures that are not full of millet and corn. These mixtures even can be used to attract a specific species of bird to the feeder.

Helpful: If squirrels steal your birdseed, choose a bird feeder that shuts its seed ports when a squirrel climbs on board. Birds can access the seed because they don't weigh enough to trigger the mechanism.

Example: Woodlink Absolute Squirrel Resistant Bird Feeder ($75).

• **In the winter, add a suet feeder.** Suet is rendered animal fat, a high-calorie meal that birds especially value during the cold months. Woodpeckers, jays, and chickadees are among the likely guests when you serve suet.

Two birds with particular food preferences...

To attract bluebirds, buy a special feeder designed to serve dried mealworms or caterpillars, available in wild-bird stores and some pet stores.

To attract orioles, buy a special feeder designed to provide fruit, such as orange halves, grapes, or jelly. (These can attract bugs as well, though orioles could help control that problem—they eat bugs in addition to fruit.) A local wild-bird supply store should have these specialty feeders if orioles are common in your area.

WATER

Buy and fill a birdbath—or just set a pan of water on your back porch. The water should be just one to three inches deep—if it's deeper, many small birds won't drink from it.

Every two or three days, pour out this water and refill. Mosquitoes lay their eggs in standing water, but their newborns take approximately a week to develop. As long as you dump this water before then, your bird water supply won't increase the mosquito population in your yard. In fact, it should reduce that population by attracting birds, such as swallows and purple martins, that will eat some of the mosquitoes already living there.

Every week or two use a scrub brush, dish soap, and water to wash out the birdbath or water pan. This lowers the odds that bird droppings in the water will spread disease among the local bird population.

COVER

Birds feel more secure when there's a spot close by where they can hide from predators and shelter from bad weather. Usually these hiding spots are in or under dense vegetation, such as thick shrubs.

Example: The native berry-producing shrubs discussed above can serve double duty, providing both food and cover.

If you have a potential source of bird food on your property that does not provide its own cover, such as a bird feeder, oak tree, or wildflowers, plant a shrub within 10 to 12 feet of this. Choose a shrub dense enough that a small bird standing underneath wouldn't be spotted through the branches by a predator flying above.

Note that birds generally do not consider birdhouses a source of cover, though some birds could view them as a place to raise young (see below).

NESTING BOXES

Bird lovers often install birdhouses in their yards, but birdhouses that look charming to people often have little appeal to birds. Bird species that build their nests on the branches of trees, not in cavities inside trees, are not attracted to birdhouses at all. And "cavity nesters," which include bluebirds, chickadees, nuthatches, owls, swallows, titmice, woodpeckers, and wrens, tend to be so particular about where they raise their young that unless you select just the right structure and put it in just the right spot, they won't take advantage either.

Before buying a birdhouse, note which cavity-nesting bird species frequent your property, then ask a local wild-bird supply store to help you choose a "nesting box" for this species and select an appropriate location for it. (Using the term "nesting box" rather than "birdhouse" signals that you're looking for something that truly appeals to birds as much or more than it appeals to you.)

Examples: Bluebirds prefer nesting boxes with entry holes one-and-a-half inches in size. Screech owls will nest only in boxes or tree cavities that are at least 10 feet above the ground.

If a box or birdhouse has a small perch beneath the entry holes, that's a warning sign that it wasn't actually designed with birds' needs in mind. Cavity-nesting birds don't need perches—the holes they nest in on trees usually don't have them, and they get into those just fine. But perches can provide handholds for predators such as racoons, increasing the odds that eggs will be stolen and eaten.

Also: If there's a dead or dying tree on your property that isn't putting your or a neighbor's house in danger, let this tree remain rather than having it taken down. Dead and dying trees often contain cavities appropriate for nesting.

Fast-Growing Evergreens

Arborvitae can be sheared into a hedge or allowed to grow into a pyramid-shaped tree. It can grow 15 feet tall and three to four feet wide. It does best in Zones 4 to 8. **Japanese cedar** can grow 50 feet tall, although shorter varieties such as Black Dragon grow only to 10 to 12 feet. Hardy in Zones 5 to 9. **Arizona Cypress** resists heat and drought and can grow to 20 feet—at a rate of up to three feet a year. Best for Zones 7 to 9. **Italian Cypress** can grow 25 feet tall and three feet wide, and tolerates ocean breezes. Does best in Zones 7 to 10. **Blue Point juniper** is low maintenance, grows more slowly than other evergreens and eventually reaches 12 feet in height and four feet in width. Hardy in Zones 4 to 9. For a map of U.S. plant-hardiness zones, go to PlantHardiness.ars.USDA.gov.

BHG.com

Use the Sun's Power to Control Soil Pest

Cover the ground with a tarp—usually a transparent polyethylene cover—to trap solar energy after watering the soil deeply. Then leave the plastic in place for at least four weeks in the hottest part of the summer. This will help control bacteria, insects and weeds. It works best on heavy soils that contain clay, loam or a mixture of both.

Texas A&M AgriLife Extension Service, AgriLife Extension.tamu.edu.

BETTER WAYS...

To Attract More Hummingbirds...

Make food for them by mixing four parts hot water to one part sugar. Boiling the water is not necessary unless you are making extra to store or your water quality is not very good. Use sugar—not honey, which can make the mixture ferment more quickly and attract ants. Do not add red dye—it may harm the birds. Change the water in your feeder every few days...or sooner if the weather is really hot. Clean the feeder occasionally to prevent mold buildup. Try adding a second feeder in late summer, when hummingbirds migrate, so that males are less likely to fight for feeding space.

FamilyHandyman.com

17

Fun Stuff

Great Games for Family and Friends

Being trapped at home during the pandemic taught us that video chatting is a surprisingly satisfying way to be with people. So whether you remain a home body or you simply have loved ones living far away, you can bring back the fun and connection of "game night" using a video-chat app such as Zoom, FaceTime, Google Duo or Google Meet.

There are plenty of online games and apps designed to be played by remote competitors, but many of these lack the social element of an in-person game night, and others are confusing or frustrating when played from different locations. The point of playing games with friends is talking and laughing together, seeing each other's faces and sharing stories, not just competing. *Here are some of the best games for socializing with friends in far-flung locations...*

• **Battleship.** You probably already know how to play this classic two-person, child-friendly game—each player tries to locate and sink the other's hidden fleet by guessing grid coordinates. Battleship works very well through a video-chat app because players don't need to touch each other's boards. Both players will need their own copy of the game to play long distance. $19.99. Hasbro.com

You also can find free, printable versions of the Battleship game grid online—enter the terms "printable," "battleship," and "game" into a search engine to locate these. You could even create your own grid using graph paper, creating the ships by coloring in squares.

Meredith Sinclair, play and lifestyle expert and regular contributor to the *Today* show. Based in Los Angeles, she is author of *Well Played: The Ultimate Guide to Awakening Your Family's Playful Spirit.* MeredithPlays.com

• **Cards Against Humanity.** This very adult card game emphasizes scoring laughs, not just scoring victories. Each round, a black card is turned over, exposing a sentence that contains blanks (or that poses a question).

Example: "Before I run for president, I must destroy all evidence of my involvement with _______."

Players then choose from among the white cards they hold in their hand, each of which features a different word or phrase. They earn points if the cards they select are deemed funniest by that round's judge (the "Card Czar") when plugged into the blanks. Cards Against Humanity is not at all appropriate for kids—the white cards are loaded with sexually suggestive, politically incorrect, and mature terms. It's generally played by groups of four or more. The judge rotates each round.

Every household taking part in the game will need the set of cards ($25)—or download and print a free deck through the game maker's website. CardsAgainstHumanity.com

• **Apples to Apples** is played in a similar way but has family-friendly editions so you can play with younger children. $19.99. MattelGames.com

• **Charades.** You no doubt already know how to play this venerable party game—one player silently acts out a word or phrase while the others try to guess it. Charades translates well to video chat because no game board or cards are required. Far-flung players will have to think up their own words to act out rather than use the traditional method of drawing slips of paper written by other participants, however.

• **Do You Know Me?** In this recently released card game, players take turns in the "hot seat" answering yes-or-no questions. Other players score points by predicting their answers. It's a wonderfully social game with lots of laughter, in part because the questions tend to be silly and personal.

Example: "If _______ won the lottery, would he share the money with the other players?"

Do You Know Me? translates well to remote play over a video chat in part because you can play it even if only one player has a copy of the game—that person can do all the question asking. It's generally played with two to eight players. This game was not created for kids—some of the questions are sexual or otherwise mature in nature—but you could carefully skip over inappropriate questions if you want to include children. $19.99. WhatDoYouMeme.com

• **Exploding Kittens.** Players try to avoid getting knocked out of the game by an exploding kitten card in this fast-paced, easy-to-learn, family-friendly card game. The game designers have developed special modified rules to assist with long-distance play—on ExplodingKittens.com, select "Instructions," then scroll down to click on "Quarantine Kittens" and download these rules. Every participating household will need its own copy of the game to play long distance. It's typically played by two to five players. $18.99.

Alternately, players can play together long distance if they each download a copy of the Exploding Kittens mobile app, available for iOS and Android for $1.99.

• **Family Feud card game.** If you've ever watched the Family Feud TV game show, you already know how to play—two teams compete to list the top survey responses to a range of topics.

Example: "Tell me something people in Florida do a lot more than people in Minnesota." Top survey responses include "Go to the beach," "Surf/swim," and "Eat fresh oranges."

This home version can be played by two teams of any size, plus one participant who serves as host rather than joining a team. The team element makes the game especially social. Only the person acting as host needs to own the game. $11 for the Platinum Edition. FamilyFeud.com

• **Heads Up!** This game was popularized by Ellen DeGeneres playing it with celebrities on her talk show. Players take turns holding their smartphone to their forehead with the screen facing outward. The free Heads Up! app then displays a word (or words, such as "dirty dancing"), which the person holding the phone cannot see. The other players provide clues until the one holding the phone figures out the word on his head. Heads Up! is fun for two or more players through a video-chat app—but if your own image is displayed on screen, close this window or cover it with a Post-It note before your turn so you don't accidentally see the word you're supposed to guess. The app is 99¢ for both Apple and Android. EllenTube.com

• **Pictionary.** In this classic artistic take on charades, participants take turns trying to draw the word or phrase listed on a card as teammates attempt to decipher their drawings. This popular game typically is played by groups of four or more. It translates very well to long-distance playing with the help of Zoom's whiteboard feature, which lets participants share digital drawings with each other on screen. (In Zoom, click the "Share Screen" button then "Whiteboard.") It helps if every household involved in the long-distance game has a copy of Pictionary. If they don't, one participant can serve as host rather than compete and privately text or e-mail the words to be drawn to players. $19.99. MattelGames.com

Or instead of buying the game, players can use the Pictionary Random Word Generator (RandomWordGenerator.com/pictionary.php).

• **Taboo.** Players provide hints intended to help a teammate figure out a "guess word"—without themselves saying any of the "forbidden words."

Example: Try to get your teammate to say "pinball" without saying "arcade," "tilt," "game," "flippers," or "roll." It's fun and social either in person or over video chat. Each household participating will need its own copy of Taboo. It is played by two teams, each of two or more players. $14.99. Hasbro.com

In a pinch those who don't own the game can find unofficial digital Taboo "cards" free online at PlayTaboo.com.

• **Trivial Pursuit.** Trivia games are very social, whether you're playing at a bar's trivia night or long distance with friends over a video-chat app. Ideally every household playing long-distance Trivial Pursuit should have a copy of the game. But if not, one player who owns the game can read all the questions and move all the pieces around the board. The game is designed for two to six players, but larger groups can play by dividing into teams. $24.99. Hasbro.com

---

Re-Create the Movie Theater Experience at Home

Jacob Palmer, head of e-commerce content for *Best Reviews*, which tests and reviews consumer products. BestReviews.com

---

Even with most theaters reopening after shutting amid the pandemic, audiences remain sparse with multiple streaming services offering both original content and blockbuster movies. Now more than ever before, you can capture the cinematic experience at home—without the overpriced Raisinets, people talking during the film, or the need to wear a face mask and social distance.

Ranging from today's best images and sound to fresh popcorn and comfortable seating, here's what you need to make your home viewing experience more cinematic...

A BIG 4K TV

A TV with a 65-, 75-, or even 85-inch screen, or a projector TV, will help immerse you in the cinematic experience. Although you can get a good smaller or lower-quality set for well under $1,000, it's worth paying extra for a big, high-quality 4K set with millions of pixels that deliver impressively clear, crisp images as long as you're watching content transmitted in 4K and you're sitting at the right distance. Although 8K sets are available and provide even sharper images, there is hardly any 8K content available yet and most people can't easily tell the difference, so there's little reason to pay $10,000 or more.

Keep in mind that 4K content currently is available mostly from streaming services, such as premium Netflix, Amazon Prime, and Hulu, rather than cable- or satellite-TV, where it's mostly limited to on-demand movies or special events and requires a special set-top box. DirecTV does have a few 4K channels.

Among the best 4K options...

• **Best big TV.** Sony Master Series Bravia OLED delivers images that provide among the very richest colors and deepest blacks of any TV on the market, although the LG OLED sets are worthy rivals. OLED stands for "Organic Light-Emitting Diode," a TV technology that excels at producing truly black blacks. Unlike many flat-screen TVs, OLEDs don't have a backlight behind the display—it's the display itself that produces light, so no unwanted light bleeds through black areas. That makes a big difference when you watch a dark movie scene in a darkened room. Sony's advanced "refresh rate" processing also helps it stand a notch above other 4K TVs—its image won't become blurry or choppy even during fast-moving action scenes. Its sound quality is very good for a flat-screen TV, but if you're looking for a real movie theater experience, it's worth adding a surround-sound system (see page 293). $2,499* for the 65-inch... or $3,499 for the 77-inch.

Helpful: Sit close to your big TV to re-create the immersive cinema experience—one rule of thumb is to sit approximately 1.5 times the screen's diagonal measurement, which is around eight feet from a 65-inch TV or 9.5 feet from a 75- or 77-inch TV.

• **Best big TV value.** Samsung QLED Q60T offers resolution and rich colors that are not far short of the Sony OLED mentioned earlier and at a much lower price. There are some sacrifices, however—the Q60T falls short of the Sony when it comes to keeping up with very fast-moving action...its picture quality degrades when viewing the screen from a sharp side angle...and its brightness levels can be uneven—this is a "QLED," or Quantum Light-Emitting Diode TV, which unlike OLED, depends on backlighting for illumination. Also, the audio is unimpressive. $998 for the 65-inch...$1,396 for the 75-inch...$2,247 for the 85-inch.

*Prices subject to change.

HOME THEATER PROJECTORS

• **Best home theater projector.** Epson Home Cinema 5050UBe offers the richest, brightest colors and deepest blacks available from a home projector—and there's nothing like projecting a film onto a big screen for re-creating the theater experience. Today's projectors are worlds away from the old Bell & Howells you once used for 8mm vacation films—these deliver 4K images virtually as sharp, bright and rich as you can get from the 4K TVs above. And with a projector, you can have a much larger image, potentially 100 to 200 inches, with a big enough room.

Projectors fare best in dark rooms—bright light can make their images seem washed out. That isn't a problem if you turn off the lights at night to re-create the theater experience, but it could be a problem during daytime viewing. This projector is far better than most in bright rooms, however, because it projects images at an enormously bright 2,600 lumens, enough to overcome most ambient light. It doesn't have speakers—a soundbar or surround-sound system is required. $3,299.

• **Best value home theater projector.** Optoma UHD50X doesn't quite match the stellar colors and deep blacks of the Epson discussed above, but it doesn't fall far short and it's less than half the price. Its images are bright enough even in a well-lit room, though, as with any projector, it does best in the dark. Its sound quality is poor, so add a soundbar or surround-sound system. $1,599.

PROJECTION SCREENS

These are available in a wide range of sizes, price points and even colors. White screens tend to do the best job of displaying light from the projector, but some gray screens are better in a lit room because they don't reflect much ambient light. Fixed screens, such as Silver Ticket Productions 150-Inch

Projector Screen, $470, remain on the wall all the time and can be stretched completely flat to avoid any distortion. Retractable screens, such as Elite Screen 84-Inch Spectrum Electric Motorized Projector Screen, $186, are nearly as flat and can roll out of the way at the push of a button.

STREAMING DEVICES

Unlike 4K TVs, most home theater projectors do not include built-in 4K streaming devices, so you will need to buy an external device to watch 4K movies and programs from streaming services such as Netflix and Amazon Prime. These external devices also could be useful if you find the streaming capabilities built into your 4K TV clunky to use or it doesn't offer access to a streaming service that you want to use. Streaming devices include Apple TV 4K, $179...Roku Ultra, $70... and Amazon Fire TV Stick 4K, $30.

AUDIO SYSTEMS

Movies in theaters don't just look great, they also sound great. *These surround-sound systems deliver an enveloping audio experience...*

• **Best surround-sound experience.** Sonos Arc 5.1 Surround Sound Set offers crystal-clear audio clarity and deep bass. This wireless system includes a soundbar, two auxiliary speakers, and a subwoofer. With the Sonos Trueplay app (iOS only), you can customize it to a room in just a few minutes. In addition, you can add speakers in other rooms and listen to music throughout your home...or keep following movie dialog when you step into the kitchen. $1,856. Additional speakers start at $169.

• **Best surround-sound system for value.** Vizio 36-Inch 5.1.4 Home Theater Sound System provides immersive movie theater–quality sound for a lower price than any other system of its quality. Like the Sonos system above, it includes a soundbar, subwoofer, and two auxiliary speakers—but while this system doesn't have to be attached with wires to your TV, its remote speakers must be connected to the subwoofer with wires. Calibrating this system to a room is less intuitive than with the Sonos, and it's not easily expandable to other rooms like the Sonos. $349.99.

HOME THEATER SEATING

Although a recliner or sofa is more comfortable than typical movie theater seats, it doesn't re-create the movie theater experience. *These home theater seats offer the best of both worlds...*

• **Best home theater seating.** Seatcraft Republic Loveseat 7000 is what movie theater seats should be—a pair of soft, comfortable top-grain leather recliners joined into a single piece of furniture reminiscent of a row of movie theater seats. The recliners work at the touch of a button, and the console between the two seats and the armrests open

More from Jacob Palmer...

Don't Forget the Popcorn!

The smell and taste of popcorn is a crucial part of the movie experience for many people. *These machines re-create that far better than a bag of microwave popcorn...*

•**Best overall.** Great Northern Popcorn Company Full Antique Style Popcorn Popper looks like an old-fashioned theater lobby popcorn popper should look—it's a five-foot-tall wheeled unit with big glass windows displaying the popcorn inside. Its popcorn tastes like it is straight from the theater, and it pops quietly so it won't distract from the film. Unlike some faux-antique popcorn poppers, it's fairly sturdy and should provide years of service. $285.

•**Best value.** Superior Popcorn Company's Old Time Countertop Popcorn Machine is attractive and makes great popcorn, too. Unlike the device above, it's a tabletop unit, not a free-standing wheeled cart. $200.

up to reveal storage and cup holders—the cup holders have soft blue LED lights so you can locate them when watching a movie in the dark. Each seat also features a USB charging port. $1,499.

• **Best value.** Flash Furniture Eclipse Series 2-Seat Push-Button Motorized Reclining Theater Seating also offers a pair of comfy, connected, motorized leather recliners. It has cup holders and hidden storage, like the Seatcraft above, but fewer flashy features like LED lighting and USB ports. $950 for the two-seater. A three-seat model also is available.

Cheer Up With These Channels on YouTube and Facebook

Andrew Selepak, PhD, program coordinator of the graduate program in social media at University of Florida College of Journalism and Communications, Gainesville. Jou.UFL.edu

---

Actor John Krasinski, best known as Jim from the TV show *The Office*, received praise during the pandemic for his YouTube channel "Some Good News." His videos were like a low-budget version of the nightly news…but segments featured people doing good deeds for neighbors and receiving pleasant surprises.

Its upbeat message proved so popular that it was bought by CBS—but it isn't the only place you can find upbeat, interesting content online. *Here's where to head on YouTube and Facebook if you'd like to escape the all-too-prevalent negativity and bickering…*

• **Facebook group/page of a place that's important to you.** Enter the name of that city or state into Facebook's search bar along with the words "old" and "photos" and a spot within the city, then click "Groups" and/or "Pages." This often turns up groups/pages where members post old pictures of the area. It's a heartwarming, nostalgic way to look back at the way things once were in places where you spent happy times or where your ancestors lived. It's also a great way to interact with people who share your fond feelings for the area. "Derry of the Past" is my personal favorite—my mother was born in Derry, Northern Ireland, and I still have family there.

• **"Today I Found Out" YouTube channel.** Brit Simon Whistler answers history and science questions that your high school textbooks didn't cover in this informative video series. Not every video is upbeat, but there is plenty of fun.

Examples: "Do People Who Get Knighted by the Queen Get Anything for It?" and "Why Doesn't the Heart Get Tired and Need to Rest Like Other Muscles?"

If you like this YouTube channel, Whistler also hosts biographical videos on the YouTube channel "Biographics."

• **Upbeat comedy.** The "Team Coco" YouTube channel features talk show host Conan O'Brien. His humor is goofy and self-deprecating, unlike many modern talk show hosts and comics who seek laughs by being overly political and critical.

Also: Talk show host Graham Norton brings on multiple guests at a time so you see celebrities interact with each other in a relaxed and entertaining way. View clips on his show's YouTube channel.

If you're looking for laughs free of topical references, enter the name of favorite talk show hosts or comics from decades past into YouTube—you can find clips and complete shows featuring everyone from Steve Allen to Sid Caesar.

• **"Rick Steves' Europe" YouTube channel.** Watching travel writer Rick Steves explore Europe isn't as fun as actually visiting Europe, but it is a way to see a different part of the world and help you make travel plans for the future.

Also: Enter the name of a place you hope to visit into YouTube along with "visiting" or "driving." The results may not have Rick Steves's insight or production values, but they still can transport you to distant parts of the globe.

• **Facebook group/page of a favorite Hollywood star of the past.** Facebook groups and pages for today's stars often are little more than marketing tools or gossip mongers, but the pages of stars from the pre-Internet era often provide a pleasant place for fans to share memories...read old interviews and articles... and see old photos and film clips.

Examples: John Wayne's official Facebook page...the Clark Gable: When Hollywood was "Golden" Facebook page.

Alternatives to TikTok

With the hugely popular short-form video app facing security concerns, you might want to look for another platform. *Instagram Reels*—you can record and edit video montages up to 15 seconds long from a single video or a series of clips. Excellent effects via augmented-reality tools. *Triller*—easy to use, although with limited effects. Lots of celebrity content. *Likee*—quite similar to TikTok. Strong emphasis on music, a thriving community and lots of content to browse. *Firework*—kind of a grown-up version of TikTok with a similar interface and tools but an emphasis on finding or creating high-quality videos with an assortment of topics and age groups represented.

LifeWire.com

BETTER WAY...

"Squinch" for Better Photos

Narrow your eyes slightly to make yourself appear more confident. You want to narrow them a bit but not so much that you appear to be squinting.

Also helpful: Have a slight smile when being photographed—this is why people are advised to say "cheese" or another word. And determine which side of your face photographs better—everyone really does have a "good side." Look at photos taken of you from both sides to figure out which you like better.

Peter Hurley, portrait photographer, New York City, quoted at FastCompany.com.

How to Get the Correct Exposure When Using a Cell-Phone Camera

If all or part of a photo you take on your smartphone is too dark or too light, try these tips. ***Identify the important part.*** Tap on the part of the image you want to be lit correctly. The camera will automatically adjust the exposure. ***Use the exposure control.*** If you want to raise or lower the exposure of the whole picture, tap the screen to bring up the exposure control and move the slider to let in more or less light. ***Use HDR.*** In your camera's settings is an option to use high dynamic range (HDR), which merges different exposures together in one image. ***Clean it up later.*** Even if you don't get your picture exactly right, you can use your photo-editing software to brighten or reduce the lighting as needed.

HowToGeek.com

Best Places to Learn Music Online

Kay Fleury, content manager for TechBoomers.com, a free website that teaches people how to improve their lives through technology. She also enjoys playing the guitar. TechBoomers.com

If you want to learn to play an instrument, this could come as music to your ears—some impressive music-instruction resources are available on the Internet, many of them for free or low cost. That's good news if you can't find an appropriate music teacher in your area...if you'd like to avoid the expense of years of lessons...or if you've grown attached to doing most everything in the comfort of your home.

Here are some of the best online music-learning resources—choose the ones that sound most appealing, or sample a few to find out which work for you...

ONLINE MUSIC COURSES

Online courses are the Internet equivalent of enrolling in college music classes but often at a fraction of the cost or even for free. Some online programs are actual college courses taught at highly regarded schools. Online courses typically have forums where students can ask questions. That's not the same as having a teacher listen to you play live, but it's better than having no feedback at all.

Coursera offers inexpensive or free online access to thousands of prerecorded courses, most of them taught at actual universities. Many of the music courses available on Coursera are courses taught at Boston's prestigious Berklee College of Music.

Example: "How to Play Guitar," a set of four courses taught by professors at Berklee, promises to teach everything needed to play songs on a guitar in about five months. Free.

Udemy also has thousands of pre-recorded courses offered on a wide range of topics. Unlike on Coursera, the instructors for many of these courses are not affiliated with universities. There are no free classes on Udemy, but prices usually are below $200 per course—or even less if you wait for a sale, which are common. Udemy.com

Example: "Learn to Play Harmonica," which features more than 23 hours of lessons by Ben Hewlett, chairman of a group called HarmonicaUK. List price is $129.99, but sale prices sometimes lower that to as little as $19.99.

MUSIC INSTRUCTION APPS AND WEBSITES

Music apps and websites tend to be more interactive than videos or online courses, and so can help you identify and overcome your musical weaknesses and provide a sense of how much progress you're really making.

MusicTheory.net is a free site that offers quality content for learning to read music, with exercises and interactive tools that enable you to practice the lessons you learn. It's also available as an iOS app that costs $2.99.

Music Tutor is a simple app that provides exercises for sight-reading proficiency—developing your speed and accuracy while reading sheet music. It's free for Android or iOS. MusicTutorApp.com

EarMaster is a versatile app that offers everything from lessons in music theory to exercises that improve rhythm, teach sheet music reading, or provide "ear training"—that's the ability to identify music elements such as pitch by listening. Some content is free, but most features require a subscription that costs $3.99 per month. It's available for iOS or on Windows or Mac computers, but not for Android.

Uberchord is a clever interactive guitar-learning app. It leads you through exercises and songs on your guitar—and provides real-time feedback about your playing. The app monitors your guitar playing and lets you know whether you're hitting the right notes. It is free, but a subscription is required to access most of the content—subscriptions cost $14.99 per month or $89.99 per year. It's available only for iOS.

Yousician is a lot like Uberchord but it provides feedback for a variety of instruments—bass, guitar, piano, vocals, or ukulele. Yousician also monitors your performance as you play songs and exercises and lets you know how you're doing and where you can improve. It's available for iOS, Android, and even on PC. As with Uberchord, the basic app is free but you'll have to pay for a subscription to access most of the content—with Yousician, "Premium+" costs $59.99 for three months...or $139.99 per year.

REMOTE MUSIC TEACHERS

Sometimes there's no substitute for a music teacher—an experienced musician who can work with you one-on-one...help you work through challenges that you can't seem to master...and provide personalized tips about how you could improve. If you can't find a music teacher you like locally, there's a world full of instructors who teach remotely over video chat.

Among the websites where you can find instructors for a wide range of musical instruments and styles: Lessonface...Live Music Tutor.

Which site is best really comes down to which happens to have the instructor who is the best fit for you, so explore both. The main way to determine this is from the profiles on the sites. The teachers don't need credentials to get on the site, but what they've done and reviews from their students are listed there, so you can choose super-vetted ones with a lot of experience, and pay more for their experience...or relative music-teaching beginners trying to make a name, and pay much less. Students sign up for classes one at a time, so one option is to continue trying different instructors until you find a favorite.

Lessonface lets instructors set their own rates—prices vary from about $15 to about $75 per 30-minute lesson. Established instructors with great reviews from other students typically charge the most, while bargains sometimes can be found by choosing instructors who have experience giving music lessons in the real world but who are new to these websites.

Live Music Tutor has fixed prices—$35 per 45-to-60-minute beginner lesson...$45 for intermediate...and $60 for advanced. Lessons for kids ages three to 12 cost $25 for 30 minutes.

YOUTUBE MUSIC INSTRUCTION VIDEOS

Of course, if you just want to dip a toe in the water of an instrument, there are a vast number of free musical instruction videos on YouTube covering almost any instrument you can imagine, from the accordion to the zither. To find these, just enter the name of an instrument and the word "lesson" into YouTube's search bar. Or enter music topics such as "music theory" or "reading music" along with the word "lesson." The main downside to learning from videos is that there's no feedback—the instructor can't hear you play, evaluate how you're doing, or offer personalized suggestions about how you can improve.

With very popular instruments, there are so many instructors and lessons on YouTube that it can be challenging to choose. *Among the best YouTube channels for learning three popular instruments...*

Best for drums: Drumeo channel features hundreds of drumming instructional videos, from "Your Very First Drum Lesson" to lessons taught by successful recording musicians, such as Jonathan "Sugarfoot" Moffett, known for his work with Michael Jackson... and Kenny Aronoff, known for his work with John Mellencamp.

Best for guitar: GuitarJamz channel offers hundreds of excellent video lessons including both the basics—one video is titled "Absolute Super Beginner Guitar Lesson"—and more advanced topics, such as how to play blues licks. There also are videos about how to play many popular songs, including some within the abilities of virtual novices, such as Tom Petty's "I Won't Back Down" and the Beatles' "Let It Be."

Best for piano/keyboard: PianoVideo Lessons channel, established in 2011, provides an extensive and well-regarded series of free video classes. The videos are designed to be used in conjunction with an inexpensive eBook—the Unit 1 eBook containing the first 16 lessons costs $19 at Courses.PianoVideo Lessons.com. No other online video tutors have the extensive material library and curated playlists offered here.

Alternative: Piano Keyboard Guide channel also offers a wide range of excellent free video lessons, no guidebook required. There are lessons for students who have never before sat at a piano up through lessons leading students through popular songs, with classics such as Frank Sinatra's "My Way" and the Beatles' "Yesterday" and recent pop hits like Harry Styles's "Adore You" and Dua Lipa's "Don't Start Now."

How to Read Shakespeare for Pleasure

If you associate the Bard with painful classroom memories, now might be a good time to revisit the plays for no better reason than to enjoy them.

Here's how: Relax—you're doing it for fun, so there's no test and no pressure. Skip around—read the parts that are most compelling, most famous, or otherwise catch your interest. And read in small doses if that's what suits you. Read as though you were the director—Shakespeare provided scant stage directions, so it's fun to ask yourself how you would make the text come alive on stage. Ignore the footnotes—nobody understands everything in a Shakespeare play, and constantly stopping to check your comprehension disrupts the narrative flow.

Emma Smith, PhD, professor of Shakespeare studies, Oxford University, UK, quoted at TheConversation.com.

DID YOU KNOW?...

Stand-up Comedian Laugh Count

A stand-up comedian has to clock in at four laughs per minute to be considered a decent comic.

Stephen Rosenfield, director, American Comedy Institute, New York City, and author of *Mastering Stand-Up.* ComedyInstitute.com

Learn to Sew

Margo Martin, executive director of the American Sewing Guild, Inc., a nonprofit national membership group organization for sewing enthusiasts, headquartered in Houston. ASG.org

---

Sewing machines flew off the shelves during the pandemic as people crafted face masks and returned to the hobby of sewing in an era of spending more time at home.

Are you ready to learn—or relearn? *Ask yourself two questions as you start your search for the best sewing machine for your needs...*

• **What kind of sewing do you want to do?** A mechanical machine that does straight and zigzag stitches is fine for simple projects such as making face masks and tote bags, although many entry-level machines today offer as many as 30 stitch types, including buttonhole, stretch stitches, blind hems and beautiful decorative stitches.

Best entry-level machines: Baby Lock Zest ($149)...Bernina Bernette 35 ($249).

• **How much do you want to spend on a sewing machine?** You can expect to pay at least $200 to $500 for a new entry-level sewing machine. Yes, you could buy a $100 machine, but it will likely not work as well and will not offer many helpful features. Advanced computerized machines can cost thousands of dollars.

A local sewing store is the best place to buy a new machine. Sewing machine dealers can answer questions to help you choose your machine, offer classes, and make repairs.

You also can buy sewing machines online and at "big box" stores such as Costco and Walmart and at craft stores such as JOANN and Michaels. But these places may not offer services such as maintenance tune-ups—particularly important for higher-end machines—and repair.

• **Consider a used machine.** If you're looking to maximize your investment, it's better to purchase a gently used, well-maintained older model of an expensive machine than an expensive new machine. Many avid sewers regularly trade up for new models, so it's not difficult to find used machines on eBay, Facebook Marketplace and within local sewing guilds and dealers.

• **Online tutorials.** The American Sewing Guild (ASG) website (ASG.org) has learn-to-sew tutorials along with many sewing education opportunities and members-only discounts on sewing products and services.

Membership: $50 to join.

YouTube has beginner sewing videos and instructions on how to operate almost every type of sewing machine.

• **Basic sewing supplies.** In addition to fabric, machine needles, and thread, you also will need straight pins, high-quality fabric scissors, disappearing ink or chalk marker, extra bobbins, a measuring tape, seam ripper, and an iron. You can purchase supplies at a local fabric store or anyplace you find them online, such as CuttingLineDesigns.com, SewingWorkshop.com, JOANN.com and Michaels.com, as well as at Amazon.com.

• **Worthwhile projects.** The public section of the ASG website under "Resources/Giving

Back" has directions for making many community service projects such as the Anti-Ouch pouch for breast cancer patients and World Wish Pillows for sick children. Being part of a sewing community such as ASG or other guilds offers sewing friends to mentor new sewing enthusiasts!

Bicycles That Won't Break the Bank

Michael Yozell, former gear editor of *Bicycling Magazine.* He is a professional bike mechanic based in Emmaus, Pennsylvania, with more than 30 years of experience, and a bike consultant to consumers and the industry.

It's easy to get sticker shock in a bike shop—some stellar bicycles cost $3,000 to $10,000. But excellent bikes for casual cyclists, with lightweight aluminum or alloy frames rather than featherweight carbon-fiber frames, can be had for $500 to $1,000.

Here are some of the best reasonably priced bikes for assorted types of road surfaces, all of which have aluminum or alloy frames and weigh 28 pounds or less…

Best for comfortable rides around town: Linus Rover 9 is ideal for easy trips on paved paths and neighborhood roads. Its upright riding position and comfortable seat let riders take in the scenery, while its 1.75-inch-wide tires provide a soft, stable ride—the wider the tire, the larger the cushion of air under the bike and the greater traction. Many bikes in this "beach cruiser" class have just one to five gears, but the 28-pound Rover 9 features a nine-speed gear system, which helps riders handle hills. $789.

Best for travel on unpaved and paved surfaces: Co-op Cycles CTY 1.1, sold by REI, is a "gravel" or "hybrid" bike—a middle ground between a road bike and a mountain bike. With 24 speeds and large wheels, it's fairly fast on pavement…but its relatively wide 1.57-inch tires and durable construction mean that it's very capable on gravel and dirt paths, too. The 28-pound CTY 1.1 has straight handlebars that create a fairly upright riding position. $599.

Best for biking adventures: Salsa Journeyman Claris 700 is capable on paved and unpaved surfaces and has a comfortable, relatively upright riding position like the gravel bike mentioned previously. But the durable 16-gear, 26-pound Journeyman also has abundant mounts for bags, luggage racks, and water bottles, making it appropriate for camping trips. And this versatile bike's standard 700c wheels can be swapped out for 2.2-inch-wide 650b wheels with mountain bike tires to convert the Claris 700 into an even more capable off-roader. $949.

Best road bike: Giant Contend 3 provides everything you need in a road bike for hundreds of dollars less than comparable offerings. Giant is the biggest bike manufacturer in the world, and its economies of scale let it undersell its competition. The Contend 3 is smooth, fast, comfortable, and durable. At 23 pounds, the 16-speed bike is impressively light and agile compared with other bikes in its price range. $820.

The Beauty of Winter Hiking

Philip Werner, former New Hampshire wilderness guide and founder and editor of the hiking website SectionHiker.com.

A coating of snow can make a hiking trail breathtakingly scenic and blissfully uncrowded. But safe winter hiking requires some additional planning and equipment. *Here's what you need to know…*

WINTER HIKING GEAR

Warmth and waterproof are the two key features to keep you safe and comfortable on cold, snowy, or icy winter hikes...

Winter hiking boots are waterproof and much more heavily insulated than other hiking boots. Many manufacturers also claim that their winter boots have soles that grip especially well on ice, but don't put too much faith in those claims—even the best soles will slip on ice. Fortunately, most winter boots also are designed to be compatible with aids such as microspikes and snowshoes that can dramatically improve traction (see below). Just three decades ago, they tended to be big and bulky, like military surplus gear, but advances in fabrics and insulation mean they're now lightweight, comfortable, and breathable. Some are designed to protect hikers in remarkably cold temperatures, as low as –40°F, but a boot rated to –20°F or below should be more than sufficient for most day hikes.

Recommended: Oboz Bridger 10-inch Men's Insulated Boot, $199*, and nine-inch Women's Insulated Boot, $195...and Salomon Toundra Pro CSWP Snow Boot for men or women, $200.

Microspikes are like tire chains for the feet. They typically attach to hiking boots with strong rubber or elastic straps, positioning metal chains and small spikes underfoot to dramatically reduce the odds of slipping on ice. The marketing materials of many winter hiking boots claim their soles grip well on ice, but don't believe it—no rubber sole grips anywhere near as well as metal spikes. Most products are relatively easy to put on and take off, so you can adjust depending on the ground conditions. They're most useful when the trail is icy, which is especially likely when earlier hikers have tamped down all the snow.

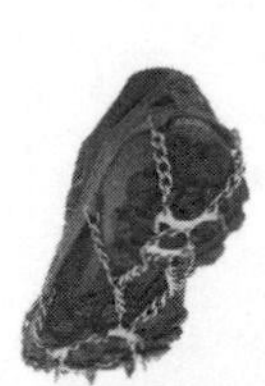

*All prices in this article reflect recent prices from major online sellers.

Recommended: Kahtoola MICROspikes Traction System, $70/pair...Hillsound Trail Crampons, $65/pair. Both fit a wide range of winter footwear and rarely slip off, a chronic problem with lesser products.

Snowshoes are like portable platforms that strap onto your boots, preventing your feet from sinking deeply into soft snow. Without snowshoes, walking in snow that's deeper than a few inches quickly becomes a tiring and unpleasant battle. Snowshoes also have metal teeth underneath to provide grip on icy surfaces.

You don't wear microspikes and snowshoes at the same time, but unless you're certain about trail conditions, it's worth having both with you so that you can switch between them as needed. Snowshoes are too bulky to fit in the typical backpack, but they can be strapped to it. They should be worn with winter hiking boots.

Recommended: Atlas Snowshoes, available in versions for men, and women, $200 to $250...MSR Evo Ascent, $200. Snowshoes come in many different sizes, shapes, and styles, however, so before buying consider trying out a few different models to determine what feels best to you. Many ski centers and REI locations rent snowshoes.

Helpful: Walking in snowshoes is awkward at first, and novices sometimes trip. Using ski poles can greatly help with balance. Walk with a slightly wider gait than normal, as if riding a horse, to reduce the odds that you'll step one snowshoe onto the other. Don't attempt to step backward or turn around quickly while wearing snowshoes—walk instead in a tight circle.

Gaiters strap onto your lower legs over the pants and boot tops to prevent snow from getting into boots when hiking or snowshoeing. "High" gaiters, which come up almost to the knee, are best when there's more than a few inches of snow on the ground. These typically have a strap that goes under the sole of the boot. Confirm that the boots you se-

lect have a gap or arch in the sole that is sufficiently wide enough to fit the strap of the gaiters you intend to purchase. Otherwise this strap would wear against the ground.

Recommended: Outdoor Research Crocodile Gaiters, available in men's and women's versions, are thick and insulating, providing an extra layer of warmth for the lower legs, around $60 for most sizes and styles...REI Backpacker Gaiters, $55, are waterproof but lightweight and breathable...as are Outdoor Research Rocky Mountain High Gaiters, available in versions for men and women, $45.

Socks worn while winter hiking should be wool or synthetic, never cotton, which absorbs moisture and will leave your feet cold and uncomfortable.

Recommended: Darn Tough Mountaineering Socks, available in men's and women's versions, $30.

Water bottles should have a mouth nearly as wide as the bottle itself—wide-mouth bottles are less likely to freeze shut on frigid hikes than are narrow-mouth bottles.

Recommended: Nalgene 32-ounce Wide Mouth Water Bottle, $11.99.

Store water bottles upside down in your backpack—after confirming that they don't leak—to further reduce the odds that the mouth will freeze shut. Wrapping bottles inside insulted gear such as a spare shirt or sock inside your backpack also reduces freezing risk. There also are insulators that keep your bottle somewhat protected from cold temps even when clipped to the outside of your backpack, saving you from having to dig through your backpack each time you want a drink.

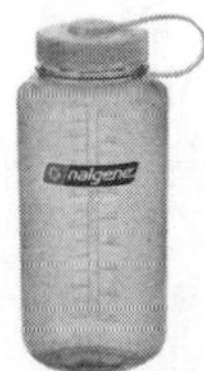

Recommended: Outdoor Research Water Bottle Parka, $32.

Naturally, you'll also need other cold-weather clothing such as jackets, hats, and gloves, but the winter gear you already own for activities such as shoveling snow or skiing might suffice. Wear multiple layers that you can remove and stow in your backpack as needed. If you hike or snowshoe aggressively, your body is likely to generate so much heat that you find yourself removing layers even though it's cold out, but it's still vital to have enough layers with you that you would be safe and comfortable if you stopped moving—whether that's to take a break and enjoy the scenery or because you're injured and must wait for help. Avoid cotton, which provides little insulation when it gets wet, and choose moisture-wicking base layers.

Pack multiple pairs of socks and gloves so that you can change these if they become wet from sweat or snow.

Remember to wear sunglasses and sunscreen. Sunlight can be as punishing to the skin and eyes in winter as in summer.

WINTER HIKING STRATEGY

- **Hike with a partner or group.** Also let a friend who isn't coming on the hike know where you'll be hiking and when to call the authorities if you fail to report in. Naturally, you should bring your phone on the hike so you can call for help if necessary, but don't depend entirely on a phone for safety—hiking trails often are in areas with poor cell reception, and cold temperatures reduce battery life, which means your phone might run out of power sooner than expected. A whistle is a simple and effective winter-hiking safety tool, calling help to your location if you get lost or hurt. If your phone battery life isn't great, it's worth bringing a portable battery pack and cord to recharge it as well.
- **Your first few winter hikes should be relatively modest distances**—half the distance or less that you could comfortably hike during warmer months. Hiking requires more effort and energy per mile in snow, especially deep snow that requires snowshoe use.
- **Carry a printed map of the trail system** even if the trail is well marked and/or you can access a trail map on your phone's GPS. Some trail markings might be obscured by snow, and GPS can be deceiving at a walking pace—the GPS might misinterpret which direction you're traveling and point you the wrong way, for example. Also, your phone's GPS can't help you if the battery runs down. Hiking on trails you already have traversed during warm months also reduces the odds

that you'll get lost, though trails can look very different under a layer of snow.

• **Drink water before beginning a winter hike—as much as a liter.** It's easy to become dangerously dehydrated on winter hikes, because you're not only sweating, you're also expelling moisture with each breath in the dry air. If you hydrate immediately before the hike, you're much less likely to become dehydrated on the trail.

Better Boating Without Buying a Boat

Peer-to-peer boat sharing is similar to using Airbnb while traveling—you rent a boat directly from the owner at sites such as Boatsetter.com and GetMyBoat.com. Boating timeshares let you buy a block of time in a company-owned fleet of boats—but be sure you understand contract terms thoroughly. Boat club memberships may be available through colleges, community centers, and city or county recreation departments—rules and prices vary widely. Chartering provides access to a wide variety of boat types, sizes, and amenities—get referrals to good local charter companies through yacht clubs, marine-supply stores, and bait-and-tackle shops.

MoneyTalksNews.com

It's Time to Get Away! Drive-to Destinations for Outdoor Fun

Donna Heiderstadt, a travel expert based in New York City who has visited nearly 100 countries and traveled to all seven continents. During her 25 years writing about travel, her work has appeared on TravelAndLeisure.com, Fodors.com, ShermansTravel.com and RobbReport.com.

How about a drive-to getaway spring or early summer to a place with outdoor activities and vacation-home rentals or resort-based cottages or cabins? *Here are 21 options in seven regions of the continental U.S....*

NEW ENGLAND

Stowe, Vermont: In April, a few ski slopes still may be open and Vermont's legendary maple syrup will be running. Hiking, mountain biking, kayaking, and trout fishing begin ramping up in May. There's also a thriving craft beer and cider scene and historic covered bridges. GoStowe.com has an inventory of vacation rentals.

Eastern Massachusetts: Walkable Boston (BostonUSA.com) is full of historical charm—The Freedom Trail and Irish Heritage Trail, postcard-perfect Back Bay, Beacon Hill, and Boston Common. Drive north to Salem, site of the 1692 witch trials (Salem.org), and south to Plymouth (SeePlymouth.com), home to the rock of 1620 Pilgrims fame. Stay at an apartment or house in and around Boston, available on Vrbo.com and Airbnb.com.

Coastal Connecticut and Rhode Island: Explore Norman Bird Sanctuary in Middletown, Rhode Island...historic Mystic Seaport in Mystic, Connecticut...the vintage Essex Steam Train and Riverboat in Essex, Connecticut...scenic beaches in Westerly, Rhode Island (SeeWesterly.com)...and Gilded Age mansions (NewportMansions.org) in Newport, Rhode Island. The 3.5-mile Newport Cliff Walk is a must—plus more than one million daffodils bloom in the city in late April and May. Book a cottage at Harborview Landing (HarborviewLanding.com) in centrally located Mystic.

MID-ATLANTIC

New York's Adirondacks: The Adirondacks (VisitAdirondacks.com) are home to 3,000 lakes and dozens of waterfalls. Six-million-acre Adirondack State Park offers hiking, biking, birding, and kayaking. Step back in time at the Great Camps...golf in Lake George (VisitLakeGeorge.com)...or hike the Saranac Lake 6ers (SarananacLake.com). Splurge on an Adirondack cabin at Lake Placid Lodge (LakePlacidLodge.com)...or rent a private cabin on Vrbo.com.

Harpers Ferry, West Virginia: This historic town makes a great base for a day trip to Washington, DC, while you vacation amid nature. Local attractions include Harpers Ferry National Historical Park (nps.gov/hafe)—home to John Brown's Fort and The Point, where the Shenandoah and Potomac rivers and three states meet. Go river rafting, hike the Appalachian Trail (AppalachianTrail.org), and enjoy a wine-tasting in Virginia's Loudoun County (VisitLoudoun.org). Check Airbnb.com for historic home, cabin, or farmhouse rentals.

Cape May, New Jersey: With its delightful Victorian architecture, circa-1859 lighthouse and two-mile oceanfront promenade, Cape May (CapeMay.com) has charm to spare. Billed as "America's Original Seaside Resort," there's the World War II Lookout Tower, fishing excursions, biking, kayaking, wine-tasting, and ghost tours. Stay at Cape Resort's Virginia Cottages (CapeResorts.com/cottages), five atmospheric Victorian homes right in town.

SOUTHEAST

Charleston to Savannah: Just 108 miles separate Charleston (CharlestonCVB.com) and Savannah (VisitSavannah.com), where historic homes and gardens plus savory Lowcountry cuisine combine to create a springtime road trip that's a feast for the senses. Stroll amid the colorful mansions of The Battery in Charleston…explore Savannah's 22 moss-draped squares…visit Civil War sites at Fort Sumter and the Secessionville Historic District…and tarry for a while in Beaufort (BeaufortSC.org), Kiawah Island (KiawahIsland.org), or Tybee Island (VisitTybee.com). Airbnb.com has beach-home rentals along the coast.

Great Smoky Mountains National Park: Spring means rushing waterfalls, wildflower meadows, and sightings of deer, elk, and even black bear. The park (nps.gov/grsm) is located in Tennessee and North Carolina. Activities include fishing, hiking, and kayaking. The park's Tennessee gateway in lively Gatlinburg (Gatlinburg.com) offers zip lining, mini golf, and a 2.1-mile scenic cable car. Book a cabin managed by CabinsOfTheSmokyMountains.com.

Natchez, Mississippi: Beat the heat with a springtime visit to Natchez (VisitNatchez.org), boasting 1,000+ structures listed on the National Register of Historic Places. In addition to grand homes, the city has five walking trails, multiple Civil War sites, Natchez Trace State Park (TNStateParks.com) for scenic hikes, and Natchez City Cemetery, known for its quirky tombstones. Sleep amid history in a home or cottage booked via Airbnb.com or Vrbo.com.

MIDWEST

Northern Michigan: Hop a ferry (after May 1) to travel back in time by horse-drawn carriage or explore by bike on car-free Mackinac Island, home to the circa-1887 Grand Hotel and 18th-century Fort Mackinac. Discover nearby towns such as Petoskey (PetoskeyArea.com), Charlevoix (VisitCharlevoix.com), and Traverse City (TraverseCity.com) to enjoy boating, birding, and golf. MackinacIsland.org lists rentals, or stay at Boyne Mountain (BoyneMountain.com).

Western Pennsylvania: Laurel Highlands (GoLaurelHighlands.com) is ideal for sightseeing. Visit Frank Lloyd Wright's Fallingwater and Kentuck Knob…pay your respects at the Flight 93 Memorial (nps.gov/flni)…and get visually swept away by the rapids of the Youghiogheny River in Ohiopyle (Ohiopyle.org). Day-trip to Pittsburgh's Phipps Conservatory and Botanical Gardens. Refuel at a craft brewery (DiscoverTheBurgh.com). Search Laurel Highlands vacation-home rentals on Vrbo.com.

Northwest Arkansas and the Ozark Mountains: There's plenty to explore amid the lakes, rivers, and woods of the Ozark Mountains in Northwest Arkansas (NorthwestArkansas.org). The region is home to several state parks (ArkansasStateParks.com) and Ozark–St. Francis National Forests (fs.usda.gov/osfnf) and hundreds of miles of hiking trails. Search for cabins on Airbnb.com, or book at The Woods Cabins (TheWoodsCabins.com).

ROCKIES

Southwest Colorado: Tour the more than 700-year-old Pueblo cave dwellings at Mesa Verde (nps.gov/meve)…ride the historic Durango and Silverton Narrow Gauge Railroad…visit the prehistoric Black Canyon (NPS.gov/blca). Telluride Resort (Telluride ResortLodging.com) makes a terrific base and has a large inventory of condo and vacation-home rentals.

Whitefish, Montana: This gateway to Glacier National Park (nps.gov/glac) is known for its surreal blue glacial lakes, scenic drives, and 700 miles of walking/hiking trails. By late May, activities such as biking, fishing, boating, hot-air ballooning, and wildlife spotting resume, although hiking trails at this elevation don't melt out until July. Whitefish (ExploreWhitefish.com) has a wide selection of rentals offering easy access to the national park.

Jackson Hole, Wyoming: Visit two national parks—Yellowstone (nps.gov/yell) with its geysers and Grand Teton (nps.gov/grte) with its majestic peaks. Enjoy spring skiing, hiking, mountain biking, and zip lining as you explore the mountain (VisitJacksonHole.com). Wildlife safaris, horseback riding, and hiking amid wildflowers are popular in spring and summer. Consider booking a cabin at Rustic Inn Creekside Resort & Spa (RusticInnAtJH.com).

SOUTHWEST

Sedona, Arizona: The views are heavenly in Sedona, where spring temperatures are ideal for hiking, biking, golfing, fishing, and four-wheeling amid the spectacular red rock formations and pine forests. This recreation mecca and artist colony is 90 minutes north of Phoenix and two hours from the Grand Canyon (nps.gov/grca). VisitSedona.com lists a variety of cabin and vacation-home rentals.

Santa Fe to Taos, New Mexico: Located 90 minutes apart, enjoy southwestern architecture, eclectic galleries, and flavorful cuisine as well as hiking, fly-fishing, rafting, horseback riding, llama trekking, and crossing the Rio Grande Gorge Bridge, set 650 feet above the river. Check SantaFe.org for rentable casitas and haciendas, or book an adobe casita at Casa Gallina (CasaGallina.net) in Taos (Taos.org).

Utah: Home to the "Mighty 5" national parks—Zion, Bryce Canyon, Canyonlands, Arches, and Capitol Reef—this region is famous for its sculptural rock formations and slot canyons. Scenic drives abound, and stargazing is excellent. Try "glamping" at Under Canvas (UnderCanvas.com) in Moab and Zion (VisitUtah.com).

WEST COAST

California's Central Coast to Yosemite: Take a 250-mile road trip that starts in the Pacific coast towns of Morro Bay (MorroBay.org) and Cambria (VisitCambriaCA.com) with beach walks and seal spotting. Next, wine-tasting in Paso Robles (TravelPaso.com), and finish by hiking or picnicking amid the grandeur of Yosemite National Park (nps.gov/yose). Check Airbnb.com and Vrbo.com for rentals in all three areas.

Willamette Valley, Oregon: The verdant Willamette Valley (OregonWineCountry.org) is the perfect spot to enjoy wine-tasting on airy outdoor patios, dine on regional farm-to-table cuisine, explore food trails, pedal through picturesque farmland, go hot-air ballooning, and hike to cascading waterfalls. Check vacation-home rental options at WillametteWines.com.

San Juan Islands, Washington: Venture offshore with a car-ferry crossing to this trio of islands—San Juan, Orcas, and Lopez—to whale watch, bird-watch, hike, bike, and kayak. Local farms, craft breweries, and wineries add an artisanal culinary element. Check Visit SanJuans.com for vacation-home options.

Tasty Toppings for 4th of July Burgers

Linda Gassenheimer, an award-winning author of several cookbooks, most recently, *The 12-Week Diabetes Cookbook*. She writes the syndicated newspaper column "Dinner in Minutes." DinnerInMinutes.com. She hosts the *Food, News and Views* WDNA radio show and podcast.

Add some fun and international flair to your burgers. These five toppings are perfect for grilled or pan-sautéed burgers—whether beef, turkey, or any other patty you put on a bun. Each recipe tops four burgers.

Greek Burger

Tzatziki is a yogurt-based Greek sauce (which you can make a few hours in advance). Feta cheese and fresh mint add extra Mediterranean flair.

½ cup peeled, seeded, and diced cucumber

½ cup plain, nonfat Greek-style yogurt

2 crushed garlic cloves

½ teaspoon dried dill

½ teaspoon lemon juice

Salt and freshly ground black pepper

½ cup crumbled feta cheese

¼ cup fresh mint leaves torn into small pieces

Mix cucumber, yogurt, garlic, dill, and lemon juice together. Sprinkle with salt and pepper to taste. Set aside.

Place cooked burgers on the bottom on the burger buns. Spoon the sauce evenly over each burger. Sprinkle the feta cheese on top and then the mint leaves.

Fajita Burger

Caramelized onion and red bell pepper are spooned over melted Cheddar for a sizzling experience.

2 Tablespoons olive oil

1 large onion, sliced (about 2 cups—any type of onion can be used)

1 large red bell pepper, seeded and sliced (about 2 cups)

½ teaspoon red pepper flakes (optional)

Salt

4 slices sharp Cheddar cheese (about ¾ ounce each)

Heat olive oil in a large skillet over medium heat. Add onion and red bell pepper, and sauté five to six minutes, stirring occasionally. Reduce heat to low, and continue to sauté about 20 minutes, stirring occasionally until the onions and peppers become soft and creamy. Add the red pepper flakes if desired, and salt to taste. Toss well. This can be made a day ahead and refrigerated. Bring to room temperature before serving.

Whether grilling or sautéing the burgers, cook one side until a crust forms, two to three minutes until the burger easily releases from the grate or skillet. Turn over, and cook two to three minutes. Place a cheese slice on top of each burger. Close the grill or cover the skillet, and cook two to three minutes more or until desired temperature. Place each burger on a hamburger bun base, and top with the onion-and-pepper mixture. Or you could even serve it wrapped in a tortilla.

Corn Salsa Burger

Charred corn kernels are the base for this spicy make-ahead salsa.

2 ears corn on the cob to make 2½ cups of kernels (frozen corn can be used, too)

1 small jalapeño pepper, seeded and chopped (about 1 Tablespoon)

¾ cup diced fresh tomatoes, well drained

½ teaspoon chipotle powder

Cilantro leaves

Salt

1½ Tablespoons mayonnaise

Remove the husk and silk from corn. Spray with vegetable oil spray. Place on the grill grates over direct heat. Turn the corn when dark spots start to appear (about one minute). Continue until all sides are spotted, about five to six minutes. Or place corn in a large skillet over medium-high heat sautéing in hot oil until slightly browned. Let cool to the touch, and cut kernels off the cob. Place the cob in a large bowl standing up—with a sharp knife, cut downward close to the cob, catching the kernels and the corn juice. Add jalapeño pepper, tomatoes, chipotle powder, cilantro leaves and salt to taste. Mix well. Add the mayonnaise, and mix to combine all ingredients. Place cooked burgers on the bottom half of a burger bun, and spoon salsa on top.

Honey-Mustard Avocado

Honey mustard lends a sweet kick, arugula leaves have a peppery finish, and avocado adds a creamy touch.

2 ripe Hass avocados

2 Tablespoons lemon juice

4 Tablespoons honey mustard

Arugula leaves (about 1 cup)

Cut avocados in half, peel, and remove the pit. Slice into thin slices, and place in a bowl. Add lemon juice to the bowl, and gently coat the avocado with the juice. (If you're using fresh lemons, you can also add the zest.) Place the cooked burgers on hamburger buns, and spread one tablespoon of honey mustard over each burger. Cover each with the avocado slices, and add arugula on top of the avocado.

Wasabi Burger

Wasabi, an Asian root vegetable, is the Japanese version of horseradish.

8 Tablespoons butter, softened to room temperature

¼ cup chopped scallions (green part only)

2 teaspoons wasabi powder

1 teaspoon reduced-sodium soy sauce

Beat butter until smooth using a hand mixer or food processor. Add scallions, wasabi powder, and soy sauce. Beat well to thoroughly mix. Roll into a log about five inches long and two inches in diameter. Wrap in plastic wrap, and refrigerate (or freeze) until firm. When needed, remove from the refrigerator, cut into four slices, and bring to room temperature. About two minutes before the burgers are fully cooked, place one slice on each burger and cover with the grill top or lid, letting the butter melt over the burger.

How to Get Beyond Small Talk

If the subject matter of your dinner parties never seems to get any deeper than the weather, it isn't because your friends are boring—they likely crave meaningful conversation as much as you do but feel hindered by social conventions. Consider using a set of conversation-starter questions such as, "If you had to change one big decision you have made, what would it be?" At a loss for such prompts? Look up Irrational Labs "No Small Talk" cards and the list of 36 "closeness-generating" questions from psychologist Arthur Aron.

Dan Ariely, PhD, the James B. Duke Professor of Psychology and Behavioral Economics at Duke University in Durham, North Carolina, writing in *The Wall Street Journal*.

6 Unsung Wine Regions in North America Worth a Visit

Donna Heiderstadt, a travel expert who has visited almost 100 countries and traveled to all seven continents. During her 24 years writing about travel, her work has appeared in leading national magazines and travel websites such as TravelAndLeisure.com, Fodors.com, ShermansTravel.com and RobbReport.com.

If asked to name North America's top wine regions, you'd most likely cite Napa and Sonoma in California and perhaps New York's Finger Lakes region. It's highly unlikely that Arizona, Virginia, or Ontario would be on your radar. But vintners in these locales are producing some delicious wines.

Bonus: Their varied settings provide scenic and sometimes historic backdrops for wine tasting. *Here are six unsung wine regions that are worth a visit...*

VERDE VALLEY & OLD TOWN SCOTTSDALE, ARIZONA

Known more for saguaro cacti than Sauvignon Blanc, this desert landscape is nevertheless producing some pretty impressive wines, thanks to enterprising vintners and the hospitable terroir of the high desert in northern Arizona's Verde Valley. A great tasting experience is available on the Verde Valley Wine Trail (VVWineTrail.com) and in a pair of historic neighborhoods—Old Town Scottsdale (ScottsdaleWineTrail.com) and Old Town Cottonwood, which is about two hours north. Each has five tasting rooms. Top labels are Burning Tree Cellars, Arizona Stronghold, Paige Springs Cellars and Merkin Vineyards.

Insider tip: Visit in May or November/early December for the best weather.

Where to stay: Plan a day trip to Cottonwood, and stay in Scottsdale with its vibrant restaurant, nightlife, and arts scenes. Book a room at Hotel Valley Ho (HotelValleyHo.com), a restored midcentury-modern gem that's walking distance from the Scottsdale Wine Trail. Rates from $235/night. Restaurants such as Postino and FnB have extensive Arizona wine offerings.

LOUDOUN COUNTY & OLD TOWN ALEXANDRIA, VIRGINIA

In northern Virginia, you can enjoy both the rich history and culinary scene in Old Town Alexandria (VisitAlexandriaVa.com), set on the Potomac River just outside Washington, DC, and the bucolic countryside of Loudoun County (VisitLoudoun.org), where horse farms are interspersed with 40-plus wineries. Old Town makes an ideal base for wine-tasting day trips, since Loudoun is only about an hour away. Enjoy sips at sustainability-focused Sunset Hills Vineyard, where solar panels power a circa-1870 barn-turned-tasting-room serving a mix of Rosé, Cabernet Franc, and red blends…Stone Tower Winery for panoramic views and premium wines such as Cabernet, Chardonnay, and Petit Verdot… Breaux Vineyards featuring 17 grape varietals and a New Orleans French Quarter–style tasting room…and Chrysalis Vineyards, home to the largest planting in the world of America's oldest native grape—the Norton varietal. Back in Alexandria, stroll King Street, which has great restaurants—Vermilion for modern farm-to-table cuisine…and shops—The Hour for vintage barware and Wine Gallery 108 for more local wines to tote home.

Insider tip: Time your stay with the Spring or Fall Wine Festival, held in May and October at George Washington's estate at Mount Vernon, to sample offerings from 20 Virginia wineries.

Where to stay: Stay at Morrison House Alexandria (MorrisonHouse.com), a 45-room property in Old Town where The Study features a few Virginia wines to complement an elevated small-plate dining menu. Rates from $185/night.

TEXAS HILL COUNTRY

Leave it to Texas to have a wine named Kick Butt Cab, which has won numerous awards for Texas Hills Vineyard in Johnson City. It's just one of more than 50 vineyards on the Texas Hill Country Wine Trail (TexasWineTrail.com), which stretches west from Austin and includes the historic, wine-centric town of Fredericksburg, home to about two dozen tasting rooms. Inviting wineries here include Becker Vineyards, known for its Malbec, Petite Sirah, and award-winning Prairie Rotie…and Grape Creek Vineyards to enjoy Tuscany-inspired architecture and wood-fired pizza as you sip a Pinot Grigio or a red blend. Fredericksburg also is a hub for German cuisine, such as the Bavarian specialties served at Ausländer.

Insider tip: If you're craving steak (this is Texas after all), book a table at Cabernet Grill to enjoy perfectly aged rib-eye or filet mignon—paired with top Texas reds.

Where to stay: Hoffman Haus (HoffmanHaus.com) is a delightfully decorated bed-and-breakfast just a block from Fredericksburg's Main Street. Rates from $155/night.

NORTH FORK OF LONG ISLAND

The Hamptons, on the South Fork of eastern Long Island, gets more hype, but the North Fork is for wine lovers. Located two hours from New York City, the region is home to more than 35 wineries and the North Fork Wine Trail (LIWines.com), which meanders from Jamesport through Mattituck, Cutchogue, Southold, and Peconic to Greenport. The North Fork is known for its Merlot, but other top varietals are Cabernet Sauvignon, Pinot Noir, Cabernet Franc and Sauvignon Blanc. Leading vineyards include Bedell Cellars, Lenz Winery, Lieb Cellars, Osprey's Dominion, and Paumanok Vineyards. Restaurants specialize in locally sourced dining—from creamy seafood chowder and crispy fried clams at Braun's Grill in Cutchogue to seasonally inspired menus at North Fork Table & Inn in Southold and creative seafood at Noah's in Greenport.

Insider tip: Visit midweek from April to November to avoid traffic, although weekends are more festive (some wineries offer live music). You can also take the ferry from New

London, Connecticut, to Orient Point, New York, and drive from there.

Where to stay: It's B&B-style at the Rose Hill Inn (Rosehill-Vineyards.com/farmhouse-inn) in Mattituck. Rates from $219/night. Or stay on the water in Greenport at the 35-room Harborfront Inn (TheHarborfrontInn.com). Rates from $230/night.

SAN DIEGO

Wine bars and tasting rooms have long proliferated in downtown San Diego, but 1870's Gold Rush Julian (VisitJulian.com) probably isn't on your radar. It's home to several wine-tasting rooms and more than a half-dozen boutique wineries, but it is better known for the sugar rush created by apple pies served daily at the Julian Pie Company and Mom's Pie House. This makes for a delicious day trip—it's about 70 minutes from San Diego. Menghini Winery, located near Volcan Mountain, has a rustic tasting room for sampling its Syrah, Cabernet, and Sauvignon Blanc. Nearby Volcan Mountain Winery is equally charming and offers tastes of Viognier, Sangiovese, Old Vine Zinfandel, and more. And don't miss Orfila Vineyards & Winery, known for its French and Italian varietals and set amid vine-covered hills in neighboring Escondido.

Where to stay: Kimpton Hotel Palomar (HotelPalomarSanDiego.com) in San Diego, which offers a complimentary nightly wine hour. Rates from $189/night.

NIAGARA-ON-THE-LAKE, ONTARIO

Toronto, with its international dining scene, is just to the north, and Niagara Falls is to the south, making the scenic slice of heaven known as Niagara-on-the-Lake (WineriesOfNiagaraOnTheLake.com) a convenient spot to enjoy both sightseeing and wine tasting. Here, you'll find 20-plus wineries producing reds, whites, and rosés—as well as the region's unique specialty, ice wine. If you've never tasted ice wine, head to Inniskillin Wines, where a variety of tours and tasting options will introduce you to the nuances of these sweet and concentrated wines made from Riesling and Cabernet Franc grapes picked when the temperature sinks to -8°C (18°F) for long enough. Neighboring Riverview Cellars is known for its Gewürztraminer, Bordeaux-style reds, and ice wines…Reif Estate Winery offers four-glass wine "flights" in its Sensory Wine Bar… and Peller Estates has gorgeous grounds and the 10Below Icewine Lounge.

Where to stay: 124 on Queen Hotel & Spa (124Queen.com), a boutique property located in Niagara-on-the-Lake's old town. Rates are from U.S. $200/night.

18

Your Success Story

Time and Money Traps That Can Rob You of Happiness

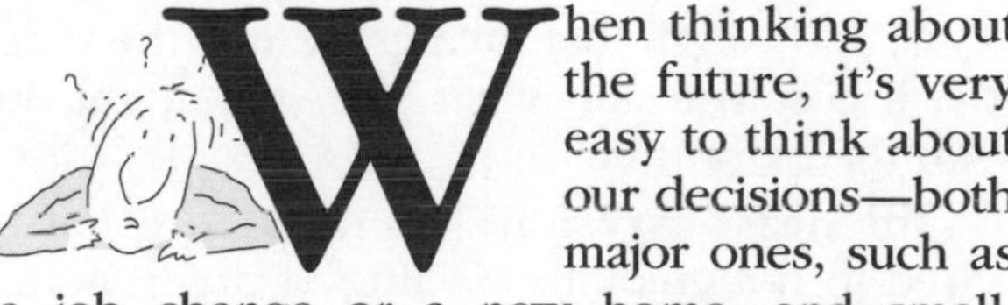

When thinking about the future, it's very easy to think about our decisions—both major ones, such as a job change or a new home, and small, everyday ones such as where to fill up your gas tank—in terms of dollars and cents, yet it is very hard to think about what it costs to give up our time to have that money. This money-focused mind-set can have seriously negative consequences for our happiness. Research shows that being willing to give up money to have more leisure time is a predictor of greater happiness, better relationships, less stress, even being more physically fit.

Researchers define "time poverty" as the feeling of having too many things to do—both professional and personal—and not enough time to do them. An astonishing 80 percent of working Americans report feeling time-poor. My research shows that the emotional impact of being time-poor can be greater than the emotional impact of being unemployed. We all should strive toward greater time-affluence, which is the opposite of time-poverty. Another way of thinking about time-affluence is that if you could write out the time spent in your ideal day in terms of social, work, and leisure, your ideal day and your actual day would be congruent with one another.

Here are a few of my favorite tips for bringing more time-affluence into your life...

ACCOUNT FOR YOUR TIME

It's critical to account for your time because it easily goes missing.

Ashley Whillans, PhD, assistant professor at Harvard Business School, Boston, and a leading scholar in the time and happiness research field. She is author of *Time Smart: How to Reclaim Your Time and Live a Happier Life*. AWhillans.com

Try this: At the end of next Tuesday (I suggest a Tuesday because Tuesdays tend to be average workdays), fill out a time diary to observe how you spend your time. What activities did you do? How positive did you feel those activities were? How meaningful? If you find that you're stuck in frustrating meetings or other activities that zap your energy 80 percent of every day, is that really how you want to spend your life?

Then think consciously about choosing time over money. We know very well, from decades of research, that a $10,000 raise will give you a half-point bump on a 10-point happiness scale. But there are many other things we can do that will give us a similar happiness boost. So think about each tiny decision you make in a day as having an income equivalent in terms of happiness. For example, just shifting your mind-set from valuing money to valuing time—in the absence of changing your behavior at all—is worth the income equivalent (in terms of happiness) of making $2,200 more personal income a year. Spending 30 minutes exercising every day will give you a mood bump that our research shows is equivalent to earning an additional $1,800 a year. For people who tend toward valuing money over time, being mindful of these dollar equivalents on activities helps improve life balance.

AVOID THESE "TIME TRAPS"

A time trap is something that makes you time-poor but that you might not even be aware you're doing. *Learning to recognize and correct for these traps can ratchet up your time-affluence…*

- **Technology trap.** The reason we're all so time-poor isn't necessarily because we're working more hours. We actually have more leisure time than we used to. The problem is that our leisure time gets broken into small, unsavory moments of free time that are easily lost because our technology is constantly pinging us. Our brains are sucked out of the present moment and thrown into the online environment, which undermines our enjoyment of the present. (I call these shredded-up bits of freedom "time confetti.") The solution is simple—when it's time for leisure, turn off your phone and choose to focus on something you really want to do rather than piddling it away on social media.

- **"Yes…Damn!" effect.** As part of human nature, we believe that we'll have more time in the future than we do in the present, so we overcommit our tomorrow even though we're very busy today ("Yes, I'll help you move next Saturday…Damn! I didn't know I'd be this busy."). To avoid this trap, ask yourself, *If I couldn't do it in the next two hours, should I really be saying yes to doing it next week?*

- **Undervalued time.** People who value money over time often will spend hours researching a purchase for days in order to save 50 bucks or will choose a flight with lots of connections in order to save $75 in airfare. It's easy to understand why we make such choices—we readily comprehend the value of $50 or $75 but have a harder time valuing the time lost. Yet such decisions do have a cost.

For example, I've calculated that habitually driving six minutes farther to save five cents per gallon of gas will, in a year, have saved $108 and cost nearly five hours of time. That puts a price on your time of $22 per hour and does not account for the opportunity cost of the happiness-inducing activities you might have spent your five hours on.

Solution: Train yourself to recognize the moments when you're making "cheaper" decisions, and weigh that savings against the time it will cost you and what else you might do with the extra time.

- **Idleness aversion.** Humans are hard-wired to not enjoy the feeling of doing nothing, sitting alone with only our thoughts. When we have an important, thinking-heavy task before us, we'll often focus instead on smaller tasks, such as reading e-mail. Responding to a message makes us feel like we're doing something proactive. It gives us a sense of self-efficacy and of being in control of our lives—even though it's not moving the needle on truly important activities.

Solution: Put "focus blocks" into your calendar, and don't let anything else in there. Thinking time is thinking time. No mail, no distractions, only heads-down stuff.

The secret to doing this successfully: Create three such blocks for your week. Set aside the first of them (say, 15 to 30 minutes on Monday morning) exclusively for planning what you'll do in the other two. Treat that time like it's the most important doctor's appointment in the world.

• **Merely urgent.** Any possible use of your time can be assessed along two axes—urgency, requiring immediate attention…and importance, contributing to your long-term goals. Ask yourself, *If I had to classify this activity, in which quadrant is it located? Is it urgent but not important? Urgent and important? Not important? Not urgent?* Being mindful of those two measures helps us avoid a lifetime of chasing after things that are urgent but ultimately unimportant, while the things that we care about but don't require immediate attention are put off forever. To make sure you get to those important-but-not-urgent tasks (writing that novel, revamping your budget), you have to schedule them in to what I call "proactive time." Maybe they go into the focus blocks described above or maybe they're their own category, but they must be sacrosanct and inviolable.

GOOD TO KNOW…

Job Apps and Sites for Older Workers

GetSetup (GetSetUp.io) hires people to teach online classes—you can work from home on your own schedule. The company employs many people ages 55 and older at a rate of $25/hour. CoolWorks (CoolWorks.com) specializes in seasonal jobs in guest services and hospitality, with pay varying by position. Rover (Rover.com) offers pet-sitting, home-sitting, and similar jobs, and says pay can be up to $1,000/month. Rent a Grandma (RentAGrandma.com) offers jobs for caregivers, chefs, child-care workers, and more. You post a résumé for potential clients to see and negotiate rates with them.

Clark.com

If you find that a task is not important and not urgent, why are you doing it? Such tasks—home repairs, for example—are great candidates for delegating or outsourcing. If you're hesitant about spending money on such a "luxury," it might help you to know that outsourcing your most unpleasant tasks is worth the happiness equivalent of an $18,000 salary increase.

How to Get Hired at Age 50 or Older

Start searching immediately...job prospects often are better when someone is newly unemployed. Use your network—it is the best way to get hired. If at all possible, find a personal contact at the company where you would like to work and make that person your entry point. Reassure a younger manager who is considering you that you are fine with the role you are applying for and expect to take the manager's direction. Never mention your age or the interviewer's age. Shorten your résumé, omitting anything from more than 10 years ago. Explain why you are not overqualified—focus on the benefits you will bring to the specific position you want. Show your comfort with technology, including social media, during the interview process—for example, refer to articles you found on the company's Twitter feed.

Money.USNews.com

Change Your Mind About How to Change Minds

Jonah Berger, PhD, professor of marketing at The Wharton School of The University of Pennsylvania. He is author of *The Catalyst: How to Change Anyone's Mind*. JonahBerger.com

Go ahead—prod people into accepting your point of view…bury them with evidence that supports your position…and carefully recount why a rethink is in their own best interest. Despite your best efforts, much of the time you'll accomplish nothing.

Whether you're trying to convince your spouse to change his/her eating habits or convince consumers to buy a new product, the tactics traditionally employed to change minds usually are ineffective. In fact, sometimes these efforts accidentally push people to dig in their heels even further. Consider all the times you've felt insulted by a manipulative advertisement…or rolled your eyes at political views voiced by someone on the other side of the aisle.

The secret of successfully changing minds often lies not in making a persuasive case but rather in removing the hidden barriers that prevent people from modifying their views. *Three of the biggest barriers and how to overcome them…*

WHEN PUSHED, PEOPLE PUSH BACK

When you try to persuade people of something, their natural reaction is to push back in an attempt to reassure themselves that they remain in control of their own opinions. These people might focus on perceived shortcomings in your argument or voice skepticism about the veracity of your facts, but this may have little to do with the merits of your case and everything to do with the threat that your attempt to convince them poses to their sense of freedom and self-control.

What to do: Rather than try to convince people of what you believe, use strategies that encourage them to convince themselves—people are far more likely to accept ideas that seem to spring from their own minds. *Among the ways to do this…*

- **Provide a carefully selected range of choices.** Offer several options that are all acceptable to you, then let the person you are trying to win over make the final selection from among these.

Example: A wife is bored with the Italian restaurant her husband chooses almost every time the couple eats out. Before their next date night, she asks if he would rather try a Mexican restaurant or a Thai restaurant or a different Italian restaurant. The husband retains control over the final decision, so there's a good chance he won't rebel against his wife's attempt to steer him away from his actual preference.

- **Warn the person that someone is trying to manipulate him/her.** This turns people's natural push-back tendencies to your advantage.

Example: A Florida antismoking campaign found success by warning teens that the tobacco industry was trying to manipulate them with its ads. Rather than push back against the antismoking campaign, as teens tend to do, they pushed back against the tobacco companies and the state's smoking rates among teens declined.

- **Ask questions rather than make challenging statements.** If you suspect that the person already knows he/she is in the wrong, don't tell him this—ask a question that encourages him to say or think it.

Example: The owner of a test-prep company who saw that many would-be business school students weren't putting sufficient hours into studying for the GMATs asked her class, "Why are you here? What's your goal?" The answer, of course, was to get into a top business school. She told the students that 250,000 people take the GMATs every year, and the top 20 MBA programs accept around 10,000 total—only 4 percent make the cut. She then asked how many hours they thought they needed to study not just to do well but to land safely in that top 4 percent.

- **Call attention to a gap between what someone is saying and what the person is doing.** Quote this person's own words back to him—people tend to agree with what they themselves have said.

Example: Your spouse dislikes a local company but does business with it anyway because of its low prices. Rather than say you don't want to work with the company, you could say, "You know, I think you were right when you said, 'These people don't respect their customers.'"

PEOPLE STICK TO STATUS QUO

One big reason that it's hard to get people to change their minds is that people don't like to change. Most people will go on buying the same brands, voting for the same political party and driving the same route to work rather than investigate other options unless it becomes painfully obvious that their initial selection is lacking. Economists estimate that the potential upside of taking action must be around 2.5 times the potential downside before the average person will make a move.

What to do: *Try one of these approaches to stress the benefits of making a change…*

• **Expose the hidden costs of not changing.** The costs of change often are more obvious than the costs of keeping things as they are—when we try something new, we often have to learn something new or buy something new, for example. But that doesn't mean the current state of affairs actually has lower costs. Perhaps people have grown so used to the way things are that they no longer notice its costs…or perhaps these costs are hidden because they're not coming out of people's pockets.

Example: Your spouse resists learning how to use a new piece of time-saving consumer technology because he believes his current way of doing things works just fine. Work out how much time he would save whenever he uses the technology, and multiply that by the number of times he would use it each year. If it saves just one minute every day, that's more than six hours a year. Tell him that if saving six hours of effort isn't important to him, then he shouldn't mind spending six hours that weekend doing chores that would normally fall to you.

• **Reframe a change as a return to the way things used to be.** This can overcome people's aversion to doing things that seem new and different.

Example: A husband doesn't want to downsize from a house to an apartment in retirement. His wife could frame the move as a return to the way things were before their first child was born, when they shared a small apartment in the city.

• **Preserve treasured memories.** Sometimes people resist change even when they know that the way things are is less than ideal because it reminds them of earlier, better times. Search for a way to preserve these positive memories yet still change.

Example: A mother doesn't want to transform a child's room into a home gym even though the child is grown and living elsewhere. She could take photos of the child's room, and hang these on the walls of the new exercise room. The photos can preserve the memories, especially since the room will be visited much more often now that it has a new purpose.

PEOPLE BALK AT EXTREME CHANGE

A common lament in our politically divided society is that we would have an easier time coming together as a country if everyone would take the time to listen to the opinions of their political opponents, rather than exclusively to media outlets and social media slanted toward the positions they already hold. A 2018 study by a Duke University sociology professor put that theory to the test. For one month, more than 1,500 politically partisan Twitter users read messages expressing views from people on the other side of the aisle.

Results: Republican participants became more conservative, and Democrats became more liberal. Not only had exposure to the other side's opinions not won them over, it had pushed them further away.

The problem isn't that people won't consider ideas different from their own—it's that they won't consider ideas vastly different from their own, at least not with their firmly held beliefs.

What to do: Seek modest progress, not massive shifts, when trying to change minds. Had that Duke study asked partisans to follow moderate Twitter messages, rather than messages from the other side of the aisle, it might have succeeded in bringing its participants a little closer. View modest change as the first stepping stone on a path to greater change.

Example: An employee is tasked with cutting costs on office supplies, but his boss is reluctant to drop the office's very reliable long-term supplier. The employee convinces the boss to try a new supplier for one small order of supplies. Once the order has arrived quickly and at a lower cost, the employee suggests more and bigger orders from the new supplier.

9 Ways to Look Better on Video Calls

Jennifer Jager, creative director of Plum Productions, a Boca Raton–based video-production company. She is host of the YouTube channel MyVideo101.com.

Is that really what I look like? Video calls are a great way to keep you connected—whether it's a chat with family and friends or a video conference—but it can be frightening to see how you look through the distortion of the camera. *Here are nine ways to look much better on a video call...*

• **Position the camera lens at your eye level or slightly above.** When a laptop computer sits on a desk or table, its camera typically angles up your face, creating a double chin and forcing conversation partners to look into your nose. The same goes for tablets and phones propped up on tables, but it doesn't necessarily apply to desktop monitors, many of which have a camera built in above the screen...or to a freestanding webcam that's attached to the top of a monitor. You'll look better if your camera is at eye level or very slightly above, so place the digital device on a stack of books and/or lower your desk chair if necessary. Positioning a camera a few inches above eye level even can have a subtle slimming effect.

• **Look at the camera lens.** It feels more natural to watch the on-screen image of the person or people you're speaking with, but looking at the lens makes it appear that you're maintaining strong eye contact.

• **Face toward the main light source.** On a bright day, face a window. Otherwise position a light in front of you but behind the camera. A shaded floor lamp is a good choice—the shade creates "diffuse" light, which is more flattering than direct light. If you don't want to reposition lights, open a blank word-processing document on the digital device you're using for the video call and then expand this document's window to fill the screen—a blank screen provides a surprising amount of illumination. The white light of screens can have an unflattering cold tint, however, so if you can easily adjust the background color of this word-processing document, choose a warmer tone. A pale orange background color will create a flattering tone for most skin tones, but try various background colors to find what makes you look best. (In Microsoft Word, try selecting "Page Color" from the "Design" tab.) If you do this, consider making the image of anyone you're talking to as small as possible so you block out as little of the light-providing word-processing document as possible.

Caution: Do not have a bright window or light behind you—that could reduce you to a virtual silhouette. Do not use overhead lighting as your main light source—that can cast harsh shadows on your face.

• **Get some distance from the camera.** A face that completely fills the screen is off-putting—like someone standing way too close. It also makes any wrinkles or skin issues more obvious.

Helpful: Position yourself far enough from the camera so that the frame includes your shoulders and the top half of your chest. Imagine where the knot of your necktie would be if you were wearing one, then place one hand horizontally below this knot. Set the bottom of the frame at the bottom of your hand.

• **Simplify your wardrobe.** Patterned and print shirts can be distracting—solid colors are the safest choice. Keep jewelry simple, too, and avoid pieces that jangle when you move. If you wear makeup, apply the amount you normally wear plus 10 percent—makeup tends to be slightly harder to see on camera. If you wear eyeglasses, look at your image on screen after you position yourself and your camera for the call. Conversation partners will find it distracting if light reflects off your glasses directly in front of your pupils. If this happens, reposition yourself and/or your camera or lighting slightly...or go without eyeglasses if that's feasible. It's no big deal if light reflects off eyeglasses near lens edges. If there's time, look at your own image on screen before the call to confirm that everything looks good.

• **Watch your posture.** Sit straight with your shoulders back. Slouching makes shirts look rumpled. Sliding down in a chair can create the impression of a double chin.

• **Include depth in your background.** Viewers will find it visually interesting if the backdrop extends well into the distance, so try to choose a big enough room where this is possible. But this is only a good idea if this large space is attractive and uncluttered. Otherwise, position yourself so an unobtrusive wall or tidy bookshelf serves as your background. If there's a bookshelf behind you, make sure there aren't any books you don't want people knowing you read.

• **Wire your computer directly into your router.** Slow Wi-Fi speeds can lead to choppy, low-resolution video and other distracting issues. If your Wi-Fi sometimes gives you trouble, you can take it out of the equation by connecting the computer directly to your router using an ethernet cable.

• **Upgrade your equipment.** The cameras built into computers, tablets, and phones are fine for most uses, but if you're willing to invest some money to improve how you look on screen, buy a highly rated external camera.

Example: Logitech C525 USB HD Webcam has an autofocus feature that keeps you in focus even if you move around during the call and an advanced light correction feature that delivers bright, crisp images even in relatively dim settings ($99).

If that's more than you're willing to spend, consider buying an external microphone. Even a cheap clip mic, available for $10 or $20 online, will be a dramatic improvement, if only because you can position it much closer to you. Headsets and earbuds with built-in microphones also can help, but I find that an external microphone is best. Taking calls in a room that has carpeting, drapes, and other soft surfaces can cut down on echoes. Improving sound quality won't literally make you look better on camera, but it is among the best ways to make people think that your video seems more professional overall...for reasons they can't quite pin down.

"Speed Bumps" Can Help Stop You from Overdosing on Your Phone

Turn off biometric unlocking: The seconds it takes to type in a password—instead of unlocking your phone with your face or thumbprint—might be long enough for you to think twice about getting sucked back into the virtual world. *Delete time-sucking apps:* Remove temptations that drain you of productivity. *Turn off notifications:* They're the siren call of technology. *Shut off the Internet:* Use apps that block access to specific sites, or schedule times when you unplug your modem.

Alexandra Samuel, PhD, technology researcher and author of *Work Smarter With Social Media.*

Create a Home Office in a Small Space

Bonnie Casamassima, MFA, adjunct professor at Savannah College of Art and Design, where she teaches the psychology of interior design. She is founder of Interweave People Place, an Atlanta-based consulting organization supporting people virtually in their homes and workplaces. InterweavePeoplePlace.com

Need to work at home, but don't have a spare room to convert into a home office? Then you'll have to carve out a workspace in a room that's also used for other purposes. *How to do it right...*

• **Create visual distinctions between work and living space.** Position a bookshelf or folding screen/room divider to function as a partition. Add an area rug to further emphasize that it's a separate area. The visual distinction will help your mind focus on work matters in the workspace...and leave work matters behind when you're in another part of the room, whether the room is a living room or a bedroom.

• **Choose a desk that shuts.** A roll-top desk or secretary desk can be closed when not in use, creating the reminder, *I'm not working right now.* Closing the desk also hides clutter.

• **Choose office storage that looks like residential furniture.** Metal filing cabinets and/or open shelving full of notebooks and folders look jarring and out of place in your living area. Instead, choose shelving that fits the room's décor and encloses messy files and other workplace clutter in attractive enclosed boxes or bins that slide easily onto these shelves. Search "storage bin" or "storage box" on Wayfair.com or ContainerStore.com to find options.

• **Storage units that serve double duty as seating or footrests can be a practical solution**—Wayfair.com has a wide selection.

Example: Lambertville Storage Ottomans, from $29.99.

• **Orient your workspace so you can see the room.** When home offices are crammed into small spaces, desks are often pushed against walls—sometimes they're even constructed inside alcoves or closets. Doing this forces people to face walls, which can undercut productivity. People become subconsciously unsettled, and stress levels increase when they cannot see the open space around them for extended stretches—the primitive part of the brain becomes concerned that a predator might sneak up even though rationally we know that isn't likely. If a desk or work table must be pushed against a wall because that's how it best fits the available space, choose one that has casters (or put furniture sliders or felt under the legs of a desk/table) so you can pull it out from the wall and face the room when you work...or orient it perpendicular to the wall or at an angle where you can at least see the room out of the corner of your eye.

Yes! You Can Publish Your Book: Here Are Five Secrets to Success

Jan Yager, PhD, who has spent her entire adult life working in book publishing, starting out at Macmillan followed by Grove Press. Her book, *How to Self-Publish Your Book*, is published by Square One Publishers. DrJanYager.com

Question: What do the following books have in common—*Joy of Cooking...A Christmas Carol...50 Shades of Grey?*

Answer: Each one started as a self-published book.

Working on your own masterpiece? *Here's how to avoid the most common traps as you make your way to self-publishing your first book...*

PITFALL #1: **You aim too high or too low.** It's great to have literary dreams but wanting to be the next Ernest Hemingway or Jane Austen can be paralyzing. On the other hand, if you treat writing your book like a hobby and fail to get it professionally edited and proofread, it could look amateurish in the end.

Solution: Start from where you are, and write the best book you can.

PITFALL #2: **Doing it all on your own.** There are numerous resources out there that can help you create a book that looks just as good as anything being released by the big publishing houses.

Solution: Hire various freelance professionals with the skills you need.

Show your book to those whose opinions you value such as colleagues in relevant fields and, if you think they can be objective, friends and family. You may also want to find a local writer's group that might offer valuable feedback. Most important, however, is to hire a professional editor and proofreader. All these eyes will help to assess proper flow and organization, catch typographical and grammatical errors, and help you find and solve other problems you didn't know your manuscript had.

Note: Don't hire the same person to both edit and proofread. These roles demand different skill sets.

Cover design is pivotal to catching readers' eyes and not looking "self-published." Unless you're artistically inclined, you will want to invest in a professionally produced cover, which typically costs anywhere from $100 to $1,000 or even more, depending on the designer's experience and base of operation. Internationally based designers in certain countries and talented design students eager to break into the cover-design field may be more affordable.

Start with referrals from any friends or colleagues who have satisfactorily self-published a book. Find designers, typesetters, editors, proofreaders, and others who will help make your book look great inside and out through Reedsy.com…Editorial Freelancers Association (The-EFA.org)…and the Society of Children's Book Writers and Illustrators (SCBWI.org), to name just a few of the many available resources.

PITFALL #3: **You plan to publish only a print version.** Some people love the feel of holding a physical book, but others prefer an e-book or an audiobook.

Solution: Publish in as many formats as possible.

All three formats—print, e-book, and audiobook—are ideal for sales. If that feels too daunting, start by picking one format based on your target audience and skill set. Once you launch your book in that first format, go on to each of the other formats when you can.

An e-book is faster and easier to format than a printed book and less costly to publish. Good resources for creating and selling your e-book include Amazon's Kindle Direct Publishing (KDP.Amazon.com)…Kobo (Kobo.com/us/en/p/writinglife)…and Barnes & Noble Press (Press.BarnesAndNoble.com).

Of course, most writers dream of one day holding their printed books in their hands. Popular self-publishing options for a print version include Amazon's Kindle Direct Publishing…Archway Publishing (ArchwayPublishing.com)…Author House (AuthorHouse.com)…BookBaby (BookBaby.com)…iUniverse.com…IngramSpark (IngramSpark.com)…and more. Depending upon the package that you select, some, such as BookBaby and Archway, will take care of everything—from editing and proofreading to interior and cover design. Others, such as IngramSpark, require that you provide them with a completely finished book.

More on printing: Thanks to print-on-demand (POD) services, books now can be printed as orders are placed. The quality usually is excellent, and it eliminates the risk of having hundreds of books sitting around that may never be sold. Some of the more popular POD services include Amazon Kindle Direct…Barnes & Noble Press…Blurb (Blurb.com)…and Ingram's Lightning Source (LightningSource.com). Depending on the length and whether the book is in black and white or color, expect to pay around $2.50 to $16 plus shipping.

A good option for new authors who want to dip their toe into audiobooks is Audiobook Creation Exchange (ACX.com), owned by Amazon. This service can connect you with a narrator if you don't want to narrate yourself. If you're hiring a narrator, you have the option of doing a royalty-only deal or paying what is called a per-finished-hour (PFH) fee. With a royalty-only deal, you split future earnings among three parties—ACX, your narrator/producer, and you. You and the narrator/producer each receive a 20 percent share of retail sales. But you could get a larger share of the earnings if you instead pay your narrator/producer a flat fee, typically $100 to $400 PFH. However, that could cost $1,000 or more.

PITFALL #4: **You don't sufficiently promote your book.** If readers don't know your book exists, they can't buy it.

Solution: Begin promoting your book in the months leading up to publication, and don't stop for at least six months to a year after publication. Better yet, keep promoting indefinitely, especially if there is something in the news that would help to revive interest in your book.

Use social-media outlets—Facebook, Linked In, Twitter, Instagram, etc.—to build excitement. Reach out to podcasters, TV news, and radio shows, and explain to them why you're the best expert on your topic or why everyone will want to read your book.

Hiring a publicist might cost $1,500 to $5,000 a month—often with a three-month minimum. If he/she has excellent connections, the money might be well-spent. Ask for referrals from fellow authors, or check out listings through *Publishing Trends* newsletter (PublishingTrends.com). If you go the DIY route, Cision has a free e-letter called HARO (Help a Reporter Out) that lists media leads (HelpAReporter.com).

Nontrade marketplaces, such as gift or novelty shops, or even through corporations, companies, associations, and book fairs, may be better suited for self-publishers because this allows for more targeted sales.

***PITFALL #5:* You let inertia or fear stand in your way of self-publishing.**

Solution: Just do it!

So many people have manuscripts squirreled away in desk drawers, or they have an idea that they want to explore. What if it's not brilliant? No matter your age, it will be an amazing accomplishment and part of your legacy to finally share your novel, nonfiction book, memoir, or cookbook with the world.

How to Start with Art at Any Age

David Wander, an artist who works in many media including, pastel, watercolor, collage, acrylic, oil on canvas, metal, and woodcarving. He is an art teacher at SAR High School in Riverdale, New York. His work has been displayed in museums and galleries around the world. DavidWanderArt.com

Many people in search of pandemic pastimes picked up paint brushes or sketch pads for the first time since high school art class. But lots of them put those art supplies back down when their early efforts looked less impressive than they had hoped. That's a shame. Learning art is like learning a foreign language—you can learn bits and pieces right from the outset, but it's likely to take months to truly communicate your thoughts. In the meantime, enjoy the process as you progress.

How to take the initial steps with three engaging art forms...

DRAWING

Drawing is a wonderful way to learn art—it helps you learn basic elements that you'll use in painting, too. Drawing is very forgiving of missteps—just use an eraser. *To get started...*

- **Learn the basics of perspective.** Translating three-dimensional objects onto a two-dimensional page is the single greatest challenge for a novice. This has been a crucial component of Western art ever since the Renaissance—it's why modern art conveys a sense of depth that Medieval art lacks.

Start by imagining that you're driving down a long, straight highway—the road seems wide around you, but far ahead it disappears into a single point, as do the power lines along the side of the highway. Now try drawing this highway. Your picture will seem to have depth—your drawing has "one-point perspective." Instructional videos are a good way to learn more on the subject.

Example: Circle Line Art School's videos about one-point, two-point and three-point perspectives are available for free on YouTube.

- **Try to see in shades of gray.** In the real world, lit objects tend to feature shaded transitions from dark to light. Your drawings will look more realistic if they include these transitions. As an exercise, create a row of 10 boxes on a white sheet of paper. Leave the box at one end completely white...shade the one at the other end as dark as you can with a pencil...then fill in the boxes in between from 10 percent dark to 90 percent dark. Next, place an apple on a table, sketch its outline, then draw lines to define the sections that are brightly lit, less brightly lit and so forth all the way down to those that are very shadowy. Use your 10 shaded boxes for reference. Pay close attention—are there areas on the apple that are surprisingly well lit, perhaps from light reflecting off the table beneath it?

- **Vary line thickness.** Beginners often give all the lines in their drawings the same thickness, or "weight." That leads to drawings that look uninteresting, like blueprints. Instead use thicker lines for the shaded side of an object and thinner lines for the brightly lit side, for example…or thicker lines for objects in the foreground and thinner for objects in the background.

• **Play with perspective and scale.** You can make your drawings more interesting by encouraging viewers to see your subjects in new ways. Draw things from unfamiliar angles…or draw them in unfamiliar sizes.

Example: Comic book artists often show cityscapes from unfamiliar angles as superheroes soar through the sky. Do a Google image search for "comic book cityscape" to see examples.

What you'll need…

• A "4B" graphite pencil, such as a Blick Studio Drawing Pencil 4B, which has softer graphite than a standard writing pencil, making it easier to draw lines that are dark and of varied thickness. $1.50. Plus a pencil sharpener if you don't already own one.

• A sketchbook with a hardback cover and unlined paper, available at any art-supply store for less than $10.

• An eraser that doesn't leave much residue, such as a Koh-I-Noor White Oblong Plastic Eraser. $0.89.

WATERCOLOR

Watercolor is the best painting option for beginners—it's simple, portable, inexpensive, and easy to clean up. Watercolors aren't just for impressionistic landscapes and seascapes. They can be used to paint any subject and in a wide range of styles—even photorealism. *To get started…*

• **Sketch first.** If you draw in a sketchbook, begin by using watercolors to add a bit of color to these sketches, no pricey canvases required. If you're not a fan of drawing, still use a pencil to make an extremely light sketch on your paper before applying any watercolors—it's easier to change these lines than to correct paint.

• **Paint in stages.** Applying lots of colors all at once is what leads to watercolor paintings that look like muddy puddles. Instead, paint the lightest parts of the image first, then let these sections dry before applying additional paint. You can use a hair dryer to speed this drying process—lay the painting flat, and hold the hair dryer far enough away that it doesn't make the paint run…or bring it closer if you want to experiment with the interesting results created by intentionally moving wet paint with blowing air. Be patient! Take as many drying breaks as necessary to avoid applying additional colors or layers of paint to a still-wet painting. Wait until the earlier paint is completely dry.

Most watercolors are translucent, so applying one color over another can combine them as if laying one color of cellophane on top of another. If you add Chinese white, an opaque white, to the watercolor it will make your colors opaque and you can paint a light over a dark.

• **Try watercolor pencils, too.** With these, you apply colored pigment by drawing, then dip a paintbrush in water and brush over the pencil lines to transform your drawing into a watercolor painting. It's a great option if you feel more comfortable drawing than painting.

What you'll need…

• A small "travel" watercolor set, such as Winsor & Newton Cotman Water Colour Sketchers' Pocket Box, $18. It includes 12 colors and a brush in a 2.6-x-5.1-x-0.9-inch plastic kit plus a mixing palette inside the lid.

• Watercolor pencils, such as Derwent Watercolour Pencils, set of 12, $16.

• A pad of watercolor paper. You can apply watercolors to any sketchbook, but watercolor paper is unlikely to fall apart because of the water. Any brand will do. Prices start at about $10.

COLLAGE

Collage is an art form where flat items such as photos, illustrations, and text clipped from magazines are combined on a surface to create something new. It's a way for novice artists to achieve visually appealing results without drawing or painting skills. There's an aspect of collage that's very modern—similar to the way people use computers to manipulate digital images. But part of this art form is quite traditional because you manipulate tactile, real-world pieces with your hands. Explore the works of collage greats such as Romare

Bearden, Max Ernst, Hanna Höch, and Kurt Schwitters online for inspiration, or enter "collages" into a Google image search to explore the many possibilities. *To get started…*

• **Collect printed images and other relatively flat items that you find compelling.** Cut images and words that interest you out of magazines and catalogs. Dig through photos or ephemera gathering dust in boxes in your attic. You could even print images you find online using Google image search.

When creating collages, I work with colored rice paper, or you could use colored tissue paper, as a way to add color quickly to a creation.

• **Affix the materials to a backing once you have an arrangement you like.** Some artists like to arrange loose pieces on a table before affixing anything to the backing… others head straight for the adhesive. Any piece of cardboard will work for the backing, though canvas boards—canvas-covered pieces of stiff backing board—are a good choice if the backing material won't be entirely covered…and/or if you intend to include some original painting.

• **"Matte medium" is a good choice for holding items in place**—it's essentially clear acrylic paint, painted on with a brush, and serves as both adhesive behind items and as a clear protective layer above them. If collage items overlap each other, apply a layer of matte medium over each. Be sure to clean the paint brush you use to apply it with soap and warm water as soon as you're done.

What you'll need: In addition to a collection of compelling flat items to use in your collages, you'll need…

• **Pieces of cardboard or canvas board for backing.** Canvas board is $1 to $2 apiece for 8-x-10-inch boards.

• **A paintbrush,** such as a one-inch or one-half-inch flat brush or #30 round brush. You don't even need to get these from art-supply stores—the paintbrushes available in home centers or hardware stores will do the trick.

• **A bottle of matte medium,** such as Liquitex Matte Medium, $25 for 32 ounces.

Turn Your Hobby into Cash by Selling on Etsy

Lauren Kilgore, accountant turned wreath maker turned Etsy expert. By sharing her knowledge of the platform as an Etsy business coach, she has helped hundreds of creative entrepreneurs find success. LaurenKilgore.com

In stressful times, being creative can be a wonderful psychological outlet, and having a new income stream can be a godsend. In fact, in the second quarter of 2020, Etsy, the online marketplace that allows individual craftspeople to sell handmade, unique, or vintage items in their own virtual "shops," saw a 100 percent spike in the number of new sellers.

As a successful Etsy shop owner with years of experience coaching other Etsy sellers on how to make the most of their shops, here is my most important advice for new people taking the plunge into selling on the platform.

MAKE YOUR PRODUCTS FINDABLE

Etsy buyers can find your offerings only by searching for them, so you've got to make your offerings as findable as possible. That means taking the time to write descriptive titles full of keywords that will be found by the site's search engine (yep, that buzzword "search engine optimization," or SEO). Two good SEO resources for Etsy sellers are Marmalead and eRank, both of which can tell you the most popular words and phrases for your items as well as how much competition you face with certain keywords, so you can consider other choices.

Imagine using your words to create a kind of funnel that moves from the overly broad (such as "socks") to narrowly specific (such as "Himalayan," "lamb's wool," or "magenta"). The idea is to reach a wide audience with the general terms, but then to include enough specifics to communicate what's unique or special about what you're selling.

A frequent mistake I see is people writing titles that are too short, robbing themselves of the potential to get more eyes on their goods by including unique descriptors. Etsy allows up to 140 characters in a title—use as many characters as you can to get in the keywords that will attract people to your products. To use an example from my own Etsy store, consider the difference in impact between a broad title such as "Christmas Wreath" and a more detailed one such as, "Christmas Wreath for Front Door, Front Porch Holiday Décor, Vintage Santa Claus."

Once a customer clicks through, you want to greet him/her with clear product descriptions and photos (more on that below). Frontload the most important keywords about your product—within the first 40 characters—to make it as easy as possible for shoppers to determine that they are interested. Include size, materials, and care instructions, but be brief and get to the point. Most customers are too rushed to wade through a lot of text, so use bulleted lists or frequent paragraph breaks to make the information easy to digest.

Another simple tip to get your stuff noticed: Fill in the "Shop Policies" and "About" forms for your shop. Etsy will automatically move sellers up in the rankings if they take those two simple steps, but I'm repeatedly surprised at how many people fail to do so. The "Policies" section tells how you'll handle returns, exchanges, delivery, disputes, and so on. It's not a place to get fancy or personal. Etsy has templates you can follow, and you should use those at a minimum. I recommend that sellers spend some time on their "About" section to really introduce themselves to their customers. Talk about your background. Did you learn at the feet of your grandfather? Do you get your ideas through travel? Are you inspired by a famous artist? Include photos of yourself in your workspace.

BE A SPECIALIST, NOT A GENERALIST

The most successful Etsy shops have clear branding and specialization, and the ones I see not doing well tend to throw everything but the kitchen sink at buyers. If you happen to be eclectically creative, great! But open multiple shops. A shop featuring hats for babies will probably do better as a baby-hats shop than as a baby-hats-and-rustic-coffee-tables-and-stained-glass-birdfeeders shop, since expectant mothers are not a natural market for rustic coffee tables or glass birdfeeders.

SET THE RIGHT PRICE

Plenty of shoppers put a filter on their Etsy searches showing the highest price first because they presume price to be a reliable proxy for quality. In other words, people don't usually come to Etsy looking for fire-sale pricing. Besides, if you don't charge enough, you simply won't survive as a business. Arriving at the right price can be tricky, but I generally advise pricing at two to three times cost. If your two-to-three-times pricing is significantly higher than the competition, examine your costs—buy smarter (preferably wholesale). While it may be useful to ask yourself, *How would my current price translate into an hourly wage?*, only you can decide whether the answer to that question is satisfactory.

POST GREAT PHOTOS

Even the world's highest-quality handcrafted product won't sell if all the customer sees is a blurry, shadowy snapshot. Your images don't have to look like the ads in *Vogue*—clarity trumps fanciness—but they do have to communicate what the product is about. Make sure there's enough lighting, and go easy on filters and effects. Your product is meant to be the center of attention, not lost in a tableau. At a certain point in developing my wreath business, I stopped obsessing about photographing my wreaths on different doors. Instead, I picked a door I liked as a background and began using it for every single wreath. Immediately my shop looked more consistent and professional. It also became much easier for customers to distinguish between the wreaths because they weren't distracted by the variety of doors. The subsequent increase in sales proved the wisdom of the simpler choice.

LEVERAGE SOCIAL MEDIA

Setting up an Etsy shop is just the first step. Next, establish a presence on social media. About half of my sales are driven by Pinterest and Facebook, and lots of Etsy shop owners use Instagram to good advantage. I usually advise that everybody should be on Pinterest and then choose between Facebook and Instagram based on which platform their buyers tend to hang out on. I hate to generalize about who's on what social-media platforms just because each product market is so unique, but as a broad rule of thumb, Instagram tends to attract a younger audience than Facebook.

Whichever you choose, create a special account for your business that's separate from your personal account and post consistently. If you're not a natural at that, use a post scheduler to batch the process weeks in advance. In your posts, stay on brand, taking the same care with look and language that you do on your Etsy shop. Show your products, but don't be pushy. Videos tend to get lots of clicks and shares, so try to think of ways to incorporate them often—show yourself working, talk about upcoming sales and events, or show creative ways for people to wrap or present your products as gifts. The people who are best at the social-media game are those who consistently offer something interesting without being repetitive and without forgetting to feature their products.

GET TO KNOW YOUR CUSTOMERS

One of the things that draws buyers to Etsy also happens to be a big potential advantage to you—boutique-style, personalized shopping. Treat your customers right, and they'll be singing your praises to their friends and family, sending more business your way. Dropping a handwritten thank-you card into a shipment can be a quick and easy way to establish rapport. Buyers particularly appreciate it when you acknowledge repeat purchasing. Customers also can be great sources of feedback and market intelligence, but you won't be able to get those things without fostering relationships whenever you can.

DON'T SELL YOURSELF SHORT

The most common self-imposed limitation I hear from people is that the markets for their crafts are already saturated. But I can almost guarantee you that they aren't. There are literally tens of millions of shoppers browsing Etsy, so there's plenty of opportunity. Think about it…in your life, do you buy only one pair of earrings? Do you buy home furnishings only from one store? Of course not. There could be thousands of other people selling what you're selling, and there's room for all of you.

MONEY MAKER…

Legitimate Work-from-Home Jobs

Amazon pays $15/hour for remote customer service, sales, marketing, and other positions. Chegg Tutors pays $20+/hour to give virtual lessons in various subjects. Tutor.com is similar. Philips pays $17 to $19/hour for customer advocates with bachelor's degrees in science, engineering, finance, or business administration—or related experience. Sykes typically pays $12/hour for home-based customer-service agents. U-Haul typically pays $12/hour for agents in customer service, sales, reservations, and roadside assistance. Working Solutions pays $9 to $30/hour for a variety of positions in consumer services, health care, retail, and travel.

Clark.com

Signs That Your Side Hustle Is Ready to Become Your Day Job

Serious growth: You've got more work than you have time for, and the trend is toward sustainable revenues. *True passion:* Your side business isn't just about money, and the work itself gives you the staying power to weather the business's ups and downs. *Self-motivation:* You don't need a boss to tell you not to blow off a day's work in favor of a beach party. *An actual plan:* You've got a good handle on growth, expansion, diversifying your client base, and a savings cushion for the early lean days. *Your full attention:* The side hustle is eclipsing your day job in terms of what takes up your waking hours, and you are feeling like something has to give. That something might be the day job.

Dean McPherson, cofounder of Paperform, a company that provides customized business forms, quoted at Forbes.com.

To Guard Against Fake News

MediaBiasFactCheck.com rates websites of all sorts, including other sites that claim to check stories for bias. Snopes.com, originally specializing in urban legends and common misconceptions, now does general fact-checking of viral misinformation, including political statements. FactCheck.org is a nonpartisan, nonprofit site focusing mainly on U.S. politics, and works with Facebook to fight viral fake news. LeadStories.com fact-checks stories that are trending online. For more resources, go to Guides.Library.UMass.edu/fakenews/fact check.

University of Massachusetts Amherst Libraries.

Top Headphones for a Better Work-at-home Experience

Powerbeats Pro Earphones are highly durable, completely wireless, stay securely in the ear and last up to nine hours on a full charge. $169. JBL LIVE 650BTNC Wireless Over-Ear Noise-Cancelling Headphones with Voice Control are well-insulated, comfortable and give a surround-sound experience. They can last 20 to 30 hours on a charge. $129. Apple AirPods Pro fit well, easily connect to iPhones, and have excellent noise cancellation. They can last 4.5 hours on a charge. $199. Bose Noise Cancelling Wireless Bluetooth Headphones 700 block external noise exceptionally well and can go for 20 hours on a single charge. $329.

Headphone tests and comparisons reported in MensHealth.com.

Great Office Chairs at Super-Low Prices

Great office chairs at super-low prices may be available through liquidators, which used to focus on furnishing businesses but now are helping people get furniture for their home offices.

Example: Executive Liquidation of Moonachie, New Jersey, emptied the offices of a major consulting firm in 2020 because of pandemic-caused lockdowns. The liquidator ended up with more than 25,000 chairs from that business and others—plus 1,000 desks and 22,000 gallons of hand sanitizer. Among chairs being sold was a $1,100 Herman Miller model at 80 percent off. Inventory at liquidators changes very often and quickly—check with firms in your area to find out what is available, and act fast if you want something they have on hand.

The Wall Street Journal.

BETTER WAY...

Take Notes by Hand In Meetings or Job Interviews

When shown videos of people in business meetings taking notes using either a cell phone or pen and paper, subjects perceived the pen-and-paper users—and the meeting—significantly more favorably. Even if you apologize for and explain the behavior, onlookers tie cell-phone use with time-wasting and social-snubbing.

Managers: To reduce this effect, discuss how technology may be used at the start of a meeting.

Cameron Piercy, PhD, assistant professor of relationships and digital media at University of Kansas, Lawrence, and leader of a study published in *Mobile Media & Communication.*

Handwriting—Not Typing—Yields the Best Learning and Memory

Scanning the brains of adults and children while they took a writing-intensive examination shows that the brain is much more active when people are writing by hand compared with when they're using a keyboard. Researchers say pressing pen to paper activates the senses, creates contact between different parts of the brain, and opens up the brain for learning and remembering.

Study by researchers at Norwegian University of Science and Technology, Trondheim, Norway, published in *Frontiers in Psychology.*

Writers' Secrets for Working from Home

Do the hard work first. Writers from Hemingway to Vonnegut chose the early part of the day for attacking the biggest tasks. There are fewer distractions, and the feeling of accomplishment can help power you through less interesting items on your to-do list. *Stick to a routine.* Writers often are fanatical when it comes to adhering to a set schedule—because they know what happens to productivity in the absence of a plan. *Embrace the isolation.* Lots of great writers shut themselves off from the rest of the household during work hours. In today's world, that means using apps such as Forest and Freedom to keep you off the Internet until leisure time. *Get exercise.* Both mind and body will suffer without some form of physical activity in your routine. Novelist Haruki Murakami commits to a rigorous running/swimming routine whenever he's writing a book. Schedule in a regular walk, a swim, or some other workout to reboot your system.

The Guardian.

How to Prevent Problems Before They Erupt

Dan Heath, senior fellow at Duke University's CASE Center in Durham, North Carolina, which supports entrepreneurs who are working for social good, and author of *Upstream: The Quest to Solve Problems Before They Happen.* HeathBrothers.com

Here are four strategies to shift from reacting to problems after they occur to avoiding them before they occur...

• **Stop allowing a minor irritation to repeatedly fly under the radar.** People often just endure seemingly trivial annoyances—it doesn't seem worth devoting the time, attention, and/or money that would be required to solve them. But that little thing you chronically bicker about with a friend or family member could expand into a major relationship rift. That odd sound your car is making could lead to a breakdown that leaves you stranded and with a costly repair bill. That mild recurring ache could develop into a major medical problem.

Even if a minor problem never escalates, the drip-drip-drip of mild irritation the problem causes over time often means that it would have been wise for you to solve it rather than let it continue.

What to do: The third time you notice a problem, take it as a sign that it isn't going to go away on its own. Consider what's at the root of the problem, and brainstorm potential permanent solutions—even if this approach takes significantly more time than the temporary fix you have been using.

Example: A husband's habit of leaving the hall light on was a recurring source of mild friction with his wife. When he finally took a moment to think about this problem, he realized that he could install a timer switch on the light, permanently removing this irritation.

• **Focus on the problems that almost emerged, not just those that did.** When a major mishap occurs, most people try to figure out what went wrong and how they can prevent it from happening again. But when people have a near miss with a major mishap, they often think, *Well, that was a close one,* count themselves fortunate, and get on with their day. But today's miss could foreshadow tomorrow's disaster—luck might not be on your side next time.

What to do: Take the time to carefully review your near misses, not just your mishaps. Some savvy hospitals have made this a standard practice, holding daily "safety huddles" during which staffers discuss errors almost made in addition to errors actually made. If you don't have a group with which you can discuss your near misses, take a quiet walk and think through whatever nearly went wrong while it's still fresh in your mind. Try to develop a plan to reduce the odds that a near miss actually could come to pass.

Example: If you nearly have an auto accident at a dangerous intersection that you regularly cross, you might want to take a different route to avoid this intersection in the future...or always wait an extra moment at this intersection to confirm that drivers coming the other way see that they have a stop sign.

- **Recognize the power of social norms to spur yourself to take preventive measures.** Most people are terrible at finding time for preventive measures. They know there are things they should be doing to reduce the odds of future problems, but they're so busy dealing with more pressing tasks that these future-focused actions never reach the top of their to-do lists.

Example: Many homeowners chronically fail to apply a pre-emergent crabgrass preventer and fertilizer to their lawns as growing season begins each year, even though doing so could significantly reduce the problems the lawn faces later in the season.

There is a glaring exception to this tendency to neglect the prevention of future problems—dental care. Most Americans brush once or twice almost every day to prevent future dental problems, even on days when they're busy or tired.

Why are people so much more responsible with problem prevention in this area than in most other facets of life? Of course, one of the reasons is that it is drilled into our consciousness that not doing this can be very harmful.

But another key factor is that it has become the social norm to take this preventive step. You wouldn't want to admit to anyone that you don't brush every day—it would make you feel weird and would seem inappropriate to others.

What to do: You can increase the odds that you will take preventive measures in other areas as well—if you can convince yourself that just about everyone else is already doing these things and that it would be embarrassing and inappropriate not to.

For your grass, if you focus on the difference between your lawn and your more diligent neighbor's lawn, you will be more likely to find the time to take preventive measures that produce a more attractive lawn.

- **Assign responsibility for preventing a potential future problem.** It's often obvious whose job it is to fix a problem that has already materialized but much less clear whose job it is to prevent that same problem from happening down the road.

Example: It's the responsibility of the police to catch criminals...but who has the primary responsibility for taking steps that could reduce future crime rates? Is it the police? Politicians? Social workers? Schools? Parents?

What to do: If you have the power to fix a problem, assign yourself responsibility for it. If you are unable to prevent a future problem on your own, try to determine who has the influence and/or skills to do so, then assign yourself responsibility for convincing that person or those people to take on this role.

Example: In 1975, a pair of researchers calculated just how massive of a problem car safety had become for kids—in America, car accidents were the leading cause of death for young children. These researchers lacked the power to fix this problem, but they thought they knew who could—pediatricians. Pediatricians had the ear of parents and were respected by politicians. The researchers published their findings in the journal *Pediatrics*, where pediatricians would see it, and the use of child car-safety seats increased dramatically. Within 10 years, all 50 states had child-seat laws, and death rates dropped dramatically.

Helpful: Not certain to whom you should assign responsibility for preventing a future problem? Sometimes the best answer is the people who are causing the problem.

Example: A mother and father were frustrated with the nightly battles required to get their kids to bed, so they sat down with those kids and explained why the entire family would benefit if this ongoing issue were resolved. They asked the kids to contribute ideas for preventing future bedtime problems. Their kids helped create a new bedtime system that featured penalties for failing to get to bed on time and rewards for going to bed on time and argument-free. The kids largely adhered to this new system, in part because they had played a role in creating it.

DON'T DO THIS, DO THAT...

What Not to Say During a Job Interview

I am a motivated self-starter. Interviewers hear this all the time. Instead, give a specific example of a time when you took the lead on a successful project. *In five years, I hope to be in your position.* This comes off as lazy and thoughtless. Instead, give specific ways you see yourself growing and advancing within the company. *I did not like my previous boss.* Admit a job was not the right fit, but do not criticize people. Explain what you hope for in a new position. *My biggest weakness is being a perfectionist.* This sounds as if you are not admitting any weaknesses. Instead, prepare a response in advance using feedback from former bosses and coworkers—then be honest about areas where you need improvement and discuss how you plan to improve.

Roundup of experts on job interviews, reported at CNBC.com.

What Women Write on Job Applications...

When women seek work in male-dominated fields, they're often tempted to avoid stereotypically feminine language when describing themselves in résumés and cover letters ("warm," "sensitive," "helpful," "interpersonal," etc.). But research shows that this strategy often backfires. While more traditionally masculine traits such as entrepreneurialism, competitiveness, and drive are indeed valued in the business world, women who present themselves in a more masculine light are seen as violating unspoken rules about how men and women should act, thus sabotaging their chances of getting hired.

Study by researchers at University of Toronto, Mississauga, Canada, published in *Academy of Management Journal.*

Disagreement Can Improve Teamwork

Quarrels within a group have traditionally been seen as slowing progress. But new research says the opposite. Groups that disagree more may be better able to solve problems than ones without conflict. This may be because disagreement forces group members to rethink or justify answers and decisions when they are challenged—leading to a better-thought-through outcome.

Study by researchers at Embry-Riddle Aeronautical University, Daytona Beach, Florida, published in *Human Factors.*

Interruptions at Work Cause Stress Levels to Spike

When researchers set up a simulated office environment and exposed study subjects to workplace stressors, they found that levels of the stress hormone cortisol were highest when workers were often interrupted by urgent messages from their bosses. And yet those participants did not report subjectively feeling like they were under great duress.

Study by researchers at ETH Zurich, Switzerland, published in *Psychoneuroendocrinology.*

How to Nurture Workplace Relationships When Working Remotely

Christopher Littlefield, a speaker and trainer based in the Washington, DC, area who specializes in employee appreciation and workplace culture. He is author of *75+ Team Building Activities for Remote Teams: Simple Ways to Build Trust, Strengthen Communications, and Laugh Together from Afar.* BeyondThankYou.com

Work from home was a novelty for many when the pandemic started, but now several companies have made it the new normal—even hiring new employees as remote workers. There are no casual conversations around the coffee machine or friendly hallway interactions. That can undermine an organization's sense of solidarity. Remote workers also are significantly more likely to perceive mistrust, incompetence, and poor decision-making, according to research by leadership training company VitalSmarts.

To avoid this problem, it's critical to make the effort for personal connections. *Here are ways to stay close to coworkers and forge bonds with new colleagues...*

- **Share digital photos from your home office.** These allow colleagues into your home and encourage them to do the same.

Examples: E-mail a photo of the mess stashed in a corner of your office where it can't be seen during Zoom calls...or of the bird perched right outside your window.

- **Transform interruptions into connections.** Kids, pets, and other residential noises can interrupt virtual meetings. When this happens to a colleague, share a quick story of a time it happened to you...and/or say hello to the child or pet who caused the disturbance. What might have been an awkward situation instead turns into a bonding moment for the two of you. Also find times to invite your children and spouse to say hello—to give colleagues a glimpse into your personal life and also give your family a view into your work life.

- **Start calls by making connections, and end them by offering appreciation.** A quick "How are you doing?" isn't sufficient to build a bond. Ask follow-up questions that express real concern or interest.

Examples: How is your family doing? What are you watching/reading that you've enjoyed? What's your favorite memory of (the current season or an upcoming holiday)? What are you doing to take care of yourself these days?

Remote workers often are starved for pats on the back. So before hanging up, provide true appreciation, not just a curt "thanks."

Examples: Say, "Before you go, I wanted to say I really appreciate all the great work you've been doing." Or immediately after the call, send a follow-up e-mail of gratitude for the good work...and perhaps even include a fun related image you find in a Google image search.

- **Send modest but relevant gifts.**

Examples: Send the type of candy that's always on the receptionist's desk with a note saying how much you've missed the treat. If you chatted about books with a colleague, send a copy of a new favorite. If you know the colleague is working late one evening, arrange for a meal to be delivered.

New employees: Ask for informal guidance. Mention to colleagues that it's difficult to figure out corporate culture remotely, and ask for a few minutes for them to fill you in. New hires often fear that asking for assistance will make them seem annoying or incompetent. In fact, research shows that asking someone for help likely will improve their opinion of, and feelings for, you—they're flattered that you value their input.

Current team members: Bring newbies into the fold. Assign "remote welcome lunches" to introduce the new person to others... hold a department Zoom in which everyone introduces themselves...assign buddies to regularly check in on the new person.

BETTER WAYS...

How to Tell If You're the Toxic Person in Your Workplace—and How to Be Better

If you tend to make everything about you—because of insecurity in general or life events that are super-stressful—make an effort to listen more and talk less in group discussions or during virtual meetings. If you give backhanded compliments, ignore coworkers or deliberately exclude certain people, recognize your behavior as anger-driven and find more productive ways to release your feelings, such as exercise before work or frequent breaks during the day. If you are jealous of the success of others, recognize that jealousy is a sign of insecurity—keep your own goals internal and focused, and share in the success of coworkers by recognizing them as a step toward the larger goals of the company.

Inc.com

Finding Treasure in That Pile of Inherited Stuff

Julie Hall, executive director of the American Society of Estate Liquidators and owner of The Estate Lady, LLC, an estate appraisal and liquidation service based in Charlotte, North Carolina. She is author of *Inheriting Clutter: How to Calm the Chaos Your Parents Leave Behind*. TheEstateLady.com

Assets and keepsakes aren't all that adult children inherit when their parents pass away. Most also are left with a lifetime of stuff—file cabinets full of paperwork, closets full of clothing, stacks of framed photos, long-forgotten boxes in basements and attics and much, much more. Coping with all this stuff is a massive task, one that often must be done even as the family grieves a parent's death.

If the heirs aren't careful, valuable or meaningful items may be discarded or sold for pennies.

Example: I once spotted an old steamer trunk in a Dumpster at an estate that I had been hired to appraise. The family was certain there was nothing of value in the trunk so they threw it away without waiting for me to arrive. There was little of value inside the trunk—but the trunk itself was made by Louis Vuitton and worth thousands of dollars.

Here's how to clear out the clutter as painlessly as possible without overlooking hidden gems...

• **Start clearing the clutter while the parent is still alive, if possible.** Not only will this reduce the size of the chore when the final cleanup occurs, it also gives the parent a chance to call attention to items that could have monetary or sentimental value.

You might face some resistance from your parent when you raise the topic of thinning out his/her stuff—if an item is still in the parent's home, the parent probably believes it might be needed again someday. Consider initially offering to remove the things that are least likely to trigger resistance, such as your old childhood belongings...things in spots that the aging parent can no longer access, such as an attic...or clearly out-of-date and nonfunctioning items.

• **Tamp down any sibling suspicions.** If you have siblings, talk to them about what you are doing and share with them what you find so that they do not become suspicious when things disappear from the parent's home without explanation.

If you remove valuables for security reasons after the parent's death, explain that you are doing so to keep them safe and will return everything when the estate is divided. Invite siblings to assist with these tasks, and provide them with an inventory, a receipt and/or digital photos.

TREASURE HUNT

• **Identify potential valuables hiding in plain sight.** Heirs often have some sense of what their parents own of value—but relying solely on that sense can be costly. Adult children often are certain that Mom owned only costume jewelry when there actually are a few "real" pieces in her jewelry box...or they think that their parents don't own valuable art or furniture when there's actually a piece worth thousands of dollars.

Example: An Oregon man discovered that the unloved painting hanging over his parents' fireplace was worth more than $100,000—he had come very close to disposing of it.

• **Check "costume" jewelry for small hallmarks**—impressions found on the back—that suggest the piece likely is made from a precious metal.

Example: If "750" or "18k" is stamped on a piece of jewelry, it suggests the piece might be 18-karat gold…"585" or "14k" suggests 14-karat gold…and "STER" or "925" suggests sterling silver. Check the backs of paintings for labels suggesting an artwork was once sold by a gallery—some oil paintings can have significant value.

These are not foolproof ways to identify value—the best option is to pay an experienced appraiser a few hundred dollars to examine parents' possessions. Choose an appraiser who is accredited by at least one of the sector's well-established professional organizations—the American Society of Appraisers (ASA)...the Appraisers Association of America (AAA)…the Certified Appraisers Guild of America (CAGA)…and/or the International Society of Appraisers (ISA)—and who has experience with the specific category of valuables in question. These organizations require ongoing training and hold their members to ethical standards.

Valuables sometimes overlooked by heirs also include…

• **Clothing and furniture from the 1930s through the 1960s.** It never occurs to most heirs that their parents' old clothes or old-but-not-antique furniture might have value, but styles from these decades are in demand.

Virtually anything made by a famous luxury brand. If an item bears the name Chanel, Gucci, Louis Vuitton, Rolex, or any high-end designer brand, it's worth having it looked at by an appraiser, even if the item is dated or broken. Sometimes even empty boxes from these companies have value.

WHERE AND HOW TO SELL IT

How should you sell items that you and your fellow heirs don't want from a parent's estate? There are a number of options, and which is best depends in part on what you're selling.

• **Estate-sale companies stage yard-sale–like events,** typically for 35 percent to 40 percent of the sale's revenues. You can find local estate-sale companies through the website of my organization, the American Society of Estate Liquidators. This is a good way to sell most household items from the typical estate, but certain items may be easier to sell or will get a better price if you sell them elsewhere such as on Facebook Marketplace or Craigslist.

• **An auction house** sometimes can get more than an estate sale for high-end pieces of jewelry, art, antiques, and collectibles worth thousands of dollars apiece. However, auction houses also charge commissions, which can vary widely. Auction houses decline many more pieces than they accept, but there's no harm in asking. Get a free auction evaluation through Heritage Auctions' website (HA.com) and/or contact auction houses in your area.

• **eBay** may bring more than an estate sale for small, easily shipped valuables that do not interest auction houses. But you or one of your fellow heirs will have to take the time to list each item on the site and manage the sale and shipping process.

• **Facebook Marketplace or Craigslist** could be the best place to sell oversized items that have value, such as pool tables, pianos, and larger-than-normal aquariums. These types of items often fail to sell at all in estate sales because most estate-sale shoppers lack the vehicles and manpower needed to transport them. But you will have to meet potential buyers at your parent's house or arrange for someone you trust to do so.

Inevitably, many household items or knickknacks from the estate won't sell. *Options for these include…*

A local nonprofit resale shop might pick up unsold potentially useful items. But many resale shops currently are overstocked and have become picky about what they'll pick up. If The Salvation Army and Goodwill say no, try lesser known shops such as those run by local hospices, religious organizations and veterans' organizations. Or you could list items to give away on sites such as Nextdoor.com, OfferUp.com, Facebook Marketplace or local Facebook community groups in your town.

Whatever remains could be thrown away. Enlist support to remove this clutter—getting it all out of the house is not a one-person job. If family members aren't available to help, ask religious and fraternal organizations that you or your parent belonged to if they can supply volunteers. Local Boy Scout and Girl Scout troops sometimes are willing to help, too. Contact the local municipal waste-removal service, and ask whether you have to make special arrangements to have a large number of garbage bags picked up. Depending on local rules and the amount of clutter, you might have to pay a private trash-hauling company or arrange for a Dumpster.

If your parent's home contains dozens of boxes of paperwork, call a shredding company, which can dispose of potentially sensitive documents quickly on site, typically for around $100. Save documents that still might be needed, such as all estate-related documents…tax and financial documents from the past seven years…and receipts and bills from the past three years.

Index

X

Z